LENIN ON THE UNITED STATES

Selections from the Writings of V. I. Lenin

Lenin
on the
United States

Selected Writings by
V. I. Lenin

INTERNATIONAL PUBLISHERS NEW YORK

The writings included in this volume have been compiled by C. Leiteizen from Lenin's *Collected Works*, published simultaneously by Progress Publishers, Moscow, and Lawrence & Wishart, London, 1963-69. Works from which English translations have been taken also were previously published in the United States and England and are protected either by U.S. Copyright or under the Universal Copyright Convention. Permission to quote any portion of the present volume, outside of reasonable usage for review purposes, should be requested from International Publishers, 381 Park Avenue South, New York, N.Y. 10016.

Library of Congress Catalog Card Number: 70-111375

Printed in the United States of America

PUBLISHER'S PREFACE

This collection affords an opportunity to study Lenin's views on specific American events and problems, and also to understand the place the United States held in his thinking at various times.

As with all of Lenin's writings, his special dialectical quality is at once apparent—in his own words, often reiterated by him: "the concrete analysis of concrete situations." Marxist generalizations based upon previous experience always served him as a theoretical base and as a guide. But they were never applied by him without first qualifying the particular times and places from which these conclusions were drawn and then studying carefully the new circumstances with their own qualifying factors.

Thus, early in this volume, we find him explaining the basic differences in the conditions and the level of the working-class movements in Britain and the United States as compared with Germany, and also between Germany and Russia, at the end of the last century. He then shows how these differences make necessary different approaches to the problems of the revolutionary movement. In the first two countries the central problem facing the Socialists was to overcome their narrowness and sectarianism by merging with the working-class movement even if it was non-socialist. In Germany and Russia, on the other hand, where Socialist parties already played an independent role, the main concern was to beware of petty-bourgeois opportunism and "parliamentary idiocy." The reader would be well-advised to apply the same Leninist approach to Lenin's comments on American events, keeping in mind the time and circumstances and the changes which have occurred since they were first made. Such a reading of the present text will make more apparent the richness of Lenin's insights and his critical mode of thought, and will enable the reader better to draw valid inferences and comparisons for the present.

It is interesting to note, for example, how Lenin compared Russia and the United States before and after the Russian revolution. In the earlier period he cited the United States as an example of advanced democracy with respect to literacy, public education, public libraries and the like (but always noting the exception with respect to the Negro people). See what can be done, he was saying, if we get rid of the Tsar and the landowners, that is, if we carry through our democratic revolution. But later, in between the two Russian revolutions of 1917 (after the democratic revolution overthrew tsarism but before Soviet power was won), notably in *State and Revolution*, he cited the United States to show that even this highest form of capitalist democracy was ruled by a dictatorship of capital. As he was to say later (in his lecture on "The State"), "the more democratic it is the cruder and more cynical is the rule of capital!" During the civil war in Russia, he denounces this same "advanced capitalist democracy" for its military intervention in the name of defending "freedom and equality—equality of the starved and over-fed." At the same time, for reasons which will be shown later, he sought economic aid from the United States.

Perhaps today, in view of the world imperialist role of the United States and the deterioration of bourgeois democracy within the country (including the educational and library systems), it no longer can be considered an "advanced capitalist democracy." Still Lenin's differentiation of both aspects of bourgeois democracy—the achievement of a significant level of democratic rights for the people as contrasted with capitalist command over and corruption of democratic institutions does suggest that the struggle to defend and extend democratic rights may well be an essential ingredient in the process of gathering the movement for the overthrow of capitalist rule.

Lenin wrote his *Imperialism: The Highest State of Capitalism* in 1916—before the United States entered the first world war and thus began its rapid ascendancy, culminating as a result of the second world war, to the prime imperialist position. Even at that time, he noted, the level of monopoly capitalism was higher in the United States than elsewhere, and the process of uneven development was leading to the demise of Britain as a world power and the rise of Germany, the United States and Japan. This process proved to be swifter than perhaps Lenin anticipated, but the essential features of the new stage of capitalist imperialism, and its relation to the socialist revolution, were clearly delineated by him.

When one considers his definition of imperialism in its five major aspects it can be seen that the subsequent emergence of American imperialism into a position of world supremacy essentially confirms his analysis, although some of the forms in which it takes place are new. Thus (1), the monopolies arising from the concentration of production and capital play an even more decisive role than during Lenin's day. Now they are fully in control of the economy, to an extent in the United States that was not thought possible 50 years ago, with critical consequences of great magnitude. Also (2) the financial oligarchy created by the merging of industrial and bank capitals in the earlier period of imperialism has not only persisted in that particular form, but has become more intensive as a result of the absorption of banking and financial functions by huge industrial corporations and, more recently, by the conglomerates. The latter represent a new form of concentrated control over vast capitals, cutting across industries and products to command a broad cross-section of the economy, especially over the new technologies and products. The net result of all these developments, old and new, is to increase greatly the role of monopoly capital and the financial oligarchy and their capacity to amass maximum profits under central control.

This super-monopoly capitalism has indeed become the leading exporter of capital (3) into practically all the continents, although its sphere of operations has been greatly limited by the emergence of the socialist world. Yet, within this restricted sphere, as a consequence largely of U.S. investments in the advanced capitalist countries as well as in the underdeveloped colonial and neo-colonial sectors, monopoly capital has been "internationalized" to a degree much beyond the level reached in Lenin's day. The cartel form (4) of division of markets, spheres of influence and control of raw materials among the world monopoly interests has perhaps been superseded by single U.S. corporations or by "multi-national" corporations (although its geographic extent, as noted, is limited by socialism and, we may add, increasingly by national liberation revolutions). However, the essential process remains an even more pronounced feature of monopoly-capitalist imperialism. At the end of the last century and for the first two decades of the 20th century (5), rival imperialisms were engaged in the division and redivision of the dependent and colonial world, with emphasis upon the seizure of colonies. This struggle now tends almost entirely to take neo-colonial forms, in an effort to contain the sweep of the national liberation revolutions. But the basic process and the objectives, as described by Lenin, remain the same within the contracting sphere of possible operations.

The emergence of the United States as the prime monopoly capital-imperialist power raises questions which impart a new significance to Lenin's polemics against Karl Kautsky. By now it does not seem necessary to argue the point that imperialism is not a "policy" that can be adopted or dropped at will, but is an actual stage of capitalist development, the consequence of the inherent characteristics of that social system when it reaches the monopoly stage. However, there is a variation of policies based upon monopoly-imperialism and directed toward the same aim of imperialist aggrandizement and domination. Thus Lenin made clear that imperialist penetration can take place in politically independent countries as well as in outright colonies, and cites the United States in Latin America as an example. In fact, this is the characteristic form of U.S. imperialism (although it has seized colonies as well), often behind a facade of liberating and democratic pronouncements which gave it a certain advantage over the more traditional colonial imperialism. Today, however, with the break-up of most of the old-style colonial empires and the emergence of the United States as the prime imperialist power, and furthermore an old hand at neo-colonialism, this has become the "modern" style of domination.

The other point which Lenin raised against Kautsky was his theory of "ultra-imperialism"—the concept that it might be possible as a result of super-combinations of monopoly on a world scale to assure peaceful accommodation among the rival capitalist groups. The principal point made by Lenin was that the further development of cartels and other forms of monopoly operating on a worldwide basis, far from assuring peaceful division and cooperation, would deepen the antagonisms among the powers. Uneven development would in any case continue and raise the necessity of a redivision of shares and spheres which could lead only to a rearrangement by force. Kautsky's theory, he held, amounted to an attempt to obscure the sharp world capitalist contradictions, thus feeding opportunism and all tendencies of compromise with imperialism. The second world war, despite the preceding high level of cartel combinations among the central world monopoly interests, fully confirmed his position.

Now it may be asked, along Kautskyian lines, whether the rise of U.S. imperialism and its monopoly groups to their commanding world position, does not indeed raise the same question in another form. The American monopoly position is so overwhelming, it may be argued, that other monopoly groups have no alternative but to submit to domination or absorption on a "partnership (multi-national) basis" by the American corporations. Indeed, there are some current opinions that inter-monopoly and inter-imperialist antagonisms no longer play a role of great importance, in view not only of the clear preponderance of power within the capitalist world held by the United States but also because of the common interest among capitalist powers in obstructing and containing further advances of socialism. Yet, it seems that the recrudescence of West German and Japanese power, after a period of dependence upon U.S. succor after the second world war, has led to the reappearance of inter-monopoly tensions and inter-imperialist antagonisms, even if these may be subdued for a time. Lesser powers like England and France are smarting at what amounts to exclusion from full participation in the consortium of world power, and the trends toward a Europe freed from U.S. hegemony persist and grow. Furthermore, another basic factor, not yet fully matured between the two wars, is the powerful world position held for socialism by the Soviet Union. This not only alerts the imperialisms to their common interest; it also offers a non-capitalist and therefore non-competing point of support for countries, large and small, which seek a counterweight to American preponderant power. Thus tensions of the inter-monopoly and inter-imperialist type, while reasserting themselves in traditional forms, are also accentuated and made more complex by a factor as yet absent during Lenin's day—the role of a powerful world socialist sector.

The same may be said with respect to the role of national liberation movements which in the current period are on a scale much beyond those following the first world war. Neo-colonialism is an effort not only to contain these revolutions before they proceed to the socialist stage: it is also the outer shell within which contending imperialist powers and monopoly groupings fight for advantage. Here, particularly in Africa and Asia, the United States has not achieved any clearly preponderant position, either against older rivals or, more to the point, against China and against the national revolutions which enjoy the support of socialist countries, despite some temporary successes in Africa. The containment of American imperialist power in Korea and its sharp rebuff in Vietnam illustrate the new truth of the current world: The United States has come to the peak of imperialist power to find that it has been denied freedom of action in a large part of the world. Within the narrower scope of world imperialism, the conflicts and antagonisms tend to grow more intense.

Another fundamental aspect of Lenin's theory of imperialism was his emphasis upon the bond between imperialism and opportunism in the labor movement. Earlier, in an article on the convention of the American Federation of Labor in 1912, he did not go beyond the views expressed by Marx and Engels regarding the "bourgeoisification" of the working class in 19th century England, when that country still held an unchallenged position in the capitalist world. He wrote about the AFL: "Alongside the rapidly growing Socialist Party [it received close to a million votes in the elections of 1912], the association is a living relic of the past: of the old craft-union, liberal-bourgeois traditions that hang full weight over America's working-class *aristocracy*" (his emphasis). At that time, he saw the prime historical causes for "the particular prominence and (temporary) strength of bourgeois labour policy in Britain and America" in the "long-standing political liberty and the exceptionally favorable conditions, in comparison with other countries, for the deep-going and widespread development of capitalism."

A few years later, in his work on *Imperialism,* his emphasis shifted. Now Lenin wrote of "the last stage of capitalism" and of imperialism as "moribund capitalism," although he did not exclude the possibility for further and significant capitalist industrial and technological development. He also expressed the view that the political content of imperialism was a turn to reaction in all respects. Obviously, then, in Lenin's thinking opportunism in the labor movement had to be considered in the new context of modern imperialism. Now, in the present stage of capitalism, he wrote, "imperialism . . . which means high monopoly profits for a handful of very rich countries, makes it economically possible to bribe the upper strata of the proletariat, and thereby fosters, gives shape to, and strengthens opportunism." Furthermore, "The intensification of antagonisms between imperialist nations for the division of the world increases the urge. And so there is created that bond between imperialism and opportunism." This is the central thought that permeates his writings on this question. It is noteworthy that Lenin considered this bond "temporary," an "abscess on a healthy body," and warned that we must not "lose sight of the forces which counteract imperialism in general, and opportunism in particular." But he went on to characterize as "the most dangerous of all . . . those who do not wish to understand that the fight against imperialism is a sham and humbug unless it is inseparably bound up with the fight against opportunism." Moribund capitalism, he said, "may remain in a state of decay for a fairly long period (if, at the worst, the cure of the opportunist abscess is protracted.)"

If anything, his view became more pronounced as the world war went on and later during the civil war and intervention following the socialist revolution. With reference to the split in the Socialist International during the war, he characterized the "social-chauvinists" (Socialists who supported the war) as "*bourgeois* within the working-class movement," representing "a stratum, or groups, or sections of the working class which *objectively* has been bribed by the bourgeoisie" (his emphasis). In 1919, in a letter addressed to the

European and American workers, he again stressed the imperialist robbery of the weak countries as the source of the "superprofits" which enables the capitalists "to bribe the top sections of the proletariat and convert it into a reformist, opportunist petty bourgeoisie that fears revolution." He finds "magnificently expressive" the title given by "the best socialists in America" to the leaders of this "bribed" sector—"labor lieutenants of the capitalist class."

Lenin was not one to mince words. His meaning is clear beyond any question. At the cornerstone of his entire philosophy is the basic Marxist proposition regarding the historic role of the proletariat in overthrowing capitalism and creating socialism. But as a great revolutionary materialist, combining theory and practice, the negative as well as the positive features in any given situation entered into his analysis. Thus, once having recognized its expression in the current movement, he sought the roots and causes of opportunism to understand better how to overcome the inner obstacles to the advance of the proletarian movement. He did not seek explanations that would satisfy the requirements and hopes of a general theory of revolution, without regard to actualities. He was not interested in painting a "rosy" picture. To those who felt there was little hope for successful revolution if it were true that concessions won under capitalism generated among the privileged minority of workers greater tendencies toward opportunism (and there was such among the Russian Socialists), Lenin replied that this position leads to false optimism for it "serves to conceal opportunism."

It seems obvious that Lenin's insistence upon the bond between imperialism and opportunism (in his definition of imperialism as monopoly capitalism) remains as pertinent today and assumes even greater significance with respect to the United States, now the super-imperialist power. The sources of maximum monopoly profits available to the big corporate interests from which concessions can be granted to sizeable sectors of labor have certainly grown—as a result of the much greater monopolization of the domestic economy and the greater world role of U.S. imperialism even within a contracted sphere of operations. The support granted by the dominant leadership of the trade unions to the Cold War and to aggression and intervention in Korea, the Dominican Republic and Vietnam, to mention only the most obvious, is too fresh in everyone's memory to need further comment here. Regarding domestic events, the trade union leaderships for the most part have at the best dragged their feet, and at the worst continued their exclusion policy toward black Americans, Puerto Ricans and Mexican-Americans.

Writing about the mass immigration to the United States earlier in this century, Lenin noted that the workers from Eastern and Southern Europe were given the most poorly paid jobs, while the longer-resident American workers provided the highest percentage of overseers and better-paid workers. Thus, he commented, "Imperialism has the tendency to create privileged sections also among the workers, and to detach them from the broad masses of the proletariat." One need only substitute for the immigrant workers of those days the black and brown workers of today, with the added factor of racism. The connection between opportunism and racism was also observed by Lenin. In his "Notebooks on Imperialism" he subheads his notes on the anti-Japanese laws in the United States, "American workers and their chauvinism" (elsewhere he makes a similar comment on the Chinese exclusion laws, and wryly comments upon Morris Hillquit's conciliatory position). He notes particularly the AFL support for such laws and that the Socialist party had also been found "wanting." With respect to the Negro, he observed that the Socialist party did "not much" and that in Mississippi it was organizing the Negroes into "special local groups!!"

While the connection between imperialism and opportunism has become more pronounced in the United States over recent years, and needs to be recognized in all its variations and dimensions, there are reasons to expect that the economic basis for this kind of class accommodation will become narrower. The objective prospects for opportunism depend to a fundamental degree upon the capacity of imperialism to feed it, and in this respect the principal trend of the present historic period is toward the further delimitation of the world scope of imperialism. Eventually, and perhaps sooner rather than later, the restrictions upon the sources of superprofits abroad are likely to have domestic repercussions of a kind that will make it more and more difficult for monopoly to assuage the class struggle at home, which has its own internal causes. Thus there may well be set into motion new class conflicts that will break through the restraints of opportunism and merge with such mass movements, today of unprecedented scope, as the opposition to the Vietnam war, the black freedom uprising, and the rebellion of the youth. The narrowing of the objective, economic base for opportunism would then be complemented by the emergence of the active forces arrayed against it, particularly within the labor movement itself. It would seem correct, therefore, to entertain the perspective that the bond between imperialism and opportunism is likely to grow weaker rather than stronger.

In the long run, in the general perspective of the current historical period, American imperialism may find it increasingly difficult to nourish opportunism in the labor movement, and thus create a crisis for opportunism itself. But it would be far from Lenin's method to assume that what is in prospect historically is necessarily expressed in current experience. How far it achieves such expression depends directly upon the struggle itself, and the awareness and effectiveness of the forces engaged in it. Accordingly, as in Lenin's day, positions that obscure the roots and forms of opportunism (which sometimes also are expressed in "left" and sectarian terms) hamper the struggle against it, which is inseparable from the struggle against imperialism.

The reader will find that Lenin was also quick to appreciate the tendencies and leaders opposing opportunism. At a distance, and under conditions of war and revolution, he was not always able to gauge properly the relation of various tendencies to the domestic issues in the United States, nor did he attempt that kind of analysis. He was more concerned with the issues involved in the world Socialist split, and greeted with enthusiasm evidences of an internationalist position. Thus, he hailed Eugene Debs for his article in *Appeal to Reason* (September 11, 1915) in which he called himself a "proletarian revolutionist" and made his famous declaration: "I am opposed to every war but one; I am for that war with heart and soul, and that is the world-wide war of the social revolution."

Throughout the war Lenin continued to link Debs' name with all in the world movement opposing the "social chauvinists." In his letter to the Socialist Propaganda League, a left-wing group of the Socialist Party, based in Boston, he welcomed its anti-war position, and sent it documents setting forth the Bolshevik views in the hope that they would be made public in the United States (there is no evidence that this was done).*

Another quality of Lenin's tactical approach can be seen in his attitude to the Industrial Workers of the World. Although he considered erroneous the IWW views on the leading role of the party and its position against participation in bourgeois parliaments and in reactionary trade unions, he urged a unitary approach. At the Second Congress of the Communist International (1920) he favored seeking its adherence to the CI because the IWW was "a profoundly proletarian and mass movement" although relatively inexperienced in political action. He urged a "very friendly" policy, even suggesting amalgamation into a single Communist party. Although the IWW as an organization did not follow this course, its outstanding leaders, notably William Haywood and Elizabeth Gurley Flynn, did become Communists, and many "Wobblies" joined the cooperatives of American workers who went to Soviet Russia to help build socialist enterprises.

Of particular interest to the American reader today are Lenin's perceptive comments on the situation of black Americans. As early as February 1913, before the first mass wave of migration from the Southern plantation to Northern industry began, he observed that traces of slavery are reflected in the deplorable conditions of the Negro in the South and that these affect the whites as well. That this was not merely an "intuitive," passing insight but came from deep study is shown by his scholarly work on American agriculture, which is reprinted here in full. Based on a detailed study of the

* In this same letter, it is of interest to note, Lenin criticized by indirection the League's negative attitude to "immediate demands" and its rejection of party centralism while fighting for party democracy, showing his sensitivity to the danger of "leftist" positions.

American Censuses of 1900 and 1910, the work is concerned primarily with the features of capitalist development in agriculture, then a central point of contention among Russian populists and Socialists. Dividing the country into three principal regions—the North, the West and the South—he singled out a half century ago those tendencies which eventually led to the high concentration of American agriculture and to the mass displacement of millions of farmers. His conclusions with respect to the role of machinery and of intensive agriculture, and his analysis of class relations among farmers, remain permanent contributions in this field.

Lenin's study of the Southern region has a special significance. It provides the first Marxist insight into the genesis of the "Negro question" after the Civil War and Reconstruction and into the imperialist era. He discerned clearly the role of the plantation-sharecropping economy as a retarding force within the capitalist structure —a "semi-feudal" formation which kept captive the majority of the Negro people within a system of especially brutal exploitation. The effects of this "remnant of slavery" were no different, in his opinion, than effects of the remnants of serfdom in Central Russia, both resulting in particularly oppressive conditions.

The theoretical extension of this interpretation is expressed succinctly in an article of 1916, dealing with the formation of advanced nation-states. "In the United States," he wrote, "the Negroes . . . account for only 11.1 per cent. They should be classed as an oppressed nation, for the equality won in the Civil War of 1861-65 and guaranteed by the Constitution of the republic was in many respects increasingly curtailed in the chief Negro areas (the South) in connection with the transition from the progressive pre-monopoly capitalism of 1860-1870 to the reactionary monopoly capitalism (imperialism) of the new era." (The years of "progressive premonopoly capitalism" comprised roughly the Civil War and Reconstruction.)

Lenin continued to press the same thought. At the Second Congress of the Communist International, in his thesis on the agrarian question, he again drew the parallel between the "former slave-owners of America" and the big landowners in Russia, Germany and other countries who were carry-overs from feudal conditions. While earlier Lenin had referred to the United States as a country free from feudal hangovers (a sort of "pure" capitalist democracy), as Marx and Engels had done before him, after his study of Southern agriculture he changed his view. He now recognized that remnants of slavery in the South, resulting in the national-type oppression of the Negro people, constrained and hampered free democratic development in much the same fashion as hangovers from feudalism in Europe.

Aside from the general import of this conclusion for the interpretation of American history as a whole, Lenin's view of the Negro as an oppressed people, has an obvious analogy to other peoples oppressed by imperialism. Many changes have occurred since Lenin developed these views, particularly the partial changeover of the Southern plantation system and the transformation of the mass of Negro sharecroppers into industrial workers. But the interpretation of the black freedom struggle in the United States as a movement of national liberation, within the specific class structure of the imperialist country itself, seems to have full validity, as the current "black revolution" confirms.

Among the first writings by Lenin to become known in the United States was his "Letter to the American Workers," which was published in December 1918 in *The Class Struggle*, a left-wing Socialist magazine. It was brought to the United States by Pytor Travin, an immigrant who had just returned to his native Russia from America. He took the Letter to John Reed who arranged for its translation and edited it. Often reprinted since then (a fully accurate version did not appear until 1934), the Letter evokes the American revolutionary tradition of the War of Independence and the Civil War to help explain the historical significance of the Bolshevik revolution. The Letter is notable for its lucid presentation of Soviet policy in the Brest-Litovsk peace with Germany, which took Russia out of the war at the cost of a heavy loss of territory. This, Lenin argued, was among the heavy sacrifices made "for the sake of power passing to the workers, for the sake of starting the world proletarian revolution." He excoriated the "scoundrels" in the world socialist movement who wanted to wait until "a path without sacrifice is found" and who sought an absolute guarantee of victory before supporting proletarian revolution.

Perhaps the clearest statement of Lenin's view of world revolutionary prospects at that time is to be found here. Since this often has been over-simplified, attention should be called to the full passage on p. 347 in the present volume, which begins: "We know that help from you will probably not come soon, comrade American workers, for the revolution is developing in different countries in different forms and at different tempos (and it cannot be otherwise)." In essence he is saying here that backward Russia was counting on the aid of world revolution to build socialism, but that revolutions in other countries could be defeated or delayed. In the meantime, Lenin explains, it is necessary to take advantage of antagonisms among the imperialist powers to advance and safeguard the socialist revolution where it has already occurred. He described the policy as "manoeuvre, stratagem, retreat, in anticipation of the moment when the rapidly maturing proletarian revolution in a number of advanced countries *completely matured*." The maturing of revolution in other countries, after initial defeats in Europe, took longer than Lenin seemed to anticipate, and in ways and places that could not be foreseen (although a few years later Lenin expected the revolution to come from the vast colonial East rather than at first from advanced Europe).

Keeping in mind the policy of "taking advantage of power antagonism" to safeguard the revolution in an economically backward and isolated country, it is easier to understand why Lenin pressed for economic aid from the United States. As early as May 1918, barely six months after the socialist revolution, we find him submitting a plan for economic relations with the United States to Colonel Raymond Robins, head of the American Red Cross Mission to Russia, for submittal to his government. Despite civil war and military intervention, he continued these efforts, including even the offer of economic concessions to foreign capitalists "as one of the means of attracting into Russia, during the period of the coexistence side by side of socialist and capitalist states, the technical help of the countries more advanced in this respect." In a reply to questions submitted by a Chicago *Daily News* correspondent in October 1919, Lenin declared: "We are decidedly for an economic understanding with America—with all countries but *especially* with America."

It was at that time that the Soviet had formulated with President Wilson's envoy, William Bullitt, a peace agreement for ending the military intervention and for economic relations. This agreement was ignored by Wilson and the other Allied statesmen as well, for they still hoped that a new counter-revolutionary offensive backed by them would overthrow Soviet power. This hope was to remain an active ingredient of U.S. policy toward the Soviet Union for many years (and other socialist states later), increasingly supplemented by the calculation that if the government itself could not be overthrown then at least it could be weakened as a result of economic discrimination and military threats against socialism. But the shape of things to come can already be discerned in Lenin's remarkable interview with Lincoln Eyre of *The World* early in 1920, when the counter-revolutionary armies in most of Russia had suffered defeat and he was certain that a new offensive from Poland, then threatening, would suffer a similar fate. Here again Lenin stressed the desire for trade with the capitalists, while sharply criticizing the "pogroms" and deportation craze against Socialists in the United States. He foretells the revival of an economically independent Europe, following its postwar dependence on the United States, and the resumption of European-Russian trade (which in fact began by 1925). In the midst of famine and of almost total economic exhaustion of Russia, he revealed what then appeared an exuberantly optimistic plan for the electrification of the country within ten years and talked of the advance that thus would be made possible toward the goal of communism. History has shown how Lenin's visionary plan became reality, while the deeply class-biased policy of the American ruling class toward Russia proved bankrupt.

Lenin's offer to grant concessions to foreign capitalists aroused the criticism of right-wing Socialists who accused him of betraying communism—by now, after so many years, a familiar strategem. In the absence of world revolution, which these same right-wing Socialists feared and obstructed—was Lenin's retort—bourgeois capital, if it could be obtained, would be useful to building up the underdeveloped economy. How far Lenin was willing to go is revealed by his offer of a 60-year concession for mineral and fishing rights in Kamchatka to an American consortium, which included the right for a naval base against Japan, then occupying a large part of the Soviet Far East. The offer was rejected, in the vain hope that Japan could be induced to pull the American chestnuts out of the Soviet fire. Although Lenin proved wrong in thinking a U.S.-Japanese war imminent (it came two decades later), here again his policy was to prevent an imperialist combination against the Soviet revolution and to open the way to trade. Actually, little came of these efforts, at least as far as the United States was concerned. Worthy of mention are only two concessions—with Armand Hammer to work the asbestos mines in the Urals, and with another group of American capitalists to construct the Grozny pipeline and a refining plant.* It took a severe economic crisis to bring about the recognition of the Soviet Union by the Roosevelt Administration in 1933, and the opening of meaningful commercial relations.

Certainly, of greater significance in many respects during the early and very difficult years of the Soviet revolution was the aid of American workers who came to Russia to help in the reconstruction. One of the most fascinating parts of this volume is the correspondence of Lenin dealing with this heroic effort. Here is revealed the importance Lenin attached to this form of international support and the painstaking care he took to assure its success. The letters show his deep concern for the comfort of these new-era pioneers—his insistence, for example, that they bring a two-year supply of food and clothing suitable to the harsh Russian conditions. Among the best known of the cooperative enterprises was the Kuzbas Autonomous Industrial

* One of the engineers participating in the latter project was an old-time Socialist, A. A. Heller, who later, together with Alexander Trachtenberg, founded International Publishers.

Colony in the Kuznetsk coal basin, in which William ("Big Bill") Haywood and H. S. Calvert, an IWW worker, played prominent roles. Many other technical teams were organized by the Societies for Technical Aid to Soviet Russia in the United States and Canada, an effort which continued until 1925. The Societies planned nearly 200 artels with 800-1,000 tractors.

Among these groups was the 22-tractor team at the Toikino State Farm in the Perm region, led by Harold Ware, an American farm expert and Communist (son of Ella Reeve "Mother" Bloor). It was singled out by Lenin for special praise, together with other American teams at state farms in the Odessa and Tambov regions, as well as a miner's group in the Donets Basin. Farms operated or aided by Americans were designated by the Soviet Government as "model farms" for the development of mechanized, collective agriculture.

Significant was the agreement negotiated with the Amalgamated Clothing Workers of America through its president, Sidney Hillman, who visited Soviet Russia in 1921 and was enthusiastic about what he saw. The agreement provided for the lease to the corporation established by the union of garment factories in Moscow, which were to be restored, supplied with equipment from the United States and put into operation. Indicative of the wide impact of the Socialist revolution in labor circles was the American Labor Alliance for Trade Relations with Russia, founded in November 1920. It received the support of 12 national unions, over a score of state federations of labor, and central labor bodies in 72 cities, altogether encompassing some two and a half million members, at a time when the total AFL membership was below five million.

To present readers, many nurtured by years of anti-Sovietism and living in the more recent Cold War ambient, Lenin's references to the enthusiasm engendered in the United States by the Russian revolution may seem exaggerated.* Actually, the enthusiastic response went considerably beyond traditional working-class and radi-

---

* See Philip S. Foner, ed., *The Bolshevik Revolution: Its Impact on American Radicals, Liberals, and Labor. A Documentary Study.* N.Y., 1967; and, among others, Christopher Lasch, *The American Liberals and the Russian Revolution.* N.Y., 1962.

cal circles. This movement reflected various levels of support, and persisted despite the extreme repressive measures of the time, including the infamous Palmer deportation raids. Among Socialists, IWWs, and other left and radical groupings the great majority came out in support of the Bolshevik revolution, no matter how they differed on the interpretation and lessons of that historic event. Lenin's reference to Soviets in America is no figment of the imagination, since it was not uncommon among the left at that time (and even later) to urge formation of councils on the Soviet model, although in time this came to be recognized as unsuitable for American conditions. In wider circles there was considerable opposition to the blockade of Soviet Russia and the military intervention, coupled with demands for commercial and diplomatic relations, often expressed by businessmen and reaching into Congress.

Here it has been possible to touch only upon some important themes that seem most pertinent for our time. The reader will find for himself in the present volume other writings of perhaps equal historical and political interest, and may be impelled to read in full the larger works from which many of these selections are taken. He is sure to find Lenin always stimulating and rewarding.

New York, November 1969

JAMES S. ALLEN

LENIN ON THE UNITED STATES

Selections from the Writings of V. I. Lenin

CORRECTIONS

p. 53, lines 13-14. Appeal to Reason was published in Girard, Kansas.

p. 56, line 25. For "Progressists" read "Progressives," i.e., supporters of the Progressive Party in the elections of 1912.

p. 436. Lenin's Introduction to *Ten Days That Shook the World* was first published in the Boni & Liveright edition of 1922.

p. 505, lines 20-21. P. P. Christensen was the presidential candidate of the Farmer-Labor Party in the elections of 1920, receiving one million votes.

p. 621, note 46, line 6. The Communist Party, USA, dates its foundation from 1919, when the Communist Labor Party and the Communist Party of America were organized after the split in the Socialist Party. The two parties fused into a single Communist Party in 1921.

p. 639, note 154, line 4 and p. 641, note 165, line 2. The correct name for the union is Amalgamated Clothing Workers of America, of which Sidney Hillman was president.

CONTENTS

LETTERS AND NOTES

From NOTEBOOKS ON IMPERIALISM

MARX ON THE AMERICAN
"GENERAL REDISTRIBUTION"

In *Vperyod* No. 12,[1] there was a reference to Marx's polemic against Kriege[2] on the agrarian question. The year was not 1848, as erroneously stated in the article by Comrade —, but 1846. Hermann Kriege, a co-worker of Marx and at the time a very young man, had gone to America in 1845 and there started a journal, the *Volkstribun*, for the propaganda of communism. But he conducted this propaganda in such a manner that Marx was obliged to protest very strongly in the name of the German Communists against Hermann Kriege's discrediting of the Communist Party. The criticism of Kriege's trend, published in 1846 in *Westphälische Dampfboot* and reprinted in Volume II of Mehring's edition of Marx's works, is of tremendous interest to present-day Russian Social-Democrats.

The point is that the agrarian question at that time had been brought to the fore by the course of the American social movement, as is the case now in Russia; it was not a question of a developed capitalist society, but, on the contrary, of the creation of the primary and fundamental conditions for a real development of capitalism. This circumstance is of particular importance for drawing a parallel between Marx's attitude towards the American ideas of "general redistribution"[3] and the attitude of Russian Social-Democrats towards the present-day peasant movement.

Kriege gave no data in his journal for a concrete study of the distinctive features of the American social system and for defining the true character of the movement of the contemporary agrarian reformers who campaigned for the abolition of rent. What Kriege did do, though (quite in the style of our "Socialist-Revolutionaries"[4]), was to clothe the question of the agrarian revolution in bombastic and high-sounding phrases: "Every poor man," wrote Kriege, "will become a useful member of human society as soon as he is given an opportunity to engage in productive work. He will be assured such an opportunity for all time if society gives him a piece of land on which he can keep himself and his family.... If this immense area (the 1,400,000,000 acres of North American public domain) is withdrawn from commerce and is secured in restricted amounts for labour,* an end will be put to poverty in America at one stroke...."

To this Marx replies: "One would have expected him to understand that legislators have no power to decree that the evolution of the patriarchal system, which Kriege desires, into an industrial system be checked, or that the industrial and commercial states of the East coast be thrown back to patriarchal barbarism."

Thus, we have before us a real plan for an American general redistribution: the withdrawal of a vast land expanse from commerce, the securing of title to the land, limitation of the extent of landownership or land tenure. And from the very outset Marx subjects this utopianism to sober criticism, he points out that the patriarchal system evolves inevitably into the industrial system, i.e., to use present-day idiom, he points out the inevitability of the development of capitalism. But it would be a great mistake to think that the utopian dreams of the participants in the movement caused Marx to adopt a negative attitude to the movement in general. Nothing of the kind. Already then, at the very beginning of his literary activity, Marx was able to extract the real and progressive content of a movement from its tawdry ideological trappings. In the second part of the criticism, entitled "The Economics [i.e., the political

---

* Recall what *Revolutsionnaya Rossiya*, beginning with issue No. 8, wrote on the passing of the land from capital to labour, on the importance of state lands in Russia, on equalised land tenure, on the bourgeois idea of drawing land into commercial transactions, etc. Precisely like Kriege!

economy]* of the *Volkstribun* and Its Attitude to Young America", Marx wrote:

"We fully recognise the historical justification of the movement of the American National Reformers. We know that this movement strives for a result which, true, would give a temporary impetus to the industrialism of modern bourgeois society, but which, as a product of the proletarian movement, and as an attack on landed property in general, especially under prevailing American conditions, must inevitably lead, by its own consequences, to communism. Kriege, who with the German Communists in New York joined the Anti-Rent *Bewegung* [movement], clothes this simple fact in bombastic phrases, without entering into the content of the movement, thereby proving that he is quite at sea as regards the connection between young America and American social conditions. We will cite another example of his outpouring of enthusiasm for humanity over the agrarians' plan for parcelling the land on an American scale.

"In issue No. 10 of the *Volkstribun*, in the article entitled 'What We Want', we read: 'The American National Reformers call the land the common heritage of all men ... and demand that the national legislature pass measures to preserve the 1,400,000,000 acres of land, not yet fallen into the hands of the grabbing speculators, as the inalienable common property of the whole of mankind.' In order to preserve for all mankind this 'inalienable common property', he accepts the plan of the National Reformers: 'to provide every peasant, whatever country he may come from, with 160 acres of American land for his subsistence'; or, as it is expressed in issue No. 14, in 'An Answer to Conze': 'Of these unappropriated public lands no one is to have a holding in excess of 160 acres, and this only provided he tills it himself.' Thus, in order to preserve the land as 'inalienable common property', and for 'the whole of mankind' besides, it is necessary immediately to begin parcelling it out. Kriege, moreover, imagines that he can

---

* Interpolations in square brackets (within passages quoted by Lenin) have been introduced by Lenin, unless otherwise indicated.—*Ed.*

rule out the necessary consequences of this allotment—concentration, industrial progress, and the like, by legislation. He regards 160 acres of land as an invariable quantity, as though the value of such an area did not vary according to its quality. The 'peasants' will have to exchange the produce of the land, if not the land itself, among themselves and with others, and, having gone thus far, they will soon find that one 'peasant', even without capital, thanks to his labour and the greater original fertility of his 160 acres, has reduced another to the position of his farm-hand. Besides, what matters it whether it is 'the land' or the produce of the land that 'falls into the hands of the grabbing speculators'? Let us seriously examine Kriege's gift to mankind. One thousand four hundred million acres are to be preserved as the 'inalienable common property of the whole of mankind', with every 'peasant' getting 160 acres. We can therefore compute the magnitude of Kriege's 'mankind': exactly 8,750,000 'peasants', who, counting five to a family, represent 43,750,000 people. We can also compute the duration of the 'for all time' during which 'the proletariat, as the representative of the whole of mankind', at least in the U.S.A., can lay claim to all the land. If the population of the U.S.A. continues to increase at its present rate, i.e., if it doubles in 25 years, then this 'for all time' will last something under 40 years; by then these 1,400,000,000 acres will have been occupied, and future generations will have nothing to 'lay claim to'. But as the free grant of land would greatly increase immigration, Kriege's 'for all time' might come to an end even sooner, particularly if it is born in mind that land for 44,000,000 people would not be an adequate outlet even for the pauperism existing in Europe today; for in Europe one out of every 10 persons is a pauper, and the British Isles alone account for 7,000,000 paupers. A similar example of naïveté in political economy is to be found in issue No. 13, in the article 'To the Women', in which Kriege says that if the city of New York gave up its 52,000 acres of land on Long Island, this would suffice to rid New York of all pauperism, misery, and crime 'at one stroke' and for ever.

"Had Kriege regarded the movement for freeing the land as an early form of the proletarian movement, necessary under certain conditions, as a movement which, by reason of the position in social life of the class from which it emanates, must necessarily develop into a communist movement; had he shown why the communist aspirations in America had to manifest themselves initially in this agrarian form, which seems to contradict all communism, there would have been nothing to object to. But he declares what is merely a subordinate form of a movement of definite, real people to be a cause of mankind in general. He represents this cause ... as the ultimate and highest aim of every movement in general, thus turning the definite aims of the movement into sheer bombastic nonsense. In the same article (issue No. 10) he continues to chant his paean: 'And so the old dreams of the Europeans would at last come true. A place would be prepared for them on this side of the ocean which they would only have to take and to fructify with the labour of their hands, so as to be able proudly to declare to all the tyrants of the world, "This is *my* cabin, which you have not built; this is *my* hearth whose glow fills your hearts with envy." '

"He might have added, This is *my* dunghill, which I, my wife, my children, my manservant, and my cattle have produced. And who are the Europeans whose 'dreams' would thus come true?- Not the communist workers, but bankrupt shopkeepers and handicraftsmen, or ruined cottars, who yearn for the good fortune of once again becoming petty bourgeois and peasants in America. And what is the 'dream' that is to be fulfilled by means of these 1,400,000,000 acres? No other than that all men be converted into private owners, a dream which is as unrealisable and as communistic as the dream to convert all men into emperors, kings, and popes."

Marx's criticism is full of caustic sarcasm. He scourges Kriege for those very aspects of his views which we now observe among our "Socialist-Revolutionaries", namely, phrase-mongering, petty-bourgeois utopias represented as the highest revolutionary utopianism, incomprehension of the real foundations of the modern economic system and its development. With remarkable penetration, Marx, who was then only the *future* economist, points to the role of exchange and commodity production. The peasants, he says, will exchange the produce of the land, if not the land itself, and that says everything! The question is dealt with in a way that is largely applicable to the Russian peasant movement and its petty-bourgeois "socialist" ideologists.

Marx, however, does not simply "repudiate" this petty-bourgeois movement, he does not dogmatically ignore it, he does not fear to soil his hands by contact with the movement of the revolutionary petty-bourgeois democrats—a fear that is characteristic of many doctrinaires. While mercilessly ridiculing the absurd ideological trappings of the movement, Marx strives in a sober, materialist manner to determine its *real* historical content, the consequences that must inevitably follow from it because of objective conditions, regardless of the will and the consciousness, the dreams and the theories, of the various individuals. Marx, therefore, does not condemn, but fully approves communist support of the movement. Adopting the dialectical standpoint, i.e., examining the movement from every aspect, taking into account both the past and the future, Marx notes the revolutionary aspect of the attack on private property in land. He recognises the petty-bourgeois movement as a peculiar initial form of the proletarian, communist movement. You will not achieve what you dream of by means of this movement, says Marx to Kriege: instead of fraternity, you will get petty-bourgeois exclusiveness; instead of inalienable peasant allotments, you will have the drawing of the land into commerce; instead of a blow at the grabbing speculators, you will witness the expansion of the basis for capitalist development. But the capitalist evil you are vainly hoping to avoid is a historical benefit, for it will accelerate social development tremendously and bring ever so much nearer new and higher forms of the communist movement. A blow struck at landed property will facilitate the inevitable further blows at property in general. The revolutionary action of the lower class for a change that will temporarily provide a restricted prosperity, and by no means for all, will facilitate the inevitable further revolutionary action of the very lowest class for a change that will really ensure complete human happiness for all toilers.

Marx's presentation of the case against Kriege should serve as a model for us Russian Social-Democrats. That the peasant movement in Russia today is of a really petty-bourgeois nature there can be no doubt. We must explain this fact by every means in our power, and we must ruthlessly and irreconcilably combat all the illusions of all the "Socialist-Revolutionaries" or primitive socialists on this score. The organisation of an independent party of the proletariat which, through all democratic upheavals, will strive for the complete socialist revolution, must be our constant aim, not to be lost sight of for a moment. But to turn away from the peasant movement for this reason would be sheer philistinism and pedantry. No, there is no doubt as to the revolutionary and democratic nature of this movement, and we must with all our might support it, develop it, make it a politically-conscious and definitely class movement, advance it, and go hand in hand with it to the end—for we go much further than the end of any peasant movement; we go to the very end of the division of society into classes. There is hardly another country in the world where the peasantry is experiencing such suffering, such oppression and degradation as in Russia. The worse this oppression has been, the more powerful will now be the peasantry's awakening, the more irresistible its revolutionary onset. The class-conscious revolutionary proletariat should support this onset with all its might, so that it may leave stand no stone of this old, accursed, feudal, autocratic, and slavish Russia; so that it may create a new generation of free and courageous people, a new republican country in which our proletarian struggle for socialism will be able freely to expand.

Vperyod No. 15,
April 20 (7), 1905

Vol. 8, pp. 323-29

PREFACE
TO THE RUSSIAN TRANSLATION OF *LETTERS*
BY JOHANNES BECKER, JOSEPH DIETZGEN,
FREDERICK ENGELS, KARL MARX, AND OTHERS
TO FRIEDRICH SORGE AND OTHERS

The collection of letters by Marx, Engels, Dietzgen, Becker and other leaders of the international working-class movement in the last century, here presented to the Russian public, is an indispensable complement to our advanced Marxist literature.

We shall not here dwell in detail on the importance of these letters for the history of socialism and for a comprehensive treatment of the activities of Marx and Engels. This aspect of the matter requires no explanation. We shall only remark that an understanding of the letters published calls for acquaintance with the principal works on the history of the International (see Jaeckh, *The International*, Russian translation in the *Znaniye* edition), and also the history of the German and the American working-class movements (see Franz Mehring, *History of German Social-Democracy*, and Morris Hillquit, *History of Socialism in the United States*), etc.

Nor do we intend here to attempt to give a general outline of the contents of this correspondence or an appreciation of the various historical periods to which it relates. Mehring has done this extremely well in his article, "Der Sorgesche Briefwechsel" (*Neue Zeit*, 25 Jahrg., Nr. 1 und 2),* which will probably be appended to the present trans-

---

* "The Sorge Correspondence", *Neue Zeit*, 25th year, Nos. 1 and 2.—*Ed.*

lation by the publisher, or else will be issued as a separate Russian publication.

Of particular interest to Russian socialists in the present revolutionary period are the lessons which the militant proletariat must draw from an acquaintance with the intimate aspects of the activities of Marx and Engels in the course of nearly thirty years (1867-95). It is, therefore, not surprising that the first attempts made in our Social-Democratic literature to acquaint readers with the letters from Marx and Engels to Sorge were also linked up with the "burning" issues of Social-Democratic tactics in the Russian revolution (Plekhanov's *Sovremennaya Zhizn* and the Menshevik *Otkliki*). And we intend to draw our readers' attention particularly to an appreciation of those passages in the published correspondence that are specially important from the viewpoint of the present tasks of the workers' party in Russia.

In their letters, Marx and Engels deal most frequently with the pressing problems of the British, American and German working-class movements. This is natural, because they were Germans who at that time lived in Britain and corresponded with their American comrade. Marx expressed himself much more frequently and in much greater detail on the French working-class movement, and particularly the Paris Commune,[5] in the letters he wrote to the German Social-Democrat Kugelmann.*

It is highly instructive to compare what Marx and Engels said of the British, American and German working-class movements. Such comparison acquires all the greater importance when we remember that Germany on the one hand, and Britain and America on the other, represent different stages of capitalist development and different forms of domination of the bourgeoisie, as a class, over the entire political life of those countries. From the scientific point of view, we have here a sample of materialist dialectics, the ability to bring to the forefront and stress the

---

* See *Letters of Karl Marx to Dr. Kugelmann*, Russian translation edited by N. Lenin, with a foreword by the editor. St. Petersburg, 1907. (See Lenin, *Collected Works*, Vol. 12, pp. 104-12.—*Ed.*)

various points, the various aspects of the problem, in application to the specific features of different political and economic conditions. From the point of view of the practical policy and tactics of the workers' party, we have here a sample of the way in which the creators of the *Communist Manifesto* defined the tasks of the fighting proletariat in accordance with the different stages of the national working-class movements in the different countries.

What Marx and Engels criticise most sharply in British and American socialism is its isolation from the working-class movement. The burden of all their numerous comments on the Social-Democratic Federation[6] in Britain and on the American socialists is the accusation that they have reduced Marxism to a dogma, to "rigid [*starre*] orthodoxy", that they consider it "a credo and not a *guide to action*",[7] that they are incapable of adapting themselves to the theoretically helpless, but living and powerful mass working-class movement that is marching alongside them. "Had we from 1864 to 1873 insisted on working together only with those who openly adopted our platform," Engels exclaimed in his letter of January 27, 1887, "where should we be today?" And in the preceding letter (December 28, 1886), he wrote, with reference to the influence of Henry George's ideas on the American working class:

"A million or two of working men's votes next November for a bona fide working men's party is worth infinitely more at present than a hundred thousand votes for a doctrinally perfect platform."

These are very interesting passages. There are Social-Democrats in our country who have hastened to utilise them in defence of the idea of a "labour congress" or something in the nature of Larin's "broad labour party".[8] Why not in defence of a "Left bloc"? we would ask these precipitate "utilisers" of Engels. The letters the quotations are taken from refer to a time when American workers voted at the elections for Henry George. Mrs. Wischnewetzky—an American woman married to a Russian and translator of Engels's works—had asked him, as may be seen from Engels's reply, to give a thorough criticism of Henry George. Engels wrote (December 28, 1886) that *the time had not yet arrived* for that, the main thing being that the workers' party should begin to organise itself, even if not on an entirely pure programme. Later on, the workers would themselves come to understand what was amiss, "would learn from their own mistakes", but "anything that might delay or prevent that national consolidation of the working men's party—on no matter what platform—I should consider a great mistake...".

It goes without saying that Engels had a perfect understanding of, and frequently mentioned, the absurdity and *reactionary character* of Henry George's ideas, from the *socialist* point of view. The Sorge correspondence contains a most interesting letter from Karl Marx dated June 20, 1881, in which he characterised Henry George as an ideologist of *the radical bourgeoisie.* "Theoretically the man is utterly backward" (*total arrière*), wrote Marx. Yet Engels was not afraid to join with this *socialist reactionary* in the elections, so long as there were people who could tell the masses of "the consequences of their own mistakes" (Engels, in the letter dated November 29, 1886).

Regarding the Knights of Labour,[9] an organisation of American workers existing at that time, Engels wrote in the same letter: "The weakest [literally: rottenest, *faulste*] side of the Knights of Labour was their *political neutrality.*... The first great step, of importance for every country newly entering into the movement, is always the constitution of the workers as an independent political party, no matter how, so long as it is a distinct workers' party."

It is obvious that from this nothing at all can be deduced in defence of a leap *from* Social-Democracy to a non-party labour congress, etc. But whoever would escape Engels's accusation of reducing Marxism to a "dogma", "orthodoxy", "sectarianism", etc., must conclude from it that a joint election campaign with radical "social-reactionaries" is sometimes permissible.

But what is more interesting, of course, is to dwell not so much on these American-Russian parallels (we had to refer to them so as to reply to our opponents), as on the *fundamental* features of the British and American working-class movements. These features are: the absence of

any big, nation-wide, *democratic* tasks facing the proletariat; the proletariat's complete subordination to bourgeois politics; the sectarian isolation of groups, of mere
handfuls of socialists, from the proletariat; not the slightest
socialist success among the working masses at the elections,
etc. Whoever forgets these fundamental conditions and
sets out to draw broad conclusions from "American-Russian
parallels", displays the greatest superficiality.

If Engels laid so much stress on the workers' economic
organisations in these conditions, it was because the most
firmly established democratic systems were under discussion, and these confronted the proletariat with purely
socialist tasks.

Engels stressed the importance of an independent workers' party, even with a poor programme, because he was
speaking of countries where there had formerly been not
even a hint of the workers' political independence and
where, in politics, the workers mostly dragged along behind
the bourgeoisie, and still do.

It would be making mock of Marx's historical method
to attempt to apply conclusions drawn from such arguments to countries or historical situations where the proletariat has formed its party prior to the liberal bourgeoisie forming theirs, where the tradition of voting for
bourgeois politicians is absolutely unknown to the proletariat, and where the immediate tasks are not socialist
but bourgeois-democratic.

Our idea will become even clearer to the reader if we
compare Engels's opinions on the British and American
movements with his opinions on the German movement.

Such opinions, of the greatest interest, abound in the
published correspondence too. And running like a scarlet
thread through all these opinions is something vastly
different—a warning against the "Right wing" of the workers' party, a merciless (sometimes—as with Marx in 1877-
79—a *furious*) war against *opportunism* in Social-Democracy.

Let us first corroborate this by quoting from the letters,
and then proceed to an appraisal of this fact.

First of all, we must here note the opinions expressed

by Marx on Höchberg and Co. In his article "Der Sorgesche Briefwechsel", Franz Mehring attempts to tone down Marx's attacks—as well as Engels's later attacks—against the opportunists and, in our opinion, rather overdoes it. As regards Höchberg and Co., in particular, Mehring insists on his view that Marx's judgement of Lassalle and the Lassalleans[10] was wrong. But, we repeat, what interests us here is not an historical assessment of whether Marx's attacks against particular socialists were correct or exaggerated, but Marx's assessment *in principle* of definite *trends* in socialism in general.

While complaining about the German Social-Democrats' compromises with the Lassalleans and Dühring (letter of October 19, 1877), Marx also condemns the compromise "with a whole gang of half-mature students and superwise diploma'd doctors [in German "doctor" is an academic degree corresponding to our "candidate" or "university graduate, class I"], who want to give socialism a 'higher, idealistic' orientation, that is to say, to replace its materialistic basis (which demands serious objective study from anyone who tries to use it) by modern mythology with its goddesses of Justice, Liberty, Equality, and Fraternity. Dr. Höchberg, who publishes the *Zukunft*, is a representative of this tendency, and has 'bought his way' into the Party—with the 'noblest' intentions, I assume, but I do not give a damn for 'intentions'. Anything more miserable than his programme of the *Zukunft* has seldom seen the light of day with more 'modest presumption'." (Letter No. 70.)

In another letter, written almost two years later (September 19, 1879), Marx rebutted the gossip that Engels and he stood behind *J. Most*, and gave Sorge a detailed account of his attitude towards the opportunists in the German Social-Democratic Party. *Zukunft* was run by Höchberg, Schramm and Eduard Bernstein. Marx and Engels *refused* to have anything to do with such a publication, and when the question was raised of establishing a new Party organ with the participation of this same Höchberg and with his financial assistance, Marx and Engels first demanded the acceptance of their nominee, Hirsch, as editor-in-chief, to exercise control over this "mixture of doctors, students and

Katheder-Socialists", and then addressed a circular letter directly to Bebel, Liebknecht and other leaders of the Social-Democratic Party, warning them that they would openly combat "such a vulgarisation [*Verluderung—an even stronger* word in German] of Party and theory", if the Höchberg, Schramm and Bernstein trend did not change.

This was the period in the German Social-Democratic Party which Mehring described in his *History*[11] as "A Year of Confusion" ("Ein Jahr der Verwirrung"). After the Anti-Socialist Law,[12] the Party did not at once find the right path, first swinging over to the anarchism of Most and the opportunism of Höchberg and Co. "These people," Marx wrote of the latter, "nonentities in theory and useless in practice, want to draw the teeth of socialism (which they have fixed up in accordance with the university recipes) and particularly of the Social-Democratic Party, to enlighten the workers or, as they put it, to imbue them with 'elements of education' from their confused half-knowledge, and above all to make the Party respectable in the eyes of the petty bourgeoisie. They are just wretched counter-revolutionary windbags."[13]

The result of Marx's "furious" attack was that the opportunists retreated and—made themselves scarce. In a letter dated November 19, 1879, Marx announced that Höchberg had been removed from the editorial committee and that all the influential leaders of the Party—Bebel, Liebknecht, Bracke, etc.—had *repudiated* his ideas. *Sozial-Demokrat,* the Social-Democratic Party organ, began to appear under the editorship of Vollmar, who at that time belonged to the revolutionary wing of the Party. A year later (November 5, 1880), Marx related that he and Engels constantly fought the "miserable" way in which *Sozial-Demokrat* was being conducted, and often expressed their opinion *sharply ("wobei's oft scharf hergeht")*. Liebknecht visited Marx in 1880 and promised that there would be an "improvement" *in all respects*.

Peace was restored, and the war never came out into the open. Höchberg withdrew, and Bernstein became a revolutionary Social-Democrat—at least until the death of Engels in 1895.

On June 20, 1882, Engels wrote to Sorge and spoke of this struggle as being a thing of the past: "In general, things in Germany are going splendidly. It is true that the literary gentlemen in the Party tried to cause a reactionary ... swing, but they failed miserably. The abuse to which the Social-Democratic workers are being everywhere subjected has made them still more revolutionary than they were three years ago.... These people [the Party literary people] wanted at all costs to beg and secure the repeal of the Anti-Socialist Law by mildness and meekness, fawning and humility, because it has made short shrift of their literary earnings. As soon as the law is repealed ... the split will apparently become an open one, and the Viereck and Höchbergs will form a separate Right wing, where they can, from time to time, be treated with, until they finally land on their backsides. We announced this immediately after the adoption of the Anti-Socialist Law, when Höchberg and Schramm published in the *Yearbook* what was a most infamous judgement of the work of the Party and demanded more cultivated [*"jebildetes"* instead of *gebildetes*—Engels is alluding to the Berlin accent of the German writers], refined and elegant behaviour of the Party."

This forecast of Bernsteinism,[14] made in 1882, was strikingly confirmed in 1898 and subsequent years.

And after that, and particularly after Marx's death, Engels, it may be said without exaggeration, was untiring in his efforts to straighten out what was being distorted by the German opportunists.

The end of 1884. The "petty-bourgeois prejudices" of the German Social-Democratic Reichstag deputies, who had voted for the steamship subsidy[15] ("Dampfersubvention", see Mehring's *History*), were condemned. Engels informed Sorge that he had to correspond a great deal on this subject (letter of December 31, 1884).

1885. Giving his opinion of the whole affair of the "Dampfersubvention", Engels wrote (June 3) that "it almost came to a split". The "philistinism" of the Social-Democratic deputies was *"colossal"*. "A petty-bourgeois socialist parliamentary group is inevitable in a country like Germany," said Engels.

1887. Engels replied to Sorge, who had written to him, that the Party was disgracing itself by electing such deputies as Viereck (a Social-Democrat of the Höchberg type). Engels excused himself, saying that there was nothing to be done, the workers' party could not find good deputies for the Reichstag. "The gentlemen of the Right wing know that they are being tolerated only because of the Anti-Socialist Law, and that they will be thrown out of the Party the very day the Party again secures freedom of action." And, in general, it was preferable that "the Party should be better than its parliamentary heroes, than the other way round" (March 3, 1887). Liebknecht is a conciliator—Engels complained—he always uses phrases to gloss over differences. But when it comes to a split, he will be with us at the decisive moment.

1889. Two international Social-Democratic congresses in Paris.[16] The opportunists (headed by the French Possibilists[17]) split away from the revolutionary Social-Democrats. Engels (who was then sixty-eight years old) flung himself into the fight with the ardour of youth. A number of letters (from January 12 to July 20, 1889) were devoted to the fight against the opportunists. Not only they, but also the Germans—Liebknecht, Bebel and others—were flagellated for their conciliatory attitude.

The Possibilists had sold themselves to the French Government, Engels wrote on January 12, 1889. And he accused the members of the British Social-Democratic Federation (S.D.F.) of having allied themselves with the Possibilists. "The writing and running about in connection with this damned congress leave me no time for anything else" (May 11, 1889). The Possibilists are busy, but our people are asleep, Engels wrote angrily. Now even Auer and Schippel are demanding that we attend the Possibilist congress. But "at last" this opened Liebknecht's eyes. Engels, together with Bernstein, wrote pamphlets (they were signed by Bernstein but Engels called them "our pamphlets") against the opportunists.

"With the exception of the S.D.F., the Possibilists have not a single socialist organisation on their side in the whole of Europe. [June 8, 1889.] They are consequently falling

back on the non-socialist trade unions" (this for the information of those who advocate a broad labour party, a labour congress, etc., in our country!). "From America they
will get one *Knight of Labour*." The   adversary was the
same as in the fight against the Bakuninists[18]: "only with
this difference that the banner of the anarchists has been
replaced by the banner of the Possibilists: the selling of
principles to the bourgeoisie for small-scale concessions,
especially in return for well-paid jobs for the leaders (on
the city councils, labour exchanges, etc.)." Brousse (the
leader of the Possibilists) and Hyndman (the leader of the
S.D.F. which had joined with the Possibilists) attacked
"authoritarian Marxism" and wanted to form the "nucleus
of a new International".

"You can have no idea of the naïveté of the Germans.
It has cost me tremendous effort to explain even to Bebel
what it all really meant" (June 8, 1889). And when the
two congresses met, when the revolutionary Social-Democrats outnumbered the Possibilists *(who had united with
the trade-unionists,* the S.D.F., a section of the Austrians,
etc.), Engels was jubilant (July 17, 1889). He was glad that
the conciliatory plans and proposals of Liebknecht and
others had failed (July 20, 1889). "It serves our sentimental
conciliatory brethren right that, for all their amicableness,
they received a good kick in their tenderest spot. This may
cure them for some time."

... Mehring was right when he said ("Der Sorgesche
Briefwechsel") that Marx and Engels did not have much
idea of "good manners": "If they did not think long over
every blow they dealt, neither did they whimper over every
blow they received." "If they think their needle pricks can
pierce my old, thick and well-tanned hide, they are mistaken,"[19] Engels once wrote. And they assumed that others
possessed the imperviousness they had themselves acquired,
Mehring said of Marx and Engels.

1893. The chastisement of the Fabians,[20] which suggests
itself when passing judgement on the Bernsteinians (for
did not Bernstein "evolve" his opportunism in England making use of the experience of the Fabians?). "The Fabians
here in London are a band of careerists who have under-

standing enough to realise the inevitability of the social
revolution, but who could not possibly entrust this gigantic
task to the raw proletariat alone, and are therefore kind
enough to set themselves at the head. Fear of the revolution is their fundamental principle. They are the 'educated'
par excellence. Their socialism is municipal socialism; not
the nation but the community is to become the owner of
the means of production, at any rate for the time being.
This socialism of theirs is then presented as an extreme but
inevitable consequence of bourgeois liberalism; hence their
tactics, not of decisively opposing the Liberals as adversar-
ies but of pushing them on towards socialist conclusions
and therefore of intriguing with them, of permeating liberalism with socialism—not of putting up socialist candidates
against the Liberals but of fastening them on to the Liberals, forcing them upon the Liberals, or getting them in
by cheating. They do not of course realise that in doing
this they are either lied to and themselves deceived or else
are lying about socialism.

"With great industry they have published, amid all sorts
of rubbish, some good propagandist writing as well, this in
fact being the best the English have produced in this field.
But as soon as they get on to their specific tactics of hush-
ing up the class struggle, it all turns putrid. Hence their
fanatical hatred of Marx and all of us—because of the
class struggle.

"These people have of course many bourgeois followers
and therefore money...."[21]

HOW THE CLASSICS ESTIMATED
INTELLECTUALIST OPPORTUNISM IN SOCIAL-DEMOCRACY

1894. The Peasant Question. "On the Continent," Engels
wrote on November 10, 1894, "success is developing the appetite for more success, and catching the peasant, in the
literal sense of the word, is becoming the fashion. First
the French, in Nantes, declare through Lafargue not
only ... that it is not our business to hasten ... the ruin
of the small peasants, which capitalism is seeing to for
us, but they add that we must directly protect the small

peasant against taxation, usury, and landlords. But we cannot co-operate in this, first because it is stupid and second because it is impossible. Next, however, Vollmar comes along in Frankfort and wants to bribe the *peasantry as a whole,* though the peasant he has to deal with in Upper Bavaria is not the debt-ridden small peasant of the Rhineland, but the middle and even the big peasant, who exploits male and female farm-hands, and sells cattle and grain in quantity. And that cannot be done without giving up the whole principle."

1894, December 4. ". . . The Bavarians, who have become very, very opportunistic and have almost turned into an ordinary people's party (that is to say, the majority of leaders and many of those who have recently joined the Party), voted in the Bavarian Diet for the budget as a whole; and Vollmar in particular has started an agitation among the peasants with the object of winning the Upper Bavarian big peasants—people who own 25 to 80 acres of land (10 to 30 hectares) and who therefore cannot manage without wage-labourers—instead of winning their farm-hands."

We thus see that for more than ten years Marx and Engels systematically and unswervingly fought opportunism in the German Social-Democratic Party, and attacked intellectualist philistinism and the petty-bourgeois outlook in socialism. This is an extremely important fact. The general public know that German Social-Democracy is regarded as a model of Marxist proletarian policy and tactics, but they do not know what constant warfare the founders of Marxism had to wage against the "Right wing" (Engels's expression) of that Party. And it is no accident that soon after Engels's death this concealed war became an open one. This was an inevitable result of the decades of historical development of German Social-Democracy.

And now we very clearly perceive the two lines of Engels's (and Marx's) recommendations, directions, corrections, threats and exhortations. The most insistent of their appeals to the British and American socialists was to merge with the working-class movement and eradicate the narrow and hidebound sectarian spirit from their organisations.

They were most insistent in teaching the German Social-Democrats to beware of succumbing to philistinism, "parliamentary idiocy" (Marx's expression in the letter of September 19, 1879), and petty-bourgeois intellectualist opportunism.

Is it not typical that our Social-Democratic gossips should have begun cackling about the recommendations of the first kind while remaining silent, holding their tongues, about the second? Is not *such* one-sidedness in appraising the letters of Marx and Engels the best indication of a certain Russian Social-Democratic ... "one-sidedness"?

At the present moment, when the international working-class movement is displaying symptoms of profound ferment and vacillation, when the extremes of opportunism, "parliamentary idiocy" and philistine reformism have evoked the other extremes of revolutionary syndicalism—the general line of Marx's and Engels's "corrections" to British and American and to German socialism acquires exceptional importance.

In countries where there are *no* Social-Democratic workers' parties, *no* Social-Democratic members of parliament, and *no* systematic and steadfast Social-Democratic policy either at elections or in the press, etc.—in such countries, Marx and Engels taught the socialists to rid themselves *at all costs* of narrow sectarianism, and *to join* with the working-class movement so as *to shake up* the proletariat *politically*. For in the last thirty years of the nineteenth century the proletariat displayed *almost no* political independence either in Britain or America. In these countries—where bourgeois-democratic historical tasks were almost entirely non-existent—the political arena was *completely* held by a triumphant and self-satisfied bourgeoisie, unequalled anywhere in the world in the art of deceiving, corrupting and bribing the workers.

To think that these recommendations, made by Marx and Engels to the British and American working-class movements, can be simply and directly applied to Russian conditions is to use Marxism not in order to achieve clarity on its *method,* not in order *to study* the concrete historical features of the working-class movement in definite countries, but in order to pay off petty, factional, and intellectualist scores.

On the other hand, in a country where the bourgeois-democratic revolution was still unconsummated, where "military despotism, embellished with parliamentary forms" (Marx's expression in his *Critique of the Gotha Programme*), prevailed, and still does, where the proletariat had long ago been drawn into politics and was pursuing a Social-Democratic policy—in such a country what Marx and Engels most of all feared was parliamentary vulgarisation and philistine derogation of the tasks and scope of the working-class movement.

It is all the more our duty to emphasise and give prominence to *this* side of Marxism, in the period of the bourgeois-democratic revolution in Russia, because in our country a vast, "brilliant" and rich liberal-bourgeois press is vociferously trumpeting to the proletariat the "exemplary"loyalty, parliamentary legality, the modesty and moderation of the neighbouring German working-class movement.

This mercenary lie of the bourgeois betrayers of the Russian revolution is not due to accident or to the personal depravity of certain past or future ministers in the Cadet* camp. It stems from the profound economic interests of the Russian liberal landlords and liberal bourgeois. And in combating this lie, this "stupefying of the masses" (*"Massenverdummung"*—Engels's expression in his letter of November 29, 1886), the letters of Marx and Engels should serve as an indispensable weapon for all Russian socialists.

The mercenary lie of the liberal bourgeois holds up to the people the exemplary "modesty" of the German Social-Democrats. The leaders of these Social-Democrats, the founders of the theory of Marxism, tell us:

"The revolutionary language and action of the French have made the hypocrisy of Viereck and Co. [the opportunist Social-Democrats in the German Reichstag Social-Democratic group] sound quite feeble" (this was said in ref-

---

* See Note 34.—*Ed.*

erence to the formation of a labour group in the French
Chamber and to the Decazeville strike, which split the
French Radicals from the French proletariat[22]). "Only
Liebknecht and Bebel spoke in the last socialist debate and
both of them spoke well. We can with this debate once
more show ourselves in decent society, which was by no
means the case with all of them. In general it is a good
thing that the Germans' leadership of the international socialist movement, particularly after they sent so many philistines to the Reichstag (which, it is true, was unavoida-
ble), is being challenged. *In Germany everything becomes
philistine in peaceful times*; and therefore the sting of
French competition is *absolutely necessary....*" (Letter of
April 29, 1886.)

These are the lessons to be learnt most thoroughly by
the Russian Social-Democratic Labour Party, which is predominantly under the ideological influence of German Social-Democracy.

These lessons are taught us not by any particular passage in the correspondence of the greatest men of the nineteenth century, but by the whole spirit and substance of
their comradely and frank criticism of the international experience of the proletariat, a criticism to which diplomacy
and petty considerations were alien.

How far all the letters of Marx and Engels were indeed
imbued with this spirit may also be seen from the following relatively specific but extremely typical passages.

In 1889 a young and fresh movement of untrained and
unskilled labourers (gas-workers, dockers, etc.) arose in
Britain, a movement marked by a new and revolutionary
spirit. Engels was delighted with it. He referred exultingly
to the part played by Tussy, Marx's daughter, who conducted agitation among these workers. "...The most re-
pulsive thing here," he says, writing from London on December 7, 1889, "is the bourgeois 'respectability' which has
grown deep into the bones of the workers. The division of
society into innumerable strata, each recognised without
question, each with its own pride but also its inborn respect for its 'betters' and 'superiors', is so old and firmly
established that the bourgeois still find it fairly easy to

get their bait accepted. I am not at all sure, for instance, that John Burns is not secretly prouder of his popularity with Cardinal Manning, the Lord Mayor, and the bourgeoisie in general than of his popularity with his own class. And Champion—an ex-lieutenant—intrigued years ago with bourgeois and especially with conservative elements, preached socialism at the parsons' Church Congress, etc. And even Tom Mann, whom I regard as the best of the lot, is fond of mentioning that he will be lunching with the Lord Mayor. If one compares this with the French, one realises what a revolution is good for after all."

No comment is needed.

Another example. In 1891 there was danger of a European war. Engels corresponded on the subject with Bebel, and they agreed that in the event of Russia attacking Germany, the German socialists must desperately fight the Russians and any allies of the Russians. "If Germany is crushed, then we shall be too, while at best the struggle will be such a violent one that Germany will only be able to maintain herself by revolutionary means, so that very possibly we shall be forced to take the helm and stage a 1793." (Letter of October 24, 1891.)

Let this be noted by those opportunists[23] who shouted from the house-tops that "Jacobin" prospects for the Russian workers' party in 1905 were un-Social-Democratic! Engels squarely suggested to Bebel the possibility of the Social-Democrats having to participate in a provisional government.

Holding such views on the tasks of Social-Democratic workers' parties, Marx and Engels naturally possessed the most fervent faith in a Russian revolution and its great world significance. We see this ardent expectation of a revolution in Russia, in this correspondence, over a period of nearly twenty years.

Take Marx's letter of September 27, 1877. He is quite enthusiastic about the Eastern crisis[24]: "Russia has long been standing on the threshold of an upheaval, all the elements of it are prepared.... The gallant Turks have hastened the explosion by years with the thrashing they have inflicted.... The upheaval will begin *secundum artem* [according to the rules of the art] with some *playing at con-stitutionalism, et puis il y aura un beau tapage* [and then there will be a fine row]. If Mother Nature is not particularly unfavourable towards us, we shall yet live to see the fun!" (Marx was then fifty-nine years old.)

Mother Nature did not—and could not very well—permit Marx to live "to see the fun". But he *foretold* the "playing at constitutionalism", and it is as though his words were written yesterday in relation to the First and Second Russian Dumas.[25] And we know that the warning to the people against "playing at constitutionalism" was the "living soul" of the boycott tactics so detested by the liberals and opportunists....

Or take Marx's letter of November 5, 1880. He was delighted with the success of *Capital* in Russia, and took the part of the members of the Narodnaya Volya organisation against the newly-arisen General Redistribution group.[26] Marx correctly perceived the anarchistic elements in their views. Not knowing and having then no opportunity of knowing the future evolution of the General Redistribution Narodniks into Social-Democrats, Marx attacked them with all his trenchant sarcasm:

"These gentlemen are against all political-revolutionary action. Russia is to make a somersault into the anarchist-communist-atheist millennium! Meanwhile, they are preparing for this leap with the most tedious doctrinairism, whose so-called *principes courent la rue depuis le feu Bakounine*."

We can gather from this how Marx would have appreciated the significance for Russia of 1905 and the succeeding years of *Social-Democracy's* "political-revolutionary action".*

There is a letter by Engels dated April 6, 1887: "On the other hand, it seems as if a crisis is impending in Russia.

---

* Incidentally, if my memory does not deceive me, Plekhanov or V. I. Zasulich told me in 1900-03 about the existence of a letter from Engels to Plekhanov concerning *Our Differences* and the character of the impending revolution in Russia. It would be interesting to know exactly whether there was such a letter, whether it still exists, and whether the time has come to publish it.[27]

The recent attentates rather upset the apple-cart. . . ." A letter of April 9, 1887, says the same thing. . . . "The army is full of discontented, conspiring officers. [Engels at that time was impressed by the revolutionary struggle of the Narodnaya Volya organisation; he set his hopes on the officers, and did not yet see the revolutionary spirit of the Russian soldiers and sailors, which was manifested so magnificently eighteen years later. . . .] I do not think things will last another year; and once it [the revolution] breaks out [*losgeht*] in Russia, then hurrah!"

A letter of April 23, 1887: "In Germany there is persecution after persecution [of socialists]. It looks as if Bismarck wants to have everything ready, so that the moment the revolution breaks out [*losgeschlagen werden*] in Russia, which is now only a question of months, Germany could immediately follow her example."

The months proved to be very, very long ones. No doubt, philistines will be found who, knitting their brows and wrinkling their foreheads, will sternly condemn Engels's "revolutionism", or will indulgently laugh at the old utopias of the old revolutionary exile.

Yes, Marx and Engels made many and frequent mistakes in determining the proximity of revolution, in their hopes in the victory of revolution (e.g., in 1848 in Germany), in their faith in the imminence of a German "republic" ("to die for the republic", wrote Engels of that period, recalling his sentiments as a participant in the military campaign for a Reich constitution in 1848-49[28]). They were mistaken in 1871 when they were engaged in "raising revolt in Southern France, for which they [Becker writes "we", referring to himself and his closest friends: letter No. 14 of July 21, 1871] sacrificed and risked all that was humanly possible. . .". The same letter says: "If we had had more means in March and April we would have roused the whole of Southern France and would have saved the Commune in Paris" (p. 29). But *such* errors—the errors of the giants of revolutionary thought, who sought to raise, and did raise, the proletariat of the whole world above the level of petty, commonplace and trivial tasks—are a thousand times more noble and magnificent and *histori-*

cally more valuable and true than the trite wisdom of official liberalism, which lauds, shouts, appeals and holds forth about the vanity of revolutionary vanities, the futility of the revolutionary struggle and the charms of counter-revolutionary "constitutional" fantasies. . . .

The Russian working class will win their freedom and give an impetus to Europe by their revolutionary action, full though it be of errors—and let the philistines pride themselves on the infallibility of their revolutionary inaction.

April 6, 1907

Written on April 6 (19), 1907

Published in 1907 in the book   Vol. 12, pp. 360-78
*Letters by Johannes Becker, Joseph
Dietzgen, Frederick Engels, Karl Marx,
and Others to Friedrich Sorge and
Others.* Published by P. G. Dauge,
St. Petersburg
Signed: *N. Lenin*

THE AGRARIAN PROGRAMME OF SOCIAL-DEMOCRACY IN THE FIRST RUSSIAN REVOLUTION, 1905-07

(Excerpts)

In Volume III of *Capital* (2. Teil, S. 156) Marx had already pointed out that the form of landed property with which the incipient capitalist mode of production is confronted *does not suit* capitalism. Capitalism *creates for itself* the required forms of agrarian relationships out of the old forms, out of feudal landed property, peasants' commune property, clan property, etc. In that chapter, Marx compares the *different methods* by which capital creates the required forms of landed property. In Germany the reshaping of the medieval forms of landed property proceeded in a reformative way, so to speak. It adapted itself to routine, to tradition, to the feudal estates that were slowly converted into Junker estates, to the routine of indolent peasants* who were undergoing the difficult transition from corvée to the condition of the Knecht and Grossbauer. In Britain this reshaping proceeded in a revolutionary, violent way; but the violence was practised for the benefit of the landlords, it was practised on the masses of the peasants, who were taxed to exhaustion, driven from the villages, evicted, and who died out, or emigrated. In America this reshaping went on in a violent way as regards the slave farms in the Southern States. There violence was applied against the slave-owning landlords. Their estates were broken up, and the large feudal estates were

---

* Cf. *Theorien über den Mehrwert*, II. Band, 1. Teil, S. 280; the condition for the capitalist mode of production in agriculture is "the substitution of a businessman [*Geschäftsmann*] for the indolent peasant".

transformed into small bourgeois farms.* As regards the
mass of "unappropriated" American lands, this role of
creating the new agrarian relationships to suit the new
mode of production (i.e., capitalism) was played by the
"American General Redistribution", by the Anti-Rent movement (*Anti-Rent-Bewegung*) of the forties, the Homestead Act.[29] etc. When, in 1846, Hermann Kriege, a German Communist, advocated the equal redistribution of the
land in America, Marx ridiculed the Socialist-Revolutionary prejudices and the petty-bourgeois theory of this qua-
si-socialism, but he *appreciated* the historical importance
of the American movement *against landed property*,** as a
movement which in a progressive way expressed the interests of the development of the productive forces and the
interests of capitalism in America.

7. UNDER WHAT CONDITIONS CAN NATIONALISATION BE BROUGHT ABOUT?

The view is often met with among Marxists that nationalisation is feasible only at a high stage of development
of capitalism, when it will have fully prepared the conditions for "divorcing the landowners from agriculture" (by
means of renting and mortgages). It is assumed that large-
scale capitalist farming must have *already* established itself
before nationalisation of the land, which cuts out rent with-

----

* See Kautsky's *Agrarian Question* (p. 132, et seq. of the German
text) concerning the growth of the small farms in the American South
as a result of the abolition of slavery.
** *Vperyod*, 1905, No. 15 (Geneva, April 7/20), article "Marx on the
American 'General Redistribution' ". (See pp. 13-19.—*Ed.*) (Second
volume of Mehring's *Collected Works of Marx and Engels*.) "We fully
recognise," wrote Marx in 1846, "the historical justification of the
movement of the American National Reformers. We know that this
movement strives for a result which, true, would give a temporary
impetus to the industrialism of modern bourgeois society, but which,
as a product of the proletarian movement, and as an attack on landed
property in general, especially under prevailing American conditions, must inevitably lead, by its own consequences, to communism.
Kriege, who with the German Communists in New York joined the
Anti-Rent *Bewegung* [movement], clothes this simple fact in bombastic
phrases, without entering into the content of the movement."

out affecting the economic organism, can be brought about.*

Is this view correct? Theoretically it cannot be substantiated; it cannot be supported by direct references to Marx; the facts of experience speak against it rather than for it.

Theoretically, nationalisation is the "ideally" pure development of capitalism in agriculture. The question whether such a combination of conditions and such a relation of forces as would permit of nationalisation in capitalist society often occur in history is another matter. But nationalisation is not only an effect of, but also a condition for, the rapid development of capitalism. To think that nationalisation is possible only at a very high stage of development of capitalism in agriculture means, if anything, the repudiation of nationalisation as a measure of *bourgeois* progress; for everywhere the high development of agricultural capitalism has already placed on the order of the day (and will in time inevitably place on the order of the day in other countries) the "socialisation of agricultural production", i.e., the socialist revolution. No measure of bourgeois progress, as a bourgeois measure, is conceivable when the class struggle between the proletariat and the bourgeoisie is very acute. Such a measure is more likely in a "young" bourgeois society, which has not yet developed its strength, has not yet developed its contradictions to the full, and has not yet created a proletariat strong enough to strive directly towards the socialist revolution. And Marx allowed the possibility of, and sometimes directly advocated, the nationalisation of the land, not only in the epoch of the bourgeois revolution in Germany in 1848, but also in 1846 for America, which, as he most accurately pointed out at that time, was only *just starting* her "industrial" development. The experience of

* Here is one of the most exact expressions of this view uttered by Comrade Borisov, an advocate of the division of the land: "...Eventually, it [the demand for the nationalisation of the land] will be put forward by history; it will be put forward when petty-bourgeois farming has degenerated, when capitalism has gained strong positions in agriculture, and when Russia will no longer be a peasant country" (Minutes of the Stockholm Congress, p. 127).[30]

various capitalist countries gives us no example of the nationalisation of the land in anything like its pure form. We
see something similar to it in New Zealand, a young capitalist democracy, where there is no evidence of highly
developed agricultural capitalism. Something similar to it
existed in America when the government passed the Homestead Act and distributed plots of land to small farmers at a nominal rent.

No. To associate nationalisation with the epoch of highly
developed capitalism means repudiating it as a measure of
bourgeois progress; and such a repudiation directly contradicts economic theory. It seems to me that in the following argument in *Theories of Surplus Value*, Marx outlines conditions for the achievement of nationalisation *other
than* those usually presumed.

After pointing out that the landowner is an absolutely
superfluous figure in capitalist production, that the purpose of the latter is "fully answered" if the land belongs
to the state, Marx goes on to say:

"That is why in theory the radical bourgeois arrives at
the repudiation of private landed property.... In practice,
however, he lacks courage, since the attack on one form
of property, private property in relation to the conditions
of labour, would be very dangerous for the other form.
Moreover, the bourgeois has territorialised himself." (*Theorien über den Mehrwert*, II. Band, 1. Teil, S. 208.)

Marx does not mention here, as an obstacle to the
achievement of nationalisation, the undeveloped state of
capitalism in agriculture. He mentions *two* other obstacles,
which speak much more strongly in favour of the idea of
achieving nationalisation in the epoch of *bourgeois revolution*.

First obstacle: the radical bourgeois *lacks the courage* to
attack private landed property owing to the danger of a
socialist attack on all private property, i.e., the danger of
a socialist revolution.

Second obstacle: "The bourgeois has territorialised himself." Evidently, what Marx has in mind is that the bourgeois mode of production has already entrenched itself in
private landed property, i.e., that this private property

has become far more bourgeois than feudal. When the bourgeoisie, as a class, *has already* become bound up with landed property on a broad, predominating scale, *has already* "territorialised itself", "settled on the land", fully subordinated landed property to itself, then a genuine *social* movement of the bourgeoisie in favour of nationalisation is *impossible*. It is impossible for the simple reason that no class ever goes against itself.

Broadly speaking, these two obstacles are removable *only* in the epoch of rising and not of declining capitalism, in the epoch of the *bourgeois* revolution, and not on the eve of the socialist revolution. The view that nationalisation is feasible only at a high stage of development of capitalism cannot be called Marxist. It contradicts both the general premises of Marx's theory and his words as quoted above. It *oversimplifies* the question of the historically concrete conditions under which nationalisation is brought about by such-and-such forces and classes, and reduces it to a schematic and bare abstraction.

The "radical bourgeois" *cannot* be *courageous* in the epoch of strongly developed capitalism. In such an epoch this bourgeoisie, in the mass, is inevitably counter-revolutionary. In such an epoch the almost complete "territorialisation" of the bourgeoisie is already inevitable. In the epoch of bourgeois revolution, however, the *objective* conditions compel the "radical bourgeois" to be courageous; for, in solving the historical problem of the given period, the bourgeoisie, as a class, cannot yet fear the *proletarian* revolution. In the epoch of bourgeois revolution the bourgeoisie has *not yet territorialised itself*: landownership is still too much steeped in feudalism in such an epoch. The phenomenon of the *mass* of the bourgeois farmers fighting against the *principal* forms of landownership and therefore arriving at the practical achievement of the *complete* bourgeois "liberation of the land", i.e., *nationalisation,* becomes possible.

Written November-December 1907

First published in 1908 (confiscated);
published in 1917 as a separate book
by the Zhizn i Znaniye Publishers

Vol. 13, pp. 275-76
and 318-21

THE AGRARIAN QUESTION IN RUSSIA
TOWARDS THE CLOSE
OF THE NINETEENTH CENTURY

(Excerpt)

The two ways I have indicated of "solving" the agrarian question in developing bourgeois Russia correspond to the two paths of development of capitalism in agriculture. I call these two paths the Prussian and the American paths. The characteristic feature of the first is that medieval relations in landowning are not liquidated at one stroke, but are gradually adapted to capitalism, which because of this for a long time retains semi-feudal features. Prussian landlordism was not crushed by the bourgeois revolution; it survived and became the basis of "Junker" economy, which is essentially capitalistic, but involves a certain degree of dependence of the rural population, such as the *Gesinde-ordnung*,* etc. As a consequence, the social and political domination of the Junkers was consolidated for many decades after 1848, and the productive forces of German agriculture developed far more slowly than in America. There, on the contrary, it was not the old slave-holding economy of the big landowners that became the basis of capitalist agriculture (the Civil War smashed the slave-owners' estates), but the free economy of the free farmer working on free land—free from all medieval fetters, from serfdom and feudalism on the one hand, and from the fetters of private property in land, on the other. Land was given away in America, out of its vast resources, at a nominal price; and it is only on a new, fully capitalist basis that private property in land has now developed there.

First published in 1918 as a separate pamphlet by the Zhizn i Znaniye Publishers

Vol. 15, pp. 139-40

---

* Regulation for Servants.—*Ed.*

INFLAMMABLE MATERIAL IN WORLD POLITICS
(Excerpt)

The sharpening of the struggle between the proletariat and the bourgeoisie is to be observed in all the advanced capitalist countries. The tendency is the same everywhere, though it manifests itself differently in accordance with the difference in historical conditions, political systems and forms of the labour movement. In America and Britain, where complete political liberty exists and where the proletariat has no revolutionary and socialist traditions that could be called living traditions, this sharpening of the struggle is expressed in the mounting movement against the trusts, in the extraordinary growth of socialism and the increasing attention it is getting from the propertied classes, and in workers' organisations, in some cases purely economic ones, that are beginning to enter upon systematic and independent proletarian political struggle. In Austria and Germany, and partly also in the Scandinavian countries, this sharpening of the class struggle shows itself in election campaigns, in party relationships, in the closer alignment of the bourgeoisie of all sorts and shades against their common enemy, the proletariat, and in the hardening of judicial and police persecution. Slowly but surely, the two opposing camps are building up their strength, consolidating their organisations, drawing apart with increasing sharpness in every sphere of public life, as if preparing, silently and intently, for the impending revolutionary battles. In the Latin countries, Italy and particularly France, the sharpening of the class struggle is expressed in especially stormy, violent, and occasionally forthright revolutionary outbreaks, when the pent-up hatred of

the proletariat for its oppressors bursts out with unexpect-
ed force, and the "peaceful" atmosphere of parliamentary
struggle gives way to episodes of real civil war.

The international revolutionary movement of the proletariat does not and cannot develop evenly and in identical
forms in different countries. The full and all-round utilisation of every opportunity in every field of activity comes
only as the result of the class struggle of the workers in
the various countries. Every country contributes its own
valuable and specific features to the common stream; but
in each particular country the movement suffers from its
own one-sidedness, its own theoretical and practical shortcomings of the individual socialist parties. On the whole we
clearly see a tremendous step forward of international socialism, the rallying of million-strong armies of the proletariat in the course of a series of practical clashes with the
enemy, and the approach of a decisive struggle with the
bourgeoisie—a struggle for which the working class is far
better *prepared* than in the days of the Commune, that last
great proletarian insurrection.

Proletary No. 33,   Vol. 15, pp. 186-87
July 23 (August 5), 1908

THE SUCCESSES OF THE AMERICAN WORKERS

The latest issue of the American labour weekly, *Appeal to Reason*,[31] received in Europe reports that its circulation has increased to 984,000 copies. The letters and demands coming in—writes the editor (No. 875, September 7, new style)—indicate beyond doubt that we shall exceed one million copies in the next few weeks.

This figure—a million copies of a socialist weekly which American courts harass and persecute shamelessly and which is growing and gaining strength under the fire of persecution—shows more clearly than long arguments the kind of revolution that is approaching in America.

Not long ago the sycophantic *Novoye Vremya*,[32] a mouthpiece of venal hacks, wrote about the "power of money" in America, relating with malicious joy the facts about the monstrous venality of Taft, Roosevelt, Wilson and, indeed, *all* presidential candidates put up by the bourgeois parties. Here is a free, democratic republic for you, hissed the venal Russian newspaper.

The class-conscious workers will reply to that calmly and proudly: we have no illusions about the significance of broad democracy. No democracy in the world can eliminate the class struggle and the omnipotence of money. It is not this that makes democracy important and useful. The importance of democracy is that it makes the class struggle broad, open and conscious. And this is not a conjecture or a wish, but a fact.

At a time when the membership of the German Social-Democratic Party has grown to 970,000 and when the circulation of an American socialist weekly has climbed to 984,000 copies, anyone who has eyes to see must acknowledge that a proletarian is powerless when alone but that millions of proletarians are all-powerful.

Pravda No. 120, September 18, 1912   Vol. 18, pp. 335-36
Signed: *M. N.*

THE RESULTS AND SIGNIFICANCE
OF THE U. S. PRESIDENTIAL ELECTIONS

Wilson, a "Democrat", has been elected President of the United States of America. He has polled over six million votes, Roosevelt (the new National Progressive Party) over four million, Taft (Republican Party) over three million, and the socialist Eugene Debs 800,000 votes.

The world significance of the U.S. elections lies not so much in the great increase in the number of socialist votes as in the far-reaching *crisis* of the *bourgeois* parties, in the amazing force with which their decay has been revealed. Lastly, the significance of the elections lies in the unusually clear and striking revelation of *bourgeois reformism* as a means of combating socialism.

In *all* bourgeois countries, the parties which stand for capitalism, i.e., the bourgeois parties, came into being a long time ago, and the greater the extent of political liberty, the more solid they are.

Freedom in the U.S.A. is most complete. And for a whole *half-century*—since the Civil War over slavery in 1860-65—*two* bourgeois parties have been distinguished there by remarkable solidity and strength. The party of the former slave-owners is the so-called Democratic Party. The capitalist party, which favoured the emancipation of the Negroes, has developed into the Republican Party.

Since the emancipation of the Negroes, the distinction between the two parties has been diminishing. The fight between these two parties has been mainly over the height of customs duties. Their fight *has not had* any *serious* importance for the mass of the people. The people have been deceived and diverted from their vital interests by means of

spectacular and meaningless *duels* between the two bourgeois parties.

This so-called bipartisan system prevailing in America
and Britain has been one of the most powerful means of
preventing the rise of an independent working-class, i.e.,
genuinely socialist, party.

And now the bipartisan system has suffered a fiasco in
America, the country boasting the most advanced capitalism! What caused this fiasco?

The strength of the working-class movement, the growth
of socialism.

The old bourgeois parties (the "Democratic" and the
"Republican" parties) have been facing towards the past,
the period of the emancipation of the Negroes. The new
bourgeois party, the National Progressive Party, is facing
towards the *future*. Its programme turns entirely on the
question whether capitalism is to be or not to be, on the
issues, to be specific, of protection for the workers and of
"trusts", as the capitalist associations are called in the
U.S.A.

The old parties are products of an epoch whose task was
to develop capitalism as speedily as possible. The struggle
between the parties was over the question *how* best to
expedite and facilitate this development.

The new party is a product of the present epoch, which
raises the issue of the very existence of capitalism. In the
U.S.A., the freest and most advanced country, this issue is
coming to the fore more clearly and broadly than anywhere
else.

The entire programme and entire agitation of Roosevelt
and the Progressives turn on how to *save capitalism* by
means of *bourgeois reforms*.

The bourgeois reformism which in old Europe manifests
itself in the chatter of liberal professors has all at once
come forward in the free American republic as a party
four millions strong. This is American style.

We shall save capitalism by reforms, says that party. We
shall grant the most progressive factory legislation. We
shall establish state control over *all* the trusts (in the
U.S.A. that means over *all* industries!). We shall establish

state control over them to eliminate poverty and enable everybody to earn a "decent" wage. We shall establish "social and industrial justice". We revere *all* reforms— *the only "reform" we don't want is expropriation of the capitalists!*

The national wealth of the U.S.A. is now reckoned to be 120 billion (thousand million) dollars, i.e., about 240 billion rubles. Approximately *one-third* of it, or about 80 billion rubles, belongs to *two* trusts, those of Rockefeller and Morgan, or is subordinated to these trusts! Not more than 40,000 families making up these two trusts are the masters of 80 million wage-slaves.

Obviously, so long as these modern slave-owners are there, all "reforms" will be nothing but a deception. Roosevelt has been *deliberately* hired by the astute multimillionaires to preach this deception. The "state control" they promise will become—if the capitalists keep their capital— a means of combating and crushing strikes.

But the American proletarian has already awakened and has taken up his post. He greets Roosevelt's success with cheerful irony, as if to say: You lured four million people with your promises of reform, dear impostor Roosevelt. Very well! Tomorrow those four million will see that your promises were a fraud, and don't forget that they are following you *only* because they feel that it is *impossible* to go on living in the old way.

Pravda No. 164, November 9, 1912
Signed: *V. I.*

Vol. 18, pp. 402-04

AFTER THE ELECTIONS IN AMERICA

We have already pointed out in *Pravda* the great importance of the Republican Party split in America and the formation of Roosevelt's Progressive Party.

Now the elections are over. The Democrats have won, and at once the consequences predicted by the socialists are beginning to tell. Roosevelt's Progressive Party, with its 4.5 million votes, is a specimen of the broad bourgeois-reformist trend which has come on the scene in sweeping American fashion.

What happens to this trend is of general interest because, in one form or another, it exists *in all* capitalist countries.

In any bourgeois-reformist trend there are two main streams: the bourgeois bigwigs and politicians, who deceive the masses with promises of reform, and the cheated masses, who feel that they cannot go on living in the old way, and follow the quack with the loudest promises. And so we find the brand-new Progressive Party in America splitting at the seams right after the elections.

The bourgeois politicians who made use of Roosevelt's quackery to dupe the masses are already yelling about a *merger* with the Republican Party. What's the idea? It is simply this: the politicians want the cushy jobs which the victorious party in America hands out to its supporters with especial brazenness. The Republican split gave the victory to the Democrats. These are now ecstatically sharing out the luscious public pie. Is it surprising that their rivals are prepared to renounce the Progressive Party and return to the *consolidated* Republican Party, which has every chance of defeating the Democrats?

Indeed, this looks very much like a cynical cheap sale of "party loyalties". But we see exactly the same thing in *all* capitalist countries; and the *less* freedom there is in a country, the dirtier and fouler is this sale of party loyalties among the bourgeois sharks, and the greater is the importance of backstairs intrigues and private connections in procuring concessions, subsidies, bonanza legal cases (for the lawyers), etc.

The other wing of any bourgeois-reformist trend—the cheated masses—has now also revealed itself in the highly original, free and lucid American style. "Scores who had voted for the Progressive Party," writes *Appeal to Reason*, the New York workers' paper, "now come to socialist editorial offices and bureaux for all kinds of information. They are mostly young people, trusting, inexperienced. They are the sheep shorn by Roosevelt, without any knowledge of politics or economics. They instinctively feel that the Socialist Party, with its one million votes, is a more serious proposition than Roosevelt's 4.5 million, and what they want to know most is whether the minimum reforms promised by Roosevelt can be implemented."

"Needless to say," the paper adds, "we are glad to give every one of these 'progressives' *any* information, and never let any of them leave without socialist literature."

The lot of capitalism is such that its sharpest operators cannot help "working"—for socialism!

Written before November 25
(December 8), 1912

First published in 1954   Vol. 36, pp. 204-05
in the magazine *Kommunist* No. 6

MORE ZEAL THAN SENSE

Each has his own preoccupations: the proletariat sees the need for peace, and the capitalists look to the "patriotic" examples provided by the Balkan War.[33] To each his own. The workers insist that in terms of human life a Balkan revolution would have cost a hundred times less than the Balkan War, and would have produced democratic results a thousand times broader and more stable.

The capitalists—both the "Right" and the liberals, all the way up to our Progressists and Cadets[34]—are straining to prove that whereas the banded capitalists in the Balkans have pocketed so much, the banded capitalists of Britain, France and Russia, as an "entente", could have made off with ever so much more.

One American "patriot", a patriot of the money-bag, managed to find out that some ships in the Greek navy had been built by Greek millionaire magnates at their own expense.

This American Guchkov or Maklakov hastened to advertise and play up the grand patriotic example in every way. He wrote: "Now if only our country's shores and all our overseas trade were protected by giant dreadnoughts called *Morgan, Astor, Vanderbilt* and *Rockefeller*! With such an example before them, the people would grumble less about the concentration of capital in the hands of billionaires and about the unequal distribution of wealth!"

Patriotic, but impractical, say the American workers laughing. Gentlemen, go ahead with your splendid scheme, we're all *for* it. Until now, the Rockefellers, Morgans, etc., over here in America have been hiring private detachments of armed men to protect their property and fight strikers.

Let the billionaires now give the people a clear picture showing that the "external" defence of the "state" is *defence of the monopolies and the profits* of the owners of our trusts! Let's see what lesson the American workers will learn as they contemplate these super-dreadnoughts named *Morgan, Rockefeller*, etc.: will it be patriotic emotion or socialist convictions? Will they become more servile to the capitalists, or will they demand with greater firmness that all trusts (manufacturers' associations), all the property of the trusts, should be handed over to the workers, to society as a whole?

... The American "patriot" has overdone it....

Written before November 26
(December 9), 1912

First published in 1954   Vol. 36, pp. 207-08
in the magazine *Kommunist* No. 6

IN AMERICA

The 32nd Annual Convention of the American Federation
of Labour, as the association of trade unions is called, has
come to a close in Rochester. Alongside the rapidly growing Socialist Party, this association is a living relic of the
past: of the old craft-union, liberal-bourgeois traditions
that hang full weight over America's working-class *aristocracy*.

On August 31, 1911, the Federation had 1,841,268 members. Samuel Gompers, a strong opponent of socialism, was
re-elected President. But Max Hayes, the socialist workers'
candidate, received 5,074 votes against Gompers's 11,974,
whereas previously Gompers used to be elected unanimously. The struggle of the socialists against the "trade
unionists" in the American trade union movement is slowly
but surely leading to the victory of the former over the
latter.

Gompers not only fully accepts the bourgeois myth of
"harmony between labour and capital", but carries on a
downright bourgeois policy in the Federation against the
socialist one, although he professes to stand for the
complete political "neutrality" of the trade unions! During
the recent presidential elections in America, Gompers
reprinted in the Federation's official publication the programmes and platforms of all three bourgeois parties
(Democrats, Republicans and Progressists) but did *not*
reprint the programme of the *Socialist* Party!!

Protests against this mode of action were voiced at the
Rochester Convention even by Gompers's own followers.

The state of affairs in the American labour movement
shows us, as it does in Britain, the remarkably clear-cut

division between purely trade unionist and socialist striv-
ings, the split between *bourgeois labour policy* and socialist
labour policy. For, strange as it may seem, in capitalist
society even the working class can carry on a bourgeois
policy, if it forgets about its emancipatory aims, puts up
with wage-slavery and confines itself to seeking alliances
now with one bourgeois party, now with another, for the
sake of imaginary "improvements" in its indentured condition.

The principal historical cause of the particular prominence and (temporary) strength of bourgeois labour policy
in Britain and America is the long-standing political liberty
and the exceptionally favourable conditions, in comparison
with other countries, for the deep-going and widespread
development of capitalism. These conditions have tended
to produce within the working class an aristocracy that
has trailed after the bourgeoisie, *betraying* its own class.

In the twentieth century, this peculiar situation in Britain
and America is rapidly disappearing. Other countries are
catching up with Anglo-Saxon capitalism, and the *mass*
of workers are learning about socialism at first hand. The
faster the growth of world capitalism, the sooner will
socialism triumph in America and Britain.

Written not later than December 6
(19), 1912

First published in 1954
in the magazine *Kommunist* No. 6   Vol. 36, pp. 214-15

RUSSIANS AND NEGROES

What a strange comparison, the reader may think. How can a race be compared with a nation?

It is a permissible comparison. The Negroes were the last to be freed from slavery, and they still bear, more than anyone else, the cruel marks of slavery—even in advanced countries—for capitalism has no "room" for other than legal emancipation, and even the latter it curtails in every possible way.

With regard to the Russians, history has it that they were "almost" freed from *serf* bondage in 1861. It was about the same time, following the Civil War against the American slave-owners, that North America's Negroes were freed from slavery.

The emancipation of the American slaves took place in a less "reformative" manner than that of the Russian slaves.

That is why today, half a century later, the Russians still show *many more* traces of slavery than the Negroes. Indeed, it would be more accurate to speak of institutions and not merely of traces. But in this short article we shall limit ourselves to a little illustration of what we have said, namely, the question of literacy. It is known that illiteracy is one of the marks of slavery. In a country oppressed by pashas, Purishkeviches and their like, the majority of the population cannot be literate.

In Russia there are *73 per cent of illiterates*, exclusive of children under nine years of age.

Among the U.S. Negroes, there were (in 1900) *44.5 per cent* of illiterates.

Such a scandalously high percentage of illiterates is a disgrace to a civilised, advanced country like the North American Republic. Furthermore, everyone knows that the position of the Negroes in America *in general* is one unworthy of a civilised country—capitalism *cannot* give either *complete* emancipation or even complete equality.

It is instructive that among the whites in America the proportion of illiterates is not more than 6 per cent. But if we divide America into what were formerly slave-holding areas (an American "Russia") and non-slave-holding areas (an American non-Russia), we shall find 11-12 per cent of illiterates *among the whites* in the former and 4-6 per cent in the latter areas!

The proportion of illiterates *among the whites* is *twice as high* in the former slave-holding areas. It is not only the Negroes that show traces of slavery!

Shame on America for the plight of the Negroes!

Written late January-early
February 1913

First published in *Krasnaya Niva*   Vol. 18, pp. 543-44
No. 3, 1925
Signed: *W.*

A "SCIENTIFIC" SYSTEM OF SWEATING

U.S. capitalism is ahead of all. The greatest development of technology and the most rapid progress are facts which make old Europe emulate the Yankees. But it is not the democratic institutions that the European bourgeoisie is borrowing from America, nor political liberty, nor yet the republican political system, but the latest methods of exploiting the workers.

The most widely discussed topic today in Europe, and to some extent in Russia, is the "system" of the American engineer, Frederick Taylor. Not so long ago Mr. Semyonov read a paper on this system in the assembly hall of the Railway Engineering Institute in St. Petersburg. Taylor himself has described his system under the title of "scientific", and his book is being eagerly translated and promoted in Europe.

What is this "scientific system"? Its purpose is to squeeze out of the worker three times more labour during a working day of the same length as before. The sturdiest and most skilful worker is put to work; a special clock registers—in seconds and fractions of a second—the amount of time spent on each operation and each motion; the most economical and most efficient working methods are developed; the work of the best worker is recorded on cinematographic film, etc.

The result is that, within the same nine or ten working hours as before, they squeeze out of the worker three times more labour, mercilessly drain him of all his strength, and are three times faster sucking out every drop of the wage-slave's nervous and physical energy. What if he dies earlier than he did before? Well, there are many others waiting at the gate!

In capitalist society, progress in science and technology means progress in the art of sweating.

Here is an example from Taylor's book.

Speaking of the operation of loading cast iron on to hand-carts for further processing, the author compares the old and the new, "scientific", system:

	Old	New system
Number of workers engaged in loading . .	500	140
Average number of tons loaded by one worker (a ton equals 61 poods*)	16	59
Average earnings of worker (rubles)	2.30	3.75
Expenditure incurred by factory owner per ton of load (kopeks)	14.4	6.4

The capitalist cuts his expenditure by *half* or more. His profits grow. The bourgeoisie is delighted and cannot praise the Taylors enough!

The workers get a wage increase at first. But hundreds of workers get the sack. Those who are left have to work four times more intensively, doing a back-breaking job. When he has been drained of all his strength, the worker will be kicked out. Only young and sturdy workers are taken on.

It is sweating in strict accordance with all the precepts of science.

Pravda No. 60, March 13, 1913
Signed: *W.*

Vol. 18, pp. 594-95

---

* Pood=36.11 lbs.—*Ed.*

OUR "ACHIEVEMENTS"

The Minister of Finance, in his explanatory note on the Budget, and all the government parties assure themselves and others that our Budget is firmly based. They refer, among other things, to the "achievements" of industry, which indubitably has been on the upgrade in the last few years.

Our industry, as well as our entire national economy, has been developing along capitalist lines. That is indisputable, and needs no proof. But anyone who limits himself to data on "development" and to the smugly boastful statement that "there is an increase of so-and-so many per cent" *shuts his eyes* to Russia's *incredible* backwardness and poverty, which these data reveal.

The output of our entire factory industry was worth 4,307 million rubles in 1908 and about 4,895 million rubles in 1911, says the Minister of Finance exultantly.

But see *what* these figures *mean*. In America a census is taken every ten years. To come upon a figure *similar* to ours, we must go back to 1860, when America still had Negro *slaves*.

In 1860 the output of America's manufacturing industry was valued at 3,771 million rubles, and in 1870 it was worth as much as 8,464 million rubles. In 1910 its value was already as high as 41,344 million rubles, i.e., almost *nine times* as much as in Russia. Russia has a population of 160 million, while America had 92 million in 1910 and 31 million in 1860!

In 1911 the Russian factory worker earned an annual average of 251 rubles, or 8.2 per cent more (in terms of the wages total) than in 1910, exults the Minister of Finance.

In America the average pay of the industrial worker in 1910 was *1,036 rubles*, i.e., more than *four times* that of his Russian counterpart. In 1860 it was *576 rubles*, i.e., double the *present* amount in Russia.

Twentieth-century Russia, the Russia of the June Third "Constitution",[35] *is in a lower position than slave-owning America.*

In Russia, annual productivity per factory worker was 1,810 rubles in 1908, while in America it was 2,860 rubles in 1860 and 6,264 rubles in 1910.

These few figures suffice as a brief illustration of *modern* capitalism and of the medieval oppression of serfdom which fetters it, and which accounts for the sorry plight of the bulk of the peasantry.

As a matter of fact, the plight of the peasantry is inevitably reducing the home market to miserable dimensions and dragging down the worker, who in 1911 earned half the amount earned by the American worker in the period of slavery. Besides, the conditions of the world market confront Russia with the alternative of either being crushed by competitors among whom capitalism is advancing at a different rate and on a truly broad basis, or of getting rid of all the survivals of serfdom.

Pravda No. 61, March 14, 1913
Signed: *V.*

Vol. 18, pp. 596-97

BIG ACHIEVEMENT OF THE CHINESE REPUBLIC

We know that the great Chinese Republic,[36] established at the cost of such sacrifice by progressive democrats among the Asian masses, recently encountered very grave financial difficulties. The six "Great" Powers, which are considered civilised nations, but which in reality follow the most reactionary policies, formed a financial consortium which suspended the granting of a loan to China.

The point is that the Chinese revolution did not evoke among the European bourgeoisie any enthusiasm for freedom and democracy—only the proletariat can entertain that feeling, which is alien to the knights of profit; it gave rise to the urge to *plunder* China, partition her and take away some of her territories. This "consortium" of the six powers (Britain, France, Russia, Germany, Japan and the United States) was trying to make China bankrupt in order to weaken and undermine the republic.

The *collapse* of this reactionary consortium is a big success for the young republic, which enjoys the sympathy of the working masses the world over. The President of the United States has announced that his government will no longer support the consortium and will officially *recognise* the Republic of China in the near future. The American banks have now *left* the consortium, and America will give China much-needed financial support, opening the Chinese market to American capital and thereby facilitating the introduction of reforms in China.

Influenced by America, Japan has also changed her policy towards China. At first, Japan would not even allow Sun Yat-sen to enter the country. Now the visit has taken place, and all Japanese democrats enthusiastically welcome an alliance with republican China; the conclusion of that *alliance* is now on the order of the day. The Japanese bourgeoisie, like the American, has come to realise that it stands to profit more from a policy of peace with China than from a policy of plundering and partitioning the Chinese Republic.

The collapse of the robber consortium is, of course, a defeat of no mean importance for Russia's reactionary foreign policy.

Pravda No. 68, March 22, 1913
Signed: *W.*

Vol. 19, pp. 29-30

THE "OIL HUNGER"

The question of the "oil hunger", the inordinate increase in the price of oil and the criminal conspiracy of the oil magnates for the purpose of fleecing the consumer, has aroused quite legitimate interest and quite understandable indignation in the Duma, and to a still greater degree outside the Duma.

The duel between the Minister of Commerce and Industry, who in a faintly disguised form *defended* the oil kings of the syndicate, and Mr. Markov the Second, who furiously and ardently expressed the hurt feelings of the noble feudal landowners—this duel (at the State Duma sitting on March 22) deserves the particular attention of the working class and all democrats. The duel throws a bright light on the relations as a whole that exist between the two "ruling" classes of Russia, the two so-called "higher" (but actually very low, despicable, plundering) classes, the class of feudal landowners and the class of financial tycoons.

It would seem at first glance that the question of the oil syndicate is an isolated one. But that is not so. Actually it is only a manifestation of the general and fundamental question of the government of Russia (or rather the plunder of Russia) by the two commanding classes. The speech by Markov the Second was a magnificent reply to the defender of the oil "kings" given from the standpoint of a *diehard* who was cheated when the prey was divided. No wonder Mr. Markov the Second could not "behold himself", could not look at himself (and his landowning friends) in the mirror at the time of his speech. I shall try to do Mr. Markov the Second a service—I will place a mirror in front of him. I will draw him a portrait of himself. I will show that the "quarrel" between Markov the Second and Khvostov, on the one hand, and the oil kings, the tycoons of the kerosene syndicate, the millionaires of Baku, on the other, is a *domestic* quarrel, a quarrel between *two* plunderers of the people's property. "The falling-out of lovers is the renewing of love." The Minister and Messrs. Nobel & Co., on the one hand, and Messrs. Khvostov, Markov and their friends in the Senate, the Council of State, etc., on the other, are *"lovers"*. But the tens of millions of workers and ruined peasants of Russia get a rough deal from this sweet and loving lot!

What lies at the bottom of the oil question?

First of all it is the shameless inflation of oil prices by the oil kings accompanied by the artificial *curtailment* of oilwell and refinery productivity by these "knights" of capitalist profit.

The chief figures illustrating these points have been quoted in the Duma, but I must repeat them in brief to make my further exposition quite clear. The price of oil was six kopeks a pood in 1902. By 1904 it had risen to fourteen kopeks. Then the price "race" became all the merrier and, after the revolution of 1905, the price of a pood of oil rose to twenty-one kopeks in 1908-09 and to *thirty-eight kopeks* in 1912.

Thus the price has increased *more than sixfold* in ten years! In the same period the extraction of oil has *decreased* from 600-700 million poods in 1900-02 to 500-585 million poods in 1908-12.

These figures are worth remembering. They deserve some thought. A reduction of output in a decade of tremendous upward leaps in world production, accompanied by *a more than sixfold* price increase.

The Minister of Commerce and Industry put forward unbelievably weak arguments in defence of these merchants and industrialists who are acting in collusion.

"There is an increased demand for fuel," he said. "There is an increased demand for oil from the automobile and aircraft industry." And he comforted us and the Russian people by saying that it is a "world-wide" phenomenon.

"What about America?" we ask. This is a question that arises naturally because everybody knows that America is Russia's only serious competitor in oil production. In 1900 Russia and America together produced over nine-tenths of the world's oil and in 1910 they produced over eight-tenths.

If it is a matter of a "world-wide" phenomenon, Mr. Minister, *the same* must also be true of America? In order to create an *impression* on inattentive listeners, the Minister, when defending the conspiring oil plunderers, quoted figures for America ... *but only for two years*! During the two past years the price of oil in America, and in Rumania, too, has doubled.

Very good, Mr. Minister! Why not make your comparison complete? If you want to draw comparisons, do so properly. Don't play with figures. You must take the figures for America *for the same period* as that for which the figures for Russia have been given. Surely it must be obvious that this is the most fundamental, the most elementary condition, the very ABC of every conscientious application of statistics!

In Russia in ten years prices have increased *more than sixfold* as compared with the lowest price, that of 1902, quoted by the Minister himself. And in America? Nothing like *such* a rise in prices has occurred. Between 1900 and 1910 the price in America *was reduced*. During recent years it has remained firm.

What, then, is the result? The price has been doubled in America and *increased sixfold* in Russia. In 1900 the output of oil in America was *less* than in Russia and in 1910 it was *three times greater* than in Russia!

This is something the Minister, in his clumsy defence of the oil millionaires' conspiracy, did not want to say. The fact is there, however. Whatever figures you take, there can be no doubt that the rise in prices in America for the past ten years has been *incomparably smaller* than in Russia, while the output has increased *tremendously* at a time of disgraceful stagnation or even a step backward in Russia.

We see immediately how little truth and how much untruth there is in our Minister's reference to the "world-wide" phenomenon of price increase. Yes, there are higher prices everywhere. Yes, there are the causes, common to all capitalism, that give rise to it.

The situation is *intolerable* in Russia, however, because in our country it is on oil that the price increase is immeasurably greater, and because in the oil industry we have stagnation instead of increased output. The situation is *absolutely intolerable* in Russia because we see, instead of a broad, free and rapid development of capitalism, stagnation and decay. High prices are therefore a hundred times more malignant in Russia.

Russia has a population of 170,000,000 and America 90,000,000, i.e., a little more than half. America now extracts *three times* more oil than we do and *eighteen times* more coal. Judging by the wages of the workers, living standards in America are *four times* higher than in Russia.

Is it not clear that the Minister's statement to the effect that the evil is a world-wide phenomenon contains a glaring untruth? The evil bears four times, if not ten times, *more heavily* on Russia.

Written not earlier than
March 26 (April 8), 1913

First published in *Pravda* No. 21,   Vol. 19, pp. 33-36
January 21, 1940

THE QUESTION OF MINISTRY
OF EDUCATION POLICY[37]
(Excerpt)

America is *not* among the advanced countries as far as the number of literates is concerned. There are about 11 per cent illiterates and among the Negroes the figure is as high as 44 per cent. But the American Negroes are *more than twice* as well off in respect of public education as the Russian peasantry. The American Negroes, no matter how much they may be, to the shame of the American Republic, oppressed, are better off than the Russian peasants—and they are better off because exactly half a century ago the people routed the American slave-owners, crushed that serpent and completely swept away slavery and the slave-owning state system, and the political privileges of the slave-owners in America.

The Kassos, Kokovtsovs and Maklakovs will teach the Russian people to copy the American example.

In 1908 there were *17,000,000* attending school in America, that is, *192 per 1,000 inhabitants—more than four times* the number in Russia. Forty-three years ago, in 1870, when America had only just *begun* to build her free way of life after *purging* the country of the diehards of slavery—forty-three years ago there were in America 6,871,522 people attending school, i.e., more than in Russia in 1904 and *almost* as many as in 1908. But even as far back as 1870 there were 178 (*one hundred and seventy-eight*) people enrolled in schools to every 1,000 inhabitants, little short of four times the number enrolled in Russia *today*.

And there, gentlemen, you have further proof that Russia *still* has to win for herself in persistent revolutionary struggle by the people *that freedom* the Americans won for themselves half a century ago.

The estimate for the Russian Ministry of Public Mis-education is fixed at 136,700,000 rubles for 1913. This amounts to only 80 kopeks per head of population (170,000,000 in 1913). Even if we accept the "sum total of state expenditure on education" that the Minister of Finance gives us on page 109 of his explanatory text to the budget, that is, 204,900,000 rubles, we still have only 1 ruble 20 kopeks per head. In Belgium, Britain and Germany the amount expended on education is two to three rubles and even three rubles fifty kopeks per head of population. In 1910, America expended 426,000,000 dollars, i.e., 852,000,000 rubles or 9 rubles 24 kopeks per head of population, on public education. Forty-three years ago, in 1870, the American Republic was spending 126,000,000 rubles a year on education, i.e., *3 rubles 30 kopeks* per head.

The official pens of government officials and the officials themselves will object and tell us that Russia is poor, that she has no money. That is true, Russia is not only poor, she is a beggar when it comes to public education. To make up for it, Russia is very "rich" when it comes to expenditure on the feudal state, ruled by landowners, or expenditure on the police, the army, on rents and on salaries of ten thousand rubles for landowners who have reached "high" government posts, expenditure on risky adventures and plunder, yesterday in Korea or on the River Yalu, today in Mongolia or in Turkish Armenia. Russia will *always* remain poor and beggarly in respect of expenditure on public education *until* the public educates itself sufficiently to cast off the yoke of feudal landowners.

Russia is poor when it comes to the salaries of school-teachers. They are paid a miserable pittance. School-teachers starve and freeze in unheated huts that are scarcely fit for human habitation. School-teachers live together with the cattle that the peasants take into their huts in winter. School-teachers are persecuted by every police sergeant, by every village adherent of the Black Hundreds,[38] by volunteer spies or detectives, to say nothing of the hole-picking and persecution by higher officials. Russia is too poor to pay a decent salary to honest workers in the field of public education, but Russia is rich enough to waste millions and tens of millions on aristocratic parasites, on military adventures and on hand-outs to owners of sugar refineries, oil kings and so on.

There is one other figure, the last one taken from American life, gentlemen, that will show the peoples oppressed by the Russian landowners and *their* government *how* the people live who have been able to achieve freedom through a revolutionary struggle. In 1870, in America there were 200,515 school-teachers with a total salary of 37,800,000 dollars, i.e., an average of 189 dollars or *377 rubles* per teacher per annum. And that was *forty years* ago! In America today there are *523,210* school-teachers and their total salaries come to 253,900,000 dollars, i.e., 483 dollars or *966 rubles* per teacher per annum. And in Russia, even at the present level of the productive forces, it would be quite possible at this very moment to guarantee a no less satisfactory salary to an army of school-teachers who are helping to lift the people out of their ignorance, darkness and oppression, if ... if the whole state system of Russia, from top to bottom, were reorganised on lines as democratic as the American system.

Written not later than
June 2 (15), 1913

First published in 1930 in the second
and third editions of Lenin's
Collected Works, Vol. XVI

Vol. 19, pp. 139-42

CAPITALISM AND TAXATION

Novy Ekonomist (No. 21 for 1913), a journal published by Mr. P. Migulin, with the Octobrists[39] and Cadets jointly collaborating, carries an interesting note about income-tax in the United States.

The bill exempts from taxation all incomes up to 4,000 dollars (8,000 rubles). Taxation is envisaged at the rate of one per cent on all incomes exceeding 4,000 dollars, two per cent on all incomes exceeding 20,000 dollars and so on, with slight increases in the percentage as incomes increase. Thus the plan is for a progressive income-tax, but with an exceedingly slow rate of progression, so that the owner of a million dollar income generally pays less than three per cent.

The plan estimates that the 425,000 people whose incomes exceed 4,000 dollars will pay 70 million dollars in taxes (about 140 million rubles) and the Octobrist-Cadet editors of *Novy Ekonomist* note with reference to this:

"Compared with the 700 million rubles import duty and the 500 million rubles excise duty, the expected revenue of 140 million rubles from income-tax is negligible and will not change the significance of indirect taxation."

It is a pity that our bourgeois liberal economists, who are in words prepared to accept a progressive income-tax and have even recorded it in their programme, have evinced no desire to make a definite and precise statement on *what* rates of income-tax *they* consider to be obligatory.

Such rates that the significance of indirect taxation would merely be changed, and if so, to what extent? Or such rates that indirect taxation would be completely abolished?

The American statistics that *Novy Ekonomist* touches upon provide an instructive illustration to this question.

It can be seen from the bill that the total income of 425,000 capitalists (if the tax provides 70 million dollars) is estimated at 5,413,000,000 dollars. This is an obvious understatement; a *hundred persons* are shown as having an income of over a million dollars and their income is shown as 150,000,000 dollars. We know that *a dozen* American multimillionaires have incomes incomparably greater. The Secretary of the Treasury in America wants to be "polite" to the multimillionaires. . . .

But even these figures, excessively "polite" to the capitalists, show a noteworthy picture. Statistics in America record only 16,000,000 families. Of these, therefore, *less than half a million* are counted as capitalists. The remaining mass of people are wage-slaves or petty farmers oppressed by capital, etc.

The statistics fix the size of the income enjoyed by the working masses in America quite accurately for a number of categories. For instance, 6,615,046 industrial workers received (in 1910) 3,427,000,000 dollars, i.e., 518 dollars (1,035 rubles) per worker. Then, 1,699,420 railway workers received 1,144,000,000 dollars (673 dollars per worker). Further, 523,210 public school-teachers received 254,000,000 dollars (483 dollars per teacher).

Combining this mass of working people and rounding off the figures we get: workers—8,800,000 with a total income of 4,800,000,000 dollars or 550 dollars each; capitalists—500,000 with a total income of 5,500,000,000 dollars or 11,000 dollars each.

Half a million capitalist families receive an income that is *greater* than that of almost 9,000,000 workers' families. What, might we ask, is the role of indirect taxation and of the planned income-tax?

Indirect taxation brings in 1,200,000,000 rubles, i.e., 600,000,000 dollars. The amount of indirect taxation is 75 rubles (37.50 dollars) per family in America. Let us compare the way in which the incomes of capitalists and workers are taxed:

	Million families	Total income	Total indirect taxes	Per cent of income paid as taxes
		(million dollars)		
Workers . . .	8.8	4,800	330	7
Capitalists . .	0.5	5,500	19	0.36

We see that the workers pay seven kopeks to the ruble in indirect taxes while the capitalists pay *one-third* of a kopek. The workers pay, proportionally, *twenty times* more than the capitalists. A system of indirect taxes inevitably creates such an "order" (a very disorderly order) in *all* capitalist countries.

If the capitalists were to pay the same percentage in taxes as the workers, the tax imposed would be *385,000,000* and not 19,000,000 *dollars*.

Does a progressive income-tax *of the sort* planned in America change much? Very little. From the capitalists 19,000,000 dollars indirect taxes plus 70,000,000 dollars income-tax would be obtained, that is, altogether 89,000,000 dollars *or only one and a half per cent of income!*

Let us divide the capitalists into middle (income 4,000 to 10,000 dollars, i.e., 8,000-20,000 rubles) and wealthy (with an income over 20,000 rubles). We get the following: middle capitalists—304,000 families with a total income of 1,813,000,000 dollars, and wealthy capitalists—121,000 families with a total income of 3,600,000,000 dollars.

If the middle capitalists paid as much as the workers pay, i.e., 7 per cent of income, the revenue would be about 130,000,000 dollars. Fifteen per cent from the income of wealthy capitalists would produce 540,000,000 dollars. The total *would more than cover all indirect taxes.* After the deduction of this tax the middle capitalists would still have an income of 11,000 rubles each and the wealthy an income of 50,000 rubles each.

We see that the demand put forward by the Social-Democrats—the *complete* abolition of all indirect taxes and their replacement by a real progressive income-tax and not one that merely plays at it—is *fully* realisable. Such a measure would, without affecting the foundations of

capitalism, give tremendous immediate relief to nine-tenths
of the population; and, secondly, it would serve as a gigantic impetus to the development of the productive forces
of society by expanding the home market and liberating
the state from the nonsensical hindrances to economic life
that have been introduced for the purpose of levying indirect taxes.

The capitalists' advocates usually point to the difficulty
of assessing big incomes. Actually, with banks, savings
societies, etc., at their present level of development, this is
a purely imaginary difficulty. The *one* difficulty is the class
avarice of the capitalists and the existence of undemocratic
institutions in the political structure of bourgeois states.

Written on June 1 (14), 1913

Published in *Pravda* No. 129,   Vol. 19, pp. 197-200
June 7, 1913
Signed: *V. Ilyin*

THE IDEAS OF AN ADVANCED CAPITALIST

One of the richest and most eminent American merchants, a certain Edward Albert *Filene*, Vice-Chairman of the International Congress of Chambers of Commerce, is now touring Paris, Berlin and other big European centres to make personal contact with the most influential people of the commercial world.

At the banquets arranged, as is fitting, by the richest people of Europe in honour of one of the American rich, the latter is developing his "new" ideas on the *world power* of the merchant. *Frankfurter Zeitung*, the organ of German finance capital, reports in detail the ideas of this "advanced" American millionaire.

"We are experiencing a great historic movement," he proclaims, "that will end in the transfer of all power over the modern world to representatives of commercial capital. We are the people who bear the greatest responsibility in the world and we should, therefore, be politically the most influential.

"Democracy is growing, the power of the masses is growing," argued Mr. Filene (rather inclined, it seems, to regard those "masses" as simpletons). "The cost of living is rising. Parliamentarism and the newspapers, distributed in millions of copies a day, are providing the masses of the people with ever more detailed information.

"The masses are striving to ensure for themselves participation in political life, the extension of franchise, the introduction of an income-tax, etc. Power over the whole world must pass into the hands of the masses, that is, *into the hands of our employees*," is the conclusion drawn by this worthy orator.

"The natural leaders of the masses should be the *industrialists and merchants*, who are learning more and more to understand the community of their interests and those of the masses." (We note in parenthesis that the cunning Mr. Filene is the owner of a gigantic commercial house employing 2,500 people, and that he has "organised" his employees in a "democratic" organisation with profit-sharing, etc. Since he considers his employees hopeless simpletons, Mr. Filene is sure that they are completely satisfied and infinitely grateful to their "father-benefactor"....)

"Wage increases, the improvement of labour conditions, that is what will bind our employees to us," said Mr. Filene, "that is what will guarantee our power over the whole world. Everybody in the world who is at all talented will come to us to enter our service.

"We need organisation and still more organisation—strong, democratic organisation, both national and international," the American exclaimed. He called upon the commercial world of Paris, Berlin, etc., to reorganise *international chambers of commerce*. They should unite the merchants and industrialists *of all* civilised countries in a single, mighty organisation. All important international problems should be discussed and settled by that organisation.

Such are the ideas of an "advanced" capitalist, Mr. Filene.

The reader will see that these ideas are a paltry, narrow, one-sided, selfishly barren *approximation* to the ideas of Marxism propounded over sixty years ago. "We" are great masters at upsetting and refuting Marx; "we", the civilised merchants and professors of political economy, have refuted him completely!... And at the same time we steal little bits and pieces from him and boast to the whole world of our "progressiveness"....

My worthy Mr. Filene! Do you really believe that the workers of the whole world are actually such simpletons?

Rabochaya Pravda No. 4,   Vol. 19, pp. 275-76
July 17, 1913
Signed: *W.*

WHAT CAN BE DONE FOR PUBLIC EDUCATION

There are quite a number of rotten prejudices current in the Western countries of which Holy Mother Russia is free. They assume there, for instance, that huge public libraries containing hundreds of thousands and millions of volumes should certainly not be reserved only for the handful of scholars or would-be scholars that uses them. Over there they have set themselves the strange, incomprehensible and barbaric aim of making these gigantic, boundless libraries available, not to a guild of scholars, professors and other such specialists, but to the masses, to the crowd, to the mob!

What a desecration of the libraries! What an absence of the "law and order" we are so justly proud of. Instead of *regulations*, discussed and elaborated by a dozen committees of civil servants inventing hundreds of formalities and obstacles to the use of books, they see to it that even *children* can make use of the rich collections; that readers can read publicly-owned books at home; they regard as the pride and glory of a public library, not the number of rarities it contains, the number of sixteenth-century editions or tenth-century manuscripts, but the *extent* to which books are distributed *among the people*, the number of new readers enrolled, the speed with which the demand for any book is met, the number of books issued to be read at home, the number of children attracted to reading and to the use of the library.... These queer prejudices are widespread in the Western states, and we must be glad that those who keep watch and ward over us protect us with care and circumspection from the influence of these prejudices, protect our rich public libraries from the mob, from the *hoi polloi*!

I have before me the report of the New York Public Library for 1911.

That year the Public Library in New York was moved from two old buildings to new premises erected by the city. The total number of books is now about two million. It so happened that the first book asked for when the reading-room opened its doors was in Russian. It was a work by N. Grot, *The Moral Ideals of Our Times*. The request for the book was handed in at eight minutes past nine in the morning. The book was delivered to the reader at nine fifteen.

In the course of the year the library was visited by 1,658,376 people. There were 246,950 readers using the reading-room and they took out 911,891 books.

This, however, is only a small part of the *book circulation* effected by the library. Only a few people can visit the library. The rational organisation of educational work is measured by the number of books issued to be read at home, by the conveniences available to *the majority of the population*.

In three boroughs of New York—Manhattan, Bronx and Richmond—the New York Public Library has *forty-two* branches and will soon have a forty-third (the total population of the three boroughs is almost *three* million). The aim that is constantly pursued is to have a branch of the Public Library within *three-quarters of a verst*, i.e., within ten minutes' walk of the house of every inhabitant, the branch library being *the centre* of all kinds of institutions and establishments for public education.

Almost *eight million* (7,914,882 volumes) were issued to readers at home, 400,000 more than in 1910. To each hundred members of the population of all ages and both sexes, 267 books were issued for reading at home in the course of the year.

Each of the forty-two branch libraries not only provides for the use of reference books in the building and the issue of books to be read at home, it is also a place for evening lectures, for public meetings and for rational entertainment.

The New York Public Library contains about 15,000 books in oriental languages, about 20,000 in Yiddish and about 16,000 in the Slav languages. In the main reading-room there are about 20,000 books standing on *open* shelves for general use.

The New York Public Library has opened a special, central, reading-room for children, and similar institutions are gradually being opened at all branches. The librarians do everything for the children's convenience and answer their questions. The number of books children took out to read at home was 2,859,888, slightly under three million (more than a third of the total). The number of children visiting the reading-room was 1,120,915.

As far as losses are concerned—the New York Public Library assesses the number of books lost at 70-80-90 per 100,000 issued to be read at home.

Such is the way things are done in New York. And in Russia?

Rabochaya Pravda No. 5,   Vol. 19, pp. 277-79
July 18, 1913
Signed: *W.*

CAPITALISM AND WORKERS' IMMIGRATION

Capitalism has given rise to a special form of migration of nations. The rapidly developing industrial countries, introducing machinery on a large scale and ousting the backward countries from the world market, raise wages at home above the average rate and thus attract workers from the backward countries.

Hundreds of thousands of workers thus wander hundreds and thousands of versts. Advanced capitalism drags them forcibly into its orbit, tears them out of the backwoods in which they live, makes them participants in the world-historical movement and brings them face to face with the powerful, united, international class of factory owners.

There can be no doubt that dire poverty alone compels people to abandon their native land, and that the capitalists exploit the immigrant workers in the most shameless manner. But only reactionaries can shut their eyes to the *progressive* significance of this modern migration of nations. Emancipation from the yoke of capital is impossible without the further development of capitalism, and without the class struggle that is based on it. And it is into this struggle that capitalism is drawing the masses of the working people of the *whole* world, breaking down the musty, fusty habits of local life, breaking down national barriers and prejudices, uniting workers from all countries in huge factories and mines in America, Germany, and so forth.

America heads the list of countries which import workers. The following are the immigration figures for America:

Ten years	1821-30	. . . .	99,000
" "	1831-40	. . . .	496,000
" "	1841-50	. . . .	1,597,000
" "	1851-60	. . . .	2,453,000
" "	1861-70	. . . .	2,064,000
" "	1871-80	. . . .	2,262,000
" "	1881-90	. . . .	4,722,000
" "	1891-1900	. . .	3,703,000
Nine "	1901-09	. . . .	7,210,000

The growth of immigration is enormous and continues to increase. During the five years 1905-09 the average number of immigrants entering America (the United States alone is referred to) was *over a million* a year.

It is interesting to note the change in the place of origin of those emigrating to America. Up to 1880 the so-called *old* immigration prevailed, that is, immigration from the old civilised countries, such as Great Britain, Germany and partly from Sweden. Even up to 1890, Great Britain and Germany provided more than half the total immigrants.

From 1880 onwards, there was an incredibly rapid increase in what is called the *new* immigration from Eastern and Southern Europe, from Austria, Italy and Russia. The number of people emigrating from these three countries to the United States was as follows:

Ten years	1871-80	. . . .	201,000
" "	1881-90	. . . .	927,000
" "	1891-1900	. . .	1,847,000
Nine "	1901-09	. . . .	5,127,000

Thus, the most backward countries in the old world, those that more than any other retain survivals of feudalism in every branch of social life, are, as it were, undergoing compulsory training in civilisation. American capitalism is tearing millions of workers of backward Eastern Europe (including Russia, which in 1891-1900 provided 594,000 immigrants and in 1900-09, 1,410,000) out of their semi-feudal conditions and is putting them in the ranks of the advanced, international army of the proletariat.

Hourwich, the author of an extremely illuminating book, *Immigration and Labour*, which appeared in English last year, makes some interesting observations. The number of

people emigrating to America grew particularly after the
1905 revolution (1905—1,000,000; 1906—1,200,000; 1907—
1,400,000; 1908 and 1909—1,900,000 respectively). Workers
who had participated in various strikes in Russia introduced
into America the bolder and more aggressive spirit of the
mass strike.

Russia is lagging farther and farther behind, losing some
of her best workers to foreign countries; America is advancing more and more rapidly, taking the most vigorous
and able-bodied sections of the working population of the
whole world.[*]

Germany, which is more or less keeping pace with the
United States, is changing from a country which released
workers into one that attracts them from foreign countries.
The number of immigrants from Germany to America in
the ten years 1881-90 was 1,453,000; but in the nine years
1901-09 it dropped to 310,000. The number of foreign
workers in Germany, however, was 695,000 in 1910-11 and
729,000 in 1911-12. Dividing these immigrants according
to occupation and country of origin we get the following:

	Foreign workers employed in Germany in 1911-12 (thousands)		
	Agriculture	Industry	Total
From Russia	274	34	308
" Austria	101	162	263
" other countries . . .	22	135	157
Total	397	331	728

The more backward the country the larger is the number
of "unskilled" agricultural labourers it supplies. The
advanced nations seize, as it were, the best paid occupations
for themselves and leave the semi-barbarian countries the
worst paid occupations. Europe in general ("other countries") provided Germany with 157,000 workers, of whom

---

[*] Other countries on the American Continent besides the United
States are also rapidly advancing. The number of immigrants entering
the United States last year was about 250,000, Brazil about 170,000
and Canada over 200,000; total 620,000 for the year.

more than eight-tenths (135,000 out of 157,000) were industrial workers. Backward Austria provided only six-tenths (162,000 out of 263,000) of the industrial workers. The most backward country of all, Russia, provided only one-tenth of the industrial workers (34,000 out of 308,000).

Thus, Russia is punished everywhere and in everything for her backwardness. But compared with the rest of the population, it is the workers of Russia who are more than any others bursting out of this state of backwardness and barbarism, more than any others combating these "delightful" features of their native land, and more closely than any others uniting with the workers of all countries into a single international force for emancipation.

The bourgeoisie incites the workers of one nation against those of another in the endeavour to keep them disunited. Class-conscious workers, realising that the break-down of all the national barriers by capitalism is inevitable and progressive, are trying to help to enlighten and organise their fellow-workers from the backward countries.

Za Pravdu No. 22,
October 29, 1913
Signed: *V. I.*

Vol. 19, pp. 454-57

CRITICAL REMARKS ON THE NATIONAL QUESTION

(Excerpts)

The question arises: what does our Bundist[40] mean when he cries out to heaven against "assimilation"? He *could not* have meant the oppression of nations, or the *privileges* enjoyed by a particular nation, because the word "assimilation" here does not fit at all, because all Marxists, individually, and as an official, united whole, have quite definitely and unambiguously condemned the slightest violence against and oppression and inequality of nations, and finally because this general Marxist idea, which the Bundist has attacked, is expressed in the *Severnaya Pravda* article in the most emphatic manner.

No, evasion is impossible here. In condemning "assimilation" Mr. Liebman had in mind, *not* violence, *not* inequality, and *not* privileges. Is there anything real left in the concept of assimilation, after all violence and all inequality have been eliminated?

Yes, there undoubtedly is. What is left is capitalism's world-historical tendency to break down national barriers, obliterate national distinctions, and to *assimilate* nations—a tendency which manifests itself more and more powerfully with every passing decade, and is one of the greatest driving forces transforming capitalism into socialism.

Whoever does not recognise and champion the equality of nations and languages, and does not fight against all national oppression or inequality, is not a Marxist; he is not even a democrat. That is beyond doubt. But it is also beyond doubt that the pseudo-Marxist who heaps abuse upon a Marxist of another nation for being an "assimilator" is simply a *nationalist philistine*. In this unhandsome category of people are all the Bundists and (as we shall shortly see) Ukrainian nationalist-socialists such as L. Yurkevich, Dontsov and Co.

To show concretely how reactionary the views held by these nationalist philistines are, we shall cite facts of three kinds.

It is the Jewish nationalists in Russia in general, and the Bundists in particular, who vociferate most about Russian orthodox Marxists being "assimilators". And yet, as the afore-mentioned figures show, out of the ten and a half million Jews all over the world, *about half* that number live in the *civilised* world, where conditions favouring "assimilation" are *strongest*, whereas the unhappy, downtrodden, disfranchised Jews in Russia and Galicia, who are crushed under the heel of the Purishkeviches (Russian and Polish), live where conditions for "assimilation" *least* prevail, where there is most segregation, and even a "Pale of Settlement", *a numerus clausus* and other charming features of the Purishkevich regime.

The Jews in the civilised world are not a nation, they have in the main become assimilated, say Karl Kautsky and Otto Bauer. The Jews in Galicia and in Russia are not a nation; unfortunately (through *no* fault of their own but through that of the Purishkeviches), they are still *a caste* here. Such is the incontrovertible judgement of people who are undoubtedly familiar with the history of Jewry and take the above-cited facts into consideration.

What do these facts prove? It is that only Jewish reactionary philistines, who want to turn back the wheel of history, and make it proceed, not from the conditions prevailing in Russia and Galicia to those prevailing in Paris and New York, but in the reverse direction—only they can clamour against "assimilation".

The best Jews, those who are celebrated in world history, and have given the world foremost leaders of democracy and socialism, have never clamoured against assimilation. It is only those who contemplate the "rear aspect" of Jewry with reverential awe that clamour against assimilation.

A rough idea of the scale which the general process of assimilation of nations is assuming under the present conditions of advanced capitalism may be obtained, for example, from the immigration statistics of the United States of America. During the decade between 1891-1900, Europe sent 3,700,000 people there, and during the nine years between 1901 and 1909, 7,200,000. The 1900 census in the United States recorded over 10,000,000 foreigners. New York State, in which, according to the same census, there were over 78,000 Austrians, 136,000 Englishmen, 20,000 Frenchmen, 480,000 Germans, 37,000 Hungarians, 425,000 Irish, 182,000 Italians, 70,000 Poles, 166,000 people from Russia (mostly Jews), 43,000 Swedes, etc., grinds down national distinctions. And what is taking place on a grand, international scale in New York is also to be seen in *every* big city and industrial township.

No one unobsessed by nationalist prejudices can fail to perceive that this process of assimilation of nations by capitalism means the greatest historical progress, the breakdown of hidebound national conservatism in the various backwoods, especially in backward countries like Russia.

In practice, the plan for "extra-territorial" or "cultural-national" autonomy could mean only one thing: *the division of educational affairs according to nationality*, i.e., the introduction of national curias in school affairs. Sufficient thought to the *real* significance of the famous Bund plan will enable one to realise how utterly reactionary it is even from the standpoint of democracy, let alone from that of the proletarian class struggle for socialism.

A single instance and a single scheme for the "nationalisation" of the school system will make this point abundantly clear. In the United States of America the division of the States into Northern and Southern holds to this day in all departments of life; the former possess the greatest traditions of freedom and of struggle against the slaveowners; the latter possess the greatest traditions of slaveownership, survivals of persecution of the Negroes, who are economically oppressed and culturally backward (44 per cent of Negroes are illiterate, and 6 per cent of whites), and so forth. In the Northern States Negro children attend the same schools as white children do. In the South there are separate "national", or racial, whichever you please, schools for Negro children. I think that this is the sole instance of actual "nationalisation" of schools.

In Eastern Europe there exists a country where things like the Beilis case are still possible, and Jews are condemned by the Purishkeviches to a condition worse than that of the Negroes. In that country a scheme for *nationalising Jewish schools* was recently mooted in the Ministry. Happily, this reactionary utopia is no more likely to be realised than the utopia of the Austrian petty bourgeoisie, who have despaired of achieving consistent democracy or of putting an end to national bickering, and have invented for the nations school-education *compartments* to keep them from bickering *over the distribution* of schools ... but have "constituted" themselves for an *eternal* bickering of one "national culture" with another.

Written October-December 1913

Published in 1913 in the journal   Vol. 20, pp. 28-30 and 37
Prosveshcheniye Nos. 10, 11 and 12
Signed: *V. Ilyin*

FOUR THOUSAND RUBLES A YEAR
AND A SIX-HOUR DAY

This is the battle-cry of the class-conscious American workers. They say: We have only one political question before us, and that is the question of the workers' earnings and their working day.

To Russian workers it may at first sight seem very strange and puzzling to have all social and political questions reduced to a single one. But in the United States of America, the most advanced country in the world, which has almost complete political liberty, where democratic institutions are most developed, and where tremendous progress has been made in labour productivity, it is quite natural that the question of socialism should come to the fore.

Thanks to the existence of complete political liberty, it is possible in America, better than in any other country, to calculate the total production of wealth and draw up a statistical report of production. That calculation, based on reliable data, shows that in America there are, in round numbers, 15,000,000 working-class families.

Together, these working-class families annually produce consumer goods to the value of sixty thousand million rubles. This works out at 4,000 rubles a year per working-class family.

But at present, under the capitalist social system, only half this vast amount of wealth, only thirty thousand millions, goes to the workers, who constitute nine-tenths of the population. The other half is pocketed by the capitalists, who, with all their apologists and hangers-on, constitute only one-tenth of the population.

In America, as in other countries, unemployment is rife and the cost of living is steadily rising. Want among the workers is becoming more and more distressful and intolerable. American statistics show that *about half* the workers are working *part time*. And what an immense amount of social labour is still being wasted owing to the preservation of senseless, backward and scattered small production, particularly in agriculture and in commerce!

Thanks to complete political liberty and the absence of feudal landlords in America, machinery is employed there on a wider scale than anywhere else in the world. The aggregate power of the machines employed in the manufacturing industry alone amounts to *eighteen million* steam h.p. At the same time, an investigation of all power resources in the form of waterfalls showed, according to the report of March 14, 1912, that by converting the power of waterfalls into electricity America could immediately obtain an additional *sixty million* h.p.!

Already a land of boundless wealth, it can at one stroke *treble* its wealth, *treble* the productivity of its social labour, and thereby guarantee to *all* working-class families a decent standard of living worthy of intelligent human beings, and a not excessively long working day of six hours.

But owing to the capitalist social system we see in most of the big cities of America—and in the rural districts too for that matter—appalling unemployment and poverty, a wanton waste of human labour side by side with the unprecedented luxury of the multimillionaires, of the rich, whose fortunes run into thousands of millions.

The American working class is rapidly becoming enlightened, and is organising in a powerful proletarian party. Sympathy for this party is growing among all the working people. Working with the aid of first-class machines, and seeing at every turn marvels of engineering and the magnificent successes of labour resulting from the organisation of large-scale production, the wage-slaves of America are beginning clearly to realise what their tasks are, and are advancing the plain, obvious and immediate demands for an income of four thousand rubles a year for every working-class family, and a six-hour day.

The aim of the American workers is quite attainable in any civilised country in the world; but to achieve it, the country must enjoy the fundamental conditions of freedom....

And there is no road to a free future other than by way of an independent working-class organisation, educational, industrial, co-operative and political.

Proletarskaya Pravda No. 19,   Vol. 20, pp. 68-70
January 1, 1914
Signed: *I.*

A LIBERAL PROFESSOR ON EQUALITY

Liberal Professor Mr. Tugan-Baranovsky is on the war-path against socialism. This time he has approached the question, not from the political and economic angle, but from that of an abstract discussion on equality (perhaps the professor thought such an abstract discussion more suitable for the religious and philosophical gatherings which he has addressed?).

"If we take socialism, not as an economic theory, but as a living ideal," Mr. Tugan declared, "then, undoubtedly, it is associated with the ideal of equality, but equality is a concept ... that cannot be deduced from experience and reason."

This is the reasoning of a liberal scholar who repeats the incredibly trite and threadbare argument that experience and reason clearly prove that men are *not* equal, yet socialism bases its ideal on equality. Hence, socialism, if you please, is an absurdity which is contrary to experience and reason, and so forth!

Mr. Tugan repeats the old trick of the reactionaries: first to misinterpret socialism by making it out to be an absurdity, and then to triumphantly refute the absurdity! When we say that experience and reason prove that men are *not* equal, we mean by equality, equality in *abilities* or *similarity* in physical strength and mental ability.

It goes without saying that in this respect men are *not* equal. No sensible person and no socialist forgets this. But *this kind* of equality has *nothing whatever* to do with socialism. If Mr. Tugan is quite unable to *think*, he is at least *able* to read; were he to take the well-known work of one of the founders of scientific socialism, Frederick Engels,

directed against Dühring,[41] he would find there a special
section explaining the absurdity of imagining that economic equality means anything else than the *abolition of classes*.
But when professors set out to refute socialism, one
never knows what to wonder at most—their stupidity,
their ignorance, or their unscrupulousness.

Since we have Mr. Tugan to deal with, we shall have to
start with the rudiments.

By political equality Social-Democrats mean *equal rights*,
and by economic equality, as we have already said, they
mean the *abolition of classes*. As for establishing human
equality in the sense of equality of strength and abilities
(physical and mental), socialists do not even think of such
things.

Political equality is a demand for equal political rights
for *all* citizens of a country who have reached a certain
age and who do not suffer from either ordinary or liberal-
professorial feeble-mindedness. This demand was first
advanced, not by the socialists, not by the proletariat, but
by the *bourgeoisie*. The well-known historical experience
of all countries of the world proves this, and Mr. Tugan
could easily have discovered this had he not called "experience" to witness solely in order to dupe students and workers, and please the powers that be by "abolishing" socialism.

The bourgeoisie put forward the demand for *equal* rights
for all citizens in the struggle against medieval, feudal,
serf-owner and caste privileges. In Russia, for example,
unlike America, Switzerland and other countries, the privileges of the nobility are preserved to this day in all spheres
of political life, in elections to the Council of State, in
elections to the Duma, in municipal administration, in
taxation, and many other things.

Even the most dull-witted and ignorant person can grasp
the fact that individual members of the nobility are *not*
equal in physical and mental abilities any more than are
people belonging to the "tax-paying", "base", "low-born"
or "non-privileged" peasant class. But in *rights*, all nobles
are *equal*, just as all the peasants are equal in their lack of
rights.

Does our learned liberal Professor Tugan now understand the difference between equality in the sense of equal rights, and equality in the sense of equal strength and abilities?

We shall now deal with economic equality. In the United States of America, as in other advanced countries, there are no medieval privileges. All citizens are equal in political rights. But are they equal as regards their *position in social production*?

No, Mr. Tugan, they are not. Some own land, factories and capital and live on the unpaid labour of the workers; these form an insignificant minority. Others, namely, the vast mass of the population, own no means of production and live only by selling their labour-power; these are proletarians.

In the United States of America there is no aristocracy, and the bourgeoisie and the proletariat enjoy *equal* political rights. But they are *not* equal in *class* status: one class, the capitalists, own the means of production and live on the unpaid labour of the workers. The other class, the wage-workers, the proletariat, own no means of production and live by selling their labour-power in the market.

The abolition of classes means placing *all* citizens on an *equal* footing with regard to the *means of production* belonging to society as a whole. It means giving all citizens *equal* opportunities of working on the publicly-owned means of production, on the publicly-owned land, at the publicly-owned factories, and so forth.

This explanation of socialism has been necessary to enlighten our learned liberal professor, Mr. Tugan, who may, if he tries hard, now grasp the fact that it is absurd to expect *equality* of strength and abilities in socialist society.

In brief, when socialists speak of equality they always mean *social* equality, equality of social status, and not by any means the physical and mental equality of individuals.

The puzzled reader may ask: how could a learned liberal professor have forgotten these elementary axioms familiar to anybody who has read any exposition of the views of socialism? The answer is simple: the *personal* qualities of

present-day professors are such that we may find among
them even exceptionally stupid people like Tugan. But the
social status of professors in bourgeois society is such that
only those are allowed to hold such posts who sell science
to serve the interests of capital, and agree to utter the most
fatuous nonsense, the most unscrupulous drivel and twad-
dle against the socialists. The bourgeoisie will forgive the
professors all this as long as they go on "abolishing"
socialism.

Put Pravdy No. 33,   Vol. 20, pp. 144-47
March 11, 1914

THE TAYLOR SYSTEM—MAN'S ENSLAVEMENT
BY THE MACHINE

Capitalism cannot be at a standstill for a single moment. It must forever be moving forward. Competition, which is keenest in a period of crisis like the present, calls for the invention of an increasing number of new devices to reduce the cost of production. But the domination of capital converts all these devices into instruments for the further exploitation of the workers.

The Taylor system is one of these devices.

Advocates of this system recently used the following techniques in America.

An electric lamp was attached to a worker's arm, the worker's movements were photographed and the movements of the lamp studied. Certain movements were found to be "superfluous" and the worker was made to avoid them, i.e., to work more intensively, without losing a second for rest.

The layout of new factory buildings is planned in such a way that not a moment will be lost in delivering materials to the factory, in conveying them from one shop to another, and in dispatching the finished products. The cinema is systematically employed for studying the work of the best operatives and increasing its intensity, i.e., "speeding up" the workers.

For example, a mechanic's operations were filmed in the course of a whole day. After studying the mechanic's movements the efficiency experts provided him with a bench high enough to enable him to avoid losing time in bending down. He was given a boy to assist him. This boy had to hand up each part of the machine in a definite and most efficient way. Within a few days the mechanic performed the work of assembling the given type of machine in *one-fourth* of the time it had taken before!

What an enormous gain in labour productivity!... But the worker's pay is not increased fourfold, but only half as much again, at the very most, and *only for a short period* at that. As soon as the workers get used to the new system their pay is cut to the former level. The capitalist obtains an enormous profit, but the workers toil four times as hard as before and wear down their nerves and muscles four times as fast as before.

A newly engaged worker is taken to the factory cinema where he is shown a "model" performance of his job; the worker is made to "catch up" with this performance. A week later he is taken to the cinema again and shown pictures of his own performance, which is then compared with the "model".

All these vast improvements are introduced *to the detriment* of the workers, for they lead to their still greater oppression and exploitation. Moreover, this rational and efficient distribution of labour is confined *to each factory*.

The question naturally arises: What about the distribution of labour in society as a whole? What a vast amount of labour is wasted at present owing to the disorganised and chaotic character of capitalist production as a whole! How much time is wasted as the raw materials pass to the factory through the hands of hundreds of buyers and middlemen, while the requirements of the market are unknown! Not only time, but the actual products are wasted and damaged. And what about the waste of time and labour in delivering the finished goods to the consumers through a host of small middlemen who, too, cannot know the requirements of their customers and perform not only a host of superfluous movements, but also make a host of superfluous purchases, journeys, and so on and so forth!

Capital organises and rationalises labour within the factory for the purpose of increasing the exploitation of the workers and increasing profit. In social production as a whole, however, chaos continues to reign and grow, leading to crises when the accumulated wealth cannot find purchasers, and millions of workers starve and die because they are unable to find employment.

The Taylor system—without its initiators knowing or wishing it—is preparing the time when the proletariat will take over all social production and appoint its own workers' committees for the purpose of properly distributing and rationalising all social labour. Large-scale production, machinery, railways, telephone—all provide thousands of opportunities to cut by three-fourths the working time of the organised workers and make them four times better off than they are today.

And these workers' committees, assisted by the workers' unions, will be able to apply these principles of rational distribution of social labour when the latter is freed from its enslavement by capital.

Put Pravdy No. 35,
March 13, 1914
Signed: *M. M.*

Vol. 20, pp. 152-54

WHAT SHOULD NOT BE COPIED
FROM THE GERMAN LABOUR MOVEMENT

Karl Legien, one of the most prominent and responsible representatives of the German trade unions, recently published a report of his visit to America in the form of a rather bulky book entitled *The Labour Movement in America.*

As a very prominent representative of the international as well as German trade union movement, K. Legien gave his visit the nature of a special occasion, one of state importance, one might say. For years he conducted negotiations on this visit with the Socialist Party of America and the American Federation of Labour, the labour-union organisation led by the famous (or rather infamous) Gompers. When Legien heard that Karl Liebknecht was going to America, he refused to go at the same time "so as to avoid the simultaneous appearance in the United States of two spokesmen whose views on the party's tactics and on the importance and value of certain branches of the labour movement did not entirely coincide".

K. Legien collected a vast amount of material on the labour-union movement in America, but failed to digest it in his book, which is cluttered up with patchy descriptions of his journey, trivial in content and trite in style. Even the labour-union rules of America, in which Legien was particularly interested, are not studied or analysed, but merely translated incompletely and without system.

There was a highly instructive episode in Legien's tour, which strikingly revealed the *two tendencies* in the international and particularly in the German labour movement.

Legien visited the chamber of deputies of the United

States, known as the Congress. Brought up in the police-ridden Prussian state, he was favourably impressed by the democratic customs of the Republic, and he remarks with understandable pleasure that in America the government provides every Congressman not only with a private office fitted with all modern conveniences, but also with a paid secretary to help him cope with a Congressman's manifold duties. The simplicity and easy manners of the Congressmen and the Speaker of the House were in striking contrast with what Legien had seen in European parliaments, and especially in Germany. In Europe, a Social-Democrat could not even think of delivering to a bourgeois parliament at an official session a speech of greeting! But in America this was done very simply, and the name of Social-Democrat did not frighten anybody ... except *that Social-Democrat himself*!

We have here an example of the American bourgeois method of killing unsteady socialists with kindness, and the German opportunist method of renouncing socialism in deference to the "kindly", suave and democratic bourgeoisie.

Legien's speech of greeting was translated into English (democracy was not in the least averse to hearing a "foreign" language spoken in its parliament); all two hundred odd Congressmen shook hands in turn with Legien as the "guest" of the Republic, and the Speaker expressed his thanks.

"The form and content of my speech of greeting," writes Legien, "were sympathetically received by the socialist press both in the United States and Germany. Certain editors in Germany, however, could not resist pointing out that my speech proved once again what an impossible task it is for a Social-Democrat to deliver a Social-Democratic speech to a bourgeois audience. Well, in my place, these editors would, no doubt, have delivered a speech against capitalism and in favour of a mass strike, but I considered it important to emphasise to this parliament that the Social-Democratic and industrially organised workers of Germany want peace among the nations, and through peace, the development of culture to the highest degree attainable."

Poor "editors", whom our Legien has annihilated with his "statesmanlike" speech! The opportunism of trade union leaders in general, and of Legien in particular, has long been common knowledge in the German labour movement, and has been duly appraised by a great many class-conscious workers. But with us in Russia, where far too much is spoken about the "model" of *European* socialism with precisely the worst, most objectionable features of this "model" being chosen, it would be advisable to deal with Legien's speech in somewhat greater detail.

When he addressed the highest body of representatives of capitalist America, this leader of a two-million-strong army of German trade unionists—namely, the Social-Democratic trade unions—this member of the Social-Democratic group in the German Reichstag, delivered a purely liberal, bourgeois speech. Needless to say, not a single liberal, not even an Octobrist, would hesitate to subscribe to a speech about "peace" and "culture".

And when German socialists remarked that this was not a Social-Democratic speech, this "leader" of capital's wage-slaves treated them with scathing contempt. What are "editors" compared to a "practical politician" and collector of workers' pennies! Our philistine Narcissus has the same contempt for editors as the police panjandrums in a certain country have for the third element.[42]

"These editors" would no doubt have delivered a speech "against capitalism".

Just think what this quasi-socialist is sneering at! He is sneering at the idea that a socialist should think it necessary to speak *against* capitalism. To the "statesmen" of German opportunism such an idea is utterly alien; they talk in such a way as *not to offend* "capitalism". Disgracing themselves by this servile renunciation of socialism, they brag of their disgrace.

Legien is not just anybody. He is a representative of the army of trade unions, or rather, the officers' corps of that army. His speech was no accident, no slip of the tongue, no casual whimsy, no blunder of a provincial German office clerk overawed by American capitalists, who were polite and revealed no trace of police arrogance. If it were *only* this, Legien's speech would not be worthy of note.

But it was obviously not that.

At the International Congress in Stuttgart,[43] half the German delegation turned out to be sham socialists of this type, who voted for the ultra-opportunist resolution on the colonial question.

Take the German magazine *Sozialistische* (??) *Monatshefte* and you will always find in it utterances by men like Legien, which are thoroughly opportunist, and have *nothing* in common with socialism, utterances touching on *all* the vital issues of the labour movement.

The "official" explanation of the "official" German party is that "nobody reads" *Sozialistische Monatshefte*, that it has no influence, etc.; but that is *not true*. The Stuttgart "incident" proved that it is not true. The most prominent and responsible people, members of parliament and trade union leaders who write for *Sozialistische Monatshefte,* constantly and undeviatingly propagate their views among the masses.

The "official optimism" of the German party has long been noted in its own camp by those people who earned Legien's appellation of "these editors"—an appellation contemptuous from the point of view of the bourgeois and honourable from the point of view of a socialist. And the more often the liberals and the liquidators[44] in Russia (including Trotsky, of course) attempt to *transplant* this amiable characteristic *to our soil*, the more determinedly must they be resisted.

German Social-Democracy has many great services to its credit. Thanks to Marx's struggle against all the Höchbergs, Dührings and Co., it possesses a strictly formulated theory, which our Narodniks vainly try to evade or touch up along opportunist lines. It has a mass organisation, newspapers, trade unions, political associations—that same mass organisation which is so definitely building up in our country in the shape of the victories the *Pravda* Marxists are winning everywhere—in Duma elections, in the daily press, in Insurance Board elections, and in the trade unions. The attempts of our liquidators, whom the workers have "removed from office", to evade the question of the growth of this mass organisation in Russia in a form adapted to Russian conditions are as vain as those of the Narodniks, and imply a similar intellectualist *breakaway* from the working-class movement.

But the merits of German Social-Democracy are merits, not because of shameful speeches like those delivered by Legien or the "utterances" (in the press) by the contributors to *Sozialistische Monatshefte,* but *despite* them. We must not try to play down the *disease* which the German party is undoubtedly suffering from, and which reveals itself in phenomena of this kind; nor must we play it down with "officially optimistic" phrases. We must lay it bare to the Russian workers, so that we may learn from the experience of the older movement, learn what should not be copied from it.

Prosveshcheniye No. 4,   Vol. 20, pp. 254-58
April 1914
Signed: *V. I.*

BRITISH PACIFISM
AND THE BRITISH DISLIKE OF THEORY
(Excerpt)

With their dislike of abstract theory and their pride in their practicality, the British often pose political issues *more directly,* thus helping the socialists of other countries to discover the actual content *beneath* the husk of wording of every kind (including the "Marxist"). Instructive in this respect is the pamphlet *Socialism and War,** published before the war by the jingoist paper, *The Clarion.* The pamphlet contains an anti-war "manifesto" by Upton Sinclair, the U.S. socialist, and also a reply to him from the jingoist Robert Blatchford, who has long adopted Hyndman's imperialist viewpoint.

Sinclair is a socialist of the emotions, without any theoretical training. He states the issue in "simple" fashion; incensed by the approach of war, he seeks salvation from it in socialism.

"We are told," Sinclair writes, "that the socialist movement is yet too weak so that we must wait for its evolution. But evolution is working in the hearts of men; we are its instruments, and if we do not struggle, there is no evolution. We are told that the movement [against war] would be crushed out; but I declare my faith that the crushing out of any rebellion which sought, from motive of sublime humanity, to prevent war, would be the greatest victory that socialism has ever gained—would shake the conscience of civilisation and rouse the workers of

---

* *Socialism and War.* The Clarion Press, 44 Warship Street, London, E. C.

the world as nothing in all history has yet done. Let us
not be too fearful for our movement, not put too much
stress upon numbers and the outward appearances of
power. A thousand men aglow with faith and determination
are stronger than a million grown cautious and respectable;
and there is no danger to the socialist movement so great
as the danger of becoming an established institution."

This, as can be seen, is a naïve, theoretically unreasoned,
but profoundly correct warning against any vulgarising
of socialism, and a call to revolutionary struggle.

What does Blatchford say in reply to Sinclair?

"It is capitalists and militarists who make wars. That
is true..." he says. Blatchford is as anxious for peace and
for socialism taking the place of capitalism as any socialist
in the world. But Sinclair will not convince him, or do
away with the facts with "rhetoric and fine phrases".
"Facts, my dear Sinclair, are obstinate things, and the German danger is a fact." Neither the British nor the German
socialists are strong enough to prevent war, and "Sinclair
greatly exaggerates the power of British socialism. The
British socialists ... are not united; they have no money,
no arms, no discipline". The only thing they can do is
to help the British Government build up the navy; there
is not, nor can there be, any other guarantee of peace.

Neither before nor since the outbreak of the war have
the chauvinists ever been so outspoken in Continental
Europe. In Germany it is not frankness that is prevalent,
but Kautsky's hypocrisy and playing at sophistry. The
same is true of Plekhanov. That is why it is so instructive
to cast a glance at the situation in a more advanced country, where nobody will be taken in with sophisms or a
travesty of Marxism. Here issues are stated in a more
straightforward and truthful manner. Let us learn from
the "advanced" British.

Sinclair is naïve in his appeal, although fundamentally
it is a very correct one; he is naïve because he ignores the
development of mass socialism over the last fifty years
and the struggle of trends within socialism; he ignores the
conditions for the growth of revolutionary action when an
objectively revolutionary situation and a revolutionary or-

ganisation exist. The "emotional" approach cannot make up for that. The intense and bitter struggle between powerful trends in socialism, between the opportunist and revolutionary trends, cannot be evaded by the use of rhetoric.

Blatchford speaks out undisguisedly, revealing the most covert argument of the Kautskyites and Co., who are afraid to tell the truth. We are still weak, that is all, says Blatchford; but his outspokenness at once lays bare his opportunism, his jingoism. It at once becomes obvious that he serves the bourgeoisie and the opportunists. By declaring that socialism is "*weak*" he *himself weakens* it by preaching an anti-socialist, bourgeois, policy.

Like Sinclair, but conversely, like a coward and not like a fighter, like a traitor and not like the recklessly brave, he, too, ignores the conditions making for a revolutionary situation.

As for his practical conclusions, his policy (the rejection of revolutionary action, of propaganda for such action and preparation of it), Blatchford, the vulgar jingoist, is in *complete* accord with Plekhanov and Kautsky.

Marxist words have in our days become a cover for a total renunciation of Marxism; to be a Marxist, one must expose the "Marxist hypocrisy" of the leaders of the Second International, fearlessly recognise the struggle of the two trends in socialism, and get to the bottom of the problems relating to that struggle. Such is the conclusion to be drawn from British relationships, which show us the *Marxist* essence of the matter, *without* Marxist words.

Written in June 1915

First published in *Pravda* No. 169,   Vol. 21, pp. 263-65
July 27, 1924

SOCIALISM AND WAR

THE ATTITUDE OF THE R.S.D.L.P. TOWARDS THE WAR

(Excerpt)

A War Between the Biggest Slave-Holders for the Maintenance and Consolidation of Slavery

To make the significance of imperialism clear, we will quote precise figures showing the partition of the world among the so-called "Great" Powers (i.e., those successful in great plunder). (See table on p. 109.—*Ed.*)

Hence it will be seen that, since 1876, most of the nations which were foremost fighters for freedom in 1789-1871, have, on the basis of a highly developed and "over-mature" capitalism, become oppressors and enslavers of most of the population and the nations of the globe. From 1876 to 1914, six "Great" Powers grabbed 25 million square kilometres, i.e., an area two and a half times that of Europe! Six Powers have enslaved *523 million* people in the colonies. For every four inhabitants in the "Great" Powers there are five in "their" colonies. It is common knowledge that colonies are conquered with fire and sword, that the population of the colonies are brutally treated, and that they are exploited in a thousand ways (by exporting capital, through concessions, etc., cheating in the sale of goods, submission to the authorities of the "ruling" nation, and so on and so forth). The Anglo-French bourgeoisie are deceiving the people when they say that they are waging a war for the freedom of nations and of Belgium; in fact they are waging a war for the purpose of retaining the colonies they have grabbed and robbed.

Partition of the World Among the "Great" Slave-Holding Powers

"Great" Powers	Colonies 1876		Colonies 1914		Metropolis 1914		Total	
	Square kilometres	Population	Square kilometres	Population	Square kilometres	Population	Square kilometres	Population
	millions		millions		millions		millions	
Britain	22.5	251.9	33.5	393.5	0.3	46.5	33.8	440.0
Russia	17.0	15.9	17.4	33.2	5.4	136.2	22.8	169.4
France	0.9	6.0	10.6	55.5	0.5	39.6	11.1	95.1
Germany . . .	—	—	2.9	12.3	0.5	64.9	3.4	77.2
Japan	—	—	0.3	19.2	0.4	53.0	0.7	72.2
United States of America	—	—	0.3	9.7	9.4	97.0	9.7	106.7
Total for the six "Great" Powers . . .	40.4	273.8	65.0	523.4	16.5	437.2	81.5	960.6

				Square kilometres	Population
Colonies belonging to *other* than Great Powers (Belgium, Holland and other states) . . .		9.9	45.3	9.9	45.3
Three "semi-colonial" countries (Turkey, China and Persia)				14.5	361.2
		Total		105.9	1,367.1
Other states and countries				28.0	289.9

Entire globe (exclusive of Arctic and Antarctic regions)

Grand Total . . 133.9 1,657.0

The German imperialists would free Belgium, etc., at once if the British and French would agree to "fairly" share their colonies with them. A feature of the situation is that in this war the fate of the colonies is being decided by a war on the Continent. From the standpoint of bourgeois justice and national freedom (or the right of nations to existence), Germany might be considered absolutely in the right as against Britain and France, for she has been "done out" of colonies, her enemies are oppressing an immeasurably far larger number of nations than she is, and the Slavs that are being oppressed by her ally, Austria, undoubtedly enjoy far more freedom than those of tsarist Russia, that veritable "prison of nations". Germany, however, is fighting, not for the liberation of nations, but for their oppression. It is not the business of socialists to help the younger and stronger robber (Germany) to plunder the older and overgorged robbers. Socialists must take advantage of the struggle between the robbers to overthrow all of them. To be able to do this, socialists must first of all tell the people the truth, namely, that this war is, in three respects, a war between slave-holders with the aim of consolidating slavery. This is a war, firstly, to increase the enslavement of the colonies by means of a "more equitable" distribution and subsequent more concerted exploitation of them; secondly, to increase the oppression of other nations within the "Great" Powers, since *both* Austria *and* Russia (Russia in greater degree and with results far worse than Austria) maintain their rule only by such oppression, intensifying it by means of war; and thirdly, to increase and prolong wage-slavery, since the proletariat is split up and suppressed, while the capitalists are the gainers, making fortunes out of the war, fanning national prejudices and intensifying reaction, which has raised its head in all countries, even in the freest and most republican.

Written in July-August 1915

Published in pamphlet form in the autumn of 1915 by the *Sotsial-Demokrat* Editorial Board in Geneva

Vol. 21, pp. 302-04

LETTER TO THE SECRETARY
OF THE SOCIALIST PROPAGANDA LEAGUE[45]

Dear Comrades!*

We are extremely glad to get your leaflet. Your appeal to the members of the Socialist Party to struggle for a new International, for clear-cut revolutionary socialism as taught by Marx and Engels, and against the opportunism, especially against those who are in favour of working class participation in a war of defence, corresponds fully with the position our party (Social-Democratic Labour Party of Russia, *Central Committee*) has taken from the beginning of this war and has always taken during more than ten years.

We send you our sincerest greetings & best wishes of success in our fight for true internationalism.

In our press & in our propaganda we differ from your programme in several points & we think it is quite necessary that we expose you briefly these points in order to make immediate and serious steps for the coordination of the international strife of the incompromisingly revolutionary Socialists especially Marxists in all countries.

We criticise in the most severe manner the old, Second (1889-1914) International, we declare it dead and not worth to be restored on old basis. But we never say in our press that too great emphasis has been heretofore placed upon so-called "Immediate Demands", and that thereby the socialism can be diluted: we say and we prove that all bourgeois parties, all parties except the working-

---

* This letter was written by Lenin in English.—*Ed.*

class revolutionary Party, are liars and hypocrites when they speak about reforms. We try to help the working class to get the smallest possible but real improvement (economic and political) in their situation and we add always that *no* reform can be durable, sincere, serious if not seconded by revolutionary methods of struggle of the masses. We preach always that a socialist party not uniting this struggle for reforms with the revolutionary methods of working-class movement can become a sect, can be severed from the masses, & that that is the most pernicious menace to the success of the clear-cut revolutionary socialism.

We defend always in our press the democracy in the party. But we never speak against the centralisation of the party. We are for the democratic centralism. We say that the centralisation of the German Labour movement is not a feeble but a strong and good feature of it. The vice of the present Social-Democratic Party of Germany consists not in the centralisation but in the preponderance of the opportunists, which should be excluded from the party especially now after their treacherous conduct in the war. If in any given crisis the small group (for instance our Central Committee is a small group) can act for directing the mighty mass *in a revolutionary direction*, it would be very good. And in *all* crises the masses can not act immediately, the masses want to be helped by the small groups of the central institutions of the parties. Our Central Committee quite at the beginning of this war, in September 1914, has directed the masses not to accept the lie about "the war of defence" & to break off with the opportunists & the "would-be-socialists-jingoes" (we call so the "Socialists" who are *now* in favour of the war of defence). We think that this centralistic measure of our Central Committee was useful & necessary.

We agree with you that we must be against craft Unionism & in favour of industrial Unionism, i.e., of big, centralised Trade Unions & in favour of the most active participation of *all* members of party in *all* economic struggles & in *all* trade union & cooperative organisations of the working class. But we consider that such people as Mr.

Legien in Germany & Mr. Gompers in the U. St. are bourgeois and that their policy is not a socialist but a nationalistic, middle class policy. Mr. Legien, Mr. Gompers & similar persons are not the representatives of working class, they represent the aristocracy & bureaucracy of the working class.

We entirely sympathise with you when in political action you claim the "mass action" of the workers. The German revolutionary & internationalist Socialists claim it also. In our press we try to define with more details what must be understood by political mass action, as f.i. political strikes (very usual in Russia), street demonstrations and civil war prepared by the present imperialist war between nations.

We do not preach unity in the *present* (prevailing in the Second International) socialist parties. On the contrary we preach *secession* with the opportunists. The war is the best object-lesson. In *all* countries the opportunists, their leaders, their most influential dailies & reviews are *for* the war, in other words, they have in reality *united* with "their" national bourgeoisie (middle class, capitalists) against the proletarian masses. You say, that in America there are also Socialists who have expressed themselves in favour of the participation in a war of defence. We are convinced, that unity with such men is an evil. *Such* unity is unity with the national middle class & capitalists, and a *division* with the international revolutionary working class. And we are for secession with nationalistic opportunists and unity with international revolutionary Marxists & working-class parties.

We never object in our press to the unity of S.P. & S.L.P. in America.[46] We always quote letters from Marx & Engels (especially to Sorge, active member of American socialist movement), where both condemn the sectarian character of the S.L.P.

We fully agree with you in your criticism of the old International. We have participated in the conference of Zimmerwald[47] (Switzerland) 5-8.IX. 1915. We have formed there a *left wing*, and have proposed *our resolution* & our draught of a manifesto. We have just published these documents in German & I send them to you (with the German translation of our small book about "Socialism & War"), hoping that in your League there are probably comrades, that know German. If you could help us to publish these things in English (it is possible only in America and later on we should send it to England), we would gladly accept your help.

In our struggle for true internationalism & against "jingo-socialism" we always quote in our press the example of the opportunist leaders of the S.P. in America, who are in favour of restrictions of the immigration of Chinese and Japanese workers (especially after the Congress of Stuttgart, 1907, & *against* the decisions of Stuttgart). We think that one can not be internationalist & be at the same time in favour of such restrictions. And we assert that Socialists in America, especially English Socialists, belonging to the ruling, and *oppressing* nation, who are not against any restrictions of immigration, against the possession of colonies (Hawaii) and for the entire freedom of colonies, that such Socialists are in reality jingoes.

For conclusion I repeat once more best greetings & wishes for your League. We should be very glad to have a further information from you & to *unite* our struggle against opportunism & for the true internationalism.

Yours *N. Lenin*

N.B. There are *two* Soc.-Dem. parties in Russia. Our party ("*Central* Committee") is against opportunism. The other party ("*Organising* Committee") is opportunist. We are *against* the unity with them.

You can write to our official address (Bibliothèque russe. For the C. K. 7 rue Hugo de Senger. 7. Genève. Switzerland). But better write to my personal address: Wl. Ulianow. Seidenweg 4a, III *Berne*. Switzerland.

Written in English
between October 31 and
November 9 (November 13 and
22), 1915

First published in 1924   Vol. 21, pp. 423-28
in *Lenin Miscellany II*

To the Secretary of the "Socialist Propaganda League"
Mr. C. W. Fitzgerald, 20 Baker Pl., Beverly,
Mass.

Dear comrades!

We are extremely glad to get your leaflet. Your appeal to the members of the Socialist Party to struggle for a new International, for clear-cut revolutionary tactics as taught by Marx & Engels, and against the opportunism, especially against those who are in favor of working class participation in a war of defense, corresponds fully with the position our party (Social Democratic Labor Party of Russia, <u>Central Committee</u>) has taken from the beginning of this war & has always taken during more than ten years.

We send you our sincerest greetings

First page of Lenin's letter to the Secretary of the Socialist Propaganda
League. November 1915
Reduced

Книгоиздательство „ЖИЗНЬ и ЗНАНІЕ".
Петроградъ, Поварской пер., д. 2. кв. 9 и 10. Телефонъ 227-42

Библіотека Обществовѣдѣнія. Кн. 42-ая.

В. ИЛЬИНЪ (Н. Ленинъ).

НОВЫЯ ДАННЫЯ
О ЗАКОНАХЪ РАЗВИТІЯ КАПИТАЛИЗМА
ВЪ ЗЕМЛЕДѢЛІИ.

ВЫПУСКЪ I.

Капитализмъ и земледѣліе въ Соед. Штатахъ Америки.

ПЕТРОГРАДЪ.
1917.

NEW DATA ON THE LAWS GOVERNING THE DEVELOPMENT OF CAPITALISM IN AGRICULTURE

Part One
Capitalism and Agriculture in the United States of America[48]

A leading country of modern capitalism is of especial interest to the study of the socio-economic structure and evolution of present-day agriculture. The U.S.A. is unrivalled either in the rate of development of capitalism at the turn of the century, or in the record level of capitalist development already attained; nor has it any rival in the vastness of the territory developed with the use of the most up-to-date machinery, which is adapted to the remarkable variety of natural and historical conditions, or in the extent of the political liberty and the cultural level of the mass of the population. That country, indeed, is in many respects the model for our bourgeois civilisation and is its ideal.

The study of the forms and laws of agricultural evolution is made easier in the U.S.A. by its decennial censuses of population, which are coupled with remarkably detailed descriptions of all industrial and agricultural enterprises. This yields a wealth of exact information that is unavailable in any other country; it helps to verify many popular notions, most of which are very loosely formulated and repeated without criticism, and usually serve to funnel bourgeois views and prejudices.

Mr. Himmer in the June (1913) issue of *Zavety* gives some data from the latest, Thirteenth (1910) Census, and on this basis reiterates the most popular and thoroughly bourgeois contention—bourgeois both as regards its theoretical basis and political significance—that "the vast majority of farms in the United States employ only family labour"; that "in the more highly developed areas agricultural capitalism is disintegrating"; that "in the great majority of areas... small-scale farming by owner-operators is becoming ever more dominant"; that it is precisely "in the older cultivated areas with a higher level of economic development" that "capitalist agriculture is disintegrating and production is breaking up into smaller units"; that "there are no areas where colonisation is no longer continuing, or where large-scale capitalist agriculture is not decaying and is not being replaced by family-labour farms", and so on and so forth.

All these assertions are monstrously untrue. They are in direct contradiction to reality. They are a sheer mockery of the truth. Their incorrectness ought to be explained in detail for a very good reason: Mr. Himmer is not the man in the street, he is not a casual contributor of a casual magazine article, but one of the most prominent economists representing the most democratic, extreme Left-wing *bourgeois* trend in Russian and European social thinking. That is precisely why Mr. Himmer's views may have, and indeed already have among some non-proletarian sections of the population, particularly wide circulation and influence. They are not merely his personal views, nor his individual mistakes, but are rather an expression— couched in the most democratic terms and heavily embellished with pseudo-socialist phraseology—of *general* bourgeois views which in the atmosphere of a capitalist society are most readily accepted both by the smug professor, treading the beaten path, and the small farmer who is more intelligent than millions of his fellows.

The theory of the non-capitalist evolution of agriculture in capitalist society, which Mr. Himmer advocates, is really the theory of the great majority of bourgeois professors and bourgeois democrats and also of opportunists in the labour movement of the whole world who are the latest variety of those selfsame bourgeois democrats. It is no exaggeration to say that this theory is an illusion, a dream, a delusion under which the whole of bourgeois society is labouring. In devoting my further exposition to the refutation of this theory, I shall try to give a complete picture of capitalism in American agriculture, because one of the main mistakes made by bourgeois economists is to isolate facts and figures, major and minor, from the general context of politico-economic relations. All my data are taken from official statistical publications of the United States of North America, including above all the volumes *Five,* devoted to agriculture, of the Twelfth and Thirteenth censuses taken in 1900 and 1910 respectively,* and also the *Statistical Abstract of the United States for 1911.* Having mentioned these sources, I shall not give references to pages or tables for each separate figure, as this would only burden the reader and needlessly encumber the text; anyone interested enough will easily find the data in question from the tables of contents in these publications.

1. GENERAL CHARACTERISTIC OF THE THREE MAIN SECTIONS. THE HOMESTEAD WEST

The vast area of the United States, which is only slightly smaller than the whole of Europe, and the great diversity of farming conditions in the various parts of the country make absolutely imperative a separate study of the major divisions, each with its peculiar economic status. American statisticians adopted five geographical divisions in 1900, and nine in 1910. (1) New England—six states on the Atlantic coast in the north-east (Maine, New Hampshire, Vermont, Massachusetts, Rhode Island, and Connecticut); (2) Middle Atlantic (New York, New Jersey, and Pennsylvania)—in 1900 these two divisions formed the North Atlantic division; (3) East North Central (Ohio, Indiana, Illinois, Michigan, and Wisconsin); (4) West North Central (Minnesota, Iowa, Missouri, North and South Dakota, Nebraska, and Kansas)—in 1900, the last two made up the

---

* *Census Reports. Twelfth Census 1900.* Vol. V. Agriculture, Wash. 1902.—*Thirteenth Census of the United States, Taken in the Year 1910.* Vol. V. Agriculture, Wash. 1913.

North Central division; (5) South Atlantic (Delaware, Maryland, District of Columbia, Virginia, West Virginia, North and South Carolina, Georgia, and Florida)—unchanged from 1900; (6) East South Central (Kentucky, Tennessee, Alabama, and Mississippi); (7) West South Central (Arkansas, Oklahoma, Louisiana, and Texas)—in 1900, the last two made up the South Central division; (8) Mountain (Montana, Idaho, Wyoming, Colorado, New Mexico, Arizona, Utah, and Nevada); and (9) Pacific (Washington, Oregon, and California)—in 1900, the last two made up the Western division.

The excessive patchwork of these divisions prompted American statisticians in 1910 to compress them into three main sections—the North (1-4), the South (5-7) and the West (8-9). We shall presently see that this division into three main sections is really most important and vital, although here, too, as in everything else, there are transitional types, so that on some basic points New England and the Middle Atlantic states will have to be considered separately.

In order to define the fundamental distinction between the three main sections, let us designate them as the *industrial* North, the *former slave-owning* South and the *homestead* West.

Here are the figures on their area, percentage of improved* land, and population:

Sections	Total land area (000,000 acres)	Percentage of improved land	Population (1910) (000,000)
The North	588	49	56
The South	562	27	29
The West	753	5	7
The U.S.A. . .	1,903	25	92

---

* The 1910 Census defines farmland as consisting of (1) improved land, (2) woodland, and (3) all other unimproved land. Improved land includes all land regularly tilled or mowed, land pastured and cropped in rotation, land lying fallow, land in gardens, orchards, vineyards, and nurseries, and land occupied by farm buildings.—*Tr.*

The North and the South have approximately the same area, while the West is nearly half as large again as either. The population of the North, however, is eight times that of the West, which, one might say, is hardly populated. How rapidly it is being settled is evident from the fact that in the 10 years between 1900 and 1910, the population in the North increased by 18 per cent; the South, by 20 per cent; and the West, by 67 per cent! There is hardly any increase in the number of farms in the North: 2,874,000 in 1900, and 2,891,000 in 1910 (+0.6 per cent); in the South the number increased by 18 per cent, from 2,600,000 to 3,100,000; and in the West, by 54 per cent, i.e., more than half as much again, from 243,000 to 373,000.

How land is being settled in the West is seen from the data on *homesteads*, which are parcels of land, mostly of 160 acres, i.e., about 65 dessiatines, allocated by the government free of charge or at a nominal price. In the 10 years between 1901 and 1910, the area occupied by homesteads in the North was 55.3 million acres (including 54.3 million, i.e., more than 98 per cent, in one division alone, namely the West North Central); the area in the South was 20 million acres (including 17.3 million in one division, the West South Central), and in the West, it was 55.3 million acres spread over both divisions. This means that the West is a solid homestead area, i.e., one where unoccupied land is given away practically free—somewhat similar to the squatter land tenure in the outlying districts of Russia, except that it is not regulated by a feudal state, but in a democratic manner (I very nearly said: in a Narodnik manner; the American Republic has implemented in a capitalist way the "Narodnik" idea of distributing unoccupied land to all applicants). The North and the South, however, *each* have only *one* homestead division, which may be regarded as a transitional type from the unsettled West to the settled North and South. Let us note, by the way, that only in two divisions of the North—the New England and the Middle Atlantic—were there absolutely no homestead grants made in the last decade. We shall later have to return to these two most highly industrialised divisions, where there is no longer any homesteading at all.

The above figures on homesteads refer only to claims that have been staked and not to those actually settled; we have no figures on the latter for the various divisions. But even if these returns are somewhat exaggerated as absolute magnitudes, they are, at any rate, a faithful reflection of the relative importance of homesteads in the various divisions. In the North in 1910 the farms totalled 414 million acres, so that homestead claims in the last 10 years came to about one-eighth of the total; in the South, about one-seventeenth (20 out of 354); and in the West, *one-half* (55 out of 111)! To lump together data on areas with hardly any land ownership at all, and data on areas where all the land is occupied, would be to make nonsense of scientific investigation.

America provides the most graphic confirmation of the truth emphasised by Marx in *Capital*, Volume III, that capitalism in agriculture does not depend on the *form* of land ownership or land tenure. Capital finds the most diverse types of medieval and patriarchal landed property—feudal, "peasant allotments" (i.e., the holdings of bonded peasants); clan, communal, state, and other forms of land ownership. Capital takes hold of all these, employing a variety of ways and methods. For agricultural statistics to be properly and rationally compiled, the methods of investigation, tabulation, etc., would have to be modified to correspond to the *forms* of capitalist penetration into agriculture; for instance, the homesteads would have to be put into a special group and their economic fate traced. Unfortunately, however, the statistics are all too often dominated by routine and meaningless, mechanical repetition of the same old methods.

How extensive agriculture is in the West, as compared with the other sections, is evident, by the way, from the data on expenditures for artificial fertilisers. In 1909, the expenditure per acre of improved land was 13 cents ($0.13) in the North; 50 cents, in the South, and only 6 cents in the West. The South has the highest figure because cotton demands great quantities of fertilisers, and the South is primarily a cotton-growing area: cotton and tobacco account for 46.8 per cent of the total value of all its farm crops; grain, only 29.3 per cent; hay and forage, 5.1 per cent. By contrast, grain leads in the North with 62.6 per cent, followed by 18.8 per cent of hay and forage, most of which is cultivated. In the West, grain accounts for 33.1 per cent of the total value of all farm crops; hay and forage, with wild grasses predominating, 31.7 per cent, while fruits, a special branch of commercial farming rapidly developing on the Pacific coast, account for 15.5 per cent of the total value.

2. THE INDUSTRIAL NORTH

By 1910, the urban population in the North reached 58.6 per cent of the total, as compared with 22.5 per cent in the South and 48.8 per cent in the West. The role of industry is evident from these figures:

	Value of products ($000,000,000)				Workers in industry (000,000)
	Crops	Live-stock	Total	Manufactures less cost of raw materials	
The North	3.1	2.1	5.2	6.9	5.2
The South	1.9	0.7	2.6	1.1	1.1
The West	0.5	0.3	0.8	0.5	0.3
The U.S.A. . .	5.5	3.1	8.6	8.5	6.6

The total crop value is here overstated because a part of the crops, such as feed, recurs in the value of the livestock products. But in any case these figures show conclusively that almost five-sixths of American manufacture is concentrated in the North, and that manufacture prevails over agriculture in that section. The South and the West, on the contrary, are predominantly agricultural.

The above table shows that the North differs from the South and the West by a comparatively greater development of industry, which creates a market and makes for the intensification of agriculture. The North—"industrial" in that sense—nevertheless still remains the largest producer of agricultural products. More than one-half, actually about three-fifths, of agricultural production is concentrated in the North. How much more intensive farming is in the North, as compared with the other sections, will be seen from the following figures on the per-acre value of all farm property—land, buildings, implements and machinery, and livestock. In 1910, it was $66 in the North, as compared with $25 in the South, and $41 in the West. The per-acre value of implements and machinery alone was $2.07 in the North, $0.83 in the South, and $1.04 in the West.

The New England and Middle Atlantic divisions stand out in this picture. As I have already pointed out there is no new homesteading in these parts. From 1900 to 1910, there was an absolute decrease in the number of farms, and in the total and in the improved acreage of the farms. Employment returns show that only 10 per cent of the population there is engaged in farming, as compared with a 33 per cent average for the U.S.A., 25 to 41 per cent for the other divisions of the North, and 51 to 63 per cent for the South. Only 6 to 25 per cent of the improved acreage in these two divisions is under cereal crops (the average for the U.S.A. is 40 per cent, and for the North, 46 per cent); 52 to 29 per cent is under grasses, mostly cultivated (as against 15 per cent and 18 per cent); and 4.6 to 3.8 per cent is under vegetables (as against 1.5 and 1.5 per cent). This is the area of the most intensive agriculture. The average expenditure for fertilisers per acre of improved land in 1909 was $1.30 and $0.62 respectively; the former being the U.S. maximum, and the latter, second only to that of one division in the South. The average value of implements and machinery per acre of improved land was $2.58, and $3.88—the maximum figures for the U.S.A. We shall later see that in these most industrialised divisions of the industrial North, agriculture is the most intensive and has the most pronounced capitalist character.

3. THE FORMER SLAVE-OWNING SOUTH

The United States of America, writes Mr. Himmer, is a "country which has never known feudalism and is free from its economic survivals" (p. 41 of his article). This is the very opposite of the truth, for the economic survivals of *slavery* are not in any way distinguishable from those of feudalism, and in the former slave-owning South of the U.S.A. these survivals *are still very powerful*. It would not be worth while to dwell on Mr. Himmer's mistake if it were merely one in a hastily written article. But all liberal and all Narodnik writings in Russia show that the very same "mistake" is being made regularly and with unusual stubbornness with regard to the Russian *labour-service* system, our own survival of feudalism.

The South of the U.S.A. was slave-owning until slavery was swept away by the Civil War of 1861-65. To this day, the Negroes, who make up no more than from 0.7 to 2.2 per cent of the population in the North and the West, constitute from 22.6 to 33.7 per cent of the population in the South. For the U.S.A. as a whole, the Negroes constitute 10.7 per cent of the population. There is no need to elaborate on the degraded social status of the Negroes: the American bourgeoisie is in no way better in this respect than the bourgeoisie of any other country. Having "freed" the Negroes, it took good care, under "free", republican-democratic capitalism, to restore everything possible, and do everything possible and impossible for the most shameless and despicable oppression of the Negroes. A minor statistical fact will illustrate their cultural level. While the proportion of illiterates in 1900 among the white population of the U.S.A. of 10 years of age and over was 6.2 per cent, among the Negroes it was as high as 44.5 per cent! More than seven times as high! In the North and the West illiteracy amounted from 4 to 6 per cent (1900), while in the South it was from 22.9 to 23.9 per cent! One can easily imagine the complex of legal and social relationships that corresponds to this disgraceful fact from the sphere of popular literacy.

What then is the economic basis that has produced and continues to support this fine "superstructure"?

It is the typically Russian, "purely Russian" *labour-service system*, which is known as *share-cropping*.

In 1910, Negroes owned 920,883 farms, i.e., 14.5 per cent of the total. Of the total number of farmers, 37 per cent were tenants; 62.1 per cent, owners; the remaining 0.9 per cent of the farms were run by managers. But among the whites 39.2 per cent were tenant farmers, and among the Negroes—75.3 per cent! The typical white farmer in America is an owner, the typical Negro farmer is a tenant. The proportion of tenants in the West was only 14 per cent: this section is being settled, with new lands unoccupied, and is an El Dorado (a short-lived and unreliable El Dorado, to be sure) for the small "independent farmer". In the North, the proportion of tenant farmers was 26.5 per cent, and in the South, 49.6 per cent! Half of the Southern farmers were tenants.

But that is not all. These are not even tenants in the European, civilised, modern-capitalist sense of the word. They are chiefly semi-feudal or—which is the same thing in economic terms—semi-slave *share-croppers*. In the "free" West, share-croppers were in the minority (25,000 out of a total of 53,000 tenants). In the old North, which was settled long ago, 483,000 out of 766,000 tenant farmers, i.e., 63 per cent, were share-croppers. In the South, *1,021,000* out of 1,537,000 tenant farmers, *i.e., 66 per cent*, were *share-croppers*.

In 1910, free, republican-democratic America had 1,500,000 share-croppers, of whom *more than 1,000,000 were Negroes*. And the proportion of share-croppers to the total number of farmers is not decreasing, but is on the contrary steadily and rather rapidly increasing. In 1880, 17.5 per cent of the farmers in the U.S.A. were share-croppers; in 1890, 18.4 per cent; in 1900, 22.2 per cent; and in 1910, 24 per cent.

American statisticians draw the following conclusions from the 1910 returns:

"In the South the conditions have at all times been somewhat different from those in the North, and many of the tenant farms are parts of plantations of considerable size which date from before the Civil War." In the South, "the system of operation by tenants—chiefly coloured tenants—has succeeded the system of operation by slave labour.... The development of the tenant system is most conspicuous in the South, where the large plantations formerly operated by slave labour have in many cases been broken up into small parcels or tracts and leased to tenants.... These plantations are in many cases still operated substantially as agricultural units, the tenants being subjected to a degree of supervision more or less similar to that which hired farm labourers are subjected to in the North" (op. cit., Vol. V, pp. 102, 104).

To show what the South is like, it is essential to add that its population is fleeing to other capitalist areas and to the towns, just as the peasantry in Russia is fleeing from the most backward central agricultural gubernias, where the survivals of serfdom have been most greatly preserved, in order to escape the rule of the notorious Markovs, to those areas of Russia which have a higher level of capitalist development, to the metropolitan cities, the industrial gubernias and the South (see *The Development of Capitalism in Russia**). The share-cropping area, both in America and in Russia, is the most stagnant area, where the masses are subjected to the greatest degradation and oppression. Immigrants to America, who have such an outstanding role to play in the country's economy and all its social life, shun the South. In 1910, the foreign-born formed 14.5 per cent of the total population of America. But in the South the figure was only 1 to 4 per cent for the several divisions, whereas in the other divisions the proportion of incomers ranged from not less than 13.9 per cent to 27.7 per cent (New England). For the "emancipated" Negroes, the American South is a kind of prison where they are hemmed in, isolated and deprived of fresh air. The South is distinguished by the immobility of its population and by the greatest "attachment to the land": with the exception of that division of the South which still has considerable homesteading (West South Central), 91 to 92

* See Lenin, *Collected Works*, Vol. 3, pp. 585-90.—*Ed.*

per cent of the population in the two other divisions of the South resided in the same division where they were born, whereas for the United States as a whole the figure was 72.6 per cent, i.e., the mobility of the population is much greater. In the West, which is a solid homestead area, only 35 to 41 per cent of the population lived in the division of their birth.

Negroes are in full flight from the two Southern divisions where there is no homesteading: in the 10 years between the last two censuses, these two divisions provided other parts of the country with almost 600,000 "black" people. The Negroes flee mainly to the towns: in the South, 77 to 80 per cent of all the Negroes live in rural communities; in other areas, only 8 to 32 per cent. Thus it turns out that there is a startling similarity in the economic status of the Negroes in America and the peasants in the heart of agricultural Russia who *"were formerly landowners' serfs"*.

4. AVERAGE SIZE OF FARMS.
"DISINTEGRATION OF CAPITALISM" IN THE SOUTH

Having examined the chief distinctive features of the three main sections of the U.S.A., as well as the general nature of their economic conditions, we can now proceed to an analysis of the data most commonly referred to. These are primarily data on the average acreage of farms. It is on the basis of these data that a great many economists, including Mr. Himmer, draw the most categorical conclusions.

Years	Average acreage per farm in the U.S.A.	
	All farmland	Improved land
1850	202.6	78.0
1860	199.2	79.8
1870	153.3	71.0
1880	133.7	71.0
1890	136.5	78.3
1900	146.2	72.2
1910	138.1	75.2

On the whole, there seems at first glance to be a reduction in the average acreage of all farmland and an uncertain fluctuation—upward and downward—in the average improved acreage. But there is a distinct break in the 1860-70 period and this I have indicated by a line. During that period there was an enormous *decrease* in the average acreage of all farmland by 46 acres (from 199.2 to 153.3) and the greatest change (from 79.8 to 71.0), also a reduction, in the average acreage of improved land.

What was the reason? Obviously, the Civil War of 1861-65 and the abolition of slavery. A decisive blow was dealt at the latifundia of the slave-owners. Further on we shall see repeated confirmation of this fact, but it is so generally known that it is surprising that it needs any proof at all. Let us separate the returns for the North and those for the South.

Average acreage per farm

Years	South		North	
	All farmland	Improved land	All farmland	Improved land
1850	332.1	101.1	127.1	65.4
1860	335.4	101.3	126.4	68.3
1870	214.2	69.2	117.0	69.2
1880	153.4	56.2	114.9	76.6
1890	139.7	58.8	123.7	87.8
1900	138.2	48.1	132.2	90.9
1910	114.4	48.6	143.0	100.3

We find that in the South the average improved acreage per farm between 1860 and 1870 greatly *decreased* (from 101.3 to 69.2), and that in the North it slightly *increased* (from 68.3 to 69.2). This means that the cause lay in the specific conditions of evolution in the South. There we find, even after the abolition of slavery, a reduction in the average acreage of farms, although the process is slow and not continuous.

Mr. Himmer's deduction is that in the South "the small-scale family farms are extending their domination, while

capital is leaving agriculture for other spheres of investment. . . . Agricultural capitalism is rapidly disintegrating
in the South Atlantic states. . .".

This is an amusing assertion likely to be matched only
in the arguments of our Narodniks on the "disintegration
of capitalism" in Russia after 1861 in consequence of the
landlords abandoning corvée for the labour-service (i.e.,
semi-corvée!) system of economy. The break-up of the slave-
worked latifundia is called the "disintegration of capitalism". The transformation of the unimproved land of yesterday's slave-owners into the small farms of Negroes, half
of whom are share-croppers (it should be borne in mind
that the proportion of share-croppers has been steadily
growing from census to census!), is called the "disintegration of capitalism". It is hardly possible to go any further
in distorting the fundamental concepts of economics!

Chapter Twelve of the 1910 Census supplies information
on typical Southern "plantations"—not of the old slave
period, but of our own day. On the 39,073 plantations
there are 39,073 "landlord farms" and 398,905 tenant
farms, or an average of 10 tenants per landlord or "master".
Plantations average 724 acres, of which only 405 acres is
improved, more than 300 acres being unimproved; not a
bad reserve for the gentlemen who were the slave-owners
of yesterday to draw on in extending their plans of exploitation. . . .

Land on the average plantation is distributed as follows: "landlord" farm—331 acres, of which 87 is improved.
"Tenant" farms, i.e., the parcels of the Negro share-croppers, who continue to work for the master and under his
eye, average 38 acres, of which 31 is improved land.

As the population and the demand for cotton increase,
the former slave-owners of the South begin to parcel out
their vast latifundia, nine-tenths of the land on which is
still unimproved, into small tracts which are either sold to
the Negroes or, more frequently, leased to them on a half-
crop basis. (From 1900 to 1910, the number of farmers
in the South who were full owners of all their farmland
increased from 1,237,000 to 1,329,000, i.e., 7.5 per cent,
while the number of share-croppers went up from 772,000

to 1,021,000, i.e., 32.2 per cent.) And yet an economist has appeared who says this is "disintegration of capitalism"....

I designate as latifundia farms with an area of 1,000 acres and over. In 1910, the proportion of such farms in the U.S.A. was 0.8 per cent (50,135 farms), and they added up to 167.1 million acres, or 19.0 per cent of the total amount of land. This is an average of 3,332 acres per latifundium. Only 18.7 per cent of their acreage was improved while for all farms the figure was 54.4 per cent. The capitalist North has the *smallest* number of latifundia: 0.5 per cent of the total number of farms accounting for 6.9 per cent of the land, 41.1 per cent of which is improved. The West has the greatest number of latifundia: 3.9 per cent of the total number of farms accounting for 48.3 per cent of the land; 32.3 per cent of the land in the latifundia is improved. But it is in the former slave-owning South that the latifundia have the *highest* proportion of unimproved land: 0.7 per cent of the farms are latifundia; they account for 23.9 per cent of the land; *only 8.5 per cent of the land* in the latifundia is improved! Incidentally, these detailed statistics clearly show that there is really no foundation for the common practice of classifying the latifundia as *capitalist* enterprises, without a detailed analysis of the specific data for each country and each area.

During the 10 years from 1900 to 1910, the total acreage of the latifundia, but only of the latifundia, showed a *decrease*. The reduction was quite substantial: from 197.8 million to 167.1 million acres, i.e., 30.7 million acres. In the South, there was a reduction of 31.8 million acres (in the North, an increase of 2.3 million, and in the West, a reduction of 1.2 million). Consequently, it is in the South, and in the slave-owning South alone, that the latifundia, with their negligible proportion (8.5 per cent) of improved land, are being broken up on a really vast scale.

The inescapable conclusion is that the only exact definition of the economic process under way is—a transition from the slave-holding latifundia, nine-tenths of which remained unimproved, to small *commercial* agriculture. It is a transition to commercial farms and not to farms worked by family labour, as Mr. Himmer and the Narodniks, together with all the bourgeois economists who sing cheap hymns to "labour", love to say. The term "family labour" has no politico-economic meaning and is indirectly misleading. It is devoid of meaning because the small farmer "labours" under any social system of economy, be it slavery, serfdom or capitalism. The term "family labour" is just an empty phrase, pure oratory which serves to cover up the *confusion* of entirely different social forms of economic organisation—a confusion from which the bourgeoisie alone stands to gain. The term "family labour" is misleading and deceives the public, for it creates the impression that *hired* labour is not employed.

Mr. Himmer, like all bourgeois economists, evades just these statistics on hired labour, although they are the most important data on the question of capitalism in agriculture and although they are to be found in the 1900 Census report, as well as in the 1910 *Abstract—Farm Crops, by States,* which Mr. Himmer himself quotes (note on p. 49 of his article).

The nature of the staple crop of the South shows that the growth of small-scale agriculture in the South is nothing but the growth of commercial farming. That crop is cotton. Cereals yield 29.3 per cent of the total crop value in the South; hay and forage, 5.1 per cent; and cotton, 42.7 per cent. From 1870 to 1910, the production of wool in the U.S.A. went up from 162 million lbs. to 321 million lbs., i.e., it doubled; wheat, increased from 236 million to 635 million bushels, i.e., less than threefold; corn, from 1,094 million to 2,886 million bushels, also less than threefold; and cotton, from 4,000,000 bales (of 500 lbs. each) to 12,000,000, i.e., threefold. The growth of the crop that is primarily commercial was faster than that of other, less commercialised, crops. In addition, there was in the main division of the South, the South Atlantic, a rather substantial development of tobacco production (12.1 per cent of the crop value in the State of Virginia); vegetables (20.1 per cent of the total crop value in the State of Delaware, 23.2 per cent in the State of Florida); fruits (21.3 per cent of the total crop value in the State of Florida); etc. The nature of all these crops implies an intensification of farming, a larger scale of operations on smaller acreages, and greater employment of hired labour.

I shall now proceed to a detailed analysis of the returns on hired labour; let us note only that the employment of hired labour is also growing in the South, although in this respect it lags behind the other sections—*less* hired labour is employed because of the *wider* practice of semi-slave share-cropping.

5. THE CAPITALIST NATURE OF AGRICULTURE

Capitalism in agriculture is usually gauged by the data on the size of farms or the number and importance of big farms (in terms of acreage). I have examined some of these data and shall return to the problem later on, but it must be said that all these are, after all, indirect indications, for acreage is not always an indication, and not by any means a direct indication, that a farm is really big as *an economic enterprise*, or that it is capitalist in character.

In this respect the data on hired labour are far more indicative and offer better proof. Agricultural censuses taken in recent years, such as the Austrian of 1902 and the German of 1907, which I shall examine elsewhere, show that the employment of hired labour in present-day agriculture—and especially in small-scale farming—is much greater than is generally believed. Nothing so obviously and categorically refutes the petty-bourgeois myth about small "family" farms as do these figures.

American statisticians have collected very extensive material on this, for each farmer's individual census form asks whether he spends anything on hired labour, and, if he does, exactly how much. In contrast to European statistics—such as those of the two countries just named—no record is made in American statistics of the number of hired labourers employed at the time by each farmer, although that could be easily discovered, and the scientific value of such information, in addition to the returns on the total expenditure on hired labour, would indeed be very great. But the worst thing is the very poor tabulation of these returns in the 1910 Census, which is in general presented much more poorly than the 1900 Census. The 1910 Census groups all farms by acreage (as does the 1900 Census) but, by contrast, it does not give any figures on the employment of hired labour by these groups. This makes it impossible for us to compare the employment of hired labour by farms with small and with large acreages. The Census merely gives the average figures for the states and the sections, i.e., data lumping together capitalist and non-capitalist farms.

I shall make a special point of going into the more elaborate data for 1900 later on; meanwhile, here are the figures for 1910; in fact they relate to 1899 and 1909.

Sections	Percentage of farms hiring labour (1909)	Increase of expenditure on hired labour 1899-1909 (per cent)	Expenditure on hired labour per acre of improved land ($)	
			1909	1899
The North	55.1	+ 70.8	1.26	0.82
The South	36.6	+ 87.1	1.07	0.69
The West	52.5	+119.0	3.25	2.07
The U.S.A. . . .	45.9	+ 82.3	1.36	0.86

The first thing that is made obvious by these figures is that agriculture is most capitalistic in the North (55.1 per cent of farms employ hired labour); then, follows the West (52.5 per cent) and, lastly, the South (36.6 per cent). That is just as it should be when any densely populated and industrial area is being compared with an area still undergoing colonisation and with an area of share-cropping. It goes without saying that figures on the proportion of farms employing hired labour are more suitable for a precise comparison of the sections than data on the expenditure on hired labour per acre of improved land. For the latter type of data to be comparable, the level of wages in the sections would have to be the same. No information on farm wages in the U.S.A. is available but in the light of the basic distinctions between the sections it is inconceivable that their wage levels are the same.

Thus, in the North and in the West—the two sections which together have two-thirds of the improved land and two-thirds of the livestock—*more than one-half* the farmers cannot manage without hired labour. The proportion is smaller in the South only because there the semi-feudal (alias semi-slave) system of exploitation in the form of share-cropping is still strong. There is no doubt that in America, as in all the other capitalist countries, a part of the handicapped farmers have to sell their labour-power. Unfortunately, American statistics do not contain any information about this, in contrast, for example, to the 1907 German statistics, in which these data have been collected and worked out in detail. According to the German statistics, hiring themselves out as labourers is the *main* occupation of 1,940,867 persons, i.e., over 30 per cent, of the 5,736,082 owners of farms (a total which includes the very small "owners"). To be sure, the mass of these farm-hands and day-labourers with a bit of land of their own belong to the poorest groups of farmers.

Let us assume that in the U.S.A., where the smallest farms (of less than three acres) are as a general rule not registered at all, only 10 per cent of the farmers sell their labour-power. Even then we find that *more than one-third* of the farmers are *directly* exploited by the landlords and capitalists (24 per cent share-croppers who are exploited by former slave-owners in feudal or semi-feudal fashion, plus 10 per cent who are exploited by the capitalists, or altogether 34 per cent). This means that of the total number of farmers a *minority*, hardly more than *one-fifth or one-quarter*, neither hire labourers nor hire themselves out or sell themselves into bondage.

Such is the actual state of affairs in the country of "model and advanced" capitalism, in the country with free distribution of millions of dessiatines of land. Here again the famous non-capitalist, small-scale "family" farming proves to be a myth.

How many hired labourers are engaged in American agriculture? Is their number increasing or decreasing in proportion to the total number of farmers and the total rural population?

It is regrettable that American statistics do not provide a direct answer to these highly important questions. Let us find an approximate answer.

Firstly, we can obtain an approximate answer from the returns on occupations (Volume IV of the Census reports). These statistics are not an American "success". They are compiled in such a routine, mechanical, incongruous manner that they contain no information on the status of the persons employed, i.e., no distinction is made between farmers, family workers, and hired labourers. Instead of making a precise economic classification, the compilers were content to use "popular" terminology, absurdly bracketing members of farmers' families and hired labourers under the head of farm workers. As we know it is *not* only in American statistics that there is complete chaos on this question.

The 1910 Census makes an attempt to bring some order into this chaos, to correct the obvious mistakes and to separate at least a part of the hired labourers (those working out) from members of the family working on the home farm. In a series of calculations the statisticians correct the total number of persons engaged in farming, reducing it by 468,100 (Vol. IV, p. 27). The number of *females* working out is set at 220,048 for 1900, and 337,522 for 1910 (an increase of 53 per cent). The number of males working out in 1910 was 2,299,444. Assuming that in 1900 the proportion of hired labourers to the total number of farm workers was the same as in 1910, the number of males working out in 1900 must have been 1,798,165. We then obtain this picture:

	1900	1910	Increase (per cent)
Total engaged in agriculture	10,381,765	12,099,825	+16
Number of farmers . . .	5,674,875	5,981,522	+ 5
Number of hired labourers	2,018,213	2,566,966	+27

That is, the percentage increase in the number of hired labourers was over five times greater than in that of farmers (27 per cent and 5 per cent). The proportion of farmers in the rural population *decreased*; the proportion of hired labourers *increased*. The proportion of independent farm operators to the total farming population dropped; the number of dependent, exploited persons increased.

In 1907, hired farm labourers in Germany numbered 4.5 million out of a total of 15 million persons working on the home farm and working out. Consequently, 30 per cent were hired labourers. In America, according to the estimate given above, the figure was 2.5 million out of 12 million, i.e., 21 per cent. It is possible that the availability of vacant land distributed free, and the high percentage of share-cropping tenants tended to lower the percentage of hired labourers in America.

Secondly, an approximate answer may be provided by the figures on expenditure on hired labour in 1899 and 1909. During the same period, the number of industrial wage-workers increased from 4.7 million to 6.6 million, i.e., 40 per cent, and their wages from $2,008 million to $3,427 million, i.e., 70 per cent. (It should be borne in mind that the rise in the cost of living cancelled out this nominal increase in wages.)

On the strength of this we may assume that the 82 per cent increase in expenditure on hired farm labour corresponds to an increase of approximately 48 per cent in the number of hired labourers. Making a similar assumption for the three main sections we obtain the following picture:

Sections	Percentage increase from 1900 to 1910		
	Total rural population	Number of farms	Number of hired labourers
The North	+ 3.9	+ 0.6	+40
The South	+14.8	+18.2	+50
The West	+49.7	+53.7	+66
The U.S.A.	+11.2	+10.9	+48

These figures also show that for the country as a whole the increase in the number of farmers is not keeping pace with the growth of the rural population, while the increase in the number of hired labourers is outstripping the growth of the rural population. In other words: the proportion of independent farm operators is decreasing, and the proportion of dependent farm workers is increasing.

It should be noted that the great difference between the increase in the number of hired labourers obtained in the first estimate (+27 per cent) and in the second (+48 per cent) is quite possible because in the former only the *professional* farm labourers were enumerated, and in the latter, *every instance* of employment of hired labour was taken into account. In farming, seasonal hired labour is highly important, and it should be the rule, therefore, that it is never enough to determine the number of hired labourers, permanent and seasonal, but that an effort must also be made to determine, as far as possible, the total expenditure on hired labour.

At any rate, both estimates definitely show a *growth* of capitalism in agriculture in the U.S.A., and an *increase* in the employment of hired labour, which is proceeding at a faster pace than the growth of the rural population and of the number of farmers.

6. AREAS OF THE MOST INTENSIVE AGRICULTURE

Having examined the general data on hired labour as the most direct indicator of capitalism in agriculture, we can now go on to a more detailed analysis of the specific *forms* assumed by capitalism in this particular branch of the economy.

We have taken a look at one area with a shrinking average acreage of farms, namely, the South, where the process signifies a transition from latifundia worked by slaves to small-scale commercial farms. There is another area where the average acreage of farms is diminishing—a part of the North: New England and the Middle Atlantic states. Here are the figures for these divisions:

	Average acreage per farm (improved land)	
	New England	Middle Atlantic states
1850	66.5	70.8
1860	66.4	70.3
1870	66.4	69.2
1880	63.4	68.0
1890	56.5	67.4
1900	42.4	63.4
1910	38.4	62.6

The average farm in New England is smaller than in any other division of the U.S.A. In two Southern divisions the average is 42 to 43 acres, and in the third, the West South Central, where homesteading is still going on, it is 61.8 acres, i.e., almost as much as in the Middle Atlantic states. It is the reduction in the average size of farms in New England and the Middle Atlantic states, "the areas with an older culture and a higher level of economic development" (Mr. Himmer, p. 60), where homesteading is no longer taking place, that has led Mr. Himmer, as it has very many other bourgeois economists, to draw the conclusion that "capitalist agriculture is disintegrating", that "production is breaking up into smaller units", that there are "no areas where colonisation is no longer continuing, or where large-scale capitalist agriculture is not decaying and is not being replaced by family-labour farms".

Mr. Himmer arrived at these conclusions, which are the very opposite of the truth, because he forgot a mere "trifle": the intensification of agriculture! It is incredible, but it is a fact. This matter requires a particularly thorough analysis because quite a few bourgeois economists, almost all in fact, contrive to forget this "trifle" when dealing with small and large-scale production in agriculture, although "in theory" they are all "aware" of and accept the intensification of farming. This is indeed one of the basic sources of all the misadventures of bourgeois (including Narodnik and opportunist) economics on the question of small "family" farms. The "trifle" they forget is this: owing to the technical peculiarities of agriculture, the process of its intensification frequently leads to a *reduction* in the improved acreage on the farm, and at the same time expands it as an *economic unit*, increasing its *output*, and making it more and more of a *capitalist* enterprise.

Let us first see whether or not there is any fundamental difference in farming techniques, in the general character of farming and degree of its intensification between New England and the Middle Atlantic states, on the one hand, and between the rest of the North and the country's other divisions, on the other.

The differences in the crops grown are shown in the following table:

Divisions	Percentage of the total crop value (1910)		
	Cereals	Hay and forage	Vegetables, fruits and similar special crops
New England	7.6	41.9	33.5
Middle Atlantic	29.6	31.4	31.8
East North Central	65.4	16.5	11.0
West North Central	75.4	14.6	5.9

The difference in farming conditions is fundamental. In the first two divisions agriculture is highly intensive; in the other two it is extensive. In the latter, cereals account for the bulk of the total crop value; in the former, they contribute not only a minor part, but sometimes a negligible part (7.6 per cent), while the special "commercial" crops (vegetables, fruits, etc.) yield a *greater* part of the crop value than cereals. Extensive agriculture has given way to intensive agriculture. Grass cultivation has become widespread. Of the 3.8 million acres under hay and forage in New England, 3.3 million acres were under *cultivated* grasses. The figures for the Middle Atlantic states are 8.5 and 7.9 million respectively. By contrast, of the 27.4 million acres under hay and forage in the West North Central states (an area of colonisation and extensive agriculture), 14.5 million, i.e., the greater part, were unimproved grasslands, etc.

Yields are considerably higher in the "intensive" states:

| Divisions | Per-acre yield in bushels | | | |
| | Corn | | Wheat | |
	1909	1899	1909	1899
New England	45.2	39.4	23.5	18.0
Middle Atlantic	32.2	34.0	18.6	14.9
East North Central . . .	38.6	38.3	17.2	12.9
West North Central . . .	27.7	31.4	14.8	12.2

The same is true of commercial livestock and dairy farming, which are especially highly developed in these divisions:

| Divisions | Average number of dairy cows per farm (1900) | Average production of milk per cow (gallons) | |
		1909	1899
New England	5.8	476	548
Middle Atlantic	6.1	490	514
East North Central	4.0	410	487
West North Central	4.9	325	371
The South (3 divisions) . . .	1.9-3.1	232-288	290-395
The West (2 divisions) . . .	4.7-5.1	339-475	334-470
The U.S.A.	3.8	362	424

This table shows that in the "intensive" states dairy farming is on a considerably *larger* scale than in all the others. The areas with the *smallest* farms (in terms of improved acreage) have the *largest* dairies. This fact is of tremendous importance, for, as everyone knows, dairy farming develops most rapidly in suburban localities and in very highly industrialised countries (or areas). Statistics from Denmark, Germany and Switzerland, which are dealt with elsewhere,* also show a *growing concentration* of dairy cattle.

* See Lenin, *Collected Works*, Vol. 5, pp. 205-22, and Vol. 13, pp. 169-216.—*Ed.*

As we have seen, hay and forage in the "intensive" states constitute a considerably greater proportion of the total crop value than cereals. Accordingly, livestock farming there develops largely on the basis of *purchased feed*. Here are the relevant figures for 1909:

Divisions	Receipts from sale of feed	Outlays on feed	Excess of receipts or outlays
	($000,000)		
New England	+ 4.3	—34.6	— 30.3
Middle Atlantic	+ 21.6	—54.7	— 33.1
East North Central	+195.6	—40.6	+155.0
West North Central	+174.4	—76.2	+ 98.2

The extensive states of the North sell feed. The intensive states buy it. It is clear that if feed is purchased *large-scale* operations of a highly capitalistic nature can be conducted on a *small* tract of land.

Let us make a comparison between the two intensive divisions of the North, New England and the Middle Atlantic states, and the most extensive division of the North, the West North Central:

Divisions	Improved land (000,000 acres)	Value of livestock ($000,000)	Receipts from sale of feed ($000,000)	Outlays on feed ($000,000)
New England + Middle Atlantic . . .	36.5	447	26	89
West North Central	164.3	1,552	174	76

We find that there is more livestock per acre of improved land in the intensive states (447 : 36=$12 per acre) than in the extensive states (1,552 : 164=$9). More capital in the form of livestock is invested in a unit of land area. And the total per-acre turnover of the feed trade (purchases+sales) is also very much greater in the intensive states (26+89= =$115 million for 36 million acres) than in the extensive states (174+76=$250 million for 164 million acres). In the intensive states farming is obviously much more *commercialised* than in the extensive states.

Expenditure on fertilisers and the value of implements and machinery are the most exact statistical expression of the degree of intensification of agriculture. Here are the figures:

Divisions	Percentage of farms with outlays on fertilisers	Average outlays per farm ($)	Average outlays per acre of improved land ($)	Average Improved acreage per farm	
			1909	1899	(1909)
The North					
New England	60.9	82	1.30	0.53	38.4
Middle Atlantic	57.1	68	0.62	0.37	62.6
East North Central . .	19.6	37	0.09	0.07	79.2
West North Central . .	2.1	41	0.01	0.01	148.0
The South					
South Atlantic	69.2	77	1.23	0.49	43.6
East South Central . .	33.8	37	0.29	0.13	42.2
West South Central . .	6.4	53	0.06	0.03	61.8
The West					
Mountain	1.3	67	0.01	0.01	86.8
Pacific	6.4	189	0.10	0.05	116.1
The U.S.A.	28.7	63	0.24	0.13	75.2

This fully brings out the difference between the extensive divisions of the North, with an insignificant proportion of farms using purchased fertilisers (2-19 per cent), and with negligible expenditure on fertilisers per acre of improved land ($0.01-$0.09)—and the intensive states, where the *majority* of farms (57-60 per cent) use purchased fertilisers and where expenditure on fertilisers is substantial. In New England, for example, the per-acre expenditure is $1.30—the *maximum* figure for all divisions (once again a case of farms with the smallest acreage and the largest expenditure on fertilisers!), which exceeds the figure for one of the divisions of the South (South Atlantic). It should be noted that in the South especially large quantities of artificial fertilisers are required by cotton, on which, as we have seen, the labour of Negro share-croppers is most widely employed.

In the Pacific states, we find a very small percentage of farms using fertilisers (6.4 per cent) but the maximum average per farm expenditure ($189)—calculated, of course, only for the farms which used fertilisers. Here we have another example of the growth of *large-scale* and capitalist agriculture with a simultaneous *reduction* of the farm acreage. In two of the three Pacific states—Washington and Oregon—the use of fertilisers is quite insignificant, a mere $0.01 per acre. It is only in the third state, California, that the figure is relatively high: $0.08 in 1899, and $0.19 in 1909. In this state, the fruit crop plays a special role, and is expanding at an extremely rapid rate along purely capitalist lines; in 1909, it accounted for 33.1 per cent of the total crop value, as against 18.3 per cent for cereals, and 27.6 per cent for hay and forage. The typical fruit-growing farm has a *smaller-than-average* acreage but the use of fertilisers and hired labour is *much greater* than average. We shall later have occasion to dwell on relationships of this type, which are typical of capitalist countries with an intensive agriculture and which are most stubbornly ignored by statisticians and economists.

But let us return to the "intensive" states of the North. Not only is expenditure on fertilisers—$1.30 per acre—in New England the highest and the average farm acreage the smallest (38.4 acres); expenditure on fertilisers is increasing at an especially rapid rate. In the 10 years between 1899 and 1909, this expenditure increased from $0.53 per acre to $1.30, i.e., two and one-half times. Consequently, here intensification of agriculture, technical progress and improvement of farming techniques are extremely rapid. To get a more graphic picture of what this means let us compare New England, the most intensive division of the North, with West North Central, the most extensive division. In the latter division, scarcely any artificial fertilisers are used at all (2.1 per cent of the farms and $0.01 per acre); its farm acreage is larger than that of any other division of America (148 acres), and is growing at a faster rate. This particular division is usually taken as the model of capitalism in American agriculture—and this Mr. Himmer also does. As I shall show in detail later on, this is incorrect. It is due to the crudest, most primitive form of extensive agriculture being confused with technically progressive intensive agriculture. In the West North Central division, the average farm is four times as big as in New England (148 acres as against 38.4), while average expenditure on fertilisers per user is only half as great: $41 as against $82.

Hence, in actual practice there are instances of a substantial *reduction* in farm acreage being accompanied by a substantial *increase* in expenditure on artificial fertilisers, so that "small" production—if we continue, as a matter of routine, to regard it as being small in terms of acreage—turns out to be "large" in terms of the capital invested in the land. This is not an exception, but the rule for any country where extensive agriculture is giving way to intensive agriculture. And this applies to *all* capitalist countries, so that when this typical, essential and fundamental characteristic of agriculture is ignored, the result is the common error of the votaries of small-scale agriculture who base their judgement only on farm acreage.

7. MACHINERY AND HIRED LABOUR IN AGRICULTURE

Let us consider another form of capital investment in land which is technically different from the form examined above—implements and machinery. All European agricultural statistics provide irrefutable evidence that the larger the farm acreage, the greater is the proportion of farms using all types of machines and the greater the number of machines used. The superiority of big farms in this highly important respect has been established beyond doubt. In this field, too, American statisticians have a rather unconventional approach: neither implements nor farm machinery are recorded separately, only their total value being given. Such data may, of course, be less exact in each individual case, but taken as a whole they allow definite comparisons between divisions and between groups of farms—comparisons which are impossible with other kinds of data.

Below are the figures for farm implements and machinery by divisions:

Divisions	Value of implements and machinery (1909)	
	Average per farm ($)	Average per acre of all farmland ($)
The North New England	269	2.58
Middle Atlantic	358	3.88
East North Central	239	2.28
West North Central	332	1.59
The South (three divisions)	72-88-127	0.71-0.92-0.95
The West (two divisions)	269-350	0.83-1.29
The U.S.A.	199	1.44

The former slave-owning South, the area of share-cropping, occupies a bottom place in the use of machinery. The value of implements and machinery per acre—for its three divisions—is one-third, one-quarter, one-fifth of the figures for the intensive states of the North. The latter lead the rest and, in particular, are far ahead of the West North Central states, America's most agricultural area and her granary, which superficial observers still frequently regard as a model area of capitalism and of the use of machinery.

It should be noted that the American statistical method of determining the value of machinery, as well as of land, livestock, buildings, etc., per acre of *all* farmland and not per acre of improved land, understates the superiority of the "intensive" areas of the North and cannot, in general, be considered correct. The difference between the divisions in regard to the proportion of improved acreage is very great: in the West, it is as low as 26.7 per cent for the Mountain states, and as high as 75.4 per cent for the East North Central states in the North. For the purposes of economic statistics, improved land is undoubtedly of much greater importance than total acreage. In New England,

improved acreage in farms and its proportion of the total
has decreased substantially, especially since 1880, probably
under the impact of competition from the free lands of the
West (i.e., free from ground-rent, from tribute to the landowning gentry). At the same time, the use of machinery
in this division is very extensive and the value of machinery per acre of *improved land* is especially high. In 1910,
it amounted to $7 per acre, while in the Middle Atlantic
states it was about $5.50 and not more than $2-3 in the
other divisions.

Again, the division with the *smallest* farms, in terms of
acreage, turns out to have the *largest* capital investments
in land in the form of machinery.

Comparing the Middle Atlantic, one of the "intensive"
divisions of the North, with the most extensive region of
the North, the West North Central, we discover that as far
as improved acreage per farm is concerned, that of the
former is *less than half that of the latter*—62.6 acres as
against 148.0—while the value of machinery used is
greater—$358 per farm against $332. The smaller farms
are thus larger enterprises in terms of machinery used.

We still have to compare the data on the intensive
nature of agriculture with the data on the employment of
hired labour. I already gave these figures in brief above, in
Chapter 5. We must now examine them in greater detail by
divisions. (See table on p. 146.)

This shows, firstly, that capitalism is undoubtedly much
more developed in the agriculture of the Northern intensive states than in that of the extensive states; secondly,
that in the former, capitalism is developing faster than in
the latter; thirdly, that the division with the smallest farms,
New England, has both the highest level of development of
capitalism in agriculture and the highest rate of its development. There the increase of expenditure on hired labour
per acre of improved land is 86 per cent; the Pacific states
come second in this respect. California, where, as I have
said, "small-scale" capitalist fruit-raising is rapidly developing, is also the leader in this respect among the Pacific
states.

The West North Central division, with the largest farm

Divisions	Percentage of farms hiring labour in 1909	Average outlays on hired labour per hiring farm ($)	Outlays on labour per acre of improved land		Increase of outlays from 1899 to 1909 (per cent)
			1909	1899	
The North New England	66.0	277	4.76	2.55	+86
Middle Atlantic	65.8	253	2.66	1.64	+62
East North Central . .	52.7	199	1.33	0.78	+71
West North Central . .	51.0	240	0.83	0.56	+48
The South South Atlantic	42.0	142	1.37	0.80	+71
East South Central . .	31.6	107	0.80	0.49	+63
West South Central . .	35.6	178	1.03	0.75	+37
The West Mountain	46.8	547	2.95	2.42	+22
Pacific	58.0	694	3.47	1.92	+80
The U.S.A.	45.9	223	1.36	0.86	+58

acreages (an average of 148 acres in 1910, counting improved land only) and with the most rapid and steady growth of farm acreages since 1850, is commonly regarded as the "model" capitalist region of American agriculture. We have now seen that this contention is profoundly erroneous. The extent to which hired labour is used is certainly the best and most direct indicator of the development of capitalism. And it tells us that America's "granary", the region of the much vaunted "wheat factories", which attract so much attention, is *less* capitalist than the industrial and intensively farmed region, where the indication of agricultural progress is not an increase in improved acreage but an *increase* in capital investments in the land, together with a simultaneous *reduction* of the acreage.

It is quite possible to imagine that with the use of machinery the improvement of the "black soil" or unploughed virgin lands in general can proceed very rapidly despite a small increase in the employment of hired labour. In the West North Central states expenditure on hired labour per acre of improved land was $0.56 in 1899, and $0.83 in 1909, an increase of only 48 per cent. In New England, where the improved area is decreasing and not increasing and where the average size of farms is decreasing and not increasing, expenditure on hired labour was not only very much higher both in 1899 ($2.55 per acre) and in 1909 ($4.76 per acre), but had grown during the period at a much faster rate (+86 per cent).

The average farm in New England is *one-fourth* the size of farms in the West North Central states (38.4 as against 148 acres), yet its average expenditure on hired labour is *greater*: $277 as against $240. Consequently, the reduction in the size of farms means in such cases that a greater amount of capital is invested in agriculture, and that the capitalist nature of agriculture is intensified; it signifies a growth of capitalism and capitalist production.

While the West North Central states, which comprise 34.3 per cent of the total improved acreage in the U.S.A., are the most typical division of "extensive" capitalist agriculture, the *Mountain* states offer an example of similar extensive farming in conditions of the most rapid colonisation. Here less hired labour is employed, in terms of the proportion of farms employing labour, but the average expenditure on hired labour is very much higher than in the West North Central division. But in the former the employment of hired labour increased at a slower rate than in any other division of America (only +22 per cent). This type of evolution was apparently due to the following conditions. In this division, colonisation and the distribution of homesteads are extremely widespread. The area under crops increased more than in any other division: by 89 per cent from 1900 to 1910. The settlers, the owners of the homesteads, naturally employ little hired labour, at any rate when starting their farms. On the other hand, hired labour must be employed on a very large scale, firstly, by some latifundia, which are especially numerous in this division as in the West in general; and secondly, by farms raising special and highly capitalist crops. In some states of this division, for instance, a very high proportion of the total crop value comes from fruits (Arizona—6 per cent, Colorado—10 per cent), and vegetables (Colorado—11.9 per cent, Nevada—11.2 per cent), and so forth.

In summing up, I must say the following: Mr. Himmer's assertion that "there are no areas where colonisation is no longer continuing, or where large-scale capitalist agriculture is not decaying and is not being replaced by family-labour farms", is a mockery of the truth, and entirely contrary to the actual facts. The New England division, where there is no colonisation at all, where farms are smallest, where farming is most intensive, shows the highest level of capitalism in agriculture and the highest rate of capitalist development. This conclusion is most essential and basic for an understanding of the process of capitalist development in agriculture in general, because the intensification of agriculture and the reduction in the average farm acreage that goes with it is not some accidental, local, casual phenomenon, but one that is *common* to all civilised countries. Bourgeois economists of every stripe make a host of mistakes when considering data on the evolution of agriculture (as in Great Britain, Denmark, and Germany) because they are not familiar enough with this general phenomenon, they have not given it enough thought and have not understood or analysed it.

8. DISPLACEMENT OF SMALL BY BIG ENTERPRISES. QUANTITY OF IMPROVED LAND

We have examined the major forms of the development of capitalism in agriculture, and have seen how extremely varied they are. The most important are: the break-up of the slave-holding latifundia in the South; the growth of large-scale extensive farming operations in the extensive area of the North; the most rapid development of capitalism in the intensive area of the North, where farms are, on the average, the smallest. The facts incontrovertibly prove that in some cases the development of capitalism is indicated by an increase in farm acreage and in others by an increase in the number of farms. In view of such a state of affairs we learn nothing from the returns on average farm acreages summarised for the country as a whole.

What then is the net result of the various local and agricultural peculiarities? An indication is given by the data on hired labour. The growing employment of hired labour is a general process transcending *all* these peculiarities. But in the vast majority of civilised countries agricultural statistics, paying tribute, intentionally or otherwise, to prevailing bourgeois notions and prejudices, either fail to furnish any systematic information on hired labour at all, or give it only for the most recent period (e.g., German Agricultural Census of 1907), so that it is impossible to make a comparison with the past. I shall show in detail elsewhere that in the elaboration and tabulation of the returns of hired labour American statistics changed markedly for the worse between 1900 and 1910.

The most common and most popular method of presenting statistical summaries in America and most other countries is to compare big and small farms by acreage. I shall now proceed to a consideration of these data.

In grouping farms by acreage, American statisticians take total acreage and not just the improved area, which would, of course, be the more correct method, and is the one employed by German statisticians. No reason is given why *seven* groups (under 20 acres, 20 to 49, 50 to 99, 100 to 174, 175 to 499, 500 to 999, 1,000 and over) are used to tabulate the returns of the 1910 Census in the United States. Statistical routine must apparently have been of paramount consideration. I shall call the 100-to-174-acre group—medium, because it consists mostly of homesteads (the official size of a homestead is 160 acres), and also because landholdings of this size usually give the farmer the greatest degree of "independence" and require the least employment of hired labour. The groups above that I shall call large or capitalistic because, as a general rule, they do not manage without hired labour. Farms with 1,000 acres and over I shall regard as latifundia—of which three-fifths is unimproved land in the North, nine-tenths, in the South, and two-thirds, in the West. Small farms are those with less than 100 acres; how much economic independence they have is evident from the fact that in three groups, from the bottom up, 51 per cent, 43 per cent and 23 per cent of the farms respectively are recorded as having no horses. It goes without saying that this characteristic should not be taken in an absolute sense and should not be applied to all divisions or to localities with specific conditions without a special analysis.

I am unable to give here the returns for all the seven groups in the main sections of the United States, for this would overload the text with an excessive number of figures. I shall, therefore, merely outline the basic distinctions between the North, the South and the West, and give the full returns only for the United States as a whole. We should not lose sight of the fact that three-fifths (60.6 per cent) of all the improved land is in the North; less than one-third (31.5 per cent), in the South; and under one-twelfth (7.9 per cent), in the West.

The most striking distinction between the three main sections is that the capitalist North has the *smallest* number of latifundia, although their number, their total acreage, and their improved acreage are on the increase. In 1910, 0.5 per cent of the farms in the North were of 1,000 acres and over; these big farms had 6.9 per cent of all the land and 4.1 per cent of the improved land. The South had 0.7 per cent of such farms, with 23.9 per cent of the total acreage and 4.8 per cent of the improved acreage. In the West there were 3.9 per cent of such farms, owning 48.3 per cent of the total acreage, and 32.3 per cent of the improved acreage. This is a familiar picture: the slave-holding latifundia of the South, and the even vaster latifundia of the West, the latter being partly the foundation of the most extensive stockraising, and partly reserve tracts of land occupied by "settlers" and resold or (less often) leased to real farmers improving the "Far West".

America demonstrates clearly that it would be imprudent to confuse the latifundia with large-scale capitalist agriculture, and that the latifundia are frequently survivals of pre-capitalist relationships—slave-owning, feudal or patriarchal. A break-up, a parcelling out of the latifundia, is taking place both in the South and in the West. In the North, the total farm acreage increased by 30.7 million acres, of which only 2.3 million is accounted for by latifundia, while 32.2 million belongs to big, capitalist farms (175 to 999 acres). In the South, the total acreage was reduced by 7.5 million. The latifundia *decreased* by 31.8 million acres. On the small farms there was an increase of 13 million, and on the medium farms, 5 million acres. In the West, the total acreage increased by 17 million; among the latifundia there was a decrease of 1.2 million; on the small farms, an increase of 2 million; medium, 5 million; large, 11 million acres.

The *improved* acreage increased in the latifundia of all three sections: substantially in the North (+3.7 million acres= +47.0 per cent), very slightly in the South (+0.3 million= +5.5 per cent), and more in the West (+2.8 million= +29.6 per cent). But in the North, the maximum increase in the improved acreage occurred on the *large* farms (175 to 999 acres); in the South, on the *small* and *medium*; in the West, on the *large* and *medium*. Hence, it is the large farms that are increasing their *share* of the improved land in the North, and the small and in part the medium farms, in the South and the West. This picture fully corresponds to what we already know about the different conditions in these sections. In the South, there is a growth of small-scale commercial farming at the expense of the disintegrating slave-holding latifundia; the process is similar in the West, except that the break-up of even larger latifundia, which had their origin *not* in slave-holding but in extensive stock ranches and pre-empted tracts, is not as pronounced. Moreover, American statisticians say the following about the Pacific division:

"The great development of small fruit and other farms on the Pacific coast, due, in part at least, to irrigation projects organised in recent years, is reflected in the increase in small farms of less than 50 acres in the Pacific division" (Vol. V, p. 264).

The North has neither slave-holding nor "primitive" latifundia, there is no disintegration of them, no growth of the small farms at the expense of the large.

The process for the United States as a whole appears as follows:

Size groups (acres)	Number of farms (000)		Ditto (per cent)		Increase or decrease
	1900	1910	1900	1910	
Under 20	674	839	11.7	13.2	+1.5
20 to 49	1,258	1,415	21.9	22.2	+0.3
50 to 99	1,366	1,438	23.8	22.6	—1.2
100 to 174	1,422	1,516	24.8	23.8	—1.0
175 to 499	868	978	15.1	15.4	+0.3
500 to 999	103	125	1.8	2.0	+0.2
1,000 and over	47	50	0.8	0.8	—
Totals	5,738	6,361	100.0	100.0	—

Thus, the number of latifundia in proportion to the total number of farms remains unchanged. The most characteristic change in the relationship between the other groups is the *reduction in the number of medium-size* farms and the strengthening of the farms at both ends. The medium-size group (100 to 174 acres) and its smaller neighbour have lost ground. The smallest and the small farms show the greatest gains, and are followed by the large-scale capitalist farms (175 to 999 acres).

Let us take a look at the total acreage.

Size groups (acres)	All farmland (000 acres)		Ditto (per cent)		Increase or decrease
	1900	1910	1900	1910	
Under 20	7,181	8,794	0.9	1.0	+0.1
20 to 49	41,536	45,378	5.0	5.2	+0.2
50 to 99	98,592	103,121	11.8	11.7	—0.1
100 to 174	192,680	205,481	23.0	23.4	+0.4
175 to 499	232,955	265,289	27.8	30.2	+2.4
500 to 999	67,864	83,653	8.1	9.5	+1.4
1,000 and over . . .	197,784	167,082	23.6	19.0	—4.6
Totals . . .	838,592	878,798	100.0	100.0	—

Here we find above all a very substantial reduction in the share of total acreage held by the latifundia. It should be borne in mind that an absolute reduction is taking place only in the South and the West, where the proportion of *un*improved land in the latifundia in 1910 was 91.5 per cent and 77.1 per cent respectively. There was also an insignificant decrease in the share of the top small group in the total acreage (—0.1 per cent in the 50-to-99-acre size group). The greatest increase was shown by the large-scale capitalist groups, the 175-to-499-acre and the 500-to-999-acre groups. There was a relatively small increase in the share of the very small groups in the acreage. The medium group (100 to 174 acres) was practically stagnant (+0.4 per cent).

Let us now take a look at the improved acreage.

Size groups (acres)	Improved land in farms (000 acres)		Ditto (per cent)		Increase or decrease
	1900	1910	1900	1910	
Under 20	6,440	7,992	1.6	1.7	+0.1
20 to 49	33,001	36,596	8.0	7.6	—0.4
50 to 99	67,345	71,155	16.2	14.9	—1.3
100 to 174	118,391	128,854	28.6	26.9	—1.7
175 to 499	135,530	161,775	32.7	33.8	+1.1
500 to 999	29,474	40,817	7.1	8.5	+1.4
1,000 and over . . .	24,317	31,263	5.9	6.5	+0.6
Totals . . .	414,498	478,452	100.0	100.0	—

The size of the *farming enterprise* is indicated with some degree of approximation and allowing for certain exceptions to which I have referred and shall refer again below —only by the improved and not the total acreage. Once again we find that while the share of the total acreage held by the latifundia substantially decreased, their share of the improved acreage *increased*. In general, all the capitalistic groups gained ground, and most of all the 500-to-999-acre group. The largest reduction was in the medium-size group (—1.7 per cent), followed by all the small groups, with the exception of the smallest, the group under 20 acres, which showed a negligible increase (+0.1 per cent).

Let us note in advance that the smallest-size group (under 20 acres) includes farms of less than 3 acres, which are not included in American statistics unless they raise at least $250 worth of products a year. For that reason these tiny farms (of less than 3 acres) have a greater volume of production and a more highly developed capitalist character than the next group up the scale. To illustrate this point here are the returns for 1900—unfortunately the corresponding returns for 1910 are not available:

Average per farm:

Size groups (1900) (acres)	Improved land (acres)	Value of all products	Outlays on hired labour	Value of implements and machinery	Value of livestock
		($)	($)	($)	($)
Under 3	1.7	592	77	53	867
3 to 10	5.6	203	18	42	101
10 to 20	12.6	236	16	41	116
20 to 50	26.2	324	18	54	172

Even the 3-to-10-acre farms, to say nothing of farms with less than 3 acres, turn out in some respects to be "larger" (outlays on hired labour, value of implements and machinery) than the 10-to-20-acre farms.* Consequently, there is good reason to attribute the increase in the share of the total improved land held by farms under 20 acres to an increase in the improved land of the pronounced capitalist-type farms of the smallest-size group.

On the whole, the returns for 1900 and 1910 on the distribution of improved land in the U.S.A. between small and large farms warrant this absolutely definite and indubitable conclusion: *the large farms are becoming stronger,*

---

* For 1900 we have returns by size groups for the number of high-income farms, i.e., farms with a product valued over $2,500. Here are these figures: among farms of less than 3 acres, the proportion of high-income farms was 5.2 per cent; 3 to 10 acres—0.6 per cent; 10 to 20 acres—0.4 per cent; 20 to 50 acres—0.3 per cent; 50 to 100—0.6 per cent; 100 to 175—1.4 per cent; 175 to 260—5.2 per cent; 260 to 500—12.7 per cent; 500 to 1,000—24.3 per cent; 1,000 and over—39.5 per cent. We find the proportion of high-income farms in all the under-20-acre groups to be *greater* than in the 20-to-50-acre group.

the medium and the small farms, weaker. Hence, *insofar* as the capitalist or non-capitalist character of agriculture can be deduced from the data relating to farms grouped by acreage, the United States in the last decade shows, as a general rule, a growth of the large-scale, capitalist farms and the obliteration of small farms.

The statistics on the increase in the number of farms and the improved acreage in each group will confirm this conclusion:

Size groups (acres)	Increase for 1900-10 (per cent)	
	Number of farms	Improved acreage
Under 20	+24.5	+24.1
20 to 49	+12.5	+10.9
50 to 99	+ 5.3	+ 5.7
100 to 174	+ 6.6	+ 8.8
175 to 499	+12.7	+19.4
500 to 999	+22.2	+38.5
1,000 and over . . .	+ 6.3	+28.6'
Overall increase	+10.9	+15.4

The largest percentage increase in the improved acreage took place in the two topmost groups. The least increase occurred in the medium-size group and the next smaller group (50 to 99 acres). In the two smallest groups the percentage increase in the improved acreage was less than the percentage increase in the number of farms.

9. CONTINUED. STATISTICS ON THE VALUE OF FARMS

American statistics, unlike European statistics, determine, for each farm and each group of farms, the value of the various elements making up the farming enterprise— the land, buildings, implements, livestock and the enterprise as a whole. These data are probably not quite as accurate as the data relating to acreage, but generally speaking they are equally reliable, and in addition give some idea of the general state of capitalism in agriculture.

In order to supplement the above analysis I shall now

take the data relating to the total value of farms with all their agricultural property, and also the data on the value of implements and machinery. I single out implements and machinery from among the various elements of the enterprise because they are a direct indication of the agricultural operations being conducted, and of how they are being conducted, i.e., whether more or less intensively, and whether they employ technical improvements to a greater or lesser extent. Here are the figures for the U.S.A.:

Percentage distribution of value

Size groups (acres)	All property on farms		Increase or decrease	Implements and machinery		Increase or decrease
	1900	1910		1900	1910	
Under 20 . . .	3.8	3.7	—0.1	3.8	3.7	—0.1
20 to 49 . . .	7.9	7.3	—0.6	9.1	8.5	—0.6
50 to 99 . . .	16.7	14.6	—2.1	19.3	17.7	—1.6
100 to 174 . . .	28.0	27.1	—0.9	29.3	28.9	—0.4
175 to 499 . . .	30.5	33.3	+2.8	27.1	30.2	+3.1
500 to 999 . . .	5.9	7.1	+1.2	5.1	6.3	+1.2
1,000 and over . .	7.3	6.9	—0.4	6.2	4.7	—1.5
Total . . .	100.0	100.0	—	100.0	100.0	—

The absolute figures show that from 1900 to 1910 the value of all farm property more than doubled; it increased from $20,440 million to $40,991 million, i.e., 100.5 per cent. The rise in the prices of farm products and rents put millions and thousands of millions of dollars into the pockets of the landowners at the expense of the working class. What were the comparative gains of the small and the big farms? The above figures supply the answer. They show that the latifundia declined (their total acreage fell from 23.6 per cent to 19.0 per cent, or 4.6 per cent), and that the *small and medium-size farms are being displaced by the large,* capitalist farms (175 to 999 acres). Adding up the figures for the small and medium farms we find that their share in the total property *decreased* from 56.4 to 52.7 per cent. Adding up the figures for the large farms and the latifundia we find that their share *increased* from

43.7 per cent to 47.3 per cent. There were absolutely identical changes in the distribution of the total value of implements and machinery between the small and large farms.

We also observe the phenomenon noted above in the figures relating to the latifundia. Their decline is limited to two sections: the South and the West. It is a decline, on the one hand, of the slave-holding latifundia, and on the other, of the primitive-squatter and the primitive-extensive latifundia. We find a *growth* of latifundia in the populated industrial North: this applies to the number of farms of this type, their total acreage, their improved acreage, their share in the total value of all farm property (2.5 per cent in 1900; 2.8 per cent in 1910), and their share in the total value of all implements and machinery.

There is moreover a growth of the role of the latifundia not only throughout the North in general but also in *both* the intensive divisions of the North in particular, where there is absolutely no colonisation, namely, New England and the Middle Atlantic states. These divisions must be analysed in greater detail because, for one thing, they have misled Mr. Himmer and many others by the particularly small average size of their farms and a reduction of that size, and, for another, these most intensive divisions are most typical of the older, long settled, civilised countries of *Europe*.

Between 1900 and 1910, the number of farms, the total acreage and the improved acreage decreased in both these divisions. In New England, there was an increase only in the number of the *smallest* farms, those under 20 acres, by 22.4 per cent (the improved land on them increased by 15.5 per cent), and in the number of latifundia—by 16.3 per cent, and their improved acreage by 26.8 per cent. In the Middle Atlantic states there was an increase in the *smallest* farms (+7.7 per cent in the number, and +2.5 per cent in the improved acreage) and also in the number of the 175-to-499-acre farms (+1.0 per cent) and the improved land on the 500-to-999-acre farms (+3.8 per cent). In both divisions, there was an *increase* in the share of the smallest farms and the share of the latifundia in the total value of all farm property and also of implements and machinery. Here are some figures which give a clearer and fuller picture of each of these divisions:

| | Percentage increase from 1900 to 1910 | | | |
| | New England | | Middle Atlantic | |
Size groups (acres)	Value of all farm property	Value of implements and machinery	Value of all farm property	Value of implements and machinery
Under 20	60.9	48.9	45.8	42.9
20 to 49	31.4	30.3	28.3	37.0
50 to 99	27.5	31.2	23.8	39.9
100 to 174	30.3	38.5	24.9	43.8
175 to 499	33.0	44.6	29.4	54.7
500 to 999	53.7	53.7	31.5	50.8
1,000 and over	102.7	60.5	74.4	65.2
Totals	35.6	39.0	28.1	44.1

This makes it clear that in both divisions *it was the latifundia* that gained most ground, showed the greatest economic gains, and made the greatest technical advance. Here the largest capitalist enterprises are *displacing* the others, the smaller farms. A minimum increase in the value of all property and also of implements and machinery is evident in the medium-size group and in the small group, but not in the smallest. Hence, it is the medium and small farms that mostly lag behind.

As for the smallest farms (under 20 acres), their advance in both divisions is *above the average*, and second only to the latifundia. We already know the reason: 31 to 33 per cent of the crop value in both these intensive divisions comes from the highly capitalist crops (vegetables, and also fruits, flowers, etc.) which yield extremely great values on very small acreages. In these divisions, cereal crops account for only 8 to 30 per cent of the crop value; and hay and forage, 31 to 42 per cent; there is a growth of dairy farming which is characterised by *smaller*-than-average acreages, but a *greater*-than-average value of produce and capital outlays on hired labour.

In the most intensive divisions, there is a decrease in the average improved acreage in farms because the average is obtained by combining the acreage of the latifundia and that of the smallest farms, the number of which is increasing more rapidly than that of the medium-size farms. The smallest farms are increasing in number faster than the latifundia. But there is a dual growth of capitalism: it increases the size of farms worked by old technical methods; and creates new enterprises raising special commercial crops on very small and tiny acreages, with an extremely great volume of production and employment of hired labour.

The net result is the greatest gains by the latifundia and the giant farms, the obliteration of the medium and small farms, and the growth of the smallest highly capitalist enterprises.

We shall presently see how the net result of such contradictory—seemingly contradictory—phenomena of capitalism in agriculture can be expressed in statistical terms.

10. DEFECTS OF CONVENTIONAL METHODS OF ECONOMIC ANALYSIS. MARX ON THE PECULIARITIES OF AGRICULTURE

The grouping of farms by acreage, total or improved, is the only kind of grouping which was used in the American Census reports for 1910, and which is used in the great majority of European countries. Generally speaking, it is indisputable that apart from fiscal, bureaucratic and administrative reasons there are scientific considerations arguing the need and correctness of this kind of grouping. Still it is obviously inadequate for it completely fails to take account of the intensification of agriculture, the increasing expenditure of capital per unit of area in the form of livestock, machinery, improved seeds, better methods of crop cultivation, etc. Meanwhile, with the exception of a very few areas and countries with a primitive or purely extensive agriculture, it is this very process that is most typical for capitalist countries everywhere. For this reason the grouping of farms by acreage in the vast majority of cases gives an oversimplified and entirely inadequate picture of agricultural development in general, and of capitalist development in agriculture in particular.

When the verbose economists and statisticians who express the most popular bourgeois views hold forth on the dissimilarity of conditions in agriculture and industry, the specific nature of the former, and so on and so forth, one is always tempted to say: Gentlemen! You yourselves are most to blame for maintaining and spreading oversimplified and crude notions of evolution in agriculture! Remember Marx's *Capital*. In it you will find references to the extreme variety of forms of land ownership, such as feudal, clan, communal (and primitive-squatter), state, etc., which capitalism encounters when it makes its appearance on the historical scene. Capital subordinates to itself all these varied forms of land ownership and remoulds them after its own fashion, and if one is to understand, evaluate and express this process in statistical terms, one must learn to modify the formulation of the question and the methods of investigation in accordance with the changing *form* of the process. Capitalism subordinates to itself all these forms of land ownership: communal-allotment holdings in Russia; squatter tracts or holdings regulated by free distribution in a democratic or a feudal state, as in Siberia or the American Far West; the slave-holding estates in the American South, and the semi-feudal landholdings of the "purely Russian" gubernias. In all these cases, the development and victory of capitalism is similar, though not identical in form. In order to study and understand the precise nature of the process one must go beyond the trite petty-bourgeois phrases about "family farming" or the routine methods of comparing acreage alone.

You will also find that Marx analyses the origin of the capitalist type of ground-rent and its relationship to its forerunners in history, such as rent in kind, labour service (corvée and its survivals); money-rent (quit-rent, etc.). But who among the bourgeois or petty-bourgeois, Narodnik, economists or statisticians has given any serious thought to applying these theoretical guiding principles of Marx's to an investigation of the rise of capitalism *from* the slave-holding economy of the American South, or *from* the corvée economy in central Russia?

Finally, you will find throughout Marx's analysis of ground-rent systematic references to the varied conditions of agriculture engendered not only by the differences in quality and location of the land, but also by the differences in *the amount of capital invested in it*. Now what does application of capital to land imply? It implies technical changes in agriculture, its intensification, the transition to higher systems of field cropping, increased use of artificial fertilisers, the wider use and improvement of implements and machinery, greater employment of hired labour, etc. A record of the acreage alone will not express all these complex and varied processes, which all combine to make up the general process of the development of capitalism in agriculture.

Russian Zemstvo statisticians, especially those of the "good old" pre-revolutionary days, won universal respect because they avoided the routine approach and took a certain scientific interest in their business, going beyond its purely fiscal, bureaucratic and administrative aspects. They were probably the first statisticians to notice the inadequacy of grouping farms by acreage alone, and, accordingly, introduced other methods of classification, such as by sown area, number of draught animals, employment of hired labour, etc. Unfortunately, the sporadic and scattered operations of our Zemstvo statistics—in the past ever what you might call an oasis in the desert of feudal obscurity, bureaucratic routine, and every kind of stupid red-tapism—have not yielded any long-term results either for Russian or European economics.

It should be noted that the grouping of the returns canvassed in modern agricultural censuses is not such a purely technical or highly specialised question as may appear at first sight. The returns contain an immense wealth of complete information on each enterprise as a unit, but due to the clumsy, thoughtless, routine approach to tabulation and grouping, this extremely valuable material is all lost, wasted, and discoloured, which often makes it practically useless for any study of the laws of agricultural evolution.

The returns make it possible to say quite categorically whether a farm is a capitalist enterprise, and to what extent; whether its farming operations are intensive, and to what degree, etc.; but when data relating to millions of farms are tabulated the most essential distinctions, features and characteristics—which ought to be most *effectively brought out*, determined and taken into account—tend to disappear, so that all the economist gets, instead of a sensible statistical review, is routine, meaningless columns of figures, a kind of statistical "game of digits".

The American Census of 1910 with which we are now concerned is an excellent example of how first-class material of surpassing wealth and completeness has been devalued and spoiled by the routine approach and scientific ignorance of the statisticians. The processing is very much worse than in the 1900 Census, and even the traditional grouping of farms by acreage has not been fully carried out, so that we have no possibility of making a comparison between the enterprises in the various groups, say, as regards their employment of hired labour, the difference in their systems of field cropping, the use of fertilisers, etc.

I am compelled, therefore, to turn to the 1900 Census. It gave, to my knowledge, the world's only example of the use of *three* different methods, instead of one, to group or "classify" (as the Americans say) the great abundance of material on more than five and a half million farms, collected in a single country, at a single time, and under a single programme.

It is true that here, too, no classification gives all the essential characteristics of the type and size of farm. Still the resultant picture of capitalist agriculture and the capitalist evolution of agriculture is, as I hope to show, very much fuller, and reflects the real situation much more correctly than can ever be the case when the conventional, one-sided and inadequate single method of classification is used. Given the opportunity for a fuller study of facts and trends, which may be safely considered common to all the capitalist countries of the world, the most serious errors and dogmas of bourgeois and petty-bourgeois, Narodnik political economy are shown up and exposed.

Since the data in question are so important I shall have to examine them in greater detail and employ statistical tables more frequently than hitherto. Realising fully that statistical tables burden the text and make reading more difficult, I have tried to keep them down to a minimum, and hope the reader will be lenient with me if I now have to increase that minimum, for on the analysis of the points examined here depends not only the general conclusion on the principal question—the trend, type, character and law of evolution of modern agriculture—but also the general assessment of the data furnished by modern agricultural statistics which are so often cited and just as often distorted.

The first grouping—"by acreage"—gives the following picture of American agriculture in 1900:

Size groups (acres)	Percentage of farms	Percentage of total acreage	Average per farm			
			Improved acreage	Outlays on hired labour ($)	Value of produce** ($)	Value of implements and machinery ($)
Under 3	0.7	—*	1.7	77	592	53
3 to 10	4.0	0.2	5.6	18	203	42
10 to 20	7.1	0.7	12.6	16	236	41
20 to 50	21.9	4.9	26.2	18	324	54
50 to 100	23.8	11.7	49.3	33	503	106
100 to 175	24.8	22.9	83.2	60	721	155
175 to 260	8.5	12.3	129.0	109	1,054	211
260 to 500	6.6	15.4	191.4	166	1,354	263
500 to 1,000	1.8	8.1	287.5	312	1,913	377
1,000 and over . . .	0.8	23.8	520.0	1,059	5,334	1,222
Average for all farms	—	—	72.3	—	656	133

It is safe to say that the statistics of any capitalist country—the inessential particulars apart—would present

---

* Less than 0.1 per cent.
** Excluding produce used as feed.

an absolutely similar picture. This is confirmed by the latest censuses in Germany, Austria, Hungary, Switzerland and Denmark. As total farm acreage increases from group to group, there is also an increase in the average improved acreage, the average value of the produce, the value of implements and machinery, the value of livestock (I have omitted these figures) and the expenditure on hired labour (earlier on I pointed out the significance of the slight exception of the under-3-acre farms and in part of the 3-to-10-acre farms).

It would seem that it could not be otherwise. The increase in expenditure on hired labour appears to confirm beyond any doubt that the division of farms into large and small on the strength of acreage is entirely in accord with their division into capitalist and non-capitalist enterprises. Nine-tenths of the usual arguments about "small-scale" agriculture are based on identification in this way and on such data.

Let us now consider the average per acre of (all) land, instead of per farm:

Per acre of all land in dollars

Size groups (acres)	Outlays on hired labour	Outlays on ferti- lisers	Value of livestock	Value of implements and machinery
Under 3 . . .	40.30	2.36	456.76	27.57
3 to 10 . . .	2.95	0.60	16.32	6.71
10 to 20 . . .	1.12	0.33	8.30	2.95
20 to 50 . . .	0.55	0.20	5.21	1.65
50 to 100 . . .	0.46	0.12	4.51	1.47
100 to 175 . . .	0.45	0.07	4.09	1.14
175 to 260 . . .	0.52	0.07	3.96	1.00
260 to 500 . . .	0.48	0.04	3.61	0.77
500 to 1,000 . . .	0.47	0.03	3.16	0.57
1,000 and over . . .	0.25	0.02	2.15	0.29

Allowing for some absolutely negligible exceptions we find a uniform decline in the characteristics of intensive farming from the lower groups to the higher.

The conclusion appears to be incontrovertible that "small-scale" production in agriculture is more intensive than large-scale production, that the smaller the "scale" of production, the greater the intensity and productivity of agriculture, and that, "consequently", capitalist production in agriculture is maintained only by the extensive, primitive nature of the economy, etc.

In fact, the same conclusions are being drawn all the time, on every hand, in all bourgeois and petty-bourgeois (opportunist-"Marxist" and Narodnik) writings, for when farms are grouped by acreage (which is not only the most common but practically the only kind of grouping done) the picture will be similar for any capitalist country, that is, it will show the same decline in the characteristics of intensive agriculture from the lower groups to the higher. There is, for instance, the celebrated work of the celebrated Eduard David—*Socialism and Agriculture*—a collection of bourgeois prejudices and bourgeois lies under the cover of quasi-socialist catchwords. It uses just that kind of data to prove the "superiority", "viability", etc., of "small-scale" production.

One factor has especially facilitated such conclusions. It is that data similar to the above are ordinarily available on the quantity of livestock; but practically nowhere are data collected on hired labour—especially in such a summarised form as expenditure on hired labour. But it is precisely the data on hired labour that reveal the incorrectness of all such conclusions. In effect, if the increase, say, in the value of livestock (or the total number of animals, which is the same thing) per unit of area down the scale is taken as evidence of the "superiority" of "small-scale" agriculture, it should be borne in mind that as we go down the scale this "superiority" turns out to be *connected* with *increasing* expenditure on hired labour! But such an increase in the expenditure on hired labour—notice that we have all along been dealing with values per unit of area, per acre, per hectare, per dessiatine—signifies a growth of the *capitalist* nature of the enterprise! But the capitalist nature of the enterprise clashes with the popular notion of "small-scale" production because small-scale production implies enterprise which is *not* based on hired labour.

This seems to create a knot of contradictions. The overall

acreage returns for the size groups indicate that the "small"
farms are non-capitalist, whereas the big farms are. Yet
the very same data show that the "smaller" the enterprise,
the more intensive it is, and the larger its expenditure on
hired labour per unit of land area!

In order to explain this let us consider another type
of grouping.

11. A MORE EXACT COMPARISON
OF SMALL AND LARGE ENTERPRISES

As I have already said, American statisticians in this
case take the value of the products raised on the farm, less
those used as feed. Taken alone, these data, which appear
to be available only in American statistics, are, of course,
less exact than the figures for acreage or livestock, and
the like. But considered as a whole, in relation to several
million farms, and especially for the purpose of determining the *relative standing* of the various groups of farms
in the country, these data undoubtedly cannot be regarded
as less suitable than the rest. At any rate, these data are
a much more direct indication than any others of the scale
of *production*, especially commercial operations, i.e., the
value of the produce raised for the market. It should be
borne in mind that any discussion of agricultural evolution
and its laws centres on a consideration of small-scale and
large-scale *production*.

What is more, in such cases the point is always the evolution of agriculture under capitalism, in connection with
capitalism, under its impact, or the like. To evaluate this
impact the greatest efforts must above all be made to draw
a line of distinction between "natural" and commercial
economy in agriculture. It is well known that "natural"
economy, i.e., production for consumption on the home
farm and not for the market, has a relatively important
part to play in agriculture, and is giving way to commercial farming at an extremely slow pace. If the accepted
principles of political economy are not to be applied me-
chanically but intelligently, the law of the displacement

of small-scale by large-scale production, for instance, can be applied *only* to commercial agriculture. It is hardly likely that anyone will object to this proposition from the theoretical standpoint. However, it is the rare economist or statistician who will make a special effort to bring out, trace and as far as possible take into account the characteristics indicative of the transformation of natural into commercial agriculture. A great step towards meeting this most important theoretical requirement is made by the classification of farms according to the money value of produce not used for feed.

Let us note that, when considering the undeniable fact that small-scale production is being displaced by large-scale production in industry, enterprises are always grouped according to the value of their product or the number of wage-workers employed. In industry, due to its technical peculiarities, the matter is much simpler. In agriculture, because relationships are so much more complicated and intertwined, it is a great deal harder to determine the scale of operations, the value of the product and the extent to which hired labour is employed. For the last-named item, it is necessary to take account of the total annual employment of hired labour and not merely the amount on hand when a census is taken, for agricultural operations are of an especially "seasonal" nature; in addition, it is necessary to list not only the permanent hired labourers but also the day-labourers who play a most important part in farming. To say that this is difficult is not to say that it is impossible. Rational methods of investigation adapted to the technical peculiarities of agriculture, including classification by output, the money value of the product, and the frequency and amount of hired labour employed, will have to be used on a much wider scale, in spite of the thick maze of bourgeois and petty-bourgeois prejudices and the efforts to embellish bourgeois realities. And it may be safely said that any step forward in the use of rational methods of investigation will serve to confirm the truth that in capitalist society small-scale production is being displaced by large-scale production both in industry and agriculture.

Let us take the 1900 returns for the groups of farms in America classified according to the value of their product:

Average per farm

Farms classified by value of product ($)		Number of farms (percentage of total)	Acreage	Improved acreage	Hired labour ($)	Implements and machinery ($)
	0	0.9	1.8	33.4	24	54
1 and under	50	2.9	1.2	18.2	4	24
50 and under	100	5.3	2.1	20.0	4	28
100 and under	250	21.8	10.1	29.2	7	42
250 and under	500	27.9	18.1	48.2	18	78
500 and under 1,000		24.0	23.6	84.0	52	154
1,000 and under 2,500		14.5	23.2	150.5	158	283
Over 2,500		2.7	19.9	322.3	786	781
Average for all farms		—	—	72.3	—	133

The farms reporting no income, i.e., with a $0 value of product, probably consist primarily of newly occupied homesteads on which their owners had not yet had time to erect buildings, acquire livestock or sow and raise a crop. In a country like America, where colonisation is still in progress on such a vast scale, special importance attaches to the question of how long a farmer has been in possession of his farm.

Leaving aside the zero-income farms, we get a picture quite similar to the one obtained above by grouping the same data according to total farm acreage. As the value of the product raised on a farm increases, there is also an increase in the average improved acreage, the average expenditure on hired labour, and the average value of implements and machinery. By and large, the more profitable farms—in terms of gross income, i.e., the value of their total product—turn out to have the larger acreage. It would appear that the new method of grouping has not yielded anything new at all.

But now let us take the averages (the value of livestock and implements, expenditure on hired labour and fertilisers) per acre instead of per farm:

Per acre of all land ($)

Farms classified by value of product ($)	Outlays on hired labour	Outlays on ferti- lisers	Value of livestock	Value of imple- ments and machinery
0	0.08	0.01	2.97	0.19
1 and under 50	0.06	0.01	1.78	0.38
50 and under 100	0.08	0.03	2.01	0.48
100 and under 250	0.11	0.05	2.46	0.62
250 and under 500	0.19	0.07	3.00	0.82
500 and under 1,000	0.36	0.07	3.75	1.07
1,000 and under 2,500	0.67	0.08	4.63	1.21
Over 2,500	0.72	0.06	3.98	0.72

The exceptions in some respects are the zero-income farms, which in general are in a very special position, and the farms with the highest incomes, which turn out to be less intensive than the next group, judging by three out of the four characteristics we have chosen. But on the whole we find a uniform *increase* in the intensity of agriculture *with the increase* in the value of the farm product.

This result is the very opposite of the one obtained when farms were grouped by acreage.

The same figures yield diametrically different conclusions, depending on the method of grouping.

As the enterprise grows in size the intensity of agriculture *declines*—if the criterion is acreage, and *increases*—if the criterion is the value of the product.

Which of these two conclusions is the correct one?

It is clear that if the land is not being improved, acreage gives *no idea at all* of the scale of agricultural operations (we must not forget that in America farms are grouped not only according to the improved acreage, but also by the total acreage and that in that country the proportion of the improved acreage ranges from 19 to 91 per cent in the farm groups, and from 27 to 75 per cent, in the geographical divisions); it gives *no correct* idea at all if besides this there are so many substantial differences between farms in the methods of cultivation, the intensity of agriculture, the methods of field cropping, quantities of fertilisers, the use of machinery, the character of livestock farming, etc.

This is known to apply to *all* capitalist countries and even to all those whose agriculture is affected by capitalism.

We see here one of the most profound and general reasons why mistaken notions about the "superiority" of small-scale agriculture are so tenacious, and why bourgeois and petty-bourgeois prejudices of this type prove to be compatible with the great progress made in the last few decades by social statistics in general, and agricultural statistics in particular. To be sure, the tenacity of these mistakes and prejudices is also a matter of the *interests* of the bourgeoisie, who seek to cover up the depth of class contradictions in contemporary bourgeois society; and everyone knows that when it comes to interests, the most incontrovertible truths are liable to be questioned.

But we are here concerned only with an examination of the theoretical sources of the erroneous notion of the "superiority" of small-scale agriculture. There is no doubt at all that of all these sources the most important one is the uncritical, routine attitude to the hackneyed methods of comparing enterprises only by their total acreage or the improved acreage.

The U.S.A. is an exception among capitalist countries in that it alone has a great deal of unoccupied, unsettled land, which is given away free. Agriculture still can and indeed does develop here through the occupation of vacant land, through the cultivation of virgin lands never before put to the plough—here it does develop in the form of the most primitive and extensive livestock and crop raising. There is nothing of the kind in the old, civilised countries of capitalist Europe. In these countries, agriculture develops *mainly* through intensive methods, not by increases in the *quantity* of land under cultivation, but by improvement in the *quality* of cultivation, by increases in the amount of capital invested in the original acreage. Those who compare farms by acreage alone lose sight of this principal trend in capitalist agriculture, a trend which is gradually becoming the principal one in the United States as well.

The principal trend in capitalist agriculture is the conversion of *small-scale* enterprise, *which remains small* in terms of acreage, *into large-scale* enterprise in terms of output, in the development of livestock raising, the quantity of fertilisers, the scale on which machinery is used, and the like.

That is why the conclusion drawn from the comparison of the various groups of enterprises by acreage—that the intensity of agriculture declines with the greater size of enterprise—is entirely incorrect. The only correct conclusion, on the contrary, is to be drawn from the comparison of the various farms by the value of their product—the bigger the enterprise, the greater is the intensity of agriculture.

For acreage is only circumstantial evidence of the scale of agricultural operations, and the broader and more rapid the intensification of agriculture, the less authentic is this "evidence". The value of the product of an enterprise is not circumstantial but direct evidence of the scale of its operations. Moreover, it is true in every case. By small-scale agriculture is always meant the kind that is *not* based on hired labour. But the transition to the exploitation of hired labour does not depend only on the extension of the acreage of an enterprise on its old technical basis—this occurs only in primitive, extensive enterprises—but also on an improvement of equipment and techniques and their modernisation, investment in the same acreage of additional capital in the form of, say, new machinery or artificial fertilisers, or of increased and improved livestock, etc.

The classification of farms by the value of their product brings together enterprises which really have *the same scale of production*, regardless of acreage. Accordingly, a highly intensive enterprise on a small tract of land falls into the same group as a relatively extensive enterprise on a large tract; both are actually large-scale in terms of production and the employment of hired labour.

On the contrary, the classification by acreage throws together large and small enterprises, because they happen to have a similar acreage; it puts into the same group enterprises with an entirely different scale of operations, those in which family labour predominates, and those in which hired labour predominates. The result is a picture of *blunted class contradictions* within capitalism, a picture which is basically incorrect and entirely misleading as to the actual state of affairs, but one the bourgeoisie is very fond of. This leads to an equally fallacious *embellishment of the condition of the small farmers*, which the bourgeoisie is just as fond of. The net result is a vindication of capitalism.

In effect, the fundamental and principal trend of capitalism is the displacement of small-scale by large-scale production, both in industry and in agriculture. But this displacement should not be interpreted *merely* as immediate expropriation. Displacement also implies the ruin of the small farmers and a worsening of conditions on their farms, a process that may go on for years and decades. This deterioration assumes a variety of forms, such as the small farmer's overwork or malnutrition, his heavy debts, worse feed and poorer care of livestock in general, poorer husbandry—cultivation, fertilisation, and the like—as well as technical stagnation on the farm, etc. If the researcher is to be absolved from the charge of wittingly or otherwise playing up to the bourgeoisie by giving a false impression of the condition of the small farmer, who is being ruined and oppressed, his task is, first and foremost, to give a precise definition of the symptoms of this ruination, which are not at all simple or uniform; his next task is to determine these symptoms, to analyse and, as far as possible, to define the extent to which they have spread and how they change with time. But present-day economists and statisticians hardly pay any attention to this vital aspect of the matter.

Just imagine that to a group of 90 small farmers who have no capital to improve their farms, who lag behind the times and are gradually being ruined the statistician adds 10 farmers who have all the capital they need and on equally small tracts of land start large-scale operations based on hired labour. The net result would be an embellished picture of the condition of all the hundred small farmers.

The U.S. Census of 1910 produced just that kind of embellished picture—and one that, objectively, favoured the bourgeoisie—primarily because it discarded the method used in 1900 of comparing the acreage grouping and the value-of-product grouping. We learn, for instance, only that expenditure on fertilisers increased immensely, namely, by 115 per cent, i.e., more than double the previous figure, while the expenditure on hired labour went up by only 82 per cent, and the total crop value by 83 per cent. This is tremendous progress. It is the progress of national agriculture as a whole. And, I dare say, some economist is likely to draw—if indeed has not yet drawn—the conclusion that this is the progress of small-scale family farming, for, generally speaking, the returns for the size groups by acreage indicate that "small-scale" agriculture has a much higher per-acre expenditure on fertilisers.

But we now know that such a conclusion would be fallacious, because the one thing the grouping of farms by acreage does is to lump together farmers on the way to ruin, or at any rate the indigent small farmers who cannot afford to buy fertilisers, and *capitalists* (even if they are small-time capitalists) who, on small tracts of land, start large-scale farming operations with the use of up-to-date, intensive methods and the employment of hired labour.

If small-scale agriculture is being generally displaced by large-scale agriculture, as the figures for the total value of farm property in 1900 and 1910 show; if, as we shall presently see, the raising of highly capitalist crops on small tracts developed at an especially fast rate in this period; if, according to the general statistics on small and large enterprises grouped by the value of their product, expenditures for fertilisers increased proportionately with the scale of the enterprise—then the conclusion inevitably follows that the "progress" in the use of fertilisers from 1900 to 1910 went to increase the preponderance of capitalist agriculture over small agriculture, which was displaced and suppressed to an even greater extent.

12. DIFFERENT TYPES OF ENTERPRISES
IN AGRICULTURE

What I have said above about the intensive, large-scale capitalist enterprises on small tracts raises this question: is there any reason to believe that the intensification of agriculture leads to a reduction of farm acreage? In other words, are there any conditions relating to modern farming techniques as such that require smaller farm acreage for greater intensity of farming?

No answer is provided either by general theoretical reasoning or by examples. In each case it is a matter of the concrete technical level of agriculture under a given set of conditions, and the actual amount of capital required by a given system of farming. In theory, any amount of capital can be invested in any acreage in any possible way, but it is obvious that "this depends" on the existing economic, technical, and cultural conditions, etc., and the whole point is the kind of conditions prevalent in a given country at a given time. Examples serve no purpose at all, because in the sphere of such complex, varied, interwoven and contradictory trends in the economics of modern agriculture, any number of examples will be found to support opposite views. What this calls for above all— and more so than in any other sphere—is a picture of the process *as a whole*, with all the trends taken into account and summed up in the form of a resultant.

The third method of grouping used by American statisticians in 1900 helps to find an answer to this question. It is classification according to the *principal source of income*. Accordingly, farms fall into one of the following groups: (1) hay and grain as the principal source of income; (2) miscellaneous: (3) livestock; (4) cotton; (5) vegetable; (6) fruit; (7) dairy produce; (8) tobacco; (9) rice; (10) sugar; (11) flowers and plants; (12) nursery products; (13) taro; and (14) coffee. The last seven groups (8-14) together make up only 2.2 per cent of the total number of farms, i.e., such an insignificant share that I shall not consider them separately. These groups (8-14) are similar to the preceding three groups (5-7) in economic characteristics and significance and constitute a single type.

Here are the data characterising the various types of farms:

Groups of farms by principal source of income	Percentage of total number of farms	Average acreage per farm	Total improved	Average per acre of all land ($)			
				Outlays on labour	Outlays on fertilisers	Value of implements and machinery	Value of livestock
Hay and grain . .	23.0	159.3	111.1	0.47	0.04	1.04	3.17
Miscellaneous . .	18.5	106.8	46.5	0.35	0.08	0.94	2.73
Livestock	27.3	226.9	86.1	0.29	0.02	0.66	4.45
Cotton	18.7	83.6	42.5	0.30	0.14	0.53	2.11
Vegetables	2.7	65.1	33.8	1.62	0.59	2.12	3.74
Fruits	1.4	74.8	41.6	2.46	0.30	2.34	3.35
Dairy produce . .	6.2	121.9	63.2	0.86	0.09	1.66	5.58
Average for all farms	100.0	146.6	72.3	0.43	0.07	0.90	3.66

It is clear that the first two groups of enterprises (hay and grain, and miscellaneous) may be classified as average both as regards the degree of their capitalist development (their expenditures for hired labour are nearest the average—0.35 to 0.47, as against an average of 0.43 for the U.S.A.) and the intensiveness of agriculture. All the characteristics of intensive operations—expenditures for fertilisers, the per-acre value of machinery and livestock—are nearest to the general average for the U.S.A.

There is no doubt that these two groups are especially typical of the majority of agricultural enterprises in general. Hay and grain, followed by a combination of various farm products ("miscellaneous" sources of income), are the chief types of agricultural enterprises in all countries. It would be extremely interesting to have more detailed data about these groups, such, for instance, as a breakdown into more and less commercialised enterprises, etc. But, as we have seen, the American Census, having made one step in that direction, did not go forward, but went back.

The next two groups, livestock and cotton, are an example of farms with the least capitalistic development (the expenditures for hired labour: 0.29 to 0.30 as against the average of 0.43), and the least intensive methods of agriculture. Their values of implements and machinery are the lowest and considerably lower than the average (0.66 and 0.53 as against 0.90). Farms whose principal source of income is livestock naturally have more livestock per acre than the average for the U.S.A. (4.45 as against 3.66), but appear to be engaged in extensive livestock raising: their expenditures for fertilisers are the minimum, they have the largest average acreage (226.9 acres) and the smallest proportion of improved acreage (86.1 out of 226.9). The cotton farms have a higher-than-average figure for fertilisers, but other indexes indicative of intensive agriculture (the per-acre value of livestock and machinery) are very low.

Finally, the last three groups—vegetables, fruit, and dairy produce—include farms which are, first, the smallest in acreage (33 to 63 acres of improved land, as against 42 to 86 and 46 to 111 in the other groups); secondly, the most capitalist: they have the heaviest expenditure on hired labour, from 2 to 6 times the average; and thirdly, the most intensive. Almost all the indexes of intensive agriculture are above the average: the expenditure on fertilisers, the value of machinery, the value of livestock (a minor exception are the fruit-growing farms which lag behind the average, but are well ahead of the farms which derive their income chiefly from hay and grain).

Let us now see what is the share of these highly capitalist farms in the country's economy. But we must first examine their intensive character in somewhat greater detail.

Take the farms whose main income is derived from vegetables. It is well known that in all capitalist countries the development of towns, factories, industrial settlements, railway stations, ports, etc., stimulates a demand for this type of product, it pushes up their prices, and increases the number of agricultural enterprises raising them for the market. The average "vegetable" farm has *less than one-third* of the improved acreage of an "ordinary" farm deriving income chiefly from hay and grain: the former is 33.8 acres, and the latter, 111.1. This means that this particular technical level with this particular accumulation of capital in agriculture requires "vegetable" farms of smaller acreage; in other words, if capital invested in agriculture is to yield a not less-than-average profit, a vegetable-raising farm should have, technology being what is it, a *smaller acreage* than a hay-and-grain farm.

But that is not all. The growth of capitalism in agriculture consists above all in a transition from natural agriculture to commercial agriculture. This is being constantly forgotten, and must be brought up again and again. Commercial agriculture, it should be noted, does not develop along the "simple" lines imagined or projected by bourgeois economists, namely, through an ever greater output of *the same* products. Not at all. Commercial agriculture very frequently develops by shifting from one type of product to another, and the shift from hay and grain to vegetables is very common. But what bearing does it have on the·question before us, that of farm acreage and the growth of capitalism in agriculture?

Such a shift signifies the *split-up* of a "large" 111.1-acre farm into more than three "small" 33.8-acre farms. The old farm produced a value of $760—the average value of its products, less the feed raised on the farm, whose chief source of income is hay and grain. Each of the new farms produces a value of $665, or a total of $665×3=$1,995, i.e., more than double the original figure.

As large-scale production displaces small-scale production, farm acreage is *reduced*.

The average expenditure on hired labour on the old farm was $76; on the new farm it is $106, or almost half as much again, while acreage is one-third or even less. Expenditure on fertilisers has gone up from $0.04 per acre to $0.59, an increase of almost 15 times; the value of implements and machinery has doubled from $1.04 to $2.12, etc.

There will, of course, be the usual objection that the number of such highly capitalist farms with specialised "commercial" crops is negligible, as compared with the total. The answer is that, first, the number and the *role*, the economic role, of such farms are much greater than is generally realised; and secondly—and this is the most important point—*it is such crops* that are developed *more rapidly* than others in the capitalist countries. That is just why a reduction in farm acreage with the intensification of agriculture so often implies an increase and not a reduction in the scale of operations, an increase and not a decrease in the exploitation of hired labour.

Here are the exact American statistics for the country as a whole. Let us take *all* the special, or "commercial", crops listed above under heads 5-14, namely, vegetables, fruit, dairy produce, tobacco, rice, sugar, flowers, nursery products, taro, and coffee. In 1900, these products were the *principal* source of income for 12.5 per cent of all farms in the U.S.A. This is one-eighth, a very small minority. Their acreage was 8.6 per cent, or one-twelfth, of the total. But to continue. Let us take the total value of the products of American agriculture (less feed). Of this value the farms in question accounted for as much as 16 per cent, i.e., their share of the value was almost double their share of the acreage.

This means that the productivity of labour and land on these farms was almost double the average.

Let us take the sum total of expenditure on hired labour in American agriculture. Of this total, 26.6 per cent, i.e., over one-quarter, fell to the farms in question. This is more than three times their share of the acreage, and more than three times the average. This means that these farms are very much more capitalist than the average.

Their share of the total value of implements and machinery is 20.1 per cent, and of the expenditures for fertilisers, 31.7 per cent, i.e., slightly less than *one-third* of the total, and nearly *four times* the average.

Consequently, an incontrovertible fact is established for the country as a whole. It is that the especially intensive farms have an especially small acreage, especially great employment of hired labour, and especially high productivity of labour; that the economic role of these farms in the nation's agriculture is two, three and more times greater than their proportion of the total number of farms, to say nothing of their share of the total acreage.

As time goes on, does the role of these highly capitalist and highly intensive crops and farms increase or decrease in comparison with other crops and farms?

The answer is provided by a comparison of the last two census reports: their role is unquestionably *increasing*. Let us take the acreage planted to the various crops. From 1900 to 1910, the acreage under grain increased by only 3.5 per cent for the U.S.A.; under beans, peas, and the like, 26.6 per cent; hay and forage, 17.2 per cent; cotton, 32 per cent; vegetables, 25.5 per cent; sugar-beets, sugar-cane, etc., 62.6 per cent.

Let us examine the crop returns. From 1900 to 1910, the grain crop went up only 1.7 per cent; beans, 122.2 per cent; hay and forage, 23 per cent; sugar-beets, 395.7 per cent; sugar-cane, 48.5 per cent; potatoes, 42.4 per cent; grapes, 97.6 per cent; there was a poor crop of berries, apples, etc., in 1910, but the orange and lemon crops, etc., were treble those of 1900.

Thus, the apparently paradoxical but nevertheless proven fact has been shown to apply to U.S. agriculture as a whole that, generally speaking, small-scale production is not only being displaced by large-scale production, but also that this displacement is taking place in the following form:

Small-scale production is being crowded out by large-scale production through the displacement of farms which are "larger" in acreage, but are less productive, less intensive and less capitalist, by farms which are "smaller" in acreage, but are more productive, more intensive, and more capitalist.

13. HOW THE DISPLACEMENT
OF SMALL-SCALE BY LARGE-SCALE PRODUCTION
IN AGRICULTURE IS MINIMISED

The objection may be raised that if the displacement of small-scale *production* "also" proceeds in the form of the intensification (and "capitalisation") of operations on the smaller-size *farms*, is the grouping by acreage of any use at all? Is this not a case of two contradictory tendencies which make any general conclusion impossible?

This objection can be met by a *complete* picture of American agriculture and its evolution; to meet it we must try to compare all three methods of grouping which present, as it were, the maximum of information social statistics has produced in the sphere of agriculture in recent years.

Such a comparison is possible. All it calls for is a table which may at first sight appear to be so abstract and complex that it may "scare" the reader away. However, it takes only a little bit of concentration to "read", understand and analyse the table.

To compare the three different groupings we need take only their *percentage ratios*. All the necessary calculations are given in the American Census report for 1900. Each grouping is tabulated under *three* main heads. By acreage we have: (1) small farms (under 100 acres); (2) medium (100 to 175 acres), and (3) large (175 and over). By value of product we have: (1) non-capitalist farms (under $500); (2) medium ($500 to 1,000), and (3) capitalist ($1,000 and over). By the principal source of income we take (1) slightly capitalist (livestock, cotton); (2) medium (hay and grain; and miscellaneous), and (3) highly capitalist (the special "commercial" crops listed above, in Chapter 12, under heads 5 to 14).

For every group we first take the percentage of farms, i.e., the number of farms in a given group expressed as a percentage ratio of the total number of farms in the U.S.A. We then take the percentage of all land, i.e., the total acreage in a given group expressed as a percentage ratio of the total acreage of all farms in the U.S.A. The acreage serves as an indicator of the extensive character of the enterprise (unfortunately, the only figures available are for *total* acreage, instead of the improved acreage only, which would have been more exact). If the percentage share of the total acreage is *higher* than the percentage share of the number of farms, for example, if 17.2 per cent of the farms have 43.1 per cent of the land, it is evident that we are dealing with large farms, larger-than-average farms, which are besides more than double the size of the average farm. The reverse is true if the percentage of land is *lower* than the percentage of farms.

Next come the indexes of *intensiveness* of agriculture: the value of implements and machinery, and the total expenditure on fertilisers. Here, too, we take the value and the expenditure in the given group expressed as a percentage share of the totals for the country as a whole. Here again, if the percentage is *higher* than the percentage of *land*, the conclusion is that intensiveness is *above* the average, etc.

Finally, in order to determine exactly the capitalist character of the enterprises, the same method is applied to the total expenditure on hired labour; while in order to determine the scale of production this is done in relation to the total value of the agricultural product for the entire country.

This has produced the following table, which I shall now proceed to explain and analyse (see table on p. 182.—*Ed.*).

Let us consider the first grouping—according to the principal source of income. Here farms are grouped, so to say, according to their line of farming, which is to some extent similar to the grouping of industrial enterprises by branches of industry. But the picture is immensely more complex in agriculture.

The first column shows the group of slightly capitalist farms. It comprises almost one-half the total number of farms—46 per cent. They own 52.9 per cent of the total acreage, i.e., they are larger than average (this group includes both the very large, extensive, livestock farms and the smaller-than-average cotton farms). Their shares of the value of machinery (37.2 per cent) and the expenditure on fertilisers (36.5 per cent) are lower than their acreage percentages, which means that their intensiveness is lower than the average. The same thing is true of the capitalist character of the enterprise (35.2 per cent) and the value of the product (45 per cent). Hence, their productivity of labour is lower than the average.

The second column shows the medium farms. Because farms which are "medium" in *every* respect fall into the

Comparison of the Three Groupings

(figures are percentages of total, sum total of each horizontal row of three figures = 100)

	By principal source of income			By farm acreage			By value of product			
	Slightly capitalist	Medium	Highly capitalist	Small	Medium	Large	Non-capitalist	Medium	Capitalist	
Number of farms	46.0	41.5	12.5	57.5	24.8	17.7	58.8	24.0	17.2	Index of extensiveness of agriculture
Total acreage	52.9	38.5	8.6	17.5	22.9	59.6	33.3	23.6	43.1	
Constant capital — Value of implements and machinery	37.2	42.7	20.1	31.7	28.9	39.4	25.3	28.0	46.7	Index of intensiveness of agriculture
Constant capital — Outlays on fertilisers	36.5	31.8	31.7	41.9	25.7	32.4	29.1	26.1	44.8	
Variable capital — Outlays on hired labour	35.2	38.2	26.6	22.3	23.5	54.2	11.3	19.6	69.1	Index of capitalist character of enterprise
Scale of production — Value of product	45.0	39.0	16.0	33.5	27.3	39.2	22.1	25.6	52.3	

medium group by *all* three methods of grouping, we find here that *all* their percentage ratios are closer to each other than in any of the other groups. The fluctuations are relatively small.

The third column shows the highly capitalist farms. I gave above a detailed analysis of what the figures in this column mean. Be it noted that *only* for this type of farm do we have accurate and comparable data both for 1900 and 1910—data testifying that these highly capitalist crops have a faster-than-average rate of development.

In what way is this more rapid development evident in the ordinary classification in use in most countries? This is shown in the next column: the small farms grouped by acreage.

This group consists of a great number of farms (57.5 per cent of the total). Its acreage is only 17.5 per cent of the total, i.e., less than one-third of the average. Hence, this is the "poorest" group, the most "land-starved" group. But then we find that it has a higher-than-average intensiveness of agriculture (the value of machinery and expenditures for fertilisers); that it is more capitalist (expenditures for hired labour); and that it has a *higher*-than-average productivity of labour (value of product): 22.3 to 41.9 per cent with 17.5 per cent of the acreage.

What is the explanation? Obviously that an especially large number of *highly capitalist* farms—see the preceding vertical column—fall into this "small"-acreage group. A *minority* of rich, capital-owning farmers conducting large-scale capitalist operations on small tracts of land are added to a majority of really small farmers who have little land and little capital. Such farmers make up only 12.5 per cent (=the percentage of highly capitalist farms) of the total in America, which means that even if they were all to be put into this one group of small-acreage farms, 45 per cent of the farmers in that group (57.5—12.5) would still be short of land and capital. Actually, of course, a part of the highly capitalist farms, even if only a small one, consists of medium and large-acreage farms, so that the figure of 45 per cent in fact *understates* the actual number of farmers who have little land and no capital.

It will be easily seen how the condition of these 45 per cent—a minimum of 45 per cent—of the farmers who are poor in land and capital is *embellished* by the inclusion into the same group of some 12, 10 or so per cent of farmers who are supplied with higher-than-average amounts of capital, machinery, money to buy fertilisers, hire labour, and the rest of it.

I shall not dwell separately on the medium and large farms of this grouping, for this would be to repeat, in slightly different words, what has been said about the small farms. For instance, if the data on the small-acreage farms put a better complexion on the oppressed condition of small-scale *production*, the data on the large-acreage farms obviously *minimise* the actual *concentration* of agriculture by large-scale production. We shall presently see an exact statistical expression of this minimised concentration.

We thus arrive at the following general proposition which may be formulated as a law applicable to the grouping of farms by acreage in any capitalist country:

The broader and more rapid the intensification of agriculture, the more the classification by acreage serves to *give a rosy picture* of the oppressed condition of small-scale production in agriculture, the condition of the small farmer who is short of *both* land *and* capital; the more it serves to *blunt* the real sharpness of the class contradiction between the prospering large-scale producer and the small-scale producer going to the wall; the more it serves to *minimise* the concentration of capital in the hands of big operators and the displacement of the small.

This is graphically confirmed by the third, and last, classification, according to the value of product. The percentage of non-capitalistic farms (or not very profitable farms in terms of gross income) is 58.8 per cent, i.e., even somewhat more than the "small" farms (57.5 per cent). They have much *more* land than the group of "small" farmers (33.3 per cent as against 17.5 per cent). But their share of the total value of the product is *one-third smaller*: 22.1 per cent as against 33.5 per cent!

What is the explanation? It is that this group does not include the highly capitalistic farms on small tracts which have *artificially and falsely* inflated the small farmers' share of the *capital* in the form of machinery, fertilisers, etc.

Thus, the oppression and dispossession—and hence the ruin—of the small *producer* in agriculture turn out to be *much more advanced* than one would suppose from the data on small *farms*.

The returns for the small and large farms, grouped by acreage, take no account of *the role of capital*, and the failure to reckon with this "trifle" in capitalist enterprise distorts the condition of the small producer, puts a false colour on it, for it "could be" tolerable "but for" the existence of capital, i.e., the power of money, and the relationship between the hired labourer and the capitalist, between the farmer and the merchant and creditor, etc.!

For that reason the concentration of agriculture as shown by the large farms is much lower than its concentration as shown by large-scale, *i.e.*, capitalist, production: 39.2 per cent of the value of the product (slightly more than double the average) is concentrated on 17.7 per cent of "large" farms, while 52.3 per cent of the total value of the product, i.e., more than *three* times the average, is concentrated on 17.2 per cent *capitalist* farms.

In the country which practises the free distribution of vast tracts of unoccupied land, and which the Manilovs consider a country of "family" farms, *more than one-half* of the total agricultural production is concentrated in about one-sixth of the *capitalist* enterprises, whose expenditure on hired labour is four times greater than the per-farm average (69.1 per cent on 17.2 per cent of the total number of farms), and is half as great again as the per-acre average (69.1 per cent of the expenditure on hired labour on farms owning 43.1 per cent of the total amount of land).

At the other pole, more than one-half, almost three-fifths, of the total number of farms (58.8 per cent) are non-capitalist. They have one-third of the land (33.3 per cent) but on it they have less than the average quantity of machinery (25.3 per cent of the value of machinery); they use less fertilisers than the average (29.1 per cent of the expenditures for fertilisers) and so its productivity is only *two-thirds of the average.* With one-third of the total acreage, this immense number of farms, which suffer the greatest oppression under the yoke of capital, produce less than one-quarter (22.1 per cent) of the total product and of its total value.

Consequently, we arrive at a general conclusion concerning the significance of classification by acreage, namely, that it is not entirely useless. The one thing that should never be forgotten is that it understates the displacement of small-scale by large-scale production, and that the understatement increases with the pace and scope of intensification of agriculture, and with the gap between the amounts of capital invested by the farms per unit of land. With modern methods of research, which produce an abundance of sound information about each farm, it would, for instance, be sufficient to combine two methods of classification—say, each of the five acreage groups could be broken down into two or three subgroups according to the employment of hired labour. If this is not done it is largely because of the fear of giving a much too naked picture of reality, a much too striking picture of the oppression, impoverishment, ruin, expropriation of the mass of small farmers, whose condition is so "conveniently" and "unnoticeably" made to look better by the "model" capitalist enterprises, which are also "small" in acreage and which are a small minority within the mass of the dispossessed. From the scientific standpoint no one would dare deny that not only land, but also capital has a part to play in modern agriculture. From the standpoint of statistical techniques, or the amount of statistical work involved, a total number of 10 to 15 groups is not at all excessive in comparison, for instance, with the 18 plus 7 groups based on acreage given in the German statistical report of 1907. This report, which classifies an abundance of material about 5,736,082 farms into the above number of acreage groups, is an example of bureaucratic routine, scientific rubbish, a meaningless juggling of figures, for there is *not a shadow* of any reasonable, rational, theoretical or practical ground for accepting such a number of groups as typical.

14. THE EXPROPRIATION OF THE SMALL FARMERS

The question of the expropriation of the small farmers is immensely important to an understanding and assessment of capitalism in agriculture in general, and it is highly characteristic of modern political economy and statistics, which are saturated through and through with bourgeois notions and prejudices, that this question is either practically not considered at all or is given the least attention.

The general statistics in all capitalist countries show that the urban population is growing at the expense of the rural, that the population is abandoning the countryside. In the U.S.A., this process is steadily advancing. The proportion of the urban population increased from 29.5 per cent in 1880 to 36.1 per cent in 1890, 40.5 per cent in 1900, and 46.3 per cent in 1910. In every part of the country the urban population is growing more rapidly than the rural population: from 1900 to 1910, the rural population in the industrial North went up by 3.9 per cent and the urban by 29.8 per cent; in the former slave-holding South, the rural population increased by 14.8 per cent, and the urban, by 41.4 per cent; in the homestead West, the figures were 49.7 and 89.6 per cent, respectively.

One should think that such a universal process would also have to be studied in the taking of agricultural censuses. A most important question from the scientific standpoint naturally arises as to what sections, strata or groups of the rural population provide the fugitives from the countryside and in what circumstances. Since highly detailed information about each agricultural enterprise and about each animal in it is collected every ten years, it would be no trouble at all to include questions as to how many and what kind of farms were sold or rented with an eye to moving into town, and how many members of households abandoned farming temporarily or for good; and in what circumstances. But no such questions are asked: the investigation does not go beyond the official stereotyped statement: "The rural population decreased from 59.5 per cent in 1900 to 53.7 per cent in 1910." The census-takers seem to have no inkling of the mass of

misery, oppression and ruin concealed behind these routine
figures. As a general rule, bourgeois and petty-bourgeois
economists turn a blind eye to the obvious connection between the flight of the population from the countryside and
the ruin of the small producers.

There is no alternative, therefore, but to try and bring
together the relatively meagre and very badly compiled
data on the expropriation of the small farmers gleaned
from the 1910 Census report.

There are the figures on the forms of farm tenure: the
number of owners, subdivided into *full* and *part* owners;
and the number of share-cropping tenants and cash-paying
tenants. These figures are tabulated for the various divisions but not the farm groups.

Here is the first picture we get from the totals for 1900
and 1910:

Total rural population increased	11.2 per cent
Total number of farms increased	10.9 ” ”
Total number of owners increased . . .	8.1 ” ”
Total number of *full* owners increased	4.8 ” ”

This picture is a clear indication of the growing expropriation of small-scale agriculture. The rural population is
increasing more slowly than the urban. The number of
farmers is increasing more slowly than the rural population; the number of owners is increasing more slowly than
the number of farmers; the number of *full* owners—more
slowly than the number of owners in general.

The proportion of owners in the total number of farmers
has been decreasing steadily over a period of several
decades, as follows:

1880	74.4 per cent
1890	71.6 ” ”
1900	64.7 ” ”
1910	63.0 ” ”

There is a corresponding growth in the proportion of
tenants, with the number of share-cropping tenants going
up faster than that of cash-paying tenants. The number of

share-cropping tenants was 17.5 per cent in 1880; then it rose to 18.4 per cent and 22.2 per cent, and finally to 24 per cent in 1910.

It is evident from the following figures that the decrease in the proportion of owners and the increase in the proportion of tenants is, on the whole, an indication of the dispossession and displacement of the small farmers:

Class of farm	Percentage of farms owning					
	domestic animals			horses		
	1900	1910	±	1900	1910	±
Owners	96.7	96.1	—0.6	85.0	81.5	—3.5
Tenants	94.2	92.9	—1.3	67.9	60.7	—7.2

According to all the returns for both census years the owners are economically stronger. The condition of the tenants is deteriorating *more rapidly* than that of the owners.

Let us examine separately the figures for the sections.

The greatest number of tenants, as I have already said, is in the South, and there tenancy has the fastest rate of growth: it rose from 47 per cent in 1900 to 49.6 per cent in 1910. Capital defeated slavery half a century ago, merely to *restore* it now in a new form as share tenancy.

In the North, the number of tenants is considerably smaller and is growing at a much slower rate: it went up from 26.2 per cent in 1900 to only 26.5 per cent in 1910. The West has the smallest number of tenants, and it is the *only* section where tenancy, instead of increasing, decreased: it fell from 16.6 per cent in 1900 to 14.0 per cent in 1910. "A very low proportion of tenant farms," says the Census report for 1910, "is also shown for the Mountain and Pacific divisions [the two divisions constituting "The West"], where it is doubtless attributable mainly to the fact that those divisions have been only recently settled and that many of the farmers in them are homesteaders who have obtained their land from the Government" free or for a very small price (Vol. V, p. 104).

This is a striking example of the peculiar characteristic of the U.S.A., to which I have repeatedly referred, namely, the availability of unoccupied, free land. This explains, on the one hand, the extremely rapid and extensive development of capitalism in America. The absence of private property in land in some parts of a vast country does not exclude capitalism—our Narodniks should make a note of this!—on the contrary, it broadens its base, and accelerates its development. Upon the other hand, this peculiarity, which is entirely unknown in the old, long-settled capitalist countries of Europe, serves in America to *cover up* the expropriation of the small farmers—a process already under way in the settled and most industrialised parts of the country.

Let us take the North. We get the following picture:

	1900	1910	+ or − per cent
Total rural population (000,000) . .	22.2	23.1	+3.9
Total number of farms (000)	2,874	2,891	+0.6
Total number of owners (000) . . .	2,088	2,091	+0.1
Total number of *full* owners (000) . .	1,794	1,749	−2.5

We see not only a relative reduction in the number of owners, not only a decline in their proportion of the total number of farmers, etc., but even an *absolute decrease* in the number of owners, against a background of growing production in the main section of the U.S.A., which embraces 60 per cent of the country's improved acreage!

It should, besides, be borne in mind that in *one* of the four divisions making up the North, namely, the West North Central, *the allotment of homesteads continues to this very day*, and that 54 million acres were allotted in the 10 years from 1901 to 1910.

The tendency of capitalism to expropriate small-scale agriculture is so strong that the American "North" shows an *absolute decrease* in the number of landowners, *in spite of* the distribution of tens of millions of acres of unoccupied, free land.

Only two factors still serve to paralyse this tendency in the U.S.A.: (1) the existence of the still unparcelled slave-holding plantations in the South, with its oppressed and downtrodden Negro population; and (2) the fact that the West is still partly unsettled. Both these factors tend to widen the future base of capitalism, and so prepare the conditions for its even more extensive and more rapid development. The sharpening of contradictions and the displacement of small-scale production are not removed but are transferred to a larger arena. The capitalist fire appears to be "damped down"—but at the price of an even greater accumulation of new and more inflammable material.

Furthermore, on the question of the expropriation of small-scale agriculture, we have the returns for the number of farms owning livestock. Here are the figures for the U.S.A.

Percentage of farms owning	1900	1910	+ or −
Domestic animals in general	95.8	94.9	−0.9
Dairy cows	78.7	80.8	+2.1
Horses	79.0	73.8	−5.2

These figures show, on the whole, a reduction in the number of owners in proportion to the total number of farmers. The increase in the percentage of those who owned dairy cows was smaller than the drop in the percentage of those who owned horses.

Let us now examine the figures for farms grouped in relation to the two major kinds of livestock.

Size groups (acres)	Percentage of farms owning dairy cows		+ or −
	1900	1910	
Under 20	49.5	52.9	+3.4
20 to 49	65.9	71.2	+5.3
50 to 99	84.1	87.1	+3.0
100 to 174	88.9	89.8	+0.9
175 to 499	92.6	93.5	+0.9
500 to 999	90.3	89.6	−0.7
1,000 and over	82.9	86.0	+3.1
Average for the U.S.A.	78.7	80.8	+2.1

We find that the greatest increase was in the number of *small* farms with dairy cows, then came the latifundia, and then the medium-size farms. There was a decrease in the percentage of farms reporting dairy cows among the big owners, with 500 to 999 acres of land.

On the whole, this seems to indicate a gain for small-scale agriculture. Let us recall, however, that in farming the ownership of dairy cattle has a twofold significance: on the one hand, it may generally indicate a higher living standard and better conditions of nutrition. On the other hand, it signifies—and rather more frequently—a development of one branch of commercial farming and cattle-breeding: the production of milk for the market in the towns and industrial centres. We saw above that farms of this type, the "dairy" farms, were classified by American statisticians under a special head, according to the principal source of income. A characteristic of this group is that it has a *smaller*-than-average total and improved acreage, but a *greater*-than-average value of output, and a *double-the-average* employment of hired labour per acre. The increasing importance of small farms in dairy farming may simply mean—and most likely does mean—a growth of *capitalist* dairy farms of the type described, on small tracts of land. For the sake of comparison here are some figures on the *concentration* of dairy cattle in America:

Sections	Average number of dairy cows per farm		Increase
	1900	1910	
The North	4.8	5.3	+0.5
The South	2.3	2.4	+0.1
The West	5.0	5.2	+0.2
Overall average	3.8	4.0	+0.2

We find that the North, which is richest of all in dairy cattle, also showed the greatest increase in wealth. Here is a distribution of this increase among the groups:

The North Size groups (acres)	Percentage increase or decrease in number of dairy cows from 1900 to 1910
Under 20	— 4 (+10.0 in the number of farms)
20 to 49	— 3 (—12.6 „ „ „ „ „)
50 to 99	+ 9 (— 7.3 „ „ „ „ „)
100 to 174	+14 (+ 2.2 „ „ „ „ „)
175 to 499	+18 (+12.7 „ „ „ „ „)
500 to 999	+29 (+40.4 „ „ „ „ „)
1,000 and over	+18 (+16.4 „ „ „ „ „)

Overall increase . . . . +14 (+ 0.6 in the number of farms)

The more rapid growth in the *number* of small farms
with dairy cattle did not prevent its more rapid *concentration* in the large enterprises.

Let us now turn to the figures on the number of farms
reporting horses. This information about draught animals
is an indication of the general pattern of farming and not
of any special branch of commercial farming.

Size groups (acres)	Percentage of farms reporting horses		Decrease
	1900	1910	
Under 20	52.4	48.9	—3.5
20 to 49	66.3	57.4	—8.9
50 to 99	82.2	77.6	—4.6
100 to 174	88.6	86.5	—2.1
175 to 499	92.0	91.0	—1.0
500 to 999	93.7	93.2	—0.5
1,000 and over	94.2	94.1	—0.1

Average for the U.S.A.   79.0   73.8   —5.2

We find that as we go down the size-group scale there is
a rising number of farms not reporting horses. With the
exception of the smallest farms (under 20 acres) which, as
we know, include a comparatively greater number of capitalistic farms than the neighbouring groups, we observe a
rapid decrease in the number of horseless farms and a
much slower increase in their number. The use of steam

ploughs and other engines on the rich farms may partly compensate for the reduction in draught animals, but such an assumption is out of the question for the mass of the poorer farms.

Finally, the growth of expropriation is also evident from the returns on the number of mortgaged farms:

Sections	Percentage of mortgaged farms		
	1890	1900	1910
The North	40.3	40.9	41.9
The South	5.7	17.2	23.5
The West	23.1	21.7	28.6
Average for the U.S.A.	28.2	31.0	33.6

The percentage of mortgaged farms is on a steady increase in all sections, and it is highest in the most populous industrialised and capitalist North. American statisticians point out (Vol. V, p. 159) that the growth in the number of mortgaged farms in the South is probably due to the "parcelling out" of the plantations, which are sold in lots to Negro and white farmers, who pay only a part of the purchase price, the rest being covered by a mortgage on the property. Consequently a peculiar *buying-up operation* is under way in the slave-holding South. Let us note that in 1910 Negroes in the U.S.A. owned only 920,883 farms, i.e., 14.5 per cent of the total; between 1900 and 1910, the number of white farms increased 9.5 per cent, and that of Negro farms, twice as fast—19.6 per cent. The Negro urge to emancipation from the "plantation owners" half a century after the "victory" over the slave-owners is still marked by an exceptional intensity.

The American statisticians also point out that the mortgaging of a farm does not always indicate lack of prosperity; it is sometimes a way of obtaining capital for land improvement; and the like. This is indisputable, but this indisputable observation should not conceal the fact—as is much too often the case with bourgeois economists— that only a well-to-do minority are in a position to obtain capital for improvements, etc., in this way, and to employ it productively; the majority are further impoverished and fall into the clutches of finance capital assuming this particular form.

Researchers could—and should—have paid much more attention to the dependence of farmers on finance capital. But although this aspect of the matter is immensely important, it has remained in the background.

The growth in the number of mortgaged farms in any case means that the actual control over them is transferred to the capitalists. It stands to reason that apart from officially recorded and notarised mortgages, a considerable number of farms are steeped in private debt, which is not covered by strict legal instruments and is not recorded by the census.

15. A COMPARATIVE PICTURE OF EVOLUTION IN INDUSTRY AND AGRICULTURE

American census statistics, for all their shortcomings, compare favourably with those of other countries because of the completeness and uniformity of the methods used. This makes it possible to compare the returns for industry and agriculture for 1900 and 1910, and to contrast the overall picture of the structure of both sectors of the economy and the evolution of this structure. One of the most popular ideas in bourgeois economics—an idea, incidentally, which Mr. Himmer repeats—is to *contrast* industry and agriculture. Let us see, in the light of a mass of precise data, what truth there is in such a contrast.

Let us begin with the number of enterprises in industry and in agriculture.

	Number of enterprises (000)		Increase (per cent)	Growth of urban and rural population (per cent)
	1900	1910		
Industry	207.5	268.5	+29.4	+34.8
Agriculture	5,737	6,361	+10.9	+11.2

The enterprises in agriculture are much more numerous and much smaller. That is an expression of its backwardness, parcellisation, and dispersion.

The number of enterprises increases much more slowly in agriculture than in industry. There are two factors in the United States which do not exist in other leading countries, and which greatly intensify and accelerate the growth in the number of enterprises in agriculture. They are, first, the continued parcelling out of the slave-holding latifundia in the South and "buying-up" by Negro and also by white farmers of small parcels from the "planters"; secondly, the availability of an immense quantity of unoccupied, free land, which is distributed by the government to all applicants. Nevertheless the number of enterprises in agriculture is increasing at a slower rate than in industry.

The reason is twofold. On the one hand, agriculture to a rather large extent retains the character of a "natural" economy, and various operations once performed by members of a peasant household are gradually branching off from agriculture—for example, the making and repair of various implements, utensils, etc.—and now constitute separate industries. On the other hand, there is a monopoly which is peculiar to agriculture and unknown to industry, and which cannot be eliminated under capitalism—the monopoly of land ownership. Even when there is no private property in land—in the United States none actually exists on very large areas to this very day—monopoly is created by the ownership of land and its occupation by individual private operators. In the country's most important regions all the land is occupied, and an increase in the number of agricultural enterprises is possible only when existing enterprises are broken up; the free formation of new enterprises alongside the old is impossible. The monopoly of land ownership is a drag on the development of agriculture, and this monopoly retards the development of capitalism in agriculture, which, therefore, is unlike industry in this respect.

We are unable to make an accurate comparison of the amounts of capital invested in industrial and in agricultural enterprises because ground-rent forms a part of the value of the land. Accordingly, we have to compare the capital invested in industry and the value of industrial products with the total value of all farm property and the value of the major farm product. Only the percentages showing increases in the total values on both sides are strictly comparable.

		$000,000		Increase (per cent)
		1900	1910	
Industry	Capital of all enterprises	8,975	18,428	105.3
	Value of products	11,406	20,671	81.2
Agriculture	Value of all farm property	20,440	40,991	100.5
	Value of all cereal crops	1,483	2,665	79.8
	Production of cereals in bushels (000,000)	4,439	4,513	1.7

We find that during the 10 years from 1900 to 1910 the value of capital invested in industry and the value of all farm property have *doubled*. The great and fundamental difference between the two is that in agriculture the major product, cereals, increased by an insignificant 1.7 per cent—while the total population increased 21 per cent.

Agriculture lags behind industry in development; this is a feature of *all* capitalist countries constituting one of the most profound causes of disproportion between the various branches of the economy, of crises and soaring prices.

Capital liberated agriculture from feudalism and drew it into commodity circulation and thereby into world economic development, lifting it from medieval backwardness and patriarchal stagnation. But capital, instead of eliminating the oppression, exploitation and poverty of the masses, produces these calamities in a new guise and restores their old forms on a "modern" basis. The contradiction between industry and agriculture, far from being eliminated by capitalism, is, on the contrary, further extended and sharpened by it. The oppression of capital, seen primarily in the sphere of trade and industry, weighs more and more heavily on agriculture.

The insignificant increase in the quantity of agricultural produce (+1.7 per cent) and the enormous increase in its value (+79.8 per cent) shows clearly, on the one hand, the role of ground-rent, the tribute extorted from society by the landowners. Because of their monopolist position, they are able to take advantage of the backwardness of agriculture, which does not keep pace with industry, and to fill their pockets with millions and millions of dollars. In the 10 years, the value of all farm property increased by $20,500 *million*, of which only $5,000 million constituted the increase in the value of buildings, livestock and equipment. The value of land—capitalised ground-rent—increased in the 10 years by *$15,000 million* (+118.1 per cent).

On the other hand, the difference in the *class* status of the small farmers and the hired labourers is here thrown into especially sharp relief. To be sure, both labour; to be sure, both are subject to exploitation by capital, though in entirely different forms. But only vulgar bourgeois democrats will for this reason put the two different classes together and speak of small-scale operations by family farms. To do so is to cover up and disguise the *social* system of the economy—its bourgeois nature—and push into the foreground a feature common to *all* earlier formations, namely, the necessity for the petty farmer to work, to engage in personal, physical labour, if he is to survive.

Under capitalism, the small farmer—whether he wants to or not, whether he is aware of it or not—becomes a commodity producer. And it is this change that is fundamental, for it alone, even when he does not as yet exploit hired labour, makes him a petty bourgeois and converts him into an antagonist of the proletariat. He sells his product, while the proletarian sells his labour-power. The small farmers, as a class, cannot but seek a rise in the prices of agricultural products, and this is tantamount to their joining the big landowners in sharing the ground-rent, and siding with the landowners against the rest of society. As commodity production develops, the small farmer, in accordance with his *class* status, inevitably becomes a *petty landed proprietor*.

There are cases even among wage-workers when a small part of them side with their masters against the whole class of wage-earners. But this is merely a *small fraction* of a class uniting with its antagonists, against the *entire* class. It is impossible to imagine any improvement of the condition of wage-earners as a class, without an improvement in the living standard of the masses, or without a sharpening of the antagonism between them and capital, which rules contemporary society, the antagonism between them and the entire class of capitalists. But it is quite possible, on the contrary, to imagine a state of affairs—indeed, such a situation is even typical of capitalism—where an improvement in the condition of the small farmers, as a class, results from their alliance with the big landlords, their participation in exacting a higher ground-rent from society as a whole, the contradictions arising between them and the mass of proletarians and semi-proletarians, who depend, entirely or at least mostly, on the sale of their labour-power.

Here is a comparison of American statistics on the number and position of wage-earners and of small farmers:

		1900	1910	Increase (per cent)
Industry	Number of wage-earners (000)	4,713	6,615	40.4
	Their wages ($000,000)	2,008	3,427	70.6
Agriculture	Number of wage-earners . . .	?	?	c. 47.1
	Their wages ($000,000)	357	652	82.3
	Number of farmers (000) . . .	5,737	6,361	10.9
	Value of their major product, cereal crops ($000,000) . . .	1,483	2,665	79.8

The workers in industry *lost*, for their wages went up by only 70.6 per cent ("only", because almost the same quantity of cereals, 101.7 per cent of the old quantity, is now 179.8 per cent of the old price!), while the number of workers increased all of 40 per cent.

The small farmers *gained*, in their capacity of petty landowners, at the expense of the proletariat. The number of small farmers increased by only 10.9 per cent (even if the small commercial farms are singled out, the increase is still only 11.9 per cent), and while the quantity of their product hardly increased at all (+1.7 per cent), its value went up 79.8 per cent.

Naturally, commercial and finance capital took the lion's share of this ground-rent, but the class status of the small farmer and the wage-earner, vis-à-vis each other, is entirely akin to the status of petty bourgeois and proletarian.

The numerical growth of wage-earners *outstrips* the growth of population (+40 per cent for the former as against +21 per cent for the latter). There is growing expropriation of the petty producers and small farmers. There is growing proletarisation of the population.*

The increase in the number of farmers—and to an even greater extent, as we already know, in the number of proprietors among them—*lags* behind the growth of the population (10.9 per cent, as against 21 per cent). The small farmers are increasingly converted into monopolists, into petty landed proprietors.

Let us now take a look at the relationship between small-scale and large-scale production in industry and in agriculture. In respect of industry the figures are not for 1900 and 1910, but for 1904 and 1910.

Industrial enterprises are divided into three main groups depending on the value of their products, the small being those with an output of less than $20,000; the medium, from $20,000 to $100,000, and the large $100,000 and over. We have no way of grouping agricultural enterprises except by acreage. Accordingly, small farms are those up to 100 acres; medium, from 100 to 175; and large, 175 and over. (See first table on p. 201.—*Ed.*)

The uniformity of evolution proves to be remarkable.

Both in industry and agriculture the proportion of medium establishments is reduced, for their number grows more slowly than that of the small and large enterprises.

Both in industry and agriculture the small enterprises increase in number at a slower rate than the large.

---

* The number of wage-earners in agriculture, or rather the growth in their number, is obtained from the following ratio: 82.3:70.6= $=X:40.4$, hence $X=47.1$.

	Groups	Number of enterprises (000)				Increase (per cent)
		1900	per cent	1910	per cent	
Industry	Small	144	66.6	180	67.2	25.0
	Medium	48	22.2	57	21.3	18.7
	Large	24	11.2	31	11.5	29.1
	Total	216	100.0	268	100.0	24.2
Agriculture	Small	3,297	57.5	3,691	58.0	11.9
	Medium	1,422	24.8	1,516	23.8	6.6
	Large	1,018	17.7	1,154	18.2	13.3
	Total	5,737	100.0	6,361	100.0	10.9

What are the changes in the economic strength or economic role of the various types of enterprises? For the industrial enterprises we have the returns on the value of their products, and for the agricultural, on the total value of all farm property.

	Groups	$000,000		$000,000		Increase (per cent)
		1900	per cent	1910	per cent	
Industry	Small	927	6.3	1,127	5.5	21.5
	Medium	2,129	14.4	2,544	12.3	19.5
	Large	11,737	79.3	17,000	82.2	44.8
	Total	14,793	100.0	20,671	100.0	39.7
Agriculture	Small	5,790	28.4	10,499	25.6	81.3
	Medium	5,721	28.0	11,089	27.1	93.8
	Large	8,929	43.6	19,403	47.3	117.3
	Total	20,440	100.0	40,991	100.0	100.5

Once again the uniformity of evolution is remarkable.

Both in industry and agriculture the relative number of small and medium enterprises is decreasing, and only the relative number of the large enterprises is increasing.

In other words, the displacement of small-scale by large-scale production is under way both in industry and in agriculture.

The difference between industry and agriculture in this case is that the proportion of small enterprises in industry increased somewhat more than the proportion of medium enterprises (+21.5 per cent, as against +19.5 per cent), while the reverse was true for agriculture. Of course, this difference is not great, and no general conclusions can be drawn from it. But the fact remains that in the world's leading capitalist country small-scale production in industry gained more ground in the last decade than medium-scale production, whereas the reverse was true for agriculture. This fact shows how little importance is to be attached to the current assertions of bourgeois economists that the law of the displacement of small-scale by large-scale production is confirmed, unconditionally and without any exception, by industry, and refuted by agriculture.

In the agriculture of the U.S.A. the displacement of small-scale by large-scale production is not merely under way, but is proceeding with greater uniformity than in industry.

In considering this, the fact demonstrated above should not be forgotten, namely, that the grouping of farms by acreage *understates* the process of displacement of small-scale by large-scale production.

As for the *degree* of concentration already achieved, agriculture is very far behind. In industry, more than eight-tenths of all production is in the hands of the large enterprises that constitute only 11 per cent of the total number. The role of the small enterprises is insignificant: two-thirds of the total number of enterprises account for only 5.5 per cent of the total production! By comparison, agriculture is still in a state of dispersion: small enterprises, comprising 58 per cent of the total number, account for one-quarter of the total value of all farm property; while 18 per cent large enterprises account for less than one-half (47 per cent). The total number of agricultural enterprises is over 20 times greater than the number in industry.

This confirms the old conclusion—if the evolution of agriculture is compared with that of industry, capitalism in agriculture is at a stage more akin to the manufactory stage than to the stage of large-scale machine industry.

Manual labour still prevails in agriculture, and the use of machinery is relatively very limited. But the data given above do not in any way prove the impossibility of socialising agricultural production, even at the present stage of its development. Those who control the banks *directly* control one-third of America's farms, and indirectly dominate the lot. In view of the modern development of associations of every kind and of communications and transport, it is undoubtedly possible to organise production under a single general plan on a million farms raising more than one-half the total value of the product.

16. SUMMARY AND CONCLUSIONS

The agricultural censuses taken in the United States in 1900 and 1910 are the last word in social statistics in this sphere of the economy. It is the best material of any available in the advanced countries, covering millions of farms and allowing precise well-founded conclusions on the evolution of agriculture under capitalism. One other particular reason why this material can be used to study the laws of the evolution is that the U.S.A. has the largest size, the greatest diversity of relationships, and the greatest range of nuances and forms of capitalist agriculture.

We find here, on the one hand, a transition from the slave-holding—or what is in this case the same, from the feudal—structure of agriculture to commercial and capitalist agriculture; and, on the other hand, capitalism developing with unusual breadth and speed in the freest and most advanced bourgeois country. We observe alongside of this remarkably extensive colonisation conducted on democratic-capitalist lines.

We find here areas which have long been settled, highly industrialised, highly intensive, and similar to most of the areas of civilised, old-capitalist Western Europe; as well as areas of primitive, extensive cropping and stock-raising, like some of the outlying areas of Russia or parts of Siberia. We find large and small farms of the most diverse types: great latifundia, plantations of the former slave-holding South, and the homestead West, and the highly capitalist North of the Atlantic seaboard; the small farms of the Negro share-croppers, and the small capitalist farms producing milk and vegetables for the market in the industrial North or fruits on the Pacific coast; "wheat factories" employing hired labour and the *homesteads* of "independent" small farmers, still full of naïve illusions about living by the "labour of their own hands".

This is a remarkable diversity of relationships, embracing both past and future, Europe and Russia. The comparison with Russia is especially instructive, by the way, in regard to the question of the consequences of a possible transfer of all land to the peasants without compensation, a measure that is progressive but undoubtedly capitalist.

The U.S.A. offers the most convenient example for the study of the general laws of capitalist development in agriculture and the variety of forms these laws assume. A study of this kind leads up to conclusions which may be summed up in the following brief propositions.

In agriculture, as compared with industry, manual labour predominates over machinery to an immeasurably greater extent. But the machine is steadily advancing, improving farming techniques, extending the scale of operations and making them more capitalist. In modern agriculture, machinery is used in the capitalist way.

Hired labour is the chief sign and indicator of capitalism in agriculture. The development of hired labour, like the growing use of machinery, is evident in *all* parts of the country, and in every branch of agriculture. The growth in the number of hired labourers outstrips the growth of the country's rural and total population. The growth in the number of farmers lags behind that of the rural population. Class contradictions are intensified and sharpened.

The displacement of small-scale by large-scale production in agriculture is going forward. This is fully proved by a comparison of the returns for 1900 and 1910 on total farm property.

However, this displacement is understated, and the condition of the small farmers is shown in bright colours because statisticians in America in 1910 confined themselves—as in fact they did almost everywhere in Europe—to grouping the farms by acreage. The wider and faster the intensification of agriculture, the higher is the degree of this understatement and the brighter the colours.

Capitalism grows not only by accelerating the development of large-acreage farms in extensive areas, but also by creating in the intensive areas enterprises on smaller tracts whose operations are on a much larger scale and are much more capitalist.

As a result, the concentration of production in the large enterprises is actually much greater—and the displacement of small-scale production actually goes farther and deeper— than is indicated by ordinary data about farms grouped by acreage. The returns of the 1900 Census, compiled with greater care and in greater detail, are more scientific and leave no doubt at all on this score.

The expropriation of small-scale agriculture is advancing. In the last few decades, the proportion of owners to the total number of farmers declined steadily, while the growth in the number of farmers lagged behind population increase. The number of full owners is declining absolutely in the North, the most important section, which yields the largest volume of farm products and has neither any vestiges of slavery nor any extensive homesteading. In the last decade, the proportion of farmers reporting livestock in general decreased; in contrast to the increased proportion of owners reporting dairy cattle there was an even greater increase in the proportion of operators without horses, especially among the small farmers.

On the whole, a comparison of corresponding data on industry and agriculture for the same period shows that although the latter is incomparably more backward, there is a remarkable similarity in the laws of evolution, and that small-scale production is being ousted from both.

Written in 1915

First published in 1917 as a   Vol. 22, pp. 13-102
separate pamphlet by the
Zhizn i Znaniye Publishers

From A SPEECH AT AN INTERNATIONAL MEETING IN BERNE

Comrades! You have heard speakers from various countries who have told you about the workers' revolutionary struggle against the war. I merely want to add another example, that of the United States of America, the biggest and richest country. Its capitalists are now making enormous profits out of the European war. And they are also campaigning for war. They are saying that America, too, must prepare to enter the war, and that hundreds of millions of the people's dollars must be siphoned off into new armaments, into armaments without end. A section of the socialists in America have also responded to this false, criminal call. Let me read a statement by Comrade *Eugene Debs*, a most popular leader of the American socialists, and the presidential candidate of the American Socialist Party.

In the September 11, 1915, issue of the American weekly, *Appeal to Reason*, he says: "*I am not a capitalist soldier; I am a proletarian revolutionist. I do not belong to the regular army of the plutocracy, but to the irregular army of the people. I refuse to obey any command to fight from the ruling class.... I am opposed to every war but one; I am for that war with heart and soul, and that is the worldwide war of the social revolution. In that war I am prepared to fight in any way the ruling class may make necessary....*"

This is what *Eugene Debs*, the American Bebel, the beloved leader of the American workers, is telling them.

This goes to show once again, comrades, that *the rallying of the working class forces is truly under way in all coun-*

tries of the world. War inflicts horrible sufferings on the people, but we must not, and we have no reason at all to, despair of the future.

Berner Tagwacht No. 33,
February 9, 1916

First published in Russian in 1929
in the second and third editions of
Lenin's *Collected Works,* Vol. XIX

Vol. 22, p. 125

SPLIT OR DECAY?

That was how *Sotsial-Demokrat* posed the alternative with regard to the German Social-Democratic Party, back in its issue No. 35,[49] when it elaborated the fundamental ideas of the Manifesto on war issued by our Party's Central Committee.[50] Notice how *the facts* bear out this conclusion.

The German Social-Democratic Party is clearly disintegrating. *Otto Rühle*, Karl Liebknecht's closest associate, quite apart from the I.S.D. group (International Socialists of Germany),[51] which has been *consistently* fighting the hypocritical Kautskyites,[52] has *openly* come out for a split. *Vorwärts*[53] had no serious, honest answer. There are actually *two* workers' parties in Germany.

Even in Britain, a statement was made by T. Russell Williams in the moderate, pacifist *Labour Leader* (the Central Organ of the Independent Labour Party), and he was supported by many local functionaries. Comrade *Ornatsky*, who has done very good internationalist work in Britain, came out in the conciliatory *Nashe Slovo* in Paris for an immediate split there. We are naturally in full agreement with *Ornatsky* in his polemic with T. Rothstein, a correspondent of *Kommunist*, who takes a Kautskyite attitude.

In France, Bourderon is a fervent opponent of any split *but*—has proposed to the Party Congress a resolution calling for outright disapproval both of the Party's Central Committee and the parliamentary group! Adoption of such a resolution would mean an immediate split in the Party.

In America, the Socialist Party appears to be united. Actually, some of its members, like Russell and others, preach "preparedness", stand for war, and want an army and navy. Others, like Eugene Debs, the Party's presidential candidate, openly preach *civil war* "in the event" of an imperialist war, rather, in connection with one.

There are now actually two parties all over the world. There are in fact already two Internationals. And if the Zimmerwald majority are afraid to recognise this, if they dream of unity with the social-chauvinists, and declare their readiness to have such unity, these "pious hopes" in practice remain nothing but hopes, expressive of inconsistency and timidity of thought. Consciousness lags behind reality.

Written February-April 1916

First published in 1931
in *Lenin Miscellany XVII*

Vol. 22, pp. 180-81

IMPERIALISM,
THE HIGHEST STAGE OF CAPITALISM
(Abridged)

During the last fifteen to twenty years, especially since the Spanish-American War (1898) and the Anglo-Boer War (1899-1902),[54] the economic and also the political literature of the two hemispheres has more and more often adopted the term "imperialism" in order to describe the present era. In 1902, a book by the English economist J. A. Hobson, *Imperialism*, was published in London and New York. This author, whose point of view is that of bourgeois social reformism and pacifism which, in essence, is identical with the present point of view of the ex-Marxist, Karl Kautsky, gives a very good and comprehensive description of the principal specific economic and political features of imperialism. In 1910, there appeared in Vienna the work of the Austrian Marxist, Rudolf Hilferding, *Finance Capital* (Russian edition, Moscow, 1912). In spite of the mistake the author makes on the theory of money, and in spite of a certain inclination on his part to reconcile Marxism with opportunism, this work gives a very valuable theoretical analysis of "the latest phase of capitalist development", as the subtitle runs. Indeed, what has been said of imperialism during the last few years, especially in an enormous number of magazine and newspaper articles, and also in the resolutions, for example, of the Chemnitz and Basle congresses which took place in the autumn of 1912,[55] has scarcely gone beyond the ideas expounded, or more exactly, summed up by the two writers mentioned above....

Later on, I shall try to show briefly, and as simply as possible, the connection and relationships between the *principal* economic features of imperialism. I shall not be able to deal with the non-economic aspects of the question, however much they deserve to be dealt with. References to literature and other notes, which, perhaps, would not interest all readers, are to be found at the end of this pamphlet.

I. CONCENTRATION OF PRODUCTION AND MONOPOLIES

The enormous growth of industry and the remarkably rapid concentration of production in ever-larger enterprises are one of the most characteristic features of capitalism. Modern production censuses give most complete and most exact data on this process.

In Germany, for example, out of every 1,000 industrial enterprises, large enterprises, i.e., those employing more than 50 workers, numbered three in 1882, six in 1895 and nine in 1907; and out of every 100 workers employed, this group of enterprises employed 22, 30 and 37, respectively. Concentration of production, however, is much more intense than the concentration of workers, since labour in the large enterprises is much more productive. This is shown by the figures on steam-engines and electric motors. If we take what in Germany is called industry in the broad sense of the term, that is, including commerce, transport, etc., we get the following picture. Large-scale enterprises, 30,588 out of a total of 3,265,623, that is to say, 0.9 per cent. These enterprises employ 5,700,000 workers out of a total of 14,400,000, i.e., 39.4 per cent; they use 6,600,000 steam horse power out of a total of 8,800,000, i.e., 75.3 per cent, and 1,200,000 kilowatts of electricity out of a total of 1,500,000, i.e., 77.2 per cent.

Less than one-hundredth of the total number of enterprises utilise *more than three-fourths* of the total amount of steam and electric power! Two million nine hundred and seventy thousand small enterprises (employing up to five workers), constituting 91 per cent of the total, utilise only 7 per cent of the total amount of steam and electric

power! Tens of thousands of huge enterprises are everything; millions of small ones are nothing.

In 1907, there were in Germany 586 establishments employing one thousand and more workers, nearly *one-tenth*
(1,380,000) of the total number of workers employed in
industry, and they consumed *almost one-third* (32 per cent)
of the total amount of steam and electric power.* As we
shall see, money capital and the banks make this superiority of a handful of the largest enterprises still more overwhelming, in the most literal sense of the word, i.e., millions of small, medium and even some big "proprietors"
are in fact in complete subjection to some hundreds of
millionaire financiers.

In another advanced country of modern capitalism, the
United States of America, the growth of the concentration
of production is still greater. Here statistics single out industry in the narrow sense of the word and classify
enterprises according to the value of their annual output.
In 1904 large-scale enterprises with an output valued at
one million dollars and over numbered 1,900 (out of
216,180, i.e., 0.9 per cent). These employed 1,400,000 workers (out of 5,500,000, i.e., 25.6 per cent) and the value of
their output amounted to $5,600,000,000 (out of
$14,800,000,000, i.e., 38 per cent). Five years later, in 1909,
the corresponding figures were: 3,060 enterprises (out of
268,491, i.e., 1.1 per cent) employing 2,000,000 workers
(out of 6,600,000, i.e., 30.5 per cent) with an output valued
at $9,000,000,000 (out of $20,700,000,000, i.e., 43.8 per
cent).**

Almost half the total production of all the enterprises
of the country was carried on by *one-hundredth part* of
these enterprises! These 3,000 giant enterprises embrace
258 branches of industry. From this it can be seen that, at
a certain stage of its development, concentration itself, as
it were, leads straight to monopoly, for a score or so of
giant enterprises can easily arrive at an agreement, and on
the other hand, the hindrance to competition, the tendency

---

* Figures taken from *Annalen des deutschen Reichs*, 1911, Zahn.
** *Statistical Abstract of the United States 1912*, p. 202.

towards monopoly, arises from the huge size of the enterprises. This transformation of competition into monopoly is one of the most important—if not the most important—phenomena of modern capitalist economy, and we must deal with it in greater detail. But first we must clear up one possible misunderstanding.

American statistics speak of 3,000 giant enterprises in 250 branches of industry, as if there were only a dozen enterprises of the largest scale for each branch of industry.

But this is not the case. Not in every branch of industry are there large-scale enterprises; and moreover, a very important feature of capitalism in its highest stage of development is so-called *combination* of production, that is to say, the grouping in a single enterprise of different branches of industry, which either represent the consecutive stages in the processing of raw materials (for example, the smelting of iron ore into pig-iron, the conversion of pig-iron into steel, and then, perhaps, the manufacture of steel goods)—or are auxiliary to one another (for example, the utilisation of scrap, or of by-products, the manufacture of packing materials, etc.).

"Combination," writes Hilferding, "levels out the fluctuations of trade and therefore assures to the combined enterprises a more stable rate of profit. Secondly, combination has the effect of eliminating trade. Thirdly, it has the effect of rendering possible technical improvements, and, consequently, the acquisition of superprofits over and above those obtained by the 'pure' [i.e., non-combined] enterprises. Fourthly, it strengthens the position of the combined enterprises relative to the 'pure' enterprises, strengthens them in the competitive struggle in periods of serious depression, when the fall in prices of raw materials does not keep pace with the fall in prices of manufactured goods."*

The German bourgeois economist, Heymann, who has written a book especially on "mixed", that is, combined, enterprises in the German iron industry, says: "Pure enter-

---

* *Finance Capital*, Russ. ed., pp. 286-87.

prises perish, they are crushed between the high price of raw material and the low price of the finished product." Thus we get the following picture: "There remain, on the one hand, the big coal companies, producing millions of tons yearly, strongly organised in their coal syndicate, and on the other, the big steel plants, closely allied to the coal mines, having their own steel syndicate. These giant enterprises, producing 400,000 tons of steel per annum, with a tremendous output of ore and coal and producing finished steel goods, employing 10,000 workers quartered in company houses, and sometimes owning their own railways and ports, are the typical representatives of the German iron and steel industry. And concentration goes on further and further. Individual enterprises are becoming larger and larger. An ever-increasing number of enterprises in one or in several different industries join together in giant enterprises, backed up and directed by half a dozen big Berlin banks. In relation to the German mining industry, the truth of the teachings of Karl Marx on concentration is definitely proved; true, this applies to a country where industry is protected by tariffs and freight rates. The German mining industry is ripe for expropriation."*

Such is the conclusion which a bourgeois economist, who by way of exception is conscientious, had to arrive at. It must be noted that he seems to place Germany in a special category because her industries are protected by high tariffs. But this is a circumstance which only accelerates concentration and the formation of monopolist manufacturers' associations, cartels, syndicates, etc. It is extremely important to note that in free-trade Britain, concentration *also* leads to monopoly, although somewhat later and perhaps in another form. Professor Hermann Levy, in his special work of research entitled *Monopolies, Cartels and Trusts*, based on data on British economic development, writes as follows:

"In Great Britain it is the size of the enterprise and its high technical level which harbour a monopolist ten-

---

* Hans Gideon Heymann, *Die gemischten Werke im deutschen Grosseisengewerbe*, Stuttgart, 1904 (S. 256, 278).

dency. This, for one thing, is due to the great investment of capital per enterprise, which gives rise to increasing demands for new capital for the new enterprises and thereby renders their launching more difficult. Moreover (and this seems to us to be the more important point), every new enterprise that wants to keep pace with the gigantic enterprises that have been formed by concentration would here produce such an enormous quantity of surplus goods that it could dispose of them only by being able to sell them profitably as a result of an enormous increase in demand; otherwise, this surplus would force prices down to a level that would be unprofitable both for the new enterprise and for the monopoly combines." Britain differs from other countries where protective tariffs facilitate the formation of cartels in that monopolist manufacturers' associations, cartels and trusts arise in the majority of cases only when the number of the chief competing enterprises has been reduced to "a couple of dozen or so". "Here the influence of concentration on the formation of large industrial monopolies in a whole sphere of industry stands out with crystal clarity."*

Half a century ago, when Marx was writing *Capital*, free competition appeared to the overwhelming majority of economists to be a "natural law" Official science tried, by a conspiracy of silence, to kill the works of Marx, who by a theoretical and historical analysis of capitalism had proved that free competition gives rise to the concentration of production, which, in turn, at a certain stage of development, leads to monopoly. Today, monopoly has become a fact. Economists are writing mountains of books in which they describe the diverse manifestations of monopoly, and continue to declare in chorus that "Marxism is refuted". But facts are stubborn things, as the English proverb says, and they have to be reckoned with, whether we like it or not. The facts show that differences between capitalist countries, e.g., in the matter of protection or

---

* Hermann Levy, *Monopole, Kartelle und Trusts*, Jena, 1909, S. 286, 290, 298.

free trade, only give rise to insignificant variations in the form of monopolies or in the moment of their appearance; and that the rise of monopolies, as the result of the concentration of production, is a general and fundamental law of the present stage of development of capitalism.

For Europe, the time when the new capitalism *definitely* superseded the old can be established with fair precision; it was the beginning of the twentieth century. In one of the latest compilations on the history of the "formation of monopolies", we read:

"Isolated examples of capitalist monopoly could be cited from the period preceding 1860; in these could be discerned the embryo of the forms that are so common today; but all this undoubtedly represents the prehistory of the cartels. The real beginning of modern monopoly goes back, at the earliest, to the sixties. The first important period of development of monopoly commenced with the international industrial depression of the seventies and lasted until the beginning of the nineties." "If we examine the question on a European scale, we will find that the development of free competition reached its apex in the sixties and seventies. It was then that Britain completed the construction of her old-style capitalist organisation. In Germany, this organisation had entered into a fierce struggle with handicraft and domestic industry, and had begun to create for itself its own forms of existence."

"The great revolution commenced with the crash of 1873, or rather, the depression which followed it and which, with hardly discernible interruptions in the early eighties, and the unusually violent, but short-lived boom round about 1889, marks twenty-two years of European economic history." "During the short boom of 1889-90, the system of cartels was widely resorted to in order to take advantage of favourable business conditions. An ill-considered policy drove prices up still more rapidly and still higher than would have been the case if there had been no cartels, and nearly all these cartels perished ingloriously in the smash. Another five-year period of bad trade and low prices followed, but a new spirit reigned in industry; the depression was no longer regarded as something to be taken for granted; it was regarded as nothing more than a pause before another boom.

"The cartel movement entered its second epoch: instead of being a transitory phenomenon, the cartels have become one of the foundations of economic life. They are winning one field of industry after another, primarily, the raw materials industry. At the beginning of the nineties the cartel system had already acquired—in the organisation of the coke syndicate on the model of which the coal syndicate was later formed—a cartel technique which has hardly been improved on. For the first time the great boom at the close of the nineteenth century and the crisis of 1900-03 occurred entirely—in the mining and iron industries at least—under the aegis of the cartels. And while at that time it appeared to be something novel, now the general public takes it for granted that large spheres of economic life have been, as a general rule, removed from the realm of free competition."*

Thus, the principal stages in the history of monopolies are the following: (1) 1860-70, the highest stage, the apex of development of free competition; monopoly is in the barely discernible, embryonic stage. (2) After the crisis of 1873, a lengthy period of development of cartels; but they are still the exception. They are not yet durable. They are still a transitory phenomenon. (3) The boom at the end of the nineteenth century and the crisis of 1900-03. Cartels become one of the foundations of the whole of economic life. Capitalism has been transformed into imperialism.

Cartels come to an agreement on the terms of sale, dates of payment, etc. They divide the markets among themselves. They fix the quantity of goods to be produced. They fix prices. They divide the profits among the various enterprises, etc.

The number of cartels in Germany was estimated at

---

* Th. Vogelstein, "Die finanzielle Organisation der kapitalistischen Industrie und die Monopolbildungen" in *Grundriss der Sozialökonomik*, VI. Abt., Tübingen, 1914. Cf., also by the same author: *Organisationsformen der Eisenindustrie und Textilindustrie in England und Amerika*, Bd. I, Lpz., 1910.

about 250 in 1896 and at 385 in 1905, with about 12,000 firms participating.* But it is generally recognised that these figures are underestimations. From the statistics of German industry for 1907 we quoted above, it is evident that even these 12,000 very big enterprises probably consume more than half the steam and electric power used in the country. In the United States of America, the number of trusts in 1900 was estimated at 185 and in 1907, 250. American statistics divide all industrial enterprises into those belonging to individuals, to private firms or to corporations. The latter in 1904 comprised 23.6 per cent, and in 1909, 25.9 per cent, i.e., more than one-fourth of the total industrial enterprises in the country. These employed in 1904, 70.6 per cent, and in 1909, 75.6 per cent, i.e., more than three-fourths of the total wage-earners. Their output at these two dates was valued at $10,900,000,000, and $16,300,000,000, i.e., 73.7 per cent and 79.0 per cent of the total, respectively.

At times cartels and trusts concentrate in their hands seven- or eight-tenths of the total output of a given branch of industry. The Rhine-Westphalian Coal Syndicate, at its foundation in 1893, concentrated 86.7 per cent of the total coal output of the area, and in 1910 it already concentrated 95.4 per cent.** The monopoly so created assures enormous profits, and leads to the formation of technical production units of formidable magnitude. The famous Standard Oil Company in the United States was founded in 1900: "It has an authorised capital of $150,000,000. It issued $100,000,000 common and $106,000,000 preferred stock. From 1900 to 1907 the following dividends were paid on the latter: 48, 48, 45, 44, 36, 40, 40, 40 per cent in the respective years, i.e., in all $367,000,000. From 1882 to 1907,

---

* Dr. Riesser, *Die deutschen Grossbanken und ihre Konzentration im Zusammenhange mit der Entwicklung der Gesamtwirtschaft in Deutschland*, 4. Aufl., 1912, S. 149; Robert Liefmann, *Kartelle und Trusts und die Weiterbildung der volkswirtschaftlichen Organisation*, 2. Aufl., 1910, S. 25.

** Dr. Fritz Kestner, *Der Organisationszwang. Eine Untersuchung über die Kämpfe zwischen Kartellen und Aussenseitern*, Berlin, 1912, S. 11.

out of total net profits amounting to $889,000,000, $606,000,000 were distributed in dividends, and the rest went to reserve capital."* "In 1907 the various works of the United States Steel Corporation employed no less than 210,180 people. The largest enterprise in the German mining industry, Gelsenkirchener Bergwerksgesellschaft, in 1908 had a staff of 46,048 workers and office employees."** In 1902, the United States Steel Corporation already produced 9,000,000 tons of steel.*** Its output constituted in 1901, 66.3 per cent, and in 1908, 56.1 per cent of the total output of steel in the United States.**** The output of ore was 43.9 per cent and 46.3 per cent, respectively.

The report of the American Government Commission on Trusts states: "Their superiority over competitors is due to the magnitude of their enterprises and their excellent technical equipment. Since its inception, the Tobacco Trust has devoted all its efforts to the universal substitution of mechanical for manual labour. With this end in view it has bought up all patents that have anything to do with the manufacture of tobacco and has spent enormous sums for this purpose. Many of these patents at first proved to be of no use, and had to be modified by the engineers employed by the trust. At the end of 1906, two subsidiary companies were formed solely to acquire patents. With the same object in view, the trust has built its own foundries, machine shops and repair shops. One of these establishments, that in Brooklyn, employs on the average 300 workers; here experiments are carried out on inventions concerning the manufacture of cigarettes, cheroots, snuff, tinfoil for packing, boxes, etc. Here, also, inventions are perfected."***** "Other trusts also employ what are called devel-

---

* R. Liefmann, *Beteiligungs- und Finanzierungsgesellschaften. Eine Studie über den modernen Kapitalismus und das Effektenwesen,* 1. Aufl., Jena, 1909, S. 212.

** Ibid., S. 218.

*** Dr. S. Tschierschky, *Kartell und Trust,* Göttingen, 1903, S. 13.

**** Th. Vogelstein, *Organisationsformen,* S. 275.

***** *Report of the Commissioner of Corporations on the Tobacco Industry,* Washington, 1909, p. 266, cited according to Dr. Paul Tafel, *Die nordamerikanischen Trusts und ihre Wirkungen auf den Fortschritt der Technik,* Stuttgart, 1913, S. 48.

opment engineers whose business it is to devise new
methods of production and to test technical improvements.
The United States Steel Corporation grants big bonuses to
its workers and engineers for all inventions that raise technical efficiency, or reduce cost of production."*

In German large-scale industry, e.g., in the chemical
industry, which has developed so enormously during these
last few decades, the promotion of technical improvement
is organised in the same way. By 1908 the process of concentration of production had already given rise to two main
"groups" which, in their way, were also in the nature of
monopolies. At first these groups constituted "dual alliances" of two pairs of big factories, each having a capital
of from twenty to twenty-one million marks—on the one
hand, the former Meister Factory in Höchst and the Casella
Factory in Frankfurt am Main; and on the other hand,
the aniline and soda factory at Ludwigshafen and the
former Bayer Factory at Elberfeld. Then, in 1905, one
of these groups, and in 1908 the other group, each concluded an agreement with yet another big factory. The
result was the formation of two "triple alliances", each
with a capital of from forty to fifty million marks. And
these "alliances" have already begun to "approach" each
other, to reach "an understanding" about prices, etc.**

Competition becomes transformed into monopoly. The
result is immense progress in the socialisation of production. In particular, the process of technical invention and
improvement becomes socialised.

This is something quite different from the old free competition between manufacturers, scattered and out of touch
with one another, and producing for an unknown market.
Concentration has reached the point at which it is possible
to make an approximate estimate of all sources of raw
materials (for example, the iron ore deposits) of a country
and even, as we shall see, of several countries, or of the
whole world. Not only are such estimates made, but these

---

* Dr. P. Tafel, ibid., p. 49.
** Riesser, op. cit., third edition, p. 547 et seq. The newspapers
(June 1916) report the formation of a new gigantic trust which com-
bines the chemical industry of Germany.

sources are captured by gigantic monopolist associations. An approximate estimate of the capacity of markets is also made, and the associations "divide" them up amongst themselves by agreement. Skilled labour is monopolised, the best engineers are engaged; the means of transport are captured—railways in America, shipping companies in Europe and America. Capitalism in its imperialist stage leads directly to the most comprehensive socialisation of production; it, so to speak, drags the capitalists, against their will and consciousness, into some sort of a new social order, a transitional one from complete free competition to complete socialisation.

Production becomes social, but appropriation remains private. The social means of production remain the private property of a few. The general framework of formally recognised free competition remains, and the yoke of a few monopolists on the rest of the population becomes a hundred times heavier, more burdensome and intolerable.

The German economist, Kestner, has written a book especially devoted to "the struggle between the cartels and outsiders", i.e., the capitalists outside the cartels. He entitled his work *Compulsory Organisation*, although, in order to present capitalism in its true light, he should, of course, have written about compulsory submission to monopolist associations. It is instructive to glance at least at the list of the methods the monopolist associations resort to in the present-day, the latest, the civilised struggle for "organisation": (1) stopping supplies of raw materials (... "one of the most important methods of compelling adherence to the cartel"); (2) stopping the supply of labour by means of "alliances" (i.e., of agreements between the capitalists and the trade unions by which the latter permit their members to work only in cartelised enterprises); (3) stopping deliveries; (4) closing trade outlets; (5) agreements with the buyers, by which the latter undertake to trade only with the cartels; (6) systematic price cutting (to ruin "outside" firms, i.e., those which refuse to submit to the monopolists. Millions are spent in order to sell goods for a certain time below their cost price; there were instances when the price of petrol was thus reduced from 40 to 22 marks, i.e., almost by half!); (7) stopping credits; (8) boycott.

Here we no longer have competition between small and large, between technically developed and backward enterprises. We see here the monopolists throttling those who do not submit to them, to their yoke, to their dictation. This is how this process is reflected in the mind of a bourgeois economist:

"Even in the purely economic sphere," writes Kestner, "a certain change is taking place from commercial activity in the old sense of the word towards organisational-speculative activity. The greatest success no longer goes to the merchant whose technical and commercial experience enables him best of all to estimate the needs of the buyer, and who is able to discover and, so to speak, 'awaken' a latent demand; it goes to the speculative genius [?!] who knows how to estimate, or even only to sense in advance, the organisational development and the possibilities of certain connections between individual enterprises and the banks...."

Translated into ordinary human language this means that the development of capitalism has arrived at a stage when, although commodity production still "reigns" and continues to be regarded as the basis of economic life, it has in reality been undermined and the bulk of the profits go to the "geniuses" of financial manipulation. At the basis of these manipulations and swindles lies socialised production; but the immense progress of mankind, which achieved this socialisation, goes to benefit ... the speculators. We shall see later how "on these grounds" reactionary, petty-bourgeois critics of capitalist imperialism dream of going *back* to "free", "peaceful", and "honest" competition.

"The prolonged raising of prices which results from the formation of cartels," says Kestner, "has hitherto been observed only in respect of the most important means of production, particularly coal, iron and potassium, but never in respect of manufactured goods. Similarly, the increase in profits resulting from this raising of prices has been limited only to the industries which produce means of production. To this observation we must add that the industries which process raw materials (and not semi-manufactures) not only secure advantages from the cartel formation in the shape of high profits, to the detriment of the finished goods industry, but have also secured a *dominating position* over the latter, which did not exist under free competition."*

The words which I have italicised reveal the essence of the case which the bourgeois economists admit so reluctantly and so rarely, and which the present-day defenders of opportunism, led by Kautsky, so zealously try to evade and brush aside. Domination, and the violence that is associated with it, such are the relationships that are typical of the "latest phase of capitalist development"; this is what inevitably had to result, and has resulted, from the formation of all-powerful economic monopolies.

I shall give one more example of the methods employed by the cartels. Where it is possible to capture all or the chief sources of raw materials, the rise of cartels and formation of monopolies is particularly easy. It would be wrong, however, to assume that monopolies do not arise in other industries in which it is impossible to corner the sources of raw materials. The cement industry, for instance, can find its raw materials everywhere. Yet in Germany this industry too is strongly cartelised. The cement manufacturers have formed regional syndicates: South German, Rhine-Westphalian, etc. The prices fixed are monopoly prices: 230 to 280 marks a car-load, when the cost price is 180 marks! The enterprises pay a dividend of from 12 to 16 per cent—and it must not be forgotten that the "geniuses" of modern speculation know how to pocket big profits besides what they draw in dividends. In order to prevent competition in such a profitable industry, the monopolists even resort to various stratagems: they spread false rumours about the bad situation in their industry; anonymous warnings are published in the newspapers, like the following: "Capitalists, don't invest your capital in the cement industry!"; lastly, they buy up "outsiders" (those outside the syndicates) and pay them compensa-

---

* Kestner, op. cit., S. 254.

tion of 60,000, 80,000 and even 150,000 marks.* Monopoly hews a path for itself everywhere without scruple as to the means, from paying a "modest" sum to buy off competitors, to the American device of employing dynamite against them.

The statement that cartels can abolish crises is a fable spread by bourgeois economists who at all costs desire to place capitalism in a favourable light. On the contrary, the monopoly created in *certain* branches of industry increases and intensifies the anarchy inherent in capitalist production *as a whole*. The disparity between the development of agriculture and that of industry, which is characteristic of capitalism in general, is increased. The privileged position of the most highly cartelised, so-called *heavy* industry, especially coal and iron, causes "a still greater lack of co-ordination" in other branches of industry—as Jeidels, the author of one of the best works on "the relationship of the German big banks to industry", admits.**

"The more developed an economic system is," writes Liefmann, an unblushing apologist of capitalism, "the more it resorts to risky enterprises, or enterprises in other countries, to those which need a great deal of time to develop, or finally, to those which are only of local importance."*** The increased risk is connected in the long run with a prodigious increase of capital, which, as it were, overflows the brim, flows abroad, etc. At the same time the extremely rapid rate of technical progress gives rise to increasing elements of disparity between the various spheres of national economy, to anarchy and crises. Liefmann is obliged to admit that: "In all probability mankind will see further important technical revolutions in the near future which will also affect the organisation of the economic system"... electricity and aviation.... "As a general rule,

---

* L. Eschwege, "Zement" in *Die Bank*, 1909, 1, S. 115 et seq.
** Jeidels, *Das Verhältnis der deutschen Grossbanken zur Industrie mit besonderer Berücksichtigung der Eisenindustrie*, Leipzig, 1905, S. 271.
*** Liefmann, *Beteiligungs- und Finanzierungsgesellschaften*, S. 434.

in such periods of radical economic change, speculation develops on a large scale.". . .*

Crises of every kind—economic crises most frequently, but not only these—in their turn increase very considerably the tendency towards concentration and towards monopoly. In this connection, the following reflections of Jeidels on the significance of the crisis of 1900, which, as we have already seen, marked the turning-point in the history of modern monopoly, are exceedingly instructive:

"Side by side with the gigantic plants in the basic industries, the crisis of 1900 still found many plants organised on lines that today would be considered obsolete, the 'pure' [non-combined] plants, which were brought into being at the height of the industrial boom. The fall in prices and the falling off in demand put these 'pure' enterprises in a precarious position, which did not affect the gigantic combined enterprises at all or only affected them for a very short time. As a consequence of this the crisis of 1900 resulted in a far greater concentration of industry than the crisis of 1873: the latter crisis also produced a sort of selection of the best-equipped enterprises, but owing to the level of technical development at that time, this selection could not place the firms which successfully emerged from the crisis in a position of monopoly. Such a durable monopoly exists to a high degree in the gigantic enterprises in the modern iron and steel and electrical industries owing to their very complicated technique, far-reaching organisation and magnitude of capital, and, to a lesser degree, in the engineering industry, certain branches of the metallurgical industry, transport, etc."**

Monopoly! This is the last word in the "latest phase of capitalist development". But we shall only have a very insufficient, incomplete, and poor notion of the real power and the significance of modern monopolies if we do not take into consideration the part played by the banks.

---

* Ibid., S. 465-66.
** Jeidels, op. cit., S. 108.

V. DIVISION OF THE WORLD
AMONG CAPITALIST ASSOCIATIONS

Monopolist capitalist associations, cartels, syndicates and trusts first divided the home market among themselves and obtained more or less complete possession of the industry of their own country. But under capitalism the home market is inevitably bound up with the foreign market. Capitalism long ago created a world market. As the export of capital increased, and as the foreign and colonial connections and "spheres of influence" of the big monopolist associations expanded in all ways, things "naturally" gravitated towards an international agreement among these associations, and towards the formation of international cartels.

This is a new stage of world concentration of capital and production, incomparably higher than the preceding stages. Let us see how this supermonopoly develops.

The electrical industry is highly typical of the latest technical achievements and is most typical of capitalism at the *end* of the nineteenth and the beginning of the twentieth centuries. This industry has developed most in the two leaders of the new capitalist countries, the United States and Germany. In Germany, the crisis of 1900 gave a particularly strong impetus to its concentration. During the crisis, the banks, which by this time had become fairly well merged with industry, enormously accelerated and intensified the ruin of relatively small firms and their absorption by the large ones. "The banks," writes Jeidels, "refused a helping hand to the very firms in greatest need of capital, and brought on first a frenzied boom and then the hopeless failure of the companies which have not been connected with them closely enough."*

As a result, after 1900, concentration in Germany progressed with giant strides. Up to 1900 there had been seven or eight "groups" in the electrical industry. Each consisted of several companies (altogether there were 28) and each was backed by from 2 to 11 banks. Between 1908 and

---

* Jeidels, op. cit., S. 232.

1912 all these groups were merged into two, or one. The following diagram shows the process:

Groups in the Electrical Industry

Prior to 1900	Felten & Guil- laume	Lah- meyer	Union A.E.G. | A.E.G. (G.E.C.)	Siemens & Halske	Schuckert & Co.	Berg- mann | Berg- mann	Kum- mer | Failed in 1900

Felten & Lahmeyer	Siemens & Halske- Schuckert

A.E.G. (G.E.C.)	Siemens & Halske-Schuckert

By
1912:   (In close "co-operation" since 1908)

The famous A.E.G. (General Electric Company), which grew up in this way, controls 175 to 200 companies (through the "holding" system), and a total capital of approximately *1,500 million* marks. Of direct agencies abroad alone, it has thirty-four, of which twelve are joint-stock companies, in more than ten countries. As early as 1904 the amount of capital invested abroad by the German electrical industry was estimated at 233 million marks. Of this sum, 62 million were invested in Russia. Needless to say, the A.E.G. is a huge "combine"—its manufacturing companies alone number no less than sixteen—producing the most diverse articles, from cables and insulators to motor-cars and flying machines.

But concentration in Europe was also a component part of the process of concentration in America, which developed in the following way:

General Electric Company

United States:	Thomson-Houston Co. establishes a firm in Europe	Edison Co. establishes in Europe the French Edison Co. which transfers its patents to the German firm
Germany:	Union Electric Co.	General Electric Co. (A.E.G.)

General Electric Co. (A.E.G.)

Thus, *two* electrical "great powers" were formed: "there are no other electrical companies in the world *completely* independent of them," wrote Heinig in his article "The Path of the Electric Trust". An idea, although far from complete, of the turnover and the size of the enterprises of the two "trusts" can be obtained from the following figures:

		Turnover (000,000 marks)	Number of employees	Net profits (000,000 marks)
America: General Electric Co. (G.E.C.)	1907	252	28,000	35.4
	1910	298	32,000	45.6
Germany: General Electric Co. (A.E.G.)	1907	216	30,700	14.5
	1911	362	60,800	21.7

And then, in 1907, the German and American trusts concluded an agreement by which they divided the world between them. Competition between them ceased. The American General Electric Company (G.E.C.) "got" the United States and Canada. The German General Electric Company (A.E.G.) "got" Germany, Austria, Russia, Holland, Denmark, Switzerland, Turkey and the Balkans. Special agreements, naturally secret, were concluded regarding the penetration of "daughter companies" into new branches of industry, into "new" countries formally not yet allotted. The two trusts were to exchange inventions and experiments.*

The difficulty of competing against this trust, actually a single world-wide trust controlling a capital of several thousand million, with "branches", agencies, representatives, connections, etc., in every corner of the world, is self-evident. But the division of the world between two powerful trusts does not preclude *redivision* if the relation of forces changes as a result of uneven development, war, bankruptcy, etc.

An instructive example of an attempt at such a redivision, of the struggle for redivision, is provided by the oil industry.

---

* Riesser, op. cit.; Diouritch, op. cit., p. 239; Kurt Heinig, op cit.

"The world oil market," wrote Jeidels in 1905, "is even today still divided between two great financial groups—Rockefeller's American Standard Oil Co., and Rothschild and Nobel, the controlling interests of the Russian oilfields in Baku. The two groups are closely connected. But for several years five enemies have been threatening their monopoly"*: (1) the exhaustion of the American oilfields; (2) the competition of the firm of Mantashev of Baku; (3) the Austrian oilfields; (4) the Rumanian oilfields; (5) the overseas oilfields, particularly in the Dutch colonies (the extremely rich firms, Samuel, and Shell, also connected with British capital). The three last groups are connected with the big German banks, headed by the huge Deutsche Bank. These banks independently and systematically developed the oil industry in Rumania, for example, in order to have a foothold of their "own". In 1907, the foreign capital invested in the Rumanian oil industry was estimated at 185 million francs, of which 74 million was German capital.**

A struggle began for the "division of the world", as, in fact, it is called in economic literature. On the one hand, the Rockefeller "oil trust" wanted to lay its hands on *everything*; it formed a "daughter company" *right in* Holland, and bought up oilfields in the Dutch Indies, in order to strike at its principal enemy, the Anglo-Dutch Shell trust. On the other hand, the Deutsche Bank and the other German banks aimed at "retaining" Rumania "for themselves" and at uniting her with Russia against Rockefeller. The latter possessed far more capital and an excellent system of oil transportation and distribution. The struggle had to end, and did end in 1907, with the utter defeat of the Deutsche Bank, which was confronted with the alternative: either to liquidate its "oil interests" and lose millions, or submit. It chose to submit, and concluded a very disadvantageous agreement with the "oil trust". The Deutsche Bank agreed "not to attempt anything which might injure American interests". Provision was made, how-

---

* Jeidels, op. cit., S. 192-93.
** Diouritch, op. cit., pp. 245-46.

ever, for the annulment of the agreement in the event of
Germany establishing a state oil monopoly.

Then the "comedy of oil" began. One of the German
finance kings, von Gwinner, a director of the Deutsche
Bank, through his private secretary, Stauss, launched a campaign *for* a state oil monopoly. The gigantic machine of
the huge German bank and all its wide "connections" were
set in motion. The press bubbled over with "patriotic"
indignation against the "yoke" of the American trust, and,
on March 15, 1911, the Reichstag, by an almost unanimous
vote, adopted a motion asking the government to introduce
a bill for the establishment of an oil monopoly. The government seized upon this "popular" idea, and the game of
the Deutsche Bank, which hoped to cheat its American
counterpart and improve its business by a state monopoly,
appeared to have been won. The German oil magnates
already saw visions of enormous profits, which would not
be less than those of the Russian sugar refiners.... But,
firstly, the big German banks quarrelled among themselves
over the division of the spoils. The Disconto-Gesellschaft
exposed the covetous aims of the Deutsche Bank; secondly,
the government took fright at the prospect of a struggle
with Rockefeller, for it was very doubtful whether Germany could be sure of obtaining oil from other sources
(the Rumanian output was small); thirdly, just at that
time the 1913 credits of a thousand million marks were
voted for Germany's war preparations. The oil monopoly
project was postponed. The Rockefeller "oil trust" came
out of the struggle, for the time being, victorious.

The Berlin review, *Die Bank*, wrote in this connection
that Germany could fight the oil trust only by establishing
an electricity monopoly and by converting water-power
into cheap electricity. "But," the author added, "the electricity monopoly will come when the producers need it,
that is to say, when the next great crash in the electrical
industry is imminent, and when the gigantic, expensive
power stations now being put up at great cost everywhere
by private electrical concerns, which are already obtaining
certain franchises from towns, from states, etc., can no
longer work at a profit. Water-power will then have to be

used. But it will be impossible to convert it into cheap electricity at state expense; it will also have to be handed over to a 'private monopoly controlled by the state', because private industry has already concluded a number of contracts and has stipulated for heavy compensation. . . . So it was with the nitrate monopoly, so it is with the oil monopoly, so it will be with the electric power monopoly. It is time our state socialists, who allow themselves to be blinded by a beautiful principle, understood, at last, that in Germany the monopolies have never pursued the aim, nor have they had the result, of benefiting the consumer, or even of handing over to the state part of the promoter's profits; they have served only to facilitate, at the expense of the state, the recovery of private industries which were on the verge of bankruptcy."*

Such are the valuable admissions which the German bourgeois economists are forced to make. We see plainly here how private and state monopolies are interwoven in the epoch of finance capital; how both are but separate links in the imperialist struggle between the big monopolists for the division of the world.

In merchant shipping, the tremendous development of concentration has ended also in the division of the world. In Germany two powerful companies have come to the fore: the Hamburg-Amerika and the Norddeutscher Lloyd, each having a capital of 200 million marks (in stocks and bonds) and possessing shipping tonnage to the value of 185 to 189 million marks. On the other hand, in America, on January 1, 1903, the International Mercantile Marine Co., known as the Morgan trust, was formed; it united nine American and British steamship companies, and possessed a capital of 120 million dollars (480 million marks). As early as 1903, the German giants and this American-British trust concluded an agreement to divide the world with a consequent division of profits. The German companies undertook not to compete in the Anglo-American traffic. Which ports were to be "allotted" to each was precisely stipulated; a joint committee of control was set up, etc.

---

* *Die Bank*, 1912, 1, S. 1036; 1912, 2, S. 629; 1913, 1, S. 388.

This agreement was concluded for twenty years, with the prudent provision for its annulment in the event of war.*

Extremely instructive also is the story of the formation of the International Rail Cartel. The first attempt of the British, Belgian and German rail manufacturers to form such a cartel was made as early as 1884, during a severe industrial depression. The manufacturers agreed not to compete with one another in the home markets of the countries involved, and they divided the foreign markets in the following quotas: Great Britain, 66 per cent; Germany, 27 per cent; Belgium, 7 per cent. India was reserved entirely for Great Britain. Joint war was declared against a British firm which remained outside the cartel, the cost of which was met by a percentage levy on all sales. But in 1886 the cartel collapsed when two British firms retired from it. It is characteristic that agreement could not be achieved during subsequent boom periods.

At the beginning of 1904, the German steel syndicate was formed. In November 1904, the International Rail Cartel was revived, with the following quotas: Britain, 53.5 per cent; Germany, 28.83 per cent; Belgium, 17.67 per cent. France came in later and received 4.8 per cent, 5.8 per cent and 6.4 per cent in the first, second and third year respectively, over and above the 100 per cent limit, i.e., out of a total of 104.8 per cent, etc. In 1905, the United States Steel Corporation entered the cartel; then Austria and Spain. "At the present time," wrote Vogelstein in 1910, "the division of the world is complete, and the big consumers, primarily the state railways—since the world has been parcelled out without consideration for their interests—can now dwell like the poet in the heavens of Jupiter."**

Let me also mention the International Zinc Syndicate which was established in 1909 and which precisely apportioned output among five groups of factories: German, Belgian, French, Spanish and British; and also the International Dynamite Trust, which, Liefmann says, is "quite a modern, close alliance of all the German explosives manufacturers who, with the French and American dynamite

---

* Riesser, op. cit., S. 125.
** Vogelstein, *Organisationsformen*, S. 100.

manufacturers, organised in a similar manner, have divided the whole world among themselves, so to speak".*

Liefmann calculated that in 1897 there were altogether about forty international cartels in which Germany had a share, while in 1910 there were about a hundred.

Certain bourgeois writers (now joined by Karl Kautsky, who has completely abandoned the Marxist position he had held, for example, in 1909) have expressed the opinion that international cartels, being one of the most striking expressions of the internationalisation of capital, give the hope of peace among nations under capitalism. Theoretically, this opinion is absolutely absurd, while in practice it is sophistry and a dishonest defence of the worst opportunism. International cartels show to what point capitalist monopolies have developed, and *the object* of the struggle between the various capitalist associations. This last circumstance is the most important; it alone shows us the historico-economic meaning of what is taking place; for the *forms* of the struggle may and do constantly change in accordance with varying, relatively specific and temporary causes, but the *substance* of the struggle, its class *content,* positively *cannot* change while classes exist. Naturally, it is in the interests of, for example, the German bourgeoisie, to whose side Kautsky has in effect gone over in his theoretical arguments (I shall deal with this later), to obscure the *substance* of the present economic struggle (the division of the world) and to emphasise now this and now another *form* of the struggle. Kautsky makes the same mistake. Of course, we have in mind not only the German bourgeoisie, but the bourgeoisie all over the world. The capitalists divide the world, not out of any particular malice, but because the degree of concentration which has been reached forces them to adopt this method in order to obtain profits. And they divide it "in proportion to capital", "in proportion to strength", because there cannot be any other method of division under commodity production and capitalism. But strength varies with the degree of economic and political development. In order to understand

---

* Liefmann, *Kartelle und Trusts*, 2. A., S. 161.

what is taking place, it is necessary to know what questions are settled by the changes in strength. The question as to whether these changes are "purely" economic or non-economic (e.g., military) is a secondary one, which cannot in the least affect fundamental views on the latest epoch of capitalism. To substitute the question of the form of the struggle and agreements (today peaceful, tomorrow warlike, the next day warlike again) for the question of the *substance* of the struggle and agreements between capitalist associations is to sink to the role of a sophist.

The epoch of the latest stage of capitalism shows us that certain relations between capitalist associations grow up, *based* on the economic division of the world; while parallel to and in connection with it, certain relations grow up between political alliances, between states, on the basis of the territorial division of the world, of the struggle for colonies, of the "struggle for spheres of influence".

VI. THE DIVISION OF THE WORLD AMONG THE GREAT POWERS

In his book, on "the territorial development of the European colonies", A. Supan,* the geographer, gives the following brief summary of this development at the end of the nineteenth century:

Percentage of Territory Belonging to the European Colonial Powers (Including the United States)

	1876	1900	Increase or decrease
Africa	10.8	90.4	+79.6
Polynesia	56.8	98.9	+42.1
Asia	51.5	56.6	+ 5.1
Australia	100.0	100.0	—
America	27.5	27.2	—0.3

"The characteristic feature of this period," he concludes, "is, therefore, the division of Africa and Polynesia." As there are no unoccupied territories—that is, territories that do not belong to any state—in Asia and America, it is

* A. Supan, *Die territoriale Entwicklung der europäischen Kolonien*, 1906, S. 254.

necessary to amplify Supan's conclusion and say that the characteristic feature of the period under review is the final partitioning of the globe—final, not in the sense that *repartition* is impossible; on the contrary, repartitions are possible and inevitable—but in the sense that the colonial policy of the capitalist countries has *completed* the seizure of the unoccupied territories on our planet. For the first time the world is completely divided up, so that in the future *only* redivision is possible, i.e., territories can only pass from one "owner" to another, instead of passing as ownerless territory to an "owner".

Hence, we are living in a peculiar epoch of world colonial policy, which is most closely connected with the "latest stage in the development of capitalism", with finance capital. For this reason, it is essential first of all to deal in greater detail with the facts, in order to ascertain as exactly as possible what distinguishes this epoch from those preceding it, and what the present situation is. In the first place, two questions of fact arise here: is an intensification of colonial policy, a sharpening of the struggle for colonies, observed precisely in the epoch of finance capital? And how, in this respect, is the world divided at the present time?

The American writer, Morris, in his book on the history of colonisation,* made an attempt to sum up the data on the colonial possessions of Great Britain, France and Germany during different periods of the nineteenth century. The following is a brief summary of the results he has obtained:

Colonial Possessions

Year	Great Britain Area (000,000 sq. m.)	Pop. (000,000)	France Area (000,000 sq. m.)	Pop. (000,000)	Germany Area (000,000 sq. m.)	Pop. (000,000)
1815-30	?	126.4	0.02	0.5	—	—
1860	2.5	145.1	0.2	3.4	—	—
1880	7.7	267.9	0.7	7.5	—	—
1899	9.3	309.0	3.7	56.4	1.0	14.7

---

* Henry C. Morris, *The History of Colonization*, New York, 1900, Vol. II, p. 88; Vol. I, p. 419; Vol. II, p. 304.

For Great Britain, the period of the enormous expansion of colonial conquests was that between 1860 and 1880, and it was also very considerable in the last twenty years of the nineteenth century. For France and Germany this period falls precisely on these twenty years. We saw above that the development of pre-monopoly capitalism, of capitalism in which free competition was predominant, reached its limit in the 1860s and 1870s. We now see that it is *precisely after that period* that the tremendous "boom" in colonial conquests begins, and that the struggle for the territorial division of the world becomes extraordinarily sharp. It is beyond doubt, therefore, that capitalism's transition to the stage of monopoly capitalism, to finance capital, *is connected* with the intensification of the struggle for the partitioning of the world.

Hobson, in his work on imperialism, marks the years 1884-1900 as the epoch of intensified "expansion" of the chief European states. According to his estimate, Great Britain during these years acquired 3,700,000 square miles of territory with 57,000,000 inhabitants; France, 3,600,000 square miles with 36,500,000; Germany, 1,000,000 square miles with 14,700,000; Belgium, 900,000 square miles with 30,000,000; Portugal, 800,000 square miles with 9,000,000 inhabitants. The scramble for colonies by all the capitalist states at the end of the nineteenth century and particularly since the 1880s is a commonly known fact in the history of diplomacy and of foreign policy.

In the most flourishing period of free competition in Great Britain, i.e., between 1840 and 1860, the leading British bourgeois politicians were *opposed* to colonial policy and were of the opinion that the liberation of the colonies, their complete separation from Britain, was inevitable and desirable. M. Beer, in an article, "Modern British Imperialism",* published in 1898, shows that in 1852, Disraeli, a statesman who was generally inclined towards imperialism, declared: "The colonies are millstones round our necks." But at the end of the nineteenth century the British heroes of the hour were Cecil Rhodes and

---

* *Die Neue Zeit*, XVI, I, 1898, S. 302.

Joseph Chamberlain, who openly advocated imperialism and applied the imperialist policy in the most cynical manner!

It is not without interest to observe that even then these leading British bourgeois politicians saw the connection between what might be called the purely economic and the socio-political roots of modern imperialism. Chamberlain advocated imperialism as a "true, wise and economical policy", and pointed particularly to the German, American and Belgian competition which Great Britain was encountering in the world market. Salvation lies in monopoly, said the capitalists as they formed cartels, syndicates and trusts. Salvation lies in monopoly, echoed the political leaders of the bourgeoisie, hastening to appropriate the parts of the world not yet shared out. And Cecil Rhodes, we are informed by his intimate friend, the journalist Stead, expressed his imperialist views to him in 1895 in the following terms: "I was in the East End of London [a working-class quarter] yesterday and attended a meeting of the unemployed. I listened to the wild speeches, which were just a cry for 'bread! bread!' and on my way home I pondered over the scene and I became more than ever convinced of the importance of imperialism. . . . My cherished idea is a solution for the social problem, i.e., in order to save the 40,000,000 inhabitants of the United Kingdom from a bloody civil war, we colonial statesmen must acquire new lands to settle the surplus population, to provide new markets for the goods produced in the factories and mines. The Empire, as I have always said, is a bread and butter question. If you want to avoid civil war, you must become imperialists."*

That was said in 1895 by Cecil Rhodes, millionaire, a king of finance, the man who was mainly responsible for the Anglo-Boer War. True, his defence of imperialism is crude and cynical, but in substance it does not differ from the "theory" advocated by Messrs. Maslov, Südekum, Potresov, David, and the founder of Russian Marxism[56] and others. Cecil Rhodes was a somewhat more honest social-chauvinist. . . .

---

* Ibid., S. 304.

To present as precise a picture as possible of the territorial division of the world and of the changes which have occurred during the last decades in this respect, I shall utilise the data furnished by Supan in the work already quoted on the colonial possessions of all the powers of the world. Supan takes the years 1876 and 1900; I shall take the year 1876—a year very aptly selected, for it is precisely by that time that the pre-monopolist stage of development of West-European capitalism can be said to have been, in the main, completed—and the year 1914, and instead of Supan's figures I shall quote the more recent statistics of Hübner's *Geographical and Statistical Tables*. Supan gives figures only for colonies; I think it useful, in order to present a complete picture of the division of the world, to add brief data on non-colonial and semi-colonial countries, in which category I place Persia, China and Turkey: the first of these countries is already almost completely a colony, the second and third are becoming such.

We thus get the following result (see table on p. 239.— *Ed.*).

We clearly see from these figures how "complete" was the partition of the world at the turn of the twentieth century. After 1876 colonial possessions increased to enormous dimensions, by more than fifty per cent, from 40,000,000 to 65,000,000 square kilometres, for the six biggest powers; the increase amounts to 25,000,000 square kilometres, fifty per cent more than the area of the metropolitan countries (16,500,000 square kilometres). In 1876 three powers had no colonies, and a fourth, France, had scarcely any. By 1914 these four powers had acquired colonies with an area of 14,100,000 square kilometres, i.e., about half as much again as the area of Europe, with a population of nearly 100,000,000. The unevenness in the rate of expansion of colonial possessions is very great. If, for instance, we compare France, Germany and Japan, which do not differ very much in area and population, we see that the first has acquired almost three times as much colonial territory as the other two combined. In regard to finance capital, France, at the beginning of the period we are considering, was also, perhaps, several times richer than Germany and Japan

Colonial Possessions of the Great Powers
(000,000 square kilometres and 000,000 inhabitants)

	Colonies				Metropolitan countries		Total	
	1876		1914		1914		1914	
	Area	Pop.	Area	Pop.	Area	Pop.	Area	Pop.
Great Britain	22.5	251.9	33.5	393.5	0.3	46.5	33.8	440.0
Russia	17.0	15.9	17.4	33.2	5.4	136.2	22.8	169.4
France	0.9	6.0	10.6	55.5	0.5	39.6	11.1	95.1
Germany	—	—	2.9	12.3	0.5	64.9	3.4	77.2
United States	—	—	0.3	9.7	9.4	97.0	9.7	106.7
Japan	—	—	0.3	19.2	0.4	53.0	0.7	72.2
Total for 6 Great Powers	40.4	273.8	65.0	523.4	16.5	437.2	81.5	960.6
Colonies of other powers (Belgium, Holland, etc.) . .							9.9	45.3
Semi-colonial countries (Persia, China, Turkey) . . .							14.5	361.2
Other countries							28.0	289.9
Total for the world							133.9	1,657.0

put together. In addition to, and on the basis of, purely economic conditions, geographical and other conditions also affect the dimensions of colonial possessions. However strong the process of levelling the world, of levelling the economic and living conditions in different countries, may have been in the past decades as a result of the pressure of large-scale industry, exchange and finance capital, considerable differences still remain; and among the six countries mentioned we see, firstly, young capitalist countries (America, Germany, Japan), whose progress has been extraordinarily rapid; secondly, countries with an old capitalist development (France and Great Britain), whose progress lately has been much slower than that of the previously mentioned countries, and thirdly, a country most backward economically (Russia), where modern capitalist imperialism is enmeshed, so to speak, in a particularly close network of pre-capitalist relations.

Alongside the colonial possessions of the great powers, we have placed the small colonies of the small states, which are, so to speak, the next objects of a possible and probable "redivision" of colonies. These small states mostly retain their colonies only because the big powers are torn by conflicting interests, friction, etc., which prevent them from coming to an agreement on the division of the spoils. As to the "semi-colonial" states, they provide an example of the transitional forms which are to be found in all spheres of nature and society. Finance capital is such a great, such a decisive, you might say, force in all economic and in all international relations, that it is capable of subjecting, and actually does subject, to itself even states enjoying the fullest political independence; we shall shortly see examples of this. Of course, finance capital finds most "convenient", and derives the greatest profit from, a *form* of subjection which involves the loss of the political independence of the subjected countries and peoples. In this respect, the semi-colonial countries provide a typical example of the "middle stage". It is natural that the struggle for these semi-dependent countries should have become particularly bitter in the epoch of finance capital, when the rest of the world has already been divided up.

Colonial policy and imperialism existed before the latest stage of capitalism, and even before capitalism. Rome, founded on slavery, pursued a colonial policy and practised imperialism. But "general" disquisitions on imperialism, which ignore, or put into the background, the fundamental difference between socio-economic formations, inevitably turn into the most vapid banality or bragging, like the comparison: "Greater Rome and Greater Britain."* Even the capitalist colonial policy of *previous* stages of capitalism is essentially different from the colonial policy of finance capital.

---

* C. P. Lucas, *Greater Rome and Greater Britain*, Oxford, 1912, or the Earl of Cromer's *Ancient and Modern Imperialism*, London, 1910.

The principal feature of the latest stage of capitalism is the domination of monopolist associations of big employers. These monopolies are most firmly established when *all* the sources of raw materials are captured by one group, and we have seen with what zeal the international capitalist associations exert every effort to deprive their rivals of all opportunity of competing, to buy up, for example, iron-fields, oilfields, etc. Colonial possession alone gives the monopolies complete guarantee against all contingencies in the struggle against competitors, including the case of the adversary wanting to be protected by a law establishing a state monopoly. The more capitalism is developed, the more strongly the shortage of raw materials is felt, the more intense the competition and the hunt for sources of raw materials throughout the whole world, the more desperate the struggle for the acquisition of colonies.

"It may be asserted," writes Schilder, "although it may sound paradoxical to some, that in the more or less foreseeable future the growth of the urban and industrial population is more likely to be hindered by a shortage of raw materials for industry than by a shortage of food." For example, there is a growing shortage of timber—the price of which is steadily rising—of leather, and of raw materials for the textile industry. "Associations of manufacturers are making efforts to create an equilibrium between agriculture and industry in the whole of world economy; as an example of this we might mention the International Federation of Cotton Spinners' Associations in several of the most important industrial countries, founded in 1904, and the European Federation of Flax Spinners' Associations, founded on the same model in 1910."*

Of course, the bourgeois reformists, and among them particularly the present-day adherents of Kautsky, try to belittle the importance of facts of this kind by arguing that raw materials "could be" obtained in the open market without a "costly and dangerous" colonial policy; and that the supply of raw materials "could be" increased enor-

---

* Schilder, op. cit., S. 38-42.

mously by "simply" improving conditions in agriculture in general. But such arguments become an apology for imperialism, an attempt to paint it in bright colours, because they ignore the principal feature of the latest stage of capitalism: monopolies. The free market is becoming more and more a thing of the past; monopolist syndicates and trusts are restricting it with every passing day, and "simply" improving conditions in agriculture means improving the conditions of the masses, raising wages and reducing profits. Where, except in the imagination of sentimental reformists, are there any trusts capable of concerning themselves with the condition of the masses instead of the conquest of colonies?

Finance capital is interested not only in the already discovered sources of raw materials but also in potential sources, because present-day technical development is extremely rapid, and land which is useless today may be improved tomorrow if new methods are devised (to this end a big bank can equip a special expedition of engineers, agricultural experts, etc.), and if large amounts of capital are invested. This also applies to prospecting for minerals, to new methods of processing up and utilising raw materials, etc., etc. Hence, the inevitable striving of finance capital to enlarge its spheres of influence and even its actual territory. In the same way that the trusts capitalise their property at two or three times its value, taking into account its "potential" (and not actual) profits and the further results of monopoly, so finance capital in general strives to seize the largest possible amount of land of all kinds in all places, and by every means, taking into account potential sources of raw materials and fearing to be left behind in the fierce struggle for the last remnants of independent territory, or for the repartition of those territories that have been already divided.

The British capitalists are exerting every effort to develop cotton growing in *their* colony, Egypt (in 1904, out of 2,300,000 hectares of land under cultivation, 600,000, or more than one-fourth, were under cotton); the Russians are doing the same in *their* colony, Turkestan, because in this way they will be in a better position to defeat their foreign competitors, to monopolise the sources of raw materials and form a more economical and profitable textile trust in which *all* the processes of cotton production and manufacturing will be "combined" and concentrated in the hands of one set of owners.

The interests pursued in exporting capital also give an impetus to the conquest of colonies, for in the colonial market it is easier to employ monopoly methods (and sometimes they are the only methods that can be employed) to eliminate competition, to ensure supplies, to secure the necessary "connections", etc.

The non-economic superstructure which grows up on the basis of finance capital, its politics and its ideology, stimulates the striving for colonial conquest. "Finance capital does not want liberty, it wants domination," as Hilferding very truly says. And a French bourgeois writer, developing and supplementing, as it were, the ideas of Cecil Rhodes quoted above,[*] writes that social causes should be added to the economic causes of modern colonial policy: "owing to the growing complexities of life and the difficulties which weigh not only on the masses of the workers, but also on the middle classes, 'impatience, irritation and hatred are accumulating in all the countries of the old civilisation and are becoming a menace to public order; the energy which is being hurled out of the definite class channel must be given employment abroad in order to avert an explosion at home'."[**]

Since we are speaking of colonial policy in the epoch of capitalist imperialism, it must be observed that finance capital and its foreign policy, which is the struggle of the great powers for the economic and political division of the world, give rise to a number of *transitional* forms of state dependence. Not only are the two main groups of countries, those owning colonies, and the colonies themselves, but also the diverse forms of dependent countries which, politically, are formally independent, but, in fact, are enmeshed in the net of financial and diplomatic de-

---

[*] See p. 237.—*Ed.*
[**] Wahl, *La France aux colonies* quoted by Henri Russier, *Le Partage de l'Océanie*, Paris, 1905, p. 165.

pendence, are typical of this epoch. We have already referred to one form of dependence—the semi-colony. An
example of another is provided by Argentina.

"South America, and especially Argentina," writes
Schulze-Gaevernitz in his work on British imperialism, "is
so dependent financially on London that it ought to be described as almost a British commercial colony."* Basing
himself on the reports of the Austro-Hungarian Consul at
Buenos Aires for 1909, Schilder estimated the amount of
British capital invested in Argentina at 8,750 million
francs. It is not difficult to imagine what strong connections British finance capital (and its faithful "friend", diplomacy) thereby acquires with the Argentine bourgeoisie,
with the circles that control the whole of that country's
economic and political life.

A somewhat different form of financial and diplomatic
dependence, accompanied by political independence, is presented by Portugal. Portugal is an independent sovereign
state, but actually, for more than two hundred years, since
the war of the Spanish Succession (1701-14), it has been
a British protectorate. Great Britain has protected Portugal and her colonies in order to fortify her own positions
in the fight against her rivals, Spain and France. In return
Great Britain has received commercial privileges, prefer-
ential conditions for importing goods and especially capital into Portugal and the Portuguese colonies, the right
to use the ports and islands of Portugal, her telegraph
cables, etc., etc.** Relations of this kind have always existed
between big and little states, but in the epoch of capitalist
imperialism they become a general system, they form part
of the sum total of "divide the world" relations and become
links in the chain of operations of world finance capital.

In order to finish with the question of the division of
the world, I must make the following additional observation. This question was raised quite openly and definitely

* Schulze-Gaevernitz, *Britischer Imperialismus und englischer
Freihandel zu Beginn des 20-ten Jahrhunderts*, Leipzig, 1906, S. 318.
Sartorius v. Waltershausen says the same in *Das volkswirtschaftliche
System der Kapitalanlage im Auslande*, Berlin, 1907, S. 46.
** Schilder, op. cit., Vol. I, S. 160-61.

not only in American literature after the Spanish-American War, and in English literature after the Anglo-Boer War, at the very end of the nineteenth century and the beginning of the twentieth; not only has German literature, which has "most jealously" watched "British imperialism", systematically given its appraisal of this fact. This question has also been raised in French bourgeois literature as definitely and broadly as is thinkable from the bourgeois point of view. Let me quote Driault, the historian, who, in his book, *Political and Social Problems at the End of the Nineteenth Century*, in the chapter "The Great Powers and the Division of the World", wrote the following: "During the past few years, all the free territory of the globe, with the exception of China, has been occupied by the powers of Europe and North America. This has already brought about several conflicts and shifts of spheres of influence, and these foreshadow more terrible upheavals in the near future. For it is necessary to make haste. The nations which have not yet made provision for themselves run the risk of never receiving their share and never participating in the tremendous exploitation of the globe which will be one of the most essential features of the next century [i.e., the twentieth]. That is why all Europe and America have lately been afflicted with the fever of colonial expansion, of 'imperialism', that most noteworthy feature of the end of the nineteenth century." And the author added: "In this partition of the world, in this furious hunt for the treasures and the big markets of the globe, the relative strength of the empires founded in this nineteenth century is totally out of proportion to the place occupied in Europe by the nations which founded them. The dominant powers in Europe, the arbiters of her destiny, are *not* equally preponderant in the whole world. And, as colonial might, the hope of controlling as yet unassessed wealth, will evidently react upon the relative strength of the European powers, the colonial question—'imperialism', if you will—which has already modified the political conditions of Europe itself, will modify them more and more."*

---

* J.-E. Driault, *Problèmes politiques et sociaux*, Paris, 1900, p. 299.

VII. IMPERIALISM, AS A SPECIAL STAGE
OF CAPITALISM

We must now try to sum up, to draw together the threads of what has been said above on the subject of imperialism. Imperialism emerged as the development and direct continuation of the fundamental characteristics of capitalism in general. But capitalism only became capitalist imperialism at a definite and very high stage of its development, when certain of its fundamental characteristics began to change into their opposites, when the features of the epoch of transition from capitalism to a higher social and economic system had taken shape and revealed themselves in all spheres. Economically, the main thing in this process is the displacement of capitalist free competition by capitalist monopoly. Free competition is the basic feature of capitalism, and of commodity production generally; monopoly is the exact opposite of free competition, but we have seen the latter being transformed into monopoly before our eyes, creating large-scale industry and forcing out small industry, replacing large-scale by still larger-scale industry, and carrying concentration of production and capital to the point where out of it has grown and is growing monopoly: cartels, syndicates and trusts, and merging with them, the capital of a dozen or so banks, which manipulate thousands of millions. At the same time the monopolies, which have grown out of free competition, do not eliminate the latter, but exist above it and alongside it, and thereby give rise to a number of very acute, intense antagonisms, frictions and conflicts. Monopoly is the transition from capitalism to a higher system.

If it were necessary to give the briefest possible definition of imperialism we should have to say that imperialism is the monopoly stage of capitalism. Such a definition would include what is most important, for, on the one hand, finance capital is the bank capital of a few very big monopolist banks, merged with the capital of the monopolist associations of industrialists; and, on the other hand, the division of the world is the transition from a colonial policy which has extended without hindrance to territories unseized by any capitalist power, to a colonial policy of monopolist possession of the territory of the world which has been completely divided up.

But very brief definitions, although convenient, for they sum up the main points, are nevertheless inadequate, since we have to deduce from them some especially important features of the phenomenon that has to be defined. And so, without forgetting the conditional and relative value of all definitions in general, which can never embrace all the concatenations of a phenomenon in its full development, we must give a definition of imperialism that will include the following five of its basic features:

(1) the concentration of production and capital has developed to such a high stage that it has created monopolies which play a decisive role in economic life; (2) the merging of bank capital with industrial capital, and the creation, on the basis of this "finance capital", of a financial oligarchy; (3) the export of capital as distinguished from the export of commodities acquires exceptional importance; (4) the formation of international monopolist capitalist associations which share the world among themselves, and (5) the territorial division of the whole world among the biggest capitalist powers is completed. Imperialism is capitalism in that stage of development at which the dominance of monopolies and finance capital is established; in which the export of capital has acquired pronounced importance; in which the division of the world among the international trusts has begun, in which the division of all territories of the globe among the biggest capitalist powers has been completed.

We shall see later that imperialism can and must be defined differently if we bear in mind, not only the basic, purely economic concepts—to which the above definition is limited—but also the historical place of this stage of capitalism in relation to capitalism in general, or the relation between imperialism and the two main trends in the working-class movement. The thing to be noted at this point is that imperialism, as interpreted above, undoubtedly represents a special stage in the development of capitalism. To enable the reader to obtain the most well-grounded idea of imperialism, we deliberately tried to quote as extensively as possible *bourgeois* economists who have to admit the particularly incontrovertible facts concerning the latest stage of capitalist economy. With the same object in view, I have quoted detailed statistics which enable one to see to what degree bank capital, etc., has grown, in what precisely the transformation of quantity into quality, of developed capitalism into imperialism, was expressed. Needless to say, of course, all boundaries in nature and in society are conventional and changeable, and it would be absurd to argue, for example, about the particular year or decade in which imperialism "definitely" became established.

In the matter of defining imperialism, however, we have to enter into controversy, primarily, with Karl Kautsky, the principal Marxist theoretician of the epoch of the so-called Second International—that is, of the twenty-five years between 1889 and 1914. The fundamental ideas expressed in our definition of imperialism were very resolutely attacked by Kautsky in 1915, and even in November 1914, when he said that imperialism must not be regarded as a "phase" or stage of economy, but as a policy, a definite policy "preferred" by finance capital; that imperialism must not be "identified" with "present-day capitalism"; that if imperialism is to be understood to mean "all the phenomena of present-day capitalism"—cartels, protection, the domination of the financiers, and colonial policy—then the question as to whether imperialism is necessary to capitalism becomes reduced to the "flattest tautology", because, in that case, "imperialism is naturally a vital necessity for capitalism", and so on. The best way to present Kautsky's idea is to quote his own definition of imperialism, which is diametrically opposed to the substance of the ideas which I have set forth (for the objections coming from the camp of the German Marxists, who have been advocating similar ideas for many years already, have been long known to Kautsky as the objections of a definite trend in Marxism).

Kautsky's definition is as follows:

"Imperialism is a product of highly developed industrial capitalism. It consists in the striving of every industrial capitalist nation to bring under its control or to annex all large areas of *agrarian* [Kautsky's italics] territory, irrespective of what nations inhabit it."*

This definition is of no use at all because it one-sidedly, i.e., arbitrarily, singles out only the national question (although the latter is extremely important in itself as well as in its relation to imperialism), it arbitrarily and *inaccurately* connects this question *only* with industrial capital in the countries which annex other nations, and in an equally arbitrary and inaccurate manner pushes into the forefront the annexation of agrarian regions.

Imperialism is a striving for annexations—this is what the *political* part of Kautsky's definition amounts to. It is correct, but very incomplete, for politically, imperialism is, in general, a striving towards violence and reaction. For the moment, however, we are interested in the *economic* aspect of the question, which Kautsky *himself* introduced into *his* definition. The inaccuracies in Kautsky's definition are glaring. The characteristic feature of imperialism is *not* industrial *but* finance capital. It is not an accident that in France it was precisely the extraordinarily rapid development of *finance* capital, and the weakening of industrial capital, that from the eighties onwards gave rise to the extreme intensification of annexationist (colonial) policy. The characteristic feature of imperialism is precisely that it strives to annex *not only* agrarian territories, but even most highly industrialised regions (German appetite for Belgium; French appetite for Lorraine), because (1) the fact that the world is already partitioned obliges those contemplating a *redivision* to reach out for *every kind* of territory, and (2) an essential feature of imperialism is the rivalry between several great powers in the striving for hegemony, i.e., for the conquest of territory, not so much directly for themselves as to weaken the adversary and undermine *his* hegemony. (Belgium is particularly important for Germany as a base for operations against Britain; Britain needs Baghdad as a base for operations against Germany, etc.)

* *Die Neue Zeit*, 1914, 2 (B. 32), S. 909, Sept. 11, 1914; cf. 1915, 2, S. 107 et seq.

Kautsky refers especially—and repeatedly—to English writers who, he alleges, have given a purely political meaning to the word "imperialism" in the sense that he, Kautsky, understands it. We take up the work by the English writer Hobson, *Imperialism*, which appeared in 1902, and there we read:

"The new imperialism differs from the older, first, in substituting for the ambition of a single growing empire the theory and the practice of competing empires, each motivated by similar lusts of political aggrandisement and commercial gain; secondly, in the dominance of financial or investing over mercantile interests."*

We see that Kautsky is absolutely wrong in referring to English writers generally (unless he meant the vulgar English imperialists, or the avowed apologists for imperialism). We see that Kautsky, while claiming that he continues to advocate Marxism, as a matter of fact takes a step backward compared with the *social-liberal* Hobson, who *more correctly* takes into account two "historically concrete" (Kautsky's definition is a mockery of historical concreteness!) features of modern imperialism: (1) the competition between *several* imperialisms, and (2) the predominance of the financier over the merchant. If it is chiefly a question of the annexation of agrarian countries by industrial countries, then the role of the merchant is put in the forefront.

Kautsky's definition is not only wrong and un-Marxist. It serves as a basis for a whole system of views which signify a rupture with Marxist theory and Marxist practice all along the line. I shall refer to this later. The argument about words which Kautsky raises as to whether the latest stage of capitalism should be called "imperialism" or "the stage of finance capital" is not worth serious attention. Call it what you will, it makes no difference. The essence of the matter is that Kautsky detaches the politics of imperialism from its economics, speaks of annexations as being a policy "preferred" by finance capital, and opposes to it another bourgeois policy which, he alleges, is possible on this very same basis of finance capital. It follows, then,

---

* Hobson, *Imperialism*, London, 1902, p. 324.

that monopolies in the economy are compatible with non-monopolistic, non-violent, non-annexationist methods in politics. It follows, then, that the territorial division of the world, which was completed during this very epoch of finance capital, and which constitutes the basis of the present peculiar forms of rivalry between the biggest capitalist states, is compatible with a non-imperialist policy. The result is a slurring-over and a blunting of the most profound contradictions of the latest stage of capitalism, instead of an exposure of their depth; the result is bourgeois reformism instead of Marxism.

Kautsky enters into controversy with the German apologist of imperialism and annexations, Cunow, who clumsily and cynically argues that imperialism is present-day capitalism; the development of capitalism is inevitable and progressive; therefore imperialism is progressive; therefore, we should grovel before it and glorify it! This is something like the caricature of the Russian Marxists which the Narodniks drew in 1894-95. They argued: if the Marxists believe that capitalism is inevitable in Russia, that it is progressive, then they ought to open a tavern and begin to implant capitalism! Kautsky's reply to Cunow is as follows: imperialism is not present-day capitalism; it is only one of the forms of the policy of present-day capitalism. This policy we can and should fight, fight imperialism, annexations, etc.

The reply seems quite plausible, but in effect it is a more subtle and more disguised (and therefore more dangerous) advocacy of conciliation with imperialism, because a "fight" against the policy of the trusts and banks that does not affect the economic basis of the trusts and banks is mere bourgeois reformism and pacifism, the benevolent and innocent expression of pious wishes. Evasion of existing contradictions, forgetting the most important of them, instead of revealing their full depth—such is Kautsky's theory, which has nothing in common with Marxism. Naturally, such a "theory" can only serve the purpose of advocating unity with the Cunows!

"From the purely economic point of view," writes Kautsky, "it is not impossible that capitalism will yet go through a new phase, that of the extension of the policy of the cartels to foreign policy, the phase of ultra-imperialism,"* i.e., of a superimperialism, of a union of the imperialisms of the whole world and not struggles among them, a phase when wars shall cease under capitalism, a phase of "the joint exploitation of the world by internationally united finance capital".**

We shall have to deal with this "theory of ultra-imperialism" later on in order to show in detail how decisively and completely it breaks with Marxism. At present, in keeping with the general plan of the present work, we must examine the exact economic data on this question. "From the purely economic point of view", is "ultra-imperialism" possible, or is it ultra-nonsense?

If the purely economic point of view is meant to be a "pure" abstraction, then all that can be said reduces itself to the following proposition: development is proceeding towards monopolies, hence, towards a single world monopoly, towards a single world trust. This is indisputable, but it is also as completely meaningless as is the statement that "development is proceeding" towards the manufacture of foodstuffs in laboratories. In this sense the "theory" of ultra-imperialism is no less absurd than a "theory of ultra-agriculture" would be.

If, however, we are discussing the "purely economic" conditions of the epoch of finance capital as a historically concrete epoch which began at the turn of the twentieth century, then the best reply that one can make to the lifeless abstractions of "ultra-imperialism" (which serve exclusively a most reactionary aim: that of diverting attention from the depth of *existing* antagonisms) is to contrast them with the concrete economic realities of present-day world economy. Kautsky's utterly meaningless talk about ultra-imperialism encourages, among other things, that profoundly mistaken idea which only brings grist to the mill of the apologists of imperialism, i.e., that the rule of

---

* *Die Neue Zeit*, 1914, 2 (B. 32), S. 921, Sept. 11, 1914. Cf. 1915, 2, S. 107 et seq.
** *Die Neue Zeit*, 1915, 1, S. 144, April 30, 1915.

finance capital *lessens* the unevenness and contradictions inherent in the world economy, whereas in reality it *increases* them.

R. Calwer, in his little book, *An Introduction to the World Economy*,* made an attempt to summarise the main, purely economic, data that enable one to obtain a concrete picture of the internal relations of the world economy at the turn of the twentieth century. He divides the world into five "main economic areas", as follows: (1) Central Europe (the whole of Europe with the exception of Russia and Great Britain); (2) Great Britain; (3) Russia; (4) Eastern Asia; (5) America; he includes the colonies in the "areas" of the states to which they belong and "leaves aside" a few countries not distributed according to areas, such as Persia, Afghanistan, and Arabia in Asia, Morocco and Abyssinia in Africa, etc.

Here is a brief summary of the economic data he quotes on these regions:

| Principal economic areas | Area (000,000 sq. km.) | Pop. (000,000) | Transport | | | Industry Output (000,000 tons) | | |
			Railways (000 km.)	Mercantile fleet (000,000 tons)	Trade (imports and exports) (000,000,000 marks)	coal	iron	Number of cotton spindles (000,000)
1) Central Europe	27.6 (23.6)**	388 (146)	204	8	41	251	15	26
2) Britain	28.9 (28.6)	398 (355)	140	11	25	249	9	51
3) Russia	22	131	63	1	3	16	3	7
4) Eastern Asia	12	389	8	1	2	8	0.02	2
5) America	30	148	379	6	14	245	14	19

We see three areas of highly developed capitalism (high development of means of transport, of trade and of indus-

---

* R. Calwer, *Einführung in die Weltwirtschaft*, Berlin, 1906.
** The figures in parentheses show the area and population of the colonies.

try): the Central European, the British and the American areas. Among these are three states which dominate the world: Germany, Great Britain, and the United States. Imperialist rivalry and the struggle between these countries have become extremely keen because Germany has only an insignificant area and few colonies; the creation of "Central Europe" is still a matter for the future, it is being born in the midst of a desperate struggle. For the moment the distinctive feature of the whole of Europe is political disunity. In the British and American areas, on the other hand, political concentration is very highly developed, but there is a vast disparity between the immense colonies of the one and the insignificant colonies of the other. In the colonies, however, capitalism is only beginning to develop. The struggle for South America is becoming more and more acute.

There are two areas where capitalism is little developed: Russia and Eastern Asia. In the former, the population is extremely sparse, in the latter it is extremely dense; in the former political concentration is high, in the latter it does not exist. The partitioning of China is only just beginning, and the struggle for it between Japan, the U.S., etc., is continually gaining in intensity.

Compare this reality—the vast diversity of economic and political conditions, the extreme disparity in the rate of development of the various countries, etc., and the violent struggles among the imperialist states—with Kautsky's silly little fable about "peaceful" ultra-imperialism. Is this not the reactionary attempt of a frightened philistine to hide from stern reality? Are not the international cartels which Kautsky imagines are the embryos of "ultra-imperialism" (in the same way as one "can" describe the manufacture of tablets in a laboratory as ultra-agriculture in embryo) an example of the division *and the redivision* of the world, the transition from peaceful division to non-peaceful division and vice versa? Is not American and other finance capital, which divided the whole world peacefully with Germany's participation in, for example, the international rail syndicate, or in the international mercantile shipping trust, now engaged in *redividing* the world on the basis of a new relation of forces that is being changed by methods *anything but* peaceful?

Finance capital and the trusts do not diminish but increase the differences in the rate of growth of the various parts of the world economy. Once the relation of forces is changed, what other solution of the contradictions can be found *under capitalism* than that of *force*? Railway statistics* provide remarkably exact data on the different rates of growth of capitalism and finance capital in world economy. In the last decades of imperialist development, the total length of railways has changed as follows:

	Railways (000 kilometres)		
	1890	1913	+
Europe	224	346	+122
U.S.	268	411	+143
All colonies	82 } 125	210 } 347	+128 } +222
Independent and semi-independent states of Asia and America	43	137	+ 94
Total	617	1,104	

Thus, the development of railways has been most rapid in the colonies and in the independent (and semi-independent) states of Asia and America. Here, as we know, the finance capital of the four or five biggest capitalist states holds undisputed sway. Two hundred thousand kilometres of new railways in the colonies and in the other countries of Asia and America represent a capital of more than 40,000 million marks newly invested on particularly advantageous terms, with special guarantees of a good return and with profitable orders for steel works, etc., etc.

Capitalism is growing with the greatest rapidity in the colonies and in overseas countries. Among the latter, *new* imperialist powers are emerging (e.g., Japan). The struggle

---

* *Statistisches Jahrbuch für das deutsche Reich, 1915*; *Archiv für Eisenbahnwesen, 1892*. Minor details for the distribution of railways among the colonies of the various countries in 1890 had to be estimated approximately.

among the world imperialisms is becoming more acute. The tribute levied by finance capital on the most profitable colonial and overseas enterprises is increasing. In the division of this "booty", an exceptionally large part goes to countries which do not always stand at the top of the list in the rapidity of the development of their productive forces. In the case of the biggest countries, together with their colonies, the total length of railways was as follows:

	(000 kilometres)		
	1890	1913	
U. S.	268	413	+145
British Empire	107	208	+101
Russia	32	78	+ 46
Germany	43	68	+ 25
France	41	63	+ 22
Total for 5 powers . . .	491	830	+339

Thus, about 80 per cent of the total existing railways are concentrated in the hands of the five biggest powers. But the concentration of the *ownership* of these railways, the concentration of finance capital, is immeasurably greater since the French and British millionaires, for example, own an enormous amount of shares and bonds in American, Russian and other railways.

Thanks to her colonies, Great Britain has increased the length of "her" railways by 100,000 kilometres, four times as much as Germany. And yet, it is well known that the development of productive forces in Germany, and especially the development of the coal and iron industries, has been incomparably more rapid during this period than in Britain—not to speak of France and Russia. In 1892, Germany produced 4,900,000 tons of pig-iron and Great Britain produced 6,800,000 tons; in 1912, Germany produced 17,600,000 tons and Great Britain, 9,000,000 tons. Germany, therefore, had an overwhelming superiority over Britain in this respect.* The question is: what means other than

* Cf. also Edgar Crammond, "The Economic Relations of the British and German Empires" in *The Journal of the Royal Statistical Society*, July 1914, p. 777 et seq.

war could there be *under capitalism* to overcome the disparity between the development of productive forces and the accumulation of capital on the one side, and the division of colonies and spheres of influence for finance capital on the other?

VIII. PARASITISM AND DECAY
OF CAPITALISM

We now have to examine yet another significant aspect of imperialism to which most of the discussions on the subject usually attach insufficient importance. One of the shortcomings of the Marxist Hilferding is that on this point he has taken a step backward compared with the non-Marxist Hobson. We refer to parasitism, which is characteristic of imperialism.

As we have seen, the deepest economic foundation of imperialism is monopoly. This is capitalist monopoly, i.e., monopoly which has grown out of capitalism and which exists in the general environment of capitalism, commodity production and competition, in permanent and insoluble contradiction to this general environment. Nevertheless, like all monopoly, it inevitably engenders a tendency to stagnation and decay. Since monopoly prices are established, even temporarily, the motive cause of technical and, consequently, of all other progress disappears to a certain extent and, further, the *economic* possibility arises of deliberately retarding technical progress. For instance, in America, a certain Owens invented a machine which revolutionised the manufacture of bottles. The German bottle-manufacturing cartel purchased Owens's patent, but pigeonholed it, refrained from utilising it. Certainly, monopoly under capitalism can never completely, and for a very long period of time, eliminate competition in the world market (and this, by the by, is one of the reasons why the theory of ultra-imperialism is so absurd). Certainly, the possibility of reducing the cost of production and increasing profits by introducing technical improvements operates in the direction of change. But the *tendency* to stagnation and decay, which is characteristic of monopoly, continues to operate, and in some branches of industry, in some countries, for certain periods of time, it gains the upper hand.

The monopoly ownership of very extensive, rich or well-situated colonies operates in the same direction.

Further, imperialism is an immense accumulation of money capital in a few countries, amounting, as we have seen, to 100,000-150,000 million francs in securities. Hence the extraordinary growth of a class, or rather, of a stratum of rentiers, i.e., people who live by "clipping coupons", who take no part in any enterprise whatever, whose profession is idleness. The export of capital, one of the most essential economic bases of imperialism, still more completely isolates the rentiers from production and sets the seal of parasitism on the whole country that lives by exploiting the labour of several overseas countries and colonies.

"In 1893," writes Hobson, "the British capital invested abroad represented about 15 per cent of the total wealth of the United Kingdom."* Let me remind the reader that by 1915 this capital had increased about two and a half times. "Aggressive imperialism," says Hobson further on, "which costs the tax-payer so dear, which is of so little value to the manufacturer and trader ... is a source of great gain to the investor.... The annual income Great Britain derives from commissions in her whole foreign and colonial trade, import and export, is estimated by Sir R. Giffen at £18,000,000 [nearly 170 million rubles] for 1899, taken at 2½ per cent, upon a turnover of £800,000,000." Great as this sum is, it cannot explain the aggressive imperialism of Great Britain, which is explained by the income of £90 million to £100 million from "invested" capital, the income of the rentiers.

The income of the rentiers is *five times greater* than the income obtained from the foreign trade of the biggest "trading" country in the world! This is the essence of imperialism and imperialist parasitism.

For that reason the term "rentier state" (Rentnerstaat), or usurer state, is coming into common use in the economic literature that deals with imperialism. The world has be-

---

* Hobson, op. cit., pp. 59, 62.

come divided into a handful of usurer states and a vast majority of debtor states. "At the top of the list of foreign investments," says Schulze-Gaevernitz, "are those placed in politically dependent or allied countries: Great Britain grants loans to Egypt, Japan, China and South America. Her navy plays here the part of bailiff in case of necessity. Great Britain's political power protects her from the indignation of her debtors."* Sartorius von Waltershausen in his book, *The National Economic System of Capital Investments Abroad*, cites Holland as the model "rentier state" and points out that Great Britain and France are now becoming such.** Schilder is of the opinion that five industrial states have become "definitely pronounced creditor countries": Great Britain, France, Germany, Belgium and Switzerland. He does not include Holland in this list simply because she is "industrially little developed".*** The United States is a creditor only of the American countries.

"Great Britain," says Schulze-Gaevernitz, "is gradually becoming transformed from an industrial into a creditor state. Notwithstanding the absolute increase in industrial output and the export of manufactured goods, there is an increase in the relative importance of income from interest and dividends, issues of securities, commissions and speculation in the whole of the national economy. In my opinion it is precisely this that forms the economic basis of imperialist ascendancy. The creditor is more firmly attached to the debtor than the seller is to the buyer."**** In regard to Germany, A. Lansburgh, the publisher of the Berlin *Die Bank*, in 1911, in an article entitled "Germany—a Rentier State", wrote the following: "People in Germany are ready to sneer at the yearning to become rentiers that is observed in France. But they forget that as far as the bourgeoisie is concerned the situation in Germany is becoming more and more like that in France."*****

---

* Schulze-Gaevernitz, *Britischer Imperialismus*, S. 320 et seq.
** Sartorius von Waltershausen, *Das volkswirtschaftliche System*, etc., Berlin, 1907, Buch IV.
*** Schilder, op. cit. S. 393.
**** Schulze-Gaevernitz, op. cit., S. 122.
***** *Die Bank*, 1911, 1, S. 10-11.

The rentier state is a state of parasitic, decaying capitalism, and this circumstance cannot fail to influence all the social-political conditions of the countries concerned, in general, and the two fundamental trends in the working-class movement, in particular. To demonstrate this in the clearest possible manner let me quote Hobson, who is a most reliable witness, since he cannot be suspected of leaning towards Marxist orthodoxy; on the other hand, he is an Englishman who is very well acquainted with the situation in the country which is richest in colonies, in finance capital, and in imperialist experience.

With the Anglo-Boer War fresh in his mind, Hobson describes the connection between imperialism and the interests of the "financiers", their growing profits from contracts, supplies, etc., and writes: "While the directors of this definitely parasitic policy are capitalists, the same motives appeal to special classes of the workers. In many towns most important trades are dependent upon government employment or contracts; the imperialism of the metal and shipbuilding centres is attributable in no small degree to this fact." Two sets of circumstances, in this writer's opinion, have weakened the old empires: (1) "economic parasitism", and (2) the formation of armies recruited from subject peoples. "There is first the habit of economic parasitism, by which the ruling state has used its provinces, colonies, and dependencies in order to enrich its ruling class and to bribe its lower classes into acquiescence." And I shall add that the economic possibility of such bribery, whatever its form may be, requires high monopolist profits.

As for the second circumstance, Hobson writes: "One of the strangest symptoms of the blindness of imperialism is the reckless indifference with which Great Britain, France and other imperial nations are embarking on this perilous dependence. Great Britain has gone farthest. Most of the fighting by which we have won our Indian Empire has been done by natives; in India, as more recently in Egypt, great standing armies are placed under British commanders; almost all the fighting associated with our African dominions, except in the southern part, has been done for us by natives."

Hobson gives the following economic appraisal of the prospect of the partitioning of China: "The greater part of Western Europe might then assume the appearance and character already exhibited by tracts of country in the South of England, in the Riviera, and in the tourist-ridden or residential parts of Italy and Switzerland, little clusters of wealthy aristocrats drawing dividends and pensions from the Far East, with a somewhat larger group of professional retainers and tradesmen and a larger body of personal servants and workers in the transport trade and in the final stages of production of the more perishable goods; all the main arterial industries would have disappeared, the staple foods and manufactures flowing in as tribute from Asia and Africa.... We have foreshadowed the possibility of even a larger alliance of Western states, a European federation of great powers which, so far from forwarding the cause of world civilisation, might introduce the gigantic peril of a Western parasitism, a group of advanced industrial nations, whose upper classes drew vast tribute from Asia and Africa, with which they supported great tame masses of retainers, no longer engaged in the staple industries of agriculture and manufacture, but kept in the performance of personal or minor industrial services under the control of a new financial aristocracy. Let those who would scout such a theory [it would be better to say: prospect] as undeserving of consideration examine the economic and social condition of districts in Southern England today which are already reduced to this condition, and reflect upon the vast extension of such a system which might be rendered feasible by the subjection of China to the economic control of similar groups of financiers, investors, and political and business officials, draining the greatest potential reservoir of profit the world has ever known, in order to consume it in Europe. The situation is far too complex, the play of world forces far too incalculable, to render this or any other single interpretation of the future very probable; but the influences which govern the imperialism of Western Europe today are moving in this direc-

tion and, unless counteracted or diverted, make towards
some such consummation."*

The author is quite right: *if* the forces of imperialism
had not been counteracted they would have led precisely
to what he has described. The significance of a "United
States of Europe" in the present imperialist situation is
correctly appraised. He should have added, however, that,
also *within* the working-class movement, the opportunists,
who are for the moment victorious in most countries, are
"working" systematically and undeviatingly in this very
direction. Imperialism, which means the partitioning of the
world, and the exploitation of other countries besides
China, which means high monopoly profits for a handful
of very rich countries, makes it economically possible to
bribe the upper strata of the proletariat, and thereby fosters, gives shape to, and strengthens opportunism. We must
not, however, lose sight of the forces which counteract
imperialism in general, and opportunism in particular, and
which, naturally, the social-liberal Hobson is unable to perceive.

The German opportunist, Gerhard Hildebrand, who was
once expelled from the Party for defending imperialism,
and who could today be a leader of the so-called "Social-
Democratic" Party of Germany, supplements Hobson well
by his advocacy of a "United States of Western Europe"
(without Russia) for the purpose of "joint" action ...
against the African Negroes, against the "great Islamic movement", for the maintenance of a "powerful army and navy",
against a "Sino-Japanese coalition",** etc.

The description of "British imperialism" in Schulze-
Gaevernitz's book reveals the same parasitical traits. The
national income of Great Britain approximately doubled
from 1865 to 1898, while the income "from abroad" increased *ninefold* in the same period. While the "merit" of
imperialism is that it "trains the Negro to habits of industry" (you cannot manage without coercion...), the "danger"

---

* Hobson, op. cit., pp. 103, 205, 144, 335, 386.
** Gerhard Hildebrand, *Die Erschütterung der Industrieherrschaft
und des Industriesozialismus*, 1910, S. 229 et seq.

of imperialism lies in that "Europe will shift the burden of physical toil—first agricultural and mining, then the rougher work in industry—on to the coloured races, and itself be content with the role of rentier, and in this way, perhaps, pave the way for the economic, and later, the political emancipation of the coloured races".

An increasing proportion of land in England is being taken out of cultivation and used for sport, for the diversion of the rich. As far as Scotland—the most aristocratic place for hunting and other sports—is concerned, it is said that "it lives on its past and on Mr. Carnegie" (the American multimillionaire). On horse racing and fox hunting alone England annually spends £14,000,000 (nearly 130 million rubles). The number of rentiers in England is about one million. The percentage of the productively employed population to the total population is declining:

	Population England and Wales (000,000)	Workers in basic industries (000,000)	Per cent of total population
1851 . .	17.9	4.1	23
1901 . .	32.5	4.9	15

And in speaking of the British working class the bourgeois student of "British imperialism at the beginning of the twentieth century" is obliged to distinguish systematically between the *"upper stratum"* of the workers and the *"lower stratum of the proletariat proper"*. The upper stratum furnishes the bulk of the membership of co-operatives, of trade unions, of sporting clubs and of numerous religious sects. To this level is adapted the electoral system, which in Great Britain is still *"sufficiently restricted to exclude the lower stratum of the proletariat proper"*! In order to present the condition of the British working class in a rosy light, only this upper stratum—which constitutes a *minority* of the proletariat—is usually spoken of. For instance, "the problem of unemployment is mainly a London problem and that of the lower proletarian stratum, *to which the politicians attach little importance...."** He should

* Schulze-Gaevernitz, *Britischer Imperialismus*, S. 301.

have said: to which the bourgeois politicians and the "socialist" opportunists attach little importance.

One of the special features of imperialism connected with the facts I am describing is the decline in emigration from imperialist countries and the increase in immigration into these countries from the more backward countries where lower wages are paid. As Hobson observes, emigration from Great Britain has been declining since 1884. In that year the number of emigrants was 242,000, while in 1900, the number was 169,000. Emigration from Germany reached the highest point between 1881 and 1890, with a total of 1,453,000 emigrants. In the course of the following two decades, it fell to 544,000 and to 341,000. On the other hand, there was an increase in the number of workers entering Germany from Austria, Italy, Russia and other countries. According to the 1907 census, there were 1,342,294 foreigners in Germany, of whom 440,800 were industrial workers and 257,329 agricultural workers.* In France, the workers employed in the mining industry are, "in great part", foreigners: Poles, Italians and Spaniards.** In the United States, immigrants from Eastern and Southern Europe are engaged in the most poorly paid jobs, while American workers provide the highest percentage of overseers or of the better-paid workers.*** Imperialism has the tendency to create privileged sections also among the workers, and to detach them from the broad masses of the proletariat.

It must be observed that in Great Britain the tendency of imperialism to split the workers, to strengthen opportunism among them and to cause temporary decay in the working-class movement, revealed itself much earlier than the end of the nineteenth and the beginning of the twentieth centuries; for two important distinguishing features of imperialism were already observed in Great Britain in the middle of the nineteenth century—vast colonial possessions and a monopolist position in the world market. Marx and

---

* *Statistik des Deutschen Reichs*, Bd. 211.
** Henger, *Die Kapitalsanlage der Franzosen*, Stuttgart, 1913.
*** Hourwich, *Immigration and Labour*, New York, 1913.

Engels traced this connection between opportunism in the working-class movement and the imperialist features of British capitalism systematically, during the course of several decades. For example, on October 7, 1858, Engels wrote to Marx: "The English proletariat is actually becoming more and more bourgeois, so that this most bourgeois of all nations is apparently aiming ultimately at the possession of a bourgeois aristocracy and a bourgeois proletariat *alongside* the bourgeoisie. For a nation which exploits the whole world this is of course to a certain extent justifiable." Almost a quarter of a century later, in a letter dated August 11, 1881, Engels speaks of the "worst English trade unions which allow themselves to be led by men sold to, or at least paid by, the middle class". In a letter to Kautsky, dated September 12, 1882, Engels wrote: "You ask me what the English workers think about colonial policy. Well, exactly the same as they think about politics in general. There is no workers' party here, there are only Conservatives and Liberal-Radicals, and the workers gaily share the feast of England's monopoly of the world market and the colonies."* (Engels expressed similar ideas in the press in his preface to the second edition of *The Condition of the Working Class in England*, which appeared in 1892.)

This clearly shows the causes and effects. The causes are: (1) exploitation of the whole world by this country; (2) its monopolist position in the world market; (3) its colonial monopoly. The effects are: (1) a section of the British proletariat becomes bourgeois; (2) a section of the proletariat allows itself to be led by men bought by, or at least paid by, the bourgeoisie. The imperialism of the beginning of the twentieth century completed the division of the world among a handful of states, each of which today exploits (in the sense of drawing superprofits from) a part of the "whole world" only a little smaller than that which England exploited in 1858; each of them occupies a monopolist position in the world market thanks to trusts, car-

* Briefwechsel von Marx und Engels, Bd. II, S. 290; IV, 433.— Karl Kautsky, *Sozialismus und Kolonialpolitik*, Berlin, 1907, S. 79; this pamphlet was written by Kautsky in those infinitely distant days when he was still a Marxist.

tels, finance capital and creditor and debtor relations; each of them enjoys to some degree a colonial monopoly (we have seen that out of the total of 75,000,000 sq. km., which comprise the *whole* colonial world, *65,000,000* sq. km., or 86 per cent, belong to six powers; *61,000,000* sq. km., or 81 per cent, belong to three powers).

The distinctive feature of the present situation is the prevalence of such economic and political conditions that are bound to increase the irreconcilability between opportunism and the general and vital interests of the working-class movement: imperialism has grown from an embryo into the predominant system; capitalist monopolies occupy first place in economics and politics; the division of the world has been completed; on the other hand, instead of the undivided monopoly of Great Britain, we see a few imperialist powers contending for the right to share in this monopoly, and this struggle is characteristic of the whole period of the early twentieth century. Opportunism cannot now be completely triumphant in the working-class movement of one country for decades as it was in Britain in the second half of the nineteenth century; but in a number of countries it has grown ripe, overripe, and rotten, and has become completely merged with bourgeois policy in the form of "social-chauvinism".*

IX. CRITIQUE OF IMPERIALISM

By the critique of imperialism, in the broad sense of the term, we mean the attitude of the different classes of society towards imperialist policy in connection with their general ideology.

The enormous dimensions of finance capital concentrated in a few hands and creating an extraordinarily dense and widespread network of relationships and connections which subordinates not only the small and medium, but also the very small capitalists and small masters, on the

---

* Russian social-chauvinism in its overt form, represented by the Potresovs, Chkhenkelis, Maslovs, etc., and in its covert form (Chkheidze, Skobelev, Axelrod, Martov, etc.), also emerged from the Russian variety of opportunism, namely, liquidationism.

one hand, and the increasingly intense struggle waged against other national state groups of financiers for the division of the world and domination over other countries, on the other hand, cause the propertied classes to go over entirely to the side of imperialism. "General" enthusiasm over the prospects of imperialism, furious defence of it and painting it in the brightest colours—such are the signs of the times. Imperialist ideology also penetrates the working class. No Chinese Wall separates it from the other classes. The leaders of the present-day, so-called "Social-Democratic" Party of Germany are justly called "social-imperialists", that is, socialists in words and imperialists in deeds; but as early as 1902, Hobson noted the existence in Britain of "Fabian imperialists" who belonged to the opportunist Fabian Society.

Bourgeois scholars and publicists usually come out in defence of imperialism in a somewhat veiled form; they obscure its complete domination and its deep-going roots, strive to push specific and secondary details into the fore-front and do their very best to distract attention from essentials by means of absolutely ridiculous schemes for "reform", such as police supervision of the trusts or banks, etc. Cynical and frank imperialists who are bold enough to admit the absurdity of the idea of reforming the fundamental characteristics of imperialism are a rare phenomenon.

Here is an example. The German imperialists attempt, in the magazine *Archives of World Economy*, to follow the national emancipation movements in the colonies, particularly, of course, in colonies other than those belonging to Germany. They note the unrest and the protest movements in India, the movement in Natal (South Africa), in the Dutch East Indies, etc. One of them, commenting on an English report of a conference held on June 28-30, 1910, of representatives of various subject nations and races, of peoples of Asia, Africa and Europe who are under foreign rule, writes as follows in appraising the speeches delivered at this conference: "We are told that we must fight imperialism; that the ruling states should recognise the right of subject peoples to independence; that an international tribunal should supervise the fulfilment of treaties concluded between the great powers and weak peoples. Further than the expression of these pious wishes they do not go. We see no trace of understanding of the fact that imperialism is inseparably bound up with capitalism in its present form and that, therefore [!!], an open struggle against imperialism would be hopeless, unless, perhaps, the fight were to be confined to protests against certain of its especially abhorrent excesses."* Since the reform of the basis of imperialism is a deception, a "pious wish", since the bourgeois representatives of the oppressed nations go no "further" forward, the bourgeois representative of an oppressing nation goes "further" *backward*, to servility towards imperialism under cover of the claim to be "scientific". That is also "logic"!

The questions as to whether it is possible to reform the basis of imperialism, whether to go forward to the further intensification and deepening of the antagonisms which it engenders, or backward, towards allaying these antagonisms, are fundamental questions in the critique of imperialism. Since the specific political features of imperialism are reaction everywhere and increased national oppression due to the oppression of the financial oligarchy and the elimination of free competition, a petty-bourgeois-democratic opposition to imperialism arose at the beginning of the twentieth century in nearly all imperialist countries. Kautsky not only did not trouble to oppose, was not only unable to oppose this petty-bourgeois reformist opposition, which is really reactionary in its economic basis, but became merged with it in practice, and this is precisely where Kautsky and the broad international Kautskian trend deserted Marxism.

In the United States, the imperialist war waged against Spain in 1898 stirred up the opposition of the "anti-imperialists", the last of the Mohicans of bourgeois democracy, who declared this war to be "criminal", regarded the annexation of foreign territories as a violation of the Constitution, declared that the treatment of Aguinaldo, leader of

---

* *Weltwirtschaftliches Archiv*, Bd. II, S. 193.

the Filipinos (the Americans promised him the independence of his country, but later landed troops and annexed it), was "Jingo treachery", and quoted the words of Lincoln: "When the white man governs himself, that is self-government; but when he governs himself and also governs others, it is no longer self-government; it is despotism."* But as long as all this criticism shrank from recognising the inseverable bond between imperialism and the trusts, and, therefore, between imperialism and the foundations of capitalism, while it shrank from joining the forces engendered by large-scale capitalism and its development—it remained a "pious wish".

This is also the main attitude taken by Hobson in his critique of imperialism. Hobson anticipated Kautsky in protesting against the "inevitability of imperialism" argument, and in urging the necessity of "increasing the consuming capacity" of the people (under capitalism!). The petty-bourgeois point of view in the critique of imperialism, the omnipotence of the banks, the financial oligarchy, etc., is adopted by the authors I have often quoted, such as Agahd, A. Lansburgh, L. Eschwege, and among the French writers Victor Berard, author of a superficial book entitled *England and Imperialism* which appeared in 1900. All these authors, who make no claim to be Marxists, contrast imperialism with free competition and democracy, condemn the Baghdad railway scheme which is leading to conflicts and war, utter "pious wishes" for peace, etc. This applies also to the compiler of international stock and share issue statistics, A. Neymarck, who, after calculating the thousands of millions of francs representing "international" securities, exclaimed in 1912: "Is it possible to believe that peace may be disturbed . . . that, in the face of these enormous figures, anyone would risk starting a war?"**

Such simple-mindedness on the part of the bourgeois economists is not surprising; moreover, *it is in their interest* to pretend to be so naïve and to talk "seriously" about peace under imperialism. But what remains of Kautsky's

---

* J. Patouillet, *L'impérialisme américain*, Dijon, 1904, p. 272.
** *Bulletin de l'Institut International de Statistique*, T. XIX, livr. II, p. 225.

Marxism, when, in 1914, 1915 and 1916, he takes up the same bourgeois-reformist point of view and affirms that "everybody is agreed" (imperialists, pseudo-socialists and social-pacifists) on the matter of peace? Instead of an analysis of imperialism and an exposure of the depths of its contradictions, we have nothing but a reformist "pious wish" to wave them aside, to evade them.

Here is a sample of Kautsky's economic criticism of imperialism. He takes the statistics of the British export and import trade with Egypt for 1872 and 1912; it seems that this export and import trade has grown more slowly than British foreign trade as a whole. From this Kautsky concludes that "we have no reason to suppose that without military occupation the growth of British trade with Egypt would have been less, simply as a result of the mere operation of economic factors". "The urge of capital to expand . . . can be best promoted, not by the violent methods of imperialism, but by peaceful democracy."*

This argument of Kautsky's, which is repeated in every key by his Russian armour-bearer (and Russian shielder of the social-chauvinists), Mr. Spectator, constitutes the basis of Kautskian critique of imperialism, and that is why we must deal with it in greater detail. We will begin with a quotation from Hilferding, whose conclusions Kautsky on many occasions, and notably in April 1915, has declared to have been "unanimously adopted by all socialist theoreticians".

"It is not the business of the proletariat," writes Hilferding, "to contrast the more progressive capitalist policy with that of the now bygone era of free trade and of hostility towards the state. The reply of the proletariat to the economic policy of finance capital, to imperialism, cannot be free trade, but socialism. The aim of proletarian policy cannot today be the ideal of restoring free competition—which has now become a reactionary ideal—but the complete elimination of competition by the abolition of capitalism."**

---

* Kautsky, *Nationalstaat, imperialistischer Staat und Staatenbund,* Nürnberg, 1915, S. 72, 70.
** *Finance Capital,* p. 567.

Kautsky broke with Marxism by advocating in the epoch of finance capital a "reactionary ideal", "peaceful democracy", "the mere operation of economic factors", for *objectively* this ideal drags us back from monopoly to non-monopoly capitalism, and is a reformist swindle.

Trade with Egypt (or with any other colony or semi-colony) "would have grown more" *without* military occupation, without imperialism, and without finance capital. What does this mean? That capitalism would have developed more rapidly if free competition had not been restricted by monopolies in general, or by the "connections", yoke (i.e., also the monopoly) of finance capital, or by the monopolist possession of colonies by certain countries?

Kautsky's argument can have no other meaning; and *this* "meaning" is meaningless. Let us assume that free competition, without any sort of monopoly, *would* have developed capitalism and trade more rapidly. But the more rapidly trade and capitalism develop, the greater is the concentration of production and capital which *gives rise* to monopoly. And monopolies have *already* arisen—precisely *out of* free competition! Even if monopolies have now begun to retard progress, it is not an argument in favour of free competition, which has become impossible after it has given rise to monopoly.

Whichever way one turns Kautsky's argument, one will find nothing in it except reaction and bourgeois reformism.

Even if we correct this argument and say, as Spectator says, that the trade of the colonies with Britain is now developing more slowly than their trade with other countries, it does not save Kautsky; for it is *also* monopoly, *also* imperialism that is beating Great Britain, only it is the monopoly and imperialism of another country (America, Germany). It is known that the cartels have given rise to a new and peculiar form of protective tariffs, i.e., goods suitable for export are protected (Engels noted this in Vol. III of *Capital*). It is known, too, that the cartels and finance capital have a system peculiar to themselves, that of "exporting goods at cut-rate prices", or "dumping", as the English call it: within a given country the cartel sells

its goods at high monopoly prices, but sells them abroad
at a much lower price to undercut the competitor, to enlarge
its own production to the utmost, etc. If Germany's trade
with the British colonies is developing more rapidly than
Great Britain's, it only proves that German imperialism
is younger, stronger and better organised than British imperialism, is superior to it; but it by no means proves the
"superiority" of free trade, for it is not a fight between
free trade and protection and colonial dependence, but between two rival imperialisms, two monopolies, two groups
of finance capital. The superiority of German imperialism
over British imperialism is more potent than the wall of
colonial frontiers or of protective tariffs: to use this as an
"argument" *in favour* of free trade and "peaceful democracy" is banal, it means forgetting the essential features
and characteristics of imperialism, substituting petty-bourgeois reformism for Marxism.

It is interesting to note that even the bourgeois economist, A. Lansburgh, whose criticism of imperialism is as petty-bourgeois as Kautsky's, nevertheless got closer to a more
scientific study of trade statistics. He did not compare one
single country, chosen at random, and one single colony with
the other countries; he examined the export trade of an
imperialist country: (1) with countries which are financially
dependent upon it, and borrow money from it; and (2) with
countries which are financially independent. He obtained
the following results:

Export Trade of Germany
(000,000 marks)

		1889	1908	Per cent increase
To countries financially dependent on Germany	Rumania	48.2	70.8	47
	Portugal	19.0	32.8	73
	Argentina	60.7	147.0	143
	Brazil	48.7	84.5	73
	Chile	28.3	52.4	85
	Turkey	29.9	64.0	114
	Total	*234.8*	*451.5*	*92*

	Great Britain	651.8	997.4	53
To countries financially independent of Germany	France	210.2	437.9	108
	Belgium	137.2	322.8	135
	Switzerland	177.4	401.1	127
	Australia	21.2	64.5	205
	Dutch East Indies	8.8	40.7	363
	Total	*1,206.6*	*2,264.4*	*87*

Lansburgh did not draw *conclusions* and therefore, strangely enough, failed to observe that *if* the figures prove anything at all, they prove that *he is wrong*, for the exports to countries financially dependent on Germany have grown *more rapidly*, if only slightly, than exports to the countries which are financially independent. (I emphasise the "if", for Lansburgh's figures are far from complete.)

Tracing the connection between exports and loans, Lansburgh writes:

"In 1890-91, a Rumanian loan was floated through the German banks, which had already in previous years made advances on this loan. It was used chiefly to purchase railway materials in Germany. In 1891, German exports to Rumania amounted to 55 million marks. The following year they dropped to 39.4 million marks and, with fluctuations, to 25.4 million in 1900. Only in very recent years have they regained the level of 1891, thanks to two new loans.

"German exports to Portugal rose, following the loans of 1888-89, to 21,100,000 (1890); then, in the two following years, they dropped to 16,200,000 and 7,400,000, and regained their former level only in 1903.

"The figures of German trade with Argentina are still more striking. Loans were floated in 1888 and 1890; German exports to Argentina reached 60,700,000 marks (1889). Two years later they amounted to only 18,600,000 marks, less than one-third of the previous figure. It was not until 1901 that they regained and surpassed the level of 1889, and then only as a result of new loans floated by the state and by municipalities, with advances to build power stations, and with other credit operations.

"Exports to Chile, as a consequence of the loan of 1889, rose to 45,200,000 marks (in 1892), and a year later dropped to 22,500,000 marks. A new Chilean loan floated by the German banks in 1906 was followed by a rise of exports to 84,700,000 marks in 1907, only to fall again to 52,400,000 marks in 1908."*

From these facts Lansburgh draws the amusing petty-bourgeois moral of how unstable and irregular export trade is when it is bound up with loans, how bad it is to invest capital abroad instead of "naturally" and "harmoniously" developing home industry, how "costly" are the millions in bakhshish that Krupp has to pay in floating foreign loans, etc. But the facts tell us clearly: the increase in exports is connected with *just these* swindling tricks of finance capital, which is not concerned with bourgeois morality, but with skinning the ox twice—first, it pockets the profits from the loan; then it pockets other profits from the *same* loan which the borrower uses to make purchases from Krupp, or to purchase railway material from the Steel Syndicate, etc.

I repeat that I do not by any means consider Lansburgh's figures to be perfect; but I had to quote them because they are more scientific than Kautsky's and Spectator's and because Lansburgh showed the correct way to approach the question. In discussing the significance of finance capital in regard to exports, etc., one must be able to single out the connection of exports especially and solely with the tricks of the financiers, especially and solely with the sale of goods by cartels, etc. Simply to compare colonies with non-colonies, one imperialism with another imperialism, one semi-colony or colony (Egypt) with all other countries, is to evade and to obscure the very *essence* of the question.

Kautsky's theoretical critique of imperialism has nothing in common with Marxism and serves only as a preamble to propaganda for peace and unity with the opportunists and the social-chauvinists, precisely for the reason that it evades and obscures the very profound and fundamental

---

* *Die Bank*, 1909, 2, S. 819 et seq.

contradictions of imperialism: the contradictions between monopoly and free competition which exists side by side with it, between the gigantic "operations" (and gigantic profits) of finance capital and "honest" trade in the free market, the contradiction between cartels and trusts, on the one hand, and non-cartelised industry, on the other, etc.

The notorious theory of "ultra-imperialism", invented by Kautsky, is just as reactionary. Compare his arguments on this subject in 1915, with Hobson's arguments in 1902.

Kautsky: "... Cannot the present imperialist policy be supplanted by a new, ultra-imperialist policy, which will introduce the joint exploitation of the world by internationally united finance capital in place of the mutual rivalries of national finance capitals? Such a new phase of capitalism is at any rate conceivable. Can it be achieved? Sufficient premises are still lacking to enable us to answer this question."*

Hobson: "Christendom thus laid out in a few great federal empires, each with a retinue of uncivilised dependencies, seems to many the most legitimate development of present tendencies, and one which would offer the best hope of permanent peace on an assured basis of inter-Imperialism."

Kautsky called ultra-imperialism or super-imperialism what Hobson, thirteen years earlier, described as inter-imperialism. Except for coining a new and clever catchword, replacing one Latin prefix by another, the only progress Kautsky has made in the sphere of "scientific" thought is that he gave out as Marxism what Hobson, in effect, described as the cant of English parsons. After the Anglo-Boer War it was quite natural for this highly honourable caste to exert their main efforts to *console* the British middle class and the workers who had lost many of their relatives on the battlefields of South Africa and who were obliged to pay higher taxes in order to guarantee still higher profits for the British financiers. And what better consolation could there be than the theory that imperial-

---

* *Die Neue Zeit*, April 30, 1915, S. 144.

ism is not so bad; that it stands close to inter- (or ultra-) imperialism, which can ensure permanent peace? No matter what the good intentions of the English parsons, or of sentimental Kautsky, may have been, the only objective, i.e., real, social significance of Kautsky's "theory" is this: it is a most reactionary method of consoling the masses with hopes of permanent peace being possible under capitalism, by distracting their attention from the sharp antagonisms and acute problems of the present times, and directing it towards illusory prospects of an imaginary "ultra-imperialism" of the future. Deception of the masses—that is all there is in Kautsky's "Marxist" theory.

Indeed, it is enough to compare well-known and indisputable facts to become convinced of the utter falsity of the prospects which Kautsky tries to conjure up before the German workers (and the workers of all lands). Let us consider India, Indo-China and China. It is known that these three colonial and semi-colonial countries, with a population of six to seven hundred million, are subjected to the exploitation of the finance capital of several imperialist powers: Great Britain, France, Japan, the U.S.A., etc. Let us assume that these imperialist countries form alliances against one another in order to protect or enlarge their possessions, their interests and their spheres of influence in these Asiatic states; these alliances will be "interimperialist", or "ultra-imperialist" alliances. Let us assume that *all* the imperialist countries conclude an alliance for the "peaceful" division of these parts of Asia; this alliance would be an alliance of "internationally united finance capital". There are actual examples of alliances of this kind in the history of the twentieth century—the attitude of the powers to China, for instance. We ask, is it "conceivable", assuming that the capitalist system remains intact—and this is precisely the assumption that Kautsky does make—that such alliances would be more than temporary, that they would eliminate friction, conflicts and struggle in every possible form?

The question has only to be presented clearly for any other than a negative answer to be impossible. This is because the only conceivable basis under capitalism for the division of spheres of influence, interests, colonies, etc., is a calculation of the *strength* of those participating, their general economic, financial, military strength, etc. And the strength of these participants in the division does not change to an equal degree, for the *even* development of different undertakings, trusts, branches of industry, or countries is impossible under capitalism. Half a century ago Germany was a miserable, insignificant country, if her capitalist strength is compared with that of the Britain of that time; Japan compared with Russia in the same way. Is it "conceivable" that in ten or twenty years' time the relative strength of the imperialist powers will have remained *un*changed? It is out of the question.

Therefore, in the realities of the capitalist system, and not in the banal philistine fantasies of English parsons, or of the German "Marxist", Kautsky, "inter-imperialist" or "ultra-imperialist" alliances, no matter what form they may assume, whether of one imperialist coalition against another, or of a general alliance embracing *all* the imperialist powers, are *inevitably* nothing more than a "truce" in periods between wars. Peaceful alliances prepare the ground for wars, and in their turn grow out of wars; the one conditions the other, producing alternating forms of peaceful and non-peaceful struggle on *one and the same* basis of imperialist connections and relations within world economics and world politics. But in order to pacify the workers and reconcile them with the social-chauvinists who have deserted to the side of the bourgeoisie, over-wise Kautsky *separates* one link of a single chain from another, separates the present peaceful (and ultra-imperialist, nay, ultra-ultra-imperialist) alliance of *all* the powers for the "pacification" of China (remember the suppression of the Boxer Rebellion) from the non-peaceful conflict of tomorrow, which will prepare the ground for another "peaceful" general alliance for the partition, say, of Turkey, on the day after tomorrow, *etc.*, *etc.* Instead of showing the living connection between periods of imperialist peace and periods of imperialist war, Kautsky presents the workers with a lifeless abstraction in order to reconcile them to their lifeless leaders.

An American writer, Hill, in his *A History of the Diplomacy in the International Development of Europe* refers in his preface to the following periods in the recent history of diplomacy: (1) the era of revolution; (2) the constitutional movement; (3) the present era of "commercial imperialism".* Another writer divides the history of Great Britain's "world policy" since 1870 into four periods: (1) the first Asiatic period (that of the struggle against Russia's advance in Central Asia towards India); (2) the African period (approximately 1885-1902): that of the struggle against France for the partition of Africa (the "Fashoda incident"[57] of 1898 which brought her within a hair's breadth of war with France); (3) the second Asiatic period (alliance with Japan against Russia), and (4) the "European" period, chiefly anti-German.** "The political patrol clashes take place on the financial field," wrote the banker, Riesser, in 1905, in showing how French finance capital operating in Italy was preparing the way for a political alliance of these countries, and how a conflict was developing between Germany and Great Britain over Persia, between all the European capitalists over Chinese loans, etc. Behold, the living reality of peaceful "ultra-imperialist" alliances in their inseverable connection with ordinary imperialist conflicts!

Kautsky's obscuring of the deepest contradictions of imperialism, which inevitably boils down to painting imperialism in bright colours, leaves its traces in this writer's criticism of the political features of imperialism. Imperialism is the epoch of finance capital and of monopolies, which introduce everywhere the striving for domination, not for freedom. Whatever the political system the result of these tendencies is everywhere reaction and an extreme intensification of antagonisms in this field. Particularly intensified become the yoke of national oppression and the striving for annexations, i.e., the violation of national independence (for annexation is nothing but the violation

---

* David Jayne Hill, *A History of the Diplomacy in the International Development of Europe*, Vol. I, p. x.
** Schilder, op. cit., S. 178.

of the right of nations to self-determination). Hilferding rightly notes the connection between imperialism and the intensification of national oppression. "In the newly opened-up countries," he writes, "the capital imported into them intensifies antagonisms and excites against the intruders the constantly growing resistance of the peoples who are awakening to national consciousness; this resistance can easily develop into dangerous measures against foreign capital. The old social relations become completely revolutionised, the age-long agrarian isolation of 'nations without history' is destroyed and they are drawn into the capitalist whirlpool. Capitalism itself gradually provides the subjugated with the means and resources for their emancipation and they set out to achieve the goal which once seemed highest to the European nations: the creation of a united national state as a means to economic and cultural freedom. This movement for national independence threatens European capital in its most valuable and most promising fields of exploitation, and European capital can maintain its domination only by continually increasing its military forces."*

To this must be added that it is not only in newly opened-up countries, but also in the old, that imperialism is leading to annexation, to increased national oppression, and, consequently, also to increasing resistance. While objecting to the intensification of political reaction by imperialism, Kautsky leaves in the shade a question that has become particularly urgent, viz., the impossibility of unity with the opportunists in the epoch of imperialism. While objecting to annexations, he presents his objections in a form that is most acceptable and least offensive to the opportunists. He addresses himself to a German audience, yet he obscures the most topical and important point, for instance, the annexation of Alsace-Lorraine by Germany. In order to appraise this "mental aberration" of Kautsky's I shall take the following example. Let us suppose that a Japanese condemns the annexation of the Philippines by the Americans. The question is: will many believe that he

---

* *Finance Capital*, p. 487.

does so because he has a horror of annexations as such, and
not because he himself has a desire to annex the Philippines? And shall we not be constrained to admit that the
"fight" the Japanese is waging against annexations can
be regarded as being sincere and politically honest only
if he fights against the annexation of Korea by Japan, and
urges freedom for Korea to secede from Japan?

Kautsky's theoretical analysis of imperialism, as well
as his economic and political critique of imperialism, are
permeated *through and through* with a spirit, absolutely
irreconcilable with Marxism, of obscuring and glossing
over the fundamental contradictions of imperialism and
with a striving to preserve at all costs the crumbling unity
with opportunism in the European working-class movement.

X. THE PLACE OF IMPERIALISM
IN HISTORY

We have seen that in its economic essence imperialism
is monopoly capitalism. This in itself determines its place
in history, for monopoly that grows out of the soil of free
competition, and precisely out of free competition, is the
transition from the capitalist system to a higher socio-
economic order. We must take special note of the four
principal types of monopoly, or principal manifestations
of monopoly capitalism, which are characteristic of the
epoch we are examining.

Firstly, monopoly arose out of the concentration of
production at a very high stage. This refers to the monopolist capitalist associations, cartels, syndicates and trusts.
We have seen the important part these play in present-
day economic life. At the beginning of the twentieth century, monopolies had acquired complete supremacy in the
advanced countries, and although the first steps towards
the formation of the cartels were taken by countries enjoying the protection of high tariffs (Germany, America),
Great Britain, with her system of free trade, revealed the
same basic phenomenon, only a little later, namely, the
birth of monopoly out of the concentration of production.

Secondly, monopolies have stimulated the seizure of the most important sources of raw materials, especially for the basic and most highly cartelised industries in capitalist society: the coal and iron industries. The monopoly of the most important sources of raw materials has enormously increased the power of big capital, and has sharpened the antagonism between cartelised and non-cartelised industry.

Thirdly, monopoly has sprung from the banks. The banks have developed from modest middleman enterprises into the monopolists of finance capital. Some three to five of the biggest banks in each of the foremost capitalist countries have achieved the "personal link-up" between industrial and bank capital, and have concentrated in their hands the control of thousands upon thousands of millions which form the greater part of the capital and income of entire countries. A financial oligarchy, which throws a close network of dependence relationships over all the economic and political institutions of present-day bourgeois society without exception—such is the most striking manifestation of this monopoly.

Fourthly, monopoly has grown out of colonial policy. To the numerous "old" motives of colonial policy, finance capital has added the struggle for the sources of raw materials, for the export of capital, for spheres of influence, i.e., for spheres for profitable deals, concessions, monopoly profits and so on, economic territory in general. When the colonies of the European powers, for instance, comprised only one-tenth of the territory of Africa (as was the case in 1876), colonial policy was able to develop by methods other than those of monopoly—by the "free grabbing" of territories, so to speak. But when nine-tenths of Africa had been seized (by 1900), when the whole world had been divided up, there was inevitably ushered in the era of monopoly possession of colonies and, consequently, of particularly intense struggle for the division and the redivision of the world.

The extent to which monopolist capital has intensified all the contradictions of capitalism is generally known. It is sufficient to mention the high cost of living and the tyranny of the cartels. This intensification of contradictions constitutes the most powerful driving force of the transitional period of history, which began from the time of the final victory of world finance capital.

Monopolies, oligarchy, the striving for domination and not for freedom, the exploitation of an increasing number of small or weak nations by a handful of the richest or most powerful nations—all these have given birth to those distinctive characteristics of imperialism which compel us to define it as parasitic or decaying capitalism. More and more prominently there emerges, as one of the tendencies of imperialism, the creation of the "rentier state", the usurer state, in which the bourgeoisie to an ever-increasing degree lives on the proceeds of capital exports and by "clipping coupons". It would be a mistake to believe that this tendency to decay precludes the rapid growth of capitalism. It does not. In the epoch of imperialism, certain branches of industry, certain strata of the bourgeoisie and certain countries betray, to a greater or lesser degree, now one and now another of these tendencies. On the whole, capitalism is growing far more rapidly than before; but this growth is not only becoming more and more uneven in general, its unevenness also manifests itself, in particular, in the decay of the countries which are richest in capital (Britain).

In regard to the rapidity of Germany's economic development, Riesser, the author of the book on the big German banks, states: "The progress of the preceding period (1848-70), which had not been exactly slow, compares with the rapidity with which the whole of Germany's national economy, and with it German banking, progressed during this period (1870-1905) in about the same way as the speed of the mail coach in the good old days compares with the speed of the present-day automobile ... which is whizzing past so fast that it endangers not only innocent pedestrians in its path, but also the occupants of the car." In its turn, this finance capital which has grown with such extraordinary rapidity is not unwilling, precisely because it has grown so quickly, to pass on to a more "tranquil" possession of colonies which have to be seized—and not only by peaceful methods—from richer nations. In the

United States, economic development in the last decades has been even more rapid than in Germany, *and for this very reason,* the parasitic features of modern American capitalism have stood out with particular prominence. On the other hand, a comparison of, say, the republican American bourgeoisie with the monarchist Japanese or German bourgeoisie shows that the most pronounced political distinction diminishes to an extreme degree in the epoch of imperialism—not because it is unimportant in general, but because in all these cases we are talking about a bourgeoisie which has definite features of parasitism.

The receipt of high monopoly profits by the capitalists in one of the numerous branches of industry, in one of the numerous countries, etc., makes it economically possible for them to bribe certain sections of the workers, and for a time a fairly considerable minority of them, and win them to the side of the bourgeoisie of a given industry or given nation against all the others. The intensification of antagonisms between imperialist nations for the division of the world increases this urge. And so there is created that bond between imperialism and opportunism, which revealed itself first and most clearly in Great Britain, owing to the fact that certain features of imperialist development were observable there much earlier than in other countries. Some writers, L. Martov, for example, are prone to wave aside the connection between imperialism and opportunism in the working-class movement—a particularly glaring fact at the present time—by resorting to "official optimism" (*à la* Kautsky and Huysmans) like the following: the cause of the opponents of capitalism would be hopeless if it were progressive capitalism that led to the increase of opportunism, or if it were the best-paid workers who were inclined towards opportunism, etc. We must have no illusions about "optimism" of this kind. It is optimism in respect of opportunism; it is optimism which serves to conceal opportunism. As a matter of fact the extraordinary rapidity and the particularly revolting character of the development of opportunism is by no means a guarantee that its victory will be durable: the rapid growth of a painful abscess on a healthy body can only cause it to burst more quickly and thus relieve the body of it. The most dangerous of all in this respect are those who do not wish to understand that the fight against imperialism is a sham and humbug unless it is inseparably bound up with the fight against opportunism.

From all that has been said in this book on the economic essence of imperialism, it follows that we must define it as capitalism in transition, or, more precisely, as moribund capitalism. It is very instructive in this respect to note that bourgeois economists, in describing modern capitalism, frequently employ catchwords and phrases like "interlocking", "absence of isolation", etc.; "in conformity with their functions and course of development", banks are "not purely private business enterprises; they are more and more outgrowing the sphere of purely private business regulation". And this very Riesser, whose words I have just quoted, declares with all seriousness that the "prophecy" of the Marxists concerning "socialisation" has "not come true"!

What then does this catchword "interlocking" express? It merely expresses the most striking feature of the process going on before our eyes. It shows that the observer counts the separate trees, but cannot see the wood. It slavishly copies the superficial, the fortuitous, the chaotic. It reveals the observer as one who is overwhelmed by the mass of raw material and is utterly incapable of appreciating its meaning and importance. Ownership of shares, the relations between owners of private property "interlock in a haphazard way". But underlying this interlocking, its very base, are the changing social relations of production. When a big enterprise assumes gigantic proportions, and, on the basis of an exact computation of mass data, organises according to plan the supply of primary raw materials to the extent of two-thirds, or three-fourths, of all that is necessary for tens of millions of people; when the raw materials are transported in a systematic and organised manner to the most suitable places of production, sometimes situated hundreds or thousands of miles from each other; when a single centre directs all the consecutive stages of processing the material right up to the manufacture of numerous varieties of finished articles; when these products are distributed according to a single plan among tens and hundreds of millions of consumers (the marketing of oil in America and Germany by the American oil trust)—then it becomes evident that we have socialisation of production, and not mere "interlocking"; that private economic and private property relations constitute a shell which no longer fits its contents, a shell which must inevitably decay if its removal is artificially delayed, a shell which may remain in a state of decay for a fairly long period (if, at the worst, the cure of the opportunist abscess is protracted), but which will inevitably be removed.

The enthusiastic admirer of German imperialism, Schulze-Gaevernitz, exclaims:

"Once the supreme management of the German banks has been entrusted to the hands of a dozen persons, their activity is even today more significant for the public good than that of the majority of the Ministers of State.... [The "interlocking" of bankers, ministers, magnates of industry and rentiers is here conveniently forgotten.] If we imagine the development of those tendencies we have noted carried to their logical conclusion we will have: the money capital of the nation united in the banks; the banks themselves combined into cartels; the investment capital of the nation cast in the shape of securities. Then the forecast of that genius Saint-Simon will be fulfilled: 'The present anarchy of production, which corresponds to the fact that economic relations are developing without uniform regulation, must make way for organisation in production. Production will no longer be directed by isolated manufacturers, independent of each other and ignorant of man's economic needs; that will be done by a certain public institution. A central committee of management, being able to survey the large field of social economy from a more elevated point of view, will regulate it for the benefit of the whole of society, will put the means of production into suitable hands, and above all will take care that there be constant harmony between production and consumption. Institutions already exist which have assumed as

part of their functions a certain organisation of economic
labour, the banks.' We are still a long way from the fulfilment of Saint-Simon's forecast, but we are on the way
towards it: Marxism, different from what Marx imagined,
but different only in form."*

A crushing "refutation" of Marx, indeed, which retreats
a step from Marx's precise, scientific analysis to Saint-
Simon's guess-work, the guess-work of a genius, but guess-
work all the same.

Written January-June 1916

First published in mid-1917   Vol. 22, pp. 195-210,
in pamphlet form, Petrograd   246-304

* *Grundriss der Sozialökonomik*, S. 146.

THE JUNIUS PAMPHLET
(Excerpt)

Only a sophist can disregard the difference between an imperialist and a national war on the grounds that one *might* develop into the other. Not infrequently have dialectics served—and the history of Greek philosophy is an example—as a bridge to sophistry. But we remain dialecticians and we combat sophistry not by denying the possibility of all transformations in general, but by analysing the *given* phenomenon in its concrete setting and development.

Transformation of the present imperialist war of 1914-16 into a national war is highly improbable, for the class that represents *progressive* development is the proletariat which is objectively striving to transform it into a civil war against the bourgeoisie. Also this: there is no very considerable difference between the forces of the two coalitions, and international finance capital has created a reactionary bourgeoisie everywhere. But such a transformation should *not* be proclaimed *impossible: if* the *European* proletariat remains impotent, say, for twenty years; *if* the present war *ends* in victories like Napoleon's and in the subjugation of a number of viable national states; *if* the transition to socialism of non-European imperialism (primarily Japanese and American) is also held up for twenty years by a war between these two countries, for example, then a great national war in Europe would be possible. It would hurl Europe *back* several decades. That is improbable. But *not* impossible, for it is undialectical, unscientific and theoret-

ically wrong to regard the course of world history as
smooth and always in a forward direction, without occa-
sional gigantic leaps back.

Further. National wars waged by colonies and semi-
colonies in the imperialist era are not only probable but
inevitable. About 1,000 million people, or *over half* of the
world's population, live in the colonies and semi-colonies
(China, Turkey, Persia). The national liberation movements
there are either already very strong, or are growing and
maturing. Every war is the continuation of politics by other
means. The continuation of national liberation politics in
the colonies will *inevitably* take the form of national wars
against imperialism. Such wars *might* lead to an imperialist war of the present "great" imperialist powers, but on
the other hand they might not. It will depend on many
factors.

Example: Britain and France fought the Seven Years'
War[58] for the possession of colonies. In other words, they
waged an imperialist war (which is possible on the basis
of slavery and primitive capitalism as well as on the basis
of modern highly developed capitalism). France suffered
defeat and lost some of her colonies. Several years later
there began the national liberation war of the North American States against Britain alone. France and Spain, then
in possession of some parts of the present United States,
concluded a friendship treaty with the States in rebellion
against Britain. This they did out of hostility to Britain,
i.e., in their own imperialist interests. French troops
fought the British on the side of the American forces. What
we have here is a national liberation war in which imperialist rivalry is an auxiliary element, one that has no serious
importance. This is the very opposite to what we see in the
war of 1914-16 (the national element in the Austro-Serbian
War is of no serious importance compared with the all-
determining element of imperialist rivalry). It would be
absurd, therefore, to apply the concept imperialism indis-
criminately and conclude that national wars are "impossible". A national liberation war, waged, for example,
by an alliance of Persia, India and China against one or
more of the imperialist powers, is both possible and prob-

able, for it would follow from the national liberation movements in these countries. The transformation of such a war into an imperialist war between the present-day imperialist powers would depend upon very many concrete factors, the emergence of which it would be ridiculous to guarantee.

Written in July 1916

Published in *Sbornik Sotsial-Demokrata*   Vol. 22, pp. 309-11
No. 1, October 1916
Signed: *N. Lenin*

A CARICATURE OF MARXISM
AND IMPERIALIST ECONOMISM

(Excerpt)

Economically, imperialism (or the "era" of finance capital—it is not a matter of words) is the highest stage in the development of capitalism, one in which production has assumed such big, immense proportions that *free competition gives way to monopoly*. That is the *economic* essence of imperialism. Monopoly manifests itself in trusts, syndicates, etc., in the omnipotence of the giant banks, in the buying up of raw material sources, etc., in the concentration of banking capital, etc. Everything hinges on economic monopoly.

The political superstructure of this new economy, of monopoly capitalism (imperialism is monopoly capitalism), is the change *from* democracy *to* political reaction. Democracy corresponds to free competition. Political reaction corresponds to monopoly. "Finance capital strives for domination, not freedom," Rudolf Hilferding rightly remarks in his *Finance Capital*.

It is fundamentally wrong, un-Marxist and unscientific, to single out "foreign policy" from policy in general, let alone counterpose foreign policy to home policy. Both in foreign and home policy imperialism strives towards violations of democracy, towards reaction. In this sense imperialism is indisputably the "negation" of *democracy in general,* of *all democracy*, and not just of *one* of its demands, national self-determination.

Being a "negation" of democracy in general, imperialism is *also* a "negation" of democracy in the national question (i.e., national self-determination): it seeks to violate democracy. The achievement of democracy is, in the same sense, and to the same degree, harder under imperialism (compared with pre-monopoly capitalism), as the achievement of a republic, a militia, popular election of officials, etc. There can be no talk of democracy being "economically" unachievable.

Kievsky was probably led astray here by the fact (besides his general lack of understanding of the requirements of economic analysis) that the philistine regards annexation (i.e., acquisition of foreign territories against the will of their people, i.e., violation of self-determination) as equivalent to the "spread" (expansion) of finance capital to a larger economic territory.

But theoretical problems should not be approached from philistine conceptions.

Economically, imperialism is monopoly capitalism. To acquire full monopoly, all competition must be eliminated, and not only on the home market (of the given state), but also on foreign markets, in the whole world. Is it *economically* possible, "in the era of finance capital", to eliminate competition even in a foreign state? Certainly it is. It is done through a rival's financial dependence and acquisition of his sources of raw materials and eventually of all his enterprises.

The American trusts are the supreme expression of the economics of imperialism or monopoly capitalism. They do not confine themselves to economic means of eliminating rivals, but constantly resort to political, even criminal, methods. It would be the greatest mistake, however, to believe that the trusts cannot establish their monopoly by purely economic methods. Reality provides ample proof that this is "achievable": the trusts undermine their rivals' credit through the banks (the owners of the trusts become the owners of the banks: buying up shares); their supply of materials (the owners of the trusts become the owners of the railways: buying up shares); for a certain time the trusts sell below cost, spending millions on this in order to ruin a competitor and then *buy up* his enterprises, his sources of raw materials (mines, land, etc.).

There you have a purely economic analysis of the power of the trusts and their expansion. There you have the purely economic path to expansion: *buying up* mills and factories, sources of raw materials.

Big finance capital of one country can always buy up competitors in another, politically independent country and constantly does so. Economically, this is fully achievable. Economic "annexation" is *fully* "achievable" without political annexation and is widely practised. In the literature on imperialism you will constantly come across indications that Argentina, for example, is in reality a "trade colony" of Britain, or that Portugal is in reality a "vassal" of Britain, etc. And that is actually so: economic dependence upon British banks, indebtedness to Britain, British acquisition of their railways, mines, land, etc., enable Britain to "annex" these countries economically without violating their political independence.

National self-determination means political independence. Imperialism seeks to violate such independence because political annexation often makes economic annexation easier, cheaper (easier to bribe officials, secure concessions, put through advantageous legislation, etc.), more convenient, less troublesome—just as imperialism seeks to replace democracy generally by oligarchy. But to speak of the *economic* "unachievability" of self-determination under imperialism is sheer nonsense.

Kievsky gets round the theoretical difficulties by a very simple and superficial dodge, known in German as *"burschikose"* phraseology, i.e., primitive, crude phrases heard (and quite naturally) at student binges. Here is an example: "Universal suffrage," he writes, "the eight-hour day and even the republic are *logically* compatible with imperialism, though imperialism far from smiles [!!] on them and their achievement is therefore extremely difficult."

We would have absolutely no objections to the *burschikose* statement that imperialism far from "smiles" on the republic—a frivolous word can sometimes lend colour to a scientific polemic!—if in this polemic on a serious issue we were given, *in addition*, an economic and political analysis of the concepts involved. With Kievsky, however, the *burschikose* phrase does duty for such an analysis or serves to conceal lack of it.

What can this mean: "Imperialism far from smiles on the republic"? And why?

The republic is one possible form of the political super-structure of capitalist society, and, moreover, under present-day conditions the most democratic form. To say that imperialism does not "smile" on the republic is to say that there is a contradiction between imperialism and democracy. It may very well be that Kievsky does not "smile" or even "far from smiles" on this conclusion. Nevertheless it is irrefutable.

To continue. What is the nature of this contradiction between imperialism and democracy? Is it a logical or illogical contradiction? Kievsky uses the word "logical" without stopping to think and therefore does not notice that in this particular case it serves to *conceal* (both from the reader's and author's eyes and mind) the *very question* he sets out to discuss! That question is the relation of economics to politics: the relation of economic conditions and the economic content of imperialism to a certain political form. To say that every "contradiction" revealed in human discussion is a logical contradiction is meaningless tautology. And with the aid of this tautology Kievsky evades the *substance* of the question: Is it a "logical" contradiction between two *economic* phenomena or propositions (1)? Or two *political* phenomena or propositions (2)? Or *economic* and *political* phenomena or propositions (3)?

For that is the heart of the matter, once we are discussing economic unachievability or achievability under one or another political form!

Had Kievsky not evaded the heart of the matter, he would probably have realised that the contradiction between imperialism and the republic is a contradiction between the economics of latter-day capitalism (namely, monopoly capitalism) and political democracy in general. For Kievsky will never prove that any major and fundamental democratic measure (popular election of officials or officers, complete freedom of association and assembly, etc.) is less contradictory to imperialism (or, if you like, more "smiled" upon) than the republic.

What we have, then, is the proposition *we* advanced in our theses: imperialism contradicts, "logically" contradicts, *all* political democracy *in general*. Kievsky does not "smile" on this proposition for it demolishes all his illogical constructions. But what can we do about it? Are we to accept a method that is supposed to refute certain propositions, but instead secretly advances them by using such expressions as "imperialism far from smiles on the republic"?

Further. Why does imperialism far from smile on the republic? And how does imperialism "combine" its economics with the republic?

Kievsky has given no thought to that. We would remind him of the following words of Engels in reference to the democratic republic. Can wealth dominate under this form of government? The question concerns the "contradiction" between economics and politics.

Engels replies: "The democratic republic officially knows nothing any more of property distinctions [between citizens]. In it, wealth exercises its power indirectly, but all the more surely. On the one hand, in the form of the direct corruption of officials, of which America provides the classical example; on the other hand, in the form of an alliance between government and stock exchange. . . ."

There you have an excellent example of economic analysis on the question of the "achievability" of democracy under capitalism. And the "achievability" of self-determination under imperialism is part of that question.

The democratic republic "logically" contradicts capitalism, because "officially" it puts the rich and the poor on an equal footing. That is a contradiction between the economic system and the political superstructure. There is the same contradiction between imperialism and the republic, deepened or aggravated by the fact that the change-over from free competition to monopoly makes the realisation of political freedoms even more "difficult".

How, then, is capitalism reconciled with democracy? By indirect implementation of the omnipotence of capital. There are two economic means for that: (1) direct bribery;

(2) alliance of government and stock exchange. (That is stated in our theses—under a bourgeois system finance capital "can freely bribe and buy any government and any official".)

Once we have the dominance of commodity production, of the bourgeoisie, of the power of money—bribery (direct or through the stock exchange) is "achievable" under any form of government and under any kind of democracy.

What, it can be asked, is altered in this respect when capitalism gives way to imperialism, i.e., when pre-monopoly capitalism is replaced by monopoly capitalism?

Only that the power of the stock exchange increases. For finance capital is industrial capital at its highest, monopoly level which has merged with banking capital. The big banks merge with and absorb the stock exchange. (The literature on imperialism speaks of the declining role of the stock exchange, but only in the sense that every giant bank is itself virtually a stock exchange.)

Further. If "wealth" in general is fully capable of achieving domination over any democratic republic by bribery and through the stock exchange, then how can Kievsky maintain, without lapsing into a very curious "logical contradiction", that the immense wealth of the trusts and the banks, which have thousands of millions at their command, cannot "achieve" the domination of finance capital over a foreign, i.e., politically independent, republic??

Well? Bribery of officials is "unachievable" in a foreign state? Or the "alliance of government and stock exchange" applies only to one's own government?

Written in August-October 1916

First published in 1924   Vol. 23, pp. 42-47
in *Zvezda* Nos. 1 and 2
Signed: *V. Lenin*

IMPERIALISM AND THE SPLIT IN SOCIALISM
(Excerpt)

Is there any connection between imperialism and the monstrous and disgusting victory opportunism (in the form of social-chauvinism) has gained over the labour movement in Europe?

This is the fundamental question of modern socialism. And having in our Party literature fully established, first, the imperialist character of our era and of the present war, and, second, the inseparable historical connection between social-chauvinism and opportunism, as well as the intrinsic similarity of their political ideology, we can and must proceed to analyse this fundamental question.

We have to begin with as precise and full a definition of imperialism as possible. Imperialism is a specific historical stage of capitalism. Its specific character is threefold: imperialism is (1) monopoly capitalism; (2) parasitic, or decaying capitalism; (3) moribund capitalism. The supplanting of free competition by monopoly is the fundamental economic feature, the *quintessence* of imperialism. Monopoly manifests itself in five principal forms: (1) cartels, syndicates and trusts—the concentration of production has reached a degree which gives rise to these monopolistic associations of capitalists; (2) the monopolistic position of the big banks—three, four or five giant banks manipulate the whole economic life of America, France, Germany; (3) seizure of the sources of *raw material* by the trusts and the financial oligarchy (finance capital is monopoly industrial capital merged with bank capital); (4) the (economic) partition of the world by the international cartels has *begun*. There are already over *one hundred* such international cartels, which command the *entire* world market and divide it "amicably" among themselves—until war *re*divides it. The export of capital, as distinct from the export of commodities under non-monopoly capitalism, is a highly characteristic phenomenon and is closely linked with the economic and territorial-political partition of the world; (5) the territorial partition of the world (colonies) *is completed*.

Imperialism, as the highest stage of capitalism in America and Europe, and later in Asia, took final shape in the period 1898-1914. The Spanish-American War (1898), the Anglo-Boer War (1899-1902), the Russo-Japanese War (1904-05) and the economic crisis in Europe in 1900 are the chief historical landmarks in the new era of world history.

The fact that imperialism is parasitic or decaying capitalism is manifested first of all in the tendency to decay, which is characteristic of *every* monopoly under the system of private ownership of the means of production. The difference between the democratic-republican and the reactionary-monarchist imperialist bourgeoisie is obliterated precisely because they are both rotting alive (which by no means precludes an extraordinarily rapid development of capitalism in individual branches of industry, in individual countries, and in individual periods). Secondly, the decay of capitalism is manifested in the creation of a huge stratum of *rentiers,* capitalists who live by "clipping coupons". In each of the four leading imperialist countries— England, U.S.A., France and Germany—capital in securities amounts to 100,000 or 150,000 *million* francs, from which each country derives an annual income of no less than five to eight thousand million. Thirdly, export of capital is parasitism raised to a high pitch. Fourthly, "finance capital strives for domination, not freedom". Political reaction *all along* the line is a characteristic feature of imperialism. Corruption, bribery on a huge scale and all kinds of fraud. Fifthly, the exploitation of oppressed nations—which is inseparably connected with annexations—and especially the exploitation of colonies by a handful of "Great" Powers, increasingly transforms the "civilised" world into a parasite on the body of hundreds of millions in the uncivilised nations. The Roman proletarian lived at the expense of society. Modern society lives at the expense of the modern proletarian. Marx specially stressed this profound observation of Sismondi.[59] Imperialism somewhat changes the situation. A privileged upper stratum of the proletariat in the imperialist countries lives partly at the expense of hundreds of millions in the uncivilised nations.

It is clear why imperialism is *moribund* capitalism, capitalism in *transition* to socialism: monopoly, which grows *out of* capitalism, is *already* dying capitalism, the beginning of its transition to socialism. The tremendous *socialisation* of labour by imperialism (what its apologists—the bourgeois economists—call "interlocking") produces the same result.

Written in October 1916

Published in *Sotsial-Demokrat*   Vol. 23, pp. 105-07
No. 2, December 1916
Signed: *N. Lenin*

AN OPEN LETTER TO BORIS SOUVARINE

(Excerpt)

This leads me to the question of a split, raised also by Souvarine. A split! That is the bogy with which the socialist leaders are trying to frighten others, and which they themselves fear so much! "What useful purpose could *now* be served by the foundation of a new International?"— Souvarine asks. "Its activity would be blighted by sterility, for numerically it would be very weak."

But the day-to-day facts show that, *precisely because they are afraid of a split,* the "activity" of Pressemane and Longuet in France, Kautsky and Ledebour in Germany, is blighted by sterility! And precisely because Karl Liebknecht and Otto Rühle in Germany were not afraid of a split, openly declaring that a split was *necessary* (cf. Rühle's letter in *Vorwärts*, January 12, 1916), and did not hesitate to carry it out—their activity is of vast importance for the proletariat, *despite their numerical weakness.* Liebknecht and Rühle are only two against 108. But these two represent millions, the exploited mass, the overwhelming majority of the population, the future of mankind, the revolution that is mounting and maturing with every passing day. The 108, on the other hand, represent only the servile spirit of a handful of bourgeois flunkeys within the proletariat. Brizon's activities, when he shares the weaknesses of the Centre or the Marsh, are blighted by sterility. And, conversely, they cease to be sterile, help to awaken, organise and stimulate the proletariat, when Brizon really demolishes "unity", when he courageously proclaims in parliament "Down with the war!", or when he publicly speaks the truth, declaring that the Allies are fighting to give Russia Constantinople.

The genuine revolutionary internationalists are numerically weak? Nonsense! Take France in 1780, or Russia in 1900. The politically-conscious and determined revolutionaries, who in France represented the bourgeoisie—the revolutionary class of that era—and in Russia today's revolutionary class—the proletariat, were extremely weak numerically. They were only a few, comprising at the most only 1/10,000, or even 1/100,000, of their class. Several years later, however, these few, this allegedly negligible minority, led the masses, millions and tens of millions of people. Why? Because this minority really represented the interests of these masses, because it believed in the coming revolution, because it was prepared to serve it with supreme devotion.

Numerical weakness? But since when have revolutionaries made their policies dependent on whether they are in a majority or minority? In November 1914, when our Party called for a split with the opportunists,* declaring that the split was the only correct and fitting reply to their betrayal in August 1914, to many that seemed to be a piece of insensate sectarianism coming from men who had completely lost all contact with real life. Two years have passed, and what is happening? In England, the split is an accomplished fact. The social-chauvinist Hyndman has been forced to leave the party. In Germany, a split is developing before everyone's eyes. The Berlin, Bremen and Stuttgart organisations have even been accorded the honour of being expelled from the party ... from the party of the Kaiser's lackeys, the party of the German Renaudels, Sembats, Thomases, Guesdes and Co. And in France? On the one hand, the party of these gentlemen states that it remains true to "fatherland defence". On the other, the Zimmerwaldists state, in their pamphlet *The Zimmerwald*

---

* See Lenin, *Collected Works*, Vol. 21, pp. 25-34.—*Ed.*

Socialists and the War, that "defence of the fatherland" is unsocialist. Isn't this a split?

And how can men who, after two years of this greatest world crisis, give diametrically opposite answers to the supreme question of modern proletarian tactics, work faithfully side by side, within one and the same party?

Look at America—apart from everything else a neutral country. Haven't we the beginnings of a split there, too: Eugene Debs, the "American Bebel", declares in the socialist press that he recognises only one type of war, civil war for the victory of socialism, and that he would sooner be shot than vote a single cent for American war expenditure (see *Appeal to Reason* No. 1032, September 11, 1915). On the other hand, the American Renaudels and Sembats advocate "national defence" and "preparedness". The American Longuets and Pressemanes—the poor souls!—are trying to bring about a reconciliation between social-chauvinists and revolutionary internationalists.

Two Internationals already exist. One is the International of Sembat-Südekum-Hyndman-Plekhanov and Co. The other is the International of Karl Liebknecht, MacLean (the Scottish school-master whom the English bourgeoisie sentenced to hard labour for supporting the workers' class struggle), Höglund (the Swedish M.P. and one of the founders of the Zimmerwald Left sentenced to hard labour for his revolutionary propaganda against the war), the five Duma members exiled to Siberia for life for their propaganda against the war,[60] etc. On the one hand, there is the International of those *who are helping their own governments wage the imperialist war,* and on the other, the International of those *who are waging a revolutionary fight against the imperialist war.* Neither parliamentary eloquence nor the "diplomacy" of socialist "statesmen" can unite these two Internationals. The Second International has outlived itself. The Third International has already been born. And if it has not yet been baptised by the high priests and Popes of the Second International but, on the contrary, has been anathemised (see Vandervelde's and Stauning's speeches), this is not preventing it from gaining strength with every passing day. The Third International will enable the proletariat to rid itself of opportunists and will lead the masses to victory in the maturing and approaching social revolution.

Written in the second half
of December (old style) 1916

First published (in abridged form)
in *La Vérité* No. 48,
January 27, 1918

Vol. 23, pp. 199-201

First published in full
in Russian in the magazine
Proletarskaya Revolutsia No. 7 (90),
1929

STATISTICS AND SOCIOLOGY
(Excerpt)

CHAPTER 1
A FEW STATISTICS

I

For a proper survey of the *whole* complex of data on national movements, we must take the *whole* population of the earth. And in so doing, two criteria must be established with the utmost accuracy and examined with the utmost fullness: first, national homogeneity or heterogeneity of the population of various states; second, division of states (or of state-like formations in cases where there is doubt that we are really dealing with a state) into politically independent and politically dependent.

Let us take the very latest data, published in 1916, and rely on two sources: one German, the *Geographical and Statistical Tables* compiled by Otto Hübner, and one English, *The Statesman's Year-Book*. The first source will have to serve as a basis, for it contains much more comprehensive data on the question that interests us; the second we shall use to check and in some, mostly minor, cases to correct the first.

We shall begin our survey with the politically independent and nationally most homogeneous states. First and foremost among these is a group of *West*-European states, i.e., situated to the west of Russia and Austria.

Here we have 17 states of which five, however, though very homogeneous in national composition, are Lilliputian in size and population. These are Luxembourg, Monaco, San Marino, Liechtenstein and Andorra, with a combined population of only 310,000. Doubtlessly, it would be much more correct not to include them among the states under examination. Of the remaining 12 states, seven are absolutely homogeneous in national composition: in Italy, Holland, Portugal, Sweden and Norway, 99 per cent of the population are of one and the same nationality; in Spain and Denmark the proportion is 96 per cent. Then come three states with a nearly homogeneous national composition: France, England and Germany. In France, the Italians make up only 1.3 per cent, in areas annexed by Napoleon III by violating and falsifying the will of their people. England's annexed territory, Ireland, has a population of 4.4 million, which is less than one-tenth of the total (46.8 million). In Germany, out of a population of 64.9 million, the non-German element, which in practically all cases is just as nationally oppressed as the Irish in England, is represented by the Poles (5.47 per cent), Danes (0.25 per cent) and the population of Alsace-Lorraine (1.87 million). However, part of the latter (the exact proportion is not known) undoubtedly incline towards Germany, due not only to language, but also to economic interests and sympathies. All in all, about 5 million of Germany's population belong to alien, unequal and even oppressed nations.

Only two small states in Western Europe are of mixed national composition: Switzerland, whose population of somewhat less than four million consists of Germans (69 per cent), French (21 per cent) and Italians (8 per cent)—and Belgium (population less than 8 million; probably about 53 per cent Flemings and about 47 per cent French). It should be observed, however, that in spite of the high national heterogeneity in these countries, there can be no question of national oppression. In both countries all nationalities are equal under the constitution; in Switzerland this equality is fully implemented in practice; in Belgium there is inequality in relation to the Flemish population, though they make up the majority, but this inequality is insignificant compared, for instance, with what the Poles have to put up with in Germany, or the Irish in

England, not to mention what has become customary in countries outside this group. That is why, incidentally, the term "state of nationalities", to which the Austrian authors Karl Renner and Otto Bauer, opportunists on the national question, have given such wide currency, is correct only in a very restricted sense. Namely, if, on the one hand, we remember the special historical place of the majority of the countries of this type (which we shall discuss later) and, on the other, if we do not allow this term to obscure the fundamental difference between genuine national equality and national oppression.

Taking all the countries we have discussed, we get a group of 12 West-European states with a total population of 242 million. Of these 242 million only about 9.5 million, i.e., only 4 per cent, represent oppressed nations (in England and Germany). If we add together those sections of the population in all these countries that do not belong to the principal nationalities, we get about 15 million, i.e., 6 per cent.

On the whole, consequently, this group of states is characterised by the following: they are the most advanced capitalist countries, the most developed both economically and politically. Their cultural level, too, is the highest. In national composition most of these countries are homogeneous or nearly homogeneous. National inequality, as a specific political phenomenon, plays a very insignificant part. What we have is the type of "national state" people so often refer to, oblivious, in most cases, to the historically conditional and transitory character of this type in the general capitalist development of mankind. But that will be dealt with in its proper place.

It might be asked: Is this type of state confined to Western Europe? Obviously not. All its basic characteristics —economic (high and particularly rapid capitalist development), political (representative government), cultural and national—are to be observed also in the advanced states of America and Asia: the United States and Japan. The latter's national composition took shape long ago and is absolutely homogeneous: Japanese make up more than 99 per cent of the population. In the United States, the

Negroes (and also the Mulattoes and Indians) account for only 11.1 per cent. They should be classed as an oppressed nation, for the equality won in the Civil War of 1861-65 and guaranteed by the Constitution of the republic was in many respects increasingly curtailed in the chief Negro areas (the South) in connection with the transition from the progressive, pre-monopoly capitalism of 1860-70 to the reactionary, monopoly capitalism (imperialism) of the new era, which in America was especially sharply etched out by the Spanish-American imperialist war of 1898 (i.e., a war between two robbers over the division of the booty).

The white population of the United States makes up 88.7 per cent of the total, and of this figure 74.3 per cent are Americans and only 14.4 per cent foreign-born, i.e., immigrants. We know that the especially favourable conditions in America for the development of capitalism and the rapidity of this development have produced a situation in which vast national differences are speedily and fundamentally, as nowhere else in the world, smoothed out to form a single "American" nation.

Adding the United States and Japan to the West-European countries enumerated above, we get 14 states with an aggregate population of 394 million, of which 26 million, i.e., 7 per cent, belong to unequal nationalities. Though this will be dealt with later, I might observe that at the turn of the century, i.e., in the period when capitalism was being transformed into imperialism, the majority of precisely these 14 advanced states made especially great strides in colonial policy, with the result that they now "dispose" of a population of over 500 million in dependent and colonial countries.

First published in 1935
in *Bolshevik* No. 2

Vol. 23, pp. 273-76

THE TASKS OF THE PROLETARIAT
IN OUR REVOLUTION

DRAFT PLATFORM FOR THE PROLETARIAN PARTY
(Excerpt)

The Situation Within the Socialist International

16. The international obligations of the working class of Russia are precisely now coming to the forefront with particular force.

Only lazy people do not swear by internationalism these days. Even the chauvinist defencists, even Plekhanov and Potresov, even Kerensky, call themselves internationalists. It becomes the duty of the proletarian party all the more urgently, therefore, to clearly, precisely and definitely counterpose internationalism in deed to internationalism in word.

Mere appeals to the workers of all countries, empty assurances of devotion to internationalism, direct or indirect attempts to fix a "sequence" of action by the revolutionary proletariat in the various belligerent countries, laborious efforts to conclude "agreements" between the socialists of the belligerent countries *on the question* of the revolutionary struggle, all the fuss over the summoning of socialist congresses *for the purpose* of a peace campaign, etc., etc.— no matter how sincere the authors of such ideas, attempts, and plans may be—amount, as far as their *objective* significance is concerned, to mere phrase-mongering, and *at best* are innocent and pious wishes, fit only to conceal the *deception* of the people by the chauvinists. The *French* social-chauvinists, who are the most adroit and accomplished in methods of parliamentary hocus-pocus, have long since broken the record for ranting and resonant pacifist and internationalist phrases *coupled with* the incredibly brazen betrayal of socialism and the International, the acceptance of posts in governments which conduct the imperialist war, the voting of credits *or loans* (as Chkheidze, Skobelev, Tsereteli and Steklov have been doing recently in Russia), opposition to the revolutionary struggle in *their own country*, etc., etc.

Good people often forget the brutal and savage setting of the imperialist world war. This setting does not tolerate phrases, and mocks at innocent and pious wishes.

There is one, and only one, kind of real internationalism, and that is—working whole-heartedly for the development of the revolutionary movement and the revolutionary struggle in *one's own* country, and supporting (by propaganda, sympathy, and material aid) *this struggle*, this, *and only this*, line, in *every* country without exception.

Everything else is deception and Manilovism.*

During the two odd years of the war the international socialist and working-class movement in *every* country has evolved three trends. Whoever ignores *reality* and refuses to recognise the existence of these three trends, to analyse them, to fight consistently for the trend that is really internationalist, is doomed to impotence, helplessness and errors.

The three trends are:

1) The social-chauvinists, i.e., socialists in word and chauvinists in deed, people who recognise "defence of the fatherland" in an imperialist war (and above all in the present imperialist war).

These people are our *class* enemies. They have gone over to the bourgeoisie.

They are the majority of the official leaders of the official Social-Democratic parties in *all* countries—Plekhanov and

---

* From the name Manilov, a character in Gogol's *Dead Souls*, represented as a type of easy-going sentimental landowner, whose name has become a synonym for an idle weak-willed dreamer and gas-bag.—*Ed.*

Co. in Russia, the Scheidemanns in Germany, Renaudel, Guesde and Sembat in France, Bissolati and Co. in Italy, Hyndman, the Fabians and the Labourites (the leaders of the "Labour Party") in Britain, Branting and Co. in Sweden, Troelstra and his party in Holland, Stauning and his party in Denmark, Victor Berger and the other "defenders of the fatherland" in America, and so forth.

2) The second trend, known as the "Centre", consists of people who vacillate between the social-chauvinists and the true internationalists.

The "Centre" all vow and declare that they are Marxists and internationalists, that they are for peace, for bringing every kind of "pressure" to bear upon the governments, for "demanding" in every way that their own government should "ascertain the will of the people for peace", that they are for all sorts of peace campaigns, for peace without annexations, etc., etc.—*and for peace with the social-chauvinists*. The "Centre" is for "unity", the Centre is opposed to a split.

The "Centre" is a realm of honeyed petty-bourgeois phrases, of internationalism in word and cowardly opportunism and fawning on the social-chauvinists in deed.

The crux of the matter is that the "Centre" is not convinced of the necessity for a revolution against one's own government; it does not preach revolution; it does not carry on a whole-hearted revolutionary struggle; and in order to evade such a struggle it resorts to the tritest ultra-"Marxist"-sounding *excuses*.

The social-chauvinists are our *class enemies*, they are *bourgeois* within the working-class movement. They represent a stratum, or groups, or sections of the working class which *objectively* have been bribed by the bourgeoisie (by better wages, positions of honour, etc.), and which help *their own* bourgeoisie to plunder and oppress small and weak peoples and to fight *for* the division of the capitalist spoils.

The "Centre" consists of routine-worshippers, eroded by the canker of legality, corrupted by the parliamentary atmosphere, etc., bureaucrats accustomed to snug positions and soft jobs. Historically and economically speaking, they are not a *separate* stratum but represent only a *transition* from a past phase of the working-class movement—the phase between 1871 and 1914, which gave much that is valuable to the proletariat, particularly in the indispensable art of slow, sustained and systematic organisational work on a large and very large scale—to a new *phase* that became *objectively* essential with the outbreak of the first imperialist world war, which inaugurated *the era of social revolution.*

The chief leader and spokesman of the "Centre" is Karl Kautsky, the most outstanding authority in the Second International (1889-1914), since August 1914 a model of utter bankruptcy as a Marxist, the embodiment of unheard-of spinelessness, and the most wretched vacillations and betrayals. This "Centrist" trend includes Kautsky, Haase, Ledebour and the so-called workers' or labour group[61] in the Reichstag; in France it includes Longuet, Pressemane and the so-called minoritaires[62] (Mensheviks) in general; in Britain, Philip Snowden, Ramsay MacDonald and many other leaders of the Independent Labour Party,[63] and some leaders of the British Socialist Party[64]; Morris Hillquit and many others in the United States; Turati, Trèves, Modigliani and others in Italy; Robert Grimm and others in Switzerland; Victor Adler and Co. in Austria; the party of the Organising Committee, Axelrod, Martov, Chkheidze, Tsereteli and others in Russia, and so forth.

Naturally, at times individuals unconsciously drift from the social-chauvinist to the "Centrist" position, and vice versa. Every Marxist knows that classes are distinct, even though individuals may move freely from one class to another; similarly, *trends* in political life are distinct in spite of the fact that individuals may change freely from one trend to another, and in spite of all attempts and efforts to *amalgamate* trends.

3) The third trend, that of the true internationalists, is best represented by the "Zimmerwald Left".[65] (We reprint as a supplement its manifesto of September 1915, to enable the reader to learn of the inception of this trend at first hand.)

Its distinctive feature is its complete break with both social-chauvinism and "Centrism", and its gallant revolutionary struggle against *its own* imperialist government and *its own* imperialist bourgeoisie. Its principle is: "Our chief enemy is at home." It wages a ruthless struggle against honeyed social-pacifist phrases (a social-pacifist is a socialist in word and a bourgeois pacifist in deed; bourgeois pacifists dream of an everlasting peace *without* the overthrow of the yoke and domination of capital) and against all *subterfuges* employed to deny the possibility, or the appropriateness, or the timeliness of a proletarian revolutionary struggle and of a proletarian socialist revolution *in connection* with the present war.

The most outstanding representative of this trend in Germany is the Spartacus group or the *Internationale* group,[66] to which Karl Liebknecht belongs. Karl Liebknecht is a most celebrated representative of this trend and of the *new*, and genuine, proletarian International.

Karl Liebknecht called upon the workers and soldiers of Germany to *turn their guns* against *their own* government. Karl Liebknecht did that openly from the rostrum of parliament (the Reichstag). He then went to a demonstration in Potsdamer Platz, one of the largest public squares in Berlin, with illegally printed leaflets proclaiming the slogan "Down with the Government!" He was arrested and sentenced to *hard labour*. He is now serving his term in a German convict prison, like *hundreds*, if not thousands, of other *true* German socialists who have been imprisoned for their anti-war activities.

Karl Liebknecht in his speeches and letters mercilessly attacked not only *his own* Plekhanovs and Potresovs (Scheidemanns, Legiens, Davids and Co.), *but also his own Centrists*, his own Chkheidzes and Tseretelis (Kautsky, Haase, Ledebour and Co.).

Karl Liebknecht and his friend Otto Rühle, two out of one hundred and ten deputies, violated discipline, destroyed the "unity" with the "Centre" and the chauvinists, and *went against all of them*. Liebknecht *alone* represents socialism, the proletarian cause, the proletarian revolution. *All* the rest of German Social-Democracy, to quote the apt words of Rosa Luxemburg (also a member and one of the leaders of the Spartacus group), is a *"stinking corpse"*.

Another group of true internationalists in Germany is that of the Bremen paper *Arbeiterpolitik*.

Closest to the internationalists in deed are: in France, Loriot and his friends (Bourderon and Merrheim have slid down to social-pacifism), as well as the Frenchman Henri Guilbeaux, who publishes in Geneva the journal *Demain*; in Britain, the newspaper *The Trade Unionist*, and *some* of the members of the British Socialist Party and of the Independent Labour Party (for instance, Russel Williams, who openly called for a break with the leaders who have *betrayed* socialism), the Scottish socialist school-teacher *MacLean,* who was sentenced to *hard labour* by the bourgeois government of Britain for his revolutionary fight against the war, and hundreds of British socialists who are in jail for the same offence. They, and they alone, are internationalists *in deed.* In the United States, the Socialist Labour Party and those within the opportunist Socialist Party who in January 1917 began publication of the paper *The Internationalist*; in Holland, the Party of the "Tribunists"[67] which publishes the paper *De Tribune* (Pannekoek, Herman Gorter, Wijnkoop, and Henriette Roland-Holst, who, although Centrist at Zimmerwald, has now joined our ranks); in Sweden, the Party of the Young, or the Left,[68] led by Lindhagen, Ture Nerman, Carleson, Ström and Z. Höglund, who at Zimmerwald was personally active in the organisation of the "Zimmerwald Left", and who is now in prison for his revolutionary fight against the war; in Denmark, Trier and his friends who have left the now purely *bourgeois* "Social-Democratic" Party of Denmark, headed by the *Minister* Stauning; in Bulgaria, the "Tesnyaki"[69]; in Italy, the nearest are Constantino Lazzari, secretary of the party, and Serrati, editor of the central organ, *Avanti!*; in Poland, Radek, Hanecki and other leaders of the Social-Democrats united under the "Regional Executive", and Rosa Luxemburg, Tyszka and other leaders of the Social-Democrats united under the "Chief Executive"; in Switzerland, those of the Left who drew up the argument for the "referendum" (January 1917) in order to fight the social-chauvinists and the "Centre" in *their own* country and who at the Zurich Cantonal Socialist Convention, held at Töss on February 11, 1917, moved a consistently revolutionary resolution against the war; in Austria, the young Left-wing friends of Friedrich Adler, who acted partly through the Karl Marx Club in Vienna, now closed by the arch-reactionary Austrian Government, which is ruining Adler's life for his heroic though ill-considered shooting at a minister, and so on.

It is not a question of shades of opinion, which certainly exist even among the Lefts. It is a question of *trend*. The thing is that it is not easy to be an internationalist in deed during a terrible imperialist war. Such people are few; but it is on such people *alone* that the future of socialism depends; they *alone* are *the leaders of the people,* and not their corrupters.

The distinction between the reformists and the revolutionaries, among the Social-Democrats, and socialists generally, was objectively bound to undergo a change under the conditions of the imperialist war. Those who confine themselves to "demanding" that the bourgeois governments should conclude peace or "ascertain the will of the peoples for peace", etc., are *actually* slipping into reforms. For, objectively, *the problem of the war* can be solved only in a *revolutionary way*.

There is no possibility of this war ending in a democratic, non-coercive peace or of the people being relieved of the burden of *billions* paid in interest to the capitalists, who have made fortunes out of the war, except through a revolution of the proletariat.

The most varied reforms can and must be demanded of the bourgeois governments, but one cannot, without sinking to Manilovism and reformism, demand that people and classes entangled by the thousands of threads of imperialist capital should *tear* those threads. And unless they are torn, all talk of a war against war is idle and deceitful prattle.

The "Kautskyites", the "Centre", are revolutionaries in word and reformists in deed, they are internationalists in word and accomplices of the social-chauvinists in deed.

First published September 1917   Vol. 24, pp. 74-80
as a pamphlet by Priboi Publishers
Signed: *N. Lenin*

"DISGRACE" AS THE CAPITALISTS
AND THE PROLETARIANS UNDERSTAND IT

Today's *Yedinstvo*[70] prints on its front page in bold type a proclamation signed by Plekhanov, Deutsch, and Zasulich. We read:

> "Every nation has a right freely to determine its own destiny. Wilhelm of Germany and Karl of Austria will never agree to this. In waging war against them, we are defending our own freedom, as well as the freedom of others. Russia cannot betray her Allies. That would bring disgrace upon her."

That is how all capitalists argue. To them non-observance of treaties *between* capitalists is a disgrace, just as to monarchs non-observance of treaties between monarchs is a disgrace.

What about the workers? Do they regard non-observance of treaties concluded by monarchs and capitalists a disgrace?

Of course not! Class-conscious workers are *for* scrapping *all* such treaties, they are for recognising only such agreements *between the workers and soldiers of all* countries as would benefit the people, i.e., not the capitalists, but the workers and poor peasants.

The workers of the world *have* a treaty of their own, namely, the Basle Manifesto of 1912[71] (signed, among others, by Plekhanov and betrayed by him). This workers' "treaty" calls it a "crime" for workers of different countries to shoot at each other for the sake of the capitalists' profits.

The writers in *Yedinstvo* argue like capitalists (so do *Rech*[72] and others), and not like workers.

It is quite true that neither the German monarch nor the Austrian will agree to freedom for every nation, as both these monarchs are crowned brigands, and so was Nicholas II. Nor, for one thing, are the English, Italian, and other monarchs (the "Allies" of Nicholas II) any better. To forget this is to become a monarchist or a defender of the monarchists.

Secondly, the *un*crowned brigands, i.e., the capitalists, have shown themselves in the present war to be no better than the monarchs. Has not American "democracy", i.e., the democratic capitalists, robbed the Philippines, and does it not rob Mexico?

The German Guchkovs and Milyukovs, if they were to take the place of Wilhelm II, would be brigands, *too*, no better than the British and Russian capitalists.

Third, will the Russian capitalists "agree" to "freedom" for nations which they themselves oppress: Armenia, Khiva, Ukraine, Finland?

By evading this question the *Yedinstvo* writers are, in effect, turning into defenders of "our own" capitalists in their predatory war with other capitalists.

The internationalist workers of the world stand for the overthrow of *all* capitalist governments, for the rejection of all agreements and understandings with any capitalists, for *universal peace* concluded by *the revolutionary workers of all* countries, a peace capable of giving real freedom to "every" nation.

Written on April 22 (May 5), 1917

Published in *Pravda* No. 39,   Vol. 24, pp. 220-21
May 6 (April 23), 1917

WAR AND REVOLUTION

(Excerpt from a Lecture)

On the question of America entering the war I shall say this. People argue that America is a democracy, America has the White House. I say: Slavery was abolished there half a century ago. The anti-slave war ended in 1865. Since then multimillonaires have mushroomed. They have the whole of America in their financial grip. They are making ready to subdue Mexico and will inevitably come to war with Japan over a carve-up of the Pacific. This war has been brewing for several decades. All literature speaks about it. America's real aim in entering the war is to prepare for this future war with Japan. The American people do enjoy considerable freedom and it is difficult to conceive them standing for compulsory military service, for the setting up of an army pursuing any aims of conquest—a struggle with Japan, for instance. The Americans have the example of Europe to show them what this leads to. The American capitalists have stepped into this war in order to have an excuse, behind a smoke-screen of lofty ideals championing the rights of small nations, for building up a strong standing army.

First published in *Pravda* No. 93,
April 23, 1929

Vol. 24, pp. 416-17

From THE SPEECH ON THE AGRARIAN QUESTION
AT THE FIRST ALL-RUSSIA CONGRESS
OF PEASANTS' DEPUTIES
MAY 22 (JUNE 4), 1917

The second step which our Party recommends is that every big economy, for example, every big landed estate, of which there are 30,000 in Russia, should be organised as soon as possible into a model farm for the *common* cultivation of the land jointly by agricultural labourers and scientifically trained agronomists, using the animals, implements, etc., of the landowner for that purpose. Without this *common* cultivation under the direction of the Soviets of Agricultural Labourers the land will not go entirely to the *working people*. To be sure, joint cultivation is a difficult business and it would be madness of course for anybody to imagine that joint cultivation of the land can be decreed from above and imposed on people, because the centuries-old habit of farming on one's own cannot suddenly disappear, and because money will be needed for it and adaptation to the new mode of life. If this advice, this view, on the common cultivation of the land with commonly owned animals and implements to be used to the best purpose jointly with agronomists—if this advice were the invention of individual political parties, the case would be a bad one, because changes are not made in the life of a people on the advice of a party, because tens of millions of people do not make a revolution on the advice of a party, and such a change would be much more of a revolution than the overthrow of the weak-minded Nicholas Romanov. I repeat, tens of millions of people will not make a revolution to order, but will do so when driven to it by dire need, when their position is an impossible one, when the joint pressure and determination of tens of millions of people break down the old barriers and are actually capable of creating a new way of life. When we advise such a measure, and advise caution in the handling of it, saying that it is becoming necessary, we are not drawing that conclusion from our programme, from our socialist doctrine alone, but because we, as socialists, have come to this conclusion by studying the life of the West-European nations. We know that there have been many revolutions over there and that they have established democratic republics; we know that in America in 1865 the slave-owners were defeated and hundreds of millions of dessiatines of land were distributed among the peasantry for nothing or next to nothing, and nevertheless capitalism dominates there more than anywhere else and oppresses the mass of the working people as badly as, if not worse than, in other countries. This is the socialist teaching, this is our study of other nations that firmly convinces us that without the common cultivation of the land by agricultural labourers using the best machinery and guided by scientifically trained agronomists there is no escape from the yoke of capitalism. But if we were to be guided only by the experience of the West-European countries it would be very bad for Russia, because the Russian people in the mass are only capable of taking a serious step along that new path when the direst need arises. And we say to you: the time has now come when that dire need for the entire Russian people is knocking at the door. The dire need I speak of is precisely this—we cannot continue farming in the old way. If we continue as before on our small isolated farms, albeit as free citizens on free soil, we are still faced with imminent ruin, for the debacle is drawing nearer day by day, hour by hour. Everyone is talking about it; it is a grim fact, due not to the malice of individuals but to the world war of conquest, to capitalism.

Published May 25, 1917   Vol. 24, pp. 502-04
in *Izvestia* of the All-Russia
Council of Peasants' Deputies
No. 14; and in December 1917
in the pamphlet *Material on the
Agrarian Question,* Priboi
Publishers

CLOSE TO THE TRUTH

Speaking at the Central Executive Committee meeting on the evening of July 4, Citizen Chaikovsky came surprisingly close to the truth.

He objected to the Soviet taking power and, among other things, advanced this what we might call "decisive" argument: we must carry on the war but cannot do it without money, and the British and Americans won't give any money if power is in the hands of "socialists"; they will only give money if the Cadets participate in the government.

That is close to the truth.

It is impossible to participate in the imperialist war without "participating" in the capitalist business of subjugating the people with loans from the capitalist gentlemen.

In order to really oppose the imperialist war, we must sever *all* ties that fetter people and bind them to capital. The workers and peasants must fearlessly take over the supervision of the banks and production and the regulation of production.

We, too, think that the British and Americans will give no money unless they have a guarantee from the Cadets. The alternative is: either serve the Cadets, serve capital, pile up imperialist loans (and put up with the fitting title of *imperialist* democrats instead of claiming to be "revolutionary" democrats); or break with the Cadets, break with the capitalists, break with imperialism, and become real revolutionaries on war issues as well.

Chaikovsky came close to the truth.

Written July 5 (18), 1917

Published in *Listok "Pravdy"*,   Vol. 25, p. 163
July 19 (6), 1917

THE IMPENDING CATASTROPHE
AND HOW TO COMBAT IT
(Excerpt)

The advantages accruing to the whole people from nationalisation of the banks—*not* to the workers especially (for the workers have little to do with banks) but to the mass of peasants and small industrialists—would be enormous. The saving in labour would be gigantic, and, assuming that the state would retain the former number of bank employees, nationalisation would be a highly important step towards making the use of the banks universal, towards increasing the number of their branches, putting their operations within easier reach, etc., etc. The availability of credit on easy terms for the *small* owners, for the peasants, would increase immensely. As to the state, it would for the first time be in a position first to *review* all the chief monetary operations, which would be unconcealed, then to *control* them, then to *regulate* economic life, and finally to *obtain* millions and billions for major state transactions, without paying the capitalist gentlemen sky-high "commissions" for their "services". That is the reason—and the only reason—why all the capitalists, all the bourgeois professors, all the bourgeoisie, and all the Plekhanovs, Potresovs and Co., who serve them, are prepared to fight tooth and nail against nationalisation of the banks and invent thousands of excuses to prevent the adoption of this very easy and very pressing measure, although *even* from the standpoint of the "defence" of the country, i.e., from the military standpoint, this measure would provide a gigantic advantage and would tremendously enhance the "military might" of the country.

The following objection might be raised: why do such advanced states as Germany and the U.S.A. "regulate economic life" so magnificently without even thinking of nationalising the banks?

Because, we reply, *both* these states are not merely capitalist, but also imperialist states, although one of them is a monarchy and the other a republic. As such, they carry out the reforms they need by reactionary-bureaucratic methods, whereas we are speaking here of revolutionary-democratic methods.

This "little difference" is of major importance. In most cases it is "not the custom" to think of it. The term "revolutionary democracy" has become with us (especially among the Socialist-Revolutionaries and Mensheviks) almost a conventional phrase, like the expression "thank God", which is also used by people who are not so ignorant as to believe in God; or like the expression "honourable citizen", which is sometimes used even in addressing staff members of *Dyen* or *Yedinstvo*, although nearly everybody guesses that these newspapers have been founded and are maintained by the capitalists in the interests of the capitalists, and that there is therefore very little "honourable" about the pseudo-socialists contributing to these newspapers.

If we do not employ the phrase "revolutionary democracy" as a stereotyped ceremonial phrase, as a conventional epithet, but *reflect* on its meaning, we find that to be a democrat means reckoning in reality with the interests of the majority of the people and not the minority, and that to be a revolutionary means destroying everything harmful and obsolete in the most resolute and ruthless manner.

Neither in America nor in Germany, as far as we know, is any claim laid by either the government or the ruling classes to the name "revolutionary democrats", to which our Socialist-Revolutionaries and Mensheviks lay claim (and which they prostitute).

In Germany there are only *four* very large private banks of national importance. In America there are only *two*. It is easier, more convenient, more profitable for the financial magnates of those banks to unite privately, surreptitiously, in a reactionary and not a revolutionary way, in a bureaucratic and not a democratic way, bribing government officials (this is the general rule both in America *and in Germany*), and preserving the private character of the banks in order to preserve secrecy of operations, to milk the state of millions upon millions in "superprofits", and to make financial frauds possible.

Both America and Germany "regulate economic life" in such a way as to create conditions of *war-time penal servitude* for the workers (and partly for the peasants) and a *paradise* for the bankers and capitalists. Their regulation consists in "squeezing" the workers to the point of starvation, while the capitalists are guaranteed (surreptitiously, in a reactionary-bureaucratic fashion) profits *higher* than before the war.

Published at the end
of October 1917 in pamphlet
form by Priboi Publishers

Vol. 25, pp. 332-34

THE STATE AND REVOLUTION
(Excerpts)

CHAPTER I
CLASS SOCIETY AND THE STATE

2. Special Bodies of Armed Men, Prisons, etc.

Engels continues:

"As distinct from the old gentile [tribal or clan] order, the state, first, divides its subjects *according to territory. . . .*"

This division seems "natural" to us, but it cost a prolonged struggle against the old organisation according to generations or tribes.

"The second distinguishing feature is the establishment of a *public power* which no longer directly coincides with the population organising itself as an armed force. This special, public power is necessary because a self-acting armed organisation of the population has become impossible since the split into classes. . . . This public power exists in every state; it consists not merely of armed men but also of material adjuncts, prisons, and institutions of coercion of all kinds, of which gentile [clan] society knew nothing. . . ."

Engels elucidates the concept of the "power" which is called the state, a power which arose from society but places itself above it and alienates itself more and more from it. What does this power mainly consist of? It consists of special bodies of armed men having prisons, etc., at their command.

We are justified in speaking of special bodies of armed men, because the public power which is an attribute of every state "does not directly coincide" with the armed population, with its "self-acting armed organisation".

Like all great revolutionary thinkers, Engels tries to draw the attention of the class-conscious workers to what prevailing philistinism regards as least worthy of attention, as the most habitual thing, hallowed by prejudices that are not only deep-rooted but, one might say, petrified. A standing army and police are the chief instruments of state power. But how can it be otherwise?

From the viewpoint of the vast majority of Europeans of the end of the nineteenth century whom Engels was addressing, and who had not gone through or closely observed a single great revolution, it could not have been otherwise. They could not understand at all what a "self-acting armed organisation of the population" was. When asked why it became necessary to have special bodies of armed men placed above society and alienating themselves from it (police and a standing army), the West-European and Russian philistines are inclined to utter a few phrases borrowed from Spencer or Mikhailovsky, to refer to the growing complexity of social life, the differentiation of functions, and so on.

Such a reference seems "scientific", and effectively lulls the ordinary person to sleep by obscuring the important and basic fact, namely, the split of society into irreconcilably antagonistic classes.

Were it not for this split, the "self-acting armed organisation of the population" would differ from the primitive organisation of a stick-wielding herd of monkeys, or of primitive men, or of men united in clans, by its complexity, its high technical level, and so on. But such an organisation would still be possible.

It is impossible because civilised society is split into antagonistic, and, moreover, irreconcilably antagonistic, classes, whose "self-acting" arming would lead to an armed struggle between them. A state arises, a special power is created, special bodies of armed men, and every revolution, by destroying the state apparatus, lays bare the class struggle and clearly shows how the ruling class strives to restore the special bodies of armed men which serve *it*, and how the oppressed class strives to create a new organisation of this kind, capable of serving the exploited instead of the exploiters.

In the above argument, Engels raises theoretically the very same question which every great revolution raises before us in practice, palpably and, what is more, on a scale of mass action, namely, the question of the relationship between "special" bodies of armed men and the "self-acting armed organisation of the population". We shall see how this question is specifically illustrated by the experience of the European and Russian revolutions.

But to return to Engels's exposition.

He points out that sometimes—in certain parts of North America, for example—this public power is weak (he has in mind a rare exception in capitalist society, and those parts of North America in its pre-imperialist days where the free colonist predominated), but that, generally speaking, it grows stronger:

> "It [the public power] grows stronger, however, in proportion as class antagonisms within the state become more acute, and as adjacent states become larger and more populous. We have only to look at our present-day Europe, where class struggle and rivalry in conquest have tuned up the public power to such a pitch that it threatens to swallow the whole of society and even the state."

This was written not later than the early nineties of the last century, Engels's last preface being dated June 16, 1891. The turn towards imperialism—meaning the complete domination of the trusts, the omnipotence of the big banks, a grand-scale colonial policy, and so forth—was only just beginning in France, and was even weaker in North America and in Germany. Since then "rivalry in conquest" has taken a gigantic stride, all the more because by the beginning of the second decade of the twentieth century the world had been completely divided up among these "rivals in conquest", i.e., among the predatory Great Powers. Since then, military and naval armaments have grown fantastically and the predatory war of 1914-17 for the domination of the world by Britain or Germany, for the division of the spoils, has brought the "swallowing" of all the forces of society by the rapacious state power close to complete catastrophe.

Engels could, as early as 1891, point to "rivalry in conquest" as one of the most important distinguishing features of the foreign policy of the Great Powers, while the social-chauvinist scoundrels have ever since 1914, when this rivalry, many times intensified, gave rise to an imperialist war, been covering up the defence of the predatory interests of "their own" bourgeoisie with phrases about "defence of the fatherland", "defence of the republic and the revolution", etc.!

CHAPTER III

THE STATE AND REVOLUTION. EXPERIENCE OF THE
PARIS COMMUNE OF 1871. MARX'S ANALYSIS

1. What Made the Communards' Attempt Heroic?

It is well known that in the autumn of 1870, a few months before the Commune, Marx warned the Paris workers that any attempt to overthrow the government would be the folly of despair. But when, in March 1871, a decisive battle was *forced* upon the workers and they accepted it, when the uprising had become a fact, Marx greeted the proletarian revolution with the greatest enthusiasm, in spite of unfavourable auguries. Marx did not persist in the pedantic attitude of condemning an "untimely" movement as did the ill-famed Russian renegade from Marxism, Plekhanov, who in November 1905 wrote encouragingly about the workers' and peasants' struggle, but after December 1905[73] cried, liberal fashion: "They should not have taken up arms."

Marx, however, was not only enthusiastic about the heroism of the Communards, who, as he expressed it, "stormed heaven". Although the mass revolutionary movement did not achieve its aim, he regarded it as a historic experience of enormous importance, as a certain advance of the world proletarian revolution, as a practical step that was more important than hundreds of programmes and arguments. Marx endeavoured to analyse this experiment, to draw tactical lessons from it and re-examine his theory in the light of it.

The only "correction" Marx thought it necessary to make to the *Communist Manifesto* he made on the basis of the revolutionary experience of the Paris Communards.

The last preface to the new German edition of the *Communist Manifesto*, signed by both its authors, is dated June 24, 1872. In this preface the authors, Karl Marx and Frederick Engels, say that the programme of the *Communist Manifesto* "has in some details become out-of-date", and they go on to say:

> "...*One thing especially was proved by the Commune, viz., that 'the working class cannot simply lay hold of the ready-made state machinery and wield it for its own purposes'....*"

The authors took the words that are in single quotation marks in this passage from Marx's book, *The Civil War in France*.

Thus, Marx and Engels regarded one principal and fundamental lesson of the Paris Commune as being of such enormous importance that they introduced it as an important correction into the *Communist Manifesto*.

Most characteristically, it is this important correction that has been distorted by the opportunists, and its meaning probably is not known to nine-tenths, if not ninety-nine-hundredths, of the readers of the *Communist Manifesto*. We shall deal with this distortion more fully farther on, in a chapter devoted specially to distortions. Here it will be sufficient to note that the current, vulgar "interpretation" of Marx's famous statement just quoted is that Marx here allegedly emphasises the idea of slow development in contradistinction to the seizure of power, and so on.

As a matter of fact, *the exact opposite is the case*. Marx's idea is that the working class must *break up*, *smash* the "ready-made state machinery", and not confine itself merely to laying hold of it.

On April 12, 1871, i.e., just at the time of the Commune, Marx wrote to Kugelmann:

"If you look up the last chapter of my *Eighteenth Brumaire*, you will find that I declare that the next attempt of the French Revolution will be no longer, as before, to transfer the bureaucratic-military machine from one hand to another, but to *smash* it [Marx's italics—the original is *zerbrechen*], and this is the precondition for every real people's revolution on the Continent. And this is what our heroic Party comrades in Paris are attempting." (*Neue Zeit*, Vol. XX, 1, 1901-02, p. 709.) (The letters of Marx to Kugelmann have appeared in Russian in no less than two editions, one of which I edited and supplied with a preface.*)

The words, "to smash the bureaucratic-military machine", briefly express the principal lesson of Marxism regarding the tasks of the proletariat during a revolution in relation to the state. And it is this lesson that has been not only completely ignored, but positively distorted by the prevailing, Kautskyite, "interpretation" of Marxism!

As for Marx's reference to *The Eighteenth Brumaire*, we have quoted the relevant passage in full above.

It is interesting to note, in particular, two points in the above-quoted argument of Marx. First, he restricts his conclusion to the Continent. This was understandable in 1871, when Britain was still the model of a purely capitalist country, but without a militarist clique and, to a considerable degree, without a bureaucracy. Marx therefore excluded Britain, where a revolution, even a people's revolution, then seemed possible, and indeed was possible, *without* the precondition of destroying the "ready-made state machinery".

Today, in 1917, at the time of the first great imperialist war, this restriction made by Marx is no longer valid. Both Britain and America, the biggest and the last representatives—in the whole world—of Anglo-Saxon "liberty", in the sense that they had no militarist cliques and bureaucracy, have completely sunk into the all-European filthy, bloody

---

* See Lenin, *Collected Works*, Vol. 12, pp. 104-12.—*Ed.*

morass of bureaucratic-military institutions which subordinate everything to themselves, and suppress everything. Today, in Britain and America, too, "the pre-condition for every real people's revolution" is the *smashing*, the *destruction* of the "ready-made state machinery" (made and brought up to "European", general imperialist, perfection in those countries in the years 1914-17).

Secondly, particular attention should be paid to Marx's extremely profound remark that the destruction of the bureaucratic-military state machine is "the pre-condition for every real *people's* revolution". This idea of a "people's" revolution seems strange coming from Marx, so that the Russian Plekhanovites and Mensheviks, those followers of Struve who wish to be regarded as Marxists, might possibly declare such an expression to be a "slip of the pen" on Marx's part. They have reduced Marxism to such a state of wretchedly liberal distortion that nothing exists for them beyond the antithesis between bourgeois revolution and proletarian revolution, and even this antithesis they interpret in an utterly lifeless way.

If we take the revolutions of the twentieth century as examples we shall, of course, have to admit that the Portuguese and the Turkish revolutions[74] are both bourgeois revolutions. Neither of them, however, is a "people's" revolution, since in neither does the mass of the people, their vast majority, come out actively, independently, with their own economic and political demands to any noticeable degree. By contrast, although the Russian bourgeois revolution of 1905-07[75] displayed no such "brilliant" successes as at times fell to the Portuguese and Turkish revolutions, it was undoubtedly a "real people's" revolution, since the mass of the people, their majority, the very lowest social groups, crushed by oppression and exploitation, rose independently and stamped on the entire course of the revolution the imprint of *their* own demands, *their* attempts to build in their own way a new society in place of the old society that was being destroyed.

In Europe, in 1871, the proletariat did not constitute the majority of the people in any country on the Continent. A "people's" revolution, one actually sweeping the majority into its stream, could be such only if it embraced both the proletariat and the peasants. These two classes then constituted the "people". These two classes are united by the fact that the "bureaucratic-military state machine" oppresses, crushes, exploits them. To *smash* this machine, *to break it up*, is truly in the interest of the "people", of their majority, of the workers and most of the peasants, is "the precondition" for a free alliance of the poor peasants and the proletarians, whereas without such an alliance democracy is unstable and socialist transformation is impossible.

As is well known, the Paris Commune was actually working its way toward such an alliance, although it did not reach its goal owing to a number of circumstances, internal and external.

Consequently, in speaking of a "real people's revolution", Marx, without in the least discounting the special features of the petty bourgeoisie (he spoke a great deal about them and often), took strict account of the actual balance of class forces in most of the continental countries of Europe in 1871. On the other hand, he stated that the "smashing" of the state machine was required by the interests of both the workers and the peasants, that it united them, that it placed before them the common task of removing the "parasite" and of replacing it by something new.

By what exactly?

Written August-September 1917

Published as a pamphlet in 1918
by Zhizn i Znaniye Publishers

Vol. 25, pp. 388-91,
413-17

DRAFT RESOLUTION
OF THE FOURTH (EXTRAORDINARY) ALL-RUSSIA CONGRESS OF SOVIETS ON WILSON'S MESSAGE[76]

The Congress expresses its gratitude to the American people, and primarily to the working and exploited classes of the United States of America, in connection with President Wilson's expression of his sympathy for the Russian people through the Congress of Soviets at a time when the Soviet Socialist Republic of Russia is passing through severe trials.

The Russian Soviet Republic, having become a neutral country, takes advantage of the message received from President Wilson to express to all peoples that are perishing and suffering from the horrors of the imperialist war its profound sympathy and firm conviction that the happy time is not far away when the working people of all bourgeois countries will throw off the yoke of capital and establish the socialist system of society, the only system able to ensure a durable and just peace and also culture and well-being for all working people.

Written on March 13 or 14, 1918

Published in *Pravda* No. 49,
March 15, 1918

Vol. 27, p. 171

From THE REPORT ON FOREIGN POLICY DELIVERED AT A JOINT MEETING OF THE ALL-RUSSIA CENTRAL EXECUTIVE COMMITTEE AND THE MOSCOW SOVIET MAY 14, 1918

The basic contradictions between the imperialist powers have led to such a merciless struggle that, while recognising its hopelessness, neither the one, nor the other group is in a position to extricate itself at will from the iron grip of this war. The war has brought out two main contradictions, which in their turn have determined the socialist Soviet Republic's present international position. The first is the battle being waged on the Western front between Germany and Britain, which has reached an extreme degree of ferocity. We have heard on more than one occasion representatives of the two belligerent groups promise and assure their own people and other peoples that all that is required is one more last effort for the enemy to be subdued, the fatherland defended and the interests of civilisation and of the war of liberation saved for all time. And the longer this terrible struggle drags on and the deeper the belligerent countries become involved, the further off is the way out of this interminable war. And it is the violence of this conflict that makes extremely difficult, well-nigh impossible, an alliance of the great imperialist powers against the Soviet Republic, which in the bare half-year of its existence has won the warm regard and the most whole-hearted sympathy of the class-conscious workers of the world.

The second contradiction determining Russia's international position is the rivalry between Japan and America. Over several decades the economic development of these countries has produced a vast amount of inflammable material which makes inevitable a desperate clash between them for domination of the Pacific Ocean and the surrounding territories. The entire diplomatic and economic history of the Far East leaves no room for doubt that under capitalist conditions it is impossible to avert the imminent conflict between Japan and America. This contradiction, temporarily concealed by the alliance of Japan and America against Germany, delays Japanese imperialism's attack on Russia, which was prepared for over a long period, which was a long time feeling its way, and which to a certain degree was started and is being supported by counter-revolutionary forces. The campaign which has been launched against the Soviet Republic (the landing at Vladivostok and the support of the Semyonov bands)[77] is being held up because it threatens to turn the hidden conflict between Japan and America into open war. It is quite likely, of course, and we must not forget that no matter how solid the imperialist groupings may appear to be, they can be broken up in a few days if the interests of sacred private property, the sacred rights of concessions, etc., demand it. It may well be that the tiniest spark will suffice to blow up the existing alignment of powers, and then the afore-mentioned contradictions will no longer protect us.

Newspaper report published
in *Pravda* Nos. 93 and 94,
May 15 and 16, 1918;
in *Izvestia* No. 95, May 15, 1918

Vol. 27, pp. 367-68

LETTER TO AMERICAN WORKERS[78]

Comrades! A Russian Bolshevik who took part in the 1905 revolution, and who lived in your country for many years afterwards, has offered to convey my letter to you. I have accepted his proposal all the more gladly because just at the present time the American revolutionary workers have to play an exceptionally important role as uncompromising enemies of American imperialism—the freshest, strongest and latest in joining in the world-wide slaughter of nations for the division of capitalist profits. At this very moment, the American multimillionaires, these modern slaveowners, have turned an exceptionally tragic page in the bloody history of bloody imperialism by giving their approval—whether direct or indirect, open or hypocritically concealed, makes no difference—to the armed expedition launched by the brutal Anglo-Japanese imperialists for the purpose of throttling the first socialist republic.

The history of modern, civilised America opened with one of those great, really liberating, really revolutionary wars of which there have been so few compared to the vast number of wars of conquest which, like the present imperialist war, were caused by squabbles among kings, landowners or capitalists over the division of usurped lands or ill-gotten gains. That was the war the American people waged against the British robbers who oppressed America and held her in colonial slavery, in the same way as these "civilised" bloodsuckers are still oppressing and holding in colonial slavery hundreds of millions of people in India, Egypt, and all parts of the world.

About 150 years have passed since then. Bourgeois civilisation has borne all its luxurious fruits. America has taken first place among the free and educated nations in level of development of the productive forces of collective human endeavour, in the utilisation of machinery and of all the wonders of modern engineering. At the same time, America has become one of the foremost countries in regard to the depth of the abyss which lies between the handful of arrogant multimillionaires who wallow in filth and luxury, and the millions of working people who constantly live on the verge of pauperism. The American people, who set the world an example in waging a revolutionary war against feudal slavery, now find themselves in the latest, capitalist stage of wage-slavery to a handful of multimillionaires, and find themselves playing the role of hired thugs who, for the benefit of wealthy scoundrels, throttled the Philippines in 1898 on the pretext of "liberating" them,[79] and are throttling the Russian Socialist Republic in 1918 on the pretext of "protecting" it from the Germans.

The four years of the imperialist slaughter of nations, however, have not passed in vain. The deception of the people by the scoundrels of both robber groups, the British and the German, has been utterly exposed by indisputable and obvious facts. The results of the four years of war have revealed the general law of capitalism as applied to war between robbers for the division of spoils: the richest and strongest profited and grabbed most, while the weakest were utterly robbed, tormented, crushed and strangled.

The British imperialist robbers were the strongest in number of "colonial slaves". The British capitalists have not lost an inch of "their" territory (i.e., territory they have grabbed over the centuries), but they have grabbed all the German colonies in Africa, they have grabbed Mesopotamia and Palestine, they have throttled Greece, and have begun to plunder Russia.

The German imperialist robbers were the strongest in organisation and discipline of "their" armies, but weaker in regard to colonies. They have lost all their colonies, but plundered half of Europe and throttled the largest number of small countries and weak nations. What a great war of "liberation" on both sides! How well the robbers of both groups, the Anglo-French and the German capitalists, together with their lackeys, the social-chauvinists, i.e., the socialists who went over to the side of *"their own"* bourgeoisie, have "defended their country"!

The American multimillionaires were, perhaps, richest of all, and geographically the most secure. They have profited more than all the rest. They have converted all, even the richest, countries into their tributaries. They have grabbed hundreds of billions of dollars. And every dollar is sullied with filth: the filth of the secret treaties between Britain and her "allies", between Germany and her vassals, treaties for the division of the spoils, treaties of mutual "aid" for oppressing the workers and persecuting the internationalist socialists. Every dollar is sullied with the filth of "profitable" war contracts, which in every country made the rich richer and the poor poorer. And every dollar is stained with blood—from that ocean of blood that has been shed by the ten million killed and twenty million maimed in the great, noble, liberating and holy war to decide whether the British or the German robbers are to get most of the spoils, whether the British or the German thugs are to be *foremost* in throttling the weak nations all over the world.

While the German robbers broke all records in war atrocities, the British have broken all records not only in the number of colonies they have grabbed, but also in the subtlety of their disgusting hypocrisy. This very day, the Anglo-French and American bourgeois newspapers are spreading, in millions and millions of copies, lies and slander about Russia, and are hypocritically justifying their predatory expedition against her on the plea that they want to "protect" Russia from the Germans!

It does not require many words to refute this despicable and hideous lie; it is sufficient to point to one well-known fact. In October 1917, after the Russian workers had overthrown their imperialist government, the Soviet government, the government of the revolutionary workers and peasants, openly proposed a just peace, a peace without annexations or indemnities, a peace that fully guaranteed equal rights to all nations—and it proposed such a peace to *all* the belligerent countries.[80]

It was the Anglo-French and the American bourgeoisie

who refused to accept our proposal; it was they who even refused to talk to us about a general peace! It was *they* who betrayed the interests of all nations; it was they who prolonged the imperialist slaughter!

It was they who, banking on the possibility of dragging Russia back into the imperialist war, refused to take part in the peace negotiations and thereby gave a free hand to the no less predatory German capitalists who imposed the annexationist and harsh Brest peace upon Russia![81]

It is difficult to imagine anything more disgusting than the hypocrisy with which the Anglo-French and American bourgeoisie are now "blaming" us *for* the Brest Peace Treaty. The very capitalists of those countries which could have turned the Brest negotiations into general negotiations for a general peace are now our "accusers"! The Anglo-French imperialist vultures, who have profited from the plunder of colonies and the slaughter of nations, have prolonged the war for nearly a whole year after Brest, and yet they "accuse" *us*, the Bolsheviks, who proposed a just peace to all countries, they accuse *us,* who tore up, published and exposed to public disgrace the secret, criminal treaties concluded between the ex-tsar and the Anglo-French capitalists.[82]

The workers of the whole world, no matter in what country they live, greet us, sympathise with us, applaud us for breaking the iron ring of imperialist ties, of sordid imperialist treaties, of imperialist chains—for breaking through to freedom, and making the heaviest sacrifices in doing so—for, as a socialist republic, although torn and plundered by the imperialists, keeping *out* of the imperialist war and raising the banner of peace, the banner of socialism for the whole world to see.

Small wonder that the international imperialist gang hates us for this, that it "accuses" us, that all the lackeys of the imperialists, including our Right Socialist-Revolutionaries and Mensheviks, also "accuse" us. The hatred these watchdogs of imperialism express for the Bolsheviks, and the sympathy of the class-conscious workers of the world, convince us more than ever of the justice of our cause.

A real socialist would not fail to understand that for the sake of achieving victory over the bourgeoisie, for the sake of power passing to the workers, for the sake of *starting* the world proletarian revolution, we *cannot* and must *not* hesitate to make the heaviest sacrifices, including the sacrifice of part of our territory, the sacrifice of heavy defeats at the hands of imperialism. A real socialist would have proved by *deeds* his willingness for "his" country to make the greatest sacrifice to give a real push forward to the cause of the socialist revolution.

For the sake of "their" cause, that is, for the sake of winning world hegemony, the imperialists of Britain and Germany have not hesitated to utterly ruin and throttle a whole number of countries, from Belgium and Serbia to Palestine and Mesopotamia. But must socialists wait with "their" cause, the cause of liberating the working people of the whole world from the yoke of capital, of winning universal and lasting peace, until a path without sacrifice is found? Must they fear to open the battle until an easy victory is "guaranteed"? Must they place the integrity and security of "their" bourgeois-created "fatherland" above the interests of the world socialist revolution? The scoundrels in the international socialist movement who think this way, those lackeys who grovel to bourgeois morality, thrice stand condemned.

The Anglo-French and American imperialist vultures "accuse" us of concluding an "agreement" with German imperialism. What hypocrites, what scoundrels they are to slander the workers' government while trembling because of the sympathy displayed towards us by the workers of "their own" countries! But their hypocrisy will be exposed. They pretend not to see the difference between an agreement entered into by "socialists" with the bourgeoisie (their own or foreign) *against the workers*, against the working people, and an agreement entered into *for the protection* of the workers who have defeated their bourgeoisie, with the bourgeoisie of one national colour *against the bourgeoisie* of another colour in order that the proletariat may take advantage of the antagonisms between the different groups of bourgeoisie.

In actual fact, every European sees this difference very well, and, as I shall show in a moment, the American people have had a particularly striking "illustration" of it in their own history. There are agreements and agreements, there are *fagots et fagots*, as the French say.

When in February 1918 the German imperialist vultures hurled their forces against unarmed, demobilised Russia, who had relied on the international solidarity of the proletariat before the world revolution had fully matured, I did not hesitate for a moment to enter into an "agreement" with the French monarchists. Captain Sadoul, a French army officer who, in words, sympathised with the Bolsheviks, but was in deeds a loyal and faithful servant of French imperialism, brought the French officer de Lubersac to see me. "I am a monarchist. My only aim is to secure the defeat of Germany," de Lubersac declared to me. "That goes without saying (*cela va sans dire*)," I replied. But this did not in the least prevent me from entering into an "agreement" with de Lubersac concerning certain services that French army officers, experts in explosives, were ready to render us by blowing up railway lines in order to hinder the German invasion. This is an example of an "agreement" of which every class-conscious worker will approve, an agreement in the interests of socialism. The French monarchist and I shook hands, although we knew that each of us would willingly hang his "partner". But for a time our interests coincided. Against the advancing rapacious Germans, *we*, in the interests of the Russian and the world socialist revolution, utilised the equally rapacious counter-interests of *other* imperialists. In this way we served the interests of the working class of Russia and of other countries, we strengthened the proletariat and weakened the bourgeoisie of the whole world, we resorted to the methods, most legitimate and essential in *every* war, of manoeuvre, stratagem, retreat, in anticipation of the moment when the rapidly maturing proletarian revolution in a number of advanced countries *completely matured*.

However much the Anglo-French and American imperialist sharks fume with rage, however much they slander us, no matter how many millions they spend on bribing the

Right Socialist-Revolutionary, Menshevik and other social-patriotic newspapers, *I shall not hesitate one second* to enter into a *similar* "agreement" with the German imperialist vultures if an attack upon Russia by Anglo-French troops calls for it. And I know perfectly well that my tactics will be approved by the class-conscious proletariat of Russia, Germany, France, Britain, America—in short, of the whole civilised world. Such tactics will ease the task of the socialist revolution, will hasten it, will weaken the international bourgeoisie, will strengthen the position of the working class which is defeating the bourgeoisie.

The American people resorted to these tactics long ago to the advantage of their revolution. When they waged their great war of liberation against the British oppressors, they had also against them the French and the Spanish oppressors who owned a part of what is now the United States of North America. In their arduous war for freedom, the American people also entered into "agreements" with some oppressors against others for the purpose of weakening the oppressors and strengthening those who were fighting in a revolutionary manner against oppression, for the purpose of serving the interests of the oppressed *people*. The American people took advantage of the strife between the French, the Spanish and the British; sometimes they even fought side by side with the forces of the French and Spanish oppressors against the British oppressors; first they defeated the British and then freed themselves (partly by ransom) from the French and the Spanish.

Historical action is not the pavement of Nevsky Prospekt, said the great Russian revolutionary Chernyshevsky.[83] A revolutionary would not "agree" to a proletarian revolution only "on the condition" that it proceeds easily and smoothly, that there is, from the outset, combined action on the part of the proletarians of different countries, that there are sure guarantees against defeats, that the road of the revolution is broad, free and straight, that it will not be necessary during the march to victory to sustain the heaviest casualties, to "bide one's time in a besieged fortress", or to make one's way along extremely narrow, impassable, winding and dangerous mountain tracks. Such a person is no revolutionary, he has not freed himself from the pedant-ry of the bourgeois intellectuals; such a person will be found constantly slipping into the camp of the counter-revolutionary bourgeoisie, like our Right Socialist-Revolu-tionaries, Mensheviks and even (although more rarely) Left Socialist-Revolutionaries.

Echoing the bourgeoisie, these gentlemen like to blame us for the "chaos" of the revolution, for the "destruction" of industry, for the unemployment and the food shortage. How hypocritical these accusations are, coming from those who welcomed and supported the imperialist war, or who entered into an "agreement" with Kerensky who continued this war! It is this imperialist war that is the cause of all these misfortunes. The revolution engendered by the war cannot avoid the terrible difficulties and suffering bequeathed it by the prolonged, ruinous, reactionary slaughter of the nations. To blame us for the "destruction" of industry, or for the "terror", is either hypocrisy or dull-witted pedantry; it reveals an inability to understand the basic conditions of the fierce class struggle, raised to the highest degree of intensity that is called revolution.

Even when "accusers" of this type do "recognise" the class struggle, they limit themselves to verbal recognition; actually, they constantly slip into the philistine utopia of class "agreement" and "collaboration"; for in revolutionary epochs the class struggle has always, inevitably, and in every country, assumed the form of *civil war*, and civil war is inconceivable without the severest destruction, terror and the restriction of formal democracy in the interests of this war. Only unctuous parsons—whether Christian or "secular" in the persons of parlour, parliamentary social-ists—cannot see, understand and feel this necessity. Only a lifeless "man in the muffler"[84] can shun the revolution for this reason instead of plunging into battle with the utmost ardour and determination at a time when history demands that the greatest problems of humanity be solved by struggle and war.

The American people have a revolutionary tradition which has been adopted by the best representatives of the American proletariat, who have repeatedly expressed their complete solidarity with us Bolsheviks. That tradition is the war of liberation against the British in the eighteenth century and the Civil War in the nineteenth century. In some respects, if we only take into consideration the "destruction" of some branches of industry and of the national economy, America in 1870 was *behind* 1860. But what a pedant, what an idiot would anyone be to deny on *these* grounds the immense, world-historic, progressive and revolutionary significance of the American Civil War of 1863-65!

The representatives of the bourgeoisie understand that for the sake of overthrowing Negro slavery, of overthrowing the rule of the slaveowners, it was worth letting the country go through long years of civil war, through the abysmal ruin, destruction and terror that accompany every war. But now, when we are confronted with the vastly greater task of overthrowing capitalist *wage*-slavery, of overthrowing the rule of the bourgeoisie—now, the representatives and defenders of the bourgeoisie, and also the reformist socialists who have been frightened by the bourgeoisie and are shunning the revolution, cannot and do not want to understand that civil war is necessary and legitimate.

The American workers will not follow the bourgeoisie. They will be with us, for civil war against the bourgeoisie. The whole history of the world and of the American labour movement strengthens my conviction that this is so. I also recall the words of one of the most beloved leaders of the American proletariat, Eugene Debs, who wrote in the *Appeal to Reason*, I believe towards the end of 1915, in the article "What Shall I Fight For" (I quoted this article at the beginning of 1916 at a public meeting of workers in Berne, Switzerland)*—that he, Debs, would rather be shot than vote credits for the present criminal and reactionary war; that he, Debs, knows of only one holy and, from the proletarian standpoint, legitimate war, namely: the war against the capitalists, the war to liberate mankind from wage-slavery.

---

* See. pp. 206-07.—*Ed.*

I am not surprised that Wilson, the head of the American multimillionaires and servant of the capitalist sharks, has thrown Debs into prison. Let the bourgeoisie be brutal to the true internationalists, to the true representatives of the revolutionary proletariat! The more fierce and brutal they are, the nearer the day of the victorious proletarian revolution.

We are blamed for the destruction caused by our revolution.... Who are the accusers? The hangers-on of the bourgeoisie, of that very bourgeoisie who, during the four years of the imperialist war, have destroyed almost the whole of European culture and have reduced Europe to barbarism, brutality and starvation. These bourgeoisie now demand we should not make a revolution on these ruins, amidst this wreckage of culture, amidst the wreckage and ruins created by the war, nor with the people who have been brutalised by the war. How humane and righteous the bourgeoisie are!

Their servants accuse us of resorting to terror.... The British bourgeoisie have forgotten their 1649, the French bourgeoisie have forgotten their 1793. Terror was just and legitimate when the bourgeoisie resorted to it for their own benefit against feudalism. Terror became monstrous and criminal when the workers and poor peasants dared to use it against the bourgeoisie! Terror was just and legitimate when used for the purpose of substituting one exploiting minority for another exploiting minority. Terror became monstrous and criminal when it began to be used for the purpose of overthrowing *every* exploiting minority, to be used in the interests of the vast actual majority, in the interests of the proletariat and semi-proletariat, the working class and the poor peasants!

The international imperialist bourgeoisie have slaughtered ten million men and maimed twenty million in "their" war, the war to decide whether the British or the German vultures are to rule the world.

If *our* war, the war of the oppressed and exploited against the oppressors and the exploiters, results in half a million or a million casualties in all countries, the bourgeoisie will say that the former casualties are justified, while the latter are criminal.

The proletariat will have something entirely different to say.

Now, amidst the horrors of the imperialist war, the proletariat is receiving a most vivid and striking illustration of the great truth taught by all revolutions and bequeathed to the workers by their best teachers, the founders of modern socialism. This truth is that no revolution can be successful unless *the resistance of the exploiters is crushed*. When we, the workers and toiling peasants, captured state power, it became our duty to crush the resistance of the exploiters. We are proud we have been doing this. We regret we are not doing it with sufficient firmness and determination.

We know that fierce resistance to the socialist revolution on the part of the bourgeoisie is inevitable in all countries, and that this resistance will *grow* with the growth of this revolution. The proletariat will crush this resistance; during the struggle against the resisting bourgeoisie it will finally mature for victory and for power.

Let the corrupt bourgeois press shout to the whole world about every mistake our revolution makes. We are not daunted by our mistakes. People have not become saints because the revolution has begun. The toiling classes who for centuries have been oppressed, downtrodden and forcibly held in the vice of poverty, brutality and ignorance cannot avoid mistakes when making a revolution. And, as I pointed out once before, the corpse of bourgeois society cannot be nailed in a coffin and buried.* The corpse of capitalism is decaying and disintegrating in our midst, polluting the air and poisoning our lives, enmeshing that which is new, fresh, young and virile in thousands of threads and bonds of that which is old, moribund and decaying.

For every hundred mistakes we commit, and which the bourgeoisie and their lackeys (including our own Mensheviks and Right Socialist-Revolutionaries) shout about to the

---

* See Lenin, *Collected Works*, Vol. 27, p. 434.—*Ed.*

whole world, 10,000 great and heroic deeds are performed, greater and more heroic because they are simple and inconspicuous amidst the everyday life of a factory district or a remote village, performed by people who are not accustomed (and have no opportunity) to shout to the whole world about their successes.

But even if the contrary were true—although I know such an assumption is wrong—even if we committed 10,000 mistakes for every 100 correct actions we performed, even in that case our revolution would be great and invincible, and *so it will be in the eyes of world history*, because, *for the first time*, not the minority, not the rich alone, not the educated alone, but the real people, the vast majority of the working people, are *themselves* building a new life, are *by their own experience* solving the most difficult problems of socialist organisation.

Every mistake committed in the course of such work, in the course of this most conscientious and earnest work of tens of millions of simple workers and peasants in reorganising their whole life, every such mistake is worth thousands and millions of "flawless" successes achieved by the exploiting minority—successes in swindling and duping the working people. For only *through* such mistakes will the workers and peasants *learn* to build the new life, learn to do *without* capitalists; only in this way will they hack a path for themselves—through thousands of obstacles—to victorious socialism.

Mistakes are being committed in the course of their revolutionary work by our peasants, who at one stroke, in one night, October 25-26 (old style), 1917, entirely abolished the private ownership of land, and are now, month after month, overcoming tremendous difficulties and correcting their mistakes themselves, solving in a practical way the most difficult tasks of organising new conditions of economic life, of fighting the kulaks, providing land for the *working people* (and not for the rich), and of changing to *communist* large-scale agriculture.

Mistakes are being committed in the course of their revolutionary work by our workers, who have already, after a few months, nationalised almost all the biggest factories and plants, and are learning by hard, everyday work the new task of managing whole branches of industry, are setting the nationalised enterprises going, overcoming the powerful resistance of inertia, petty-bourgeois mentality and selfishness, and, brick by brick, are laying the foundation of *new* social ties, of a *new* labour discipline, of a *new* influence of the workers' trade unions over their members.

Mistakes are committed in the course of their revolutionary work by our Soviets, which were created as far back as 1905 by a mighty upsurge of the people. The Soviets of Workers and Peasants are a new *type* of state, a new and higher *type* of democracy, a form of the proletarian dictatorship, a means of administering the state *without* the bourgeoisie and *against* the bourgeoisie. For the first time democracy is here serving the people, the working people, and has ceased to be democracy for the rich as it still is in all bourgeois republics, even the most democratic. For the first time, the people are grappling, on a scale involving one hundred million, with the problem of implementing the dictatorship of the proletariat and semi-proletariat—a problem which, if not solved, makes socialism *out of the question.*

Let the pedants, or the people whose minds are incurably stuffed with bourgeois-democratic or parliamentary prejudices, shake their heads in perplexity about our Soviets, about the absence of direct elections, for example. These people have forgotten nothing and have learned nothing during the period of the great upheavals of 1914-18. The combination of the proletarian dictatorship with the new democracy for the working people—of civil war with the widest participation of the people in politics—such a combination cannot be brought about at one stroke, nor does it fit in with the outworn modes of routine parliamentary democracy. The contours of a new world, the world of socialism, are rising before us in the shape of the Soviet Republic. It is not surprising that this world does not come into being ready-made, does not spring forth like Minerva from the head of Jupiter.

The old bourgeois-democratic constitutions waxed eloquent about formal equality and right of assembly; but our proletarian and peasant Soviet Constitution casts aside the hypocrisy of formal equality. When the bourgeois republicans overturned thrones they did not worry about formal equality between monarchists and republicans. When it is a matter of overthrowing the bourgeoisie, only traitors or idiots can demand formal equality of rights for the bourgeoisie. "Freedom of assembly" for workers and peasants is not worth a farthing when the best buildings belong to the bourgeoisie. Our Soviets have *confiscated* all the good buildings in town and country from the rich and have *transferred all* of them to the workers and peasants for *their* unions and meetings. This is *our* freedom of assembly—for the working people! This is the meaning and content of our Soviet, our socialist Constitution!

That is why we are all so firmly convinced that no matter what misfortunes may still be in store for it, our Republic of Soviets is *invincible*.

It is invincible because every blow struck by frenzied imperialism, every defeat the international bourgeoisie inflict on us, rouses more and more sections of the workers and peasants to the struggle, teaches them at the cost of enormous sacrifice, steels them and engenders new heroism on a mass scale.

We know that help from you will probably not come soon, comrade American workers, for the revolution is developing in different countries in different forms and at different tempos (and it cannot be otherwise). We know that although the European proletarian revolution has been maturing very rapidly lately, it may, after all, not flare up within the next few weeks. We are banking on the inevitability of the world revolution, but this does not mean that we are such fools as to bank on the revolution inevitably coming on a *definite* and early date. We have seen two great revolutions in our country, 1905 and 1917, and we know revolutions are not made to order, or by agreement. We know that circumstances brought *our* Russian detachment of the socialist proletariat to the fore not because of our merits, but because of the exceptional backwardness of Russia, and that *before* the world revolution breaks out a number of separate revolutions may be defeated.

In spite of this, we are firmly convinced that we are invincible, because the spirit of mankind will not be broken by the imperialist slaughter. Mankind will vanquish it. And the first country to *break* the convict chains of the imperialist war was *our* country. We sustained enormously heavy casualties in the struggle to break these chains, but we *broke* them. We are *free from* imperialist dependence, we have raised the banner of struggle for the complete overthrow of imperialism for the whole world to see.

We are now, as it were, in a besieged fortress, waiting for the other detachments of the world socialist revolution to come to our relief. These detachments *exist*, they are *more numerous* than ours, they are maturing, growing, gaining more strength the longer the brutalities of imperialism continue. The workers are breaking away from their social-traitors—the Gomperses, Hendersons, Renaudels, Scheidemanns and Renners. Slowly but surely the workers are adopting communist, Bolshevik tactics and are marching towards the proletarian revolution, which alone is capable of saving dying culture and dying mankind.

In short, we are invincible, because the world proletarian revolution is invincible.

N. Lenin

August 20, 1918

Pravda No. 178,   Vol. 28, pp. 62-75
August 22, 1918

From A SPEECH AT A MEETING
AT THE FORMER MICHELSON WORKS
AUGUST 30, 1918

What government replaced the tsar? The Guchkov-Milyukov government, which set about convening a Constituent Assembly in Russia.[85] What was behind these activities supposed to be in favour of the people liberated from their millennial oppression? It was that Guchkov and other champions were backed by a gang of capitalists pursuing their own imperialist ends. And when Kerensky, Chernov and Co. were in the saddle, this government, tottering and without any foundation, was only concerned with the vested interests of their friends, the bourgeoisie. Power in fact passed into the hands of the kulaks, and the working people got nothing. We find the same thing in other countries. Take America, the freest and most civilised country. There you have a democratic republic. But what do we find? The brazen rule of a handful, not even of millionaires, but multimillionaires, while the people are in slavery and servitude. Where is your much-vaunted equality and fraternity if the mills, factories, banks, and all the country's wealth belong to the capitalists, and side by side with the democratic republic you have feudal servitude for millions of workers and unrelieved destitution?

No, wherever "democrats" are in power, you have real, barefaced robbery. We know the true nature of the so-called democracies.

Izvestia No. 188,   Vol. 28, p. 90
September 1, 1918

We know very well what an immense workers' movement
has sprung up in other countries as well. We saw how
Gompers went to Italy and, with Entente money and the
help of all the Italian bourgeoisie and social-patriots, toured
every town in Italy calling upon the Italian workers to
carry on the imperialist war. We saw the Italian socialist
papers carry articles about this in which all that was left
was Gompers's name, after the censor had deleted everything else; or articles which jeered: "Gompers is banquet-
ing and tongue-wagging." And the bourgeois papers admitted Gompers was hissed everywhere. The bourgeois papers
wrote: "The Italian workers are behaving as if they would
allow only Lenin and Trotsky to tour Italy." During the
war the Italian Socialist Party has made tremendous strides
forward, that is, to the left. We know there have been too
many patriots among the workers in France; they were
told that Paris and French territory were in grave danger.
But there, too, the workers' attitude is changing. There
were cries of "Hurrah for the Socialist Republic!" at the
last congress,[86] when a letter was read about what the
Allies, the British and French imperialists, were doing. And
yesterday news was received that a meeting had been held
in Paris attended by two thousand metalworkers, which
hailed the Soviet Republic in Russia. We see that of the
three socialist parties in Great Britain, only one, the Independent Socialist Party, is not openly supporting the

Bolsheviks, whereas the British Socialist Party and the Socialist Labour Party of Scotland have definitely proclaimed their support for the Bolsheviks. Bolshevism is also beginning to spread in Britain. And the Spanish parties are hailing the Russian Bolsheviks at their congresses[87] although they had formerly sided with British and French imperialism and had had only one or two men on the outbreak of the war with even a remote conception of what internationalists were. Bolshevism has become the world-wide theory and tactics of the international proletariat! (*Applause.*) It has accomplished a thoroughgoing socialist revolution for all the world to see. To be for or against the Bolsheviks is actually the dividing line among socialists. As a result of what Bolshevism has done, a programme for the creation of a workers' state is the vital question of the day. Workers who had no idea of what was going on in Russia, because they only read the bourgeois papers which were full of lies and slander, began to realise, on seeing the workers' government winning one victory after another over its counter-revolutionaries, that our tactics and the revolutionary form of action of our workers' government was the only way out of this war. Last Wednesday there was a demonstration in Berlin, and the workers expressed their disgust with the Kaiser by trying to march past his palace; then they proceeded to the Russian Embassy to express their solidarity with the actions of the Russian Government.

Newspaper reports published
October 23, 1918 in *Pravda* No. 229
and *Izvestia* No. 231

Published in full in 1919   Vol. 28, pp. 116-17
in the book *All-Russia
Central Executive Committee,
Fifth Convocation. Verbatim
Report,* Moscow

From THE SPEECH ON THE INTERNATIONAL
SITUATION DELIVERED AT THE SIXTH
(EXTRAORDINARY) ALL-RUSSIA CONGRESS
OF SOVIETS OF WORKERS', PEASANTS',
COSSACKS' AND RED ARMY DEPUTIES
NOVEMBER 8, 1918

In recent months, and in recent weeks, the international situation has began to change sharply; now German imperialism is almost completely defeated. All designs on the Ukraine which the German imperialists fostered among their working people proved to be empty promises. It turned out that American imperialism was ready, and a blow was struck at Germany. A totally different situation has arisen. We have been under no illusions. After the October Revolution we were considerably weaker than imperialism and even now we are weaker than international imperialism. We must repeat this now so as not to deceive ourselves: following the October Revolution we were weaker and could not fight. Now we are weaker too and must do everything we can to avoid a clash with imperialism.

That we were able to survive a year after the October Revolution was due to the split of international imperialism into two predatory groups: Anglo-French-American on the one hand, and German on the other, which were locked in mortal combat, and which had no time for us. Neither group could muster large forces against us, which they would have done had they been in a position to do so. They were blinded by the bloodthirsty atmosphere of war. The material sacrifices required to carry on the war demanded the utmost concentration of their efforts. They had no time for us, not because by some miracle we were stronger than the imperialists—no, that would be nonsense—but only because international imperialism had split into two predatory groups which were at each other's throats. Only thanks to this the Soviet Republic was able to openly declare war on the imperialists of all countries, depriving them of their capital in the shape of foreign loans, slapping them in the face and openly emptying their plunder-laden pockets.

An end has come to the period of declarations which we then made over the correspondence started by the German imperialists, even though world imperialism could not tear into us as it should have done in line with its hostility and thirst for capitalist profits, which had been fantastically expanded by the war. Until the moment of the Anglo-American imperialists' victory over the other group they were fully occupied fighting among themselves, and so had no chance to launch a decisive campaign against the Soviet Republic. There is no longer a second group. Only one group of victors remains. This has completely altered our international position, and we must take this change into account. The facts show how this change bears on the development of the international situation. The workers' revolution is now winning in the defeated countries; everyone can clearly see what tremendous advances it has made. When we took power in October we were nothing more in Europe than a single spark. True, the sparks began to fly, and they flew from us. This is our greatest achievement, but even so, these were isolated sparks. Now most countries within the sphere of German-Austrian imperialism are aflame (Bulgaria, Austria and Hungary). We know that from Bulgaria the revolution has spread to Serbia. We know how these worker-peasant revolutions passed through Austria and reached Germany. Several countries are enveloped in the flames of workers' revolution. In this respect our efforts and sacrifices have been justified. They were not reckless adventures, as our enemies slanderously claimed, but an essential step towards world revolution, which had to be taken by the country that had been placed in the lead, despite its underdevelopment and backwardness.

This is one result, and the most important from the point of view of the final outcome of the imperialist war. The other result is the one to which I referred earlier, that Anglo-American imperialism is now exposing itself in the same way as Austro-German did in its time. We can see that if, at the time of the Brest-Litovsk negotiations,[88] Germany had been somewhat level-headed, able to keep herself in check and to refrain from making gambles, she would have been able to maintain her domination and undoubtedly could have secured an advantageous position in the West. She did not do this because when a machine like a war involving millions and tens of millions, a war which inflamed chauvinist passions to the utmost, a war bound up with capitalist interests totalling hundreds of billions of rubles—when such a machine has gathered full speed there are no brakes that can stop it. This machine went farther than the German imperialists themselves desired, and they were crushed by it. They were stuck; they ended up like a man who had gorged himself to death. And now, before our very eyes, British and American imperialism is in this extremely ugly, but, from the viewpoint of the revolutionary proletariat, extremely useful position. You might have thought they would have had much greater political experience than Germany. Here are people used to democratic rule, not to the rule of some Junker[89] or other, people who went through the hardest period of their history hundreds of years ago. You might have thought these people would have retained their presence of mind. If we were to speak as individuals, from the point of view of democracy in general, as bourgeois philistines, professors, who have understood nothing from the struggle between imperialism and the working class, whether or not they were capable of level-headedness, if we reasoned from the point of view of democracy in general, then we would have to say that Britain and America are countries with a centuries-old tradition of democracy, that the bourgeoisie there would be able to hold their ground. If by some means they were to succeed now in holding on, this would at any rate be for a fairly long period. But it seems that the same thing is happening to them as happened to the militarist-despotic Germany. In this imperialist war there is a tremendous difference between Russia and the republican coun-

tries. The imperialist war is so steeped in blood, so predatory and bestial, that it has effaced even these important
differences, and in this respect it has brought the freest
democracy of America to the level of semi-militarist, despotic Germany.

We see that Britain and America, countries which had
greater opportunities than others for remaining democratic
republics, have overdone things as savagely and insanely
as Germany did in her time, and so they are heading, just
as quickly, and perhaps even faster, towards the end so
successfully arrived at by German imperialism. It swelled
out fantastically over three-quarters of Europe, became
distended and then burst, leaving behind it an awful stench.
Now British and American imperialism is racing to the
same end. You only have to take a cursory glance at the
armistice and peace terms which the British and Americans,
the "liberators" of the people from German imperialism,
are presenting to the defeated nations. Take Bulgaria. You
would have thought that a country like Bulgaria could hold
no terror for the Anglo-American imperialist colossus.
Nevertheless, the revolution in this small, weak, absolutely
helpless country caused the Anglo-Americans to lose their
heads and present armistice terms that are tantamount to
occupation. In this country where a peasants' republic has
been proclaimed, in Sofia, an important railway junction,
the whole railway is now in the hands of Anglo-American
troops. They are forced to fight this little peasants' republic.
From the military point of view this is a walkover. People
who take the view of the bourgeoisie, of the old ruling
class, of old military relations, merely smile contemptuous-
ly. What does this pigmy Bulgaria signify in comparison
with the Anglo-American forces? Nothing from the military
standpoint, but a great deal from the revolutionary standpoint. This is not a colony where they are used to exter-
minating the defeated people in their millions. The British
and Americans consider this is only establishing law and
order, bringing civilisation and Christianity to African sav-
ages. But this is not Central Africa. Here the soldiers, no
matter how strong their army, become demoralised when
they come up against a revolution. Germany is proof enough

of this. In Germany, at any rate as regards discipline, the soldiers were model army men. Yet when the Germans marched into the Ukraine, factors other than discipline came into play. The starving German soldier marched for bread, and it would have been unrealistic to demand that he should not steal too much bread. Moreover, we know that in this country he was most of all infected by the spirit of the Russian revolution. The German bourgeoisie were well aware of this and it caused Wilhelm to panic. The Hohenzollerns are mistaken if they imagine that Germany will shed a single drop of blood for them. This is the result of the policy of bellicose German imperialism. The same thing is repeating itself in regard to Britain. The Anglo-American army is already becoming demoralised; this began as soon as it launched the ferocious campaign against Bulgaria. And this is only the beginning. Austria followed Bulgaria. Permit me to read you some of the clauses of the terms dictated by the Anglo-American imperialist victors. These are the people who most of all shouted to the working people that they were conducting a war of liberation, that their chief aim was to crush Prussian militarism which threatened to spread the despotic regime over all countries. They shouted loudest that they were conducting a war of liberation. This was a deception. You know that bourgeois lawyers, these parliamentarians who have spent their whole lives learning the art of deception without blushing, find it easy to deceive each other— but they don't get away with it when they have to deceive the workers in the same way. British and American politicians and parliamentarians are past masters at this art. But they will not get away with deception. The working people, whom they incited in the name of freedom, will come to their senses straight away, and even more so when, on a mass scale, not from proclamations (which help, but do not really move the revolution), but from their own experience, they see they are being deceived, when they become aware of the peace terms with Austria.

These are peace terms now being forced on a comparatively weak, disintegrating state by people who shouted that the Bolsheviks were traitors because they signed the Brest-

Litovsk Peace Treaty. When the Germans wanted to send their soldiers to Moscow, we said we would rather all die in battle than agree to this. (*Applause*.) We told ourselves great sacrifices would have to be made in the occupied areas, but everybody knows how Soviet Russia helped and kept them supplied with necessities. Now the democratic troops of Britain and France will have to serve to "maintain law and order", and this when there are Soviets of Workers' Deputies in Bulgaria and Serbia, when there are Soviets of Workers' Deputies in Vienna and Budapest. We know what kind of order this means. It means that the Anglo-American troops are to be the throttlers and executioners of the world revolution.

Comrades, when the Russian serf troops were sent to suppress the Hungarian Revolution in 1848, they were able to get away with it because they were serfs; they were able to get away with it in relation to Poland. But people who have known freedom for a century and who were incited to hate German imperialism because it was a beast which had to be destroyed, must understand that Anglo-American imperialism is the same sort of beast whom it would be only right to destroy as well!

And now history, with its usual malicious irony, has arrived at the point where, after the exposure of German imperialism, it is the turn of Anglo-French imperialism to utterly expose itself. We declare to the Russian, German and Austrian working people that these are not the Russian serf troops of 1848! They will not get away with it! They are out to stop people getting from capitalism to freedom and to suppress the revolution. We are absolutely convinced that this bloated monster will fall into the same abyss as did the German imperialist monster.

Newspaper reports published
in *Izvestia* No. 244, November 9, 1918
and in *Pravda* No. 243, November 10,
1918

First published in full in 1919   Vol. 28, pp. 154-59
in the book *Extraordinary
Sixth All-Russia Congress of
Soviets. Verbatim Report.* Moscow

THE VALUABLE ADMISSIONS OF PITIRIM SOROKIN
(Excerpt)

Furthermore, faith in "democracy" *in general*, as a universal panacea, and failure to understand that this democracy is *bourgeois* democracy, historically limited in its usefulness and its necessity, have for decades and centuries been particularly characteristic of the petty bourgeoisie of all countries. The big bourgeois is case-hardened; he knows that under capitalism a democratic republic, like every other form of state, is nothing but a machine for the suppression of the proletariat. The big bourgeois *knows* this from his most intimate acquaintance with the real leaders and with the most profound (and therefore frequently the most concealed) springs of *every* bourgeois state machine. The petty bourgeois, owing to his economic position and his conditions of life generally, is less able to appreciate this truth, and even cherishes the illusion that a democratic republic implies "pure democracy", "a free people's state", the non-class or supra-class rule of the people, a pure manifestation of the will of the people, and so on and so forth. The tenacity of these prejudices of the petty-bourgeois democrat is inevitably due to the fact that he is farther removed from the acute class struggle, the stock exchange, and "real" politics; and it would be absolutely un-Marxist to expect these prejudices to be eradicated very rapidly by propaganda alone.

World history, however, is moving with such furious rapidity, is smashing everything customary and established with a hammer of such immense weight, by crises of such unparalleled intensity, that the most tenacious prejudices are giving way. The naïve belief in a Constituent Assembly and the naïve habit of contrasting "pure democracy" with "proletarian dictatorship" took shape naturally and inevitably in the mind of the "democrat in general". But the experiences of the Constituent Assembly supporters in Archangel, Samara, Siberia and the South could not but destroy even the most tenacious of prejudices.[90] The idealised democratic republic of Wilson *proved* in practice to be a form of the most rabid imperialism, of the most shameless oppression and suppression of weak and small nations. The average "democrat" in general, the Menshevik and the Socialist-Revolutionary, thought: "How can we even dream of some allegedly superior type of state, some Soviet government? God grant us even an ordinary democratic republic!" And, of course, in "ordinary", comparatively peaceful times he could have kept on cherishing this "hope" for many a long decade.

Now, however, the course of world events and the bitter lessons derived from the alliance of all the Russian monarchists with Anglo-French and American imperialism are proving *in practice* that a democratic republic is a bourgeois-democratic republic, which is already out of date from the point of view of the problems which imperialism has placed before history. They show that there is no *other* alternative: *either* Soviet government triumphs in every advanced country in the world, *or* the most reactionary imperialism triumphs, the most savage imperialism, which is throttling the small and weak nations and reinstating reaction all over the world—Anglo-American imperialism, which has perfectly mastered the art of using the form of a democratic republic.

One or the other.

There is no middle course. Until quite recently this view was regarded as the blind fanaticism of the Bolsheviks.

But it turned out to be true.

If Pitirim Sorokin has relinquished his seat in the Constituent Assembly, it is not without reason; it is a symptom of a change of front on the part of a whole class, the petty-bourgeois democrats. A split among them is inevitable: one section will come over to our side, another section will remain neutral, while a third will deliberately join forces with the monarchist Constitutional-Democrats, who are selling Russia to Anglo-American capital and seeking to crush the revolution with the aid of foreign bayonets. One of the most urgent tasks of the present day is to take into account and make use of the turn among the Menshevik and Socialist-Revolutionary democrats from hostility to Bolshevism first to neutrality and then to support of Bolshevism.

Written on November 20, 1918

Published in *Pravda* No. 252,   Vol. 28, pp. 188-90
November 21, 1918
Signed: *N. Lenin*

The change in international politics was inevitably followed by a change in the position of the petty-bourgeois democrats. A change of heart is now occurring in their camp. In the Menshevik[91] appeal we find a call to renounce alliance with the propertied classes, a call to go and fight British and American imperialism addressed by the Mensheviks to their friends, people from among the petty-bourgeois democrats who had concluded an alliance with the Dutov men, the Czechs[92] and the British. It is now clear to everybody that, except for British and American imperialism, there is no force that can put up any sort of stand against the Bolshevik power. Similar vacillations are going on among the S.R.s[93] and the intellectuals, who most of all share the prejudices of the petty-bourgeois democrats and were swayed by patriotic sentiments. The same sort of thing is going on among them too.

Our Party's job now is to be guided by class relations when choosing tactics, and to be perfectly clear whether this is just chance, spinelessness, groundless vacillation, or, on the contrary, a process with deep social roots. The answer is quite obvious if we examine this question as a whole from the standpoint of theoretically established relations between the proletariat and the middle peasants, and from the standpoint of the history of our revolution. This change of front is *not due to chance* or *something personal*. It involves millions and millions of people whose status in Russia is either that of middle peasants or something equivalent. The change of front involves all the petty-bourgeois democrats, who opposed us with a bitterness amounting almost to fury because we had to break down all their patriotic sentiments. But history has veered round to bring patriotism back towards us now. It is evident that the Bolsheviks cannot be overthrown except by foreign bayonets. Up till now the petty bourgeoisie had cherished the illusion that the British, French and Americans stood for real democracy. But now that illusion is being completely dispelled by the peace terms that are being imposed on Austria and Germany. The British are behaving as if they had made a special point of proving the correctness of the Bolshevik views on international imperialism.

Hence voices are being raised in the parties that fought us, as in the Plekhanovite camp, for instance, saying: "We were mistaken, we thought that German imperialism was our chief enemy and that the Western countries—France, Britain and America—would bring us a democratic system." Yet now it appears that the peace terms these Western countries offer are a hundred times more humiliating, rapacious and predatory than our peace terms at Brest-Litovsk. It appears that the British and Americans are acting as the hangmen of Russian freedom, as gendarmes, playing the part of the Russian butcher Nicholas I, and are doing it no less effectively than the kings who played the hangmen in throttling the Hungarian revolution. This part is now being played by Wilson's agents. They are crushing the revolution in Austria, they are playing the gendarme, they are issuing an ultimatum to Switzerland: "You'll get no bread from us if you don't join the fight against the Bolshevik Government." They tell Holland: "Don't you dare allow Soviet ambassadors into your country, or we'll blockade you." Theirs is a simple weapon—the noose of famine. That is what they are using to strangle the peoples.

The history of recent times, of the war and post-war period, has developed with extraordinary speed, and it goes to show that British and French imperialism is just as infamous as German imperialism. Don't forget that even in America, where we have the freest and most democratic of all republics, that does not prevent its imperialists from behaving just as brutally. Internationalists are not only lynched, they are dragged into the street by the mob, stripped naked, tarred and burned.

Pravda Nos. 264 and 265, December 5 and 6, 1918

Vol. 28, pp. 208-09

THE PROLETARIAN REVOLUTION
AND THE RENEGADE KAUTSKY

(Excerpt)

The proletarian revolution is impossible without the forcible destruction of the bourgeois state machine and the substitution for it of a *new one* which, in the words of Engels, is "no longer a state in the proper sense of the word".[94]

Because of his renegade position, Kautsky, however, has to befog and belie all this.

Look what wretched subterfuges he uses.

First subterfuge. "That Marx in this case did not have in mind a form of government is proved by the fact that he was of the opinion that in Britain and America the transition might take place peacefully, i.e., in a democratic way."

The *form of government* has absolutely nothing to do with it, for there are monarchies which are not typical of the bourgeois *state,* such, for instance, as have no military clique, and there are republics which are quite typical in this respect, such, for instance, as have a military clique and a bureaucracy. This is a universally known historical and political fact, and Kautsky cannot falsify it.

If Kautsky had wanted to argue in a serious and honest manner he would have asked himself: Are there historical laws relating to revolution which know of no exception? And the reply would have been: No, there are no such laws. Such laws only apply to the typical, to what Marx once termed the "ideal", meaning average, normal, typical capitalism.

Further, was there in the seventies anything which made England and America exceptional *in regard to what we are now discussing*? It will be obvious to anyone at all familiar with the requirements of science in regard to the problems of history that this question must be put. To fail to put it is tantamount to falsifying science, to engaging in sophistry. And, the question having been put, there can be no doubt as to the reply: the revolutionary dictatorship of the proletariat is *violence* against the bourgeoisie; and the necessity of such violence is *particularly* called for, as Marx and Engels have repeatedly explained in detail (especially in *The Civil War in France* and in the preface to it), by the existence of *militarism and a bureaucracy*. But it is precisely these institutions that were *non-existent* in Britain and America in the seventies, when Marx made his observations[95] (they *do* exist in Britain and in America *now*)!

Kautsky has to resort to trickery literally at every step to cover up his apostasy!

And note how he inadvertently betrayed his cloven hoof when he wrote: "peacefully, *i.e., in a democratic way*"!

In defining dictatorship, Kautsky tried his utmost to conceal from the reader the fundamental feature of this concept, namely, revolutionary *violence*. But now the truth is out: it is a question of the contrast between *peaceful* and *violent revolutions*.

That is the crux of the matter. Kautsky has to resort to all these subterfuges, sophistries and falsifications only to *excuse* himself from *violent* revolution, and to conceal his renunciation of it, his desertion to the side of the *liberal* labour policy, i.e., to the side of the bourgeoisie. That is the crux of the matter.

Kautsky the "historian" so shamelessly falsifies history that he "forgets" the fundamental fact that pre-monopoly capitalism—which actually reached its zenith in the seventies—was by virtue of its fundamental *economic* traits, which found most typical expression in Britain and in America, distinguished by a, relatively speaking, maximum fondness for peace and freedom. Imperialism, on the other hand, i.e., monopoly capitalism, which finally matured

only in the twentieth century, is, by virtue of its fundamental *economic* traits, distinguished by a minimum fondness for peace and freedom, and by a maximum and universal development of militarism. To "fail to notice" this
in discussing the extent to which a peaceful or violent revolution is typical or probable is to stoop to the level of
a most ordinary lackey of the bourgeoisie.

Written October-November 1918

Published in pamphlet form in 1918   Vol. 28, pp. 237-39
by Kommunist Publishers, Moscow

From A SPEECH TO THE THIRD
WORKERS' CO-OPERATIVE CONGRESS
DECEMBER 9, 1918

The Western nations once regarded us and all our revolutionary movement as a curiosity. They used to say: "Let the people have their fling; we shall wait and see how it all works out.... Queer people, those Russians!" Now the "queer Russians" have shown the world what their "fling" means. (*Applause*.)

Now that the German revolution has broken out,[96] a foreign consul said to Zinoviev: "It's hard to say at this point who has made better use of the Brest-Litovsk Peace, you or we."

He said this because everyone was saying it. Everyone saw that this was just the beginning of the great world revolution. And this great revolution was started by the backward and "queer" Russian people.... History certainly has strange ways: that a backward country should have the honour of leading a great world movement, which is seen and understood by the bourgeoisie of the whole world. This conflagration has swept Germany, Belgium, Switzerland and Holland.

This movement is spreading from day to day, the revolutionary Soviet Government is daily gaining in strength. That is why the bourgeoisie have now taken an entirely different attitude to matters. Now that the axe is about to fall on world capitalism, there can be no question at all of any independence for individual parties. America provides the most glaring example. America is one of the most democratic countries, it is a great democratic social republic. Where else, if not in that country—which has all the electoral rights and all the rights of a free state—

could we expect a correct solution to all legal questions?
Yet we know what has happened to a clergyman there, in
that democratic republic: he was tarred and whipped until
his blood flowed in the dust. This took place in a free
country, in a democratic republic. This was allowed to
happen by the "humane", "philanthropic" Tiger Wilsons
and Co. What are these Wilsons now doing with Germany,
a defeated country? The pictures of world relations are
displayed before us in full view! We see the substance of
what the Wilsons offer their friends from these pictures,
which carry such overwhelming conviction. The Wilsons
would have instantly proved our point. These gentlemen—
the free multimillionaires, the "most humane" people in
the world—would have instantly broken their friends'
habit of talking, even of dreaming, of "independence" in
any form. They would have squarely put before you the
alternative: either you stand for the capitalist system or
you stand for the Soviets. They would have said: do this,
because we say so, we, your friends, the British, the Americans— the Wilsons, and the French—Clemenceau's friends.

That is why it is quite hopeless to expect any vestige
of independence to remain. This cannot be, and it is no
use dreaming of it. There can be no middle course once
it is a question of protecting property on the one hand,
and once the proletariat has found its way on the other.
The branches of the tree of life must either be closely
intertwined with capital, or even more closely with the
Soviet Republic. It is absolutely clear to everyone that socialism has entered the period of its realisation. It is quite
clear to everyone that it is absolutely impossible to maintain or retain petty-bourgeois positions through universal
suffrage. The Wilsons may nurture such illusions, rather,
they do not nurture such illusions but try to embellish
their own aims by fostering such illusions, but you won't
find many people nowadays who believe these fairy-tales.
If such people do exist, they are a historical rarity or a
museum piece. (*Applause*.)

The differences you have had from the outset about
preserving the "independence" of the co-operative move-

ment are nothing but vain efforts which must peter out without any hope of a positive solution. This struggle is not serious and it clashes with the principles of democracy. Although this is not surprising because the Wilsons are also "democrats". They say that it remains for them to establish one final union because they have so many dollars they can buy up the whole of Russia, and the whole of India, and the whole world. Wilson presides over their company, their pockets are bulging with dollars and that is why they talk about buying up Russia and India and everything else. But they forget that basic international issues are settled in an entirely different manner, that only some people, in a definite environment, may be impressed by their statements. They forget that the resolutions daily adopted by the strongest class in the world—the kind our own Congress is sure to adopt unanimously—greet only the dictatorship of the proletariat all over the world. By adopting such a resolution our Congress takes the road which does not and cannot lead to the kind of "independence" being discussed here today. You are aware that Karl Liebknecht has shown some opposition not only to the petty-bourgeois peasants, but also to the co-operative movement. You know that just for this Scheidemann and company consider him a dreamer and fanatic, yet you addressed a message of greetings to him, just as you sent greetings to MacLean. By voicing solidarity on these matters with the great world leaders you have burnt your boats. You must keep a firm stand because at the moment you are standing up not only for yourselves, not only for your own rights, but also for the rights of Liebknecht and MacLean. I have often heard the Russian Mensheviks condemn conciliation, and inveigh against those who came to terms with the Kaiser's lackeys. Nor were the Mensheviks alone in erring that way. The whole world pointed at us, hurling this stern charge: "Conciliators." Now that the world revolution has started, and they have to deal with Haase and Kautsky, we have the right to describe our position in the words of the good Russian proverb: "Let's stand back, and see how well we are placed."

We know our shortcomings, and they are easily pointed out. But to the onlooker everything appears to be quite different from what it actually is. At one time, you know, everyone in the other parties condemned our behaviour and our policy, and now whole parties are siding with us, and want to work with us. The wheel of the world revolutionary movement has now turned to such an extent that we need not fear any kind of conciliation whatsoever. And I am sure that our Congress will find the right way out of the situation. There is only one way out: a merger of the co-operative movement with the Soviet government. You know that Britain, France, America and Spain regarded our actions as experiments; they have now changed their tune: they now have to look to their own affairs at home. Of course, physically, materially and financially they are considerably stronger than we are, but in spite of their outward polish we know they are rotten inside; they are stronger than we are at present with the strength that was Germany's when the Brest-Litovsk Peace Treaty was concluded. But what do we see now? Everyone recoiled from us then. Now, every month we spend in strengthening the Soviet Republic we spend in defending not only ourselves, but also the cause started by Liebknecht and MacLean, and we already see that Britain, France, America and Spain have been infected with the same disease and are fired with the same flame as Germany, the flame of the universal and world-wide struggle of the working class against imperialism. (*Prolonged applause.*)

Brief report published
in *Izvestia* No. 270,
December 10, 1918

Published in full in 1919

Vol. 28, pp. 334-37

From A SPEECH AT A PRESNYA DISTRICT
WORKERS' CONFERENCE
DECEMBER 14, 1918

Britain, America and Japan are now fighting for a share of the spoils. Everything has been divided. Wilson is President of the world's most democratic republic. But what is he saying? People there are shot in the streets by jingoist crowds for one word in favour of peace. A clergyman who had never been a revolutionary was dragged out into the street and severely beaten for preaching peace. Where the wildest terror reigns troops are now being used to crush the revolution, to threaten suppression of the German revolution. The revolution in Germany broke out just recently, only a month ago; the burning issue there is a Constituent Assembly or Soviet government. All the bourgeoisie there are for the Constituent Assembly, and all the socialists—those who served the Kaiser as lackeys, who did not dare start a revolutionary war—they, too, want a Constituent Assembly. Germany is split into two camps. The socialists now favour the Constituent Assembly, while Liebknecht, who spent three years in prison, stands, like Rosa Luxemburg, at the head of *Die Rote Fahne*.[97] An issue of the newspaper was received in Moscow yesterday. It had a very difficult and eventful journey. In it you will find a number of articles—all the authors, who are revolutionary leaders, describe how the bourgeoisie are cheating the people. Freedom in Germany was in the hands of the capitalists. They published only their own newspapers, and now *Die Rote Fahne* says that only the workers have the right to use national wealth. Although the revolution in Germany is only a month old, the country is split into two camps. All the traitor socialists are clamouring for a Constituent Assembly, while the genuine, honest socialists are saying: "We all stand for the power of the workers and the soldiers." They are not saying "and the peasants", because in Germany many peasants also hire labourers, and so they are saying "for the workers and the soldiers". They say instead "for the small peasants". Soviet power there has already become a form of government.

Brief report published   Vol. 28, p. 360
in *Pravda* No. 275,
December 18, 1918

From A REPORT AT THE SECOND ALL-RUSSIA TRADE UNION CONGRESS JANUARY 20, 1919

The trade unions have never embraced more than one-fifth of the wage-workers in capitalist society, even under the most favourable circumstances, even in the most advanced countries, after decades and sometimes even centuries of development of bourgeois-democratic civilisation and culture. Only a small upper section were members, and of them only a very few were lured over and bribed by the capitalists to take their place in capitalist society as workers' leaders. The American socialists called these people "labour lieutenants of the capitalist class". In that country of the freest bourgeois culture, in that most democratic of bourgeois republics, they saw most clearly the role played by this tiny upper section of the proletariat who had virtually entered the service of the bourgeoisie as its deputies, who were bribed and bought by it, and who came to form those groups of social-patriots and defence advocates of which Ebert and Scheidemann will always remain the perfect heroes.

Newspaper reports published
in *Pravda* Nos. 15 and 16,
January 22 and 24, 1919

Vol. 28, p. 421

LETTER TO THE WORKERS OF EUROPE AND AMERICA

Comrades, at the end of my letter to American workers dated August 20, 1918, I wrote that we are in a besieged fortress so long as the other armies of the world socialist revolution do not come to our aid. I added that the workers are breaking away from their social-traitors, the Gomperses and Renners. The workers are slowly but surely coming round to communist and Bolshevik tactics.

Less than five months have passed since those words were written, and it must be said that during this time, in view of the fact that workers of various countries have turned to communism and Bolshevism, the maturing of the world proletarian revolution has proceeded very rapidly.

Then, on August 20, 1918, only our Party, the Bolshevik Party, had resolutely broken with the old, Second International of 1889-1914 which so shamefully collapsed during the imperialist war of 1914-18. Only our Party had unreservedly taken the new path, from the socialists and social-democracy which had disgraced themselves by alliance with the predatory bourgeoisie, to communism; from petty-bourgeois reformism and opportunism, which had thoroughly permeated, and now permeate, the official Social-Democratic and socialist parties, to genuinely proletarian, revolutionary tactics.

Now, on January 12, 1919, we already see quite a number of communist proletarian parties, not only within the boundaries of the former tsarist empire—in Latvia, Finland and Poland, for example—but also in Western Europe—Austria, Hungary, Holland and, lastly, Germany. The *foundation* of a genuinely proletarian, genuinely internationalist, genuinely revolutionary Third International, the *Communist International*, became *a fact* when the German Spartacus League, with such world-known and world-famous leaders, with such staunch working-class champions as Liebknecht, Rosa Luxemburg, Clara Zetkin and Franz Mehring, made a clean break with socialists like Scheidemann and Südekum, social-chauvinists (socialists in words, but chauvinists in deeds) who have earned eternal shame by their alliance with the predatory, imperialist German bourgeoisie and Wilhelm II. It became a fact when the Spartacus League changed its name to the Communist Party of Germany. Though it has not yet been officially inaugurated, the Third International actually exists.

No class-conscious worker, no sincere socialist can now fail to see how dastardly was the betrayal of socialism by those who, like the Mensheviks and "Socialist-Revolutionaries" in Russia, the Scheidemanns and Südekums in Germany, the Renaudels and Vanderveldes in France, the Hendersons and Webbs in Britain, and Gompers and Co. in America, supported "their" bourgeoisie in the 1914-18 war. That war fully exposed itself as an imperialist, reactionary, predatory war both on the part of Germany and on the part of the capitalists of Britain, France, Italy and America. The latter are now beginning to quarrel over the spoils, over the division of Turkey, Russia, the African and Polynesian colonies, the Balkans, and so on. The hypocritical phrases uttered by Wilson and his followers about "democracy" and "union of nations" are exposed with amazing rapidity when we see the capture of the left bank of the Rhine by the French bourgeoisie, the capture of Turkey (Syria, Mesopotamia) and part of Russia (Siberia, Archangel, Baku, Krasnovodsk, Ashkhabad, and so on) by the French, British and American capitalists, and the increasing animosity over the division of the spoils between Italy and France, France and Britain, Britain and America, America and Japan.

Beside the craven, half-hearted "socialists" who are thoroughly imbued with the prejudices of bourgeois democracy, who yesterday defended "their" imperialist governments and today limit themselves to platonic "protests" against military intervention in Russia—beside these there is a growing number of people in the Allied countries who have taken the communist path, the path of MacLean, Debs, Loriot, Lazzari and Serrati. These are men who have realised that if imperialism is to be crushed and the victory of socialism and lasting peace ensured, the bourgeoisie must be overthrown, bourgeois parliaments abolished, and Soviet power and the dictatorship of the proletariat established.

Then, on August 20, 1918, the proletarian revolution was confined to Russia, and "Soviet government", i.e., the system under which *all* state power is vested in Soviets of Workers', Soldiers' and Peasants' Deputies, still seemed to be (and actually was) only a Russian institution.

Now, on January 12, 1919, we see a mighty "Soviet" movement not only in parts of the former tsarist empire, for example, in Latvia, Poland and the Ukraine, but also in West-European countries, in neutral countries (Switzerland, Holland and Norway) and in countries which have suffered from the war (Austria and Germany). The revolution in Germany—which is particularly important and characteristic as one of the most advanced capitalist countries—at once assumed "Soviet" forms. The whole course of the German revolution, and particularly the struggle of the Spartacists, i.e., the true and only representatives of the proletariat, against the alliance of those treacherous scoundrels, the Scheidemanns and Südekums, with the bourgeoisie—all this clearly shows how history has *formulated* the question in relation to Germany:

"Soviet power" or the bourgeois parliament, no matter under what signboard (such as "National" or "Constituent" Assembly) it may appear.

That is how *world history* has formulated the question. Now, this can and must be said without any exaggeration.

"Soviet power" is the second historical step, or stage, in the development of the proletarian dictatorship. The first step was the Paris Commune. The brilliant analysis of its nature and significance given by Marx in his *The Civil War in France* showed that the Commune had created a *new type* of state, a *proletarian state*. Every state, including the most democratic republic, is nothing but a machine for the suppression of one class by another. The proletarian state is a machine for the suppression of the bourgeoisie by the proletariat. Such suppression is necessary because of the furious, desperate resistance put up by the landowners and capitalists, by the entire bourgeoisie and all their hangers-on, by all the exploiters, who stop at nothing when their overthrow, when the expropriation of the expropriators, begins.

The bourgeois parliament, even the most democratic in the most democratic republic, in which the property and rule of the capitalists are preserved, is a machine for the suppression of the working millions by small groups of exploiters. The socialists, the fighters for the emancipation of the working people from exploitation, had to utilise the bourgeois parliaments as a platform, as a base, for propaganda, agitation and organisation *as long as our struggle was confined to the framework of the bourgeois system.* Now that world history has brought up the question of destroying the whole of that system, of overthrowing and suppressing the exploiters, of passing from capitalism to socialism, it would be a shameful betrayal of the proletariat, deserting to its class enemy, the bourgeoisie, and being a traitor and a renegade to confine oneself to bourgeois parliamentarism, to bourgeois democracy, to present it as "democracy" in general, to obscure its *bourgeois* character, to forget that as long as capitalist property exists universal suffrage is an instrument of the bourgeois state.

The three trends in world socialism, about which the Bolshevik press has been speaking incessantly since 1915, stand out with particular distinctness today, against the background of the bloody struggle and civil war in Germany.

Karl Liebknecht is a name known to the workers of all countries. Everywhere, and particularly in the Allied countries, it is the symbol of a leader's devotion to the interests of the proletariat and loyalty to the socialist revolution. It is the symbol of really sincere, really self-sacrificing and ruthless struggle against capitalism. It is the symbol of uncompromising struggle against imperialism not in words, but in deeds, of self-sacrificing struggle precisely in the period when "one's own" country is flushed with imperialist victories. With Liebknecht and the Spartacists are all those German socialists who have remained honest and really revolutionary, all the best and dedicated men among the proletariat, the exploited masses who are seething with indignation and among whom there is a growing readiness for revolution.

Against Liebknecht are the Scheidemanns, the Südekums and the whole gang of despicable lackeys of the Kaiser and the bourgeoisie. They are just as much traitors to socialism as the Gomperses and Victor Bergers, the Hendersons and Webbs, the Renaudels and Vanderveldes. They represent that top section of workers who have been bribed by the bourgeoisie, those whom we Bolsheviks called (applying the name to the Russian Südekums, the Mensheviks) "agents of the bourgeoisie in the working-class movement", and to whom the best socialists in America gave the magnificently expressive and very fitting title: "labour lieutenants of the capitalist class." They represent *the latest*, "modern", *type* of socialist treachery, for in all the civilised, advanced countries the bourgeoisie rob—either by colonial oppression or by financially extracting "gain" from formally independent weak countries—they rob a population many times larger than that of "their own" country. This is the economic factor that enables the imperialist bourgeoisie to obtain superprofits, part of which is used to bribe the top section of the proletariat and convert it into a reformist, opportunist petty bourgeoisie that fears revolution.

Between the Spartacists and the Scheidemann men are the wavering, spineless "Kautskyites", who in words are "independent", but in deeds are entirely, and all along the line, *dependent* upon the bourgeoisie and the Scheidemann men one day, upon the Spartacists the next, some following the former and some the latter. These are people without ideas, without backbone, without policy, without honour, without conscience, the living embodiment of the bewilderment of philistines who stand for socialist revolution in words, but are actually incapable of understanding it when it has begun and, in renegade fashion, defend "democracy" in general, that is, *actually* defend *bourgeois* democracy.

In every capitalist country, every thinking worker will, in the situation varying with national and historical conditions, perceive these three main trends among the socialists and among the syndicalists, for the imperialist war and the incipient world proletarian revolution engender identical ideological and political trends all over the world.

* * *

The foregoing lines were written before the brutal and dastardly murder of Karl Liebknecht and Rosa Luxemburg by the Ebert and Scheidemann government. Those butchers, in their servility to the bourgeoisie, allowed the German whiteguards, the watchdogs of sacred capitalist property, to lynch Rosa Luxemburg, to murder Karl Liebknecht by shooting him in the back on the patently false plea that he "attempted to escape" (Russian tsarism often used that excuse to murder prisoners during its bloody suppression of the 1905 revolution). At the same time those butchers protected the whiteguards with the authority of the government, which claims to be quite innocent and to stand above classes! No words can describe the foul and abominable character of the butchery perpetrated by alleged socialists. Evidently, history has chosen a path on which the role of "labour lieutenants of the capitalist class" must be played to the "last degree" of brutality, baseness and meanness. Let those simpletons, the Kautskyites, talk in their newspaper *Freiheit* about a "court" of representatives of "all" "socialist" parties (those servile souls insist that the Scheidemann executioners are socialists)! Those heroes of philistine stupidity and petty-bourgeois cowardice even fail to understand that the courts are organs of state power, and that the issue in the struggle and civil war now being waged in Germany is precisely one of who is to hold this power—the bourgeoisie, "served" by the Scheidemanns as executioners and instigators of pogroms, and by the Kautskys as glorifiers of "pure democracy", or the proletariat, which will over-throw the capitalist exploiters and crush their resistance.

The blood of the best representatives of the world pro-letarian International, of the unforgettable leaders of the world socialist revolution, will steel ever new masses of workers for the life-and-death struggle. And this struggle will lead to victory. We in Russia, in the summer of 1917, lived through the "July days", when the Russian Schei-demanns, the Mensheviks and Socialist-Revolutionaries, also provided "state" protection for the "victory" of the whiteguards over the Bolsheviks, and when Cossacks shot the worker Voinov in the streets of Petrograd for distri-buting Bolshevik leaflets. We know from experience how quickly such "victories" of the bourgeoisie and their henchmen cure the people of their illusions about bour-geois democracy, "universal suffrage", and so forth.

* * *

The bourgeoisie and the governments of the Allied coun-tries seem to be wavering. One section sees that demorali-sation is already setting in among the Allied troops in Rus-sia, who are helping the whiteguards and serving the blackest monarchist and landlord reaction. It realises that continuation of the military intervention and attempts to defeat Russia—which would mean maintaining a million-strong army of occupation for a long time—is the surest and quickest way of carrying the proletarian revolution to the Allied countries. The example of the German occu-pation forces in the Ukraine is convincing enough of that.

Another section of the Allied bourgeoisie persists in its policy of military intervention, "economic encirclement" (Clemenceau) and strangulation of the Soviet Republic. The entire press in the service of that bourgeoisie, i.e., the majority of the capitalist-bought daily newspapers in Brit-ain and France, predicts the early collapse of the Soviet government, draws lurid pictures of the horrors of the famine in Russia, lies about "disorders" and the "insta-bility" of the Soviet Government. The whiteguard armies of the landowners and capitalists, whom the Allies are helping with officers, ammunition, money and auxiliary detachments, are cutting off the starving central and northern parts of Russia from the most fertile regions, Siberia and the Don.

The distress of the starving workers in Petrograd and Moscow, in Ivanovo-Voznesensk and other industrial centres is indeed great. If the workers did not understand that they are defending the cause of socialism in Russia and throughout the world they would never be able to bear the hardships, the torments of hunger to which they are doomed by the Allied military intervention (often covered up by hypocritical promises not to send their "own" troops, while continuing to send "black" troops, and also ammunition, money and officers).

The "Allied" and whiteguard troops hold Archangel, Perm, Orenburg, Rostov-on-Don, Baku and Ashkhabad, but the "Soviet movement" has won Riga and Kharkov, Latvia and the Ukraine are becoming Soviet republics. The workers see that their great sacrifices are not in vain, that the victory of Soviet power is approaching, spreading, growing and gaining strength the world over. Every month of hard fighting and heavy sacrifice strengthens the cause of Soviet power throughout the world and weakens its enemies, the exploiters.

The exploiters are still strong enough to murder and lynch the finest leaders of the world proletarian revolution, to increase the sacrifices and suffering of the workers in occupied or conquered countries and regions. But the exploiters all over the world are not strong enough to prevent the victory of the world proletarian revolution, which will free mankind from the yoke of capital and the eternal menace of new imperialist wars, which are inevitable under capitalism.

N. Lenin

January 21, 1919

Pravda No. 16,   Vol. 28, pp. 429-36
January 24, 1919

THESES AND REPORT ON BOURGEOIS DEMOCRACY AND THE DICTATORSHIP OF THE PROLETARIAT DELIVERED AT THE FIRST CONGRESS OF THE COMMUNIST INTERNATIONAL

MARCH 4, 1919

(Excerpt)

8. "Freedom of the press" is another of the principal slogans of "pure democracy". And here, too, the workers know—and socialists everywhere have admitted it millions of times—that this freedom is a deception while the best printing-presses and the biggest stocks of paper are appropriated by the capitalists, and while capitalist rule over the press remains, a rule that is manifested throughout the world all the more strikingly, sharply and cynically the more democracy and the republican system are developed, as in America for example. The first thing to do to win real equality and genuine democracy for the working people, for the workers and peasants, is to deprive capital of the possibility of hiring writers, buying up publishing houses and bribing newspapers. And to do that the capitalists and exploiters have to be overthrown and their resistance suppressed. The capitalists have always used the term "freedom" to mean freedom for the rich to get richer and for the workers to starve to death. In capitalist usage, freedom of the press means freedom of the rich to bribe the press, freedom to use their wealth to shape and fabricate so-called public opinion. In this respect, too, the defenders of "pure democracy" prove to be defenders of an utterly foul and venal system that gives the rich control over the mass media. They prove to

be deceivers of the people, who, with the aid of plausible, fine-sounding, but thoroughly false phrases, divert them from the concrete historical task of liberating the press from capitalist enslavement. Genuine freedom and equality will be embodied in the system which the Communists are building, and in which there will be no opportunity for amassing wealth at the expense of others, no objective opportunities for putting the press under the direct or indirect power of money, and no impediments in the way of any workingman (or groups of workingmen, in any numbers) for enjoying and practising equal rights in the use of public printing-presses and public stocks of paper.

9. The history of the nineteenth and twentieth centuries demonstrated, even before the war, what this celebrated "pure democracy" really is under capitalism. Marxists have always maintained that the more developed, the "purer" democracy is, the more naked, acute and merciless the class struggle becomes, and the "purer" the capitalist oppression and bourgeois dictatorship. The Dreyfus case[98] in republican France, the massacre of strikers by hired bands armed by the capitalists in the free and democratic American republic—these and thousands of similar facts illustrate the truth which the bourgeoisie are vainly seeking to conceal, namely, that actually terror and bourgeois dictatorship prevail in the most democratic of republics and are openly displayed every time the exploiters think the power of capital is being shaken.

10. The imperialist war of 1914-18 conclusively revealed even to backward workers the true nature of bourgeois democracy, even in the freest republics, as being a dictatorship of the bourgeoisie. Tens of millions were killed for the sake of enriching the German or the British group of millionaires and multimillionaires, and bourgeois military dictatorships were established in the freest republics. This military dictatorship continues to exist in the Allied countries even after Germany's defeat. It was mostly the war that opened the eyes of the working people, that stripped bourgeois democracy of its camouflage and showed the people the abyss of speculation and profiteer-

ing that existed during and because of the war. It was in the name of "freedom and equality" that the bourgeoisie waged the war, and in the name of "freedom and equality" that the munition manufacturers piled up fabulous fortunes. Nothing that the yellow Berne International[99] does can conceal from the people the now thoroughly exposed exploiting character of bourgeois freedom, bourgeois equality and bourgeois democracy.

11. In Germany, the most developed capitalist country of continental Europe, the very first months of full republican freedom, established as a result of imperialist Germany's defeat, have shown the German workers and the whole world the true class substance of the bourgeois-democratic republic. The murder of Karl Liebknecht and Rosa Luxemburg is an event of epoch-making significance not only because of the tragic death of these finest people and leaders of the truly proletarian, Communist International, but also because the class nature of an advanced European state—it can be said without exaggeration, of an advanced state on a world-wide scale—has been conclusively exposed. If those arrested, i.e., those placed under state protection, could be assassinated by officers and capitalists with impunity, and this under a government headed by social-patriots, then the democratic republic where such a thing was possible is a bourgeois dictatorship. Those who voice their indignation at the murder of Karl Liebknecht and Rosa Luxemburg but fail to understand this fact are only demonstrating their stupidity, or hypocrisy. "Freedom" in the German republic, one of the freest and advanced republics of the world, is freedom to murder arrested leaders of the proletariat with impunity. Nor can it be otherwise as long as capitalism remains, for the development of democracy sharpens rather than dampens the class struggle which, by virtue of all the results and influences of the war and of its consequences, has been brought to boiling point.

Throughout the civilised world we see Bolsheviks being exiled, persecuted and thrown into prison. This is the case, for example, in Switzerland, one of the freest bourgeois republics, and in America, where there have been anti-

Bolshevik pogroms, etc. From the standpoint of "democracy in general", or "pure democracy", it is really ridiculous that advanced, civilised, and democratic countries, which are armed to the teeth, should fear the presence of a few score men from backward, famine-stricken and ruined Russia, which the bourgeois papers, in tens of millions of copies, describe as savage, criminal, etc. Clearly, the social situation that could produce this crying contradiction is in fact a dictatorship of the bourgeoisie.

Theses published March 6, 1919   Vol. 28, pp. 460-63
in *Pravda* No. 51; report first
published in 1920 in the German
and in 1921 in the Russian
editions of the Minutes of
the First Congress of the
Communist International

"We knew perfectly well," Lenin continued, "that to achieve success in the struggle that had been started the greatest possible cohesion of the exploited masses and all elements of the entire working population was essential, and this inevitably brought us face to face with the question of forms of organisation. We remembered very well the part the Soviets had played in 1905, and revived them as the most suitable means of uniting the working people in their struggle against the exploiters. Before the revolution in Germany we always said that the Soviets were the most suitable organs of government for Russia. At that time we could not say that they were equally suitable for the West, but events have shown that they are. We see that Soviets are gaining popularity in the West, and that the fight for them is going on not only in Europe, but also in America. Soviet-type councils are being set up everywhere, and sooner or later they will take power into their own hands.

"The present situation in America, where such councils are being set up, is extremely interesting. Perhaps the movement there will not develop as it is developing in this country, but the important thing is that there, too, the Soviet form of organisation has gained extensive popularity. This form has superseded all other forms of proletarian organisation. The anarchists were formerly opposed to all government but after they had got to know the Soviet form they accepted it, and thereby demolished the whole theory of anarchism, which repudiates every form of government. Two years ago the compromising idea of collaboration with the bourgeoisie was dominant in our Soviets. A certain amount of time was required to clear the minds of the masses of the old rubbish that prevented them from understanding what was going on. This could be achieved only when the Soviets had undertaken the practical work of building the state. The masses of the workers in Germany are now in the same position, and their minds, too, must be cleared of the same old rubbish, although in that country the process is more intense, cruel and bloody than in Russia."

Severnaya Kommuna No. 58,   Vol. 29, p. 20
March 14, 1919

REPLIES TO WRITTEN QUESTIONS AT A SESSION OF THE PETROGRAD SOVIET

MARCH 12, 1919

(Excerpt)

Some workers, printers, for instance, say that capitalism was good, there were a lot of newspapers whereas now there are few, in those days they earned a decent wage and they do not want any socialism. There were quite a number of branches of industry that depended on the rich classes or on the production of articles of luxury. Under capitalism quite a number of workers in big cities lived by producing articles of luxury. In the Soviet Republic we shall have to leave these workers unemployed for a time. We shall say to them, "Get down to some other, useful work." And the worker will say, "I did delicate work, I was a jeweller, it was clean work, I worked for gentlement; now the muzhik is in power, the gentlemen have been scattered and I want to go back to capitalism." Such people will preach going back to capitalism, or, as the Mensheviks say, going forward to healthy capitalism and sound democracy. A few hundred workers are to be found who will say, "We lived well under a healthy capitalism." The people who lived well under capitalism were an insignificant minority—we defend the interests of the majority that lived badly under capitalism. (*Applause.*) Healthy capitalism led to world slaughter in the countries with the greatest freedom. There can be no healthy capitalism, there can be capitalism of the sort obtaining in the freest republic, one like the American republic, cultured, rich, technically developed; and that democratic and most republican capitalism led to the most savage world slaughter over the plunder of the whole world. Out of fifteen million workers you will find a few thousand who lived well under capitalism. In the rich countries there are more such workers because they work for a greater number of millionaires and multimillionaires. They served that handful and received particularly high wages from them. Take hundreds of British millionaires—they have accumulated thousands of millions because they have plundered India and a large number of colonies. It meant nothing to them to make gifts to 10,000 or 20,000 workers, giving them double or higher wages so that they would work well for them. I once read the reminiscences of an American barber whom a multimillionaire paid a dollar a day to shave him. And that barber wrote a whole book praising that multimillionaire and his own wonderful life. For a daily visit of one hour to his financial majesty he received a dollar, was satisfied and did not want anything but capitalism. We have to be on our guard against such an argument. The vast majority of workers were not in such a position. We, the Communists of the whole world, defend the interests of the vast majority of working people, and it was a small minority of working people whom the capitalists bribed with high wages and made them the loyal servants of capital. Under serfdom there were people, peasants, who said to the landowners, "We are your slaves (that was after emancipation), we shall not leave you." Were there many of them? An insignificant few. Can you deny that there was a struggle against serfdom by reference to them? Of course not. And today communism cannot be denied by reference to the minority of workers who earned good money on bourgeois newspapers, on the production of articles of luxury and for their personal services to multimillionaires.

First published in 1950   Vol. 29, pp. 28-30

THE ACHIEVEMENTS AND DIFFICULTIES OF THE SOVIET GOVERNMENT

(Excerpt)

The real test to which our revolution is being subjected is that we, in a backward country, succeeded in capturing power before the others, succeeded in establishing the Soviet form of government, the power of the working and exploited people. Shall we be able to hold on at least until the masses in the other countries make a move? If we are not prepared to make fresh sacrifices and do not hold out, it will be said that our revolution was historically unjustified. But democrats in civilised countries who are armed to the teeth dread the presence of a hundred or so Bolsheviks in a free republic with a hundred million population, in the way America does. Bolshevism is so infectious! And it turns out that the democrats cannot cope with a hundred immigrants from starving, ruined Russia who might talk about Bolshevism! The masses sympathise with us! The bourgeoisie have only one path of salvation, and that is, while their hand still grasps the sword, while they still control the guns, to turn these guns against Soviet Russia and to crush her in a few months, because later on nothing will crush her. This is the situation we are in; this is what determined the military policy of the Council of People's Commissars during the past year; and this is why, pointing to the facts, to the results, we have a right to say that we have stood the test only because the workers and peasants, though utterly exhausted by war, are creating a new army under still more arduous conditions and are displaying new heroism.

Published in pamphlet form
by the Petrograd Soviet of Workers'
and Red Army Deputies,
March-April 1919

Vol. 29, p. 68

AN APPEAL TO THE RED ARMY
(Excerpt)

Comrades, Red Army men! The capitalists of Britain, America and France are waging war against Russia. They are taking revenge on the Soviet workers' and peasants' republic for having overthrown the power of the landowners and capitalists and thereby set an example to all the nations of the globe. The capitalists of Britain, France and America are helping with money and munitions the Russian landowners who are bringing troops from Siberia, the Don and North Caucasus against Soviet power for the purpose of restoring the rule of the tsar and the power of the landowners and capitalists. But this will not happen. The Red Army has closed its ranks, has risen up and driven the landowners' troops and whiteguard officers from the Volga, has recaptured Riga and almost the whole of the Ukraine, and is marching towards Odessa and Rostov. A little more effort, a few more months of fighting the enemy, and victory will be ours. The Red Army is strong because it is consciously and unitedly marching into battle for the peasants' land, for the rule of the workers and peasants, for Soviet power.

The Red Army is invincible because it has united millions of working peasants with the workers who have now learned to fight, have acquired comradely discipline, who do not lose heart, who become steeled after slight reverses, and are more and more boldly marching against the enemy, convinced he will soon be defeated.

Recording made at the   Vol. 29, p. 244
end of March 1919

From THE REPORT ON THE DOMESTIC
AND FOREIGN SITUATION
OF THE SOVIET REPUBLIC

EXTRAORDINARY PLENARY MEETING OF THE MOSCOW
SOVIET OF WORKERS' AND RED ARMY DEPUTIES
APRIL 3, 1919

We now come to the international situation. I say that
the imperialists of Britain, France and America are making
their last attempt to bring us to our knees, but they will
fail. Difficult as the situation is, we can say with confidence that we shall defeat international imperialism. We
shall defeat the multimillionaires of the whole world. There
are two reasons why we shall beat them. First, because
they are wild beasts who are so absorbed in fighting among
themselves that they continue to bite each other and fail
to see that they are on the brink of a precipice; secondly,
because Soviet power is growing uninterruptedly all over
the world. Not a day passes but what we read about this
in the newspapers. Today we read a message wirelessed
from an American press office in Lyons to the effect that
the Committee of Ten has now been reduced, and that
there are now only four—Wilson, Lloyd George, Clemenceau and Orlando. These are the leaders of four nations,
but even they cannot reach an agreement. Britain and
America do not want France to have the coal profits. They
are wild beasts who have plundered the whole world and
are now quarrelling over the prey. These four men have
shut themselves up in close conclave so that, God forbid,
rumours may not get about—they are all such great dem-

ocrats—but they themselves set rumours afloat by sending out wireless messages about not agreeing to give up the coal profits. A French comrade who saw the French prisoners of war told me that these prisoners say: "We were told that we must go to Russia to fight the Germans because the Germans had destroyed our country. But now there is an armistice with Germany; whom are we going to fight?" They were not told a word about that. The number of people who are asking themselves this question is day by day growing into millions and millions. These people have experienced the horrors of the imperialist war, and they say: "What are we going to fight for?" In the past, the Bolsheviks taught them what they were fighting for in underground leaflets; but now the imperialists send out wireless messages saying that Britain does not agree to allow France to have the coal profits. Thus, as a French journalist expressed it, they are rushing from room to room in a vain effort to solve the problem. They are trying to decide who should get most, and they have been fighting each other for five months. These wild beasts have lost their self-control, and will go on fighting until nothing is left of them except their tails. And we say that our international position, which at first was so precarious that they could have crushed us in several weeks, is now, when they are quarrelling over the loot and are beginning to fly at each other's throats—now our position is much better. They promised the soldiers that if they conquered Germany they would receive untold benefits. They are arguing whether to compel Germany to pay sixty or eighty milliard. This is an extremely important question of principle, an extremely interesting one, especially if the workers or peasants are told about it. But if they go on arguing for long they will not get even one milliard. This is what is most interesting!

Pravda Nos. 76 and 77,   Vol. 29, pp. 267-68
April 9 and 10, 1919

DECEPTION OF THE PEOPLE WITH SLOGANS OF FREEDOM AND EQUALITY

SPEECH AT THE FIRST ALL-RUSSIA CONGRESS ON ADULT EDUCATION
MAY 19, 1919

(Excerpts)

In my "Letter to American Workers",[100] I spoke, among other things, about the American revolutionary people fighting to liberate themselves from England in the eighteenth century, when they were waging one of the first and greatest wars for real liberation in human history, one of the few really revolutionary wars in human history —and this great revolutionary American people, in fighting for their liberation, entered into agreements with the bandits of Spanish and French imperialism, who at that time had colonies in neighbouring parts of America. In alliance with these bandits, the American people fought the English and liberated themselves from them. Have you ever met any literate person anywhere in the world, have you seen any socialists, Socialist-Revolutionaries, representatives of democracy, or whatever it is they call themselves—even the Mensheviks—have you ever heard that any of these have the temerity publicly to blame the American people for this, to say that they violated the principle of democracy, freedom, and so forth? Such a crank has not yet been born. But today, we get people here who call themselves by these titles, and even claim a right to belong to the same International that we belong to, and say that it is merely a piece of Bolshevik mischievousness—and everybody knows that the Bolsheviks are mischievous—to organise their own International and refuse to join the good, old, common to all, united, Berne International!

But I have digressed somewhat from my subject and must return to it. Today, in all countries, the word "Bolshevik" and the word "Soviet" have ceased to be regarded as queer terms, as they were only recently, like the word "Boxer", which we repeated without understanding what it meant. The word "Bolshevik" and the word "Soviet" are now being repeated in all the languages of the world. Every day the class-conscious workers see that the bourgeoisie of all countries release a flood of lies about Soviet power in the millions of copies of their newspapers, but they learn from this vituperation. Recently I read some American newspapers. I read the speech of a certain American parson who said that the Bolsheviks were immoral, that they had nationalised women, that they are robbers and plunderers. And I also read the reply of the American Socialists. They are distributing at five cents a copy the Constitution of the Soviet Republic of Russia, of this "dictatorship", which does not provide "equality of labour democracy". They reply by quoting a clause of the Constitution of these "usurpers", "robbers" and "tyrants" who disrupt the unity of labour democracy. Incidentally, in welcoming Breshkovskaya on the day she arrived in America the leading capitalist newspaper in New York carried a headline in letters a yard long stating: "Welcome, Granny!" The American Socialists reprinted this and wrote: "She is in favour of political democracy—is there anything surprising, American workers, in the fact that the capitalists praise her?" She stands for political democracy. Why should they praise her? Because she is opposed to the Soviet Constitution. "Well," said the American Socialists, "here is a clause from the Constitution of these robbers." And they always quote the same clause which says that those who exploit the labour of others shall not have the right to elect or be elected. This clause from our Constitution is known all over the world. And it is because Soviet power frankly states that all must be subordinated to the dictatorship of the proletariat, that it is a new type of state organisation—it is precisely for this reason that it has won the sympathies of the workers all over the world. This new state organisation is being born in travail because it is far more difficult, a million times more difficult, to overcome our disruptive, petty-bourgeois laxity than to suppress the tyrannical landowners or the tyrannical capitalists, but the effort bears a million times more fruit in creating the new organisation which knows no exploitation. When proletarian organisation solves this problem, socialism will triumph completely. And it is to this that you must devote all your activities both in the schools and in the field of adult education. Notwithstanding the extremely difficult conditions that prevail, and the fact that the first socialist revolution in history is taking place in a country with a very low level of culture, notwithstanding this, Soviet power has already won the recognition of the workers of other countries. The phrase "dictatorship of the proletariat" is a Latin phrase, and the working people who heard it for the first time did not know what it meant, and did not know how it could be instituted. Now this Latin phrase has been translated into the modern languages and we have shown that the dictatorship of the proletariat is Soviet power, the government under which the workers organise themselves and say that their organisation is superior to every other. No idler, no exploiter can belong to this organisation. This organisation has but one object, and that is, to overthrow capitalism. No false slogans, no fetishes like "freedom" and "equality", will deceive us. We recognise no freedom, no equality, no labour democracy if it conflicts with the cause of emancipating labour from the yoke of capital. This is what we incorporated in the Soviet Constitution, and we have already won for it the sympathies of the workers of all countries. They know that in spite of the difficulty with which the new order is being born, and in spite of the severe trials and even defeats which may fall to the lot of some of the Soviet republics, no power on earth can compel mankind to turn back. (*Stormy applause.*)

Published in the pamphlet: Vol. 29, pp. 349-50,
N. Lenin, *Two Speeches at*   374-76
the First All-Russia
Congress on Adult Education,
Moscow, 1919

A GREAT BEGINNING

(Excerpt)

If we get down to brass tacks, however, has it ever happened in history that a new mode of production has taken root immediately, without a long succession of setbacks, blunders and relapses? Half a century after the abolition of serfdom[101] there were still quite a number of survivals of serfdom in the Russian countryside. Half a century after the abolition of slavery in America the position of the Negroes was still very often one of semi-slavery. The bourgeois intellectuals, including the Mensheviks and Socialist-Revolutionaries, are true to themselves in serving capital and in continuing to use absolutely false arguments—before the proletarian revolution they accused us of being utopian; after the revolution they demand that we wipe out all traces of the past with fantastic rapidity!

Published in July 1919
as a separate pamphlet
in Moscow
Signed: N. Lenin

Vol. 29, p. 425

THE STATE

(Excerpt from a Lecture)

Whichever party we take in Russia or in any of the more civilised countries, we find that nearly all political disputes, disagreements and opinions now centre around the conception of the state. Is the state in a capitalist country, in a democratic republic—especially one like Switzerland or the U.S.A.—in the freest democratic republics, an expression of the popular will, the sum total of the general decision of the people, the expression of the national will, and so forth; or is the state a machine that enables the capitalists of those countries to maintain their power over the working class and the peasantry? That is the fundamental question around which all political disputes all over the world now centre. What do they say about Bolshevism? The bourgeois press abuses the Bolsheviks. You will not find a single newspaper that does not repeat the hackneyed accusation that the Bolsheviks violate popular rule. If our Mensheviks and Socialist-Revolutionaries in their simplicity of heart (perhaps it is not simplicity, or perhaps it is the simplicity which the proverb says is worse than robbery) think that they discovered and invented the accusation that the Bolsheviks have violated liberty and popular rule, they are ludicrously mistaken. Today every one of the richest newspapers in the richest countries, which spend tens of millions on their distribution and disseminate bourgeois lies and imperialist policy in tens of millions of copies—every one of these newspapers repeats these basic arguments and accusations against Bolshevism, namely, that the U.S.A., Britain and Switzerland are advanced states based on popular rule, whereas the Bolshevik republic is a state of bandits in which liberty is unknown, and that the Bolsheviks have violated the idea of popular rule and have even gone so far as to disperse the Constituent Assembly. These terrible accusations against the Bolsheviks are repeated all over the world. These accusations lead us directly to the question—what is the state? In order to understand these accusations, in order to study them and have a fully intelligent attitude towards them, and not to examine them on hearsay but with a firm opinion of our own, we must have a clear idea of what the state is. We have before us capitalist states of every kind and all the theories in defence of them which were created before the war. In order to answer the question properly we must critically examine all these theories and views.

I have already advised you to turn for help to Engels's book *The Origin of the Family, Private Property and the State*. This book says that every state in which private ownership of the land and means of production exists, in which capital dominates, however democratic it may be, is a capitalist state, a machine used by the capitalists to keep the working class and the poor peasants in subjection; while universal suffrage, a Constituent Assembly, a parliament are merely a form, a sort of promissory note, which does not change the real state of affairs.

The forms of domination of the state may vary: capital manifests its power in one way where one form exists, and in another way where another form exists—but essentially the power is in the hands of capital, whether there are voting qualifications or some other rights or not, or whether the republic is a democratic one or not—in fact, the more democratic it is the cruder and more cynical is the rule of capitalism. One of the most democratic republics in the world is the United States of America, yet nowhere (and those who have been there since 1905 probably know it) is the power of capital, the power of a handful of multimillionaires over the whole of society, so crude and so openly corrupt as in America. Once capital exists, it dominates the whole of society, and no democratic republic, no franchise can change its nature.

The democratic republic and universal suffrage were an immense progressive advance as compared with feudalism: they have enabled the proletariat to achieve its present unity and solidarity, to form those firm and disciplined ranks which are waging a systematic struggle against capital. There was nothing even approximately resembling this among the peasant serfs, not to speak of the slaves. The slaves, as we know, revolted, rioted, started civil wars, but they could never create a class-conscious majority and parties to lead the struggle, they could not clearly realise what their aims were, and even in the most revolutionary moments of history they were always pawns in the hands of the ruling classes. The bourgeois republic, parliament, universal suffrage—all represent great progress from the standpoint of the world development of society. Mankind moved towards capitalism, and it was capitalism alone which, thanks to urban culture, enabled the oppressed proletarian class to become conscious of itself and to create the world working-class movement, the millions of workers organised all over the world in parties—the socialist parties which are consciously leading the struggle of the masses. Without parliamentarism, without an electoral system, this development of the working class would have been impossible. That is why all these things have acquired such great importance in the eyes of the broad masses of people. That is why a radical change seems to be so difficult. It is not only the conscious hypocrites, scientists and priests that uphold and defend the bourgeois lie that the state is free and that it is its mission to defend the interests of all; so also do a large number of people who sincerely adhere to the old prejudices and who cannot understand the transition from the old, capitalist society to socialism. Not only people who are directly dependent on the bourgeoisie, not only those who live under the yoke of capital or who have been bribed by capital (there are a large number of all sorts of scientists, artists, priests, etc., in the service of capital), but even people who are simply under the sway of the prejudice of bourgeois liberty, have taken up arms against Bolshevism all over the world because when the Soviet Republic was founded it rejected these bourgeois lies and openly declared: you say your state is free, whereas in reality, as long as there is private property, your state, even if it is a democratic republic, is nothing but a machine used by the capitalists to suppress the workers, and the freer the state, the more clearly is this expressed. Examples of this are Switzerland in Europe and the United States in America. Nowhere does capital rule so cynically and ruthlessly, and nowhere is it so clearly apparent, as in these countries, although they are democratic republics, no matter how prettily they are painted and notwithstanding all the talk about labour democracy and the equality of all citizens. The fact is that in Switzerland and the United States capital dominates, and every attempt of the workers to achieve the slightest real improvement in their condition is immediately met by civil war. There are fewer soldiers, a smaller standing army, in these countries— Switzerland has a militia and every Swiss has a gun at home, while in America there was no standing army until quite recently—and so when there is a strike the bourgeoisie arms, hires soldiery and suppresses the strike; and nowhere is this suppression of the working-class movement accompanied by such ruthless severity as in Switzerland and the U.S.A., and nowhere does the influence of capital in parliament manifest itself as powerfully as in these countries. The power of capital is everything, the stock exchange is everything, while parliament and elections are marionettes, puppets.... But the eyes of the workers are being opened more and more, and the idea of Soviet government is spreading farther and farther afield, especially after the bloody carnage[102] we have just experienced. The necessity for a relentless war on the capitalists is becoming clearer and clearer to the working class.

Whatever guise a republic may assume, however democratic it may be, if it is a bourgeois republic, if it retains private ownership of the land and factories, and if private capital keeps the whole of society in wage-slavery, that is, if the republic does not carry out what is proclaimed in the Programme of our Party and in the Soviet Constitution, then this state is a machine for the suppression of some people by others. And we shall place this machine in the hands of the class that is to overthrow the power of capital. We shall reject all the old prejudices about the state meaning universal equality—for that is a fraud: as long as there is exploitation there cannot be equality. The landowner cannot be the equal of the worker, or the hungry man the equal of the full man. This machine called the state, before which people bowed in superstitious awe, believing the old tales that it means popular rule, tales which the proletariat declares to be a bourgeois lie—this machine the proletariat will smash. So far we have deprived the capitalists of this machine and have taken it over. We shall use this machine, or bludgeon, to destroy all exploitation. And when the possibility of exploitation no longer exists anywhere in the world, when there are no longer owners of land and owners of factories, and when there is no longer a situation in which some gorge while others starve, only when the possibility of this no longer exists shall we consign this machine to the scrap-heap. Then there will be no state and no exploitation. Such is the view of our Communist Party. I hope that we shall return to this subject in subsequent lectures, return to it again and again.

First published in   Vol. 29, pp. 484-88
Pravda No. 15, January 18, 1929

ANSWERS TO AN AMERICAN
JOURNALIST'S QUESTIONS[103]

I answer the five questions put to me on condition of the fulfilment of the written promise that my answers will be printed in full in over a hundred newspapers in the United States of America.[104]

1. The governmental programme of the Soviet Government was not a reformist, but a revolutionary one. Reforms are concessions obtained from a ruling class that retains its rule. Revolution is the overthrow of the ruling class. Reformist programmes, therefore, usually consist of many items of partial significance. Our revolutionary programme consisted properly of one general item—removal of the yoke of the landowners and capitalists, the overthrow of their power and the emancipation of the working people from those exploiters. This programme we have never changed. Some partial measures aimed at the realisation of the programme have often been subjected to change; their enumeration would require a whole volume. I will only mention that there is one other general point in our governmental programme which has, perhaps, given rise to the greatest number of changes of partial measures. That point is—the suppression of the exploiters' resistance. After the Revolution of October 25 (November 7), 1917 we did not close down even the bourgeois newspapers and there was no mention of terror at all. We released not only many of Kerensky's ministers, but even Krasnov who had made war on us. It was only after the exploiters, i.e., the capitalists, had begun developing their resistance that we began to crush that resistance systematically, applying even terror. This was the proletariat's response to such actions

of the bourgeoisie as the conspiracy with the capitalists of Germany, Britain, Japan, America and France to restore the rule of the exploiters in Russia, the bribery of the Czechoslovaks[105] with Anglo-French money, the bribery of Mannerheim, Denikin and others with German and French money, etc. One of the latest conspiracies leading to "a change"—to put it precisely, leading to increased terror against the bourgeoisie in Petrograd—was that of the bourgeoisie, acting jointly with the Mensheviks and Socialist-Revolutionaries; their conspiracy concerned the surrender of Petrograd, the seizure of Krasnaya Gorka by officer-conspirators, the bribing by British and French capitalists of employees of the Swiss Embassy and of many Russian employees, etc.

2. The activities of our Soviet Republic in Afghanistan, India and other Moslem countries outside Russia are the same as our activities among the numerous Moslems and other non-Russian peoples inside Russia. We have made it possible, for instance, for the Bashkirian people to establish an autonomous republic within Russia, we are doing everything possible to help the independent, free development of every nationality, the growth and dissemination of literature in the native language of each of them, we are translating and propagandising our Soviet Constitution which has the misfortune to be more pleasing to more than a thousand million inhabitants of the earth who belong to colonial, dependent, oppressed, underprivileged nations than the constitutions of the West-European and American bourgeois-"democratic" states that perpetuate private property in land and capital, i.e., strengthen the oppression of the working people of their own countries and of hundreds of millions of people in the colonies of Asia, Africa, etc., by a small number of "civilised" capitalists.

3. As far as the United States and Japan are concerned, our first political objective is to repulse their shameless, criminal, predatory invasion of Russia that serves only to enrich their capitalists. We have many times made solemn proposals of peace to both these countries, but they have not even answered us and continue to make war on us, helping Denikin and Kolchak, plundering Murmansk and

Archangel, ruining and laying waste to, especially, Eastern Siberia, where the Russian peasants are offering heroic resistance to the capitalist bandits of Japan and the United States of America.

We have one further political and economic objective in respect of all peoples—including those of the United States and Japan—fraternal alliance with the workers and all working people of all countries without exception.

4. We have, on many occasions, given a precise, clear and written exposition of the terms upon which we agree to conclude peace with Kolchak, Denikin and Manner-heim—for instance to Bullitt[106] who conducted negotiations with us (and with me personally in Moscow) on behalf of the United States Government, in a letter to Nansen,[107] etc. It is not our fault that the governments of the United States and other countries are afraid to publish those documents in full and that they hide the truth from the people. I will mention only our basic condition; we are prepared to pay all debts to France and other countries provided there is a real peace and not peace in words alone, i.e., if it is formally signed and ratified by the governments of Great Britain, France, the United States, Japan and Italy—Deni-kin, Kolchak, Mannerheim and the others being mere pawns in the hands of those governments.

5. More than anything else I should like to state the following to the American public:

Compared to feudalism, capitalism was an historical advance along the road of "liberty", "equality", "democracy" and "civilisation". Nevertheless capitalism was, and remains, a system of *wage-slavery*, of the enslavement of millions of working people, workers and peasants, by an insignificant minority of modern slave-owners, landowners and capitalists. Bourgeois democracy, as compared to feudalism, has changed the form of this economic slavery, has created a brilliant screen for it but has not, and could not, change its essence. Capitalism and bourgeois democracy are wage-slavery.

The gigantic progress of technology in general, and of means of transport in particular, and the tremendous growth of capital and banks have resulted in capitalism becoming mature and overmature. It has outlived itself. It has become the most reactionary hindrance to human progress. It has become reduced to the absolute power of a handful of millionaires and multimillionaires who send whole nations into a bloodbath to decide whether the German or the Anglo-French group of plunderers is to obtain the spoils of imperialism, power over the colonies, financial "spheres of influence" or "mandates to rule", etc.

During the war of 1914-18 tens of millions of people were killed or mutilated for that reason and for that reason alone. Knowledge of this truth is spreading with indomitable force and rapidity among the working people of all countries, the more so because the war has everywhere caused unparalleled ruin, and because interest on war debts has to be paid *everywhere,* even by the "victor" nations. What is this interest? It is a tribute of thousands of millions to the millionaire gentlemen who were kind enough to allow tens of millions of workers and peasants to kill and maim one another to settle the question of the division of profits by the capitalists.

The collapse of capitalism is inevitable. The revolutionary consciousness of the masses is everywhere growing; there are thousands of signs of this. One small sign, unimportant, but impressive to the man in the street, is the novels written by Henri Barbusse (*Le Feu, Clarté*) who was a peaceful, modest, law-abiding petty bourgeois, a philistine, a man in the street, when he went to the war.

The capitalists, the bourgeoisie, can at "best" put off the victory of socialism in one country or another at the cost of slaughtering further hundreds of thousands of workers and peasants. But they cannot save capitalism. The *Soviet Republic* has come to take the place of capitalism, the Republic which gives power to the working people and only to the working people, which entrusts the proletariat with the guidance of their liberation, which abolishes private property in land, factories and other means of production, because this private property is the source of the exploitation of the many by the few, the source of mass poverty, the source of predatory wars between nations, wars that enrich only the capitalists.

The victory of the world Soviet republic is certain.

A brief illustration in conclusion: the American bourgeoisie are deceiving the people by boasting of the liberty, equality and democracy of their country. But neither this nor any other bourgeoisie nor any government in the world can accept, it is afraid to accept, a contest with our government on the basis of real liberty, equality and democracy; let us suppose that an agreement ensured our government and any other government freedom to exchange ... pamphlets published in the name of the government in any language and containing the text of the laws of the given country, the text of its constitution, and an explanation of its superiority over the others.

Not one bourgeois government in the world would dare conclude such a peaceful, civilised, free, equal, democratic treaty with us.

Why? Because all of them, with the exception of Soviet governments, keep in power by the oppression and deception of the masses. But the great war of 1914-18 exposed the great deception.

Lenin

July 20, 1919

Pravda No. 162,   Vol. 29, pp. 515-19
July 25, 1919

Those who say that the Bolsheviks violate freedom and who propose the formation of a united socialist front, that is, an alliance with those who vacillated, and twice in the history of the Russian revolution went over to the side of the bourgeoisie—these people are very fond of accusing us of resorting to terror. They say that the Bolsheviks have introduced a system of terror in administration, and if Russia is to be saved, the Bolsheviks must renounce it. This reminds me of a witty French bourgeois who, in his bourgeois manner, said with reference to the abolition of the death penalty, "Let the murderers be the first to abolish the death penalty." I recall this when people say, "Let the Bolsheviks renounce the terror." Let the Russian capitalists and their allies, America, France and Britain, that is, those who first imposed terror on Soviet Russia, let them renounce it! They are the imperialists who attacked us and are still attacking us with all their military might, which is a thousand times greater than ours. Is it not terror for all the Entente countries, all the imperialists of Britain, France and America, to keep in their capitals servitors of international capital—whether their names are Sazonov or Maklakov—who have organised tens and hundreds of thousands of the dissatisfied, ruined, humiliated and indignant representatives of capital and the bourgeoisie? You must have heard about the plots among the military, you must have read about the latest plot in Krasnaya Gorka, which nearly led to the loss of Petrograd; what was this but a manifestation of terror on the part of the bourgeoisie of the whole world, which will commit any violence, crime and atrocity in order to reinstate the exploiters in Russia and stamp out the flames of the socialist revolution, which is now threatening even their own countries? There is the source of terror, that is where the responsibility lies! That is why we are sure that those who preach renunciation of terror in Russia are nothing but conscious, or unwitting, tools and agents of the imperialist terrorists, who are trying to crush Russia with their blockades and aid to Denikin and Kolchak. But their cause is a hopeless one.

Russia is the country assigned by history the role of trail-blazer of the socialist revolution, and that is just why so much struggle and suffering has fallen to our lot. The capitalists and imperialists of other countries realise that Russia is up in arms, and that the future not only of Russian but of international capital is being decided in Russia. That is why in all their press—in all the bourgeois world press which they have bribed with their many millions—they spread the most incredible slanders about the Bolsheviks.

They are attacking Russia in the name of the selfsame principles of "Liberty, Equality and Bentham". If you come across someone in this country who thinks that when he speaks of freedom and equality and of their violation by the Bolsheviks, he is championing something that is quite independent, the principles of democracy in general, ask him to have a look at the capitalist press of Europe. What is the screen being used by Denikin and Kolchak, what is the screen being used by European capitalists and the bourgeoisie in their efforts to crush Russia? Liberty and equality—that is all they talk about! When the Americans, British and French seized Archangel, when they sent their troops to the South, they did so in defence of liberty and equality. That is the kind of slogan they use as camouflage, and that is why the proletariat of Russia has risen against world capital in this fierce struggle. Such is the purpose of these slogans of freedom and equality which all agents of the bourgeoisie use to deceive the people, and which intellectuals who really side with the workers and peasants have to expose.

We see that as the attempts of the Entente imperialists

become more desperate and vicious they meet with ever greater resistance on the part of the proletariat of their own countries. The first attempt at an international strike by workers in Britain, France and Italy against their governments that was made on July 21 had as its slogan, "Hands off Russia, and an honest peace with the Republic". This strike failed. Separate strikes broke out in Britain, France and Italy. In America and Canada, everything that looks like Bolshevism is fiercely persecuted. In the last few years, we have gone through two great revolutions. We know how hard it was for the vanguard of the Russian working people in 1905 to rise in the struggle against tsarism. We know that after the first bloody lesson of January 9, 1905, the strike movement developed slowly and laboriously until October 1905, when the mass strike scored its first success in Russia. We know how hard the going was. This was proved by the experience of two revolutions, although the situation in Russia was more revolutionary than in other countries. We know with what difficulty the forces for the struggle against capitalism are mobilised in a series of strikes. That is why we are not surprised by the failure of this first international strike of July 21. We know that there is much greater resistance and opposition to the revolution in the European countries than over here. We know that in fixing July 21 as the date for an international strike, the workers of Britain, France and Italy had to overcome incredible difficulties. It was an experiment unparalleled in history. It is not surprising that it failed. But we also know that the working people of the leading and most civilised countries are on our side despite the European bourgeoisie's rabid hatred of us, that they understand our cause, and whatever the hardships of the revolution and the trials ahead, whatever the atmosphere of lies and deception in the name of the "freedom and equality" of capital, equality of the starved and the overfed, whatever the atmosphere, we know that our cause is the cause of the workers of all countries, and that is why this cause will inevitably defeat international capital.

Pravda No. 170,
August 3, 1919

Vol. 29, pp. 536-39

HOW THE BOURGEOISIE UTILISES RENEGADES
(Excerpt)

... To show what Kautsky's disquisitions on the subject of "terrorism" are worth, whom, *which class,* they *serve,* I shall cite in full a short article by a *liberal* writer. It is a letter to *The New Republic* (June 25, 1919), a liberal American journal which, generally speaking, expresses the petty-bourgeois viewpoint. However, it is preferable to Kautsky's in not presenting that viewpoint either as revolutionary socialism or Marxism.

This is the full text of the letter:

MANNERHEIM AND KOLCHAK

Sir: The Allied governments have refused to recognise the Soviet Government of Russia because, as they state:

1. The Soviet Government is—or was—pro-German.
2. The Soviet Government is based on terrorism.
3. The Soviet Government is undemocratic and unrepresentative of the Russian people.

Meanwhile the Allied governments have long since recognised the present whiteguard Government of Finland under the dictatorship of General Mannerheim, although it appears:

1. That German troops aided the whiteguards in crushing the Socialist Republic of Finland, and that General Mannerheim sent repeated telegrams of sympathy and esteem to the Kaiser. Meanwhile the Soviet Government was busily undermining the German Government with propaganda among troops on the Russian front. The Finnish Government was infinitely more pro-German than the Russian.

2. That the present Government of Finland on coming into power executed in cold blood within a few days' time 16,700 members of the old Socialist Republic, and imprisoned in starvation camps 70,000 more. Meanwhile the total executions in Russia for the year ended November 1, 1918, were officially stated to have been 3,800, including many

corrupt Soviet officials as well as counter-revolutionists. The Finnish Government was infinitely more terroristic than the Russian.

3. That after killing and imprisoning nearly 90,000 socialists, and driving some 50,000 more over the border into Russia—and Finland is a small country with an electorate of only about 400,000—the white-guard government deemed it sufficiently safe to hold elections. In spite of all precautions, a majority of socialists were elected, but General Mannerheim, like the Allies after the Vladivostok elections, allowed not one of them to be seated. Meanwhile the Soviet Government had disenfranchised all those who do no useful work for a living. The Finnish Government was considerably less democratic than the Russian.

And much the same story might be rehearsed in respect to that great champion of democracy and the new order, Admiral Kolchak of Omsk, whom the Allied governments have supported, supplied and equipped, and are now on the point of officially recognising.

Thus every argument that the Allies have urged against the recognition of the Soviets, can be applied with more strength and honesty against Mannerheim and Kolchak. Yet the latter are recognised, and the blockade draws ever tighter about starving Russia.

Stuart Chase

Washington, D. C.

This letter written by a bourgeois liberal effectively exposes all the vileness of the Kautskys, Martovs, Chernovs, Brantings and other heroes of the Berne yellow International and their betrayal of socialism.

For, first, Kautsky and all these heroes lie about Soviet Russia on the question of terrorism and democracy. Secondly, they do not assess developments from the standpoint of the class struggle as it is actually developing on a world scale and in the sharpest possible form, but from the standpoint of a petty-bourgeois, philistine longing for what might have been if there had been no close link between bourgeois democracy and capitalism, if there were no whiteguards in the world, if they had not been supported by the world bourgeoisie, and so on and so forth. Thirdly, a comparison of this American letter with the writings of Kautsky and Co. will clearly show that Kautsky's *objective* role is servility to the bourgeoisie.

The world bourgeoisie supports the Mannerheims and Kolchaks in an attempt to stifle Soviet power, alleging that it is terrorist and undemocratic. Such are the facts. And Kautsky, Martov, Chernov and Co. are only singing songs about terrorism and democracy in chorus with the bourgeoisie, for the world bourgeoisie is singing this song to deceive the workers and strangle the workers' revolution. The personal honesty of "socialists" who sing the same song "sincerely", i.e., because they are extremely dull-witted, does not in any way alter the objective role played by the song. The "honest opportunists", the Kautskys, Martovs, Longuets and Co., have become "honest" (in their unprecedented spinelessness) *counter-revolutionaries*.

Such are the facts.

An American liberal realises—not because he is theoretically equipped to do so, but simply because he is an attentive observer of developments in a sufficiently broad light, on a world scale—that the *world bourgeoisie has organised and is waging a civil war against the revolutionary proletariat* and, accordingly, is supporting Kolchak and Denikin in Russia, Mannerheim in Finland, the Georgian Mensheviks, those lackeys of the bourgeoisie, in the Caucasus, the Polish imperialists and Polish Kerenskys in Poland, the Scheidemanns in Germany, the counter-revolutionaries (Mensheviks and capitalists) in Hungary, etc., etc.

But Kautsky, like the inveterate reactionary philistine he is, continues snivelling about the fears and horrors of civil war! All semblance of revolutionary understanding, and all semblance of historical realism (for it is high time the inevitability of imperialist war being turned into civil war were realised) have disappeared. This is, furthermore, directly abetting the bourgeoisie, it is *helping* them, and Kautsky is *actually on the side of the bourgeoisie* in the civil war that is being waged, or is obviously being prepared, throughout the world.

Published in September 1919   Vol. 30, pp. 29-32

TO THE AMERICAN WORKERS

Comrades,

About a year ago, in my letter to the American workers (dated August 20th, 1918)[108] I exposed to you the situation in Soviet Russia and the problems facing the latter. That was before the German revolution. The events which since took place in the world's history proved how right the Bolsheviks were in their estimation of the imperialist war of 1914-18 in general and of the Entente imperialism in particular. As for the Soviet power it has become familiar and dear to the minds and hearts of the working masses of the whole world. Everywhere the working people, in spite of the influence of the old leaders with their chauvinism and opportunism penetrating them through and through, become aware of the rottenness of the bourgeois parliaments and of the necessity of the Soviet power, the power of the working people, the dictatorship of the proletariat, for the sake of the emancipation of humanity from the yoke of capital. And Soviet power will win in the whole world, however furiously, however frantically the bourgeoisie of all countries rages and storms. The bourgeoisie inundates Russia with blood, waging war upon us and inciting against us the counter-revolutionaries, those who wish the yoke of capital to be restored. The bourgeoisie inflicts upon the working masses of Russia unprecedented sufferings through the blockade and through the help it gives to counter-revolution, but we have already defeated Kolchak and we are carrying on the war against Denikin with the firm assurance of our coming victory.

N. Lenin

September 23, 1919

* * *

I am often asked whether those American opponents of the war against Russia—not only workers, but mainly bourgeois—are right, who expect from us, after peace is concluded, not only resumption of trade relations, but also the possibility of receiving concessions in Russia. I repeat once more that they are right. A durable peace would be such a relief to the working people of Russia that they would undoubtedly agree to certain concessions being granted. The granting of concessions under reasonable terms is desirable also for us, as one of the means of attracting into Russia, during the period of the coexistence side by side of socialist and capitalist states, the technical help of the countries which are more advanced in this respect.

N. Lenin

September 23, 1919

Published in English on
December 27, 1919 in the
magazine *Soviet Russia* No. 30

First published in Russian
in *Pravda* No. 308,
November 7, 1930

Vol. 30, pp. 38-39

ANSWERS TO QUESTIONS
PUT BY A *CHICAGO DAILY NEWS* CORRESPONDENT

October 5, 1919

I beg to apologise for my bad English. I am glad to answer your few questions.

1. What is the present policy of the Soviet Government on the question of peace?
2. What, in general outline, are the peace terms put forward by Soviet Russia?

Our peace policy is the former, that is, we have accepted the peace proposition of Mr. Bullitt.[109] We have never changed our peace conditions (question 2), which are formulated with Mr. Bullitt.

We have many times officially proposed peace to the Entente before coming of Mr. Bullitt.

3. Is the Soviet Government prepared to guarantee absolute non-intervention in the internal affairs of foreign states?

We are willing to guarantee it.

4. Is the Soviet Government prepared to prove that it represents the majority of the Russian people?

Yes, the Soviet Government is the most democratic government of all governments in the world. We are willing to prove it.

5. What is the position of the Soviet Government in respect of an economic understanding with America?

We are decidedly for an economic understanding with America—with all countries but *especially* with America.

If necessary we can give you the full text of our peace conditions as formulated by our government with Mr. Bullitt.

Wl. Oulianoff (*N. Lenin*)

Published in the *Chicago Daily News* No. 257, October 27, 1919

First published in Russian in 1942

Vol. 30, pp. 50-51

ADDRESS TO THE SECOND ALL-RUSSIA CONGRESS OF COMMUNIST ORGANISATIONS OF THE PEOPLES OF THE EAST
NOVEMBER 22, 1919
(Excerpt)

Everyone knows that the social revolution is maturing in Western Europe by leaps and bounds, and that the same thing is happening in America and in Britain, the countries ostensibly representing culture and civilisation, victors over the Huns, the German imperialists. Yet when it came to the Treaty of Versailles, everyone saw that it was a hundred times more rapacious than the Treaty of Brest which the German robbers forced upon us, and that it was the heaviest blow the capitalists and imperialists of those luckless victor countries could possibly have struck at themselves. The Treaty of Versailles opened the eyes of the people of the victor nations, and showed that in the case of Britain and France, even though they are democratic states, we have before us not representatives of culture and civilisation, but countries ruled by imperialist predators. The internal struggle among these predators is developing so swiftly that we may rejoice in the knowledge that the Treaty of Versailles is only a seeming victory for the jubilant imperialists, and that in reality it signifies the bankruptcy of the entire imperialist world and the resolute abandonment by the working people of those socialists who during the war allied themselves with the representatives of decaying imperialism and defended one of the groups of belligerent predators. The eyes of the working people have been opened because the Treaty of Versailles was a rapacious peace and showed that France and Britain had actually fought Germany in order to strengthen their rule over the colonies and to enhance their imperialist might. That internal struggle grows broader as time goes on. Today I saw a wireless message from London dated November 21, in which American journalists—men who cannot be suspected of sympathising with revolutionaries— say that in France an unprecedented outburst of hatred towards the Americans is to be observed, because the Americans refuse to ratify the Treaty of Versailles.

Britain and France are victors, but they are up to their ears in debt to America, who has decided that the French and the British may consider themselves victors as much as they like, but that she is going to skim the cream and exact usurious interest for her assistance during the war; and the guarantee of this is to be the American Navy which is now being built and is overtaking the British Navy in size. And the crudeness of the Americans' rapacious imperialism may be seen from the fact that American agents are buying white slaves, women and girls, and shipping them to America for the development of prostitution. Just think, free, cultured America supplying white slaves for brothels! Conflicts with American agents are occurring in Poland and Belgium. That is a tiny illustration of what is taking place on a vast scale in every little country which received assistance from the Entente. Take Poland, for instance. You find American agents and profiteers going there and buying up all the wealth of Poland, who boasts that she is now an independent power. Poland is being bought up by American agents. There is not a factory or branch of industry which is not in the pockets of the Americans. The Americans have become so brazen that they are beginning to enslave that "great and free victor", France, who was formerly a country of usurers, but is now deep in debt to America, because she has lost her economic strength, and has not enough grain or coal of her own and cannot develop her material resources on a large scale, while America insists that the tribute be paid unreservedly and in full. It is thus becoming increasingly apparent that

France, Britain and other powerful countries are economically bankrupt. In the French elections the Clericals have
gained the upper hand. The French people, who were deceived into devoting all their strength supposedly to the
defence of freedom and democracy against Germany, have
now been rewarded with an interminable debt, with the
sneers of the rapacious American imperialists and, on top
of it, with a Clerical majority consisting of representatives
of the most savage reaction.

Bulletin of the C.C., R.C.P.(B.)
No. 9, December 20, 1919

Vol. 30, pp. 155-57

From THE POLITICAL REPORT
OF THE CENTRAL COMMITTEE AT THE EIGHTH
ALL-RUSSIA CONFERENCE OF THE R.C.P.(B.)
DECEMBER 2, 1919

...It is specifically those countries that always have been and still are regarded as the most democratic, civilised and cultured that conducted a war against Russia by the most brutal means, without even a shade of legality. The Bolsheviks are accused of violating democracy—this is the most popular argument against us among the Mensheviks and Socialist-Revolutionaries and in the entire European bourgeois press. But not one of those democratic states has taken or would dare to take the risk under the laws of its own country of declaring war on Soviet Russia. Parallel to this there is a protest, outwardly unnoticeable but nevertheless a profound protest on the part of the working-class press which asks where, in their constitution, in the constitution of France, Britain or America, are to be found laws permitting the conduct of war without having declared war and without having consulted parliament? The press of Britain, France and America has proposed to arraign their heads of state for a crime against the state, for declaring war without the permission of parliament. Such proposals have been made, although it is true that it was in papers that come out not more than once a week and are probably confiscated not less than once a month and have a circulation of a few hundred or a few thousand copies. The leaders of the responsible government parties could afford to ignore such papers. But here we have to consider two different tendencies; the ruling classes throughout the world

publish well-known capitalist dailies in millions of copies
and these are packed with unprecedented lies and slander
against the Bolsheviks. But down below, the working-class
masses learn about the falsity of that whole campaign from
the soldiers who have returned from Russia. That is why
it became necessary for the Entente to withdraw its forces
from Russia.

Bulletin of the C.C., R.C.P.(B.)   Vol. 30, pp. 172-73
No. 9, December 20, 1919

DRAFT RESOLUTION
OF THE EIGHTH ALL-RUSSIA CONFERENCE
OF THE R.C.P.(B.) ON FOREIGN POLICY[110]

The Russian Socialist Federative Soviet Republic wishes to live in peace with all peoples and devote all its efforts to internal development so as to put production, transport and government affairs in order on the basis of the Soviet system; this has so far been prevented by the intervention of the Entente and the starvation blockade.

The workers' and peasants' government has made repeated peace proposals to the Entente powers—the message from the People's Commissariat of Foreign Affairs to the American representative, Mr. Poole, on August 5, 1918; to President Wilson on October 24, 1918; to all Entente governments through representatives of neutral countries on November 3, 1918; a message from the Sixth All-Russia Congress of Soviets on November 7, 1918; Litvinov's Note in Stockholm to all Entente representatives on December 23, 1918; then there were the messages of January 12, January 17 and February 4, 1919, and the draft treaty drawn up jointly with Bullitt on March 12, 1919; and a message through Nansen on May 7, 1919.

The Seventh Congress of Soviets fully approves these many steps taken by the Council of People's Commissars and the People's Commissariat of Foreign Affairs, once more confirms its lasting desire for peace and again proposes to the Entente powers, Britain, France, the United States of America, Italy and Japan, individually and collectively, to begin immediately negotiations on peace; the Congress instructs the All-Russia Central Executive Committee, the Council of People's Commissars and the People's Commissariat of Foreign Affairs to continue this peace policy systematically (or: to continue this peace policy systematically, taking all appropriate measures to ensure its success).

Written on December 2, 1919

First published in 1932

Vol. 30, pp. 191-92

From THE REPORT
OF THE ALL-RUSSIA CENTRAL EXECUTIVE
COMMITTEE
AND THE COUNCIL OF PEOPLE'S COMMISSARS
DELIVERED AT THE SEVENTH ALL-RUSSIA
CONGRESS OF SOVIETS
DECEMBER 5, 1919

Examining the history of the Entente intervention and its political lesson for us from this point of view, I would say that it could be divided into three main stages, each of which has successively given us full and lasting victory.

The first stage, naturally the most convenient and easiest for the Entente countries, involved their attempt to settle matters with Soviet Russia by using their own troops. Of course, after the Entente countries had defeated Germany they had armies of millions of men who had not yet openly declared for peace and who did not immediately recover from the fright given them by the bogey of German imperialism, which had been used to scare them in all the Western countries. At that time, of course, from the military point of view, and from the point of view of foreign policy, it would have been easy for the Entente countries to take a tenth part of their armies and dispatch them to Russia. Note that they completely dominated at sea, that they had complete naval supremacy. Troop transportation and supplies were always completely under their control. Had the Entente countries, who hated us as only the bourgeoisie can hate the socialist revolution, then been able to fling even a tenth part of their armies against us with any success, there cannot be the slightest doubt that Soviet

Russia would have been doomed and would have met the same fate as Hungary.

Why did the Entente countries fail to achieve this? They landed troops in Murmansk. The drive into Siberia was undertaken with the aid of Entente troops, and Japanese troops continue to hold a distant slice of Eastern Siberia, while there were military units, even if not big ones, from all the Entente states in all parts of Western Siberia. Then French troops were landed in the South of Russia. That was the first stage of international intervention in our affairs, the first attempt, so to speak, to crush the Soviets with troops from the Entente's own countries, i.e., with the aid of workers and peasants of the more advanced countries, who were splendidly equipped; generally speaking the Entente countries lacked nothing in the way of technical and material means for the campaign. There were no obstacles confronting them. How, then, are we to explain the failure of that attempt? It ended in the Entente countries having to withdraw their troops, because they proved incapable of waging a struggle against revolutionary Soviet Russia. That, comrades, has always been our main and principal argument. From the very outset of the revolution we have said that we constitute a party of the international proletariat, and that, however great the difficulties facing the revolution, there would come a time when, at the most decisive moment, the sympathy, the solidarity of the workers oppressed by international imperialism would make itself felt. For this we were accused of being utopians. But experience has shown that while we cannot always and in all cases rely on action by the proletariat, at any rate we may say that during these two years of the world's history we have been proved correct a thousand times. The attempt by the British and French to crush Soviet Russia with their own troops, an attempt that promised them certain and very easy success in a minimum of time, ended in failure; the British troops have left Archangel, and the French troops that had landed in the South have all been sent home. Despite the blockade, despite the ring drawn around us, news does reach us from Western Europe, we do get British and French newspapers, even if only sporadically, from which we learn that letters sent by British soldiers from Archangel Region have somehow reached Britain and been published there. We know that the name of the Frenchwoman, Comrade Jeanne Labourbe, who engaged in communist activity among French soldiers and workers and was shot in Odessa, became known to the entire French proletariat and became a battle-cry, a name around which all French workers united for action against international imperialism despite the apparently insurmountable factional trends of syndicalism. The words of Comrade Radek, who fortunately, as today's reports state, has been liberated by Germany and whom we shall perhaps see soon, that the soil of Russia, aflame with the fire of revolution, would prove inaccessible to the Entente troops—these words, which seemed to be just a writer's flight of fancy, were actually realised. Despite all our backwardness, despite all the burden of our struggle, the troops of Britain and France proved incapable of fighting us on our own soil. The result was a victory for us. The first time that they tried to send massive military forces against us—and without them victory is impossible—the only result was that, thanks to their correct class instinct, the French and British soldiers brought home from Russia the very ulcer of Bolshevism that the German imperialists were fighting when they expelled our envoys from Berlin. They thought they would protect themselves in this way against the ulcer of Bolshevism, which now spreads over the whole of Germany in the shape of a strengthened labour movement. The victory we won in compelling the evacuation of the British and French troops was the greatest of our victories over the Entente countries. We deprived them of their soldiers. Our response to the unlimited military and technical superiority of the Entente countries was to deprive them of it through the solidarity of the working people against the imperialist governments.

This revealed how superficial and uncertain it is to judge these so-called democratic countries by accepted criteria. Their parliaments have stable bourgeois majorities. This they call "democracy". Capital dominates and weighs down everything and they still resort to military censorship. And

they call that "democracy". Among the millions of copies
of their newspapers and magazines you would be hard put
to find any but an insignificant few that contain even a
hint of anything favourable about the Bolsheviks. That is
why they say: "We are protected against the Bolsheviks,
there is order in our countries", and they call it "democracy". How could it happen that a small section of British
soldiers and French sailors were able to compel the withdrawal of the Entente troops from Russia? There is something wrong here. It means that even in Britain, France
and America the mass of the people are for us; it means
that all these external features, as socialists who refuse to
betray socialism have always asserted, are a deception; it
means that the bourgeois parliamentary system, bourgeois
democracy, bourgeois freedom of the press are merely
freedom for the capitalists, freedom to bribe public opinion,
to exert pressure on it by all the power of money. That is
what socialists always said until the imperialist war scattered
them to their national camps and turned each national
group of socialists into lackeys of their own bourgeoisie.
That was said by socialists before the war, that was always
said by the internationalists and Bolsheviks during the
war—and it all proved to be absolutely correct. All the
external features, all the window-dressings, are a fraud;
and this is becoming increasingly obvious to the people.
They all shout about democracy, but in no parliament in
the world did they dare to say that they were declaring
war on Soviet Russia. That is why we read in the numerous
French, British and American publications now available
the proposal to "place the heads of state in the dock for
having violated the Constitution, for waging war on Russia
without declaring war". When and where was it sanctioned,
what article of the Constitution, what parliament sanctioned it? Where did they gather their parliamentary
representatives together, even after taking the precaution
to imprison all Bolsheviks and near-Bolsheviks, to use the
expression of the French press? Even under those conditions they did not dare to state in their parliaments that
they were fighting Russia. That was why the splendidly
armed, previously undefeated troops of Britain and France

were unable to defeat us and departed from Archangel Region in the North, and from the South.

That was our first and chief victory, because it was not only a military victory, it was not really a military victory at all—it was actually a victory of that international solidarity of the working people for which we began the whole revolution, and which we pointed to and said that, however numerous the trials we would have to undergo, all these sacrifices would be repaid a hundredfold by the development of the world revolution, which is inevitable. It was apparent from the fact that in the sphere where the grossest material factors play the greatest part, namely, in the military sphere, we defeated the Entente countries by depriving them of the workers and peasants in soldiers' uniforms.

The first victory was followed by the second period of Entente intervention in our affairs. Each nation is headed by a group of politicians who possess wonderful experience, and that is why, after losing this stake, they placed another, taking advantage of their dominant position in the world. There is not a single country, not a single bit of the earth's surface, which is not in fact totally dominated by British, French and American finance capital. That was the basis for the new attempt they made, namely, to compel the small countries surrounding Russia, many of which had been liberated and had been able to declare themselves independent only during the war—Poland, Estonia, Finland, Georgia, the Ukraine, etc.—to compel these small states to go to war against Russia on British, French and American money.

You may remember, comrades, that our newspapers reported a speech by Churchill, the well-known British Cabinet Minister, in which he said that 14 states would attack Russia and that September would see the fall of Petrograd, and December that of Moscow. I heard that Churchill then disclaimed this report, but it was taken from the Swedish *Folkets Dagblad—Politiken* of August 25. But even if this source proved unreliable we know full well that Churchill and the British imperialists acted precisely in this way. We are perfectly well aware that everything was done to

exert pressure on Finland, Estonia and other small countries, in order to persuade them to wage war on Soviet
Russia. I happened to read a leading article in *The Times,*
the most influential bourgeois newspaper in Britain, a leader written when Yudenich's troops, obviously supplied,
equipped and conveyed on board Entente transports, were
a few versts from Petrograd, and Detskoye Selo had been
taken. The article was a veritable onslaught, in which the
maximum pressure was exerted—military, diplomatic and
historical. British capital flung itself on Finland and faced
her with an ultimatum: The eyes of the whole world are
on Finland, said the British capitalists, the entire fate of
Finland depends on whether she understands her role,
whether she will help to crush the filthy, dirty, bloody
wave of Bolshevism and liberate Russia. And in return for
this "great and moral" work, for this "noble, civilised"
work, Finland was promised so many million pounds, such-
and-such a piece of territory, and such-and-such benefits.
And what was the result? There was a time when Yudenich's troops were a few versts away from Petrograd, when
Denikin stood to the north of Orel, when the slightest assistance to them would have quickly settled the fate of
Petrograd to the advantage of our enemies, in a minimum
of time and at negligible cost.

The entire pressure of the Entente countries was brought
to bear on Finland, a country that is up to its neck in debt
to them. And not only in debt: Finland cannot carry on
for one month without the aid of these countries. But how
did the "miracle" of our having won the battle against such
an enemy happen? And win it we did. Finland did not
enter the war, Yudenich was defeated, so was Denikin, and
that at a time when joint action by them would most
surely, most swiftly have settled the whole struggle to the
advantage of international capitalism. We won the battle
with international imperialism in this most serious and
desperate trial of strength. But how did we do it? How
could such a "miracle" have taken place? It took place
because the Entente backed the same card as all capitalist
states, which operate wholly and solely by deception and
pressure; that was why everything they did aroused such

resistance that the result was to our advantage. We were very poorly armed, worn out, and we said to the Finnish workers, whom the Finnish bourgeoisie had crushed, "You must not fight against us." The Entente countries appeared strong in their armaments, with all their outward might, with the food they were in a position to supply to these countries, and demanded that they fight against us. We won this battle. We won because the Entente countries had no troops of their own to fling against us, they had to resort to the forces of the small nations, but here, not only the workers and peasants, but even the considerable section of that very bourgeoisie that had crushed the working class did not in the end go against us.

When the Entente imperialists spoke of democracy and independence, these nations had the impudence from the Entente viewpoint, and foolishness from our viewpoint, to take these promises seriously and to understand independence as really implying independence, and not a means of enriching the British and French capitalists. They thought that democracy meant living as free men, and not that all American multimillionaires would be able to plunder their country, or that every tinpot aristocrat of an officer should be able to behave like a swine and turn into a brazen black-marketeer prepared, for the sake of a few hundred per cent profit, to do the filthiest of jobs. That was how we won! The Entente encountered opposition to its pressure on these small countries, on each of these 14 countries. The Finnish bourgeoisie who employed White Terror to crush tens of thousands of Finnish workers know that this will not be forgotten, and that the German bayonets that made it possible no longer exist—these Finnish bourgeois hate the Bolsheviks as intensely as an exploiter would hate the workers who kicked him out. Nevertheless the Finnish bourgeoisie said to themselves, "If we follow the instructions of the Entente, that means we shall undoubtedly lose all hope of independence." And this independence was given to them by the Bolsheviks in November 1917, when Finland had a bourgeois government. The attitude of wide sections of the Finnish bourgeoisie, therefore, proved to be one of vacillation. We won the battle with the Entente countries because they counted on the small nations and at the same time repelled them.

This experience confirms, on an enormous, global scale, what we have always said. There are two forces on earth that can decide the destiny of mankind. One force is international capitalism, and should it be victorious it will display this force in countless atrocities as may be seen from the history of every small nation's development. The other force is the international proletariat that is fighting for the socialist revolution through the dictatorship of the proletariat, which it calls workers' democracy. Neither the vacillating elements here in Russia, nor the bourgeoisie of the small countries believed us; they called us utopians or bandits or even worse, for there is no stupid and monstrous accusation that they will not fling at us. But when they faced up squarely to the issue of either going with the Entente countries and helping them to crush the Bolsheviks, or of helping the Bolsheviks by neutrality, we proved to have won the battle and to have got that neutrality. We had no treaties, whereas Britain, France and America had all sorts of promissory notes, all sorts of treaties; nevertheless the small nations did as we wanted them to; they did so not because the Polish, Finnish, Lithuanian or Latvian bourgeoisie derived satisfaction from conducting their policy in a way that suited the Bolsheviks—that, of course, is nonsense—but because our definition of the historical forces involved was correct, namely, that either brute capital would be victorious, and then, even if it were in the most democratic republic, it would crush all the small nations of the world—or the dictatorship of the proletariat would be victorious, which is the sole hope of all working people and of the small, downtrodden and weak nations. It turned out that we were right not only in theory, but also in practical world politics. When this battle for the troops of Finland and Estonia took place we won it, although they could have crushed us with insignificant forces. We won the battle despite the Entente countries having thrown the enormous weight of their financial pressure, their military might, and their food supplies into the fray in order to compel Finland to take action.

That, comrades, was the second stage of international intervention, our second historic victory. First, we won the workers and peasants away from Britain, France and America. These troops could not fight against us. Secondly, we won away from them these small countries, all of which are against us, and in which not Soviet but bourgeois rule dominates. They displayed friendly neutrality towards us and acted contrary to the desires of that mighty world force, the Entente, for it was a beast that wanted to crush them.

We witness here on a world scale the same thing that happened to the Siberian peasants, who believed in the Constituent Assembly and helped the Socialist-Revolutionaries and Mensheviks to join forces with Kolchak and to strike at us. When they learned to their own cost that Kolchak represented the dictatorship of the very worst exploiters, a plunderous dictatorship of landowners and capitalists which was worse than that of the tsar, they organised the tremendous number of revolts in Siberia about which comrades have given us reliable information, and which now guarantee the complete return to us of Siberia, this time politically conscious. What happened to the Siberian peasant, with all his backwardness and political ignorance, has now happened on a broader scale, on a world scale, to all the small nations. They hated the Bolsheviks; some of them had suppressed the Bolsheviks with a bloody hand, with furious White Terror, but when they saw their "liberators", the British officers, they understood the meaning of British and American "democracy". When representatives of the British and American bourgeoisie appeared in Finland and Estonia, the acts of suppression they began were more brazen than those of the Russian imperialists had been, because the Russian imperialists had belonged to an older period and did not know how to suppress properly, whereas these people do know, and go about it thoroughly.

That is why this victory at the second stage is a far more lasting one than is apparent at the moment. I am not exaggerating at all, and consider exaggerations to be extremely dangerous. I have not the slightest doubt that further attempts will be made by the Entente to set against us now one, now another of the small states that are our neighbours. Such attempts will occur because the small states are wholly dependent on the Entente, because all this talk about freedom, independence and democracy is sheer hypocrisy, and the Entente may compel them once again to raise their hand against us. But if this attempt was foiled at such a convenient moment when it was so easy to wage a struggle against us, we may, I think, say definitely that in this respect the main difficulty is undoubtedly behind us. We are entitled to say this, and to say it without the slightest exaggeration, fully conscious that the Entente countries possess a tremendous advantage in strength. We have won a lasting victory. Attempts will be made against us, but we shall defeat them with greater ease, because the small states, despite their bourgeois system, have become convinced by experience, not theory—these gentlemen are theory-proof—that the Entente is a more brazen and predatory brute than the one they have in their minds when they think of the Bolsheviks, the bogey used to scare children and cultured philistines all over Europe.

Comrades, from what I have said about our international successes it follows—and, I think, it is not necessary to dwell at length on this—that we must repeat our peace proposal in a manner that is calm and business-like to the maximum degree. We must do this because it is a proposal we have made many times, and each time we gained something in the eyes of every educated man, even if he was our enemy, that made him blush with shame. That was the case when Bullitt came here, was received by Comrade Chicherin, talked with him and with me, and when we concluded a preliminary agreement on peace in the course of a few hours. And he assured us (those gentlemen like to boast) that America is everything, and who would worry about France in face of America's strength? But when we signed the agreement the French and British ministers did this. (*Lenin makes an expressive gesture with his foot. Laughter.*) Bullitt was left with a useless piece of paper and he was told, "Who would have thought you were naïve and foolish enough to believe in the democracy of Britain and France?" (*Applause.*) The result is that in the same issue I read the full text of the agreement with Bullitt in French—and it was published in all the British and American newspapers. The result is that they are showing themselves to the whole world to be either rogues or infants—let them take their choice! (*Applause.*) All the sympathies even of the petty bourgeoisie, even of those bourgeois who have any sort of an education and who recall how they once fought their own tsars and kings, are on our side, because we signed the hardest possible peace terms in a business-like manner and said, "The price of the blood of our workers and soldiers is too high for us; we shall pay you businessmen a heavy tribute as the price of peace; we consent to a heavy tribute to preserve the lives of our workers and peasants." That is why I think there is no reason for us to dwell long on this, and in conclusion I shall read a draft resolution that will express, in the name of the Congress of Soviets, our unwavering desire to pursue a policy of peace. (*Applause.*)

Published in *Pravda* Nos. 275, 276 and 277, December 7, 9 and 10, 1919

Vol. 30, pp. 209-17, 221-22

INTRODUCTION TO THE BOOK BY JOHN REED: *TEN DAYS THAT SHOOK THE WORLD*

INTRODUCTION TO THE AMERICAN EDITION

With the greatest interest and with never slackening attention I read John Reed's book, *Ten Days That Shook the World*. Unreservedly do I recommend it to the workers of the world. Here is a book which I should like to see published in millions of copies and translated into all languages. It gives a truthful and most vivid exposition of the events so significant to the comprehension of what really is the Proletarian Revolution and the Dictatorship of the Proletariat. These problems are widely discussed, but before one can accept or reject these ideas, he must understand the full significance of his decision. John Reed's book will undoubtedly help to clear this question, which is the fundamental problem of the international labor movement.

Nikolai Lenin

Written at the end of 1919

First published in Russian in 1923 in the book: Dzhon Rid, *10 dnei kotoriye potryasli mir*, Moscow

Collected Works, Vol. 36, p. 519

From **THE REPORT ON THE WORK OF THE
ALL-RUSSIA CENTRAL EXECUTIVE COMMITTEE
AND THE COUNCIL OF PEOPLE'S COMMISSARS
DELIVERED AT THE FIRST SESSION OF THE
ALL-RUSSIA CENTRAL EXECUTIVE COMMITTEE,
SEVENTH CONVOCATION
FEBRUARY 2, 1920**

Democracy is most clearly manifested in the fundamental question of war and peace. All the powers are preparing a fresh imperialist war, and this is seen daily by the workers of the world. Any day now America and Japan will hurl themselves at each other; Britain grabbed so many colonies after her victory over Germany that the other imperialist powers will never resign themselves to this. A new fanatical war is being prepared, and the people are aware of this. And just at this moment Russia, with her huge forces, who is accused of intending to fling those forces against a small state as soon as she has finished with Yudenich, Kolchak and Denikin—Russia has concluded a democratic peace with Estonia.[111] Furthermore, the terms of the peace treaty provide for a number of territorial concessions on our part which do not completely correspond to the strict observance of the principle of self-determination of nations, and prove in practice that the question of frontiers is of secondary importance to us; the question of peaceful relations, however, the question of our ability to await the development of the conditions of life of each nation, is not only an important question of principle, it is also a matter in which we have succeeded in winning the confidence of nations hostile to us. It is no accident that we have achieved this in relation to Estonia; it is evidence that the weak proletarian republic, existing in isolation and apparently helpless, has begun to win to its side countries dependent on the imperialist states—and they constitute the vast majority. That is why our peace with Estonia is of such great historical significance. No matter how the Entente strives to start a war—even if it succeeds in turning peace once again into war—the fact will remain, firmly established in history, that despite all the pressure of international capital we were able to inspire greater confidence in a small country ruled by the bourgeoisie than the so-called democratic, but in reality predatory, imperialist bourgeoisie.

We by chance came to possess some very interesting documents showing how our policy compared with that of the allegedly democratic, but in actual fact predatory, powers of the whole world, which please permit me to read to you. These documents were furnished by a white-guard officer or official named Oleinikov who was commissioned by one whiteguard government to hand over some highly important documents to another. But he handed them over to us instead.[112] (*Applause.*) It proved possible to send these documents to Russia, and I shall read them to you, although it will take some time to do so. Nevertheless, they are very interesting for they very clearly reveal the hidden springs of policy. The first document is a telegram to Minister Gulkevich from Sazonov:

Paris, October 14, 1919, No. 668.

S. D. Sazonov conveys his respects to Konstantin Nikolayevich, and has the honour to enclose for his information copies of a telegram from B. A. Bakhmetev, No. 1050, and a telegram from I. I. Sukin, No. 23, on the situation in the Baltic Provinces.

Then comes a more interesting document—a telegram from Washington dated October 11:

Received October 12, 1919. File No. 3346.
Bakhmetev to the Minister.
Washington, October 11, 1919, No. 1050.
Further to my telegram No. 1045.
(In code) The State Department acquainted me verbally with the instructions given to Gade. He is appointed the Commissar of the American Government in the Baltic Provinces of Russia. He is not accredited

to any Russian Government. His mission is to observe and inform. His behaviour must not lead the local population to expect that the American Government could agree to support separatist trends going beyond autonomy. On the contrary, the American Government trusts that the population of the Baltic Provinces will help their Russian brothers in their work of general state importance. The instructions are based on the interpretation of the agreement of the Allied governments with the Supreme Ruler as outlined in my memorandum of June 17 to the government. Gade has been given extracts from the recent speeches of the President in which he fulminates against Bolshevism.

So, the American Government intimates that its representative can issue any kind of instructions but may not support independence, i.e., may not guarantee the independence of these states. This is what directly or indirectly came to light, and Estonia could not be kept in ignorance of the fact that she was being deceived by the Great Powers. Of course, everyone could have guessed this, but now we have the documents and they will be published:

Received October 12, 1919. File No. 3347.
Sukin to the Minister.
Omsk, October 9, 1919, No. 28.
(In code) Knox has given the Supreme Ruler the message of the British War Office in which the latter warns of the inclination of the Baltic states to conclude a peace with the Bolsheviks who guarantee them immediate recognition of their independence. At the same time the British War Office raises the question of the advisability of paralysing this pledge by satisfying, in its turn, the wishes of the states indicated. We replied to Knox by referring to the principles outlined in the Note of the Supreme Ruler to the Powers on June 4, and, in addition, we pointed out that the conclusion of a peace between the Baltic states and the Bolsheviks would be undoubtedly fraught with danger since this would permit the release of part of the Soviet forces and would clear the way to the infiltration of Bolshevism in the West. The mere fact that they are ready to talk peace is in our opinion evidence of the utter demoralisation of the parties of these self-governing entities which cannot protect themselves from the penetration of aggressive Bolshevism.

Expressing the conviction that the Powers could not approve of the further spread of Bolshevism, we pointed to the necessity of withdrawing all aid from the Baltic states since this would be a real means of exerting influence by the Powers, and is more advisable than competition in promises with the Bolsheviks, who now have nothing to lose.

In transmitting the above, I would request you to make similar representations in Paris and London; we are making a special approach to Bakhmetev.

Received October 9, 1919. File No. 3286.
Sablin to the Minister.
London, October 7, 1919, No. 677.
(In code) In a letter to Guchkov, the Director of Military Operations of the War Office, to whom Guchkov made an offer of our
shipping in order to facilitate the delivery of supplies to Yudenich by
the British, states that in the opinion of the War Office Yudenich has
all that he requires at the moment, and that Britain is experiencing
some difficulty in providing further supplies. He adds, however, that
as we have shipping, we could arrange supplies for Yudenich on a
commercial basis, providing we obtain credits. At the same time General Radcliffe admits that Yudenich's army must be properly equipped
since it is "the only force among the Baltic states able to engage in
active operations against the Bolsheviks".

Minister to Bakhmetev in Washington.
Paris, September 30, 1919, No. 2442.
(In code) From a strictly confidential Swedish source I learn that
the American envoy in Stockholm, Morris, is talking about growing
sympathy in America towards the Bolsheviks and of intentions to cease
aid to Kolchak in order to enter into contacts with Moscow in the
interests of American trade. Such statements on the part of an official
representative make a strange impression.

Received October 5, 1919. File No. 3244.
Bakhmetev to the Minister.
Washington, October 4, 1919, No. 1021.
Further to your telegram No. 2442.
(In code) The State Department informed me in confidence that it
is true that the envoy in Stockholm, Morris, and particularly Hapgood
in Copenhagen, are well known for their Left sympathies, but that they
have no influence or authority here, and that the government is obliged
to admonish them from time to time, categorically pointing out that
American policy is one of the undeviating support of our government
in the struggle against the Bolsheviks.

Here are all the documents which we shall publish and
which clearly show how the battle went on around Estonia, how the Entente, Britain and France, together with
Kolchak and America, all brought pressure to bear on
Estonia with the one aim of preventing the signing of a
peace treaty with the Bolsheviks, and how the Bolsheviks,
pledging themselves to territorial concessions and guaran-
teeing independence, won this trial of strength. I state that
this victory is of gigantic historical significance, because
it has been gained without the use of force. This victory
over world imperialism is a victory that is bringing the
Bolsheviks the sympathy of the whole world. This victory

by no means denotes that universal peace will be concluded immediately; but it does show that we represent the
peace interests of the majority of the world's population
against the imperialist war-mongers. Such an assessment
of the situation has induced bourgeois Estonia, an opponent of communism, to conclude peace with us. Since we,
a proletarian state, a Soviet republic, are concluding a
peace treaty, since we are acting in a spirit of peace towards bourgeois governments oppressed by the great magnates of imperialism, we must be able to decide from this
how our international policy is to be shaped.

The main task we set ourselves is to defeat the exploiters and to win to our side the waverers—this is a task of
historic significance. Among the waverers are a whole
number of bourgeois states which, as bourgeois states,
detest us, but which, on the other hand, as oppressed
states, prefer peace with us. This explains the peace with
Estonia. This peace is, of course, only a first step, and its
influence will only be felt in the future, but that it will be
felt is a fact. Up to now we have negotiated with Latvia
only through the Red Cross,[113] and the same is true of
our negotiations with the Polish Government. I repeat—
the peace with Estonia is bound to influence events because
the basis is identical; the same attempts are being made
to goad Latvia and Poland into making war on Russia as
were made in the case of Estonia. Perhaps these attempts
will prove successful, and since war with Poland is possible, we must be vigilant, but we are certain—this has
been demonstrated by our main achievements—that we
can conclude peace and make concessions which permit
the development of any form of democracy. This is now
especially important because the Polish question is particularly acute. We have received a number of communications indicating that apart from bourgeois, conservative,
landowning Poland, apart from the pressure being exerted
by all capitalist parties in Poland, all the Entente powers
are doing their utmost to incite Poland to make war
against us.

As you know, the Council of People's Commissars has
issued an appeal to the working people of Poland.[114] We

are going to ask you to endorse this appeal as a means of fighting that campaign of calumny in which Polish landowning circles are engaged. We shall submit an additional text of an appeal to the working people of Poland. This appeal will be a blow to the imperialist powers, who are doing their utmost to incite Poland against us; for us the interests of the majority of the people take first place.

I shall now acquaint you with a telegram intercepted by us yesterday, which illustrates the attempts of American capital to present us in a certain light and thereby drag us into a war with Poland. The telegram says (*reads*). I have said and heard nothing of the sort, but they are able to lie because it is not for nothing that they spend their money on spreading lying rumours that have a definite aim. Their bourgeois government guarantees them this. (*Continues reading the telegram.*) This telegram was sent from Europe to America and was paid for out of capitalist funds; it serves as a shameless means of provoking a war with Poland. American capital is doing its utmost to bring pressure to bear on Poland and does this unashamedly, making it appear that the Bolsheviks want to finish with Kolchak and Denikin in order to throw all their "iron troops" against Poland.

It is important that we should here and now endorse the decision of the Council of People's Commissars, and then we must do what we did previously in relation to other states, and also what we did in regard to the troops of Kolchak and Denikin. We must immediately appeal to the Polish people and explain the real state of affairs. We know full well that this method of ours has a most positive effect in tending to disrupt the ranks of our enemy. And in the end, this method will lead on to the path we need, the path on to which it has led the working population of all countries. This policy must make a definite beginning—no matter how difficult this may prove—and once a beginning is made, we shall carry it through to completion.

Brief reports published
on February 3, 1920
in *Pravda* No. 23
and in *Izvestia* No. 23

Vol. 30, pp. 319-25

IN REPLY TO QUESTIONS PUT BY KARL WIEGAND, BERLIN CORRESPONDENT OF UNIVERSAL SERVICE[115]

1. Do we intend to attack Poland and Rumania?

No. We have declared most emphatically and officially, in the name of the Council of People's Commissars and the All-Russia Central Executive Committee, our peaceful intentions. It is very much to be regretted that the French capitalist government is instigating Poland (and presumably Rumania, too) to attack us. This is even mentioned by a number of American radios from Lyons.

2. What are our plans in Asia?

They are the same as in Europe: peaceful coexistence with all peoples; with the workers and peasants of all nations awakening to a new life—a life without exploiters, without landowners, without capitalists, without merchants. The imperialist war of 1914-18, the war of the capitalists of the Anglo-French (and Russian) group against the German-Austrian capitalist group for the partition of the world, has awakened Asia and has strengthened there, as everywhere else, the urge towards freedom, towards peaceful labour and against possible future wars.

3. What would be the basis of peace with America?

Let the American capitalists leave us alone. We shall not touch them. We are even ready to pay them in gold for any machinery, tools, etc., useful to our transport and industries. We are ready to pay not only in gold, but in raw materials too.

4. What are the obstacles to such a peace?

None on our part; imperialism on the part of the American (and of any other) capitalists.

5. What are our views of the deportation of Russian revolutionaries from America?

We have accepted them. We are not afraid of revolutionaries here in this country. As a matter of fact, we are not afraid of anybody, and if America is afraid of a few more hundred or thousand of its citizens, we are ready to begin negotiations with a view of receiving any citizens whom America thinks dangerous (with the exception of criminals, of course).

6. What possibilities are there of an economic alliance between Russia and Germany?

Unfortunately, they are not great. The Scheidemanns are bad allies. We stand for an alliance with all countries without exception.

7. What are our views upon the allied demand for the extradition of war criminals?

If we are to speak seriously on this matter of war guilt, the guilty ones are the capitalists of all countries. Hand over to us all your landed proprietors owning more than a hundred hectares and capitalists having a capital of more than 100,000 francs, and we shall educate them to useful labour and make them break with the shameful, base and bloody role of exploiters and instigators of wars for the partition of colonies. Wars will then soon become absolutely impossible.

8. What would be the influence of peace with Russia upon the economic conditions in Europe?

Exchange of machinery for grain, flax and other raw materials—I ask, can this be disadvantageous for Europe? Clearly, it cannot be anything but beneficial.

9. What is our opinion regarding the future development of the Soviets as a world force?

The future belongs to the Soviet system all the world over. The facts have proved it. One has only to count by quarterly periods, say, the growth in the number of pamphlets, books, leaflets and newspapers standing for or sympathising with the Soviets published in any country. It cannot be otherwise. Once the workers in the cities, the workers, landless peasants and the handicraftsmen in the villages as well as the small peasants (i.e., those who do not exploit hired labour)—once this enormous majority of working people have understood that the Soviet system gives all power into their hands, releasing them from the yoke of landlords and capitalists—how could one prevent the victory of the Soviet system all over the world? I, for one, do not know of any means of preventing it.

10. Has Russia still to fear counter-revolution from without?

Unfortunately, it has, for the capitalists are stupid, greedy people. They have made a number of such stupid, greedy attempts at intervention and one has to fear repetitions until the workers and peasants of all countries thoroughly *re-educate* their own capitalists.

11. Is Russia ready to enter into business relations with America?

Of course she is ready to do so, and with all other countries. Peace with Estonia, to whom we have conceded a great deal, has proved our readiness, for the sake of business relations, to give even industrial concessions on certain conditions.

February 18, 1920

V. Ulyanov (N. Lenin)

Published on February 21, 1920
in the *New York Evening Journal*
No. 12671

First published in Russian on   Vol. 30, pp. 365-67
April 22, 1950
in *Pravda* No. 112

TALK WITH LINCOLN EYRE,
CORRESPONDENT OF *THE WORLD* (U.S.A.)[116]

Allies Playing "Chess Game"

Of the Allies' reported decision to lift the blockade[117] Lenin said:

It is hard to see sincerity behind so vague a proposal, coupled as it seems to be with preparations to attack us afresh through Poland. At first glance the Supreme Council's proposition looks plausible enough—the resumption of commercial relations through the medium of the Russian co-operatives. But the co-operatives do not any longer exist, having been linked up with our Soviet distribution organs. Therefore what is meant when the Allies talk of dealing with the co-operatives? Certainly it is not clear.

Therefore I say that closer examination convinces us that this Paris decision is simply a move in the Allied chess game the motives of which are still obscure.

Lenin paused a moment, then added with a broad grin:

Far obscurer, for instance, than Marshal Foch's intended visit to Warsaw.

I asked if he deemed the probability of a Polish offensive serious (it must be recalled that in Russia the talk was of a drive by the Poles against the Bolsheviks, not vice versa).

Beyond doubt, Lenin replied. Clemenceau and Foch are very, very serious gentlemen, and the one originated and the other is going to carry out this offensive scheme. It is a grave menace, of course, but we have faced graver ones. It does not cause us fear so much as disappointment that the Allies should still pursue the impossible. For a

Polish offensive can no more settle the Russian problem for them than did Kolchak's and Denikin's. Poland has many troubles of her own, remember. And it is obvious that she can get no help from any of her neighbours, including Rumania.

Yet peace seems nearer than before, I suggested.

Yes, that's true. If peace is a corollary of trade with us, the Allies cannot avoid it much longer. I have heard that Millerand, Clemenceau's successor, expresses willingness to envisage commercial relations with the Russian people. Perhaps this heralds a change of front among the French capitalists. But Churchill is still strong in England, and Lloyd George, who probably wants to do business with us, dare not risk an open rupture with the political and financial interests supporting the Churchill policy.

United States Oppresses Socialists

And America?

It is hard to see clearly what is going on there. Your bankers seem to fear us more than ever. At any rate, your government is instituting more violently repressive measures not only against the socialists but against the working class in general than any other government, even the reactionary French. Apparently it is persecuting foreigners. And yet, what would America be without her foreign workers? They are an absolute necessity to your economic development.

Still, some American manufacturers appear to have begun to realise that making money in Russia is wiser than making war against Russia, which is a good sign. We shall need American manufactures—locomotives, automobiles, etc.—more than those of any other country.

And your peace terms?

It is idle to talk further about them, Lenin returned emphatically. All the world knows that we are prepared to make peace on terms the fairness of which even the most imperialistic capitalists could not dispute. We have

reiterated and reiterated our desire for peace, our need
for peace and our readiness to give foreign capital the
most generous concessions and guarantees. But we do
not propose to be strangled to death for the sake of peace.

I know of no reason why a socialist state like ours cannot do business indefinitely with capitalist countries. We
don't mind taking the capitalist locomotives and farming
machinery, so why should they mind taking our socialist
wheat, flax and platinum. Socialist grain tastes the same
as any other grain, does it not? Of course, they will have
to have business relations with the dreadful Bolsheviks,
that is, the Soviet Government. But it should not be harder
for American steel manufacturers, for instance, to
deal with the Soviets than it was for them to deal with
Entente governments in their war-time munition deals.

Europe Dependent on Russia

That is why this talk of reopening trade with Russia
through co-operatives seems to us insincere, or, at least,
obscure—a move in a game of chess rather than a frank,
straightforward proposition that would be immediately
grasped and acted upon. Moreover, if the Supreme Council really means to lift the blockade, why doesn't it tell
us of its intentions? We are without official word from
Paris. What little we know is derived from newspaper
dispatches picked up by our wireless. . . .

The statesmen of the Entente and the United States do
not seem to understand that Russia's present economic
distress is simply a part of the world's economic distress.
Until the economic problem is faced from a world standpoint and not merely from the standpoint of certain nations or a group of nations, a solution is impossible. Without Russia, Europe cannot get on her feet. And with
Europe prostrate, America's position becomes critical.
What good is America's wealth if she cannot buy with it
that which she needs? America cannot eat or wear the
gold she has accumulated, can she? She can't trade profitably, that is, on a basis that will be of real value to her,
with Europe until Europe is able to give her the things

she wants in exchange for that which she has to give. And Europe cannot give her those things until she is on her feet economically.

World Needs Russian Goods

In Russia we have wheat, flax, platinum, potash and many minerals of which the whole world stands in desperate need. The world must come to us for them in the end, Bolshevism or no Bolshevism. There are signs that a realisation of this truth is gradually awakening. But meanwhile not only Russia but all Europe is going to pieces, and the Supreme Council still indulges in tergiversation. Russia can be saved from utter ruin and Europe too, but it must be done soon and quickly. And the Supreme Council is so slow, so very slow. In fact, it has already been dissolved, I believe, in favour of a Council of Ambassadors, leaving nothing settled and with only a League of Nations[118] which is non-existent, still-born, to take its place. How can the League of Nations possibly come to life without the United States to give it backbone!

I inquired as to whether the Soviet Government was satisfied with the military situation.

Very much so, Lenin replied promptly. The only symptoms of further military aggression against us are those I spoke of in Poland. If Poland embarks on such an adventure there will be more suffering on both sides, more lives needlessly sacrificed. But even Foch could not give the Poles victory. They could not defeat our Red Army even if Churchill himself fought with them.

Here Lenin threw back his head and laughed grimly. Then he went on in a graver vein:

We can be crushed, of course, by any one of the big Allied powers if they can send their own armies against us. But that they dare not do. The extraordinary paradox is that weak as Russia is compared with the Allies' boundless resources, she has not only been able to shatter every armed force, including British, American and French

troops that they have managed to send against her, but
to win diplomatic and moral victories as well over the
cordon sanitaire countries. Finland refused to fight against
us. We have peace with Estonia and peace with Serbia*
and Lithuania is at hand. Despite material inducements
offered to and sinister threats made against these small
countries by the Entente, they preferred to establish pacific relations with us.

Internal Situation Hopeful

This assuredly demonstrates the tremendous moral force
we hold. The Baltic states, our nearest neighbours, appreciate that we alone have no designs against their independence and well-being.

And Russia's internal situation?

It is critical but hopeful. With spring the food shortage
will be overcome to the extent at least of saving the cities
from famine. There will be sufficient fuel then too. The
reconstruction period is under way, thanks to the Red
Army's stupendous performances. Now parts of that army
are transformed into armies of labour, an extraordinary
phenomenon only possible in a country struggling toward
a high ideal. Certainly it could not be done in capitalist
countries. We have sacrificed everything to victory over
our armed antagonists in the past; and now we shall turn
all our strength to economic rehabilitation. It will take
years, but we shall win out in the end.

When do you think communism will be complete in Russia?
The question was a poser, I thought, but Lenin replied immediately:

We mean to electrify our entire industrial system
through power stations in the Urals and elsewhere. Our
engineers tell us it will take ten years When the electrification is accomplished it will be the frst important
stage on the road to the communist organisation of public

---

* This was an error in the newspaper text. Serbia was not at
war with Soviet Russia. Apparently Lenin spoke of Latvia.—*Ed.*

economic life. All our industries will receive their motive power from a common source, capable of supplying them all adequately. This will eliminate wasteful competition in the quest of fuel, and place manufacturing enterprise on a sound economic footing, without which we cannot hope to achieve a full measure of interchange of essential products in accordance with communist principles.

Incidentally, in three years we expect to have 50,000,000 incandescent lamps burning in Russia. There are 70,000,000 in the United States, I believe, but in a land where electricity is in its infancy more than two-thirds of that number is a very high figure to achieve. Electrification is to my mind the most momentous of the great tasks that confront us.

Scores socialist leaders

At the close of our talk Lenin delivered himself, not for publication, however, of some cutting criticism of certain socialist leaders in Europe and America which revealed his lack of faith in the ability or even the desire of these gentry to promote world revolution effectively. He evidently feels that Bolshevism will come to pass in spite of, rather than because of, the "official" chieftains of socialism.

The World No. 21368, February 21, 1920

Published according to the newspaper text

From A SPEECH DELIVERED AT THE FIRST ALL-RUSSIA CONGRESS OF WORKING COSSACKS MARCH 1, 1920

A big tussle is developing among the bourgeois countries themselves. America and Japan are on the verge of flinging themselves at each other's throats because Japan sat snug during the imperialist war and has grabbed nearly the whole of China, which has a population of four hundred million. The imperialist gentlemen say, "We are in favour of a republic, we are in favour of democracy; but why did the Japanese grab more than they should under our very noses?" Japan and America are on the verge of war, and there is absolutely no possibility of preventing that war, in which another ten million will be killed and twenty million crippled. France, too, says, "Who got the colonies?—Britain." France was victorious, but she is up to her ears in debt; she is in a hopeless position, whereas Britain has piled up wealth. Over there, new combinations and alliances are already being engineered. They want to fling themselves at each other's throats again over the division of colonies. And an imperialist war is again brewing and cannot be prevented. It cannot be prevented, not because the capitalists, taken individually, are vicious—individually they are just like other people—but because they cannot free themselves of the financial meshes in any other way, because the whole world is in debt, in bondage, and because private property has led and always will lead to war.

Pravda Nos. 47, 48 and 49,
March 2, 3 and 4, 1920

Vol. 30, pp. 393-94

PRELIMINARY DRAFT THESES
ON THE AGRARIAN QUESTION

FOR THE SECOND CONGRESS
OF THE COMMUNIST INTERNATIONAL

(Excerpt)

6) The revolutionary proletariat must immediately and unreservedly confiscate all landed estates, those of the big landowners, who, in capitalist countries—directly or through their tenant farmers—systematically exploit wage-labour and the neighbouring small (and, not infrequently, part of the middle) peasantry, do not themselves engage in manual labour, and are in the main descended from the feudal lords (the nobles in Russia, Germany, and Hungary, the restored seigneurs in France, the lords in Britain, and the former slave-owners in America), or are rich financial magnates, or else a mixture of both these categories of exploiters and parasites.

Under no circumstances is it permissible for Communist parties to advocate or practise compensating the big landowners for the confiscated lands, for under present-day conditions in Europe and America this would be tantamount to a betrayal of socialism and the imposition of new tribute upon the masses of working and exploited people, to whom the war has meant the greatest hardships, while it has increased the number of millionaires and enriched them.

As to the mode of cultivation of the land that the victorious proletariat confiscates from the big landowners, the distribution of that land among the peasantry for their use has been predominant in Russia, owing to her economic backwardness; it is only in relatively rare and exceptional cases that state farms have been organised on the former estates which the proletarian state runs at its own expense, converting the former wage-labourers into workers for the state and members of the Soviets, which administer the state. The Communist International is of the opinion that in the case of the advanced capitalist countries it would be correct to keep *most* of the big agricultural enterprises intact and to conduct them on the lines of the "state farms" in Russia.

It would, however, be grossly erroneous to exaggerate or to stereotype this rule and never to permit the free grant of *part* of the land that belonged to the expropriated expropriators to the neighbouring small and sometimes middle peasants.

First, the objection usually raised to this, namely, that large-scale farming is technically superior, often amounts to an indisputable theoretical truth being replaced by the worst kind of opportunism and betrayal of the revolution. To achieve the success of this revolution, the proletariat should not shrink from a temporary decline in production, any more than the bourgeois opponents of slavery in North America shrank from a temporary decline in cotton production as a consequence of the Civil War of 1863-65. What is most important to the bourgeois is production for the sake of production; what is most important to the working and exploited population is the overthrow of the exploiters and the creation of conditions that will permit the working people to work for themselves, and not for the capitalists. It is the primary and fundamental task of the proletariat to ensure the proletarian victory and its stability. There can, however, be no stable proletarian government unless the middle peasantry is neutralised and the support is secured of a very considerable section of the small peasantry, if not all of them.

Second, not merely an increase but even the preservation of large-scale production in agriculture presupposes the existence of a fully developed and revolutionarily conscious rural proletariat with considerable experience of trade union and political organisation behind it. Where this condition does not yet exist, or where this work cannot expediently be entrusted to class-conscious and competent industrial workers, hasty attempts to set up large state-conducted farms can only discredit the proletarian government. Under such conditions, the utmost caution must be exercised and the most thorough preparations made when state farms are set up.

Third, in all capitalist countries, even the most advanced, there still exist survivals of medieval, semi-feudal exploitation of the neighbouring small peasants by the big landowners as in the case of the *Instleute** in Germany, the *métayers* in France, and the sharecroppers in the United States (not only Negroes, who, in the Southern States, are mostly exploited in this way, but sometimes whites too). In such cases it is incumbent on the proletarian state to grant the small peasants free use of the lands they formerly rented, since no other economic or technical basis exists, and it cannot be created at one stroke.

The implements and stock of the big farms must be confiscated without fail and converted into state property, with the absolute condition that, *after* the requirements of the big state farms have been met, the neighbouring small peasants may have the use of these implements gratis, in compliance with conditions drawn up by the proletarian state.

In the period immediately following the proletarian revolution, it is absolutely necessary, not only to confiscate the estates of the big landowners at once, but also to deport or to intern them all as leaders of counter-revolution and ruthless oppressors of the entire rural population. However, with the consolidation of the proletarian power in the countryside as well as in the cities, systematic efforts should be made to employ (under the special control of highly reliable communist workers) those forces within this class that possess valuable experience, knowhow, and organising skill, to build large-scale socialist agriculture.

Written in early June 1920

Published in July 1920   Vol. 31, pp. 159-61

---

* Tenant farmers.—*Ed.*

THESES ON THE FUNDAMENTAL TASKS
OF THE SECOND CONGRESS
OF THE COMMUNIST INTERNATIONAL
(Excerpts)

13. In particular, the conditions of the working-class press in most advanced capitalist countries strikingly reveal the utter fraudulency of liberty and equality under bourgeois democracy, as well as the necessity of systematically combining legal work with illegal work. Both in vanquished Germany and in victorious America, the entire power of the bourgeoisie's machinery of state and all the machinations of the financial magnates are employed to deprive the workers of their press, these including legal proceedings, the arrest (or murder by hired assassins) of editors, denial of mailing privileges, the cutting off of paper supplies, and so on and so forth. Besides, the news services essential to daily newspapers are run by bourgeois telegraph agencies, while advertisements, without which a large newspaper cannot pay its way, depend on the "good will" of the capitalists. To sum up: through skulduggery and the pressure of capital and the bourgeois state, the bourgeoisie is depriving the revolutionary proletariat of its press.

To combat this, the Communist parties must create a new type of periodical press for mass distribution among the workers: first, legal publications, which, without calling themselves communist and without publicising their links with the Party, must learn to make use of any legal opportunity, however slight, just as the Bolsheviks did under the tsar, after 1905; secondly, illegal leaflets, even

the briefest and published at irregular intervals, but reprinted at numerous printshops by workers (secretly, or,
if the movement has become strong enough, by the revolutionary seizure of printshops), and providing the proletariat with outspoken revolutionary information and
revolutionary slogans.

Preparations for the dictatorship of the proletariat are
impossible without a revolutionary struggle, into which
the masses are drawn, for the freedom of the communist
press.

18. The Second Congress of the Third International
considers erroneous the views on the Party's relation to
the class and to the masses, and the view that it is not
obligatory for Communist parties to participate in bourgeois parliaments and in reactionary trade unions. These
views have been refuted in detail in special decisions of
the present Congress, and advocated most fully by the
Communist Workers' Party of Germany,[119] and partly by
the Communist Party of Switzerland, by *Kommunismus*,
organ of the East-European Secretariat of the Communist
International in Vienna, by the now dissolved secretariat
in Amsterdam, by several Dutch comrades, by several
Communist organisations in Great Britain, as, for example,
the Workers' Socialist Federation, etc., and also by the
Industrial Workers of the World in the U.S.A. and the
Shop Stewards' Committees in Great Britain,[120] etc.

Nevertheless, the Second Congress of the Third International considers it possible and desirable that those of
the above-mentioned organisations which have not yet
officially affiliated to the Communist International should
do so immediately; for in the present instance, particularly
as regards the Industrial Workers of the World in the
U.S.A. and Australia, as well as the Shop Stewards' Committees in Great Britain, we are dealing with a profoundly
proletarian and mass movement, which in all essentials
actually stands by the basic principles of the Communist
International. The erroneous views held by these organisations regarding participation in bourgeois parliaments
can be explained, not so much by the influence of elements

coming from the bourgeoisie, who bring their essentially petty-bourgeois views into the movement—views such as anarchists often hold—as by the political inexperience of proletarians who are quite revolutionary and connected with the masses.

For this reason, the Second Congress of the Third International requests all Communist organisations and groups in the Anglo-Saxon countries, even if the Industrial Workers of the World and the Shop Stewards' Committees do not immediately affiliate to the Third International, to pursue a very friendly policy towards these organisations, to establish closer contacts with them and the masses that sympathise with them, and to explain to them in a friendly spirit—on the basis of the experience of all revolutions, and particularly of the three Russian revolutions of the twentieth century—the erroneousness of their views as set forth above, and not to desist from further efforts to amalgamate with these organisations to form a single Communist party.

Published in July 1920

Vol. 31, pp. 196-97, 199-201

From THE REPORT TO THE SECOND CONGRESS
ON THE INTERNATIONAL SITUATION
AND THE FUNDAMENTAL TASKS OF THE
COMMUNIST INTERNATIONAL
JULY 19, 1920

This domination by a handful of capitalists achieved full development when the whole world had been partitioned, not only in the sense that the various sources of raw materials and means of production had been seized by the biggest capitalists, but also in the sense that the preliminary partition of the colonies had been completed. Some forty years ago, the population of the colonies stood at somewhat over 250,000,000, who were subordinated to six capitalist powers. Before the war of 1914, the population of the colonies was estimated at about 600,000,000, and if we add countries like Persia, Turkey, and China, which were already semi-colonies, we shall get, in round figures, a population of a thousand million people oppressed through colonial dependence by the richest, most civilised and freest countries. And you know that, apart from direct political and juridical dependence, colonial dependence presumes a number of relations of financial and economic dependence, a number of wars, which were not regarded as wars because very often they amounted to sheer massacres, when European and American imperialist troops, armed with the most up-to-date weapons of destruction, slaughtered the unarmed and defenceless inhabitants of colonial countries.

The first imperialist war of 1914-18 was the inevitable outcome of this partition of the whole world, of this domination by the capitalist monopolies, of this great power wielded by an insignificant number of very big banks—

two, three, four or five in each country. This war was waged for the repartitioning of the whole world. It was waged in order to decide which of the small groups of the biggest states—the British or the German—was to obtain the opportunity and the right to rob, strangle and exploit the whole world. You know that the war settled this question in favour of the British group. And, as a result of this war, all capitalist contradictions have become immeasurably more acute. At a single stroke the war relegated about 250,000,000 of the world's inhabitants to what is equivalent to colonial status, viz., Russia, whose population can be taken at about 130,000,000, and Austria-Hungary, Germany and Bulgaria, with a total population of not less than 120,000,000. That means 250,000,000 people living in countries, of which some, like Germany, are among the most advanced, most enlightened, most cultured, and on a level with modern technical progress. By means of the Treaty of Versailles, the war imposed such terms upon these countries that advanced peoples have been reduced to a state of colonial dependence, poverty, starvation, ruin, and loss of rights: this treaty binds them for many generations, placing them in conditions that no civilised nation has ever lived in. The following is the post-war picture of the world: at least *1,250 million* people are at once brought under the colonial yoke, exploited by a brutal capitalism, which once boasted of its love for peace, and had some right to do so some fifty years ago, when the world was not yet partitioned, the monopolies did not as yet rule, and capitalism could still develop in a relatively peaceful way, without tremendous military conflicts.

Today, after this "peaceful" period, we see a monstrous intensification of oppression, the reversion to a colonial and military oppression that is far worse than before. The Treaty of Versailles has placed Germany and the other defeated countries in a position that makes their economic existence physically impossible, deprives them of all rights, and humiliates them.

How many nations are the beneficiaries? To answer this question we must recall that the population of the

United States—the only full beneficiary from the war, a country which, from a heavy debtor, has become a general creditor—is no more than 100,000,000. The population of Japan—which gained a great deal by keeping out of the European-American conflict and by seizing the enormous Asian continent—is 50,000,000. The population of Britain, which next to the above-mentioned countries gained most, is about 50,000,000. If we add the neutral countries with their very small populations, countries which were enriched by the war, we shall get, in round figures, some 250,000,000 people.

Thus you get the broad outlines of the picture of the world as it appeared after the imperialist war. In the oppressed colonies—countries which are being dismembered such as Persia, Turkey and China, and in countries that were defeated and have been relegated to the position of colonies—there are 1,250 million inhabitants. Not more than 250,000,000 inhabit countries that have retained their old positions, but have become economically dependent upon America, and all of which, during the war, were militarily dependent, once the war involved the whole world and did not permit a single state to remain really neutral. And, finally, we have not more than 250,000,000 inhabitants in countries whose top stratum, the capitalists alone, benefited from the partition of the world. We thus get a total of about 1,750 million comprising the entire population of the world. I would like to remind you of this picture of the world, for all the basic contradictions of capitalism, of imperialism, which are leading up to revolution, all the basic contradictions in the working-class movement that have led up to the furious struggle against the Second International, facts our chairman has referred to, are all connected with this partitioning of the world's population.

Of course, these figures give the economic picture of the world only approximately, in broad outline. And, comrades, it is natural that, with the population of the world divided in this way, exploitation by finance capital, the capitalist monopolies, has increased many times over.

Not only have the colonial and the defeated countries

been reduced to a state of dependence; within each victor state the contradictions have grown more acute; all the capitalist contradictions have become aggravated. I shall illustrate this briefly with a few examples.

Let us take the national debts. We know that the debts of the principal European states increased no less than *sevenfold* in the period between 1914 and 1920. I shall quote another economic source, one of particular significance—Keynes, the British diplomat and author of *The Economic Consequences of the Peace*, who, on instructions from his government, took part in the Versailles peace negotiations, observed them on the spot from the purely bourgeois point of view, studied the subject in detail, step by step, and took part in the conferences as an economist. He has arrived at conclusions which are more weighty, more striking and more instructive than any a Communist revolutionary could draw, because they are the conclusions of a well-known bourgeois and implacable enemy of Bolshevism, which he, like the British philistine he is, imagines as something monstrous, ferocious, and bestial. Keynes has reached the conclusion that after the Peace of Versailles, Europe and the whole world are heading for bankruptcy. He has resigned, and thrown his book in the government's face with the words: "What you are doing is madness." I shall quote his figures, which can be summed up as follows.

What are the debtor-creditor relations that have developed between the principal powers? I shall convert pounds sterling into gold rubles, at a rate of ten gold rubles to one pound. Here is what we get: the United States has assets amounting to 19,000 million, its liabilities are nil. Before the war it was in Britain's debt. In his report on April 14, 1920, to the last congress of the Communist Party of Germany, Comrade Levi very correctly pointed out that there are now only two powers in the world that can act independently, viz., Britain and America. America alone is absolutely independent financially. Before the war she was a debtor; she is now a creditor only. All the other powers in the world are debtors. Britain has been reduced to a position in which her assets total 17,000 million, and her liabilities 8,000 million. She is already half-way to becoming a debtor nation. Moreover, her assets include about 6,000 million owed to her by Russia. Included in the debt are military supplies received by Russia during the war. When Krasin, as representative of the Russian Soviet Government, recently had occasion to discuss with Lloyd George the subject of debt agreements, he made it plain to the scientists and politicians, to the British Government's leaders, that they were labouring under a strange delusion if they were counting on getting these debts repaid. The British diplomat Keynes has already laid this delusion bare.

Of course, it is not only or even not at all a question of the Russian revolutionary government having no wish to pay the debts. No government would pay, because these debts are usurious interest on a sum that has been paid twenty times over, and the selfsame bourgeois Keynes, who does not in the least sympathise with the Russian revolutionary movement, says: "It is clear that these debts cannot be taken into account."

In regard to France, Keynes quotes the following figures: her assets amount to 3,500 million, and her liabilities to 10,500 million! And this is a country which the French themselves called the world's money-lender, because her "savings" were enormous; the proceeds of colonial and financial pillage—a gigantic capital—enabled her to grant thousands upon thousands of millions in loans, particularly to Russia. These loans brought in an enormous revenue. Notwithstanding this and notwithstanding victory, France has been reduced to debtor status.

A bourgeois American source, quoted by Comrade Braun, a Communist, in his book *Who Must Pay the War Debts?* (Leipzig, 1920), estimates the ratio of debts to national wealth as follows: in the victor countries, Britain and France, the ratio of debts to aggregate national wealth is over 50 per cent; in Italy the percentage is between 60 and 70, and in Russia 90. As you know, however, these debts do not disturb us, because we followed Keynes's excellent advice just a little before his book appeared— we annulled all our debts. (*Stormy applause.*)

In this, however, Keynes reveals the usual crankiness of the philistine: while advising that all debts should be annulled, he goes on to say that, of course, France only stands to gain by it, that, of course, Britain will not lose very much, as nothing can be got out of Russia in any case; America will lose a fair amount, but Keynes counts on American "generosity"! On this point our views differ from those of Keynes and other petty-bourgeois pacifists. We think that to get the debts annulled they will have to wait for something else to happen, and will have to try working in a direction other than counting on the "generosity" of the capitalists.

These few figures go to show that the imperialist war has created an impossible situation for the victor powers as well. This is further shown by the enormous disparity between wages and price rises. On March 8 of this year, the Supreme Economic Council, an institution charged with protecting the bourgeois system throughout the world from the mounting revolution, adopted a resolution which ended with an appeal for order, industry and thrift, provided, of course, the workers remain the slaves of capital. This Supreme Economic Council, organ of the Entente and of the capitalists of the whole world, presented the following summary.

In the United States of America food prices have risen, on the average, by 120 per cent, whereas wages have increased only by 100 per cent. In Britain, food prices have gone up by 170 per cent, and wages 130 per cent; in France, food prices—300 per cent, and wages 200 per cent; in Japan, food prices—130 per cent, and wages 60 per cent (I have analysed Comrade Braun's figures in his pamphlet and those of the Supreme Economic Council as published in *The Times* of March 10, 1920).

In such circumstances, the workers' mounting resentment, the growth of a revolutionary temper and ideas, and the increase in spontaneous mass strikes are obviously inevitable since the position of the workers is becoming intolerable. The workers' own experience is convincing them that the capitalists have become prodigiously enriched by the war and are placing the burden of war costs and debts upon the workers' shoulders. We recently learnt by cable that America wants to deport another 500 Communists to Russia so as to get rid of "dangerous agitators".

Even if America deports to our country, not 500 but 500,000 Russian, American, Japanese and French "agitators" that will make no difference, because there will still be the disparity between prices and wages, which they can do nothing about. The reason why they can do nothing about it is because private property is most strictly safeguarded, is "sacred" there. That should not be forgotten, because it is only in Russia that the exploiters' private property has been abolished. The capitalists can do nothing about the gap between prices and wages, and the workers cannot live on their previous wages. The old methods are useless against this calamity. Nothing can be achieved by isolated strikes, the parliamentary struggle, or the vote, because "private property is sacred", and the capitalists have accumulated such debts that the whole world is in bondage to a handful of men. Meanwhile the workers' living conditions are becoming more and more unbearable. There is no other way out but to abolish the exploiters' "private property".

In his pamphlet *Britain and the World Revolution*, valuable extracts from which were published by our *Bulletin of the People's Commissariat of Foreign Affairs* of February 1920, Comrade Lapinsky points out that in Britain coal export prices have doubled as against those anticipated by official industrial circles.

In Lancashire things have gone so far that shares are at a premium of 400 per cent. Bank profits are at least 40-50 per cent. It should, moreover, be noted that, in determining bank profits, all bank officials are able to conceal the lion's share of profits by calling them, not profits but bonuses, commissions, etc. So here, too, indisputable economic facts prove that the wealth of a tiny handful of people has grown prodigiously and that their luxury beggars description, while the poverty of the working class is steadily growing. We must particularly note the further circumstance brought out very clearly by Comrade Levi in the report I have just referred to, namely, the change in the value of money. Money has everywhere depreciated as a result of the debts, the issue of paper currency, etc. The same bourgeois source I have already mentioned, namely, the statement of the Supreme Economic Council of March 8, 1920, has calculated that in Britain the depreciation in the value of currency as against the dollar is approximately one-third, in France and Italy two-thirds, and in Germany as much as 96 per cent.

This fact shows that the "mechanism" of the world capitalist economy is falling apart. The trade relations on which the acquisition of raw materials and the sale of commodities hinge under capitalism cannot go on; they cannot continue to be based on the subordination of a number of countries to a single country—the reason being the change in the value of money. No wealthy country can exist or trade unless it sells its goods and obtains raw materials.

Thus we have a situation in which America, a wealthy country that all countries are subordinate to, cannot buy or sell. And the selfsame Keynes who went through the entire gamut of the Versailles negotiations has been compelled to acknowledge this impossibility despite his unyielding determination to defend capitalism, and all his hatred of Bolshevism. Incidentally, I do not think any communist manifesto, or one that is revolutionary in general, could compare in forcefulness with those pages in Keynes's book which depict Wilson and "Wilsonism" in action. Wilson was the idol of philistines and pacifists like Keynes and a number of heroes of the Second International (and even of the "Two-and-a-Half" International[121]), who exalted the "Fourteen Points"[122] and even wrote "learned" books about the "roots" of Wilson's policy; they hoped that Wilson would save "social peace", reconcile exploiters and exploited, and bring about social reforms. Keynes showed vividly how Wilson was made a fool of, and all these illusions were shattered at the first impact with the practical, mercantile and huckster policy of capital as personified by Clemenceau and Lloyd George. The masses of the workers now see more clearly than ever, from their own experience—and the learned pedants could see it just by reading Keynes's book—that the "roots" of Wilson's policy lay in sanctimonious piffle, petty-bourgeois phrase-mongering, and an utter inability to understand the class struggle.

In consequence of all this, two conditions, two fundamental situations, have inevitably and naturally emerged. On the one hand, the impoverishment of the masses has grown incredibly, primarily among 1,250 million people, i.e., 70 per cent of the world's population. These are the colonial and dependent countries whose inhabitants possess no legal rights, countries "mandated" to the brigands of finance. Besides, the enslavement of the defeated countries has been sanctioned by the Treaty of Versailles and by existing secret treaties regarding Russia, whose validity, it is true, is sometimes about as real as that of the scraps of paper stating that we owe so many thousands of millions. For the first time in world history, we see robbery, slavery, dependence, poverty and starvation imposed upon 1,250 million people by a legal act.

On the other hand, the workers in each of the creditor countries have found themselves in conditions that are intolerable. The war has led to an unprecedented aggravation of all capitalist contradictions, this being the origin of the intense revolutionary ferment that is ever growing. During the war people were put under military discipline, hurled into the ranks of death, or threatened with immediate wartime punishment. Because of the war conditions people could not see the economic realities. Writers, poets, the clergy, the whole press were engaged in nothing but glorifying the war. Now that the war has ended, the exposures have begun: German imperialism with its Peace of Brest-Litovsk has been laid bare; the Treaty of Versailles, which was to have been a victory for imperialism but proved its defeat, has been exposed. Incidentally, the example of Keynes shows that in Europe and America tens and hundreds of thousands of petty bourgeois, intellectuals, and simply more or less literate and educated people, have had to follow the road taken by Keynes, who resigned and threw in the face of the government a book exposing it. Keynes has shown what is taking place and will take place in the minds of thousands and hundreds of thousands of people when they realise that all the speeches about a "war for liberty", etc., were sheer deception, and that as a result only a handful of people were enriched, while the others were ruined and reduced to slavery. Is it not a fact that the bourgeois Keynes declares that, to survive and save the British economy, the British must secure the resumption of free commercial intercourse between Germany and Russia? How can this be achieved? By cancelling all debts, as Keynes proposes. This is an idea that has been arrived at not only by Keynes, the learned economist; millions of people are or will be getting the same idea. And millions of people hear bourgeois economists declare that there is no way out except annulling the debts; therefore "damn the Bolsheviks" (who have annulled the debts), and let us appeal to America's "generosity"! I think that, on behalf of the Congress of the Communist International, we should send a message of thanks to these economists, who have been agitating for Bolshevism.

If, on the one hand, the economic position of the masses has become intolerable, and, on the other hand, the disintegration described by Keynes has set in and is growing among the negligible minority of all-powerful victor countries, then we are in the presence of the maturing of the two conditions for the world revolution.

We now have before us a somewhat more complete picture of the whole world. We know what dependence upon a handful of rich men means to 1,250 million people who have been placed in intolerable conditions of existence. On the other hand, when the peoples were presented with the League of Nations Covenant, declaring that the League had put an end to war and would henceforth not permit anyone to break the peace, and when this Covenant, the last hope of working people all over the world, came into force, it proved to be a victory of the first order for us. Before it came into force, people used to say that it was impossible not to impose special conditions on a country like Germany, but when the Covenant was drawn up, everything would come out all right. Yet, when the Covenant was published, the bitterest opponents of Bolshevism were obliged to repudiate it! When the Covenant came into operation, it appeared that a small group of the richest countries, the "Big Four"—in the persons of Clemenceau, Lloyd George, Orlando and Wilson—had been put on the job of creating the new relations! When the machinery of the Covenant was put into operation, this led to a complete breakdown.

We saw this in the case of the wars against Russia. Weak, ruined and crushed, Russia, a most backward country, fought against all the nations, against a league of the rich and powerful states that dominate the world, and emerged victorious. We could not put up a force that was anything like the equal of theirs, and yet we proved the victors. Why was that? Because there was not a jot of unity among them, because each power worked against the other. France wanted Russia to pay her debts and become a formidable force against Germany; Britain wanted to partition Russia, and attempted to seize the Baku oilfields and conclude a treaty with the border states of Russia. Among the official British documents there is a Paper which scrupulously enumerates all the states (fourteen in all) which some six months ago, in December 1919, pledged themselves to take Moscow and Petrograd. Britain based her policy on these states, to whom she granted loans running into millions. All these calculations have now misfired, and all the loans are unrecoverable.

Such is the situation created by the League of Nations. Every day of this Covenant's existence provides the best propaganda for Bolshevism, since the most powerful adherents of the capitalist "order" are revealing that, on every question, they put spokes in one another's wheels. Furious wrangling over the partitioning of Turkey, Persia, Mesopotamia and China is going on between Japan, Britain, America and France. The bourgeois press in these countries is full of the bitterest attacks and the angriest statements against their "colleagues" for trying to snatch the booty from under their noses. We see complete discord at the top, among this handful, this very small number of extremely rich countries. There are 1,250 million people who find it impossible to live in the conditions of servitude which "advanced" and civilised capitalism wishes to impose on them: after all, these represent 70 per cent of the world's population. This handful of the richest states —Britain, America and Japan (though Japan was able to plunder the Eastern, the Asian countries, she cannot constitute an independent financial and military force without support from another country)—these two or three countries are unable to organise economic relations, and are directing their policies towards disrupting policies of their colleagues and partners in the League of Nations. Hence the world crisis; it is these economic roots of the crisis that provide the chief reason of the brilliant successes the Communist International is achieving.

First published in full in 1921
in the book *The Second Congress of
the Communist International. Verbatim
Report.* Published by the Communist
International, Petrograd

Vol. 31, pp. 216-26

Comrades, in my report on the domestic and the external position of the Republic, which you wished to hear,
I shall naturally have to devote most of my remarks to
the war with Poland and its causes. It was this war which
in the main determined the Republic's domestic and external position during the past six months. Now that the
preliminaries for a peace with Poland have just been
signed, it is possible and necessary to take a general look
at this war and its significance and try to give thought to
the lessons we have all learnt from the war which has
just ended, though nobody knows whether it has ended
for good. I would therefore like first to remind you that
it was on April 26 of this year that the Poles began their
offensive. The Soviet Republic solemnly and formally proposed a peace to the Poles, the Polish landowners and the
Polish bourgeoisie, on terms more favourable than those
we have offered them now, despite the tremendous reverses our troops suffered at Warsaw, and the even greater
reverses during the retreat from Warsaw. At the end of
the April of this year, the Poles held a line between 50
and 150 versts to the east of the one they now regard as
the line of a preliminary peace; though at that time the
line was manifestly an unfair one, we solemnly proposed
peace to them on behalf of the All-Russia Central Executive Committee, since, as you all of course know and remember, the Soviet government was mainly concerned at
the time with ensuring the transition to peaceful construction. We had no reason for wishing to resort to arms

in settling questions in dispute between ourselves and the Polish state. We were fully aware that the Polish state was, and still is, a state of the landowners and capitalists, and that it is fully dependent on the capitalists of the Entente countries, in particular on France. Though at the time Poland controlled, not only the whole of Lithuania but also Byelorussia, to say nothing of Eastern Galicia, we considered it our duty to do everything possible to avert a war, so as to give the working class and the peasantry of Russia at least a brief respite from imperialist and civil wars, and at last enable them to get down in earnest to peaceful work. The events that ensued have happened all too frequently: our straightforward and public offer of peace on the line the Poles actually held was taken as a sign of weakness. Bourgeois diplomats of all countries are unaccustomed to such frank statements and our readiness to accept a peace along a line so disadvantageous to us was taken and interpreted as proof of our extreme weakness. The French capitalists succeeded in inciting the Polish capitalists to go to war. You will remember how, after a brief interval following upon the Polish offensive, we replied by dealing a counter-blow and almost reached Warsaw, after which our troops suffered a heavy defeat, and were thrown back.

For over a month and right down to the present, our troops were retreating and suffered reverses, for they were utterly worn out, exhausted by their unparalleled advance from Polotsk to Warsaw. But, I repeat, despite this difficult situation, peace was signed on terms less advantageous to Poland than the earlier ones. The earlier frontier lay 50 versts to the east, whereas it is now 50 versts to the west. Thus, though we signed a peace at a time favourable only to the enemy, when our troops were on the retreat and Wrangel was building up his offensive, we signed a peace treaty on more favourable terms. This once again proves to you that when the Soviet Government proposes peace, its words and statements have to be treated seriously; otherwise what will happen is that we shall offer peace on terms less favourable to us, and get this peace on better terms. This is a lesson the Polish landowners and capitalists will not, of course, forget; they realise that they have gone too far; the peace terms now give them less territory than was offered previously. This is not the first lesson either. You all probably remember that, in the spring of 1919, a representative of the U. S. Government came to Moscow and proposed a preliminary peace with us and with all the whiteguard commanders at the time: Kolchak, Denikin and others, a peace which would have been extremely unfavourable to us. When he returned and reported on our peace terms, they were not considered advantageous, and the war went on. You are aware of the outcome of the war. This is not the first time that the Soviet state has proved that it is considerably stronger than it appears, and that our diplomatic Notes do not contain the boasts and threats that are usual with all bourgeois governments; consequently, rejecting an offer of peace from Soviet Russia means getting that peace some time later on terms that are far worse. Such things are not forgotten in international politics; after proving to the Polish landowners that they have now obtained a peace worse than the one which we originally offered, we shall teach the Polish people, the Polish peasants and workers, to weigh and compare the statements of their government and ours.

Many of you may have read in the newspapers the American Government's Note, in which it declares: "we do not wish to have any dealings with the Soviet Government because it does not honour its obligations." This does not surprise us, because it has been said for many years, the only outcome being that all their attempts to invade Soviet Russia have ended in disaster. The Polish newspapers, nearly all of which are in the pay of the landowners and the capitalists—there this is called freedom of the press—assert that the Soviet government cannot be trusted, since it is a government of tyrants and frauds. All Polish newspapers say the same thing, but the Polish workers and peasants compare these words with the facts, and the facts show that we demonstrated our attachment to peace the very first time we made our peace offer; by concluding peace in October we proved this again. You

will not find proof of this kind in the history of any bourgeois government, a fact that cannot but leave its impress
on the minds of the Polish workers and peasants. The
Soviet Government signed a peace when it was not to
its advantage to do so. It is only in this way that we shall
teach the governments that are controlled by the landowners and capitalists to stop lying; only in this way shall
we destroy the faith the workers and peasants have in
them. We must give more thought to this than to anything
else. Soviet power in Russia is surrounded by countless
enemies, and yet these enemies are impotent. Think of the
course and outcome of the Polish war. We now know that
the French capitalists stood behind Poland, that they
supplied Poland with money and munitions, and sent them
French officers. We quite recently received information
that African troops, namely, French colonial troops, had
appeared on the Polish front. This means that the war
was waged by France with aid from Britain and America.
At the same time, France recognised the lawful government of Russia in the person of Wrangel—so Wrangel too
was backed by France, who provided him with the means
to equip and maintain an army. Britain and America are
also aiding Wrangel's army. Consequently, three allies
stood against us: France, supported by the world's wealthy
countries, Poland, and Wrangel—yet we have emerged
from this war by concluding a favourable peace. In other
words, we have won. Anyone who examines the map will
see that we have won, that we have emerged from this
war with more territory than we had before it started.
But is the enemy weaker than we are? Is he weaker in
the military sense? Has he got fewer men and munitions?
No, he has more of everything. This enemy is stronger
than we are, and yet he has been beaten. This is what we
must give thought to in order to understand Soviet Russia's position with respect to all other countries.

Published in 1920 in the book: Vol. 31, pp. 318-21
Verbatim Reports of the Plenary
Sessions of the Moscow Soviet of
Workers', Peasants' and Red Army
Deputies

OUR FOREIGN AND DOMESTIC POSITION
AND THE TASKS OF THE PARTY

From A SPEECH DELIVERED TO THE MOSCOW GUBERNIA
CONFERENCE OF THE R.C.P.(B.), NOVEMBER 21, 1920

The entry of the socialist country into trade relations
with capitalist countries is a most important factor ensuring our existence in such a complex and absolutely exceptional situation.

I have had occasion to observe a certain Spargo, an
American social-chauvinist close to our Right Socialist-
Revolutionaries and Mensheviks, one of the leaders of the
Second International and member of the American Socialist Party, a kind of American Alexinsky, and author of a
number of anti-Bolshevik books, who has reproached us—
and has quoted the fact as evidence of the complete collapse of communism—for speaking of transactions with
capitalist powers. He has written that he cannot imagine
better proof of the complete collapse of communism and
the breakdown of its programme. I think that anybody
who has given thought to the matter will say the reverse.
No better proof of the Russian Soviet Republic's material
and moral victory over the capitalists of the whole world
can be found than the fact that the powers that took up
arms against us because of our terror and our entire system have been compelled, against their will, to enter into
trade relations with us in the knowledge that by so doing
they are strengthening us. This might have been advanced
as proof of the collapse of communism only if we had
promised, with the forces of Russia alone, to transform

the whole world, or had dreamed of doing so. However, we have never harboured such crazy ideas and have always said that our revolution will be victorious when it is supported by the workers of all lands. In fact, they went half-way in their support, for they weakened the hand raised against us, yet in doing so they were helping us.

Published in 1920 in the pamphlet: Vol. 31, p. 414
*Current Questions of the Party's
Present Work*. Published by the
Moscow Committee, R.C.P.(B.)

From A SPEECH DELIVERED AT A MEETING
OF CELLS' SECRETARIES OF THE MOSCOW
ORGANISATION OF THE R.C.P.(B.)
NOVEMBER 26, 1920

In one of his books, Spargo, the American Socialist, a man who is something like our Alexinsky, and has a vindictive hate of the Bolsheviks, speaks of concessions as proof of the collapse of communism. Our Mensheviks say the same thing. The challenge has been made, and we are ready to take it up. Let us consider the question in terms of the facts. Who has got the worse of it, we or the European bourgeoisie? For three years they have been calumniating us, calling us usurpers and bandits; they have had recourse to all and every means to overthrow us, but have now had to confess to failure, which is in itself a victory for us. The Mensheviks assert that we are pledged to defeating the world bourgeoisie on our own. We have, however, always said that we are only a single link in the chain of the world revolution, and have never set ourselves the aim of achieving victory by our own means. The world revolution has not yet come about, but then we have not yet been overcome. While militarism is decaying, we are growing stronger; not we, but they have had the worse of it.

They now want to subdue us by means of a treaty. Until the revolution comes about, bourgeois capital will be useful to us. How can we speed up the development of our economy whilst we are an economically weaker country? We can do that with the aid of bourgeois capital. We now have before us two drafts of concessions. One of them is for a ten-year concession in Kamchatka. We were recently visited by an American multimillionaire, who told us very frankly of the reasons behind the treaty, viz., that America wants to have a base in Asia in case of a war against Japan. This multimillionaire said that if we sold Kamchatka to America, he could promise us such enthusiasm among the people of the United States that the American Government would immediately recognise the Soviets of Russia. If we gave them only the lease, there would be less enthusiasm. He is now on his way to America, where he will make it known that Soviet Russia is a far cry from what people believed her to be.

We have till now been more than a match for the world bourgeoisie, because they are incapable of uniting. The Treaties of Brest-Litovsk and Versailles have both divided them. An intense hostility is now developing between America and Japan. We are making use of this and are offering a lease of Kamchatka instead of giving it away gratis; after all, Japan has taken a huge expanse of our territory in the Far East, this by force of arms. It is far more to our advantage to run no risk, grant a lease of Kamchatka, and receive part of its products, the more so for our being unable, in any case, to run or exploit it. The treaty has not been signed, but it is already being spoken of in Japan with the utmost anger. Through this treaty we have aggravated the differences between our enemies.

Pravda No. 269,   Vol. 31, pp. 430-31
November 30, 1920

From A SPEECH DELIVERED AT A MEETING OF ACTIVISTS OF THE MOSCOW ORGANISATION OF THE R.C.P.(B.) DECEMBER 6, 1920

Are there any radical antagonisms in the present-day capitalist world that must be utilised? Yes, there are three principal ones, which I should like to enumerate. The first, the one that affects us closest, is the relations between Japan and America. War is brewing between them. They cannot live together in peace on the shores of the Pacific, although those shores are three thousand versts apart. This rivalry arises incontestably from the relation between their capitalisms. A vast literature exists on the future Japanese-American war. It is beyond doubt that war is brewing, that it is inevitable. The pacifists are trying to ignore the matter and obscure it with general phrases, but no student of the history of economic relations and diplomacy can have the slightest doubt that war is ripe from the economic viewpoint and is being prepared politically. One cannot open a single book on this subject without seeing that a war is brewing. The world has been partitioned. Japan has seized vast colonies. Japan has a population of fifty million, and she is comparatively weak economically. America has a population of a hundred and ten million, and although she is many times richer than Japan she has no colonies. Japan has seized China, which has a population of four hundred million and the richest coal reserves in the world. How can this plum be kept? It is absurd to think that a stronger capitalism will not deprive a weaker capitalism of the latter's spoils. Can the Americans remain indifferent under such circumstances? Can strong capitalists remain side by side with weak capitalists and not be expected to grab everything they can from the latter? What would they be good for if they did not? But that being the case, can we, as Communists, remain indifferent and merely say: "We shall carry on propaganda for communism in these countries." That is correct, but it is not everything. The practical task of communist policy is to take advantage of this hostility and to play one side off against the other. Here a new situation arises. Take the two imperialist countries, Japan and America. They want to fight and will fight for world supremacy, for the right to loot. Japan will fight so as to continue to plunder Korea, which she is doing with unprecedented brutality, combining all the latest technical inventions with purely Asiatic tortures. We recently received a Korean newspaper which gives an account of what the Japanese are doing. Here we find all the methods of tsarism and all the latest technical perfections combined with a purely Asiatic system of torture and unparalleled brutality. But the Americans would like to grab this Korean titbit. Of course, defence of country in such a war would be a heinous crime, a betrayal of socialism. Of course, to support one of these countries against the other would be a crime against communism; we Communists have to play one off against the other. Are we not committing a crime against communism? No, because we are doing that as a socialist state which is carrying on communist propaganda and is obliged to take advantage of every hour granted it by circumstances in order to gain strength as rapidly as possible. We have begun to gain strength, but very slowly. America and the other capitalist countries are growing in economic and military might at tremendous speed. We shall develop far more slowly, however we muster our forces.

We must take advantage of the situation that has arisen. That is the whole purpose of the Kamchatka concessions. We have had a visit from Vanderlip, a distant relative of the well-known multimillionaire, if he is to be believed; but since our intelligence service in the Cheka, although splendidly organised, unfortunately does not yet extend to the United States of America, we have not yet established the exact kinship of these Vanderlips. Some even say there is no kinship at all. I do not presume to judge: my knowledge is confined to having read a book by Vanderlip, not the one that was in our country and is said to be such a very important person that he has been received with all the honours by kings and ministers—from which one must infer that his pocket is very well lined indeed. He spoke to them in the way people discuss matters at meetings such as ours, for instance, and told them in the calmest tones how Europe should be restored. If ministers spoke to him with so much respect, it must mean that Vanderlip is in touch with the multimillionaires. His book reveals the outlook of a man of business who knows nothing else but business and who, after observing Europe, says: "It looks as if nothing will come of it and everything will go to the devil." The book is full of hatred of Bolshevism, but it does take up the matter of establishing business contacts. It is a most interesting book from the point of view of agitation too, better than many a communist book, because its final conclusion is: "I'm afraid this patient is incurable—though we have lots of money and the means for his treatment."

Well, Vanderlip brought a letter to the Council of People's Commissars. It was a very interesting letter, for, with the utter frankness, cynicism and crudity of an American tightfist, the writer of the letter said: "We are very strong now, in 1920, and in 1923 our navy will be still stronger. However, Japan stands in the way of our growing might and we shall have to fight her, and you cannot fight without oil. Sell us Kamchatka, and I can vouch that the enthusiasm of the American people will be so great that we shall recognise you. The presidential elections in March will result in a victory for our party. If, however, you let us have only the lease of Kamchatka, I assure you there will be no such enthusiasm." That is almost literrally what he said in his letter. Here we have an unblushing imperialism, which does not even consider it necessary to veil itself in any way because it thinks it is magnificent just as it is. When this letter was received, we said that

we must grasp at the opportunity with both hands. That
he is right, economically speaking, is shown by the fact
that in America the Republican Party is on the eve of
victory. For the first time in the history of America, people
in the South have voted against the Democrats. It is therefore clear that here we have the economically correct
reasoning of an imperialist. Kamchatka belonged to the
former Russian Empire. That is true. Who it belongs to
at the present moment is not clear. It seems to be the
property of a state called the Far Eastern Republic, but
the boundaries of that state have not been precisely fixed.
True, certain documents are being drawn up on the subject, but, first, they have not yet been drawn up, and,
second, they have not yet been ratified. The Far East is
dominated by Japan, who can do anything she pleases
there. If we lease to America Kamchatka, which legally
belongs to us but has actually been seized by Japan, we
shall clearly be the gainers. That is the basis of my political reasoning, and on that basis we at once decided to conclude an immediate agreement with America. Of course,
we have to bargain, as no businessman will respect us if
we do not. Comrade Rykov accordingly began to bargain,
and we drafted an agreement. But when it came to the
actual signing, we said: "Everybody knows who we are,
but who are you?" It transpired that Vanderlip could provide no guarantee, whereupon we said that we were ready
to accommodate. Why, we said, this is merely a draft,
and you said yourself that it would come into force when
your party gained the upper hand; it has not gained the
upper hand as yet, so we shall wait. Things worked out
as follows: we drew up a draft of the treaty, as yet un-
signed, giving Kamchatka—a big slice of the territory of
the Far East and North-East Siberia—to America for a period of sixty years, with the right to build a naval harbour in a port that is ice-free the year round, and has
oil and coal.

A draft agreement is not binding in any way. We can
always say that it contains unclear passages, and back
out at any moment. In that case we shall only have lost
time in negotiating with Vanderlip, and a few sheets of

paper; yet we have already gained something. One has only to take the reports from Europe to see that. There is hardly a report from Japan which does not speak of the great concern caused by the expected concessions. "We shall not tolerate it," Japan declares, "it infringes our interests." Go ahead then, and defeat America; we have no objections. We have already set Japan and America at loggerheads, to put it crudely, and have thereby gained a point. We have also gained as far as the Americans are concerned.

Who is Vanderlip? We have not established who he is —but it is a fact that in the capitalist world telegrams are not dispatched all over the world about rank-and-file citizens. And when he left us, telegrams went to all corners of the earth. Well, he went about saying that he had obtained a good concession and, wherever he went, began to praise Lenin. That was rather funny, but let me tell you that there is a bit of politics in this funny situation. When Vanderlip had concluded all his negotiations here, he wanted to meet me. I consulted representatives of the appropriate departments and asked whether I should receive him. They said, "Let him leave with a sense of satisfaction." Vanderlip came to see me. We talked about all these things, and when he began to tell me that he had been in Siberia, that he knew Siberia and came of a worker's family, just like most American multi-millionaires, and so on, that they valued only practical things, and that they believed a thing only when they saw it, I replied, "Well, you are a practical people, and when you see the Soviet system you will introduce it in your own country." He stared at me in amazement at this turn in the conversation, and said to me in Russian (the whole conversation had been in English), "Mozhet byt."* I asked in surprise where he had got his knowledge of Russian. "Why, I covered most of Siberia on horseback when I was twenty-five." I will tell you of a remark by Vanderlip which belongs to the sphere of the humorous. At parting he said: "I shall have to tell them in

---

* Perhaps.—*Ed.*

America that Mr. Lenin has no horns." I did not grasp
his meaning at once, as I don't understand English very
well. "What did you say? Will you please repeat that?"
He is a spry old fellow; pointing to his temple, he said,
"No horns here." There was an interpreter present who
said, "That is exactly what he says." In America they are
convinced that I have horns here, that is, the bourgeois
say that I have been marked by the devil. "And now I
shall have to tell them that you have no horns," said
Vanderlip. We parted very amicably. I expressed the hope
that friendly relations between the two states would be
a basis not only for the granting of a concession, but also
for the normal development of reciprocal economic assistance. It all went off in that kind of vein. Then telegrams
came telling what Vanderlip had said on arriving home
from abroad. Vanderlip had compared Lenin with Washington and Lincoln. Vanderlip had asked for my auto-
graphed portrait. I had declined, because when you present a portrait you write, "To Comrade So-and-so", and
I could not write, "To Comrade Vanderlip". Neither was
it possible to write: "To the Vanderlip we are signing a
concession with", because that concession agreement
would be concluded by the Administration when it took
office. I did not know what to write. It would have been
illogical to give my photograph to an out-and-out imperialist. Yet these were the kind of telegrams that arrived;
this affair has clearly played a certain part in imperialist
politics. When the news of the Vanderlip concessions
came out, Harding—the man who has been elected President, but who will take office only next March—issued
an official denial. declaring that he knew nothing about
it, had no dealings with the Bolsheviks and had heard
nothing about any concessions. That was during the elections, and, for all we know, to confess, during elections,
that you have dealings with the Bolsheviks may cost you
votes. That was why he issued an official denial. He had
this report sent to all the newspapers that are hostile to
the Bolsheviks and are on the pay roll of the imperialist
parties. The political advantages we can gain in respect
of America and Japan are perfectly clear to us. This re-

port is significant because it concretely shows the kind of concessions we want to sign, and on what terms. Of course this cannot be told to the press. It can be told only to a Party meeting. We must not be silent in the press about this agreement. It is to our advantage, and we must not say a single word that may hamper the conclusion of such an agreement because it promises us tremendous advantages and a weakening of both U.S. and Japanese imperialism with regard to us.

All this deal means deflecting the imperialist forces away from us—while the imperialists are sighing and waiting for an opportune moment to strangle the Bolsheviks, we are deferring that moment. When Japan was becoming involved in the Korean venture, the Japanese said to the Americans: "Of course, we can beat the Bolsheviks, but what will you give us for it? China? We shall take her anyway, whereas here we have to go ten thousand versts to beat the Bolsheviks, with you Americans in our rear. No, that is not politics." Even then the Japanese could have beaten us in a few weeks, had there been a double-track railway and America's aid in transport facilities. What saved us was the fact that while Japan was busy gobbling up China she could not advance westward, through all of Siberia, with America in her rear; moreover, she did not want to pull America's chestnuts out of the fire.

A war between the imperialist powers would have saved us even more. If we are obliged to put up with such scoundrels as the capitalist robbers, each of whom is ready to knife us, it is our prime duty to make them turn their knives against each other. Whenever thieves fall out, honest men come into their own. The second gain is purely political. Even if this concession agreement does not materialise, it will be to our advantage. As for the economic gain, it will provide us with part of the products. If the Americans received part of the products, it would be to our advantage. There is so much oil and ore in Kamchatka that we are obviously not in a position to work them.

I have shown you one of the imperialist antagonisms

we must take advantage of—that which exists between
Japan and America. There is another—the antagonism
between America and the rest of the capitalist world.
Practically the entire capitalist world of "victors" emerged
from the war tremendously enriched. America is
strong; she is everybody's creditor and everything depends on her; she is being more and more detested; she is
robbing all and sundry and doing so in a unique fashion.
She has no colonies. Britain emerged from the war with
vast colonies. So did France. Britain offered America a
mandate—that is the language they use nowadays—for
one of the colonies she had seized, but America did not
accept it. U.S. businessmen evidently reason in some other
way. They have seen that, in the devastation it produces
and the temper it arouses among the workers, war has
very definite consequences, and they have come to the
conclusion that there is nothing to be gained by accepting a mandate. Naturally, however, they will not permit
this colony to be used by any other state. All bourgeois
literature testifies to a rising hatred of America, while in
America there is a growing demand for an agreement with
Russia. America signed an agreement with Kolchak giving him recognition and support but here they have already come to grief, the only reward for their pains being
losses and disgrace. Thus we have before us the greatest
state in the world, which by 1923 will have a navy stronger than the British, and this state is meeting with growing enmity from the other capitalist countries. We must
take this trend of things into account. America cannot
come to terms with the rest of Europe—that is a fact
proved by history. Nowhere has the Versailles Treaty been
analysed so well as in the book by Keynes, a British representative at Versailles. In his book Keynes ridicules
Wilson and the part he played in the Treaty of Versailles. Here, Wilson proved to be an utter simpleton, whom
Clemenceau and Lloyd George twisted round their little
fingers. Thus everything goes to show that America cannot come to terms with the other countries because of
the profound economic antagonism between them, since
America is richer than the rest.

We shall therefore examine all questions of concessions from this angle: if the least opportunity arises of aggravating the differences between America and the other capitalist countries, it should be grasped with both hands. America stands in inevitable contradiction with the colonies, and if she attempts to become more involved there she will be helping us ten times as much. The colonies are seething with unrest, and when you touch them, whether or not you like it, whether or not you are rich—and the richer you are the better—you will be helping us, and the Vanderlips will be sent packing. That is why to us this antagonism is the main consideration.

The third antagonism is that between the Entente and Germany. Germany has been vanquished, crushed by the Treaty of Versailles, but she possesses vast economic potentialities. Germany is the world's second country in economic development, if America is taken as the first. The experts even say that as far as the electrical industry is concerned she is superior to America, and you know that the electrical industry is tremendously important. As regards the extent of the application of electricity, America is superior, but Germany has surpassed her in technical perfection. It is on such a country that the Treaty of Versailles has been imposed, a treaty she cannot possibly live under. Germany is one of the most powerful and advanced of the capitalist countries. She cannot put up with the Treaty of Versailles. Although she is herself imperialist, Germany is obliged to seek for an ally against world imperialism, because she has been crushed. That is the situation we must turn to our advantage. Everything that increases the antagonism between America and the rest of the Entente or between the entire Entente and Germany should be used by us from the viewpoint of the concessions. That is why we must try and attract their interest; that is why the pamphlet Milyutin promised to bring, and has brought and will distribute, contains the decrees of the Council of People's Commissars written in a way that will attract prospective concessionaires. The booklet contains maps with explanations. We shall get it translated into all languages and encourage its distribution with the aim of setting Germany against Britain, because concessions will be a lifeline to Germany. We shall likewise set America against Japan, the entire Entente against America, and all Germany against the Entente.

These, then, are the three antagonisms that are upsetting the imperialists' apple-cart. That is the crux of the matter; that is why, from the political standpoint, we should be heart and soul—or rather with all our wits—in favour of concessions.

First published in 1923   Vol. 31, pp. 442-50

From THE REPORT ON CONCESSIONS DELIVERED
TO THE R.C.P.(B.) GROUP AT THE EIGHTH
CONGRESS OF SOVIETS
DECEMBER 21, 1920

Comrades, I think you have made a fully correct decision by preferring the discussion on concessions to be held first in the Party group. To the best of our knowledge, the question of concessions has everywhere aroused considerable concern and even anxiety, not only in Party circles and among the working-class masses but also among the masses of the peasantry. All comrades have pointed out that, since the decree of November 23 of this year, the questions most frequently raised and the written questions submitted at most meetings held on a variety of subjects have dealt with concessions, and the general tone of the questions, as well as of talk on the subject, has been one of apprehension: we have driven out our own capitalists, and now we want to admit others. I believe that this apprehension, this widespread interest in concessions—displayed, not only by Party comrades but by many others—is a good sign, which shows that in three years of incredibly hard struggle the workers' and peasants' state power has become so strong and our experience of the capitalists has become so fixed in the mind that the broad masses consider the workers' and peasants' state power stable enough to manage without concessions; they also consider their lesson learnt well enough to avoid any deals with the capitalists unless there is a dire necessity to do so. This sort of supervision from below, this kind of apprehension emanating from the masses, and this kind of anxiety among non-Party circles show the highly vigilant attention that is being paid to relations between us and the capitalists. I believe that on this score we should absolutely welcome this apprehension as revealing the temper of the masses.

Yet I think that we shall come to the conclusion that, in the question of concessions, we cannot be guided by this revolutionary instinct alone. When we have analysed all aspects of the question we shall see that the policy we have adopted—the policy of offering concessions—is the correct one. I can tell you briefly that the main subject of my report—or rather the repetition of a talk I had very recently in Moscow with several hundred leading executives, because I have not prepared a report and cannot present it to you—the main subject of this talk is to offer proof of two premises: first, that any war is merely the continuation of peacetime politics by other means, and second, that the concessions which we are giving, which we are forced to give, are a continuation of war in another form, using other means. To prove these two premises, or rather to prove only the second because the first does not require any special proof, I shall begin with the political aspect of the question. I shall dwell on those relations existing between the present-day imperialist powers, which are important for an understanding of present-day foreign policy in its entirety, and of our reasons for adopting this policy.

The American Vanderlip sent a letter to the Council of People's Commissars in which he said that the Republicans, members of the Republican Party of America, the party of the banking interests, which is linked with memories of the war against the Southern States for liberation, were not in power at the time. He wrote this before the November elections, which he hoped the Republicans would win (they have won them) and have their own president in March. The Republicans' policy, he went on, would not repeat the follies that had involved America in European affairs, they would look after their own interests. American interests would lead them to a clash with Japan, and they would fight Japan. It might interest you to know, he went on, that in 1923 the U.S. navy would be stronger than Britain's. To fight, they needed control of oil, without which they could not wage a modern war. They not only needed oil, but also had to take steps to ensure that the enemy did not get any. Japan was in a bad way in that respect. Somewhere near Kamchatka there is an inlet (whose name he had forgotten) with oil deposits, and they did not want the Japanese to get that oil. If we sold them that land, Vanderlip could vouch that the Americans would grow so enthusiastic that the U.S. would immediately recognise our government. If we offered a concession, and did not sell them the land, he could not say that they would refuse to examine the project, but he could not promise the enthusiasm that would guarantee recognition of the Soviet Government.

Vanderlip's letter is quite outspoken; with unparalleled cynicism he outlines the point of view of an imperialist who clearly sees that a war with Japan is imminent, and poses the question openly and directly—enter into a deal with us and you will get certain advantages from it. The issue is the following: the Far East, Kamchatka and a piece of Siberia are *de facto* in the possession of Japan insofar as her troops are in control there, and circumstances made necessary the creation of a buffer state, the Far Eastern Republic. We are well aware of the unbelievable sufferings that the Siberian peasants are enduring at the hands of the Japanese imperialists and the atrocities the Japanese have committed in Siberia. The comrades from Siberia know this; their recent publications have given details of it. Nevertheless, we cannot go to war with Japan and must make every effort, not only to put off a war with Japan but, if possible, to avert it because, for reasons known to you, it is beyond our strength. At the same time Japan is causing us tremendous losses by depriving us of our links with world trade through the Pacific Ocean. Under such conditions, when we are confronted with a growing conflict, an imminent clash between America and Japan—for a most stubborn struggle has been going on for many decades between Japan and America over the Pacific Ocean and the mastery of its shores, and the entire diplomatic, economic and trade history of the Pa-

cific Ocean and its shores is full of quite definite indications that the struggle is developing and making war between America and Japan inevitable—we return to a situation we were in for three years: we are a Socialist Republic surrounded by imperialist countries that are far stronger
than us in the military sense, are using every means
of agitation and propaganda to increase hatred for the
Soviet Republic, and will never miss an opportunity for
military intervention, as they put it, i.e., to strangle Soviet
power.

If, remembering this, we cast a glance over the history
of the past three years from the point of view of the international situation of the Soviet Republic, it becomes
clear that we have been able to hold out and have been
able to defeat the Entente powers—an alliance of unparalleled might that was supported by our whiteguards
—only because there has been no unity among these powers. We have so far been victorious only because of the
most profound discord among the imperialist powers, and
only because that discord has not been a fortuitous and internal dissension between parties, but a most deep-seated
and ineradicable conflict of economic interests among the
imperialist countries which, based on private property in
land and capital, cannot but pursue a predatory policy
which has stultified their efforts to unite their forces
against the Soviets. I take Japan, who controlled almost
the whole of Siberia and could, of course, have helped
Kolchak at any time. The main reason she did not do so
was that her interests differ radically from those of America, and she did not want to pull chestnuts out of the fire
for U.S. capital. Knowing this weakness, we could of
course pursue no other policy than that of taking advantage of this enmity between America and Japan so as to
strengthen ourselves and delay any possibility of an
agreement between Japan and America against us; we have
had an instance of the possibility of such an agreement:
American newspapers carried the text of an agreement
between all countries who had promised to support Kolchak.

That agreement fell through, of course, but it is not

impossible that an attempt will be made to restore it at the first opportunity. The deeper and more formidable the communist movement grows, the greater will be the number of new attempts to strangle our Republic. Hence our policy of utilising the discord among the imperialist powers so as to hamper an agreement or to make one temporarily impossible. This has been the fundamental line of our policy for three years; it necessitated the conclusion of the Peace of Brest-Litovsk, as well as the signing, with Bullitt, of a peace treaty and an armistice agreement most disadvantageous to us. This political line of conduct enjoins us to grasp at a proposal on the granting of concessions. Today we are giving America Kamchatka, which in any case is not actually ours because it is held by Japanese troops. At the moment we are in no condition to fight Japan. We are giving America, for economic exploitation, a territory where we have absolutely no naval or military forces, and where we cannot send them. By doing so we are setting American imperialism against Japanese imperialism and against the bourgeoisie closest to us, the Japanese bourgeoisie, which still maintains its hold on the Far Eastern Republic.

Thus, our main interests were political at the concessions negotiations. Recent events, moreover, have shown with the greatest clarity that we have been the gainers from the mere fact of negotiations on concessions. We have not yet granted any concessions, and shall not be able to do so until the American president takes office, which will not be before March; besides, we reserve the possibility of renouncing the agreement when the details are being worked out.

It follows, therefore, that in this matter the economic interest is secondary, its real value lying in its political interest. The contents of the press we have received goes to show that we have been the gainers. Vanderlip himself insisted that the concessions plan should be kept secret for the time being, until the Republican Party had won the elections. We agreed not to publish either his letter or the entire preliminary draft. However, it appeared that such a secret could not be kept for long. No sooner had

Vanderlip returned to America than exposures of various kinds began. Before the elections Harding was candidate for the presidency: he has now been elected. The selfsame Harding published in the press a denial of the report that he was in touch with the Soviets through Vanderlip. That denial was categorical, almost in the following words: I don't know Vanderlip and recognise no relations with the Soviets. The reason behind this denial is quite obvious. On the eve of the elections in bourgeois America, it might have meant losing several hundred thousand votes for Harding to become known as a supporter of an agreement with the Soviets, and so he hastened to announce in the press that he did not know any Vanderlip. As soon as the elections were over, however, information of a quite different kind began to come in from America. In a number of newspaper articles Vanderlip came out in full support of an agreement with the Soviets and even wrote in one article that he compared Lenin to Washington. It turns out, therefore, that in the bourgeois countries we have propagandists for an agreement with us, and have won these propagandists from among representatives of exploiters of the worst type, such as Vanderlip, and not in the person of the Soviet ambassador or among certain journalists.

When I told a meeting of leading executives what I am now telling you, a comrade just back from America, where he had worked in Vanderlip's factories, said he had been horrified; nowhere had he seen such exploitation as at Vanderlip's factories. And now in the person of this capitalist shark we have won a propagandist for trade relations with Soviet Russia, and even if we do not get anything except the proposed agreement on concessions we shall still be able to say that we have gained something. We have received a number of reports, secret ones, of course, to the effect that the capitalist countries have not given up the idea of launching a new war against Soviet Russia in the spring. We have learnt that preliminary steps are being taken by some capitalist states, while whiteguard elements are, it may be said, making preparations in all countries. Our chief interest, therefore, lies in achieving

the re-establishment of trade relations, and for that purpose we need to have at least a section of the capitalists
on our side.

In Britain the struggle has been going on for a long
time. We have gained by the mere fact that among those
who represent the worst capitalist exploitation we have
people who back the policy of restoring trade relations
with Russia. The agreement with Britain—a trade agreement—has not yet been signed. Krasin is now actively
negotiating it in London. The British Government has submitted its draft to us and we have presented our coun-
terdraft, but all the same we see that the British Government is dragging out the negotiations and that there is a
reactionary military group hard at work there which is
hindering the conclusion of trade agreements and has so
far been successful. It is our prime interest and prime
duty to support anything that can strengthen the parties
and groups working for the conclusion of this agreement
with us. In Vanderlip we have gained such a supporter,
not by mere chance or because Vanderlip is particularly
enterprising or knows Siberia very well. The causes here
lie much deeper and are linked with the development of
the interests of British imperialism, which possesses a
huge number of colonies. This rift between American and
British imperialism is deep, and it is our imperative duty
to base ourselves on it.

I have mentioned that Vanderlip is particularly know-
ledgeable in respect of Siberia. When our talks were
coming to a close, Comrade Chicherin pointed out that Vanderlip should be received because it would have an excellent effect on his further actions in Western Europe. Of
course, the prospect of talking to such a capitalist shark
was not of the pleasantest, but then I had had to talk very
politely, by way of duty, even to the late Mirbach, so I
was certainly not afraid of a talk with Vanderlip. It is interesting that when Vanderlip and I exchanged all sorts
of pleasantries and he started joking and telling me that
the Americans are an extremely practical people and do
not believe what they are told until they see it with their
own eyes, I said to him, half in banter: "Now you can see

how good things are in Soviet Russia and you can introduce the same in America." He answered me, not in English but in Russian: "Mozhet byt."* "Why, you even
know Russian?" He answered: "A long time ago I travelled five thousand versts through Siberia and the country interested me greatly." This humorous exchange of
pleasantries with Vanderlip ended by his saying as he was
leaving, "Yes, it is true Mr. Lenin has no horns and I
must tell that to my friends in America." It would have
seemed simply ridiculous had it not been for the further
reports in the European press to the effect that the Soviets are a monster no relations can be established with.
We were given an opportunity to throw into that swamp
a stone in the person of Vanderlip, who favours the re-
establishment of trade relations with us.

There has not been a single report from Japan that has
not spoken of the extraordinary alarm in Japanese commercial circles. The Japanese public say that they will
never go against their own interests, and are opposed to
concessions in Soviet Russia. In short, we have a terrific
aggravation of the enmity between Japan and America
and thus an undoubted slackening of both Japanese and
American pressure on us.

At the meeting of executives in Moscow where I had to
mention the fact, the following question was asked. "It
appears," one of the comrades wrote, "that we are driving Japan and America to war, but it is the workers and
peasants who will do the fighting. Although these are imperialist powers, is it worthy of us socialists to drive two
powers into a war against each other, which will lead to
the shedding of workers' blood?" I replied that if we were
really driving workers and peasants to war that would be
a crime. All our politics and propaganda, however, are
directed towards putting an end to war and in no way
towards driving nations to war. Experience has shown
sufficiently that the socialist revolution is the only way
out of eternal warfare. Our policy, therefore, is not that
of involving others in a war. We have not done anything

---

* Perhaps.—*Ed.*

justifying, directly or indirectly, a war between Japan and America. All our propaganda and all our newspaper articles try to drive home the truth that a war between America and Japan would be just as much an imperialist war as the one between the British and the German groups in 1914, and that socialists should think, not of defending their respective countries but of overthrowing the power of the capitalists; they should think of the workers' revolution. Is it the correct policy for us to use the discord between the imperialist bandits to make it more difficult for them to unite against us, who are doing everything in our power to accelerate that revolution, but are in the position of a weak socialist republic that is being attacked by imperialist bandits? Of course, it is the correct policy. We have pursued that policy for four years. The Treaty of Brest-Litovsk was the chief expression of this policy. While the German imperialists were offering resistance, we were able to hold out even when the Red Army had not yet been formed, by using the contradictions existing between the imperialists.

Such was the situation in which our concessions policy in respect to Kamchatka emerged. This type of concession is quite exceptional. I shall speak later of the way the other concessions are taking shape. For the moment I shall confine myself to the political aspect of the question. I want to point out that the relations between Japan and America show why it is to our advantage to offer concessions or to use them as an inducement. Concessions presume some kind of re-establishment of peaceful agreements, the restoration of trade relations; they presume the possibility for us to begin direct and extensive purchases of the machinery we need. We must turn all our efforts to achieving this. That has not yet been done.

We have been told that the concessionaires will create exclusive conditions for their workers, and supply them with better clothes, better footwear, and better food. That will be their propaganda among our workers, who are suffering privation and will have to suffer privation for a long time to come. We shall then have a socialist re-

public in which the workers are poverty-stricken and next
to it a capitalist island, in which the workers get an excellent livelihood. This apprehension is frequently voiced at
our Party meetings. Of course, there is a danger of that
kind, and it shows that concessions are a continuation of
war and do not constitute peace. We have, however, experienced far greater deprivations and have seen that workers from capitalist countries nevertheless come to our
country, knowing that the economic conditions awaiting
them in Russia are far worse; surely, then, we ought to
be able to defend ourselves against such propaganda with
counter-propaganda; surely we should be able to show
the workers that capitalism can, of course, provide better
conditions for certain groups of its workers, but that this
does not improve the conditions of the rest of the workers.
And lastly, why is it that at every contact with bourgeois
Europe and America we, not they, have always won? Why
is it that to this day it is they who fear to send delegations
to us, and not we to them? To this day we have always
managed to win over to our side at least a small part of
the delegations, despite the fact that such delegations
consisted in the main of Menshevik elements, and that
they were people who came to us for short periods. Should
we be afraid of being unable to explain the truth to the
workers?! We should be in a bad way if we had such
fears, if we were to place such considerations above the
direct interest which is a matter of the greatest significance
as far as concessions are concerned. The position of
our peasants and workers remains a difficult one. It must
be improved. We cannot have any doubt on that score.
I think we shall agree that the concessions policy is a
policy of continuation of the war, but we must also agree
that it is our task to ensure the continued existence of an
isolated socialist republic surrounded by capitalist enemies, to preserve a republic that is infinitely weaker than
the capitalist enemies surrounding it, thereby eliminating
any possibility of our enemies forming an alliance among
themselves for the struggle against us, and to hamper their
policies and not give them an opportunity to win a victory. It is our task to secure for Russia the necessary ma-

chinery and funds for the restoration of the economy; when we have obtained that, we shall stand so firmly on our own feet that no capitalist enemies can overawe us. That is the point of view which has guided us in our policy on concessions, the policy I have outlined.

First published in 1930   Vol. 31, pp. 463-71,
                                                        485-86

INTERNATIONAL WORKING WOMEN'S DAY
(Excerpt)

And so on this international working women's day countless meetings of working women in all countries of the world will send greetings to Soviet Russia, which has been the first to tackle this unparalleled and incredibly hard but great task, a task that is universally great and truly liberatory. There will be bracing calls not to lose heart in face of the fierce and frequently savage bourgeois reaction. The "freer" or "more democratic" a bourgeois country is, the wilder the rampage of its gang of capitalists against the workers' revolution, an example of this being the democratic republic of the United States of North America. But the mass of workers have already awakened. The dormant, somnolent and inert masses in America, Europe and even in backward Asia were finally roused by the imperialist war.

Published in a Supplement to
Pravda No. 51, March 8, 1921
Signed: *N. Lenin*

Vol. 32, p. 162

IN DEFENCE OF THE TACTICS
OF THE COMMUNIST INTERNATIONAL

From THE SPEECH AT THE THIRD CONGRESS
OF THE COMMUNIST INTERNATIONAL
JULY 1, 1921

I have been speaking too long as it is; hence I wish to say only a few words about the concept of "masses". It is one that changes in accordance with the changes in the nature of the struggle. At the beginning of the struggle it took only a few thousand genuinely revolutionary workers to warrant talk of the masses. If the party succeeds in drawing into the struggle not only its own members, if it also succeeds in arousing non-party people, it is well on the way to winning the masses. During our revolutions there were instances when several thousand workers represented the masses. In the history of our movement, and of our struggle against the Mensheviks, you will find many examples where several thousand workers in a town were enough to give a clearly mass character to the movement. You have a mass when several thousand non-party workers, who usually live a philistine life and drag out a miserable existence, and who have never heard anything about politics, begin to act in a revolutionary way. If the movement spreads and intensifies, it gradually develops into a real revolution. We saw this in 1905 and 1917 during three revolutions, and you too will have to go through all this. When the revolution has been sufficiently prepared, the concept "masses" becomes different: several thousand workers no longer constitute the masses. This word begins to denote something else. The concept of "masses" undergoes a change so that it implies the majority, and not simply a majority of the workers alone, but the majority of all the exploited. Any other kind of interpretation is impermissible for a revolutionary, and any other sense of the word becomes incomprehensible. It is possible that even a small party, the British or American party, for example, after it has thoroughly studied the course of political development and become acquainted with the life and customs of the non-party masses, will at a favourable moment evoke a revolutionary movement (Comrade Radek has pointed to the miners' strike as a good example). You will have a mass movement if such a party comes forward with its slogans at such a moment and succeeds in getting millions of workers to follow it. I would not altogether deny that a revolution can be started by a very small party and brought to a victorious conclusion. But one must have a knowledge of the methods by which the masses can be won over. For this thoroughgoing preparation of revolution is essential. But here you have comrades coming forward with the assertion that we should immediately give up the demand for "big" masses. They must be challenged. Without thoroughgoing preparation you will not achieve victory in any country. Quite a small party is sufficient to lead the masses. At certain times there is no necessity for big organisations.

But to win, we must have the sympathy of the masses. An absolute majority is not always essential; but what is essential to win and retain power is not only the majority of the working class—I use the term "working class" in its West-European sense, i.e., in the sense of the industrial proletariat—but also the majority of the working and exploited rural population. Have you thought about this? Do we find in Terracini's speech even a hint at this thought? He speaks only of "dynamic tendency" and the "transition from passivity to activity". Does he devote even a single word to the food question? And yet the workers demand their victuals, although they can put up with a great deal and go hungry, as we have seen to a certain extent in Russia. We must, therefore, win over to our side not only the majority of the working class, but also the majority of the working and exploited rural population. Have you prepared for this? Almost nowhere.

First published in 1922 in the book: *Third World Congress of the Communist International. Verbatim Report.* Petrograd, 1922

Vol. 32, pp. 475-77

THE HOME AND FOREIGN POLICY OF THE REPUBLIC

From A REPORT OF THE ALL-RUSSIA
CENTRAL EXECUTIVE COMMITTEE AND THE COUNCIL
OF PEOPLE'S COMMISSARS TO THE NINTH ALL-RUSSIA
CONGRESS OF SOVIETS
DECEMBER 23, 1921

Today we see how the representatives of the most moderate bourgeoisie, who are definitely and without doubt far removed from socialist ideas, to say nothing of "that awful Bolshevism", change their tune; this concerns even people like the famous writer Keynes, whose book has been translated into all languages, who took part in the Versailles negotiations, and who devoted himself heart and soul to helping the governments—even he, subsequently, has had to change his tune, to give it up, although he continues to curse socialism. I repeat, he does not mention, nor does he wish even to think about Bolshevism—but he tells the capitalist world: "What you are doing will lead you into a hopeless situation", and he even proposes something like the annulment of all debts.

That is excellent, gentlemen! You should have followed our example long ago.

Only a few days ago we read a short report in the newspapers to the effect that one of the most experienced, exceedingly skilful and astute leaders of a capitalist government, Lloyd George, is, it appears, beginning to propose a similar step; and that seemingly the U.S.A. wishes to reply by saying: "Sorry, but we want to be repaid in full." That being so, we say to ourselves that things are not going too

well in these advanced and mighty states since they are
discussing such a simple measure so many years after the
war. This was one of the easiest things we did—it was
nothing to some of the other difficulties we overcame.
(*Applause*.) When we see the growing confusion on this
question we say that we are not afraid of their propaganda; although we by no means forget either the dangers
surrounding us or our economic and military weakness
compared to any one of these states, who, jointly, quite
openly and frequently express their hatred for us. Whenever we express somewhat different views as to whether
the existence of landowners and capitalists is justified they
do not like it, and these views are declared to be criminal
propaganda. I simply cannot understand this, for the same
sort of propaganda is conducted legally in all states that
do not share our economic views and opinions. Propaganda which calls Bolshevism monstrous, criminal, usurpa-
tory—this monster defies description—this propaganda is
conducted openly in all these countries. Recently I had a
meeting with Christensen, who was a candidate for the
U.S. Presidency on behalf of the farmers' and workers'
party there. Do not be misled by this name, comrades. It
does not in the least resemble the workers' and peasants'
party in Russia. It is a purely bourgeois party, openly and
resolutely hostile to any kind of socialism, and is recognised as being perfectly respectable by all bourgeois parties. This Danish-born American, who received almost a
million votes at the presidential elections (and this, after
all, is something in the United States), told me how in Denmark, when he tried to say among people "dressed like I
am", and he was well dressed, like a bourgeois, that the
Bolsheviks were not criminals, "they nearly killed me".
They told him that the Bolsheviks were monsters, usurpers, and that they were surprised that anyone could mention such people in decent society. This is the type of propaganda atmosphere surrounding us.

We see, nevertheless, that a certain equilibrium has
been created. This is the objective political situation,
quite independent of our victories, which proves that we
have fathomed the depth of the contradictions connected

with the imperialist war, and that we are gauging them more correctly than ever before and more correctly than other powers, who, despite all their victories, despite all their strength, have not yet found a way out, nor see any. That is the substance of the international situation which accounts for what we now see. We have before us a highly unstable equilibrium but one that is, nevertheless, certain, obvious, indisputable. I do not know whether this is for long, and I do not think that anyone can know. That is why, for our part, we must display the utmost caution. And the first precept of our policy, the first lesson that emerges from our governmental activities for the past year, the lesson which must be learned by all workers and peasants, is to be on the alert, to remember that we are surrounded by people, classes, governments who openly express the utmost hatred for us. We must remember that we are always a hair's breadth away from invasion. We shall do all in our power to prevent this misfortune. It is doubtful that any nation has experienced such a burden of the imperialist war as we have. Then we bore the burden of the Civil War forced on us by the ruling classes, who fought for the Russia of the émigrés, the Russia of the landowners, the Russia of the capitalists. We know, we know only too well, the incredible misfortunes that war brings to the workers and peasants. For that reason our attitude to this question must be most cautious and circumspect. We are ready to make the greatest concessions and sacrifices in order to preserve the peace for which we have paid such a high price. We are ready to make huge concessions and sacrifices, but not any kind and not for ever. Let those, fortunately not numerous, representatives of the war parties and aggressive cliques of Finland, Poland and Rumania who make great play of this—let them mark it well. (*Applause.*)

Anyone who has any political sense or acumen will say that there has not been—nor can there be—a government in Russia other than the Soviet Government prepared to make such concessions and sacrifices in relation to nationalities within our state, and also to those which had joined the Russian Empire. There is not, and cannot be, another government which would recognise as clearly as we do and declare so distinctly to one and all that the attitude of old Russia (tsarist Russia, Russia of the war parties) to the nationalities populating Russia was criminal, that this attitude was impermissible, that it aroused the rightful and indignant protest and discontent of the oppressed nationalities. There is not, and cannot be, another government which would so openly admit this, which would conduct this anti-chauvinist propaganda, a propaganda that recognises the guilt of old Russia, tsarist Russia, Kerensky Russia—a government which would conduct propaganda against the forcible incorporation of other nationalities into Russia. This is not mere words—this is an obvious political fact, absolutely indisputable and plain for all to see. As long as no nationalities engage in intrigues against us which bind them to the imperialist oppression, as long as they do not help to crush us, we shall not be deterred by formalities. We shall not forget that we are revolutionaries. (*Applause.*) But there are facts incontrovertibly and indisputably showing that in Russia, that has defeated the Mensheviks and Socialist-Revolutionaries, the smallest, completely unarmed nationality, however weak it may be, may and must absolutely rest assured that we have nothing but peaceful intentions towards it, that our propaganda about the criminality of the old policy of the old governments is not weakening, and that we are as firm as ever in our desire at all costs, and at the price of enormous sacrifices and concessions, to maintain peace with all nationalities that belonged to the former Russian Empire, but who did not wish to remain with us. We have proved this. And we shall prove this no matter how great the curses rained on us from all sides. It seems to us that we have given excellent proof of it, and we declare to the meeting of representatives of the workers and peasants of Russia, to the many millions of workers and peasants, that we shall do our utmost to preserve peace in the future, that we shall not shrink from great sacrifices and concessions in order to safeguard this peace.

There are, however, limits beyond which one cannot go. We shall not permit peace treaties to be flouted. We shall not permit attempts to interfere with our peaceful work. On no account shall we permit this, and we shall rise to a man to defend our existence. (*Applause.*)

Comrades, what I have just said is perfectly clear and comprehensible to you, and you could not expect anything else from anyone reporting to you on our policy. You know that such, and no other, is our policy. But, unfortunately, there are now two worlds: the old world of capitalism, that is in a state of confusion but which will never surrender voluntarily, and the rising new world, which is still very weak, but which will grow, for it is invincible. This old world has its old diplomacy, which cannot believe that it is possible to speak frankly and forthrightly. This old diplomacy thinks there must be a trap of some sort here. (*Applause, laughter.*) When this economically and militarily all-powerful old world sent us—that was some time ago—Bullitt, a representative of the United States Government, who came to us with the proposal that we should conclude peace with Kolchak and Denikin on terms that were most unfavourable to us—we said that we held so dear the blood of the workers and peasants shed for so long in Russia that although the terms were extremely unfavourable we were prepared to accept them, because we were convinced that the forces of Kolchak and Denikin would disintegrate from within. We said this quite frankly, with the minimum of diplomatic subtlety, and so they concluded that we must be trying to dupe them. And Bullitt, who had held these friendly, round-table conversations with us, was met with reproach and compelled to resign as soon as he got home. I am surprised that he has not yet been thrown into gaol, in keeping with the imperialist custom, for secretly sympathising with the Bolsheviks. (*Laughter, applause.*) But the upshot was that we, who at that time had proposed peace to our disadvantage, obtained peace on much more favourable terms. That was something of a lesson. I know that we can no more learn the old diplomacy than we can remould ourselves; but the lessons in diplomacy that we have given since then and that have been learned by the other powers must have had some effect; they must have remained in the memory of some people. (*Laughter.*) Hence, our straightforward statement that our workers and peasants prized above all the blessings of peace, but that there were limits to the concessions they were prepared to make to preserve it, was taken to mean that they had not for a moment, not for a second, forgotten the hardships they had suffered in the imperialist war and the Civil War. This reminder, which I am sure this Congress, and the whole mass of workers and peasants, all Russia, will endorse and express—this reminder will surely have some effect and play a certain role, no matter how the powers take it, no matter what diplomatic ruse their old diplomatic habits make them suspect.

This, comrades, is what I think must be said about our international situation. A certain unstable equilibrium has been reached. Materially—economically and militarily— we are extremely weak; but morally—by which, of course, I mean not abstract morals, but the alignment of the real forces of all classes in all countries—we are the strongest of all. This has been proved in practice; it has been proved not merely by words but by deeds; it has been proved once and, if history takes a certain turn, it will, perhaps, be proved many times again. That is why we say that having started on our work of peaceful development we shall exert every effort to continue it without interruption. At the same time, comrades, be vigilant, safeguard the defence potential of our country, strengthen our Red Army to the utmost, and remember that we have no right to permit an instant's slackening where our workers and peasants and their gains are concerned. (*Applause.*)

Pravda No. 292,
December 25, 1921

Vol. 33, pp. 146-51

NOTES OF A PUBLICIST
(Excerpt)

The development of the German and Italian Communist Parties since the Third Congress of the Comintern has shown that the mistakes committed by the Lefts at that Congress have been noted and are being rectified—little by little, slowly, but steadily; the decisions of the Third Congress of the Communist International are being loyally carried out. The process of transforming the old type of European parliamentary party—which in fact is reformist and only slightly tinted with revolutionary colours—into a *new type* of party, into a genuinely revolutionary, genuinely Communist Party, is an extremely arduous one. This is demonstrated most clearly, perhaps, by the example of France. The process of changing the *type* of Party work in everyday life, of getting it out of the humdrum channel; the process of converting the Party into the vanguard of the revolutionary proletariat without permitting it to become divorced from the masses, but, on the contrary, by linking it more and more closely with them, imbuing them with revolutionary consciousness and rousing them for the revolutionary struggle, is a very difficult, but most important one. If the European Communists do not take advantage of the intervals (probably very short) between the periods of particularly acute revolutionary battles—such as took place in many capitalist countries of Europe and America in 1921 and the beginning of 1922—for the purpose of bringing about this fundamental, internal, profound reorganisation of the whole structure of their Parties and of their work, they will be committing the gravest of crimes. Fortunately, there is no reason to fear this. The quiet, steady, calm, not very rapid, but profound work of creating genuine Communist Parties, genuine revolutionary vanguards of the proletariat, has begun and is proceeding in Europe and America.

Written late in February 1922

First published in *Pravda* No. 87,   Vol. 33, pp. 209-10
April 16, 1924

ON THE SIGNIFICANCE OF MILITANT MATERIALISM

(Excerpt)

Pod Znamenem Marksisma, which sets out to be an organ of militant materialism, should devote much of its space to atheist propaganda, to reviews of the literature on the subject and to correcting the immense shortcomings of our governmental work in this field. It is particularly important to utilise books and pamphlets which contain many concrete facts and comparisons showing how the class interests and class organisations of the modern bourgeoisie are connected with the organisations of religious institutions and religious propaganda.

All material relating to the United States of America, where the official, state connection between religion and capital is less manifest, is extremely important. But, on the other hand, it becomes all the clearer to us that so-called modern democracy (which the Mensheviks, the Socialist-Revolutionaries, partly also the anarchists, etc., so unreasonably worship) is nothing but the freedom to preach whatever is to the advantage of the bourgeoisie, to preach, namely, the most reactionary ideas, religion, obscurantism, defence of the exploiters, etc.

Pod Znamenem Marksizma No. 3,   Vol. 33, pp. 231-32
March 1922
Signed: *N. Lenin*

A FLY IN THE OINTMENT

Citizen O. A. Yermansky has written a very good, useful book: *The Taylor System and the Scientific Organisation of Labour* (Gosizdat, 1922). It is a revised edition of his book, *The Taylor System*, which first appeared in 1918. The book has been substantially enlarged; very important supplements have been added: I. "Productive Labour and Culture"; II. "The Problem of Fatigue". One of the most important sections, earlier entitled "Labour and Leisure", only 16 pages long, has now been enlarged to 70 pages (Chapter III: "Human Labour").

The book gives a detailed exposition of the Taylor system and, this is especially important, both its positive and *negative aspects,* and also the principal scientific data on the physiological intake and output in the human machine. On the whole the book is quite suitable, I think, as a standard textbook for all trade union schools and for all secondary schools in general. To learn how to work is now the main, the truly national task of the Soviet Republic. Our primary and most important task is to attain universal literacy, but we should in no circumstances limit ourselves to this target. We must at all costs go beyond it and adopt everything that is truly valuable in European and American science.

Citizen Yermansky's book has one serious flaw which may make it unacceptable as a textbook. It is the author's verbosity. He repeats the same thing again and again without any conceivable need. I suppose the author may be vindicated to some extent by the fact that he was not trying to write a textbook. However, he says on p. VIII that he regards the popular exposition of scientific questions as one of the merits of his book. He is right. But popular exposition should also shun repetition. The people have no time to waste on bulky volumes. Without good reason, Citizen Yermansky's book is much too bulky. That is what prevents it from being a popular book. . . .*

Written after September 10, 1922

First published in 1928

Vol. 33, pp. 368-69

---

* Here the manuscript breaks off.—*Ed.*

(*Stormy, prolonged applause. All rise.*) Comrades, permit me to confine myself to a few words of greeting. We should first of all, of course, send our greetings to the Red Army, which has recently given further proof of its valour by capturing Vladivostok and clearing the entire territory of the last of the republics linked with Soviet Russia. I am sure that I am expressing the general opinion when I say that we all welcome this new feat of the Red Army, and also the fact that apparently a very important step has been taken towards bringing the war to a close; the last of the whiteguard forces have been driven into the sea. (*Applause.*) I think that our Red Army has rid us for a long time of the possibility of another whiteguard attack on Russia or on any of the republics that are directly or indirectly, closely or more or less remotely, connected with us.

At the same time, however, in order to avoid adopting a tone of inordinate self-adulation, we must say that the strength of the Red Army and its recent victory were not the only factors in this; other factors were the international situation and our diplomacy.

Some time ago Japan and the United States signed a pact to support Kolchak. But that was so long ago that many people have probably forgotten it completely. But that was the case. We have made such pacts impossible now, and, due to our efforts, the Japanese, in spite of their military strength, declared that they would withdraw, and have kept their promise; our diplomacy must also be given credit for this. I shall not drag out my brief greeting by saying what brought us that success. I shall only say that in the near future our diplomats will once again have to display their skill in a matter of immense importance, and one in which we are vitally interested. I have in mind the Middle East Conference that Great Britain is convening in Lausanne on November 13.[123] I am sure that there, too, our diplomats will prove their mettle, and that we shall be able to vindicate the interests of all our federated republics, and of the R.S.F.S.R. At all events, we shall succeed in revealing to the masses where and what the obstacle is, and to what extent it is an obstacle to the legitimate desires and aspirations not only of ourselves, but of all countries interested in the question of the Straits.

I shall limit my utterances on foreign politics to these brief remarks and shall now deal with the proceedings of this session.

I think that here we have achieved no small success in spite of the fact that to some people the questions dealt with may at first sight appear to be not so very important. Take the first code of laws that you have already passed—the Code of Labour Laws. Our adoption of a code of laws which firmly lays down the principles of labour legislation such as the eight-hour day at a time when in all other countries the working class is being heavily attacked is a tremendous achievement for Soviet rule. True, there are people who, perhaps, would desire something more from this code; but I think that such a desire would be totally unjustified.

We must bear in mind that compared with all the countries where fierce capitalist competition is raging, where there are millions and tens of millions of unemployed, and where the capitalists are forming vast combinations and are launching an offensive against the working class—if we compare ourselves with those countries, we are the least cultured, our productivity of labour is the lowest, and we are the least efficient. This is, I would say, a very unpleasant thing to have to admit. I think, however, that precisely because we do not disguise such things with platitudes and stereotyped catchwords, but candidly admit them, precisely because we all admit, and are not afraid to proclaim from this rostrum, that we are exerting more efforts than any other country to rectify all this, we shall succeed in catching up with these countries faster than they ever dreamed possible.

This will not be done at a fantastic speed, of course, it will naturally take us several years of laborious effort to achieve it. It goes without saying that nothing can be done overnight. We have been in existence for five years, we have seen at what speed social relations change, and have learned to appreciate what time means; and we must go on learning what it means. Nobody believes that any important change can be achieved at a fantastic speed; but we do believe in real speed, speed compared with the rate of development in any period in history you like to take— especially if progress is guided by a genuinely revolutionary party; and this speed we shall achieve at all costs.

Pravda No. 247,
November 1, 1922

Vol. 33, pp. 390-92

LETTERS AND NOTES

TO ISAAC A. HOURWICH

Cracow. February 27, 1914

Dear Colleague,

I have long since received your book, *Immigration and Labour*,[124] and have been looking for your address to send you my thanks. But it proved far from easy to find your address. I got it only today, and hasten to express my gratitude to you for sending me the book. I have already written an article[125] about it, and on the basis of it, in our St. Petersburg Social-Democratic newspaper *Pravda*, and intend to write again. I believe that this work provides a mass of valuable material for the study of capitalism, being at the same time something of an application of the best methods of our Zemstvo statisticians on *Western* soil.

The comrade who sent me your address (Mr. John El lert) has written to tell me that you could use your influence to help obtain all kinds of material from the Bureau of the Census in Washington. May I, therefore, ask you to do me a favour, provided of course that this will not give you too much trouble or interfere with your work.

When I made a study of American agricultural statistics (Vol. V. *Agriculture—Census of 1900*) in Paris, I found a great deal of interesting matter. Now, in Cracow, I am unable to obtain these publications. Cahan, editor of the Jewish socialist paper in New York, who was over here a year ago, promised to have them[126] sent, but has apparently forgotten to do so.

They say that when requested by the right people the American Bureau of the Census will send its publications free of charge even to foreign countries. If that is so, could you put in a word? (I could send the Bureau of the Census library my books, *The Development of Capitalism in Russia* and the *Agrarian Question*[127]). What I need *most* is *Agriculture*, Vol. V, Census of 1900, and *the same volume of the Census of 1910* (if that is not yet out, then the bulletins).

If that is impossible, would you be so kind as to send a postcard to Mr. John *Ellert* (c/o *Novy Mir*. 140. East 4th Street, New York)—I shall send him the money to buy the things I need most.

I thank you once again for the book, and hope you will pardon the trouble.

With Social-Democratic greetings,

N. Lenin (*V. Ulyanov*)

Address: Wl. Ulianow. 51. Ulica Lubomirskiego. *Krakau* (Galizien). Austria.

Sent to New York

First published in 1930
in *Lenin Miscellany XIII*   Vol. 36, pp. 271-72

TO ALEXANDRA KOLLONTAI

November 9, 1915

Dear A. M.,

Only yesterday did we get your letter of October 18 from Milwaukee. Letters take a terribly long time! You have not yet received my letter (and Nos. 45-46 and 47 of *Sotsial-Demokrat*) about Zimmerwald,[128] and containing all the replies to your questions; yet that letter was written more than a month ago. Try at any rate to calculate where you will be (approximately, in six weeks' time) and give us addresses (for letters to you), so that they arrive nearer.

As regards the New York *Volkszeitung*, Grimm assured me today that they are quite Kautskian! Is that the case? I think our *German* pamphlet* might help you to determine the "strength" of their internationalism. Have you had it? (500 copies were sent to you.)

In a few days we are publishing here (in German, and then *we hope* to put it out in French and, if we can manage the money, in Italian) a little pamphlet on behalf of the *Zimmerwald Left*. Under this name we should like to launch into international circulation, as widely as possible, our Left group at Zimmerwald (the C.C. + the Polish Social-Democrats + the Letts + the Swedes + the Norwegians + 1 German + 1 Swiss) with its *draft resolution* and *manifesto* (printed in No. 45-46 of *Sotsial-Demokrat*). The little pamphlet (20-30-35 thousand letters and spaces) will contain these two documents and a small introduction. We rely on you to publish it in America *in English too* (for it is hopeless to do this in England: it has to be brought there *from* America) and, if possible, in other languages. This is

---

* Reference is to the pamphlet *Socialism and War* (*The Attitude of the R.S.D.L.P. Towards the War*) (see Lenin, *Collected Works*, Vol. 21, pp. 295-338).—*Ed.*

to be the first publication by the *nucleus of Left* Social-
Democrats of *all* countries, who have a clear, exact and
full *reply* to the question of what is to be done and in
which direction to go. It would be most important if you
could succeed in publishing this in America, circulating it
as widely as possible and *establishing firm publishing links*
(*Charles Kerr* (N.B.) at Chicago; the *Appeal to Reason** at
Kansas, etc.), for it is generally most important for us to
come out in various languages (you could do *a great deal*
in this respect).

As regards money, I see with distress from your letter
that so far you have not managed to collect anything for
the Central Committee. Perhaps this "Manifesto of the
Left" will help....

I never doubted that Hillquit would be for Kautsky and
even *to the right* of him, because I saw him at Stuttgart
(1907)[129] and *heard* how *afterwards* he defended the prohi-
bition against bringing yellow people into America (an "internationalist")....

The Zimmerwald Manifesto[130] itself is *inadequate*; Kautsky and Co. are ready to put up with it, on *condition* that
there is "not a step further". We *don't* accept this, because
it is *complete hypocrisy*. So that if there are people in
America who are afraid *even* of the Zimmerwald Manifesto, you can brush them aside, and bring in only those
who are *more Left than the Zimmerwald Manifesto*.

I shake you by the hand and wish you every success!

Yours,

Lenin

(Ulianow. Seidenweg. 4ᵃ. III. *Bern*)

Sent from Berne to New York

First published in 1924
in *Lenin Miscellany II*   Vol. 35, pp. 210-11

---

* Try establishing contact with them—if only in writing, should
you not get to Kansas. Their little paper is sometimes *not bad*. Be
sure to sound them out with our resolution of the "Zimmerwald
Left". And what is Eugene *Debs*? He sometimes writes in a revolutionary way. Or is he also a wet rag *à la* Kautsky?

Write *when* you will *again* be in New York, and for *how many*
days. Try *everywhere* to see (if only for 5 minutes) the local *Bolsheviks*,
to "refresh" them and *get them in touch with us*.

TO MAXIM GORKY

January 11, 1916

Dear Alexei Maximovich,

I am sending you at the *Letopis* address, not for *Letopis* but for the publishing house, the manuscript of a pamphlet and request you to publish it.[131]

I have tried in as popular a form as possible to set forth new data about America which, I am convinced, are particularly suitable for popularising Marxism and substantiating it by means of facts. I hope I have succeeded in setting out these important data clearly and comprehensibly for the new sections of the reading public which are multiplying in Russia and need an explanation of the world's economic evolution.

I should like to continue, and subsequently also to publish, a second part—about Germany.

I am setting to work on a pamphlet about imperialism.[132]

Owing to war-time conditions I am in extreme need of earnings, and would therefore ask, if it is possible and will not embarrass you too much, to speed up publication of the pamphlet.

Yours with respect,

V. Ilyin

The address is Mr. Wl. Oulianoff, Seidenweg, *4-a*, *Berne*, (Suisse).

Sent to Petrograd

First published in 1925
in *Lenin Miscellany III*

Vol. 35, p. 212

TO ALEXANDRA KOLLONTAI

March 19, 1916

Dear A. M.,

We have received your letter, and once again congratulate you on your success.

I was terribly irritated by the fact that "noble" France had (actually!) *confiscated* some of my registered letters to you in America. Well, we can't help that, can we? Now you must do *your very best* about contacts with America.

You did write me that while in America you received *Internationale Flugblätter*[133] No. 1 in German, and that you would try to publish it in English! And now there's *not a word* about it?

What does it mean?!

Is that to say that no sympathisers are to be found in America and that *Internationale Flugblätter cannot* be published in English?

This is incredible!

But if that is so, it should be published in Norway (in English). Would you undertake to translate it, and how much will it cost to publish it?

I also wrote to you in America that I had received a Socialist Propaganda League leaflet from Boston, Mass. (signed by 20 Socialists *with addresses*, mostly in Massachusetts). This League is internationalist, with a programme clearly tending to the left.

I sent them *the longest* letter in English[134] (and *Internationale Flugblätter* in German). There has been no reply. I wonder if "noble" France has confiscated the lot.

If you received *nothing* and know *nothing* about them, I shall send you their address and a copy of my letter. Will you undertake to send it on to America?

And what of the Socialist *Labour* Party? After all, they are internationalists (even if there is something narrowly sectarian about them). Have they got their copy of *Internationale Flugblätter*? Have you any contacts with *them*?

Furthermore, you also wrote that you had *started* negotiations with *Charles* H. Kerr. What's the result? He did promise to publish a *part* of our pamphlet (by Lenin and Zinoviev).[135]

Now you say nothing more about it.... How are we to understand this?

Internationale Korrespondenz[136] reported that the *New Review* in America had undertaken to publish articles by the Zimmerwald Left. Is that true? Do you know the *New Review*?

Reply as soon and as circumstantially as you can. You will, of course, find out *everything* in great detail about *direct* mail steamers from Norway to America.

As for Höglund and the Norwegians, *I am still* unable to find out whether or not they have received *Internationale Flugblätter*, whether or not they have published it in Swedish and Norwegian, whether or not they have *officially* affiliated to the Zimmerwald Left (like the Rev. Soc. *Verband* of Roland-Holst). Please take the trouble to find out, get things done, give them a piece of your mind, make them do it, follow it through! Let Bukharin inform you of the contents of our special letter to him about the Zimmerwald people, and please see that this is done.

Regards,
Yours,
Lenin

My address is: Herrn Uljanow (Schuhladen Kammerer). Spiegelgasse. 12. *Zürich*. I.

P.S. What interesting books and pamphlets have you brought along? Schlüter's history of Chartism? What else?

P.S. Am sending you our "theses" (from *Vorbote* No. 2). Drive this home to the Scandinavians.

Sent from Zurich to Christiania (Oslo)

First published in 1924
in *Lenin Miscellany II*

Vol. 36, pp. 373-74

TO ALEXANDRA KOLLONTAI

Dear A. M.,

Thank you very much for your letter. I shall send you the address of the Socialist Propaganda League, unless I have left it behind in Berne: in that case I shall send it over from Berne (i.e., in 2 or 3 weeks' time).

Do you think *Appeal to Reason* would refuse to reprint *Internationale Flugblätter* No. 1? Is it worth trying?

Will the Socialist *Labour* Party agree to publish, if *we pay* the costs? Are these people hopeless sectarians or not? Have you any connections with them? Why *don't they send us* copies of their papers in the *Internationale Sozialistische Kommission*?[137] (I saw some quite by chance.) Or are they maniacs with an *idée fixe* about a special "economic" organisation of workers?

You ask how desirable it is that the Norwegian party should send its official representative to the conference? Of course, it is 1,000 times better to have a class-conscious and intelligent *Left-winger* from among the youth, than a Right-winger or a 1/2-Kautskyite from the party.

That is clear. Use your influence on these lines, if you can.

I am very much distressed that we do not see eye to eye on self-determination. Let's try to argue this out in detail *without a squabble* (which someone is trying very hard to stir up for us on this score).... *Entre nous*, perhaps Alexander will show you my reply to N. I. Bukharin's remarks (for the time being this discord must remain strictly confidential, but I trust to your discretion).

This question ("self-determination") is of the utmost importance. Besides, it is *organically* bound up with the question of *annexations*.

The best of everything,

Yours,
Lenin

P.S. I sent Alexander a great big letter a few days ago. Has he got it?

Written after March 19, 1916
Sent from Zurich to Christiania

First published in 1924   Vol. 36, pp. 375-76
in *Lenin Miscellany II*

NOTE TO PRESS BUREAU, COUNCIL OF PEOPLE'S COMMISSARS

April 27, 1918

Press Bureau

Comrade Axelrod,
Please, be so kind as to help the bearer, Comrade Gomberg, to collect all the materials (printed) about our revolution. This is of tremendous *public* importance because on this depends the information of America and the whole world.

Greetings!
Lenin

First published in 1959   *Lenin Miscellany XXXVI*,
p. 40

TO RAYMOND ROBINS

April 30, 1918

Dear Mr. Robins,

I thank you very much for your letter. I am sure that the new democracy, i.e., proletarian democracy, will be established in all countries and will break down all obstacles and the imperialist-capitalist system in the Old World and the New.

With cordial greetings and gratitude,

Yours truly,

Lenin

First published in Russian
in 1957 in the book
Dokumenty vneshnei politiki SSSR,
Vol. I

Lenin Miscellany XXXVI,
pp. 40-41

TO RAYMOND ROBINS

To Colonel Robins

14 May, 1918

Dear Mr. Robins:

I enclose the preliminary plan of our economic relations with America. This preliminary plan was elaborated in the Council of Export Trade in our highest Council of National Economy.

I hope this preliminary can be useful for you in your conversation with the American Foreign Office and American Export Specialists.

With best thanks,

yours truly,

(signed) *Lenin*

First published in English in 1920 in the book: *Russian-American Relations. March 1917-March 1920. Documents and Papers*, New York, p. 204

First published in Russian in 1957 in the book: *Dokumenty vneshnei politiki SSSR*, Vol. I

CONCERNING JACK TANNER'S SPEECH
AT THE SECOND CONGRESS OF THE COMINTERN

Tanner's speech (Shop Stewards) has made it quite clear that:

1) a place should be made *within* the Third International for *sympathisers*;

2) a *special* reservation should be made for Britain and America to the effect that in spite of our contradictions on parliamentarism we propose that

(a) the mass movement in the form of the I.W.W. and the Shop Stewards should remain affiliated with the Third International; and

(b) the question should be thoroughly discussed once again and a practical test should be made to *improve* the socialist parties which had agitated among the masses *insufficiently* and *did not know* how to establish ties with them.

Lenin

Written on July 23, 1920

First published in 1959

Lenin Miscellany XXXVI,
pp. 114-15

TO ALL PEOPLE'S COMMISSARS
AND MEMBERS OF COLLEGIUMS

August 17, 1920

Comrade *Louis Fraina*, an American Communist, who is staying in Moscow and who is the author of some extremely valuable writings (about Bolshevism, its history and tactics)in English,

will need *several* comrades able to *interpret* from Russian into English to work with him permanently.

Non-Party members will do.

I request you to find the right people with a *good* knowledge of English, and to inform *our secretariat* accordingly.

V. Ulyanov (Lenin)

Chairman, Council of People's Commissars

First published in 1957

Inostrannaya literatura
No. 11, 1957, p. 21

TO N. I. BUKHARIN

Comrade Bukharin,

I think we *should* publish in Russian De Leon's *Two Pages*, *etc.*,[138] with Fraina's foreword and notes. I shall also write a few words.

If you agree, *will you give the word* through the State Publishing House.

If you don't, let's discuss it.

Lenin

Written in the late summer of 1920

First published in 1924 in the   Vol. 36, p. 528
magazine *Zhizn* No. 1

РОССІЙСКАЯ
ФЕДЕРАТИВНАЯ
соціалистическая
СОВѢТСКАЯ РЕСПУБЛИКА.

ПРЕДСѢДАТЕЛЬ
СОВѢТА
НАРОДНЫХЪ КОМИССАРОВЪ.

Москва, Кремль.
27 VIII 1920
№

To Comrade
Edward Martin.

Dear comrade,

I understand that You are ill having
worked too hard for the Communist
International. Comrade John Reed spoke
about it with me.

I beg You to accept my best wishes,
my sincerest thanks to You & my assurance
that I am ready to do my possible in order to help
You.

With best wishes Yours
W. Ulianoff (Lenin).

Lenin's letter to Edward Martin. August 27, 1920
Reduced

TO COMRADE EDWARD MARTIN

August 27, 1920

Comrade Edward Martin

Dear Comrade,
  I understand that you are ill having worked too hard for the Communist International. Comrade John Reed spoke about it with me.
  I beg you to accept my best wishes, my sincerest thanks to you and my assurance that I am ready to do my possible in order to help you.

With best wishes,
Yours,

Wl. Oulianoff (Lenin)

Written in English
First published in 1957

Inostrannaya literatura
No. 11, 1957, pp. 17-18

NOTE TO M. V. KOBETSKY

(Excerpt)

Comrade Kobetsky,
Your *report* (i.e., the doctor's report which you sent in) and this note[139] should be translated into English and sent abroad.

October 18

Lenin

First published in 1957

Inostrannaya literatura
No. 11, 1957, p. 19

TO N. P. GORBUNOV

February 21, 1921

Comrade Gorbunov,

Martens, our former representative in America, is here. He needs help. See him today. You will find him at the Luxe[140] through my telephone operators.

1) Electrotechnical textbooks at *Goelro.*

Call up Krzhizhanovsky.

2) About the American workers (in Russia)[141] with *Anixt.*

3) About a tour of the plants and factories

$\left\{ \begin{array}{l} \text{?Find out through Rykov.} \\ \text{?Who could arrange it.} \end{array} \right\}$

4) About technical aid groups for us in America (with the S.T.D*?

or also with the Supreme Economic Council and the People's Commissariat for Foreign Trade? find out who can arrange this).

5) Resettlement of various persons and groups in this country from America

(great *care* must be taken. Is there any commission on this question?[142]).

Lenin

First published in 1959

Lenin Miscellany XXXVI, pp. 199-200

---

* Scientific and Technical Department.—*Ed.*

TO WASHINGTON VANDERLIP

Moscow, March 17, 1921

Mr. Washington B. Vanderlip

Dear Sir,

I thank you for your kind letter of the 14th inst., and am very glad to hear of President Harding's favourable views as to our trade with America. You know what value we attach to our future American business relations. We fully recognise the part played in this respect by your syndicate and also the great importance of your personal efforts.[143] Your new proposals are highly interesting and I have asked the Supreme Council of National Economy to report to me at short intervals about the progress of the negotiations. You can be sure that we will treat every reasonable suggestion with the greatest attention and care. It is on production and trade that our efforts are principally concentrated and your help is to us of the greatest value.

If you have to complain of some officials please send your complaint to the respective People's Commissariat who will investigate the matter and report, if necessary. I have already ordered special investigation concerning the person you mention in your letter.

The Congress of the Communist Party[144] has taken so much of my time and forces that I am very tired and ill. Will you kindly excuse me if I am unable to have an interview with you just now. I will beg Comrade Chicherin to speak with you shortly.

Wishing you much success, I remain

Yours truly,

Wl. Oulianoff (Lenin)

Written in English

First published in 1932

Lenin Miscellany XX,
pp. 189-90

TO L. K. MARTENS

June 22, 1921

Comrade Martens,

I must reproach you for sending the papers about the American colonies in Russia through the wrong channels.

I read them only on June 20. You should not have sent them through Bukharin, but should have set out the proposals in Russian, about 20 lines all told, and sent them on to the Council of Labour and Defence, with a personal copy for me and a brief letter.

The delay was due to the records being sent through the wrong channels.

Now about the substance of the matter. I am in favour, *if* the American workers and settlers in general will bring along:

1) Food supplies for two years (you write that this has been done before, which means that it can be done again);

2) Clothing for the same period;

3) Implements of labour.

Point 1 (and 2) are the most important. The $200 are less important. Given Point 1, I agree to *support* the project *in every way*.

In order to expedite matters, please make a draft C.L.D. resolution and hand it in at the C.L.D. today (before 3 p.m., if you can make it). We shall decide at 6 p.m. today[145]; if you cannot make it, hand it in at the C.L.D. at 6 p.m. anyway, we shall set up a commission and decide on Friday, June 24.

The draft resolution: (1) the terms—the three listed above; (2) management (you + one American worker + 1

man from the People's Commissariat for Labour?); (3)
our assistance (we provide the land, timber, mines, etc.);
(4) financial terms (specify).

Please reply by bearer.

V. Ulyanov (*Lenin*)
Chairman, Council
of People's Commis-
sars

P.S. After writing this letter I discovered that the question was on today's C.L.D. agenda. Please work out the
points I have indicated.

First published in 1932   *Lenin Miscellany XX*,
                                            pp. 200-01

TO L. K. MARTENS

Comrade Martens,

I request you to give full and resolute assistance in the organisation of Garment Factory No. 36 by the American workers.

Eliminate all red tape in obtaining all the necessary materials and especially pipes, armatures to them (T-joints, sleeves, etc.) and electrical wire.

Please help the group of workers to obtain housing; this must be done without any red tape on the part of the Housing Department.

The factory must be built and run in within the shortest possible time. The carelessness and red tape in this whole business is outrageous.

Chairman of the Council
of Labour and Defence

Written on June 27, 1921

First published in 1932

Lenin Miscellany XX,
p. 201

TO V. M. LIKHACHOV

Comrade Likhachov,
    Chairman of the Moscow City Economic Council

Please give the fullest and most resolute assistance in the work of the group of American workers in organising Garment Factory No. 36.

Please issue the necessary instructions to the chief of Moskvoshvei,* Comrade Seryakov.

Eliminate all red tape in obtaining materials, especially pipes, and armatures to them and electrical wire.

There can be no excuse for any unwarranted delay or red tape in this case.

Help the group of workers to obtain housing without any unwarranted delay on the part of the Housing Department.

The factory must be completed and run in as soon as possible.

Chairman of the Council
of Labour and Defence

Written on June 27, 1921
First published in 1932

Lenin Miscellany XX,
p. 201

---

* Moscow Garment Board.—*Ed.*

TO M. M. BORODIN

Comrade Borodin

Dear Comrade,
  Could you get me some material on the American third party, the workers' and farmers' or the Farmer-Labour Party, or the Non-partisan League, its activity in the State of North Dakota, which it controls.[146] I should like to have some of the most important documents relating to this party and its activity in North Dakota or, which is better, in addition to these documents, a short memo from you on the question. May I ask you to write me soon to say if you can do this and when.

V. Ulyanov (Lenin)
Chairman, Council of People's Commissars

Written on July 13, 1921

First published in 1959

Lenin Miscellany XXXVI,
p. 287

TO L. K. MARTENS

To *Martens*

I have a telegram from Riga about the Congress of Societies for Technical Aid to Soviet Russia[147] of the United States and Canada which, the New York *Golos Rossii* says, was held in New York in early July.

The Congress, says this report, sent a telegram of greetings to Martens and the People's Commissars announcing its decision to organise technical teams immediately for dispatch to Soviet Russia.

I think I should send them the following telegram:

"Having learned, from the New York *Golos Rossii*, of your Congress and its telegram of greetings to Soviet Russia, I should like to express deep gratitude on behalf of the Council of People's Commissars.

"May I add personally that we are extremely in need of technical assistance from the United States and Canada. If teams are sent without preliminary agreement as to the site of settlement, factory, etc., the team should have supplies of food, clothing, etc., for two years. Each team should be prepared both for agricultural and industrial operations. It would be better to start by sending delegates to make an on-the-spot examination of the land tracts for settlement, forest tracts, mines, factories, etc., which are to be leased."

Lenin
Chairman, Council of People's Commissars

The signatures of Martens and the People's Commissar for Labour are required; those of Bogdanov and Chicherin are also desirable.

Written on August 2, 1921
First published in 1933

Lenin Miscellany XXIII,
pp. 38-39

TELEPHONE MESSAGE TO V. A. SMOLYANINOV

Smolyaninov

In view of the detailed and formal protest lodged by Comrade Chicherin against the dispatch of the enclosed telegram[148] please call an additional conference consisting of Comrade Martens, a representative of the People's Commissariat for Labour who is informed on the question, and a representative of the People's Commissariat for Foreign Affairs, also informed on the question. A total of four persons, including yourself.

Please have the conference[149] discuss Chicherin's objections and pay especial attention to the demand stated in the telegram that food should be brought for two years.

I think that if we were to add a few words about the fight against hardships and privation in Russia and the uselessness of sending people over who are unable to bear them, the telegram would be only to the good. Please send me a very short resolution in writing not later than tomorrow night.

Lenin

Dictated by telephone on
August 4, 1921

First published in 1959

Lenin Miscellany XXXVI,
p. 302

TO G. V. CHICHERIN AND L. B. KAMENEV[150]

In view of the fact that the low-down American hucksters are trying to create the impression that we could be expected to cheat,

I propose that we should immediately telegraph them officially on behalf of the government, over the signatures of Kamenev and Chicherin (and if necessary Kalinin's and mine as well),

the following:

We shall deposit with a New York bank an amount in gold constituting 120 per cent of what they will supply in the course of a month for one million starving children and sick persons. But our terms in that case are such that, considering such a complete material guarantee, the Americans must absolutely abstain not only from political but also from administrative interference, and must make no claims whatsoever, since this voids all the terms of the treaty giving them the least right to interfere even administratively. On the spot check-ups will be made by parity commissions (representing our government and them).

This proposal will show the hucksters just where they stand and subsequently disgrace them in the eyes of the whole world.

We should not forget that we have never had rationing of any kind in the countryside. If we are to make no mistake in this matter, I suggest we invite someone from the People's Commissariat for Food to discuss the matter.

Lenin

August 13, 1921

First published in 1959

Lenin Miscellany XXXVI,
p. 309

TO V. V. KUIBYSHEV

September 19, 1921

Comrade Kuibyshev,
I have just had a call from
Rutgers,
Calvert
and Haywood
representing the American workers' colony group who wish to take the Nadezhdinsk Works and *several* enterprises in Kuznetsk basin.

They want their representative (with an interpreter) to attend the *Council of Labour and Defence* on Friday. I think we should let them come.

I also draw your attention to and request you to inform all members of the commission and subcommissions of the following:

1) The Nadezhdinsk Works, in their opinion, is both economically and technically *connected* with a group of enterprises in Kuzbas, for it will provide tractors for their farms; tractors and all other farming implements for the peasants; repair of machinery for their group's enterprises in Kuzbas, etc., equipment for water transport, communications with Siberia, etc.

2) In Kuznetsk basin they are taking 12,000 dessiatines of land and *several* enterprises, wishing to set up a large and *complete* economic whole.

3) They want *only* 300,000 dollars in cash. It would be wrong to think otherwise.

4) In addition they want grain and clothing, in order to start the necessary building operations *at once*. They say

work should be started *this very* winter to have time to finish it by the spring of 1922.

5) They stress that they will have a clearcut *administrative* set-up for their workers' group; and the whole group (3,000-6,000 workers) selected from among the *best* workers, mostly young and unmarried men, who have had *practical* experience in their line, and had lived in a climate similar to that of Russia (Canada and the Northern United States).

6) They want to be directly subordinate to the Council of Labour and Defence. Something like an autonomous state trust consisting of a workers' association.

They say, by the way, that 200 American lumberjacks are living here in the "émigré house". Most of them are without work. They are itching to get to work. If you send about 30 of them to the Nadezhdinsk Works and 15 to Kuznetsk basin *at once*—with full equipment and food, they will start building log cabins *immediately* (the rest of the 200 will go there later). They want us to hurry up with sending them off.

They say that Gerbek (I did not quite catch the English pronunciation of the name) from the Urals *Industrial Bureau* had *agreed* to their plan verbally, and the Siberians (the Siberian Industrial Bureau), in writing.

They intend to take along 10-15 per cent of Russian-speaking workers. They could take more.

Please take all this into account.

V. Ulyanov (Lenin)
Chairman, Council of Labour and Defence

First published in 1933   *Lenin   Miscellany   XXIII*,
                                                                pp. 39-41

LETTER TO V. V. KUIBYSHEV
AND A DRAFT PLEDGE OF AMERICAN WORKERS
GOING TO RUSSIA

Comrade Kuibyshev,

Here is a draft statement which Rutgers and *all* his men, every single worker inclusive, must sign (in the event a contract is signed[151]).

If you agree tell them about it.

You must find (for all your talks) a reliable *interpreter*, who knows *both* languages *well*.

Besides, the contract must be extremely precise.

It should be drawn up by our own *lawyer* (a Communist). I think it should be called a contract of *lease for management* of a number of factories, etc.

The technical expertise should be signed by *Styunkel* and several other solid experts.

With communist greetings,

Lenin

Are the leaders and organisers of the enterprise willing to sign and get everyone coming from America to Russia to sign the following pledge?

1. We pledge ourselves to arrange and *collectively* guarantee that only men willing and able consciously to bear the hardships inevitable in the rehabilitation of industry in a very backward and incredibly devastated country *will arrive* in Russia.

2. Those coming to Russia pledge themselves to work with maximum intensiveness and with productivity of la-

bour and discipline on a higher level than capitalist standards, otherwise Russia will be unable to outstrip or even
catch up with capitalism.

3. We pledge ourselves to refer all conflicts without exception, whatever their nature, to the final decision of the
supreme Soviet power in Russia and conscientiously to
abide by all its decisions.

4. We pledge to bear in mind the extreme nervousness
of the starved and exhausted Russian workers and peasants
in the vicinity of our enterprise and to help them in every
way to establish friendly relations and overcome suspicion
and envy.

Written on September 22, 1921

First published in
Torgovo-Promyshlennaya
Gazeta No. 17, January 20, 1929

Lenin Miscellany XXIII,
p. 42

TELEGRAM TO L. K. MARTENS

Yekaterinburg

Telegraph Martens [in] Nizhni Tagil that Rutgers insists on an immediate decision on the matter of leasing a part of Kuznetsk basin and the Nadezhdinsk Works to the group of American workers saying the urgency springs from the need for a representative of Calvert's group to go to America immediately. I am at a loss, in view of your request to put it off until your return, for I should not like to decide without you. Let us know: first, when you are arriving in Moscow; second, your opinion in essence of Rutgers's haste; do you believe it absolutely imperative to make an immediate decision or advise to insist that Rutgers should await your return? In spite of your telegram Rutgers says that you agree with him.

Lenin
Chairman of the C.L.D.

Written on September 27, 1921
First published in 1933

Lenin Miscellany XXIII,
p. 43

TO V. V. KUIBYSHEV

October 12, 1921

Comrade Kuibyshev,

Please let me have the following additional explanations on the Rutgers case[152]:

1) Everyone seems to think we shall have to spend 300,000 dollars.

But § 4 (a) says:

"The Soviet Government allocates 100 dollars *for each worker coming to settle*",

while §5 (a) and (b) say that 2,800+3,000=5,800 are due to settle.

Doesn't that make our expenditure 600,000 dollars?

Or should we add clearly: 100 dollars for *3,000* men for the Nadezhdinsk Works and nothing more?

2) Why is there no written statement from all three, Rutgers, Haywood and Calvert, that they are *willing to sign* the enclosed pledge?[153]

Please order this today without fail in *English*.

3) End of § 8 (our pledge to repay expenses) should be set out more clearly in a special §: "The Soviet Government undertakes to reimburse expenses only on the following principles and in the following cases."

4) Is there any sign of an ultimatum in the amendments made by Rutgers and the others to the text adopted by the Supreme Economic Council Presidium?

Please send me your reply (+the English pledge) and *return this letter* to *Molotov*, C.C. Secretary, *tomorrow, Thursday, October 13*.

With communist greetings,

Lenin

First published in 1959   *Lenin Miscellany XXXVI*, p. 331

LETTER TO MEMBERS OF THE POLITBUREAU WITH A DRAFT RESOLUTION OF THE R.C.P.(B.) C.C. AND C.L.D. ON S. RUTGERS'S PROPOSALS

In my opinion we cannot accept Rutgers's proposals now, in their present shape. But let's try the following: make him *alter the group* (Rutgers+Haywood+Calvert). And amend the financial terms. I suggest the following resolution:

Rejecting Comrade Rutgers's proposals in their present form, i.e., the proposals of Comrade Bogdanov and the members of the Supreme Economic Council Presidium who voted with him,

The Central Committee (followed by the Council of Labour and Defence, as is the Soviet practice) expresses the insistent desire that Comrade Rutgers's group should not regard this refusal as final, but should rework its proposals on the following principles: (α) change the composition of the group, the leading group of initiators, by co-opting 5-8 prominent members of the American trade union movement or other labour organisations; (β) reduce our government's expenditures down to a maximum of $300,000; ($\gamma$) reduce and specify our expenditures in the event the contract is cancelled.

Lenin

Written between October
12 and 15, 1921

First published in 1959

Lenin Miscellany XXXVI,
p. 333

TO SIDNEY HILLMAN

October 13, 1921

Comrade Hillman,

I thank you with all my heart for your help. Thanks to you an agreement was rapidly achieved on organisation of help for Soviet Russia by the American workers.[154] Particularly important is the fact that the organisation of this aid has now been arranged in respect also of those workers who are *not* Communists. Throughout the world, and particularly in the most advanced capitalist countries, millions of workers do not at the present time share the views of the Communists, but nonetheless are ready to help Soviet Russia, to help and feed the starving, if only some of them, and to help the cause of restoring the economy of the Russian Socialist Federative Soviet Republic. Such workers repeat with complete conviction the words —and what is more important not only repeat the words but give them practical expression in life—of the leaders of the Amsterdam Trade Union International (unquestionably hostile to communism), namely, that any victory of the international bourgeoisie over Soviet Russia would mean the greatest possible victory of world reaction over the working class in general.

Soviet Russia is exerting all her strength to overcome starvation, ruin and dislocation. The financial aid of the workers of the whole world is infinitely important for us in this respect, side by side with moral help and political help. America, naturally, is at the head of the states where the workers can help us, are already helping us and will help—I am profoundly convinced—on a far greater scale.

Devoted to the cause, the energetic advanced workers of America will be taking the lead of all the workers of a number of industrial countries who are bringing Soviet Russia their technical knowledge, and their determination to make sacrifices in order to help the Workers' and Peasants' Republic to restore its economy. Among the peaceful means of struggle against the yoke of international finance capital, against international reaction, there is no other means with such rapid and certain promise of victory as aid in the restoration of the economy of Soviet Russia.

With best greetings to all workers who are bringing aid, in one form or another, to Soviet Russia.

N. Lenin

First published in 1930   Vol. 35, pp. 526-27
in the second and third editions of
Lenin's *Collected Works*, Vol. XXVII

TO THE MEMBERS OF THE CENTRAL COMMITTEE
OF THE R.C.P.(B.)

Attention, all members of the C.C.:

Reinshtein informed me yesterday that the American millionaire *Hammer*, who is Russian born (is in prison on a charge of illegally procuring an abortion; actually it is said, in revenge for communism), is prepared to give the Urals workers *1,000,000 poods of grain* on very easy terms (5 per cent) and to take *Urals valuables* on commission for sale in America.

This Hammer's son (and partner), a doctor, is in Russia, and has brought Semashko $60,000 worth of surgical instruments as a gift. The son has visited the Urals with Martens and has decided to help rehabilitate the Urals industry.

An official report will soon be made by *Martens*.

Lenin

October 14, 1921

First published in 1959   *Lenin Miscellany XXXVI*,
p. 336

TO L. K. MARTENS

October 15, 1921

Comrade Martens,

Can Hammer (Reinshtein told me about him) be persuaded to

undertake the financing of the Rutgers group to save the Urals, and *improve* the composition of the group? by including, say, four American *businessmen*?

Let me have an answer to this right away.

Second. Will Hammer take an interest in a scheme to electrify the Urals, so that Hammer should provide not only the grain, but also the electrical equipment (naturally on a loan basis).

Rutgers's plan must be *corrected* (try to do this through Hammer), and not just rejected.

With communist greetings,
Lenin

First published in 1959

Lenin Miscellany XXXVI,
p. 337

TO L. K. MARTENS

Comrade Martens,

If Hammer is in earnest about his plan to supply 1,000,000 poods of grain to the Urals (and your written confirmation of Reinshtein's words indicates that he is, and that the plan is not just so much hot air),

you must try to give the whole the precise juridical form of a contract or concession.[155]

Let it be a *concession*, even if a fictitious one (asbestos or any other Urals valuable or what have you). What we want to show and have in print (later, when *performance begins*) is that the Americans have gone in for *concessions*. This is important politically. Let me have your reply.

With communist greetings,
Lenin

Written on October 19, 1921
First published in 1959

Lenin Miscellany XXXVI,
p. 341

TO L. K. MARTENS

Comrade Martens,

I think this reply of Rutgers's[156] leads to a *positive decision of the whole business*.

The C.C. will decide today or tomorrow.

Please draw up a *list* of candidates[157] and let me have it and your opinion of them (and your respective proposals) at 8.30 today.

With communist greetings,
Lenin

Written on October 19, 1921

First published in 1959

Lenin Miscellany XXXVI,
p. 341

NOTE TO V. M. MIKHAILOV
WITH A DRAFT RESOLUTION OF THE R.C.P.(B.) C.C.
ON AN AGREEMENT WITH THE RUTGERS GROUP

October 19, 1921

Comrade Mikhailov,

I enclose the reply of the Rutgers group to the C.L.D. decision (i.e., the C.C. resolution).

I think this is tantamount to an *acceptance* of our terms.

I enclose, therefore, a draft *C.C. resolution* and request you to *circulate* it among the Politbureau members *right away. This is very urgent.*

With communist greetings,
Lenin

In view of the fact that the sponsoring group (Comrades Rutgers, Haywood and Calvert) have accepted the terms set out in the *C.L.D.* decision of October 17, the C.C. resolves and instructs the C.L.D. to decree:

The *C.L.D.* decrees:

1) The agreement with the group shall be deemed concluded;

2) Comrade Bogdanov shall immediately draft and submit to the chairman of the C.L.D. telegrams with the most urgent instructions to start stockpiling firewood, timber, etc.;

3) The Presidium of the Supreme Economic Council shall within two days work out the final text of the amended contract to be submitted for the approval of the C.L.D. on Friday, October 21, 1921;

4) On Saturday, October 22, Comrade Rutgers shall be paid $5,000 in accordance with the contract, immediately after its approval by the C.L.D. on October 21.

Further, without recording this as a C.L.D. decision, the C.C. instructs Comrade Bogdanov and the Kuibyshev Commission, and the Council of Labour and Defence to amend the contract in such a way as (1) to give the C.L.D. the right to participate in the selection of additional candidates to the Organising Committee *before* and *for* final approval of this list; (2) to keep the *total* amount of *all* manner of expenditures by the Soviet Government *under* $300,000; (3) to *prevent* the Soviet Government in the event the contract is annulled *from incurring* any financial obligations (or incurring only such as would be recognised as lawful by the R.S.F.S.R. court or the *Central Executive Committee* of the R.S.F.S.R.).[158]

Lenin

First published in 1959   *Lenin Miscellany XXXVI*,
pp. 342-43

TELEGRAM
TO THE SIBERIAN INDUSTRIAL BUREAU

S.I.B., copy: Siberian Revolutionary Committee

Agreement [with] Rutgers has been reached. Under the contract, we undertake to stockpile [by the] spring 50,000 logs[159] for operations [in] Kuzbas. Take necessary steps [for] performance without fail. Cable reports of measures taken (01290).

*Lenin**

Chairman, Council of People's Commissars

Sent on October 21, 1921

First published in 1933

Lenin Miscellany XXIII,
p. 45

---

* The telegram is also signed by P. A. Bogdanov, Chairman of the Supreme Economic Council.—*Ed*.

TO V. V. KUIBYSHEV

Comrade Kuibyshev,

Here is a copy of a telephone message from Comrade Reinshtein to me.

In re § 3: please let me have a memo as to your *final agreement* with Rutgers.

Have you the *text* of the contract? Let me have it right away.

In re § 1: the business is *very* urgent. Please show § 1 to Comrade Bogdanov and let me have his (and if necessary your own) opinion *as soon as possible*: what's the hitch?

Let us have the agreement with *Hammer as soon as possible*, and *conclude* the concession contract.

With communist greetings,
Lenin

Written on October 24, 1921

First published in 1933   *Lenin Miscellany XXIII*, p. 43

NOTE TO V. M. MIKHAILOV
WITH DRAFT TELEGRAM TO L. B. KRASIN

October 28, 1921

Comrade Mikhailov,

Please *urgently* circulate it among members of Polit-bureau (if they approve, co-ordinate with Bogdanov and Chicherin and dispatch this very day).

Considering that it is of tremendous importance for Krasin to be able to go to America before the Washington Conference[160];

considering that it is *equally* important to make American capital take an interest in our oil, I *propose* that the following telegram (naturally, in code) should be sent to Krasin[161] *this very day*:

"Agree to appropriate up to one hundred thousand dollars to pay for the prospecting operations of the Foundation Company, provided our workers and specialists participate and all details of prospecting handed to us. Consider it tremendously important to attract American capital to build a paraffine separation plant and oil pipeline in Grozny. Please get on with this business at maximum speed and with utmost energy because it is especially important to have your trip made before the Washington Conference opens."

Lenin

First published in 1959

Lenin Miscellany XXXVI,
pp. 352-53

NOTES TO P. P. GORBUNOV
AND TELEGRAM TO L. B. KRASIN

1)

P. P. Gorbunov
Commissariat for Foreign Affairs

Please check up and inform me precisely
1) *when* the Politbureau's decision *in favour* of the Foundation Company's proposal was sent to Krasin.
2) Let me have a *copy* of the text you sent about this.

Lenin

November 7, 1921

P.S. Return this telegram.

Lenin

2)

Comrade Gorbunov,
Please send this to *Krasin* in code:

Your cable of November 1 virtually hysterical. You forget that even you did not propose that we should give in to Leslie Urquhart at once, whereas the Politbureau resolution is very well considered and is not a refusal. As for the Foundation Company, full consent and instructions to hasten were sent you on October 29. A much faster exchange of telegrams between us must be arranged: the Foreign Trade apparatus is on the whole rather sluggish.

Lenin

Written on November 7, 1921
First published in 1959   *Lenin Miscellany XXXVI*,
                                                    pp. 357-58

TO N. P. GORBUNOV
(Excerpt)

1) Send *Frye*'s[162] letter according to my marking and check up *on return*;

2) Remind me when it comes back;

3) The rest to be referred to the *Commissariat for Agriculture*; see that it is *not mislaid* and is *speedily* returned to me.

Lenin

Written on November 15, 1921

First published in 1945

Lenin Miscellany XXXV, p. 293

TO V. V. KUIBYSHEV

Comrade Kuibyshev,

The main thing in the Rutgers business now is to try to *improve* the composition of the Organising Committee.

I shall try to inquire from the Finnish Communists through *Kuusinen*. Will you (and Bogdanov) also try to find new *reliable* candidates through comrades who have a good knowledge of the American labour movement. We shall co-opt them to the Organising Committee.

Written in late November 1921

First published in 1933

Lenin Miscellany XXIII,
pp. 45-46

TO COMRADES BALLISTER AND KARR

December 5, 1921

Dear Comrades,

I send you my book about the evolution of agriculture in the United States.[163]

I should be very much obliged if I could have the opinion of Comrade Karr, if my book can be read by him with the aid of an English or German translator.

I should like also to receive from Comrade Ballister, if possible, official publications of the Census of 1920 (I have analysed in my book two censuses: 1900 and 1910).

If any publisher would like to publish my book in English in Un. States, I should like to write a short preface.

Sincerely yours,
Lenin

Written in English
First published in 1945

Lenin Miscellany XXXV,
pp. 298-99

TO G. B. KRASNOSHCHOKOVA

1)

December 3

Comrade Krasnoshchokova,
   It appears that Beatty who visited me is the author of the book *Red Heart of Russia*?
   Could I have it for a couple of days to page through? Has Beatty written any other books or pamphlets? Or a couple of her articles on various topics?
   If it's not too much trouble, I should very much like to have them.

With communist greetings,
Lenin

Written on December 3, 1921

2)

December 15

Comrade Krasnoshchokova,

   Here are my corrections.[164]
   I am not well at all and beg to be excused: I just glanced at the thing and am scribbling this in a hurry. I hope Mrs. Beatty will excuse me, and also for postponing our meeting for a photograph.

With communist greetings,
Lenin

Written on December 15, 1921

First published in 1957

Inostrannaya literatura
No. 11, 1957, p. 26

TELEGRAM TO SIDNEY HILLMAN

Rusaminco, President Hillman
New York

Heartiest greetings to all active workers on behalf economic reconstruction Soviet Russia—RAIC[165] and amalgamated stop Every precaution taken to insure investments American workers against loss. Double your efforts, you are on the right road.

President Sovnarcom
Lenin

Written in English on February 9, 1922

First published in 1959

Lenin Miscellany XXXVI,
pp. 423-24

TO G. V. CHICHERIN

March 14, 1922

Comrade Chicherin,

I have read your letter of March 10. I think yours is an excellent exposition of the pacifist programme.

The whole point now is to have the skill to expound it and our commercial proposals loudly and clearly *before* the fold-up[166] (if "they" do try to fold it up in haste).

You and your delegation have enough skill to do this.

I think you have made some 13 points (I enclose your letter with my remarks), which are excellent.

We shall have everyone intrigued by saying: "We have a most extensive and comprehensive programme!" If they prevent us from making it public, we shall *publish* it with our protest.

In every case we make this "little" reservation: we are Communists and have *our own* communist programme (the Third International); *nevertheless* we consider it to be our duty as *businessmen to support* (even if the odds are 10,000 to 1) the *pacifists in the other*, i.e., bourgeois, camp (taking account of *its* Second and Two-and-a-Half Internationals).

This will be "genteel" and have teeth, and will help to demoralise the enemy.

If we adopt such tactics we shall win out, even if Genoa is a failure. We shall *not accept* any unprofitable deal.

With communist greetings,

Yours,

Lenin

March 14

P.S. Comrade Chicherin,

Why not add even more bite ("very politely") and say the following:

We propose (§ 14) abolition of *all* war debts and (§ 15) *revision* (on the basis of the 13§§) of the Versailles and *all* military treaties,

but not through the majority riding roughshod over the minority, but on the basis of an *agreement*, because *in this case* we are businessmen and *cannot* put forward any other principle *here* than the commercial one! We don't want to have it all our own way with the United States through a majority; we are businessmen; we want to *persuade* it!! A *poll of all* the states and an *attempt to persuade* those who do not agree. This is both genteel and unacceptable to the bourgeois. We shall disgrace and humiliate them in a very "genteel" way.

Here is a variant: submission of a minority of countries (in population) to the majority can be proposed *separately* within each of the two camps: the bourgeois and the Soviet (the one recognising private property, and the other not recognising it).

Let us put forward both the project and the variant.

Les rieurs seront avec nous!

* an additional point: an exemption to be made for smallholders *insofar as* it can be precisely proved that these are not fictitious but actual toiling smallholders.

MARGINAL NOTES ON A
LETTER FROM G. V. CHICHERIN

To Comrade Lenin

March 10, 1922

Esteemed Vladimir Ilyich,

I earnestly request you to read through the proposals made below and let me have your instructions. We have to put forward "a broad pacifist programme", that is one of the most important elements of our forthcoming act[167]; we have not, however, got one. We have only the separate fragmentary points in the first directives of the Central Committee. I am here making a first attempt to approach the task.

The chief difficulty is that the present international political and economic forms serve as permanent fig-leaves covering the predatory acts of the imperialists; in particular, these forms serve as a weapon against us. The League of Nations is simply a tool of the Entente that has already been used against us. You have yourself pointed out that arbitration between the bourgeois and Soviet governments is impossible; nevertheless arbitration is an indispensable weapon in the pacifist arsenal. The internationalisation of the Chinese Eastern Railway is a euphemism for its alienation from us and from China and its seizure by the Entente. A foreign bank of issue in Russia and the introduction of the dollar into Russia, like the introduction of a universal single gold unit in general, would be the most effective weapon for complete economic bondage to America.

We have to introduce something new into the customary modern international forms to prevent those forms being turned into a tool of imperialism. This new something is provided by our experience and our creative activity as well as by the creative action of life itself in the process of the growing ruin and break-up of the imperialist world. The world war has resulted in the intensification of the liberation movement of all oppressed and colonial peoples. World states are coming undone at the seams. Our international programme must bring all oppressed colonial peoples into the international scheme. The right of all peoples to secession or to home rule must be recognised. The African Conference of 1885 resulted in the horrors of the Belgian Congo, because the European powers at that conference indulged in philanthropy towards the Negroes and that philanthropy turned out to be a fig-leaf covering the most barbaric exploitation. The novelty of our international scheme must be that the Negro and all other colonial peoples participate on ‖ 1)

an equal footing with the European peoples in conferences and com- ‖

true!

missions and have the right to prevent interference in their internal

affairs. Another novelty is the obligatory participation of working-class 2)
organisations. The demand for trade unions to take part in a future European congress was very popular in British working-class literature during the world war. We have actually realised this by including three members of the Central Council of Trade Unions in our delegation. We must lay down that one-third of the votes in the international organisation we are going to propose should belong to the working-class organisations represented in each delegation. These two novelties, however, are not sufficient to protect the oppressed peoples and countries from the domination of the imperialists because the upper stratum of the colonial peoples may well be puppets in the same way as treacherous labour leaders are. The inclusion of these two opens up the way for future struggles. Working-class organisations will be confronted with the task of struggling for the liberation of the colonial peoples, for aid to Soviet power and against imperialist depredation. The leaders, however, will try to betray them. Therefore another thing to be

3)   established is the <u>principle of non-intervention on the part of interna-</u>
<u>tional conferences and congresses</u> in the internal affairs of various peo-
ples. Voluntary co-operation and aid for the weak on the part of the
strong must be applied without subordinating the former to the latter.

      As a result we have a very bold and completely new proposal—A
WORLD CONGRESS with all peoples of the world participating on a
completely equal footing, on the basis of the declaration of the right
to self-determination, the right to complete secession or home rule for
all oppressed peoples, and also with the participation of working-class
organisations to the extent of one-third of the entire congress. The purpose of the congress will not be <u>compulsion</u> of the minority but <u>com-</u>

4)   <u>plete agreement</u>. The congress will help by its moral authority. In
e-
sely   practice it will set up <u>technical commissions</u> for the implementation of
our extensive economic programme of world-wide reconstruction.

      All the projects for a League of Nations or Association of Nations
contain only two types of proposals concerning methods of compulsion
to ensure the fulfilment of League decisions—either the establishment
of composite armies with contingents from all states or the investment
of a punitive mandate in a certain power or several such powers. In
the first case we would have something incompetent because a composite army made up of contingents from numerous countries is of no
use. In the second case the League of Nations or Association of Nations
is nothing but an excuse to justify fresh conquests by the more influential powers. And so it is essential to eliminate completely the element of compulsion or punitive expeditions and leave to the World

cor-
rect!   Congress only its moral authority, allowing it to be an arena for dis_
cussions aimed at reaching agreement. The prevention of war is a matter for arbitration. There are two types of arbitration—the voluntary
appeal of the two parties to an arbiter, to the Hague Tribunal, for
instance—in such cases the decision of the arbiter is binding—or the
second method, an example of which is to be found in the article on
arbitration contained in the treaty between Great Britain and the
United States according to which, in the event of there being a danger
of war, special commissions of conciliation are set up to which the two
parties must appeal but whose decision is merely advisory although for
a definite period, for instance a year, the proceedings of the commission
continue; this second method has as its purpose the postponement of
the beginning of military action to enable the passions of both parties to
subside in the legally established interval and lessen the conflict. In the
first case appeal to the arbiter is not obligatory but decisions are binding. In the second case appeal to the arbiter is obligatory but decisions
are not binding, and the parties are bound only for the legally established period.

      At the present moment we cannot avoid one of these alternatives.
The proposed World Congress could take over the Hague Tribunal

with its advisory arbitration and other services. We shall consider that the only court of arbitration between a capitalist state and the
(5)
Soviet state can be that in which an equal number of members is

appointed by each party so that half the members will be imperialists and half will be Communists. At the same time we shall propose a
(6)
general reduction of armaments based on those theses we have estab-

lished with the Revolutionary Military Council of the Republic; developing the traditions of the Hague and Geneva Conventions we shall propose adding a number of prohibitions to the rules of war—

the abolition of submarines, chemical gases, mortars, flame-throwers and armed air battles.

The technical commissions set up by the World Congress will guide

the implementation of a broad programme of world-wide rehabilitation. This programme will not be imposed by force. It will be a voluntary proposal that appeals to the advantage of every participant. Aid will be given to the weak. In this way world railways, river and

sea routes must be laid down. The internationalisation of those routes will be a matter of gradual development since the compulsion of those who resist will not be allowed. International technical commissions will propose to individual countries economic and technical aid for the creation of super-main lines, for the regulation of traffic on international rivers, for the use of international harbours and for the technical improvement of world sea routes. We shall propose that the capital of the advanced countries be used to build a super-main line

London-Moscow-Vladivostok (Peking) and we shall explain that it

will open up the incalculable wealth of Siberia for the use of all. In general, aid from the strong for the weak will be the basic principle of world rehabilitation which must be based on economic geography and the planned distribution of resources. A world gold unit can make its appearance only as a result of the improvement of the economically weak countries with the aid of the strong; this improvement is to the interest of all since world ruin affects the strong countries as well, giving rise to unparalleled unemployment, even in America. The strong, by helping the weak, are opening up for themselves markets and sources of raw materials. Proceeding from these premises we shall propose the planned distribution of the gold that is at the moment

lying idle in the vaults of the American banks. This planned distribution of gold in all countries must be combined with the planned distribution of orders, trade, supplies of deficient materials, in general,

with all-round economic aid for the ruined countries. This aid may take the form of loans, since under a planned economy the return

of the money would begin in a few years. Under this heading we place
the Barter Institute plan (Keynes), or the Zentralstelle, or national
trade centres. If Germany opposes us by a single Zentralstelle in place
of individual merchants it will be bad for us since it would be a
means of imposing bad goods on us at high prices. If, however, the
Zentralstellen are <u>instruments</u> for the <u>planned, world-wide distribution</u>
of essential commodities and a means of <u>rendering aid to weak</u>
countries by the strong, they would be <u>essential components of an
extensive programme</u> of economic reconstruction. The grain sent to
us by America is the beginning of the international distribution of
food. Within the Entente there was a partially planned distribution
of fuel during the war; one of the chief elements of the broad programme should be the systematic distribution of oil and coal, but in
this case, too, the element of compulsion and repression must be
eliminated. The international technical commissions must elaborate,
in very general outline, a programme for the planned distribution
of fuel and energy resources. All these points, taken together, provide
a picture of what is theoretically possible under the bourgeois system,
but which in historically conditioned reality will come up against
national egoism and the predatory acts of the capitalist oligarchy.

With communist greetings,
Georgi Chicherin

Written on March 14, 1922
First published in 1959

Lenin Miscellany XXXVI,
pp. 454-55, 451-54

TO G. M. KRZHIZHANOVSKY

1)

March 31, 1922

Gleb Maximilianovich,

I enclose what I have received today.[168] I remember you telling me about Steinmetz that he is a world figure. Before you told me about him I had never even heard his name.

Shall I send a kind reply? Shouldn't I make some practical proposition in my reply? After all, he has offered his assistance. In view of this shouldn't I specify some *concrete* types of assistance?

Have all the works on electrification been sent to him?

Do you think it is worth publishing his letter and my reply?[169]

Please return the enclosure and this letter with your advice. I think I should also consult Martens. We must give more thought to the best way of replying.

Yours,

Lenin

2)

April 2, 1922

Comrade Krzhizhanovsky,

Here is the draft of a reply to Steinmetz. Please return it with your remarks or additions.

With communist greetings,

Lenin

First published in 1959

Lenin Miscellany XXXVI,
p. 463

TO A. I. RYKOV

Comrade *Rykov*
Copy to Comrade *Tsyurupa*
Copy to the Managing Dept., C.P.C.

This business of a concession granted to *Rutgers* and a group of American workers,[170] as *Martens* informs me, is in a very bad state. This requires a check-up and serious attention. It is an exceptional concession granted by us to American workers by special permission of the Politbureau.

The whole undertaking may go to pieces without special support and check-ups.

Please ask *Martens* for information and strictly check up on the whole course of this business.

Lenin

Dictated by telephone
on April 5, 1922

First published in 1959

Lenin Miscellany XXXVI,
p. 467

TO A. I. RYKOV

Comrade *Rykov*
Copy to Comrade *Tsyurupa*
Copy to the Managing Dept., C.P.C.

Please pay attention to the concession of the American *Hammer*,[171] who, as *Reinshtein*, who knows him personally, has informed me, is now in Russia.

According to *Martens*, we've already made one great blunder, to put it mildly, namely: the *goods* sent to America under the contract with *Hammer* by the People's Commissariat of Foreign Trade turned out to be of bad quality. We must demand information about this business both from the P.C.F.T. and the Supreme Economic Council and also from Comrade *Reinshtein*, who knows *Hammer* personally. We must see to it that our obligations under this concession are performed with undeviating strictness and accuracy, and in general we must pay greater attention to the whole business.

Lenin

Dictated by telephone
on April 5, 1922

First published in 1959

Lenin Miscellany XXXVI,
pp. 467-68

TO CHARLES P. STEINMETZ

Moscow. April 10, 1922

Dear Mr. Steinmetz,

I thank you cordially for your friendly letter of February 16, 1922.[172] I must admit to my shame that I heard your name for the first time only a few months ago from Comrade Krzhizhanovsky, who was the Chairman of our State Commission for Working out a Plan for the Electrification of Russia and is now Chairman of the State General Planning Commission. He told me of the outstanding position which you have gained among the electrical engineers of the whole world.

Comrade Martens has now made me better acquainted by his accounts of you. I have seen from these accounts that your sympathies with Soviet Russia have been aroused, on the one hand, by your social and political views. On the other hand, as a representative of electrical engineering and particularly in one of the technically advanced countries, you have become convinced of the necessity and inevitability of the replacement of capitalism by a new social order, which will establish the planned regulation of economy and ensure the welfare of the entire mass of the people on the basis of the electrification of entire countries. In all the countries of the world there is growing—more slowly than one would like, but irresistibly and unswervingly—the number of representatives of science, technology, art, who are becoming convinced of the necessity of replacing capitalism by a different socio-economic system, and whom the "terrible difficulties"* of the struggle of Soviet Russia

---
* These words were written by Lenin in English.—*Ed.*

against the entire capitalist world do not repel, do not frighten away but, on the contrary, lead to an understanding of the inevitability of the struggle and the necessity of taking what part in it they can, helping the new to overcome the old.

In particular, I want to thank you for your offer to help Russia with your advice, suggestions, etc. As the absence of official and legally recognised relations between Soviet Russia and the United States makes the practical realisation of your offer extremely difficult both for us and for you, I will allow myself to publish both your letter and my reply, in the hope that many persons who live in America, or in countries connected by commercial treaties both with the United States and with Russia, will then help you (by information, by translations from Russian into English, etc.) to give effect to your intention of helping the Soviet Republic.

With very best greetings,

Yours fraternally,

Lenin

Sent to New York

Published in *Pravda* No. 85,   Vol. 35, pp. 552-53
April 19, 1922

TO G. Y. ZINOVIEV

May 11, 1922

To Comrade Zinoviev or his deputy
Petrograd

I beg you to help the comrade Armand Hammer; it is extremely important for us that his first concession would be a full success.

Yours,

V. Ulyanov (Lenin)

Written in English

First published in 1959

Lenin Miscellany XXXVI,
pp. 480-81

TO G. Y. ZINOVIEV

May 22, 1922

Comrade Zinoviev,

Today, Reinshtein showed me a letter from *Armand Hammer* of whom I wrote you (an American, a millionaire's son, one of the first to have taken a concession from us which is *highly profitable* to us). He says that in spite of my letter, his colleague *Mishell* (Hammer's colleague) has bitterly complained about "the *rudeness* and *red tape* on the part of *Begge*, who received him in Petrograd".

I am going to complain about Begge's behaviour to the Central Committee. This is the limit! In spite of my special letter to you and *your deputy*, they acted *to the contrary*!!

I was informed of nothing: neither of their disagreement with me, *nor of anything else.*

Please make a special check-up and investigation of this case.

Did my letter (telephone message) to you or your deputy ever reach Begge?

If it did, it's Begge's fault.

If not, one of your secretaries must be to blame.

Whose fault is it? This must be found out. Could you *influence* Begge and *clear up the matter*?[173]

Lenin

First published in 1959

Lenin Miscellany XXXVI,
p. 491

TO J. V. STALIN

Urgent
Confidential

To Comrade Stalin with a request to circulate among the members of the Politbureau (and in particular to Comrade Zinoviev).

On the strength of this information from Comrade Reinshtein[174] I give my special recommendation to Armand *Hammer* and B. *Mishell* and request all members of the Central Committee to extend their *particular* support to these persons and their enterprise. This is a small path leading to the American "business" world, and it should be used in *every possible way*. Please inform my secretary (Fotieva or Lepeshinskaya) *by telephone* about any objections to allow me to clear up the matter (and get a final decision through the Politbureau) before my departure, that is, within the next few days.[175]

May 24, 1922   *Lenin*

P.S. May 27. I delayed sending this until a reply from Comrade Zinoviev. It came in on May 26.

Lenin

First published in 1959   *Lenin Miscellany XXXVI*,
p. 493

TO V. A. TRIFONOV

To Comrade *Trifonov, Deputy Chief of the C.F.A.*

I have been informed of the considerable successes achieved by the American tractor expedition for the mechanical cultivation of land in the Toikino State Farm, Okhansk Uyezd, Perm Gubernia.[176]

The Perm Gubernia Executive Committee reports that they would have scored an even greater success but for the shortage of gasoline and lubricating oil (it is reported that kerosene is being supplied instead of gasoline).

Please issue urgent orders to your subordinate organ (Perm District Oil Office) handling the distribution and sale of oil products in the area to supply the American expedition working in the Toikino State Farm with the necessary quantity of gasoline and lubricating oil on the easiest possible terms.

Send a copy of your order to Comrade Smolyaninov.

Chairman of the Council
of People's Commissars

Written on October 10, 1922

First published in 1959

Lenin Miscellany XXXVI,
p. 501

TO THE CHAIRMAN OF THE PERM GUBERNIA EXECUTIVE COMMITTEE

October 20, 1922

Chairman of the Perm
Gubernia Executive Committee

The American tractor team, led by Comrade Harold Ware, which is working in Okhansk Uyezd, on the territory of Perm Gubernia, has achieved considerable results, although it has been working only a short time. Altogether, up to 1,500 dessiatines has been ploughed up, of which almost 1,000 dessiatines has been sown to winter grain crops.

But for the usual drawbacks in our practice, the said group would have undoubtedly succeeded in achieving even greater results.

Your report, however, mentions the shortage of gasoline and lubricating oil, and the shortage of building workers, but says nothing about what the Gubernia Executive Committee has done to straighten things out.

It is absolutely intolerable that such a useful undertaking does not meet with every possible support, especially on the part of local organisations, which are in a better position to analyse any obstacles and help to remove them.

Please give the maximum support to this group, and, in particular, help implement their proposals for the efficient use of tractors, supply of gasoline, establishment of a repair shop, housing construction, etc.

The assistance being extended to us by the American agricultural groups is most desirable and timely. Our task in all this is mainly to help them carry out their ideas with the least possible delay.

Please inform me of the results of your measures through Comrade Smolyaninov, and also of any specially important current needs which you are unable to meet yourself.

V. Ulyanov (Lenin)
Chairman, Council of People's Commissars

First published in 1959   *Lenin Miscellany XXXVI,*
p. 503

TO THE SOCIETY OF FRIENDS OF SOVIET RUSSIA
(IN THE UNITED STATES)[177]

October 20, 1922

Dear Comrades,

I have just verified by special inquiry to the Perm Gubernia Executive Committee the extremely favourable information that was published in our newspapers about the work of the members of your Society, headed by Harold Ware, with the tractor team at the Toikino State Farm, Perm Gubernia.

In spite of the immense difficulties, particularly in view of the extreme remoteness of that locality from the centre, and also the devastation caused by Kolchak during the Civil War, you have achieved successes that must be regarded as truly outstanding.

I hasten to express to you my profound gratitude and to ask you to publish this in your Society's journal, and, if possible, in the general press of the United States.

I am sending a recommendation to the Presidium of the All-Russia Central Executive Committee that it should recognise this state farm as a model farm, and render it special and extraordinary assistance in building and also in supplying petrol, metal, and other materials necessary for a repair shop.

Once again on behalf of our Republic I express to you our profound gratitude, and ask you to bear in mind that no form of assistance is as timely and as important for us as that which you are rendering.

Lenin
Chairman, Council of People's Commissars

Pravda No. 240,
October 24, 1922

Vol. 33, p. 380

TO THE SOCIETY FOR TECHNICAL AID
FOR SOVIET RUSSIA[178]

October 20, 1922

Dear Comrades,

Extremely favourable information has appeared in our press about the work of members of your Society at the state farms in Kirsanov Uyezd, Tambov Gubernia, and at Mitino Station, Odessa Gubernia, and also about the work of the group of miners in the Donets Basin.

In spite of the enormous difficulties, and particularly in view of the devastation caused by the Civil War, you have achieved successes that must be regarded as outstanding.

I hasten to express to you my profound gratitude and to ask you to publish this in your Society's journal, and, if possible, in the general press in the United States.

I am sending a recommendation to the Presidium of the All-Russia Central Executive Committee that it should recognise the most successful farms as model farms, and render them the special and extraordinary assistance necessary for the successful promotion of their work.

Once again on behalf of our Republic I express to you our profound gratitude, and ask you to bear in mind that the work you are doing to cultivate land with the aid of tractors is particularly timely and important for us.

It gives me particular satisfaction to be able to congratulate you on your proposal to organise 200 agricultural communes.

Lenin

Chairman, Council of People's Commissars

Pravda No. 240,
October 24, 1922

Vol. 33, p. 381

TO THE PRESIDIUM OF THE ALL-RUSSIA
CENTRAL EXECUTIVE COMMITTEE

October 24, 1922

A number of newspaper articles have carried accounts of the absolutely extraordinary success scored by some American agricultural communes and teams who had brought their tractors along with them. It has been established in a special check-up that excellent work has been done by the tractor team led by Harold Ware in the Toikino State Farm, Perm Gubernia. Besides, the Industrial Immigration Department of the Supreme Economic Council is also in possession of information concerning the work of agricultural communes in Kirsanov Uyezd, Tambov Gubernia, and in the village of Migayevo, Tiraspol Uyezd, Odessa Gubernia.

The American Society for Technical Aid to Russia is now organising nearly 200 artels with 800-1,000 tractors for dispatch to Russia. If this goes through, we shall have at least one model farm with American machinery in each uyezd, which I believe to be of great importance.

With the object of encouraging this undertaking, I have written a letter of thanks to the American Society of Friends of Soviet Russia, and the American Society for Technical Aid to Soviet Russia, telling them that no type of aid was as important to us or as timely as that which they were extending to our agriculture. In these letters I tell them that I am sending a recommendation to the Presidium of the All-Russia Central Executive Committee that they should declare the Perm and other leading farms model ones and give them special and extra-

ordinary assistance, both in respect of building operations, and in the supply of gasoline, metal, and other materials necessary for the extension of operations and the
starting of repair shops.

Please consider this question and grant my request.[179]

V. Ulyanov (Lenin)
Chairman, Council of People's Commissars

First published in 1959   *Lenin Miscellany XXXVI*,
p. 504

TO COMRADE MÜNZENBERG, SECRETARY OF THE INTERNATIONAL WORKERS' AID[180]

Supplementing your report at the Fourth Congress of the Comintern, I should like in a few words to point out the significance of the organisation of aid.

The assistance given to the starving by the international working class helped Soviet Russia in considerable measure to endure the painful days of last year's famine and to overcome it. At the present time we have to heal the wounds inflicted by the famine, provide in the first place for many thousands of orphaned children, and restore our agriculture and industry which have suffered heavily as a result of the famine.

In this sphere, too, the fraternal aid of the international working class has already begun to operate. The American tractor column near Perm, the agricultural groups of the American Technical Aid, the agricultural and industrial undertakings of the International Workers' Aid, the allocation of and subscriptions to the first proletarian loan, through the Workers' Aid to Soviet Russia—all these are very promising beginnings in the cause of workers' fraternal aid to promote the economic restoration of Soviet Russia.

The work of economic assistance, so happily begun by the International Workers' Aid to Soviet Russia, should be supported in every possible way by the workers and toilers of the whole world. Side by side with the continuing strong political pressure on the governments of the bourgeois countries over the demand for recognition of the Soviet government, widespread economic aid by the world proletariat is at present the best and most practical support of Soviet Russia in her difficult economic war against the imperialist concerns, and the best support for her work of building a socialist economy.

V. Ulyanov (Lenin)

Moscow, December 2, 1922

First published in 1924 in the book *Tri goda mezhdunarodnoi rabochei pomoshchi. 1921-24,* Moscow, Mezhrabpom Publishers

Vol. 35, pp. 559-60

From NOTEBOOKS ON IMPERIALISM[181]

THE ANNALS OF THE AMERICAN ACADEMY

The Annals of the American Academy of Political & 30
Social Science. Vol. LVII-LIX (*1915*)

<table>
<tr>
<td>

For later
reference

</td>
<td>

(consists of separate booklets+a biblio-
graphy, etc., Vol LIX (*May* 1915): *The
American Industrial Opportunity*. A Collec-
tion of articles).

</td>
</tr>
</table>

> Summary of Wage Rates in
> American Industry
> 1/10 $1,000 and over (p. 115)
> 2/10 $750 to $1,000
> 7/10 Under $750

Inter alia, an article by *William S. Kies,* "Branch Banks
and Our Foreign Trade" (p. 301).

"Forty English banks operating in foreign countries
have 1,325 branches; in South America, five German
banks have forty branches and five English banks have
seventy branches.... England and Germany have put
into Argentine, Brazil, and Uruguay, in the last twenty-
five years, approximately four thousand million dollars,
and as a result enjoy together 46 per cent of the total
trade of these three countries."*
     ((Then follows a description of New York's attempt to
     get a foot in....))

---

* See Lenin, *Collected Works*, Vol. 22, p. 245.—*Ed.*

| N.B. | A special analysis of the question of the U.S. "opportunity" of increasing trade, etc., with *South America* on the occasion of the war. |

200,000 million francs
40,000 million dollars
$\left. \begin{array}{l} =160,000 \\ \text{million} \\ \text{marks} \end{array} \right\}$

cf. p. 2
here**

p. 331 (in another article)... "Sir George Paish in the last annual of the *Statist* estimated that upwards of $40,000,000,000 of the capital has been supplied to the less developed countries by the five lending nations of the world, Great Britain, Germany, France, Belgium, and Holland."*

From another article about "South American Markets":

N.B.

"Another fundamental proposition, and the most important of all for increasing trade with South America, is the investment of capital from the United States in loans and in construction and similar enterprises. The country, whose capital is invested in a South American country, is going to get most of the contracts for materials, used in construction enterprises, railway building, and the like, as well as the contracts for public improvements carried on by the governments. England's investments in Argentine railways, banks, and loans are the living evidence of this fact." (314)

110 corporations have a capital of $7,300 million, and 626,984 shareholders.

idem for *1910*, inter alia "Stocks and the Stock Market". American stocks total=$34,500 million (and without dupli-

---

* Ibid.—*Ed.*
** See Lenin, *Collected Works*, 4th Russian edition, Vol. 39, pp. 40-41.—*Ed.*

cations about)=$24,400 million, the fortunes totalling=
=$107,100 million.

Lenin, *Collected Works*,
4th Russian Edition,
Vol. 39, pp. 22-24

PATOUILLET, *AMERICAN IMPERIALISM*

Joseph *Patouillet, L'impérialisme américain*. Dijon, 1904. *9)*
(Thesis.) (388 pp.).

> A thesis. An altogether raw piece of work. No scien-
> tific value at all, *except* for copious quotations and a
> *summary* of certain facts. Juridical twaddle prevails,
> economic aspect weak.

The author (at the beginning) quotes Hobson (*Imperialism*) and borrows what is most widely known.

The author treats *British imperialism* (p. 33 et seq.) and
German imperialism (p. 36 et seq.) as a fact (see Sections I
and II of Chapter Two).

A couple of words about Japanese and Russian imperialism (p. 39 *in fine*).

p. 43: "To practise imperialism is to want the keys
to the world, but not the military keys, as under the
Roman Empire, but the great economic and commercial keys. It is not to seek a territorial rounding off ‖ ?
but the conquest and occupation of the major junctures
of the world's trade routes; it is not to seek great
colonies, but those that are conveniently situated, in
order to throw around the globe a fine network of
stations, coal depots and cables" (quote from *De
Lapradelle*, "L'Impérialisme et l'Américanisme aux
Etats-Unis", *Revue du droit publique*, 1900, v. XIII,
pp. 65-66. Quoted from Patouillet, p. 43).

Driault (*Les problèmes politiques*, pp. 221-22): "The rout
of Spain was a revelation. . . . It had appeared to be settled
that the world balance was a matter for decision by five or

six major European powers: then an outsider butted into the problem" (p. 49).

10)   "Thus, the war over Cuba was an economic war in the sense that its object was to corner the island's sugar market; similarly, the annexation of the Hawaiian Islands and the Philippines was caused by a desire to get hold of the coffee and sugar produced by these tropical countries" (p. 51). (*Idem*, pp. 62-63)....

"Thus, the conquest of marketing outlets, and the quest for tropical products are the primary cause of this policy of colonial expansion, which is known as Imperialism. All these colonies will also furnish excellent strategic points whose value we shall indicate: ... they had to have bases ... in order to assure themselves Asian markets..." (p. 64).

Percentage of exports from the United States

Total exports $ millions		Europe	North America	South America	Asia	Oceania	Africa
	1870	79.35	13.03	4.09	2.07	0.82	0.64
	1880	86.10	8.31	2.77	1.39	0.82	0.61
857.8	1890	79.74	10.98	4.52	2.30	1.92	0.54
1,394.5	1900	74.60	13.45	2.79	4.66	3.11	1.79
	1902	72.96	14.76	2.75	4.63	2.48	2.42

there are a great many, a mass of indications of a forthcoming struggle over the Pacific Ocean

The Hawaiian Islands—halfway from Panama to Hongkong.

The Philippines—a step towards Asia and *China* (p. 118). *Idem* 119-120-122.

The war with Spain over Cuba was justified by the interests of *liberty*, Cuba's liberation, etc. (p. 158 et seq.).

sic!   The Constitution demands equality of all taxes, etc., in all the United States. "They interpreted" this to mean that this *did not apply* to the colonies because they were territory "*belonging* to the United States", *not* "a part of the United States" (p. 175). The rights of the colonies (they say) will be extended "*gradually*" (p. 190) (*no* equality for them)....

Canada. Her economic subjection is paving the way for her political "incorporation" (p. 198).

"Germany" (sic) wants to "oppose" the United States of America with a "United States of Europe" (p. 205)....

11

"... Beginning from 1897, Wilhelm II repeatedly voiced the idea of a policy of unification to fight overseas competition, a policy based on a European customs entente, a sort of continental blockade against the United States" ... (205) ... "In France, the establishment of a European *Zollverein* was put forward by M. Paul Leroy-Beaulieu" (206).

A United States of Europe (and Wilhelm II)

"... The agreement between the European states may after all be one of the happy consequences of American imperialism" (206).

"happy consequence"

In America, the events have led to a struggle between the *"anti-imperialists"* and the imperialists (p. 268, Book II, Chapter I: "Imperialists and Anti-Imperialists").... Imperialism, they say, contradicts freedom, etc., leads to colonial bondage, etc. (*all the democratic arguments: a series of quotations*). One American anti-imperialist quotes *Lincoln:* "When the white man governs himself, that is self-government; but when he governs himself and also governs others, it is no longer self-government; it is despotism"* (272).

Phelps. United States Intervention in Cuba. New York, 1898, and others declared the Cuban war to be *"criminal"*, etc.

Chapter III, p. 293, is entitled: United States Present Policy: the Combination of Imperialism and the Monroe Doctrine: they combined it and put their own interpretation on it!!!

The South Americans object (p. 311 et seq.) to such an interpretation of the Monroe Doctrine, namely, that America should belong to the *North* Americans. They fear the United States and want independence. The United States is

12

* See p. 269.—*Ed.*

"*eyeing*" South America and is fighting against *Germany's growing influence there....*

(Cf. Novikov's bibliography, see specifically.*)

In annexing the Philippines, the United States cheated Chief *Aguinaldo*, by promising his country freedom (p. 373): the annexation was described as "jingo treachery".**

N.B. ‖ Atkinson. *Criminal Aggression, By Whom Committed*? Boston, 1899.
The North American Review, September 1899. *Filipino*. "Aguinaldo's Case Against the United States". ‖

N.B. ‖ There is a growing urge in South America for a *rapprochement* with *Spain*, the Congress in *Madrid* in 1900 (Spanish-American) was attended by delegates from 15 South American states (p. 326) (*). Growing ties with Spain, her influence, "Latin" sympathies, etc.(**)

---

sic! ‖ p. 379: "The era of national wars has evidently passed"... ‖
(wars over markets, etc.).

N.B. ‖ (*) *Revue des deux mondes*. 1901 (15.11). ‖
(**) Slogan: "Spanish-American Alliance".

Lenin, *Collected Works*,
4th Russian Edition,
Vol. 39, pp. 185-88

SUMMARY OF J. HOBSON'S *IMPERIALISM*

(Excerpt)

pp. 82-84. America's domestic market is saturated, capital no longer finds room for investment.

---

* See Lenin, *Collected Works*, 4th Russian edition, Vol. 39, p. 189.—*Ed.*

** See p. 269.—*Ed.*

"It is this sudden demand for foreign markets for manufactures and for investments which is avowedly responsible for the *adoption of Imperialism* as a political policy and practice by the Republican Party to which the great industrial and financial chiefs belong, and which belongs to them. The adventurous enthusiasm of President Roosevelt and his 'manifest destiny' and 'mission of civilisation' party must not deceive us. *It is Messrs. Rockefeller*, Pierpont Morgan, Hanna, Schwab, and their associates *who need Imperialism* and who are fastening it upon the shoulders of the great Republic of the West. They need Imperialism because they desire to use the public resources of their country to find profitable employment for the capital which otherwise would be superfluous.

N.B.

"It is not indeed necessary to own a country in order to do trade with it or to invest capital in it, and doubtless the United States can find some vent for their surplus goods and capital in European countries. But these countries are for the most part able to make provision for themselves: most of them have erected tariffs against manufacturing imports, and even Great Britain is being urged to defend herself by reverting to Protection. The big American manufacturers and financiers will be compelled to look to China and the Pacific and to South America for their most profitable chances. Protectionists by principle and practice, they will insist upon getting as close a monopoly of these markets as they can secure, and the competition of Germany, England, and other trading nations will drive them to the establishment of special political relations with the markets they most prize. Cuba, the Philippines, and Hawaii are but the *hors d'œuvre* to whet an appetite for an ampler banquet. Moreover, the powerful hold upon politics which these industrial and financial magnates possess forms a separate stimulus, which, as we have shown, is operative in Great Britain and elsewhere; the public expenditure in pursuit of an imperial career will be a separate immense source of profit to these men, as financiers negotiating loans,

N.B.

shipbuilders and owners handling subsidies, contrac-
tors and manufacturers of armaments and other
imperialist appliances."

Lenin, *Collected Works*,
4th Russian Edition,
Vol. 39, pp. 389-90

SOCIALISTS AND NEGROES IN AMERICA

Attitude to
Negroes
N.B.
Socialists
and *Negroes*

The Socialist Party and the Negroes
in America: *pp. 382-83: Industrial Workers of the World* stand *for* the Negroes.
The attitude of the Socialist Party is
"*not altogether unanimous*". Only the
1901 appeal for the Negroes. Not
much!!!

*Negroes and
Socialists!!*

Ibidem, p. 592: in the state of Mississippi the Socialists are organising
the Negroes into "special local
groups"!!

Lenin, *Collected Works*,
4th Russian Edition,
Vol. 39, p. 570

ABOUT DEBS

about
Debs

Die Neue Zeit, 1913-14, 32, 1, pp. 1007-8. *Debs*
in the *International Socialist Review* (March
1913) stands *for* the unity of the Socialist Party+
the Socialist Labour Party (Debs is the founder
of the *Industrial Workers of the World*) and the
alliance of the Industrial Workers of the World
against the American Federation of Labour. Debs
is fiercely attacked by the *New Yorker Volkszeitung*, 7. 3. 1913, which says that Debs has been
abusing his "privilege to talk nonsense" (sic!),

that the Industrial Workers of the World=
naught, that the American Federation of La-
bour=the "American labour movement", and
that it is "impossible to educate the labour movement of a country in a progressive spirit by
setting up revolutionary organisations with radical programmes" (sic!). . . . (Obviously, they have
the usual picture over there too: the *New Yorker
Volkszeitung*=the "orthodox", the Kautskyites,
whereas *Debs* is a revolutionary but without any
clearcut theory, and is not a Marxist.)

Lenin, *Collected Works*,
4th Russian Edition,
Vol. 39, p. 572

THE JAPANESE AND THE CHAUVINISM OF AMERICAN WORKERS

Die Neue Zeit, 1913 (31,2), pp. 410-12 (issue dated
20.4.1913).

> N.B.
> workers' chauvinism

*Erwin Gudde. New Exceptional Law
against Japanese in the United States*
(Date: San Francisco, 21. 5. 1913).
This law prohibiting the Japanese
from purchasing land (they are allowed
to lease land only for three years) was
signed by the Governor on 19.5.1913, in
spite of Woodrow Wilson's insistence.

American
workers
and their
chauvinism

This is "an exceptional law of the
worst kind" (410), "a policy even worse
than the Prussian policy towards the
Poles" (412).

In respect
of the
Japanese

N.B.

And the workers of America are guilty of "*chauvinism*" (N.B.) (412). "The gentlemen of the American Federation of Labour not only want to deprive the 'yellows' of all rights, but want to drive them out of the country altogether" (411).

Workers side with the imperialists

The Soc. Party likewise!!!

This exceptional law "is proof that the population of California, and above all its working class, are doing yeoman service for the American *imperialists*, who for years have been preparing for a war against Japan. *The Socialist Party, too, has been found wanting in this matter*" (411).

This law is "only a link in a long chain of laws" (412).

Lenin, *Collected Works*, 4th Russian Edition, Vol. 39, p. 606

A. B. HART, *THE MONROE DOCTRINE*

A. B. Hart: *The Monroe Doctrine*, Boston, 1916.

This seems to be a rather interesting story of U.S. foreign policy.

A bibliography is appended.

p. 373: the "anti-imperialists" are defeated, 1898.

303-04: a table (highly instructive) of America's development as a state from 1823 to 1915. (The growth of U.S. imperialism, etc.)

314: "The most striking change in the conditions of nations is the building up of large units. Consolidation applies not simply to banks and factories and railroads, but to world powers." The next century will see five Great Powers: Great Britain, Germany, Russia, China and the United States (!!)....

The growth of protectorates and "influence" (and financial interests! 332). The United States in Central America!—332.

N.B. "*fixed* policy of protectorates" (335).

359: *Roland Greene Usher, Pan-Americanism, A Fore-cast of the Inevitable Clash Between the United States and Europe's Victor*, New York, 1915 (p. 419).

The author castigates it, but goes on to defend the "doctrine" of—"protectorates" (369), "to safeguard American capital" (369)!!

$\Sigma\Sigma$ (402) *for* militarism!! (*N.B.*) (especially § 5)—especially (!!!) against Germany and Japan (403). *N.B.*

EUGEN VON PHILIPPOVICH, *MONOPOLY*
Eugen von Philippovich. Monopoly...

In the United States (1912) a total of *180* company owners and their directors (18 banks) held *746* directorates in *134* corporations with a Σ capital of $25,325 million (=101,300 million marks). "This is probably one-third of the American national wealth" (159 pp.).

180 persons (families?) $25,000 million

A.E.G. (Allgemeine Elektrizitäts Gesell-schaft). Capital (1912)=*378 million marks*. On its Board are *32 men* with almost *500 directorates* in various enterprises.

Lenin, *Collected Works*, 4th Russian Edition, Vol. 39, pp. 734-35

EXCERPTS FROM WIRTH'S *MODERN UNIVERSAL HISTORY*

"In the old days, there was always some room for expansion; all the Western nations found enough place for development each in its own 'new Europe', and rivalry merely led to fruitful

(3(

N.B.

|| competition. But North America now wants to have nothing more to do with immigrants; Australia is already closing its doors; Siberia offers privileges only to the subjects of one definite state, while South Africa has been making horribly obvious the grim fact that emigration is no longer of any help to us in securing a place in the world which has become so crowded, that the Europeans have to strangulate each other. There is still a great deal of land, but the once small states have become great powers, the former great powers have become world powers, and they have to worry about providing enough space for their future population right away. The Yankees will not let us have any Brazilian lands, while the French envy the Italians their arid wastes of Tripoli. The embittered struggle for existence increases the hostility between Europeans and leads to attempts at mutual destruction. This, in turn, goes to benefit the East (215).

N.B.

N.B.

N.B.

In the chapter: "The War over Cuba":

"The Yankees started out by preaching the equality of all men and striving for an ideal state abounding in peaceful and self-satisfied happiness. They finally arrived at the conclusion that men were inveterately unequal and ended up with a violent policy of conquest. They started out with freedom in all things, freedom in trade and relations, and tolerance for other creeds, races and states. They now have the harshest protective tariffs, mounting hostility for Catholics, and decided aggressiveness in respect of alien races and states. They started out by depriving the Chinese of the rights of citizenship, and prohibited their entry; then they destroyed, not juridically but in fact, the rights of the blacks for whom they had waged such a futile and absurd fight during their great Civil War, and, to cap it all, they have used all manner of petty means to restrict the flow of white immigrants

#

N.B.

N.B.

ha-ha!!

37)

which they were so eager to have in the past. The increasingly tighter system of self-isolation goes hand in hand with the world policy of the States. It needs only a dictatorship to crown this progressive exclusiveness and centralisation" (252). . . .

⧧ *Idem*, p. 345. "The war (civil war) was in essence meaningless, because •the Negro, over whom it was fought, is now once again well on the way to being deprived of all his rights."

N.B.

The growth of friction between Germany and the United States (Samoa), Germany and Britain, Britain and France (Fashoda), the growth of armaments. . . . "Imperialism is the household word used to denote this general aggressive mood" (253).

Lenin, *Collected Works*,
4th Russian Edition,
Vol. 39, pp. 499-500

NOTES

[1] Lenin's article "On Our Agrarian Programme" published in the newspaper *Vperyod* (Forward).   p. 13

[2] Marx's article "The Anti-Kriege Circular".   p. 13

[3] *"General redistribution"*—a popular peasant slogan under the tsars, demanding a general sharing out of landed property.   p. 13

[4] *Socialist-Revolutionaries* (S.R.s)—a party of petty-bourgeois democrats formed in Russia in late 1901 and early 1902; it published the newspaper *Revolutsionnaya Rossiya* (Revolutionary Russia).

The S.R.s put forward the slogan of "equalitarian labour use of the land" and insisted that the transfer of landed estates to the peasants and an "equalitarian" redistribution of land at certain intervals would lead to the "socialisation of land" and socialism. In several of his works, Lenin showed these views to be wrong and proved that "equalitarian labour use of the land", if implemented, would not lead to socialism but would merely eliminate the survivals of feudal relationships and accelerate the development of capitalism in agriculture.

After the defeat of the 1905-07 revolution, a considerable section of the S.R.s and the party leadership accepted bourgeois liberalism. After the bourgeois-democratic revolution of February 1917, the S.R. leadership took part in the bourgeois Provisional Government, which tried to suppress the peasant movement. The S.R.s fully supported the bourgeoisie and the big landowners in their fight against the working class, which was preparing the socialist revolution. After the October Socialist Revolution, the S.R.s joined the counter-revolutionaries—the bourgeoisie and the landowners—in fighting the Soviet people.   p. 14

[5] The Paris Commune of 1871.   p. 21

[6] The *Social-Democratic Federation* of Britain was founded in 1884. Among its members were reformists (Hyndman, etc.) and anarchists, and a group of Marxist Social-Democrats (Harry Quelch, Tom Mann, Edward Aveling, Eleanor Marx, and others), who constituted the Left wing of the British socialist movement.

Frederick Engels sharply criticised the Social-Democratic Federation for its dogmatism and sectarianism, its isolation from the mass working-class movement in Britain and for ignoring its peculiarities.

In 1907, the Federation took the name of the Social-Democratic Party, which in 1911 merged with Leftist elements of the Independent Workers' Party to form the British Socialist Party. In 1920, most of its members took part in founding the Communist Party of Great Britain. p. 22

7 A letter from Engels to F. A. Sorge dated November 29, 1886. p. 22

8 The idea of a "labour congress" and a "broad labour party" was put forward by the liquidators, an opportunist trend in Russia after the defeat of the 1905-07 revolution. Larin was a leader of the liquidators.

They were so called because they wanted the illegal revolutionary party of the working class disbanded and replaced by a "broad" opportunist petty-bourgeois labour party, on the lines of the British Labour Party; it was not to have any programme and its highest organ was to be a "labour congress" attended by Social-Democrats, Socialist-Revolutionaries and anarchists. It was to abandon the revolutionary struggle against tsarism and confine itself to legal activity sanctioned by the tsarist government. Lenin exposed this very harmful attempt to liquidate the Social-Democratic Labour Party and to dissolve the vanguard of the working class in the petty-bourgeois mass. The liquidators failed to carry any section of the working class with them. The Prague Conference of the R.S.D.L.P., held in January 1912, expelled the liquidators from the Party. p. 22

9 An American working-class organisation founded in Philadelphia in 1869. It remained a secret organisation, practising a mystical ritual until 1881, when it came out into the open but retained some secret rites. Membership was open to skilled and unskilled workers from all industries, without regard to sex, race, nationality or creed. Its main purpose was to enlighten the workers and defend their interests through working-class solidarity. The leadership was opposed to the participation of workers in political struggle and to the establishment of a political working-class party; it considered co-operatives to be the best way of eliminating the evils of capitalism.

It flourished in the 1880s, when the U.S.A. was swept by a broad wave of strikes. By 1886, it had almost 700,000 members, including 60,000 Negroes. But the leadership opposed a nation-wide workers' strike for an 8-hour day, and helped to break the strike by forbidding its members to take part. In spite of the ban, the rank and file took part in the strike. Because of the leadership's opportunist policy it lost ground among the masses after 1886, and broke up in the late nineties. p. 23

10 *Lassalleans*—members of the General Association of German Workers, a political organisation of German workers, founded at the congress of workers' societies in Leipzig in 1863 with the active participation of Lassalle. The very fact of its formation was of positive significance, but Lassalle, who was elected president, led

the Association along the opportunist path. It confined its aims to the struggle for universal suffrage and peaceful parliamentary activity. The Lassalleans regarded the peasantry as a reactionary mass and favoured the counter-revolutionary path of Germany's unification "from above", through dynastic wars waged by Prussia. The Association existed until 1875.

The advance of the labour movement and increased government reprisals led, at the 1875 Gotha Congress, to the merger of the Association and the Marxist Social-Democratic Workers' Party of Germany, which was founded by Wilhelm Liebknecht and August Bebel. In the new Socialist Labour Party of Germany, the Lassalleans constituted the opportunist wing.   p. 25

11 *Geschichte der deutschen Sozialdemokratie* (A History of German Social-Democracy), by Franz Mehring.   p. 26

12 The Anti-Socialist Law was introduced in Germany by the Bismarck government in 1878. It banned the Socialist Party, all mass labour organisations and the labour press. German Social-Democrats, led by August Bebel and Wilhelm Liebknecht, conducted illegal activities on a large-scale, with the result that the party's influence in the working class was actually enhanced. In the 1890 elections to the Reichstag, the Social-Democrats polled nearly 1,500,000 votes, and the government was forced to repeal the law that very year. p. 26

13 From Marx's letter to F. A. Sorge of September 19, 1879.   p. 26

14 An anti-Marxist trend among international Social-Democrats which arose in Germany in the late nineteenth century and which got its name from Eduard Bernstein, the opportunist German Social-Democrat.   p. 27

15 In late 1884, Reichschancellor Bismarck demanded, in the interests of Germany's predatory colonial policy, that the Reichstag should approve subsidies to private shipping companies to establish steamship lines to East Asia, Australia and Africa. Following the debate in the Reichstag, the Right wing of the Social-Democratic group voted in favour of the East Asia and Australia lines, and said they would vote for the Africa and other lines, if the orders for new ships went to German shipyards. This motion was negatived, and only then did the group vote against the subsidies as such.

Engels censured this opportunist stand in a letter to Sorge dated December 31, 1884.   p. 27

16 The *International Socialist Workers' Congress* was held in Paris July 14-20, 1889, on the initiative of the French socialists and with the support of socialists from other countries. Opportunists from among the French Possibilists and the Social-Democratic Federation of Britain tried to control the preparations for and the Congress itself. They were vigorously opposed by Engels, who took active part in preparing the Congress. Engels and the revolutionary Marxists exposed the moves of the Possibilists and the leaders of the S.D. Federation, and thwarted their efforts to seize the leader-

ship of the international working-class movement. The socialist parties were united internationally on the basis of revolutionary Marxism. Although the International Socialist Workers' Congress did not adopt any formal decision to inaugurate the Second International, it was in actual fact its constituent congress.

The Possibilists and the leaders of the Social-Democratic Federation of Britain held a congress of opportunists in Paris.   p. 28

[17] *Possibilists* (Paul Brousse, Benoit Malon, etc.)—a petty-bourgeois reformist trend in the French socialist movement. When the French Workers' Party split up at the Ste. Etienne Congress in 1882, the Possibilists founded their Workers' Social-Revolutionary Party. They opposed the revolutionary programme and tactics of the proletariat and proposed that the workers should only strive to attain the "possible", hence their name.   p. 28

[18] *Bakuninists*—followers of the anarchist Mikhail Bakunin, who joined the International Working Men's Association (the First International), which was founded by Marx in 1864, but tried to disrupt the working-class movement by fighting Marxism tooth and claw and setting up a secret anarchist alliance within the First International. Bakunin and his followers were expelled from the First International by a decision of its Hague Congress in 1872.   p. 29

[19] A quotation from Engels's letter to Florence Kelley-Wischnewetzky of May 2, 1888.   p. 29

[20] *Fabians*—members of the Fabian Society, a British reformist organisation, founded in 1884. It derived its name from the Roman commander, Fabius Maximus (d. 203 B.C.), surnamed Cunctator, i.e., the Delayer, for his tactics of harassing Hannibal's army without risking a pitched battle. Among the members of the Fabian Society were bourgeois intellectuals, including Sidney and Beatrice Webb, Bernard Shaw, etc.

The Fabians denied the need for class struggle by the proletariat or the socialist revolution, insisting that the transition from capitalism to socialism could be made only through petty reform and gradual social change. The Fabian Society served as a conductor of bourgeois influence within the working class. Lenin said it was "an extreme opportunist trend". In 1900, the Fabian Society was affiliated with the Labour Party. Fabian "socialism" is one of the ideological sources of the Labourites.   p. 29

[21] A quotation from Engels's letter to F. A. Sorge dated January 18, 1893.   p. 30

[22] *Decazeville strike*—a French miners' strike in Decazeville in January 1886, which was suppressed by government troops. Mass protests were organised by French socialists against the actions of the government and the employers. Bourgeois deputies, including the Radicals, supported the reprisals against the miners. As a result, the workers' deputies left the Radicals and formed an independent workers' group in the Chamber of Deputies. Engels watched these

developments in France and attached great importance to "this first bold and independent action by the French proletariat in the Chamber".   p. 34

23 Reference is to the Russian Mensheviks, who during the 1905-07 revolution opposed Social-Democratic participation in the Provisional Revolutionary Government.

Mensheviks—an opportunist trend among Russian Social-Democrats. In the elections to the central organs of the Russian Social-Democratic Labour Party (R.S.D.L.P.), at its Second Congress in 1903, the revolutionary Social-Democrats, led by Lenin, won a majority (Russ. *bolshinstvo*, hence the name Bolshevik) and the opportunists were left in the minority (Russ. *menshinstvo*, hence Menshevik).

During the 1905-07 revolution, the Mensheviks opposed the hegemony of the working class in the revolution, and its alliance with the peasantry, and demanded an accord with the liberal bourgeoisie, which, they said, should lead the revolution. When reaction set in after the defeat of the 1905-07 revolution, most of the Mensheviks became liquidators: they wanted the illegal revolutionary working-class party disbanded. After the bourgeois-democratic revolution of February 1917, the Mensheviks took part in the bourgeois Provisional Government, supporting its imperialist policy and fighting the socialist revolution which was then being prepared.

After the Socialist Revolution in October 1917, the Mensheviks fought against the Soviet people on the side of the counter-revolutionary capitalists and landowners.   p. 35

24 The Russo-Turkish war of 1877-78.   p. 35

25 The *State Duma*—the representative assembly which the tsarist government was forced to set up after the 1905 revolution. It was nominally a legislative body, but did not exercise real power. Elections to it were not direct, equal or general. The electoral rights of the labouring classes, and also of the non-Russian nationalities, were whittled down, while a sizable section of the workers and peasants had no electoral rights at all. Under the electoral law of December 11 (24), 1905, one big landowner vote was equal to 3 urban capitalist votes, 15 peasant votes and 45 workers' votes.

The First Duma (April-July 1906) and the Second Duma (February-June 1907) were dissolved by the tsarist government. After its June 3, 1907 coup, the government issued a new electoral law, which made even greater inroads into the rights of the workers, peasants and urban petty bourgeoisie and gave the ultra-reactionary bloc of big landowners and capitalists complete control of the Third (1907-12) and Fourth (1912-17) Dumas.   p. 36

26 In August 1879, the illegal revolutionary organisation Zemlya i Volya (Land and Freedom) was split into two parties: Narodnaya Volya (People's Will) and Chorny Peredel (General Redistribution).

Members of the Narodnaya Volya group (Narodovoltsi)—Zhelyabov, Perovskaya, Mikhailov, Morozov, Figner, Frolenko, etc.—took the path of political struggle, believing the overthrow of the autocracy and the winning of political freedom to be their main task. Their programme called for a "permanent people's representation" elected on the basis of universal suffrage, democratic freedoms and transfer of the land to the people. They fought tsarism mainly by terroristic acts. The Narodovoltsi were wrong in believing that a handful of revolutionaries could terrorise, disorganise and destroy the autocracy, without massive support from a revolutionary movement. They made several attempts to assassinate high-ranking officials and on March 1, 1881 assassinated Alexander II. The tsarist government countered with savage reprisals and in the later eighties the group was broken up.

By contrast, members of the General Redistribution group underrated the importance of political struggle against tsarism and believed propaganda to be their main task. Some (Plekhanov, Axelrod, Zasulich, Deutsch and Ignatov) subsequently became Marxists, and in 1883 set up abroad the first Russian Marxist organisation, the Emancipation of Labour group.   p. 36

[27] Engels wrote about Plekhanov's book, *Our Differences*, and about the nature of the impending revolution in Russia, in a letter to Vera Zasulich dated April 23, 1885.   p. 36

[28] Engels's essay, "To Die for the Republic", from his series, *The German Campaign for an Imperial Constitution*.   p. 37

[29] The *Homestead Act of 1862* gave all U.S. citizens the right to receive from the state, free of charge or for a nominal price, a tract of land up to 160 acres, which became the farmer's property not more than five years later.   p. 40

[30] The *Stockholm (Unity) Congress* of the R.S.D.L.P. held from April 10 to 25 (April 23-May 8), 1906. The agrarian question was one of the principal items on its agenda.   p. 41

[31] *Appeal to Reason*—an American socialist weekly founded in 1895. It took an internationalist stand during the First World War, and ceased publication in 1919.   p. 47

[32] *Novoye Vremya* (New Times)—a monarchist newspaper published in Russia from 1868 to 1917.   p. 47

[33] The *First Balkan War* (October 1912-April 1913). The Balkan states —Bulgaria, Greece, Serbia and Montenegro—formed an alliance and started military operations against Turkey to liberate Macedonia and other areas inhabited by Slavs and Greeks. Turkey was defeated and under the peace treaty, signed in London in May 1913, lost a considerable part of her possessions. Macedonia was divided between Bulgaria, Serbia and Greece, a big part of Thrace went to Bulgaria, while Albania was declared an "independent" state under a German prince.   p. 54

[34] *Progressists, Progressist Party*—a party of the Russian monarchist bourgeoisie founded in November 1912. What they want, wrote Lenin, is "a moderate constitution with narrowly restricted rights

based on a bicameral system and an anti-democratic suffrage. They want a 'strong authority' that would pursue 'patriotic' policy of conquering with sword and fire new markets for 'national industry' ". Their leadership included Moscow big businessmen Ryabushinsky and Konovalov. After the Socialist Revolution of October 1917, the Progressists joined the counter-revolutionaries in their war against the Soviet people.

Cadets, Constitutional-Democratic Party—the chief party of the liberal-monarchist bourgeoisie in Russia, which was founded in October 1905. The Cadets wanted a constitutional monarchy. During the first Russian revolution of 1905-07, they styled themselves "the people's freedom" party, although they actually betrayed the people's interests and conducted secret negotiations with the tsarist government on how to crush the revolution. While acting as the "opposition" in the Duma, the Cadets wanted the tsarist government to allow them to take power, and supported it on key domestic and foreign policy issues.

During the imperialist war of 1914-17, the Cadet leaders, Milyukov and others, were the chief ideologists of the policy of aggrandisement conducted by Russian imperialism. After the February revolution of 1917, they joined the bourgeois Provisional Government and fought the workers' and peasants' revolutionary movement, defended big landed property, and tried to make the people continue the imperialist war. After the socialist revolution in October 1917, the Cadets joined the counter-revolutionaries in their war against the Soviet people.   p. 54

[35] On June 3, 1907, the tsarist government staged a coup: it dissolved the Second Duma, arrested the Social-Democratic deputies, and issued a new electoral law which gave many more seats to the landowners and capitalists and whittled down the small number of workers' and peasants' seats. It withdrew electoral rights from the native population of the Asian part of Russia and the Turkic people of Astrakhan and Stavropol gubernias, and halved the representation of the people of Poland and the Caucasus. The Third Duma convened in November 1907 on the basis of this electoral law consisted of ultra-reactionaries and dyed-in-the-wool monarchists.   p. 63

[36] The Chinese Republic established as a result of the revolution of 1911.   p. 64

[37] Lenin drafted the speech, "The Question of Ministry of Education Policy", for a Bolshevik deputy in the State Duma. It was made on June 4 (17), 1913 by Deputy Badayev, in the debate on the report of the Budgetary Commission on the Ministry of Public Education estimates for 1913. Badayev delivered the greater part of the speech almost word for world but never finished it; he was ruled out of order when he said: "Doesn't this government deserve to be driven out by the people?"   p. 70

[38] The *Black Hundreds* were monarchist gangs organised by the tsarist police to fight the revolutionary movement. They assassinated revolutionaries, attacked progressive intellectuals, and organised anti-Jewish pogroms.   p. 72

[39] *Octobrists, Union of October Seventeenth*—a monarchist party of big capitalists, founded in November 1905, following the promulgation of the tsar's manifesto of October 17, 1905, promising constitutional liberties in Russia. The party was hostile to the people and was formed to safeguard the vested interests of big capitalists and land-owners who ran their estates on capitalist lines. It supported the tsar's reactionary domestic and foreign policy. After the socialist revolution in Russia, the Octobrists joined the Cadets in organising the armed struggle against the Soviet people with the aid of foreign imperialists.   p. 73

[40] *Bund*—an abbreviation for the General Jewish Workers' Union in Lithuania, Poland and Russia, which was founded in 1897, its members being in the main Jewish handicraftsmen in Russia's western provinces. The Bundists followed an opportunist, Menshevist policy. They were under the strong influence of the nationalistic Jewish bourgeoisie and wanted to isolate Jewish workers from workers of other nationalities in Russia. After the Socialist Revolution in October 1917, the Bund leadership joined the bourgeois and landowner counter-revolutionaries in fighting against Soviet power. The Bund dissolved itself in 1921.   p. 86

[41] Engels's *Anti-Dühring. Herr Eugen Dühring's Revolution in Science*.
                                                                    p. 94

[42] Lenin is referring to the tsarist bureaucracy's attitude towards the democratic Zemstvo intellectuals—doctors, technicians, statisticians, teachers, agriculturists, etc., called the "third element" in a speech made in 1900 by the Samara Deputy Governor-General Kondoidi. The expression was subsequently used in literature to designate the Zemstvo democratic intelligentsia.   p. 102

[43] The *International Socialist Congress* held in Stuttgart in August 1907. In the debate on the colonial question, Van Kol, representing the Dutch socialists, and the German opportunists, Bernstein and David, speaking on behalf of the majority of the German delegation, motioned the inclusion in the resolution on the colonial question of the following clause, which Lenin called "monstrous". It said: "The Congress does not condemn in principle, and for all time, every colonial policy which, under a socialist regime, may become a work of civilisation." Lenin said: "In reality this proposition was tantamount to a direct retreat towards bourgeois policy and a bourgeois world outlook that justifies colonial wars and atrocities. . . . The Congress quite rightly deleted the above-quoted words from the resolution and substituted for them a condemnation of colonial policy that was sharper than that contained in former resolutions."   p. 103

[44] See Note 8.   p. 103

[45] The letter to the Secretary of the Socialist Propaganda League is in response to a League leaflet which Lenin received in November 1915 from its Secretary, Fitzgerald. The leaflet was signed by 20 American Socialists.   p. 111

[46] The *Socialist Party of America*—a reformist, opportunist party founded in 1901. During the First World War, its Right-wing majority supported the policy of U.S. imperialism. The revolutionary minority, which took an internationalist stand, opposed the war and subsequently formed the core of the Communist Party of the United States, which was founded in 1921.

The *Socialist Labour Party of America* was founded in 1876 through the merger of the North American Section of the First International, the Social-Democratic Labour Party and a number of socialist groups. Most of its members were foreign-born. It did not have extensive ties with the proletarian masses and was of a sectarian nature. During the First World War it inclined to internationalism.   p. 113

[47] *Zimmerwald* (Switzerland) was the scene of an international conference in September 1915 of internationalist socialists from 11 European countries, including Russia, Germany, France, Italy, etc. Lenin said it was the "first step" in developing the international movement against the imperialist war.

The conference was the scene of a struggle between the group of real internationalists led by Lenin (Zimmerwald Left) and the Centrist majority. The Zimmerwald Left tabled its own draft manifesto and a draft resolution on the world war and the tasks of Social-Democrats. They stressed the need for a complete break with social-chauvinism, and urged the people to wage a revolutionary struggle against their imperialist governments.

The majority rejected the proposals of the Zimmerwald Left and approved a manifesto which, while censuring the imperialist governments for starting the world war, said nothing of the revolutionary tasks facing the working class. The manifesto served as a basis for the formation of the Zimmerwald Association and the election of the International Socialist Commission, its Executive.

The Zimmerwald Left elected a bureau, which after the conference continued the work to unify the revolutionary internationalist groups.   p. 113

[48] The work was written in 1915. In early 1916, Lenin, while in Berne, sent the manuscript of the book to Maxim Gorky for publication in Petrograd. It was published in 1917.

The notes—variants of the plan and extracts from the statistical tables of the U.S. census reports for 1900 and 1910—were published in *Lenin Miscellany XIX* in 1932.

Lenin did not carry out his intention of writing the second part of the book, which was to have dealt with Germany.   p. 115

[49] *Sotsial-Demokrat* (Social-Democrat)—an illegal newspaper, the Central Organ of the R.S.D.L.P., which appeared from 1908 to 1917.

Lenin refers to his article, "Dead Chauvinism and Living So-cialism", published in *Sotsial-Demokrat* No. 35, December 12, 1914. (See Lenin, *Collected Works*, Vol. 21.) p. 208

50 Written by Lenin and published on November 1, 1914, in *Sotsial-Demokrat* No. 33, under the title "The War and Russian Social-Democracy". (See Lenin, *Collected Works*, Vol. 21.) p. 208

51 *International Socialists of Germany* (I.S.D.)—a group of Left-wing Social-Democrats which emerged during the First World War and joined the Zimmerwald Left. It was out of touch with the masses and soon broke up. p. 208

52 *Kautskyites*—the followers of Karl Kautsky, leader of the Centrists among the German Social-Democrats and in the Second Interna-tional.

Centrism—an opportunist trend in the international working-class movement, whose representatives took a middle-of-the-road stand between the avowed opportunists and the revolutionary Left wing, hence their name. During the First World War, the Centrists supported the policy of the social-chauvinists, but also proclaimed pacifist slogans, thereby diverting the workers from their revolu-tionary struggle against imperialist war and spreading the illusion that "a democratic peace without annexations" could be had while the imperialists remained in power. p. 208

53 *Vorwärts* (Forward)—a daily, the Central Organ of the German Social-Democrats. During the First World War it took a social-chauvinist stand, supported the German Government's imperialist policy, and fought against internationalist Social-Democrats. p. 208

54 The *Spanish-American War of 1898*—the imperialist war fought by the United States against Spain with the object of seizing her colonies. It started in April 1898. After several battles Spain ad-mitted defeat and gave up the last of her colonies in Latin Amer-ica: Cuba, Puerto Rico, and also the Philippines and Guam.

Under the peace treaty concluded in December 1898 Puerto Rico, Guam and the Philippines became U.S. colonies. Cuba was nomi-nally recognised as an independent republic, but the Platt Amend-ment inserted in her constitution gave the U.S.A. the right of armed intervention in Cuba's internal affairs. The U.S. Government and monopolies became the virtual masters of Cuba.

The peoples of Cuba, the Philippines, and Puerto Rico, who had long fought against the Spanish colonialists, continued their strug-gle for independence against their new masters.

The *Anglo-Boer War of 1899-1902*—the war Britain fought against the Boers of the South African republics of Transvaal and the Or-ange Free State to turn them into British colonies and lay hands on their rich deposits of gold and diamonds. The Boers gallantly fought against the colonialists, but were hopelessly outnumbered: there were 10 British soldiers to each Boer guerrilla fighter. Under the peace treaty, which the leaders of the Boers were forced to sign in May 1902, the Boer republics lost their independence and were turned into British colonies. They were subsequently included in the Union of South Africa, a British dominion formed in 1910.   p. 210

55 The *Chemnitz Congress*—a congress of German Social-Democrats held in Chemnitz in September 1912.

The *Basle Congress*—an International Socialist Congress (Extraordinary Congress of the Second International) convoked in November 1912 to protest against the Balkan War, which had broken out, and the impending imperialist world war. The Congress adopted a resolution (Manifesto) calling on the socialists of all countries to "prevent the breaking out of war...." The proletariat considers "it a crime *to shoot each other* down in the interest and for the profit of capitalism, for the sake of dynastic honour and of diplomatic secret treaties". But in case war should break out notwithstanding, socialists "shall be bound to intervene for its being brought to a speedy end, and to employ all their forces for utilising the economic and political crisis created by the war in order to rouse the masses of the people and to hasten the downbreak of the predominance of the capitalist class".

When the imperialist world war broke out in July 1914, most of the socialist leaders of the Second International betrayed the cause of socialism; they refused to fulfil the Basle resolution, and sided with their imperialist governments. The Russian Bolsheviks, led by Lenin, the Liebknecht and Luxemburg group in Germany, John MacLean and other internationalists in Britain and some groups in other socialist parties remained true to the principles of internationalism and, in conformity with the Basle Manifesto, called on the workers of their countries to fight their imperialist governments and the imperialist war.   p. 210

56 G. V. Plekhanov.   p. 237

57 Fashoda—a populated locality on the White Nile in Eastern Sudan, and the scene of an incident in the imperialist struggle for colonial possessions in Africa which nearly sparked off a war between Britain and France.

In July 1898, a detachment of French expeditionary troops occupied Fashoda and hoisted the French flag. In September, British troops, sent to Africa to conquer the Sudan, approached Fashoda, and demanded that the French evacuate it. The latter refused, whereupon Britain adopted a belligerent posture and threatened to fight. In November, the French Government backed down and ordered its detachment to withdraw. Under the agreement concluded between Britain and France in 1899, Eastern Sudan became a condominium of Britain and Egypt, which in fact made it a British colony.   p. 278

58 The *Seven Years' War* (1756-63)—a war fought by Prussia and Britain against Austria, France, Russia and Sweden, and from 1762, also against Spain.   p. 288

[59] See Marx, "The Eighteenth Brumaire of Louis Bonaparte." Preface to the Second Edition.   p. 298

[60] For their speeches against the imperialist war, the Bolshevik deputies to the State Duma, Badayev, Petrovsky, Samoilov, Muranov and Shagov, were arrested by the tsarist government in 1915 and sentenced to hard labour.   p. 301

[61] The *Workers' or labour group—Arbeitsgemeinschaft*—an organisation of German Centrists formed in March 1916 by Reichstag deputies who had broken away from the Social-Democratic group in the Reichstag. They formed the core of the Centrist Independent Social-Democratic Party of Germany, which was formed in 1917; it vindicated social-chauvinists and favoured continuing the alliance with them.   p. 310

[62] *Minoritaires* or *Longuetists* (the followers of Jean Longuet)—a minority of the French Socialist Party, which was formed in 1915 and held Centrist views. The Longuetists were left in a minority at the French Socialist Party Congress in Tours in December 1920, where the Lefts won out. Together with the avowed opportunists they split away from the party and joined the so-called Two-and-a-Half International; they returned to the Second International when the former broke up.   p. 310

[63] The *Independent Labour Party*—a reformist party founded by the leaders of the "new trade unions" in 1893, during a revival of the strike struggle and a mounting drive of the working class for independence from the bourgeois parties. The party united the membership of the "new trade unions" and a number of old trade unions intellectuals and representatives of the petty bourgeoisie who were under the influence of the Fabians. It was led by James Keir Hardie. From the very outset, the party adopted bourgeois-reformist positions and concentrated on parliamentary struggle and parliamentary deals with the Liberals. Lenin wrote that it was "actually an opportunist party that has always depended on the bourgeoisie".

When the First World War broke out, the I.L.P. issued an anti-war manifesto, but shortly afterwards it took a social-chauvinist stand.   p. 310

[64] The *British Socialist Party* (B.S.P.) was founded in Manchester in 1911 through the merger of the Social-Democratic Party and other socialist groups. The B.S.P. spread Marxist ideas and was "not opportunist and *really* independent of the Liberals" (Lenin). It was somewhat sectarian because it was small and its ties with the masses weak.

During the imperialist world war of 1914-18 a sharp struggle was fought within the party between the internationalist trend (Albert Inkpin, Theodore Rothstein, John MacLean, William Gallacher, etc.) and the social-chauvinist trend headed by Hyndman. Some elements of the internationalist trend were inconsistent and took a Centrist stand on a number of issues.

In February 1916, a group of B.S.P. members founded the newspaper, *The Call*, which had an important part to play in uniting the internationalists. The B.S.P. annual conference held in Salford in April 1916 condemned the social-chauvinist stand of Hyndman and his followers, and they left the party.

The B.S.P. welcomed the Great October Socialist Revolution in Russia. Its members played a great part in the British working people's movement in defence of Soviet Russia against foreign intervention. In 1919, the majority of its organisations (98 against 4) came out in favour of joining the Communist International. The B.S.P., together with the Communist Unity Group, played the chief role in forming the Communist Party of Great Britain. At the first unity congress in 1920, the overwhelming majority of local B.S.P. organisations joined the ranks of the Communist Party.   p. 310

[65] See Note 47.   p. 310

[66] The *Internationale* group (Spartacus League)—an organisation set up in the early stages of the First World War by German Left-wing Social-Democrats, Karl Liebknecht, Rosa Luxemburg, Franz Mehring, Clara Zetkin, etc. They fought against German imperialism and exposed before the working class the German Social-Democratic leaders who had gone over to the imperialist side. For their revolutionary activities, they were fiercely persecuted by the German Government. Rosa Luxemburg and other members of the group took a wrong stand on a number of theoretical and political questions and their mistakes were criticised by Lenin in his articles, "The Junius Pamphlet", "A Caricature of Marxism and Imperialist Economism", etc. In 1916, the *Internationale* group took the name of Spartacus League. In December 1918, its members founded the Communist Party of Germany.   p. 311

[67] *Tribunists*—a Left-wing group of the Dutch Social-Democratic Labour Party, which in 1907 began to publish the newspaper *De Tribune*. In 1909, they were expelled from the Dutch Social-Democratic Labour Party and formed the Social-Democratic Party of Holland. In 1918, they took part in forming the Communist Party of Holland.   p. 312

[68] The *Party of the Young, or the Left*—the name used by Lenin to denote the Left-wing trend among the Swedish Social-Democrats. During the imperialist world war of 1914-1918, the Young took an internationalist stand and sided with the Zimmerwald Left. In May 1917, they formed the Left-wing Social-Democratic Party of Sweden. Its congress in 1919 decided to join the Communist International. In 1921, the party's revolutionary wing formed the Swedish Communist Party.   p. 312

[69] *Tesnyaki*—the revolutionary Social-Democratic Labour Party of Bulgaria, founded in 1903 after the split within the Social-Democratic Party. The founder and leader of the Tesnyaki was Dmitry Blagoyev; subsequent leaders, Blagoyev's disciples, were G. Dimi-

trov, V. Kolarov and others. In 1914-18, they opposed the imperialist war, and in 1919 joined the Communist International and formed
the Bulgarian Communist Party.   p. 312

[70] *Yedinstvo* (Unity)—a newspaper, organ of the extreme Right group
of Menshevik defencists headed by Plekhanov, started in 1917. It
fully supported the Provisional Government and fiercely fought the
Bolshevik Party.   p. 314

[71] See Note 55.   p. 314

[72] *Rech* (Speech)—the Central Organ of the Cadet Party, published in
Petrograd from 1906 to 1917. After the February revolution of 1917,
the newspaper supported the Provisional Government's imperialist
policy and urged violence against the Bolshevik Party.   p. 314

[73] That is, after the Moscow workers' armed uprising in December
1905. For more details about the Russian revolution of 1905-07 see
Note 75.   p. 326

[74] The Portuguese bourgeois revolution of 1910, which overthrew the
monarchy and proclaimed a bourgeois republic; and the Turkish
revolution of 1908-09, as a result of which Turkey became a constitutional monarchy.   p. 329

[75] The revolution broke out on January 9, 1905. On that day the workers of Petersburg, together with their wives and children, set out
for the Winter Palace to present a petition to the tsar, describing
their intolerable condition and absolute lack of rights. The tsar
responded by ordering the fusillade of the peaceful demonstration.
Thousands of unarmed workers, women, children and old people
were killed and wounded in the streets.

The working class of all Russia countered the tsarist government's atrocity with demonstrations, strikes and armed action. The
workers, who led the revolution, fought for the overthrow of the
autocracy and wanted a democratic republic, abolition of landed
estates and introduction of an eight-hour working day. In the
summer of 1905, the workers of Ivanovo-Voznesensk set up the
first Soviet of Workers' Deputies, and the workers of other industrial areas followed suit.

The peasantry joined in the struggle against the tsarist and landowner system with a demand that all landed estates should be
handed over to the people. In June 1905, an uprising broke out
aboard the battleship *Potyomkin* of the Black Sea fleet.

A nation-wide political strike was staged in October 1905. It
brought to a halt all plants, factories, and railways all over the
vast country. The general strike showed the great strength of the
working class. On October 17, the tsar was forced to issue a manifesto promising a constitution and "granting" freedom of speech,
assembly, the press, etc. The tsar's promises turned out to be a
fraud, and were never kept.

An armed uprising began in Moscow in December 1905. For nine
days, the factory workers, led by Moscow's Social-Democrats—the

Bolsheviks—heroically fought on the barricades against the tsar's troops, which used artillery. Only when army units were brought up from Petersburg was the tsarist government able to defeat the workers.

In 1906, more than one million workers took part in strikes. In the first half of 1906, the peasant movement spread to more than half the districts.

The tsarist government crushed the revolutionary movement with great savagery. Punitive expeditions, on a rampage in all major industrial centres and areas of peasant uprisings, killed thousands of workers and peasants.

The first Russian revolution was defeated but it was historic. Lenin said that for the people of tsarist Russia the 1905-07 revolution was "a dress rehearsal", without which the working class could not have won out in October 1917. The Russian revolution of 1905-07 had a great impact on the development of the revolutionary movement in Asia, including Persia, Turkey, China and India. p. 329

[76] Approved by the Fourth (Extraordinary) All-Russia Congress of Soviets, convoked in March 1918 to ratify the Brest Peace Treaty.

The resolution was in reply to a message from President Woodrow Wilson of the United States. It was an attempt to prevent Soviet Russia from concluding peace with Germany, to get her to side with the Entente and to use the Russian Army to divert German troops from the Western front. p. 331

[77] In the spring of 1918, the imperialists of Great Britain, the U.S.A., France, and Japan began their intervention against Soviet Russia. British and American troops were landed at Murmansk and Archangel in the North of Russia. In the Far East, a joint attack was mounted by Japan, which landed a force in Vladivostok on April 5, 1918, and the bands of the counter-revolutionary Cossack chieftain, Semyonov, who was supplied with Japanese arms.

On July 2, 1918, the Supreme Allied Council decided to step up the intervention in Siberia. The Allies, it said, must "take advantage of an opportunity of gaining control of Siberia ... which may never return".

Fresh Japanese units and also Canadian and French troops were landed in Vladivostok in early August, followed a few days later by the 27th and 31st regiments of the U.S. Army. The American General Graves arrived on September 1 on board the troopship *Thomas*. According to U.S. sources, the American forces landed at Vladivostok totalled about 9,000 men. Under the overall command of the Japanese General Otani the army of interventionists started its offensive against Soviet Russia.

While being united in their desire to overthrow the Soviets and subjugate Russia, the interventionists squabbled over the bearskin that was still on the bear's back. The contradictions between the U.S.A. and Japan were especially aggravated. The U.S. forces wanted to take control of the Far Eastern railways, but Japan objected. The Americans were also discontented with the fact that the Japanese had considerably more troops (72,000) in the Far East than the Americans.

The Red Army routed the forces of the imperialists in the Far East, in the North and South of Russia, the Volga area and Siberia. All the interventionist armies were driven off Soviet territory. p. 333

[78] Written by Lenin on August 20, 1918, and delivered to the U.S.A. in spite of the blockade and intervention. In December 1918, it appeared in abridged form in a magazine published by internationalist socialists in New York, and then in pamphlet form, as a reprint from the magazine. It has been repeatedly reprinted in the American press. p. 334

[79] In 1898, the U.S. imperialists, under the pretext of "aiding" the Filipino people, who in 1896 had staged an uprising against Spanish colonial oppression and proclaimed an independent Philippine Republic, declared war on Spain and landed their forces in the Philippines. Defeated Spain ceded the Philippines to the U.S.A. In February 1899, the U.S. imperialists started military operations against the Philippine Republic. By 1901, the resistance of the Filipino people was overcome and the country became a U.S. colony. p. 335

[80] The Second All-Russia Congress of Soviets of Workers' and Soldiers' Deputies, which opened in Petrograd on October 25 (November 7), 1917, announced that the bourgeois Provisional Government had been overthrown and that power was in the hands of the Soviets.

It heard Lenin's report on peace. He motioned his *Decree on Peace*, which proposed that all belligerent nations and their governments should immediately start negotiations on a just and democratic peace without annexations, i.e., without any seizure of foreign territories, forcible annexations of other peoples, or indemnities.

None of the imperialist governments taking part in the war responded to the Soviet Government's call for peace talks. The imperialist war continued. p. 336

[81] The *Brest Peace Treaty* was signed between Soviet Russia and the countries of the Quadruple Alliance (Germany, Austria-Hungary, Bulgaria and Turkey) on March 3, 1918. The terms were extremely unfavourable for Russia. Under it, Germany and Austria-Hungary were to establish their control over Poland, the greater part of the Baltic provinces, and a part of Byelorussia. The Ukraine was to be separated from Soviet Russia and turned into a German dependency. The towns of Kars, Batum, and Ardagan were to go to Turkey. In August 1918, Germany imposed on Soviet Russia a supplementary treaty and financial agreement which contained more rapacious terms.

The treaty was abrogated after the November 1918 revolution which overthrew the monarchy in Germany. p. 337

[82] *Secret treaties* concluded by tsarist Russia with the imperialist powers were made public by Soviet Russia's People's Commissariat for Foreign Affairs in December 1917 and early 1918, in virtue of a decision of the Second All-Russia Congress of Soviets. More than 100 treaties and a great quantity of secret correspondence between the tsarist and provisional governments, on the one hand, and on the other, France, Poland, Germany, Austria-Hungary and other states were extracted from the archives of the former Russian Ministry of Foreign Affairs, deciphered and published, first in the newspapers and then in nine separate volumes. The publication of the secret treaties had a tremendous part to play in exposing the imperialist nature of the First World War. p. 337

[83] Lenin is referring to the following extract from N. G. Chernyshevsky's review of Henry Charles Carey's book, *Letters to the President on the Foreign and Domestic Policy of the Union, and Its Effects*: "The path of history is not paved like Nevsky Prospekt; it runs across fields, either dusty or muddy, and cuts through swamps or forest thickets. Anyone who fears being covered with dust or muddying his boots, should not engage in social activity." p. 340

[84] *Man in the muffler*—a character in Chekhov's story of that name, the epitome of everything that is inert, conservative, and hostile to anything novel or progressive. p. 341

[85] The bourgeois Provisional Government, formed in Russia after the February 1917 revolution, announced on March 2 (15), 1917 its intention to convoke a Constituent Assembly but the elections were repeatedly deferred, as the Provisional Government put off its convocation.

It was finally convened on January 5, 1918, after the October Socialist Revolution, when the majority of the people were behind the socialist revolution and the Soviet government. But because the elections had been held in early October 1917, there was a sharp discrepancy between the political temper of the broad masses and the composition of the Assembly. The vast majority of the people —workers, peasants and soldiers—demanded that the Constituent Assembly should recognise Soviet power and the Soviet decrees on land and peace. Most of the deputies belonged to parties which had lost popular support and refused to submit to the popular will, and the Constituent Assembly was dissolved. p. 349

[86] Congress of the French Socialist Party held in Paris on October 6-11, 1918. p. 350

[87] The decision of the Third Spanish Socialist Congress and the Eighth Congress of Spanish Workers to send a message of solidarity with the Soviet Republic. p. 351

[88] The negotiations in Brest-Litovsk in January-March 1918, on the peace treaty with Germany. p. 354

[89] A Prussian landed proprietor.   p. 354

[90] Lenin lists the towns and areas occupied by the Russian counter-
revolutionary armed forces and the Anglo-American-French-Japa-
nese interventionists in 1918-19.   p. 359•

[91] See Note 23.   p. 361

[92] The counter-revolutionary revolt of the Czechoslovak Corps engineered by the Entente imperialists with the active participation of
the Mensheviks and Socialist-Revolutionaries. The Corps was formed
in Russia before the October Socialist Revolution from among
Czech and Slovak prisoners of war. In the summer of 1918, it
numbered over 60,000 men. After the establishment of the Soviet
power, the Corps was financed by the Entente which intended to
use it to fight the Soviet Republic. The agreement of March 26,
1918 allowed the Corps to leave Russia via Vladivostok on the
condition that it surrendered its arms. But at the end of May the
counter-revolutionary command of the Corps violated the agreement and, taking its cue from the Entente imperialists, provoked an
armed revolt. The U.S., British and French governments openly
supported the revolt in every possible way and French officers took
a direct part in it. Working hand in glove with the Russian whiteguards and landowners, the Czech whites occupied a large part of
the Volga area, the Urals and Siberia, everywhere restoring the
rule of the bourgeoisie. In the Czech-occupied areas whiteguard
governments were set up with the participation of the Mensheviks
and Socialist-Revolutionaries.

Most of the Czech and Slovak prisoners of war sympathised with
the Soviet power and did not fall for the anti-Soviet propaganda of
their commanders. Seeing that they had been deceived, they deserted
and refused to fight against the Soviet power. Some 12,000 Czechs
and Slovaks fought in the ranks of the Red Army.

The Volga area was liberated by the Red Army in the autumn
of 1918, and the revolt was finally suppressed along with that of
Kolchak.   p. 361

[93] See Note 4.   p. 361

[94] See Engels's letter to A. Bebel of March 18-28, 1875.   p. 364

[95] Marx and Engels said in several of their works that they thought
in certain circumstances a peaceful transition to socialism was possible in Britain and America. In his speech on the Hague Congress
of the First International delivered at a meeting in Amsterdam on
September 8, 1872, Marx said: "We know that the institutions,
mores and traditions of various countries have to be taken into
account; and we do not deny that there are countries, like America,
Britain, and, if I had had a better knowledge of your institutions,
I might well have added Holland, too, in which the workers may
attain their aim by peaceful means. But even if that is so, we must
also recognise that force must be the lever of our revolution in most

countries of the continent; force will have to be used for some time
to come in order to establish the rule of labour for good."   p. 365

[96] The revolution which broke out in Germany in November 1918, when
Councils of workers' and soldiers' deputies were formed as a result
of a series of revolutionary acts by the German workers' and sea-
men's uprisings in Kiel. They took power in Hamburg, Lübeck, Bremen and Kiel. A mammoth demonstration was staged by workers
in Berlin on November 9, 1918, Wilhelm II was overthrown and
a republic was proclaimed.

Social-Democrats Ebert, Scheidemann, etc., headed the new government (Council of People's Representatives), whose aim was to retain
capitalism and curb the revolution. The Councils were stripped of all
power. When the workers' uprising broke out in Berlin in January
1919, it was drowned in blood by Social-Democrat Noske's troops.
The leaders of the German Communist Party, Karl Liebknecht and
Rosa Luxemburg, were arrested and brutally murdered in January
1919. The strike movement in the Ruhr was stamped out by fierce
reprisals. The Bavarian Soviet Republic was strangulated in March
1919.

The German revolution was defeated. Power passed into the
hands of the bourgeoisie.   p. 367

[97] *Die Rote Fahne* (The Red Flag)—a daily founded by Karl Liebknecht
and Rosa Luxemburg as the organ of the Spartacus League. It subsequently became the Central Organ of the Communist Party of Germany. It was published in Berlin from November 9, 1918, and was
banned when Hitler came to power in 1933, but continued to be
printed secretly.   p. 371

[98] The *Dreyfus case*—in 1894, Dreyfus, an officer of the French General Staff and a Jew by nationality, was falsely accused of espio-
nage and high treason, and sentenced by a military court to life imprisonment. The case was trumped up by the reactionary militarists
and was used by the clericals and the royalists to attack the republic and fan anti-Semitism. Socialists, republicans, and all progressives in France, including Emile Zola, Anatole France, and Jean
Jaurès, demanded a retrial. This brought on an acute political struggle which lasted for several years. Because of public pressure Dreyfus was finally pardoned and released in 1899, but only in 1906
was he cleared and reinstated in the army by a court of cassation.
      p. 383

[99] The *Berne International* was the name of the Second International
as reconstituted by a conference of social-chauvinist and Centrist
parties in Berne in February 1919.   p. 384

[100] See pp. 334-48.   p. 394

[101] Serfdom was abolished in Russia on February 19, 1861.   p. 397

[102] The imperialist world war of 1914-18.   p. 401

[103] The article was in reply to the following five questions submitted to Lenin by the United Press Agency: 1) Has the Russian Soviet Republic made any major or minor changes in the government's initial domestic and foreign policy programme and the economic programme, when and what kind? 2) What are the tactics of the Russian Soviet Republic in respect of Afghanistan, India and other Moslem countries outside Russia? 3) What political and economic aims do you set yourself in respect of the United States and Japan? 4) On what terms are you prepared to conclude peace with Kolchak, Denikin, and Mannerheim? 5) What else would you like to convey to American public opinion?   p. 403

[104] The promise was not kept: the United Press Agency sent Lenin's article to the newspapers without his answer to the fifth question.

In October 1919, Lenin's answer to the fifth question was carried by the Left-wing socialist magazine, *The Liberator,* in an article entitled "A Statement and a Challenge".   p. 403

[105] A reference to the counter-revolutionary uprising of the Czechoslovak Corps organised by the Allied imperialists with the support of the Mensheviks and the Socialist-Revolutionaries. For more details, see Note 92.   p. 404

[106] The Soviet Government negotiated with William Bullitt in Moscow in March 1919; he was assigned by U.S. President Wilson to negotiate on a peace. The Soviet Government put forward a number of addenda and specifications to the U.S. and British proposals and the final text of an agreement was then drafted. All governments existing in Russia were to remain on their territories, trade relations were to be restored, the Soviet Government was to be granted free transit on all railways and the use of all ports which had belonged to the former Russian Empire, etc. On the Soviet Government's proposal a clause was inserted in the agreement to the effect that *directly* after the agreement was signed (and not after the Russian army was demobilised, as the Allies proposed) all foreign troops would be withdrawn from Russia and all military support of the anti-Soviet governments would cease.

The Soviet proposals were not accepted by the governments of the U.S.A. and Britain, for in the spring of 1919 Kolchak's army had launched an offensive and they were hoping that Soviet Russia would be defeated. Wilson refused to see Bullitt, while Lloyd George declared in Parliament that he had not empowered anyone to negotiate with the Bolsheviks.   p. 405

[107] A radiogramme sent on May 7, 1919 by the People's Commissar for Foreign Affairs, Chicherin, to the well-known polar explorer and public figure, Fridtjof Nansen. It was in reply to Nansen's letter to Lenin radioed on May 4, 1919. Nansen proposed the setting up of an international commission to help Russia with food and medicines. He said the Allied governments had agreed to assist such a commission, provided military operations in Russia were halted. In his radiogramme to Nansen, Chicherin, on behalf of the Soviet Government, accepted the plan but rejected the Allies' terms as an

attempt to preserve the counter-revolutionary whiteguard governments on the fringes of Russia. The Soviet Government agreed to
negotiate on a cessation of military operations only simultaneously
with a discussion of all matters relative to the ending of the intervention and the Civil War. The Allied governments did not reply
to the Soviet Government's proposal.   p. 405

[108] See pp. 334-48.   p. 414

[109] See Note 106.   p. 416

[110] The foreign policy resolution was motioned by Lenin at the Eighth
All-Russia Conference of the R.C.P.(B.) on December 2, 1919, and
approved. It was read out by Lenin on December 5 in his report
to the Seventh All-Russia Congress of Soviets and adopted unanimously as a peace proposal to the Allies. The resolution was published in the press on December 6 and sent to the Allied governments on December 10, 1919. The governments of Britain, France,
U.S.A. and Italy refused to examine the peace proposal of the Seventh Congress of Soviets.   p. 423

[111] Soviet Russia and Estonia opened their peace talks on December
5, 1919, and signed the peace treaty in Yuriev (Tarty) on February
2, 1920.   p. 437

[112] The documents Lenin mentions were received from a whiteguard
officer, Oleinikov, who came over to the Soviet side. He was carry-
ing them via Sweden from S.D. Sazonov in Paris to Yudenich.
Among those mentioned in the documents were: Sazonov—tsarist
and Kolchak Foreign Minister and a representative of Kolchak and
Denikin in Paris; Gulkevich—Kolchak's envoy in Sweden; Bakh-
metev—Kolchak's Ambassador to Washington; Sukin—chief of the
Foreign Ministry in Omsk; Sablin—Kolchak's chargé d'affaires in
London; Knox—general, representing the British Government with
Kolchak.   p. 438

[113] The reference is to negotiations conducted by the Red Cross on the
exchange of prisoners of war, return of refugees, etc.   p. 441

[114] A statement by the Council of People's Commissars of the R.S.F.S.R.
on the Principles of Soviet Policy in Respect of Poland. It was
adopted on January 28, 1920, and broadcast and published in the
central press. On February 2, the first session of the Seventh All-
Russia Central Executive Committee adopted a message to the Polish people, exposing the imperialist slander that Soviet Russia had
predatory intentions with respect to Poland, and stressing the Soviet Government's undeviating desire for peace and friendly, good-
neighbour relations with an independent Poland.   p. 441

[115] After the Red Army's victory over Kolchak and Denikin, the American press, expressing the mood of business circles, twice asked
Lenin for an interview. On February 18, 1920, Lenin replied to the
questions put by Karl Wiegand, the Berlin correspondent of Universal Service. Lenin's answers were wired to Berlin and from there

on to New York on February 21, 1920. That same evening, they were published in the *New York Evening Journal.* Lenin's answers were reprinted in the German communist and socialist press.p. 443

[116] Lenin was interviewed in English by Lincoln Eyre, a correspondent of the American newspaper, *The World*, in mid-February 1920. The hour-long interview began in Lenin's study and continued in his Kremlin flat. The headlines are *The World*'s.   p. 446

[117] A press report on January 18, 1920 said the Allied governments intended to lift their blockade of Soviet Russia and to allow trade with her. A decision of the Supreme Allied Council on January 16, 1920 stressed that "these arrangements imply no change in the policy of the Allied governments towards the Soviet Government".
                                                                        p. 446

[118] An international organisation operating between the wars. It was set up at the Paris Peace Conference of the victor powers in 1919. The Covenant of the League was a part of the Versailles Peace Treaty. It had 44 members, including the major imperialist powers, but not the U.S.A. The League was a centre where armed intervention against Soviet Russia was organised. It did not conduct any effective peace-keeping operations, and folded up with the outbreak of the Second World War, but was formally dissolved only in April 1946.   p. 449

[119] The *Communist Workers' Party of Germany*—a group of "Leftists" who split away from the Communist Party of Germany in 1919 and formed an independent organisation in 1920. It was semi-anarchist, had no influence in the working class and finally degenerated into an anti-Communist sect.   p. 457

[120] The *Workers' Socialist Federation*—a small organisation which emerged in Britain in 1918 on the basis of the Workers' Electoral Rights' Federation, and consisted mainly of women. In January 1921, the Federation merged with the Communist Party of Great Britain.
    The *Industrial Workers of the World*—a mass working-class organisation founded in America in 1905. Among its founders were prominent leaders of the American labour movement, Daniel De Leon, Eugene Debs, and William Haywood. The I. W. W. had a big part to play in the history of the American labour movement. During the First World War (1914-18) it led a number of mass anti-war manifestations by the American working class, exposing the policy of the reactionary leaders of the American Federation of Labour and the Right-wing Socialists. Some I.W.W. leaders— Haywood among them—subsequently joined the Communist Party of the U.S.A. But some I.W.W. activities were markedly anarchist and syndicalist: it ignored the political struggle of the proletariat, denied the party's leading role and the need for the dictatorship of the proletariat; refused to work among members of trade unions within the American Federation of Labour. The I.W.W. eventually

became a sectarian organisation without any influence in the labour movement.

The *Shop Stewards' Committees*—elective labour organisations in various industries, which were particularly widespread during the First World War, when the labour movement was growing and there was discontent with the reformist policy of the trade union leaders. The shop stewards united in shop, district and city committees, led a number of major working-class actions against the imperialist war and for better living conditions.

After the October Socialist Revolution, during the foreign armed intervention, the shop stewards' committees actively supported Soviet Russia. Many leaders of the shop stewards' committees, among them William Gallacher, Harry Pollitt and Arthur MacManus, joined the Communist Party of Great Britain. p. 457

[121] Set up in Vienna in February 1912 by a conference of Centrist parties and groups which had temporarily withdrawn from the Second International under the pressure of revolutionary-minded workers. In 1923, the two were reunited. p. 466

[122] President Wilson's programme announced in January 1918 as a basis for peace between the Allies and the Austro-German coalition.

Wilson's 14 points were designed to weaken the effect on the masses in the belligerent countries of the Decree on Peace adopted after Lenin's report by the Second Congress of Soviets on October 26 (November 8) 1917, which proposed to all nations and belligerent governments the immediate conclusion of a peace without annexations or indemnities.

Wilson's 14 points proposed a limitation on armaments, freedom of the seas, establishment of a League of Nations, etc. Most of the points were never implemented. p. 466

[123] A conference on Middle East questions, then in preparation, was held at Lausanne from November 1922 to July 1923. Called on the initiative of Britain, France, and Italy, it was attended by Japan, Rumania, Yugoslavia, Greece, Turkey, and had observers from the U.S.A. Soviet Russia was also to have attended, but on October 14, 1922, the British Government announced that Russia would be allowed to discuss only one item of the agenda, namely, the Straits (the Dardanelles and Bosporus).

The Soviet delegation to the Lausanne Conference motioned a proposal that commercial navigation in the Bosporus, the Sea of Marmara and the Dardanelles should be absolutely free, but that both in peace and war time the Dardanelles and the Bosporus should be closed to the warships and aircraft of all states, with the exception of Turkey. The Soviet proposal was rejected. The Conference adopted the British proposal giving warships free transit through the Straits. p. 516

[124] Isaac A. Hourwich, *Immigration and Labour. The Economic Aspects of European Immigration to the United States*, New York and London, 1912. p. 521

[125] "Capitalism and Workers' Immigration" (see pp. 82-85). p. 521

[126] Census Reports. Twelfth Census 1900, Vol. V. Agriculture. Washington, 1902. Thirteenth Census of the United States, taken in the year 1910, Vol. V; Agriculture, Washington, 1913. Lenin received one of the volumes from America in May 1914, and the other shortly before the outbreak of the imperialist war. They formed the basis of his *New Data on the Laws Governing the Development of Capitalism in Agriculture. Part I. Capitalism and Agriculture in the United States of America* (see pp. 115-205). p. 521

[127] 1. *The Development of Capitalism in Russia. The Process of the Formation of a Home Market for Large-scale Industry* (see Lenin, *Collected Works*, Vol. 3); 2. *The Agrarian Programme of Social-Democracy in the First Russian Revolution, 1905-1907* (ibid., Vol. 13). p. 522

[128] See Note 47. p. 523

[129] Reference is to the *International Socialist Congress in Stuttgart*—the Seventh Congress of the Second International, which was held on August 18-24, 1907, and was attended by nearly 900 delegates, representing the socialist parties and working-class organisations of 25 nations. It discussed the following: 1) the colonial question; 2) relations between political parties and trade unions; 3) labour immigration and emigration; 4) women's electoral rights, and 5) militarism and international conflicts.

It was the scene of a struggle of the revolutionary wing of the international socialist movement represented by the Russian Bolsheviks, led by Lenin, and the German Left-wing Social-Democrats Rosa Luxemburg and others, against the opportunists (Vollmar, Bernstein, Van Kol, etc.). The opportunists were defeated and the resolutions formulated the principal tasks facing the socialist parties in a spirit of revolutionary Marxism. p. 524

[130] See Note 47. p. 524

[131] The magazine *Letopis* (Chronicle) ran a publishing house, Parus (Sail), and to this Lenin sent his *New Data on the Laws Governing the Development of Capitalism in Agriculture. Part I. Capitalism and Agriculture in the United States of America.* p. 525

[132] Lenin's *Imperialism, the Highest Stage of Capitalism.* p. 525

[133] *Internationale Flugblätter* (International Leaflets) No. 1 was published in November 1915 by the bureau of the Zimmerwald Left, and carried its draft resolution and Manifesto. It could not be published in English in the United States. p. 526

[134] See pp. 111-114. p. 526

[135] Nothing came of the talks with Charles Kerr, a publisher of socialist literature, concerning the publication in English of the pamphlet *Socialism and War* in America. p. 527

[136] *Internationale Korrespondenz* (International Correspondence)—a

German social-chauvinist weekly dealing with foreign affairs and the labour movement. Published in Berlin from 1914 to 1918. p. 527

137 *Internationale Sozialistische Kommission* (I.S.K.)—the executive of the Zimmerwald Association, which was elected at the Zimmerwald Conference in September 1915. p. 529

138 The reference is to the book by the American revolutionary socialist Daniel De Leon, *Two Pages from Roman History. I. Plebs Leaders and Labour Leaders. II. Warning of the Gracchi*, published by the National Executive Committee, Socialist Labour Party, New York, 1915, 89 pp. De Leon's book was not published in Russian. p. 536

139 The medical report on John Reed's illness and death which Lenin received from the secretary of the Executive Committee of the Comintern, M. V. Kobetsky, on October 18, 1920. It was published in the newspaper *The Call* on November 3, 1920.

Lenin refers to the announcement of John Reed's death published in *Pravda* on October 19, which read: "On the night of October 16-17 Comrade John Reed, member of the Executive Committee of the Communist International and representative of the United Communist Party of America, died of typhus." p. 538

140 A hotel in Moscow. p. 539

141 In 1921, groups of American workers volunteered to go to Soviet Russia to help in economic rehabilitation. A great part of them were Russians who had emigrated to America before the October Revolution. It was L. K. Martens who put before the Soviet Government the question of their coming to Russia. p. 539

142 The commission was established by decision of the Council of Labour and Defence on February 25, 1921. Apart from considering the questions of worker re-emigrants the commission was "to collect jointly with the People's Commissariat for Labour (Comrade Martens) information on admission of emigrant workers coming back from abroad (the number to be admitted and the terms)." p. 539

143 In the autumn of 1920, Washington Vanderlip, a representative of the American Vanderlip Syndicate, came to Moscow for talks on fisheries concessions, prospecting and extraction of oil in Kamchatka and the rest of Siberia east of longitude 160°E. At the end of October, a treaty was drafted on a 60-year concession. The Soviet Government had an option on all the concession enterprises within 35 years, and upon expiration of the treaty all the enterprises, complete with plant, were to become the property of the R.S.F.S.R. But the Vanderlip Syndicate did not get any support either from the government or influential financial groups in the U.S.A. and the agreement was not signed. p. 540

144 The Tenth Congress of the R.C.P.(B.) was held on March 8-16, 1921. p. 540

[145] The Council of Labour and Defence examined the question of American industrial emigration on June 22, 1921. It was recognised as desirable that "industrial enterprises or groups of enterprises should be developed under lease to groups of American workers and industrially developed farmers under contractual terms assuring them of a measure of economic autonomy". p. 541

[146] For details see p. 505. p. 545

[147] The Society was formed by Russian emigrants in New York in May 1919. Its branches were set up in other parts of the United States and Canada. The aim of the Society was to send skilled workers and technicians to help Russia restore her economy.

From late 1921 to October 1922, the Society sent to Soviet Russia seven agricultural, two building and one miners' communes and several groups which brought $500,000 worth of plant, seeds and foodstuffs. By 1923, the Society numbered more than 20,000 members and had 75 branches. Russia continued to receive economic help from the Society until 1925.

Lenin saw the activities of the Society as a vivid manifestation of proletarian internationalism and the fraternal solidarity of the working people. p. 546

[148] Lenin's draft telegram to the American Society for Technical Aid to Soviet Russia (see p. 546). p. 547

[149] Held on August 6, 1921. Because the votes were split, a poll was taken of the members of the Council of People's Commissars, the majority of whom were in favour of sending the telegram.

On Lenin's proposal, the following was inserted in the text: "Account must be taken of the difficulties in Russia which have to be overcome, the food supply snags, etc. The men who come to Russia must be prepared for all this. It is necessary to be guided by the instructions of the Industrial Emigration Department of the Supreme Economic Council, which are being sent to you. It would be better to start by sending delegates to make an on-the-spot examination over here of the land tracts for settlement, and the forest tracts, mines, factories, etc., which are to be leased." p. 547

[150] A letter written in connection with the negotiations in Riga between a Soviet government delegation and the American Relief Administration (A.R.A.), which was headed by the U.S. Secretary of Commerce, Hoover, on the extension of help to the starving people of the Volga area. The agreement was concluded on August 20, 1921. p. 548

[151] On September 23, 1921, the Council of Labour and Defence decided it was desirable to conclude an agreement with an American workers' group leasing to them the Nadezhdinsk Works in the Urals and certain other enterprises in the Kuznetsk coal basin, and instructed a commission consisting of representatives of the Supreme Economic Council, the People's Commissariat for Labour and the People's Commissariat for Agriculture to produce the final draft agreement. In these negotiations with the Soviet Government, the

American workers were represented by Rutgers, Haywood and Calvert. p. 551

152 The chairman of the commission to draft the agreement with the American workers' group (see Note 151) was Kuibyshev, a member of the Presidium of the Supreme Economic Council; on October 11, he sent Lenin a progress report and the draft agreement approved by the Presidium of the Supreme Economic Council on October 10, 1921. Lenin's subsequent references are to this draft. p. 554

153 The reference is to a draft pledge which American workers wishing to come to Soviet Russia were to sign. For the text of the draft pledge see pp. 551-52. p. 554

154 A draft agreement between the Soviet Government and the Russian-American Trade and Industrial Corporation (later renamed Russian-American Industrial Corporation) signed on October 12, 1921. The Corporation was set up by the United Garment Workers of America, which offered to lease several garment factories in Moscow, restore them, purchase equipment for them in the United States and put them into operation. p. 556

155 The agreement between the Soviet Government and the American Amalgamated Drug and Chemical Corporation, which was represented by Hammer, on the delivery to Russia of one million poods of wheat was concluded in Moscow on October 27, 1921.

Under another agreement, approved by the Council of People's Commissars on November 1, 1921, the American Amalgamated Drug and Chemical Corporation received a concession for the working of asbestos mines in Alapayevsk District in the Urals, this being the first concession on the territory of the R.S.F.S.R. p. 560

156 Rutgers's letter to the Council of Labour and Defence of October 11, 1921, replying, on behalf of the sponsoring group of American workers coming to Soviet Russia, to all the remarks made by Martens, who disagreed with Rutgers's proposals. p. 561

157 The candidates for the board of the sponsoring group of American workers. p. 561

158 A draft resolution written by Lenin and adopted by the Political Bureau of the Central Committee of the R.C.P.(B.) on October 20, 1921. In November 1921, the Soviet Government concluded an agreement with an American workers' group (the Rutgers group) under which they were to bring with them specified quantities of materials, implements of production and food, with the Soviet Government earmarking the amount of $300,000 for the purchase of machinery and implements abroad. That was the origin of the "Kuzbas Autonomous Industrial Colony", which occupied a part of the Kuznetsk coal basin. p. 563

159 To build houses for the American workers. p. 564

160 Held from November 12, 1921 to February 6, 1922, convened on the

initiative of the U.S.A., and attended by Great Britain, Belgium, Holland, Italy, China, Portugal, U.S.A., France and Japan. Its purpose was to complete the redivision of colonial possessions and spheres of influence in the Far East and the Pacific. The major documents signed at the conference were: Four-Power Treaty (U.S.A., Britain, Japan and France) on the protection of territorial rights in the Pacific area; Nine-Power Treaty on the open door principle in China; and Five-Power Treaty (U.S.A., Britain, Japan, France and Italy) limiting naval armaments.   p. 566

[161] In his telegram from London dated October 19, 1921, Krasin reported on the start of his talks with the American Foundation Company, which was prepared to build a paraffine separation plant and an oil pipeline to link Grozny with the Black Sea, provided the prospecting was done by the Company's engineers. Krasin proposed the allocation of the necessary funds.

Lenin's draft telegram to Krasin was approved by the Political Bureau of the Central Committee of the R.C.P.(B.) on October 28, 1921.   p. 566

[162] A letter received by Lenin from the United States:

October 4, 1921

To Premier Nicklay Lennin.

Dear Sir: Enclosed find copy of my United States patent for Plant Protector, which, along with my compliments, permit me to present to you and your people, in testimony of the warm sympathy and gratitude I feel for your people who came to our relief with their fleet of warships during our civil war from 1861 to 1865, which so surprised the British fleet, which had anchored in New York harbor to shell New York City, that they hoisted their anchors and faded away. The great masses of America have not forgotten this. I'm a veteran of the Civil War and was left on the field for dead; recovered and a prisoner for nine months. I'm in my 81st year of age, and know what war is. With the present of my Plant Protector I also extend to you the right to give to your people who may be living, at present, outside of your jurisdiction the benefit of my Protector at your discretion, free. All I wish in return, is that it may benefit your people, and that you acknowledge the receipt of it and send me your photograph.... With kindest wishes for the realisation of your most ardent hopes for yourself and people, I remain your sincere friend.

Robert B. Frye.
2731 Orman Avenue,
Pueblo, Colorado, U.S.A.   p. 568

[163] *New Data on the Laws Governing the Development of Capitalism in Agriculture. Part I. Capitalism and Agriculture in the United States of America.* See p. 115-205.   p. 570

[164] Lenin's corrections in the report written by the American correspondent Bessie Beatty of her interview with Lenin in early December 1921.   p. 571

165 The Russian-American Industrial Corporation (RAIC, Rusaminco) was set up by the United Garment Workers of America with funds collected by American workers to help in the economic rehabilitation of Soviet Russia.   p. 572

166 Assuming that the International Economic Conference (Genoa Conference) is broken up.   p. 573

167 Chicherin refers to the proposals to be advanced by the Soviet delegation at the International Economic Conference (Genoa Conference) which was held from April 10 to May 19, 1922.   p. 574

168 A letter received by Lenin from the well-known American scientist and electrical engineer, Charles P. Steinmetz:

                              Steinmetz, Charles P.
                                        Schenectady, N. Y., Feb. 16. 1922
Mr. W. Lenin,
My Dear Mr. Lenin:
    Mr. B. W. Lassoff's return to Russia gives me an opportunity to express to you my admiration of the wonderful work of social and industrial regeneration which Russia is accomplishing under such terrible difficulties.
    I wish you the fullest success and have every confidence that you will succeed. Indeed, you must succeed, for the great work which Russia has started must not be allowed to fail.
    If in technical and more particularly in electrical engineering matters I can assist Russia in any manner with advice, suggestion or consultation, I shall always be very pleased to do so as far as I am able.
                                        Fraternally yours
                                        Charles P. Steinmetz
                                                        p. 579

169 Steinmetz's letter (see Note 168) and Lenin's reply (see pp. 582-83) were published in *Pravda* No. 85, April 19, 1922.   p. 579

170 See pp. 549-55 and 561-65 and also Notes 151, 152, 156, and 158.
                                                                p. 580

171 See pp. 558, 559, 560, 565.   p. 581

172 See Note 168.   p. 582

173 In reply to this letter Lenin received a telephone message from Zinoviev in Petrograd and a written explanation from Begge, an agent of the People's Commissariat for Foreign Trade, stating that Mishell's complaint was due to a misunderstanding and promising to straighten out things right away.   p. 585

174 Reinshtein's report giving details about Dr. J. Hammer and his son Dr. Armand Hammer, and their American Amalgamated Drug and Chemical Corporation.   p. 586

[175] Lenin's proposal to support A. Hammer and B. Mishell's initiatives was adopted by the Political Bureau of the Central Committee of the R.C.P.(B.) on June 2, 1922.   p. 586

[176] A tractor team sent by the American Society for Technical Aid to Soviet Russia.   p. 587

[177] *The Society of Friends of Soviet Russia* was set up in the U.S.A. in 1921 to organise industrial aid to Soviet Russia and tell the truth about the country to counter the false reports in the American bourgeois press. In 1921, the Society collected money to help the famine-stricken Volga area. The U.S. Government hampered the Society's activity and harassed its members.

In the summer of 1922, having collected almost $2 million, the Society dispatched a 22-tractor team to Soviet Russia. It went to the Toikino State Farm (Perm Gubernia), where it did good work in teaching the peasants to cultivate land collectively with the aid of tractors. *Pravda* No. 233 of October 15, 1922, carried an article by Harold Ware, entitled "The American Tractor Team", describing its operations. Lenin fully appreciated the work done by the team and on November 9, 1922, the Presidium of the All-Russia Central Executive Committee, on Lenin's proposal, adopted the following resolution:

"The Perm and other most outstanding farms directed by the teams of the American Society for Technical Aid to Russia shall be known as model farms."   p. 590

[178] See Note 147.   p. 591

[179] See Note 177.   p. 593

[180] An international proletarian organisation set up in 1921 to help famine-stricken areas after a crop failure on the Volga. Clara Zetkin was its President, and Münzenberg, its Secretary-General. It did great work in collecting money and food for the starving, supplying distress areas with medicines, organising children's homes, etc. In 1922, it started to set up a number of industrial and agricultural enterprises in Soviet Russia, thereby promoting the country's economic regeneration. It subsequently became a powerful organisation and gave a great deal of aid to the international labour movement.
p. 594

[181] First published in 1939, *Notebooks on Imperialism* contain the preparatory material for *Imperialism, the Highest Stage of Capitalism*, which Lenin wrote in 1916. Lenin made extracts from and summarised hundreds of books, articles and statistical abstracts in English, French, German and other languages.   p. 597

NAME INDEX

A

Adler, Friedrich (1879-1960)—
Austrian reformist and Social-Democrat. Editor of
the Swiss Social-Democrat
Volksrecht (People's Right)
in 1910-11, and later a
secretary of the Austrian
Social-Democratic Party. In
1916, assassinated the Austrian Prime Minister, Count
Karl von Stürgkh. An
organiser of the Centrist
Two-and-a-Half International
(1921-23)—313

Adler, Victor (1851-1918)—
organiser and leader of the
Austrian Social-Democrats;
subsequently a reformist
leader of the Second International. During the First
World War took a Centrist
stand, preached "class peace"
and fought revolutionary action by the working class—
310

Agahd, E.—German petty-bourgeois economist—269

Aguinaldo, Emilio (b. 1869)—
leader of the Philippine uprising against the Spanish colonialists in 1896-98. President
of the Philippines in 1899—
268, 604

Alexinsky, Grigory Alexeyevich
(b. 1879)—Social-Democrat in
his early political activity.
During the First World War,
a social-chauvinist, writing in
a number of bourgeois newspapers. Fled abroad in April

1918, and joined the extreme
reactionary camp—475, 477

Anixt, Abram Moiseyevich (1887-
1941)—member of the Com-
munist Party of the Soviet
Union from 1919; in 1919-22
member of the Collegium of
the People's Commissariat of
Labour and Deputy People's
Commissar of Labour—539

Atkinson, Edward (1827-1905)—
American economist—604

Auer, Ignaz (1846-1907)—German
Social-Democrat; in 1875,
secretary of the Socialist
Labour Party of Germany,
and several times a deputy of
the Reichstag. Subsequently a
reformist, and a leader of the
opportunist wing of German
Social-Democracy—28

Axelrod, Pavel Borisovich (1850-
1928)—Menshevik leader, and
a leader of the liquidators
in the years of reaction
(1907-10). A social-chauvinist
during the First World War.
Took a hostile attitude to the
October Revolution; emigrated and called for armed
intervention against Soviet
Russia—266, 310

Axelrod, T. L. (1888-1938)—
chief of the Press Bureau of
the Council of People's Commissars from October 1917 to
July 1918 and the Comintern's
Press Bureau in 1920-21.
Later worked in the press—
531

B

Bakhmetev, B. A.—representative of Kolchak's counter-revolutionary government in the United States in 1919—438, 439, 440

Bakunin, Mikhail Alexandrovich (1814-1876)—leader of the Russian revolutionary movement and founder and ideologist of anarchism. Took part in the 1848-49 revolution in Germany. A member of the First International where he attacked Marxism.

Marx and Engels waged a resolute struggle against Bakunin's anarchist views—36

Ballister, D. (Mainor Robert) (1884-1952)—prominent American Socialist, journalist and painter; met the October Revolution with enthusiasm. While in Moscow, edited *The Call*, a newspaper distributed among the British and American interventionist forces; returned to the United States in 1920, joined the Communist Party and became one of its leaders—570

Barbusse, Henri (1873-1935)—well-known French writer, Communist, and outstanding anti-fascist—406

Bauer, Otto (1882-1938)—leader of the Austrian Social-Democrats and the Second International; the author of the opportunist theory of "cultural-national autonomy". In 1918-19, Foreign Minister of the Austrian bourgeois Republic. In 1919, 1927 and 1934 took active part in crushing the revolutionary action of the Austrian workers—87, 305

Beatty, Bessie (1886-1947)—American writer, visited Russia in 1917 and witnessed the October Revolution; met with Lenin in 1918 and 1921. Her book *The Red Heart of Russia* was imbued with sympathy for the revolutionary masses. In 1921 she travelled on the "October Revolution" agitation train through the famine-stricken Volga country.

During the last years of her life she worked as a radio commentator—571

Bebel, August (1840-1913)—founder and prominent leader of German Social-Democracy and the international working-class movement, a turner by trade. Active opponent of revisionism and reformism within the German working-class movement—26, 28, 34, 35, 206, 301

Becker, Johann Philipp (1809-1886)—leader of the German and international working-class movement, and a friend and associate of Marx and Engels—20, 37

Beer, Max (1864-1943)—German Social-Democrat, historian of socialism—236

Begge, Karl Mikkelevich (1884-1938)—member of the R.S.D.L.P. from 1902; member of the Collegium and an agent of the Commissariat for Foreign Trade in Petrograd in 1922—585

Bentham, Jeremy (1748-1832)—English bourgeois sociologist, theoretician of utilitarianism. He declared man of bourgeois society to be the model of man in general, and bourgeois society a system ensuring universal happiness. Marx called him "an oracle of the ordinary bourgeois intelligence of the 19th century" (Marx, *Capital*, Vol. I, Moscow, 1965, p. 609)—409

Berard, Victor (1864-1931)— French petty-bourgeois economist, publicist and philologist—269

Berger, Victor Louis (1860-1929) —American Right-wing socialist and a founder of the Socialist Party of America; pacifist during the imperialist world war; in 1916, actively supported U.S. imperialism in its fight against Mexico—309, 378

Bernstein, Eduard (1950-1932)— leader of the opportunist wing of German Social-Democracy and the Second International, a theoretician of revisionism; in 1896-98 published a series of articles entitled "Problems of Socialism", attacking the key propositions of revolutionary Marxism: the doctrine of socialist revolution, the dictatorship of the proletariat and the inevitable transition from capitalism to socialism—25, 26, 27, 28, 29

Bismarck, Otto (1815-1898)— Prince, monarchist, Prussian statesman; Reichschancellor from 1871 to 1890; carried out the forcible unification of Germany under Prussian rule—37

Bissolati, Leonida (1857-1920)— founder of the Italian Socialist Party, headed its Right wing; expelled from its ranks in 1912 and founded the Social-Reformist Party; social-chauvinist during the imperialist world war—309

Blatchford, Robert (1851-1943)— British socialist reformist, journalist and writer; in the early stages of the First World War contributed to the ultra-chauvinist organs of the British press; in 1916 joined Hyndman in founding the sectarian, chauvinist National Socialist Party—105, 106, 107

Bogdanov, Pyotr Alexeyevich (1882-1939)—member of the Bolshevik Party from 1905; in 1921-25, Chairman of the Supreme Economic Council and member of the Council of People's Commissars—546, 555, 564, 565, 566, 569

Borisov (Suvorov, S. A.) (1869- 1918)—Social-Democrat and delegate to the Fourth Unity Congress of the R.S.D.L.P. (1906), a rapporteur on the agrarian question; defended the demand for a distribution of landed property and its transfer into the ownership of the peasants— 41

Borodin, Mikhail Markovich (Grusenberg) (1884-1951)— member of the Party from 1903; emigrated to the U.S.A. in 1907; in 1918, returned to Russia and worked at the People's Commissariat of Foreign Affairs and the Comintern until 1922; from 1927, worked for TASS, the Supreme Economic Council and other organisations—545

Bourderon, Albert (b. 1858)— French Socialist, leader of the Left wing of the French syndicalist movement; took part in the Zimmerwald Conference, occupying a Centrist stand. After 1916 was in opposition to the revolutionary working-class movement— 208, 312

Bracke, Wilhelm (1842-1880)–

part in setting up the Industrial Workers of the World. In 1918, for his opposition to the imperialist war, was sentenced to 10 years in jail. Welcomed the Great October Socialist Revolution with enthusiasm—49, 206, 209, 301, 342, 343, 376, 524, 606, 607

De Leon, Daniel (1852-1914)— leader of the U.S. working-class movement, leader and ideologist of the American Socialist Labour Party; fought opportunism and betrayal of U.S. trade union leaders. Founder and one of the leaders of the Industrial Workers of the World—536

Denikin, Anton Ivanovich (1872-1947)—tsarist army general; with the aid of British, American and French imperialists set up the dictatorship of the bourgeoisie and landowners in the South of Russia and the Ukraine (1919); started offensive against Moscow in the summer and autumn of 1919; routed by the Red Army in early 1920—404, 405, 409, 413, 414, 430, 437, 442, 447, 473, 508

Deutsch, Lev Grigoryevich (1855-1941)—participant in the Narodnik and later the Social-Democratic movement in Russia. In 1883, one of the organisers of the first Russian Marxist group, Emancipation of Labour. After the Second Congress of the R.S.D.L.P. (1903), a Menshevik; liquidator in the years of reaction (1907-10); social-chauvinist during the First World War. Withdrew from political activity after the October Revolution—314

Dietzgen, Joseph (1828-1888)— —German worker, Social-Democrat, philosopher, who independently arrived at the basic principles of dialectical materialism—20

Disraeli, Benjamin (Lord Beaconsfield) (1804-1881)—prominent British statesman and writer, leader of the Conservative Party; Prime Minister (1868, 1874-80)—236

Dontsov, Dmitro—Ukrainian nationalist, whiteguard émigré after the October Revolution—87

Dreyfus, Alfred (1859-1935)— Jew, French General Staff officer, in 1894 sentenced to life imprisonment on a trumped-up charge of high treason; verdict revised and Dreyfus cleared after years of struggle waged by progressive French forces—383

Driault, Edouard—French bourgeois historian—245

Dühring, Karl Eugen (1833-1921) —German philosopher and economist; his views, an eclectic mixture of idealism and vulgar materialism, were scathingly criticised by Engels in his *Anti-Dühring*—25, 94, 103

Dutov, Alexander Ilyich (1864-1921)—colonel of the tsarist General Staff, chief of the Orenburg Cossack troops; organised several counter-revolutionary uprisings against Soviet power in the Urals (1917-20)—361

E

Ebert, Friedrich (1871-1925)— one of the leaders of the Right wing of the German

of Statistics of the British Board of Trade—258

Gompers, Samuel (1850-1924)—leader of the U.S. trade union movement, and opponent of socialism. From 1882 until his death, he was President of the American Federation of Labour. Conducted a policy of class collaboration with the capitalists and opposed the revolutionary struggle of the working class—56, 100, 348, 350, 374, 375, 378

Gorbunov, Nikolai Petrovich (1892-1938)—member of the Communist Party from 1917. After the October Socialist Revolution worked as Secretary and then as Business Secretary of the Council of People's Commissars—539, 568

Gorbunov, P. P. (1885-1937)—in 1921-22, Business Secretary of the People's Commissariat for Foreign Affairs—567

Gorky, Maxim (Peshkov, Alexei Maximovich) (1868-1936)—great Russian writer. After the October Socialist Revolution Gorky did a great deal to rally intellectuals in support of the Soviet power. He was one of the founders of the Soviet Writers' Union and its President until his death—525

Gorter, Herman (1864-1927)—Dutch Left-wing Social-Democrat, poet and publicist. In 1907, was one of the founders of *De Tribune*, the organ of the Left wing of the Dutch Social-Democratic Workers' Party. During the First World War—internationalist. From 1918 to 1921, member of the Communist Party of Holland where he

took an ultra-Left, sectarian position. In 1921, withdrew from the Communist Party and from active politics—312

Grimm, Robert (1881-1958)—leader of the Swiss Social-Democrats. During the First World War, Centrist and chairman of the Zimmerwald and Kienthal conferences. In 1945-46, President of the Swiss National Council—310, 523

Grot, Nikolai Yakovlevich (1852-1899)—idealist philosopher, and President of the Moscow Psychological Society—80

Guchkov, Alexander Ivanovich (1862-1936)—representative of the big commercial and industrial bourgeoisie in Russia, monarchist and leader of the bourgeois Octobrist Party. After the bourgeois-democratic revolution in February 1917, member of the Provisional Government. After the October Socialist Revolution, a whiteguard in emigration actively fighting the Soviet power—54, 315, 349, 440

Guesde, Jules (1845-1922)—one of the organisers and leaders of the French socialist movement and the Second International. Took a social-chauvinist attitude from the outset of the First World War and was a member of the bourgeois government in France—300, 309

Guilbeaux, Henri (1885-1938)—French Socialist, poet and journalist. During the first World War, Centrist and publisher of the pacifist magazine *Demain*. In 1916, took part in the work of the Kienthal Conference. From the early 1920s, lived in Ger-

decisions of the Fifth Congress of the Comintern; rejoined the Social-Democratic Party in 1926—301, 312, 527

Hohenzollern—dynasty, ruled German Empire from 1871 to 1918—356

Hourwich, Isaac A. (1860-1924)—economist. In 1889, emigrated from Russia to America where he was active in the trade union and Social-Democratic movement. Lenin commended his books *The Economic Condition of the Russian Village* (in Russian) and *Immigration and Labour* (1912). In the early years of the 20th century he became a revisionist 83, 264, 521

Hübner, Otto (1818-1877)—economist and statistician, compiled and published geographical statistical annuals—238, 303

Huysmans, Camille (b. 1871)—Belgian politician, and member of the Belgian Socialist Party Bureau. In 1904-19, Secretary of the International Socialist Bureau of the Second International; Centrist; member of several Belgian governments, Prime Minister in 1946-47; President of the Chamber of Deputies from 1936 to 1939 and from 1954 to 1959. Lately advocated contacts between socialist parties and the C.P.S.U. and re-establishment of unity of the international working-class movement—283

Hyndman, Henry Mayers (1842-1921)—British socialist and reformist. In 1881, founded the Democratic Federation, which in 1884 was reorganised as the Social-Democratic Federation. He was one of the leaders of the British Socialist Party, which he left in 1916 after the Party Conference held in Salford had condemned his social-chauvinist stand—29, 105, 200, 301, 309

I

Ilyin, V.—see *V. I. Lenin*—525

J

Jaeckh, Gustav (1866-1907)—German Social-Democrat and journalist; author of a book on the history of the First International—20

Jeidels, Otto—German economist specialising in the study of finance capital—224, 225, 226, 229

Junius—see *Luxemburg, Rosa*—287

K

Kalinin, Mikhail Ivanovich (1875-1946)—outstanding leader of the C.P.S.U. and the Soviet state; member of the Communist Party from 1898; member of the Political Bureau of the C.P.S.U. (B.) from 1925; Chairman of the All-Russia Central Executive Committee from 1919 and later of the Presidium of the Supreme Soviet of the U.S.S.R. —548

Kamenev, Lev Borisovich (Rosenfeld) (1883-1936)—member of the R.S.D.L.P. from 1901; joined the Bolsheviks after the Second Congress of the R.S.D.L.P. (1903); during the years of reaction (1907-10) advocated reconciliation with the liquidators, otzovists and Trotskyites; after the February revolution of 1917, opposed Lenin's *April Theses* and the Party's course towards socialist revolution; in October 1917, together with Zinoviev, revealed the C.C. decision to stage an armed uprising. After the October Revolution, repeatedly opposed the Party's Leninist policy; in 1925, one of the organisers of the New Opposition; in 1926, one of the leaders of the anti-Party, Trotsky-Zinoviev bloc; in 1934, expelled from the Party for anti-Party activity—548

Karr, John (b. 1880)—representative of the U.S. Communist Party in the Comintern (in 1921)—570

Kasso, Lev Aristidovich (1865-1914)—rabid reactionary and big landowner; tsarist Minister of Public Education (1910-14); used harsh reprisals against revolutionary students and progressive teachers—70

Kautsky, Karl (1854-1938)—leader of the German Social-Democrats and the Second International; initially a Marxist, he later became the ideologist of the most dangerous and harmful variety of opportunism, Centrism (Kautskianism); editor of *Die Neue Zeit* (New Times), the German Social-Democrats' theoretical journal.

After the October Revolution, he opposed proletarian revolution and the dictatorship of the proletariat—87, 106, 107, 208, 210, 223, 233, 248, 249, 250, 251, 252, 254, 265, 268, 269, 270, 271, 272, 274, 275, 276, 277, 278, 279, 280, 283, 299, 310, 313, 364, 365, 369, 378, 379, 411, 412, 413, 523, 524, 529

Kelley-Wischnewetzky, Florence (1859-1932)—American socialist, translator of Engels's book *The Condition of the Working Class in England* into English; active in the American co-operative movement—22

Kerensky, Alexander Fyodorovich (b. 1881)—Socialist-Revolutionary; after the February 1917 bourgeois-democratic revolution, a Minister and later Prime Minister of the Provisional Government and the supreme commander-in-chief; after the October Revolution, actively fought against Soviet power, and fled abroad in 1918—307, 341, 349, 403, 413, 507

Kestner, Fritz—German bourgeois economist; studied the development of trusts in capitalist society and their fight against unorganised capitalist enterprises—218, 221, 222

Keynes, John Maynard (1883-1946)—British bourgeois economist and politician; representative of the British Government at the Paris Peace Conference (1919); soon resigned because he considered the Treaty of Versailles injurious to the European economy; set out his views in *The Economic Consequences of the Peace*—462, 463, 464, 466, 467, 468, 486, 504, 578

Khvostov, Alexei Nikolayevich (1872-1918)—big landowner; Governor of Vologda and then of Nizhni-Novgorod (1906-10); ill-famed for his reactionary stand; Deputy to the Fourth

L

Lafargue, Paul (1842-1911)—outstanding leader of the French and international working-class movement, a talented publicist, one of the first followers of scientific communism in France, and a close friend and associate of Karl Marx and Frederick Engels; together with Jules Guesde he founded the French Workers' Party, and was editor of its organ, *L'Egalité* (Equality); actively fought against opportunism in the Second International; defended and spread the ideas of Marxism in the sphere of political economy, philosophy, history, linguistics, and fought against reformism and revisionism—30

Lansburgh, Alfred (b. 1872)—German bourgeois economist, publisher of *Die Bank* (1908-35), which carried several of his studies of finance capital—259, 269, 272, 273, 274

Lapinsky, P. L. (Levinson, Y.) (1879-1937)—Polish Communist, economist and publicist. In the 1920s, was on diplomatic work. In the 1930s, engaged in scientific and publicist work—465

Larin, Y. (Lurye, Mikhail Alexandrovich) (1882-1932)—Social-Democrat, Menshevik; in 1906, supported the opportunist idea of convoking a "labour congress" to set up a legal "broad labour party", which implied elimination of the R.S.D.L.P. and establishment of a non-Party organisation; in August 1917, joined the Communist Party, and after the October Socialist Revolution worked in Soviet government and economic agencies—22

Lassalle, Ferdinand (1825-1864) —German petty-bourgeois socialist; one of the founders of the General Association of German Workers (1863) which had a positive effect on the working-class movement. But Lassalle, who was elected its President, directed it along an opportunist path; Marx and Engels sharply criticised the theoretical and political views of the Lassalleans—25

Lazzari, Constantino (1854-1927) —prominent Italian socialist; one of the founders of the Italian Workers' Party (1882), and the Italian Socialist Party (1892); General Secretary of the Italian Socialist Party from 1912 to 1919—312, 376

Ledebour, Georg (1850-1947)—one of the leaders of the German Social-Democrats, Centrist and deputy of the Reichstag; in 1917, took part in setting up the Centrist Independent Social-Democratic Party of Germany—299, 310, 311

Legien, Karl (1861-1920)—German Right-wing Social-Democrat, German trade union leader, revisionist; from 1893 to 1920 (intermittently), deputy of the Reichstag from the Social-Democratic Party; took an extreme social-chauvinist stand during the First World War; supported the policy of the bourgeoisie and fought against the proletarian revolutionary movement—100, 101, 102, 103, 104, 113, 311

Lenin, N.—see *Lenin, V. I.*—21,

114, 348, 381, 414, 415, 417, 436, 445, 522, 557

Lenin, V. I. (1870-1924)—350, 386, 407, 483, 484, 494, 496, 522, 524, 527, 530, 546, 547, 550, 553, 554, 555, 557, 558, 559, 560, 561, 563, 564, 565, 566, 567, 568, 570, 571, 572, 573, 579, 580, 581, 583, 584, 585, 586, 589, 590, 591, 593, 595

Lepeshinskaya, Natalia Stepanovna (1890-1923)—worked in Lenin's secretariat—586

Leroy-Beaulieu, Pierre-Paul (1843-1916)—French liberal economist and sociologist, author of several works against scientific socialism—603

Levi, Paul (1883-1930)—German Left-wing Social-Democrat, member of the Spartacus League; during the First World War took an internationalist stand; member of the Communist Party of Germany since its foundation (1919); expelled from the Party in 1921 for opportunist, factionalist activity and subsequently returned to the Social-Democratic Party—462, 465

Levy, Hermann (b. 1881)—German bourgeois economist, professor of Heidelberg University; from 1921, professor of the Higher Technical School in Berlin; author of several works on finance capital—214, 215

Liebknecht, Karl (1871-1919)—outstanding leader of the German and international working-class movement; one of the founders of the Communist Party of Germany; in January 1919, was savagely murdered by counter-revolu-

tionaries—100, 208, 299, 301, 311, 369, 370, 371, 375, 377, 378, 379, 384

Liebknecht, Wilhelm (1826-1900) —prominent leader of the German and international working-class movement, one of the founders and leaders of the German Social-Democratic Party; from 1875 to his last days, member of the Central Committee of the German Social-Democratic Party and executive editor of its central organ, *Vorwärts*; took active part in the First International and the establishment of the Second International—26, 28, 29, 34

Liebman, F. (Hersch, Peisakh) (b. 1882)—one of the leaders of the Bund, the Jewish petty-bourgeois nationalist party; Centrist during the First World War—86

Liefmann, Robert (1874-1941)— German bourgeois economist; author of several works on economic and social problems —218, 219, 224, 233

Likhachov, V. M. (1882-1924)— member of the R.S.D.L.P. from 1902, Bolshevik. After the October Revolution was in charge of the Administrative Department of the Moscow Soviet; in 1921-22, Chairman of the Moscow Economic Council—544

Lincoln, Abraham (1809-1865)— outstanding American statesman, President of the United States from 1861 to 1865; led the struggle of the Northern States against the slaveholding South, for abolition of Negro slavery—269, 484, 603

Lindhagen, Karl (1860-1946)— Swedish Social-Democrat, internationalist during the First World War; from 1917 to 1921, member of the Communist Party of Sweden; in 1921, expelled from the Party for opposing the decisions of the Second Congress of the Comintern—312

Litvinov, Maxim Maximovich (1876-1951)—Communist, prominent Soviet diplomat; from 1918, member of the Collegium of the People's Commissariat for Foreign Affairs; from 1921, Deputy People's Commissar for Foreign Affairs; from 1930 to 1939, People's Commissar for Foreign Affairs; later held responsible posts in the Commissariat—423

Lloyd George, David (1863-1945) —British statesman, leader of the Liberal Party; from 1916 to 1922, Prime Minister; made efforts to build up British imperialist positions in the Middle East and the Balkans, and crushed the national liberation movement in the colonies and dependent countries; after the October Revolution, one of the sponsors and organisers of the armed intervention and blockade aimed against the Soviet state—392, 447, 463, 466, 469, 486, 504

Longuet, Jean (1876-1938)— publicist and member of the French Socialist Party and the Second International; during the First World War, headed the Centrist minority within the French Socialist Party—299, 301, 310, 413

Loriot, Fernand (1870-1930)— French socialist; during the First World War, internationalist and adherent of the Zim-

merwald Left; took part in founding the Communist Party of France—312, 376

Lubersac, Jean de—French lieutenant, monarchist; member of the French military mission in Russia in 1917 and 1918; Lenin's talk with him occurred on February 27, 1918 —339

Luxemburg, Rosa (1871-1919)— outstanding leader of the German, Polish and international working-class movement, leader of the Left wing of the Second International. From the outbreak of the First World War, took an internationalist stand; one of the initiators of the founding in Germany of the *Internationale* group, which was subsequently renamed the Spartacus group and then the Spartacus League; after the November 1918 revolution in Germany, took a leading part in the Constituent Congress of the Communist Party of Germany; in January 1919, was savagely murdered by a band of counter-revolutionaries—311, 312, 371, 375, 379, 384

M

MacDonald, James Ramsay (1866-1937)—British politician, founder and leader of the Independent Labour Party and the Labour Party; conducted an extreme opportunist policy, advocated the theory of class collaboration and the gradual growth of capitalism into socialism; in 1924 and from 1929 to 1931, Prime Minister—310

MacLean, John (1879-1923)—

prominent leader of the British labour movement; during the First World War, adopted an internationalist stand and engaged in active revolutionary anti-war propaganda; in April 1916, elected to the leadership of the British Socialist Party; in his later years withdrew from active politics—301, 312, 369, 370, 376

Maklakov, Vasily Alexeyevich (b. 1870)—big landowner, deputy of the Second, Third and Fourth Dumas, member of the Cadet Party's Central Committee; after the February 1917 revolution, Ambassador of the bourgeois Provisional Government to Paris, and later whiteguard émigré —54, 70, 408

Mann, Tom (1856-1941)—well-known leader of the British working-class movement; a Communist from 1920—35

Mannerheim, Carl Gustaf (1867-1951)—reactionary Finnish statesman; in 1918, commanded the counter-revolutionary whiteguard Finnish army which joined forces with the German interventionists in crushing the workers' revolution in Finland; one of the leaders of anti-Soviet ventures undertaken by Finnish reactionaries; from August 1944 to March 1946, President of Finland; retired under the pressure of democratic forces —404, 405, 411, 412, 413

Manning, Henry Edward (1808-1892)—cardinal, advocate of stronger temporal power of the Pope of Rome—35

Markov II, Nikolai Yevgenyevich (b. 1876)—big landowner, monarchist, and active member of the ultra-reactionary Union of the Russian People, leader of the extreme Right-wing group in the Third and Fourth Dumas; emigrated after the February 1917 revolution—66, 67, 125

Martens, Ludwig Karlovich (1875-1948)—prominent Soviet executive, scientist in machine building and thermal power engineering; member of the R.S.D.L.P. from 1893. In 1899 he emigrated to Germany and later to Britain. From January 1919, representative of the R.S.F.S.R. in the U.S.A. In 1921, after unsuccessful attempts to normalise relations with the U.S.A., was expelled from that country. On return to Soviet Russia he became a member of the Presidium of the Supreme Economic Council—539, 541, 543, 546, 547, 553, 558, 559, 560, 561, 579, 580, 581, 582

Martin, Edward—delegate of the American Communist Labour Party to the Second Congress of the Communist International—537

Martov, L. (*Tsederbaum, Yuli Osipovich*) (1873-1923)—leader of the Menshevik opportunist trend among Russian Social-Democrats; took a Centrist attitude during the First World War; after the October Revolution, opposed Soviet power; emigrated in 1920—266, 283, 310, 412, 413

Marx, Karl (1818-1883)—13, 14, 17, 18, 19, 20, 21, 22, 23, 24, 25, 26, 27, 29, 30, 31, 32, 33, 34, 35, 36, 39, 40, 42, 43, 78, 86, 103, 105, 111, 113, 120, 160, 161, 215, 216, 265, 286,

man, held several ministerial posts; Prime Minister from 1917 to 1919—392, 469

Ornatsky—see Chicherin, G. V.—208

Owens, Michael Joseph (1859-1923)—American inventor of the bottle-making machine—257

P

Paish, Sir George (1867-1957)—British bourgeois economist; statistician; author of several works on world economic and political problems—600

Pannekoek, Anton (1873-1960)—Dutch Social-Democrat; in 1918-21, member of the Dutch Communist Party; took part in the work of the Comintern; took an ultra-Left sectarian stand; in 1921 withdrew from the Communist Party and from politics—312

Phelps, Edward John (1822-1900)—American lawyer and diplomat—603

Plekhanov, Georgi Valentinovich (1856-1918)—outstanding leader of the Russian and international working-class movement, first propagandist of Marxism in Russia, founder of the first Russian Marxist group, the Emancipation of Labour. After the Second Congress of the R.S.D.L.P. (1903), Menshevik; during the First World War, took a social-chauvinist attitude; took a negative stand on the October Revolution but did not take part in fighting Soviet power—36, 106, 107, 301, 307, 308, 311, 314, 320, 326, 329, 362

Poole, Dewitt (1885-1952)—

American diplomat; from July 1917, Consul in Moscow; from November 1918 to June 1919, American chargé d'affaires to the whiteguard Provisional Government of the Northern Region—423

Potresov, Alexander Nikolayevich (1869-1934)—Menshevik leader; during the years of reaction (1907-10), led the liquidators; social-chauvinist during the First World War; whiteguard émigré after the October Revolution—237, 266, 307, 311, 320

Pressemane, Adrian (1879-1929)—French socialist; in 1912, permanent representative of the French Socialist Party in the International Socialist Bureau; Centrist during the First World War—299, 301, 310

Purishkevich, Vladimir Mitrofanovich (1870-1920)—big landowner, monarchist; in 1905-07, founder of the Black-Hundred pogrom organisations set up to fight the revolutionary movement; after the October Revolution, actively fought Soviet power—58, 87, 89

R

Radcliffe, Percy de Blaquiere (1874-1934)—British major-general; Director of Military Operations, War Office (1918-22)—440

Radek, Karl Berngardovich (pseudonym—K. R.) (1885-1939)—from the turn of the century took part in the Social-Democratic movement of Galicia, Poland and Germany; during the First World War, internationalist, but inclined to Centrism; took a wrong stand on the right of nations to self-determination; joined the Communist Party in 1917; during the discussion of the Peace of Brest-Litovsk, Left Communist; from 1923, active leader of the Trotskyite opposition, for which was expelled from the Party by the 15th Congress in 1927; reinstated in 1930, but once again expelled in 1936 for anti-Party activity—312, 502

Reed, John (1887-1920)—American working-class leader, writer and publicist; in 1917, came to Russia; his book, *Ten Days That Shook the World*, deals with the events of the October Socialist Revolution, which he wholeheartedly accepted; Lenin wrote a foreword to his book. Reed was one of the founders and first leaders of the U.S. Communist Party; in 1920, took part in the work of the Second Congress of the Comintern; died in Moscow, buried by the Kremlin Wall—436, 537

Reinshtein, Boris I. (1866-1947) —joined the revolutionary movement in 1884; emigrated to the United States, worked in the American Socialist Labour Party and represented it in the Second International; in 1917, returned to Russia and, in April 1918, was admitted to the Bolshevik Party; worked mainly in the Comintern and in the Red International of Labour Unions—558, 559, 560, 565, 581, 585, 586

Renaudel, Pierre (1871-1935)— opportunist leader of the French Socialist Party; social-chauvinist during the First World War; in 1933, expelled

from the Socialist Party—301, 309, 348, 375, 378

Renner, Karl (1870-1950)— Austrian politician, leader and theoretician of the Austrian Right-wing Social-Democrats; social-chauvinist during the First World War; in 1919-20, Chancellor of Austria; in 1945-50, President of Austria —305, 348, 374

Rhodes, Cecil John (1853-1902) —reactionary British statesman and politician, actively conducted British colonial policy and preached imperialist expansion; chief perpetrator of the Anglo-Boer War (1899-1902)—236, 237, 243

Riesser, Jacob (1853-1932)— German economist and banker—218, 228, 232, 278, 282, 284

Robins, Raymond (b. 1873)— colonel, American public figure; in 1917-18, chief of the American Red Cross mission in Russia; sympathised with Soviet power, and met Lenin. After the Second World War worked to strengthen friendship between the peoples of the U.S.S.R. and the U.S.A.— 532, 533

Rockefeller—dynasty of American multimillionaires—51, 54, 229, 230, 605

Roland-Holst, Henriette (1869-1952)—Dutch Socialist and author; worked to organise women's unions; adhered to the Left wing of the Dutch Social-Democrats, who from 1907 were grouped around *De Tribune*; at the outbreak of the First World War she took a Centrist stand, then joined the internationalists; in 1918-27, member of the Communist Party of Hol-

geois Cabinet—301, 375, 378

Viereck, *Louis* (1851-1921)— German Social-Democrat, opportunist; lived in the U.S.A. from 1896; during the First World War published pro-German articles in the American press—27, 28, 33

Vogelstein, *Theodor*—German economist and author of "The Financial Organisation of Capitalist Industry and the Rise of Monopolies"—217, 219, 232

Voinov, *Ivan Avksentyevich* (1884-1917)—worker, Bolshevik and active contributor to the Bolshevik newspapers, *Pravda* and *Borba*. Killed by cadets in Petrograd on July 19 (6), 1917, as he was distributing the *Listok Pravdy* (Pravda Leaflet)—380

Vollmar, *Georg Heinrich* (1850-1922)—leader of the opportunist wing in the German Social-Democratic Party; since the beginning of the 90s, an ideologist of reformism and revisionism. A social-chauvinist during the First World War—26, 31

W

Ware, *Harold* (1890-1935)— member of the U.S. Communist Party from the time of its foundation in 1919, agronomist by profession.

In the summer of 1922 he visited Soviet Russia as head of a tractor team he had organised. Afterwards visited the Soviet Union several times, consulting the organisation of big state farms—588, 590, 592

Washington, *George* (1732-99)— outstanding American states-

man, and commander-in-chief of the colonial forces in their war for independence against Britain (1755-83); the first President of the United States (1789-97)—484, 494

Webb, *Beatrice* (1858-1943) and *Sidney* (1859-1947)—well-known British public figures and founders of the Fabian Society; authors of several books on the history and theory of the British labour movement. Took a social-chauvinist attitude during the First World War. After the October Socialist Revolution, the Webbs greatly sympathised with the Soviet Union —375, 378

Wiegand, *Karl*—Berlin correspondent of the Universal Service news agency—443

Wijnkoop, *David* (1877-1941)— Dutch Social-Democrat, later Communist; in 1907, founder and later editor-in-chief of the newspaper *De Tribune*, the organ of the Left wing of the Dutch Social-Democratic Workers' Party; during the First World War, internationalist—312

Wilhelm II (*Hohenzollern*) (1859-1941)—Emperor of Germany and King of Prussia (1888-1918)—314, 315, 356, 375, 603

Williams, *T. Russell*—British Socialist, member of the British Independent Labour Party; took an anti-militarist stand during the First World War, and criticised the policy of the leaders of the Second International—208, 312

Wilson, *Woodrow* (1856-1924) —American statesman, President of the U.S.A. from 1913 to 1921. One of the organisers of the armed intervention against Soviet Russia—47, 49, 331, 343, 359, 362, 368, 369, 371, 375, 392, 607

Wischnewetzky—see *Kelley-Wischnewetzky, Florence*—22

Wrangel, Pyotr Nikolayevich (1878-1928)—Russian army general, one of the leaders of the counter-revolution in the South of Russia during the Civil War. In April 1920, succeeded A. I. Denikin as commander-in-chief of the counter-revolutionary armed forces in the South of Russia. In the autumn of 1920 Wrangel's forces were routed by the Red Army—472, 474

Y

Yermansky, Osip Arkadyevich (1866-1941)—Social-Democrat and Menshevik; broke with Mensheviks in 1921; engaged in public work and scientific research—513, 514

Yudenich, Nikolai Nikolayevich (1862-1933)—tsarist general and one of the inspirers of counter-revolution after the establishment of Soviet power. In 1919, made two attempts to capture Petrograd but was defeated by the Red Army—430, 437, 440

Yurkevich, Lev (1885-1918)—Ukrainian nationalist and petty-bourgeois Socialist—87

Z

Zasulich, Vera Ivanovna (1849-1919)—prominent participant in the Narodnik and later the Social-Democratic movement in Russia; a Menshevik leader after the Second Congress of the R.S.D.L.P. (1903); social-chauvinist during the First World War—36, 314

Zetkin, Clara (1857-1933)—outstanding leader of the German and international working-class movement; one of the founders of the Communist Party of Germany. Elected by the Third Congress of the Comintern to its Executive Committee; headed the Comintern's International Women's Secretariat; from 1924, permanent Chairman of the Executive Committee of the International Organisation of Help to the Revolutionary Fighters—375

Zinoviev, Grigory Yevseyevich (*Radomyslsky*) (1883-1936)—member of the R.S.D.L.P. from 1901; joined Bolsheviks after the Second Congress of the R.S.D.L.P. (1903); repeatedly opposed Lenin and the Party's policy; advocated compromise with the liquidators, otzovists and Trotskyites in the years of the Stolypin reaction (1907-10); together with Kamenev revealed the Central Committee's decision to stage an armed uprising (October 1917); an organiser of the New Opposition (1925); a leader of the anti-Party Trotsky-Zinoviev block (1926); expelled from the Party for anti-Party activities (1934)—367, 527, 584, 585, 586